Ornamental Grasses and Grasslike Plants

A. J. Oakes

An **avi** Book
Published by Van Nostrand Reinhold
New York

Library of Congress Catalog Card Number 89-16575
ISBN 0-442-23931-9

Printed in the United States of America

Van Nostrand Reinhold
115 Fifth Avenue
New York, New York 10003

Van Nostrand Reinhold International Company Limited
11 New Fetter Lane
London EC4P 4EE, England

Van Nostrand Reinhold
480 La Trobe Street
Melbourne, Victoria 3000, Australia

Nelson Canada
1120 Birchmount Road
Scarborough, Ontario M1K 5G4, Canada

16 15 14 13 12 11 10 9 8 7 6 5 4 3 2 1

Library of Congress Cataloging in Publication Data

Oakes, Albert J. (Albert Jackson), 1915–
  Ornamental grasses and grasslike plants / A. J. Oakes.
  p. cm.
  Includes bibliographical references.
  ISBN 0-442-23931-9
  1. Ornamental grasses. 2. Plants, Ornamental. I. Title.
II. Title: Grasslike plants.
SB431.7.025 1990
635.9′ 349—dc20

89-16575
CIP

Contents

Preface

The Gramineae, or grass family, is second in size only to the Compositeae, or sunflower family. It is among the most important plant families in the world. The major food crops of the world are found in the grass family. From time immemorial, grasses have provided food and shelter for humanity, domesticated livestock, and wildlife; without grasses, these forms of life might cease to exist. The grass family is large in size, diverse in habit, and ubiquitous in distribution. Earth would be bleak and bare, indeed, in the absence of this life-sustaining plant family. In addition to its economic and industrial value, the grass family has some ornamental value. It provides us with physical sustenance and gives us much pleasure and satisfaction in its ornamental forms.

The purpose of this book is to point out the value and usefulness of grasses as ornamentals and to delineate their attributes and uses in the home, in the garden, and in the landscape. Ornamental grasses serve a unique and significant purpose in ornamental horticulture. Horticulturists, other plant scientists, and nursery personnel are more fully aware of the value and usefulness of grasses as ornamentals than is the general public. It is mainly for this reason that this work is directed toward the home gardener and the scientist alike, in the hope of enhancing reader appreciation of the role grasses play in ornamental horticulture. Information about adaptation, habitat, description, cultivation, and uses of selected forms of grasses in the home, the home garden, and the landscape is provided in Chapter 1, "Ornamental Grasses." Although grasses, in their diverse forms, have not attained the economic significance of other ornamentals, they do contribute significantly to ornamental horticulture. Species and cultivars of temperate and tropical origin are included in this book. Their usefulness extends throughout the United States, including Alaska and Hawaii.

Bamboo is the largest member of the grass family. This diverse group of grasses is quite variable in form, size, color, texture, hardiness, and growth habit. The ornamental value of certain forms of bamboo renders them worthy of use in ornamental horticulture. The uniqueness of bamboo, coupled with its ornamental value, is given separate treatment in Chapter 2, "Bamboo."

Certain plants in other plant families, which are grasslike in appearance and share the same habitat, are also of ornamental value. Those species are included in Chapter 3, "Grasslike Plants."

No work involving ornamental grasses would be complete without a discussion of certain rushes and sedges from two closely related plant families— the Cyperaceae, or sedge family, and Juncaceae, or rush family. They are included in Chapter 4, "Rushes and Sedges." Certain forms within these plant families are similar to grasses in appearance, adaptation, growth habit, and usefulness as ornamentals. Nurseries usually include rushes and sedges with ornamental grasses in the trade.

Ornamental grasses, including bamboo, grasslike plants, and rushes and sedges, all have a place in ornamental horticulture. Each class of these ornamentals makes its own unique contribution to landscape improvement. Their prudent use, together and with other ornamentals, adds diversity and beauty to the home, home garden, and landscape.

Acknowledgments

I have made judicious use of much information in the published works of my colleagues—that is, botany texts, monographs, taxonomic revisions, floras, floristic studies, and manuals. These publications have greatly benefited me in making my task practicable, and this is gratefully acknowledged. The "Manual of Grasses of the United States" (Hitchcock and Chase, 1951) was particularly valuable; it formed the basis for the description of most grasses. The works of McClure (1946 and 1957), Young (1945, 1946), and Young and Haun (1961) provided valuable information on bamboo. Valuable sources of information on grasslike plants were the works of Anderson and Woodson (1935), Brackett (1923), Buell (1935), Fernald (1970), Hauke (1963), Hotchkiss and Dozier (1949), Kral (1966), Robinson and Fernald (1908), Shinners (1957), Small (1933), and Hortus Third (1977). The works of Fernald (1970), Mackenzie (1931–1935), Svenson (1929, 1957a, 1957b), and Hortus Third (1977) were valuable sources of information on rushes and sedges.

I drew liberally from the artwork of Hitchcock (1936), Hitchcock and Chase (1951), Meredith (1955), and Reed (1970) for illustrations of grasses. The artwork of McClure (1957) and Young (1954) was used to illustrate bamboo. Grasslike plants and rushes and sedges were illustrated by using the artwork of Abrams and Ferris (1923), Britton and Brown (1896, 1913), Correll and Correll (1982), Gates (1934), Godfrey and Wooten (1979), Hitchcock and others (1969), and Mackenzie (1940).

The National Herbarium, Washington, DC, and the Friesner Herbarium, Butler University, Indianapolis, were used in taxonomic studies.

Special thanks are due my wife, May Ritz Oakes, whose support helped me to complete this work. Her contribution is duly acknowledged with appreciation and gratitude.

REFERENCES

Abrams, Leroy, and Roxana Stinchfield Ferris. 1923. *An Illustrated Flora of the Pacific States.* Vol. 1. Stanford, CA: Stanford Univ. Press.

Anderson, Edgar, and Robert E. Woodson. 1935. *The Species of Tradescantia Indigenous to the United States.* Contributions to Arnold Arboretum. Jamaica Plain, MA: Arnold Arboretum.

Brackett, Amelia. 1923. Revision of the American Species of Hypoxis. *Rhodora* 25 (296):120–163.

Britton, N. L., and Addison Brown. 1896. *An Illustrated Flora of the Northern United States, Canada and the British Possessions.* Vol. 1. New York: Charles Scribner's Sons.

———. 1913. *An Illustrated Flora of the Northern United States, Canada and the British possessions.* 2nd ed., Vol. 1. New York: Charles Scribner's Sons.

Buell, M. F. 1935. Acorus calamus in America. *Rhodora* 37(442):367–369.

Correll, D. S., and Helen B. Correll. 1982. *Flora of the Bahama Archipelago.* Vaduz, Hirschberg: Strauss and J. Cramer Gmbh.

Fernald, M. L. 1950. *Gray's Manual of Botany.* 8th ed. New York: American Book Company.

Fernald, M. L. 1970. *Gray's Manual of Botany.* (Corrected printing) 8th ed. New York; D. Van Nostrand Company.

Gates, F. C. 1934. *Wild flowers in Kansas.* Kansas State Board of Agriculture Rept. Vol. 51, No. 204-B. Topeka: Kansas State Printing Plant.

Godfrey, R. K., and Jean W. Wooten. 1979. *Aquatic and wetland plants of southeastern United States. Monocotyledons.* Athens, GA: Univ. of Georgia Press.

Hauke, R. L. 1963. A taxonomic monograph of the genus Equisetum subgenus Hippochaete. Beich. *Nova Hedwigia* 8:1–123.

Hitchcock, A. S. 1936. *Manual of the grasses of the West Indies.* USDA Misc. Pub. 243. Washington, DC: Govt. Printing Office.

Hitchcock, A. S., and Agnes Chase. 1951. *Manual of the grasses of the United States.* USDA Misc. Pub. 200, 2nd ed. (Revised) Washington, DC: Govt. Printing Office.

Hitchcock, C. Leo., Arthur Cronquest, Marion Ownbey, and J. W. Thompson. 1969. *Vascular plants of the Pacific Northwest.* Pt. 1. Seattle, WA: Univ. of Washington Press.

Hortus Third. 1977. *A concise dictionary of plants cultivated in the United States and Canada.* New York: Macmillan Publishing Company.

Hotchkiss, N., and H. L. Dozier. 1949. Taxonomy and distribution of North American cat-tails. *American Midland Naturalist* 41:237–254.

Kral, Robert. 1966. Xyris (Xyridaceae) of the continental United States and Canada. *Sida* 2(3):177–260.

Mackenzie, K. K. 1931–1935. Cyperaceae-Cariceae. *North American Flora* 18: 1–478. New York: The New York Bot. Garden.

———. 1940. *North American Cariceae.* Vols. 1 and 2. New York: The New York Bot. Garden.

Malme, Gustaf Oskar Anderson. 1973. Xyris L. *North American Flora* 19(1):3–15. New York: The New York Bot. Garden.

McClure, F. A. 1946. The genus Bambusa and some of its first-known species. *Blumea,* Suppl. 3:90–116.

McClure, F. A. 1957. *Bamboos of the genus* Phyllostachys *under cultivation in the United States with a key for their identification.* USDA Handbook No. 114. Washington, DC: Govt. Printing Office.

McClure, F. A. 1966. *The bamboos—A fresh perspective.* Cambridge, MA: Harvard Univ. Press.

Meredith, D. B. D., Hon. Ed. 1955. *The grasses and pastures of South Africa.* Cape Town, CP: Central News Agency.

Reed, Clyde F. 1970. *Selected weeds of the United States.* USDA Handbook No. 366. Washington, DC: Govt. Printing Office.

Robinson, B. L., and M. L. Fernald. 1908. *Gray's new manual of botany.* 7th ed. New York: American Book Company.

Shinners, L. H. 1957. Sisyrinchium Bermudiana L. instead of Sisyrinchium angustifolium Miller. *Rhodora* 59(702):159–160.

Small, J. K. 1933. *Manual of the southeastern flora.* New York: J. K. Small.

Svenson, H. K. 1929. Monographic studies in the genus Eleocharis. *Rhodora* 31(68):152–163; 31(369):167–191.

———. 1957a. Cyperaceae (Fuirena). *North American Flora* 18(9):505–507.

———. 1957b. Eleocharis R. Br. *North American Flora* 18(9):509–540.

Young, Robert A. 1945. Bamboos for American Horticulture. I, II. *Natl. Hort. Mag.* 24(3):171–196, 24(4):274–291.

Young, Robert A. 1946. Bamboos for American Horticulture. III, IV, V. *Natl. Hort. Mag.* 25(1):40–64, 25(3):257–283, 25(4):352–365.

———. 1954. Flavor qualities of some edible oriental bamboos. *Econ. Bot.* 8(4):377–386.

Young, Robert A., and J. R. Haun. 1961. *Bamboos in the United States: Description, Culture, Utilization,* USDA Handbook No. 193. Washington, DC: Govt. Printing Office.

1

Ornamental Grasses

Grasses are ubiquitous; they dominate the wild flora throughout many parts of the globe. They occur in pure or mixed stands in a vast array of climates, topography, and soils, from near sea level to alpine regions beyond the tree line. Some species occur in pure stands in the wild to the exclusion of other plants, whereas other grasses form compatible mixed stands among themselves or with other grasslike plants or broad-leaved species. Aquatic forms, including tufted and mat-forming types, occur naturally at low elevations in wet, marshy areas, including bayous, bogs, floodplains, and swamps. These aquatic grasses are usually capable of growing in wet soil, in mud, or directly in water. Small cespitose or stoloniferous, drought-tolerant grasses are commonly found in hot, dry regions. Some of these forms escape extended drought periods by producing their seed crops during interims between droughts. Certain grasses manage survival in drought regions by producing a drastically reduced leaf area and by folding their leaves up, thereby greatly reducing transpiration. The extensive root system of some drought-tolerant grasses aids in their survival in arid regions.

Many grass species occur at low and middle elevations, whereas fewer species are found in alpine regions. Small, hardy, alpine, mat-forming species are adapted to the glaciated soils of mountainous regions. These are usually shade-tolerant forms capable of thriving in wet rock crevices. Hardy species are common in middle and upper temperate zones, whereas warm-season forms are native to low elevations in low latitudes. Warm-season species are common in tropical and subtropical zones and in the warmer parts of the lower temperate zone (i.e., zone 10). Woodland grasses, tolerant of shade, occur in open woods on dry, moist, or wet soils. There are gradations in shade tolerance among woodland grasses; similar gradations in shade tolerance occur among cultivated ornamental grasses. Full sunlight usually blisters and discolors the variegated foliage of some grasses. This is why cultivated ornamentals with variegated foliage are best suited to shaded sites. Certain species occur naturally in freshwater marshes; other species inhabit brackish sites; and yet others are common in saltwater marshes. Certain cultivated ornamental grasses have been characterized as to their salt tolerance. Some species that occur along seacoasts are tolerant of both atmospheric and edaphic salinity, whereas other types are tolerant of saline soils only.

Many grass species, forms, and types are suitable and useful in landscape beautification. Plant size, invasiveness, and competitiveness, or the lack of these traits in certain species, often limits their use as ornamentals. Some forms are domineering in size and gregarious in growth habit, which tends to limit their use in ornamental horticulture. Excessive invasiveness and competitiveness may be demonstrated in the use of mat-forming species such as Bermuda grass, *Cynodon dactylon,* or limpograss, *Hemarthria altissima,* when grown as ground cover in naturalized areas. Large, aquatic, tufted forms, such as common reed (*Phragmites australis*), or smaller types, such as rhizomatous reedgrass (*Calamagrostis arundinaceae*), or yet smaller, tufted, rattlesnake mannagrass (*Glyceria canadensis*), may eventually dominate wet, swampy areas in which they are established. Common reed may or may not be desirable in some situations because of its excessive size, invasiveness, and competitiveness. Invasiveness is defined as the ability of a species to invade an area in which it was not planted or established. Competitiveness is defined as the ability of a species to coexist successfully with other species in an area in which they occur simultaneously.

Many ornamental grasses with rhizomes or stolons or both are commonly used in ornamental horticulture and in the home garden. The presence of these attributes in certain species may be advantageous in some situations but detrimental in others. Certain rhizomatous ornamental grasses are useful for specific purposes when used in certain sites in landscape improvement. Rhizomatous Canada bluegrass, *Poa compressa,* is useful as ground cover in naturalized areas, whereas rhizomatous variegated ribbongrass, *Phalaris arundinacea* var. *picta,* and *Phalaris arundinacea* var. *variegata,* are ideal grasses for the water garden. The invasiveness of the latter precludes its use in rock garden and border plantings; in fact, rhizomatous and stoloniferous grasses are not recommended for the rock garden under any circumstances. Stoloniferous grasses, such as striped St. Augustine grass, *Stenotaphrum secundatum* 'Variegatum,' and *Oplismenus hirtellus* 'Vittatus,' are ideal house plants when grown in hanging baskets, but they are unsuited for the rock garden or as edging plants in foreground borders. Stoloniferous mannagrass, *Glyceria maxima,* and its variegated cultivars are at home in bogs, swamps, or water gardens, but they are unsuited for border plantings. The corms of cormose buffelgrass, *Cenchrus ciliaris,* are beneficial in enabling this warm-season species to survive extended droughts when grown as ground cover in full sun or in dry sites.

Cormose, rhizomatous, and stoloniferous grasses do play an important role in landscape development and improvement; however, they are necessarily relegated to specific uses in appropriate sites or locations. Rhizomatous and stoloniferous grasses are usually invasive in varying degrees, which limits their usefulness as ornamentals. Such forms do have a prominent place and function in ornamental horticulture, however; their use in landscape improvement should not be overlooked. Some grasses are too small and weak, unobtrusive, or unattractive for use as ornamentals.

Certain species used as ornamentals are partially or completely sterile, thus relying on some form of vegetative propagation. Whether certain species are either completely or partially sterile may or may not pose a problem in their culture. Usually their sterility is not detrimental to their culture and use as ornamentals. Vegetative propagation usually entails more time and labor than does seeding, although this by no means should preclude the use of these species in landscape improvement. Many ornamental grasses are propagated both by seeding and by vegetative methods. One chief advantage that results from vegetative propagation is that of maintaining the size, shape, color, and inflorescence type and color of the parent plant, which is not always achievable in sexual reproduction. Grasses propagated vegetatively, usually by plant division, usually develop to maturity much faster than those reproduced by seeding; this may be another worthwhile advantage of this method of propagation. The fact that some ornamental grasses are usually propagated vegetatively should not influence or limit their use as ornamentals. Pampas grass, *Cortaderia selloana* and its many cultivars, among many other ornamental grasses, may be propagated either by seeding or vegetatively by plant division. Propagation of this species and its many variants by plant division is recommended for the home garden. Other ornamentals, by contrast, produce prodigious quantities of seeds that may become weedy upon germination. These weedy forms may become a nuisance in some situations; however, when used in the proper manner, they cease to be a nuisance.

Despite the potential or actual weediness of some grasses, they usually possess some admirable attributes that, when used appropriately, will overshadow their undesirability as weedy forms. Bermuda grass, for example, spreads by its prodigious seed production and by its numerous stolons; despite this, however, it is useful in heavy traffic areas, on sports fields, on golf courses, in naturalized areas, and along highway banks and median strips, where it serves as ground cover and as an erosion-control plant. Similarly, other weedy grasses, such as foxtail barley (*Hordeum jubatum*), and broomsedge (*Andropogon virginicus*), are used for canal and highway beautification. Tufted foxtail barley is noted for its colorful flower heads, which are particularly attractive both in color and in their undulating movement caused by the slightest breeze or by fast-moving vehicles on highways. So-called weedy grasses should not be completely condemned or ignored, as they usually have some redeeming quality that either overcomes their weediness or qualifies them as beneficial for specific purposes. Bermuda grass and limpograss are both strongly stoloniferous, gregarious, sod-forming grasses unsuited for border or rock garden plantings but well suited for ground cover and erosion control. One definition of a weed is "a plant growing out of place." By applying this definition to the example given above, it is evident that, in one situation, the grasses are considered weedy, whereas in another they are considered beneficial. Some species included in this book are no doubt weedy forms and might not be recommended for cultivation as ornamentals. These weedy forms, along with those cited previously and including *Andropogon virginicus* (broomsedge) and *Phalaris arundinaceae* var. *picta* (ribbongrass), among others, have redeeming attributes that overcome their undesirable weediness when used in the right place for the right purpose. Certain species included in this book occur in selected lists of weeds of the United States and the world's worst weeds. The weediness of these species should not entirely preclude their use in ornamental horticulture and garden and landscape improvement.

Despite the shortcomings of certain grass species from an ornamental viewpoint, many forms are useful in ornamental horticulture and landscape improvement. Both tufted and mat-forming types are useful as ornamentals; in addition, those with corms, rhizomes, and stolons are also useful. Evergreen, semievergreen, and deciduous grasses are included among those of ornamental value. Aquatic, semiaquatic, and terrestrial forms are valuable as ornamentals. Grasses adapted to tropical and temperate climates, aptly referred to as warm-season and hardy species, respectively, are also valuable as ornamentals. Growth habit (i.e., tufted versus mat-forming) constitutes another variable attribute found among ornamental grasses.

Ornamental types differing in winter hardiness are available for ornamental usage. Winter hardiness of perennial types is an important attribute in which, fortunately, considerable variation is present among ornamental forms. Ornamental grasses are available that exhibit variable degrees of tolerance to drought, moisture, heat, sun, and shade. Foliage color and texture (i.e., leaf width and inflorescence shape, size, and color) are important ornamental characteristics that are present in certain grasses available for use in ornamental horticulture. Considerable variation exists among ornamental grasses in their flowering pattern. Some forms flower in the spring (April–May), some during summer (June–July), and others in late summer and early fall, continuing until frost. Some types flower throughout the growing season, such as sea oats, *Uniola paniculata;* other types flower twice annually (i.e., spring and fall), whereas others, such as basketgrass, *Oplismenus hirtellus,* flower only sporadically. Some ornamental types fail to flower at all, and some bamboo species do not flower until they are several years old. Some tropical grasses, such as canegrass, *Lasiacis divaricata,* and uvagrass, *Gynerium sagittatum,* blossom only during the winter months. At least one ornamental species, *Holcus lanatus,* flowers twice daily. Flowering of some forms is influenced by whether or not the grasses are grown in the garden or indoors. The presence of shade and the duration of the growing season also influence flowering of some species. Some types that flower profusely when grown outdoors fail to flower when grown indoors. Many tropical perennial species, such as vetivergrass, *Vetiveria zizanioides,* when started indoors in early spring and later transferred outside, will flower in late summer but will fail to perenniate.

Ornamental grasses are used in many different ways in developing and improving the home garden and in ornamental horticulture in general. Public awareness of the garden uses of ornamental grasses perhaps came about in part through their use in dried floral arrangements. The economic importance of ornamental grasses in the trade is small compared to that of other ornamentals; however, with the increased awareness of their value in ornamental horticulture, it is growing.

TYPES AND KINDS

Ornamental grasses may be arbitrarily divided into two groups: those used in the home and those used in the home garden. The former are used as potted specimens, cut flowers, and in dried floral arrangements, either dyed or in natural color. Those for the home garden are used in single, group, and massed plantings in the following garden types: bog, cut-flower, pebble and rock, vegetable, and water, and in peat beds. They are employed as accent, ground-cover, and specimen plants. Erosion control, hedges, screens, windbreaks, lawns, or lawn substitutes are among other uses of ornamental grasses in the home garden. Certain types are grown primarily for their colorful foliage, other types for their flowers, and yet others for both their flowers and foliage. Some types are grown mainly as a curiosity, others for cut flowers and dried specimens, and others for their fragrance. Often the same species are used advantageously as both house and garden plants.

Ornamental grasses vary considerably. Ornamental grasses are available that are suitable for almost any climate and situation. They are comprised of annuals, biennials, and perennials, varying in size from minuscule forms to large, treelike bamboos. Growth habit varies from decumbent mat-forming types to erect cespitose forms. Plant forms include mat-forming and mound-forming types, irregular, open spreading, upright-arching, upright-narrow, and upright-open. Ornamental grasses include cormose, rhizomatous, and stoloniferous forms. Tropical warm-season and cool-season hardy forms are available, which include evergreen, semievergreen, and deciduous types. Aquatic, semiaquatic, and terrestrial types are included among ornamental grasses. Differences in texture, foliage, and inflorescence color exist among species, cultivars, and individual plants. The variation within and among species is exploited in the use of ornamental grasses in ornamental horticulture. Examples of the kinds of ornamental grasses demonstrate their diversity and usefulness.

Annuals, such as Job's tears, *Coix lacryma-jobi,* complete their life cycle in one year or one growing season; biennials (e.g., foxtail barley, *Hordeum jubatum*) complete their life cycle in two seasons; perennials (e.g., carpet grass, *Axonopus compressus*) live for three or more seasons. A horticultural annual is a perennial from a warm climate grown as an annual in a cold climate; buffelgrass, *Cenchrus ciliaris,* is an example.

Tremendous variation in size exists among ornamental grasses. An example of extreme variation in size is that of the minuscule onion couch, which is small enough for sink gardens, versus large, treelike bamboos (e.g., *Arundinaria* and *Phyllostachys* species). Erect cespitose grasses such as broomsedge (*Andropogon virginicus*) grow in clumps, whereas decumbent stoloniferous types (e.g., Bermuda grass) are mat forming.

Species that demonstrate the various forms of ornamental grasses include irregular *Elymus giganteus;* mound-forming *Eragrostis curvula;* open-spreading *Hemarthria altissima;* upright-arching *Oryza sativa;* upright-narrow *Elymus villosus;* and upright-open *Hordeum jubatum.* Cormose grasses are exemplified by such forms as bulbous oatgrass, *Arrhenatherum elatius* var. *bulbosum* and buffelgrass, *Cenchrus ciliaris.* Such grasses have solid, hard, swollen, lower-stem extremities or so-called bulbs, usually below ground level, that aid the plants in surviving extended periods of drought and low temperatures. Perennial rhizomatous grasses usually have horizontal stems or rootstocks, usually underground, from which a succession of stems arise at the apex (e.g., bahiagrass, *Paspalum notatum,* and creeping softgrass, *Holcus mollis*). Stoloniferous perennial grasses such as Rhodesgrass, *Chloris gayana,* have aboveground shoots or runners that root at the nodes, giving rise to new plants. Warm-season tropical grasses include those types of tropical origin that withstand little frost, if any, in contrast to cool-season, hardy forms of temperate origin that thrive in temperate zones. Truly tropical grasses, such as certain *Bambusa* species or *Gynerium sagittatum,* do not withstand any frost whatsoever. Evergreen grasses, such as switchcane, *Arundinaria gigantea* ssp. *tecta,* remain green and live through more than one growing season, whereas semievergreen types, such as bulbous oatgrass, *Arrhenatherum elatius* var. *bulbosum,* remains partially green and functional through more than one season. The foliage of deciduous perennial grasses, such as giant reed, *Arundo donax,* is killed to ground level each winter; such grasses are not evergreen.

Additional attributes and refinements of ornamental grasses include winter hardiness, degree of density of cespitose forms, expressed as densely tufted or loosely tufted, and tolerance of wet soils. Winter hardiness of each species in this book is indicated by plant-hardiness zones defined by the U.S. Department of Agriculture (Appendix 5); descriptions of winter hardiness are included with the species descriptions. Densely tufted grasses are exemplified by purple three-awn grass, *Aristida purpurea.* Perennial quaking grass exemplifies loosely tufted forms. Rice, which grows directly in mud or water, is a good example of an aquatic grass; incidentally, rice is also cultivated to a limited extent as a terrestrial plant. Semiaquatic grasses grow in mud or wet soil; rice cutgrass, *Leersia oryzoides,* is an example of a semiaquatic grass. Most grasses are terrestrial; that is, they grow in ordinary soil.

Ornamental grasses exhibit considerable variation in texture (i.e., leaf width). The texture of species with leaves up to 0.4 in./10 mm wide is considered to be fine; those with leaves 0.4–0.6 in./10–15 mm wide are medium; and those with leaves wider than 0.7 in./15 mm are coarse. Spear grasses, *Stipa* species, are usually fine in texture, in contrast to bushgrass, *Calamagrostis epigejos,* of medium texture and giant reed, *Arundo donax,* of coarse texture. The wide variation in foliage and inflorescence color lends impetus to the use of ornamental grasses in the home garden and in landscape improvement.

Differences in tolerance of shade, wet or dry soils, and disease and insect damage among ornamental grasses are exploited in their use in ornamental horticulture. Species of *Calamagrostis, Dactylis, Deschampsia, Hakonechloa,* and *Melina,* among others, demonstrate variable degrees of shade tolerance. Certain ornamental grasses are adapted to dry soils, whereas others thrive best in wet soil. Speargrasses, *Stipa* species, exemplify forms that prefer dry soils, and Japanese silvergrass and plumegrass prefer wet soils. Intraspecific differences in tolerance to damage from leaf fungi is demonstrated by clones of tall oatgrass. Some clones suffer severe damage from leaf fungi in the class *Hyphomycete,* whereas other clones are tolerant. Certain lines of maize, *Zea mays,* suffer severe damage from the corn earworm, whereas other lines are somewhat immune.

GARDEN TYPES

Several things should be considered simultaneously in the correct use of ornamental grasses in improving the landscape or garden. First, perhaps, is the desired type of garden, whether it is a formal or informal garden, or a bog, rock, water, or cut-flower garden. The same plants used in a small bog garden certainly would not be suitable in perennial mixed borders or in rock gardens. Similarly, stoloniferous or strongly rhizomatous grasses should not be included in rock garden plantings, as their invasiveness and competitiveness with other species would result in a tangled mass requiring much labor and cost to maintain. Scree, rock, and water gardens require constant, intensive, and costly maintenance, which most people wish to avoid. Bog gardens and naturalized areas, on the other hand, require very little or no maintenance and are far less expensive, resulting in more satisfaction for the effort and money expended.

A definition and interpretation of the word *garden* might be helpful. The term *garden* is used more commonly in Europe than in the United States. Europeans use the terms *front garden, side garden,* and *back garden* to refer to areas in the front, on either side, and at the rear of the house, respectively. The term *garden* is also used in North America. However, the word *yard* is usually heard (i.e., front yard, side yard, or backyard). The terms *garden* and *yard* both describe the same area. One notable difference between American and European gardens is their size; American gardens are usually larger. Land is at a premium in Europe, where it is used more intensively than in the United States. Thumbnail-size minigardens are a common sight in many European countries. These tiny gardens are less common in the United States, where we tend to have more space, except in some metropolitan areas.

It is difficult to describe a typical home garden in the United States. Home gardens of various types, shapes, and sizes are common throughout the world, occurring in vastly different climates and habitats. The usual concept of the home garden is one that comprises a lawn and adjacent borders and flower beds arranged in various patterns. The borders and flower beds usually contain annual, biennial, and perennial flowering ornamentals and shrubs. The lawn most likely comprises the major portion of the garden's total area. The most formal portion of the garden is usually near the house, and less formal portions are further away. The entire garden may be surrounded by large flowering shrubs and trees. The trees and large shrubbery complete the landscape by augmenting the lawn, borders, and flower beds while simultaneously competing with the flowering plants and the lawn for moisture, soil nutrients, and sunlight. Differences in the sizes and shapes of gardens allow more diversity in design and the choice of plants in landscaping them.

Climate has a pronounced effect on the type of home garden developed and, perhaps more specifically, on the ornamental plants it contains. Rainfall amount and distribution, maximum and minimum temperature, including the windchill factor, which affects winter hardiness, and sunlight are major climatic factors that influence the type of garden developed and the plants it contains. The types of home gardens developed in the vastly different climates of New England, the Gulf Coast, the Northwest, and the Southwest are quite different, primarily because of climatic differences among the regions. Furthermore, the climatic differences determine, to a large degree, the kinds of ornamentals adapted to each region. Examples include the bluegrasses, *Poa* species, used as lawns in the middle Atlantic states, versus St. Augustine grass, *Stenotaphrum secundatum,* which is recommended for the Southwest. Another contrast is in the species used in rock gardens in different climates. For example, dwarf, hardy *Alopecurus alpinus* is adapted to zones 2–4, whereas large blue fescue (*Festuca amethystina*), is adapted to zones 4–8. Rock gardens usually do not fare well in the cool, wet Northwest, nor do water gardens flourish in the hot, dry Southwest. Minimum winter temperature, which influences winter hardiness, is a major factor dictating the use of certain perennial ornamental grasses in home gardens in different regions. Job's tears, *Coix lacryma-jobi,* and little quaking grass, *Briza minor,* are adapted to zones 5–10; however, the former requires a much longer growing season than the latter. Also the length of growing season affects plant growth and development. As a result, Job's tears thrives much better in zone 10 than in zone 5, and little quaking grass does equally well in either zone.

The particular habitat influences, to a great extent, the type of garden that is best for the home. Some sites in sunny locations are flat, with hard soil; other sites may be on steep slopes in shaded locations; and yet other sites may require terracing in order to establish a garden. Gardens developed on flat, level terrain are easier and cheaper to establish and maintain than those located on steep slopes requiring terracing or those in low, wet sites, in which bog or water gardens are usually established. Dry, flat, sunny sites in warm, arid climates are ideal for rock gardens, in contrast to shaded wet areas in moderate- or high-rainfall belts in cool climates. The same species of ornamental flowers and grasses suited for hard, rocky, pebbly, dry soil located in sunny, hot, dry sites are not adapted for use in fertile loamy or clay soils located in shaded, moist sites. Shade from large surrounding trees or tall buildings also has a profound influence on the type of ornamentals used in developing the garden, including the lawn. Shade-tolerant, flowering plants, including ornamental and lawn grasses, are required for shaded locations. Gardens on steep slopes are usually developed to conform to the terrain. This usually consists of terraces comprised of a series of retaining walls. Rhizomatous and stoloniferous ornamental grasses are useful in preventing erosion in gardens on steep slopes. Terraced gardens are usually very dry and either cold or warm, depending on their exposure. It is preferable to develop terraced gardens with a southern exposure, especially in temperate and cold climates. The exposure of a garden site also influences, to some extent, the type of ornamentals employed. Soils in garden sites with a southern exposure usually warm up in the spring before those with a northern exposure. Furthermore, they may remain warm longer in the fall with the onset of cooler weather, thus perceptibly extending the growing season of some species. A closely correlated factor is that of soil type; sandy and loamy soils are warmer than clay or clay loams. Furthermore, the former usually warm up in the spring earlier than the latter and remain warm longer in the autumn. The combination of soil type (sandy) and exposure (southern) influences, to some extent at least, the range of ornamentals used and the duration of their attractiveness. Soil acidity and alkalinity also influence the types of ornamentals used, including ornamental grasses. Gardens in the cool climates of New England and the Pacific Northwest are quite different from those of the warm, dry climate of the Southwest. This reflects the adaptation of certain ornamental grasses to different climates.

Gardens of various types, designs, and sizes are in common usage. They include formal and informal, bog, pebble and rock, vegetable, cut-flower, sink and water gardens, and peat beds. Each is defined and described according to its use and function.

The connotation of the term *informal garden* is that of the normal home garden in which flowering plants are grown for their beauty and attractiveness. The designs and planting patterns are quite variable, depending upon individual taste.

A *formal garden* is defined as an area in which ornamentals are established in a precise order conforming to a particular design. The plantings in formal gardens are established in an orderly, balanced, usually symmetrical design. Many aspects of landscape design and improvement are considered in the development of formal gardens. The design and development of formal gardens usually require the assistance of professional landscape artists. Formal gardens require much planning and labor to establish; they are usually costly to develop and maintain. Such gardens, requiring high maintenance costs, are less common than those of the average home garden. Considerable skill, labor, money, and professionalism are involved in the development and maintenance of formal gardens. Much information on this subject is available in ornamental literature.

Bog gardens, peat beds, and water gardens are all characterized as being wet; they may be located on sites ranging from full sun to deep shade. Low, wet, marshy, shaded sites are ideal for the location of bog or water gardens. Bog gardens by definition are wet, spongy, and usually acid sites. They provide a perfect habitat for aquatic ornamental grasses, grasslike plants such as cattails and rushes or sedges, most of which are acid and shade tolerant and capable of growing in wet soil, in mud, or directly in water. Variegated aquatic forms are particularly useful in shaded bog gardens, since their foliage is not harmed by direct sunlight. Not all locations are adaptable for the development of bog or water gardens, nor are they suitable for rock gardens, for that matter. Nevertheless, bog gardens play a significant role in landscape design and improvement in their proper setting.

Peat beds, like water gardens and bog gardens, are usually situated in low, wet, marshy sites. A peat bed is formed by the partial decay of plants in low, wet sites; it is usually acid in nature. The same types of plants found in bog and water gardens are equally at home in the peat bed (i.e., aquatic forms that are capable of growing in wet soil, mud, or directly in water). Peat beds located in shaded sites on acid soils require plants that are acid and shade tolerant. Peat beds alone or in combination with bog and water gardens also contribute to landscape improvement in their own unique way.

Pebble and rock gardens are most common in arid regions of the sunbelt. Rock gardens usually consist primarily of pebbles, small stones, and larger rocks. It is preferable but not always possible to locate the rock garden so that it will have a southern exposure, especially in northern regions. Screes randomly located in a pebble or rock garden are an added attraction. It is preferable that soils in rock gardens be either neutral or slightly acid or alkaline. Xerophytic plants such as cacti and other small, fleshy species are ideal for rock gardens. Small, delicate forms are best; however, larger types with extensive root systems also are well suited for this particular environment. Combinations of drought-tolerant shrubs and fleshy desert plants with certain ornamental grasses provide an interesting display in the rock garden. Stoloniferous and rhizomatous grasses should not be used in the rock garden, however, as they compete with and crowd out other plants, usually forming a miniature jungle, which requires much time and labor to clean up. Despite the attractiveness and adaptation of such forms, they only cause trouble in the end in rock gardens. Such grasses are adaptable and useful elsewhere in landscape improvement.

Tufted, drought-tolerant grasses capable of growing in full sun are best suited for the rock garden. They are often used in conjunction with ground covers; their form, texture, and color either harmonize or contrast with surrounding plants. Examples of small forms include the red color of *Imperata cylindrica* 'Rubra' in contrast to the glaucous foliage of *Poa glauca*. The unique inflorescences of *Briza* and *Chloris* species provide an added dimension to rock garden plantings. Foliage of broad-leaved uniola, the fescues, and fountain grass are outstanding examples of the use of grasses noted for their attractive foliage in rock gardens. Natal grass provides an unusual display of flowers in such sites, as do pampas grass and all its variants. No rock garden is complete in the absence of pampas grass. Even multicolored varieties of corn are an asset to the rock garden. Grasses are generally used in mixed plantings with other species. Their use provides a pleasing contrast to columnar or cylindrical cactaceous plants, in addition to low-lying plants, including fleshy forms. Species useful in the rock garden are listed in Appendix 1, column 12.

Shades of green, such as metallic bluish green and olive green, among cultivars of *Festuca ovina* var. *glauca,* and among *Elymus* species provide pleasing contrasts to the dark green foliage of other rock garden plants. Variegated cultivars of *Cortaderia selloana, Dactylis glomerata, Hakonechloa macra, Miscanthus sinensis,* and *Zea mays* add a variety of color to the rock garden. These plants are upright-narrow or upright-open, in contrast to low-growing ground covers and other spreading species. Rock gardens are often covered with small pebbles or stones of various colors. The variegated foliage of grasses provides a pleasing contrast in color to the pebbles or other ground cover. Raised beds in shaded sites provide an ideal site for viviparous forms such as *Festuca vivipara* and *Poa bulbosa* var. *vivipara*. Drought-tolerant, elegant *Stipa* species and vetivergrass are additional tufted forms for the rock garden. The admixture of grasses in the rock garden results in a pleasing variety of color, texture, and plant form. Their use complements other rock garden plants, and vice versa.

A cut-flower garden is defined as an area in which flowering ornamentals with attractive inflorescences are grown primarily for use as cut flowers. A broader interpretation of the cut-flower garden could include other flowering plants, such as accent and specimen plants, potted plants grown outside, those included in borders and flower beds, and even those used in naturalized sites. The soil moisture and fertility requirements, along with those of light, cannot be defined with a great degree of precision for the cut-flower garden. This is especially true in view of the vast array of ornamental grasses adapted for use in it.

Both urban and rural dwellers often develop what are commonly known as sink gardens. These consist of old, discarded bathtubs, barrels (both metal and wooden), sinks, stoves, wooden kegs, buckets, or other similar containers that are used to establish these miniature gardens. They are fascinating to develop and maintain, and they afford the home gardener endless pleasure. Such gardens are usually developed by plant hobbyists or by others who do not have sufficient space for larger gardens. Fortunately, a few dwarf ornamental grasses are suitable in size for such small gardens.

Many vegetable gardens are quite often interplanted with ornamental flowering plants, including certain ornamental grasses. As with the cut-flower garden, soil moisture, fertility, and light requirements cannot be precisely defined. Ornamental grasses interplanted in the vegetable garden are usually small or medium-sized annuals that are compatible with, but not necessarily competitive with, the vegetables. They are chosen primarily for their attractive inflorescences, although their size, texture, and foliage color may also be considered. Rhizomatous and stoloniferous grasses should not be used in the vegetable garden. They would compete unduly with the vegetables and interfere with annual changes made with the vegetable crops. Grasses interplanted in the vegetable garden are generally used as cut flowers. The judicious use of selected ornamental grasses in the vegetable garden provides diversity and interest. The grasses are enhanced by the vegetables, and vice versa.

A water garden may be the main focus of attention for some home gardeners, or it may constitute a portion of the overall garden plan for others. Water gardens, peat beds, and bog gardens are all characterized as being wet and requiring water-loving plants. Such situations require aquatic and semiaquatic plants, which are usually acid tolerant.

A water garden consists of a natural or artificially created pond, pool, lake, or a slow-moving stream planted with aquatic and subaquatic plants arranged in either a systematic or a haphazard manner. It is ideally located in either deep shade or in open, wooded sites. Added attractions usually include fountains, birdbaths, miniature waterfalls, or divided streams, with occasional dams forming pools around and in which aquatic and semiaquatic plants abound. Still water is usually best for aquatic plants. Pools and ponds may be developed by damming small, slow-flowing streams or from natural springs. Water gardens that are large and elaborate or small and simple may be developed. Fortunately, water gardens are low-maintenance gardens, requiring little or no watering, weeding, pruning, fertilizing, spraying, or other maintenance procedures associated with growing terrestrial plants. One of the main problems encountered with growing aquatic plants is that of restraining overvigorous species. Periodically picking off dead or yellowish leaves maintains the attractiveness of aquatics.

Hardy aquatics are planted in the spring just as new growth begins. Tender tropical aquatics are planted after the weather and water temperatures are warm and stabilized at a steady, warm level suitable for the plants. Aquatic and semiaquatic ornamentals, including grasses and grasslike plants in water gardens, should be tolerant of shade and acid soils and capable of growing in wet soil, mud, or directly in water. Grasses with unusual foliage, especially variegated forms, are ideal for use in water gardens. Aquatic ornamental grasses thrive best in rich, fertile soil, either moist or wet soil, mud, or directly in water. The lower portion of common reed is below water level, although the major portion of the erect plant is above water level. The large leaves of water lilies float on the surface of the water, as opposed to the erect plants of *Carex, Cyperus, Juncus,* and *Scirpus* species, all of which are grasslike plants. Certain ornamental grasses capable of growing directly in water include *Alopecurus aequalis, Calamagrostis* species, *Glyceria* species, *Leersia* species, *Oryza sativa, Spartina* species, and *Zizania aquatica.* Additional species are given in Appendix 1, column 13. Other species, such as *Deschampsia caespitosa* and *Elymus* species, do well in wet soil or mud. Giant reed, *Arundo donax, Coix lacryma-jobi* 'Aurea Zebrina,' *Miscanthus* species and *Stenotaphrum secundatum* 'Variegatum' thrive in moist or wet soil. Some submerged aquatics, such as *Vallisneria spiralis,* are also useful in the water garden.

Floating aquatics not in the grass family, such as *Azolla, Eichhornia,* and *Pistia,* should also be considered as water garden plants. True sedges, *Carex* species, *Cyperus* species, flowering rush, *Butomus umbellatus,* and cattails are also suitable for planting in shallow water. Plants for the water garden range in size from small *Leersia* species to large forms, such as *Arundo donax, Miscanthus* species, and *Phragmites australis.* The use of variegated cultivars of *Calamagrostis, Glyceria, Phalaris,* and *Spartina* add a new dimension in color to the water garden. Diversity in plant form is demonstrated by the use of erect forms, such as common reed, when planted with water lilies, or by low-growing, striped, St. Augustine grass grown as an edging plant near the pool. The use of aquatic and subaquatic grasses in the water garden grown in admixtures with other aquatics lends diversity in plant form, color, and texture not achieved by any other plants. Their use in water garden plantings usually improves the appearance and diversity of water garden flora. Bog gardens and peat beds may be considered valuable adjuncts to the water garden.

ADAPTATION

Ornamental grasses are used in many ways in the home garden. However, there are many uses for ornamental grasses and their grasslike relatives that go beyond that of their use in the home garden and its immediate surroundings. Ornamental grasses are used as ground cover and in naturalizing difficult sites in many areas; they are useful in parks, sports fields, along streets and highways, and in zoos. Certain ornamental grasses provide food and protection for wildlife. Other grasses and grasslike plants are useful in improving the landscape in many areas in which improvement is needed. Some species occur naturally in difficult sites, where they serve a useful purpose, but other species could be introduced and used to further improve the landscape in certain areas. Some of same species that are used in formal plantings are also useful in difficult sites and in locations other than the home garden.

Certain ornamental grasses have been characterized as being adapted to the following difficult conditions:

acid or alkaline soils
brackish-water, freshwater,
  and saltwater marshes

dry soils
infertile soils
rocky soils

saline soils   shaded sites
wet soils   extremely cold situations
seashore sand dunes

Grasses and grasslike plants used in these sites are useful in the following ways: as accent or specimen plants; to provide ground cover and prevent erosion on steep slopes, stream banks, and seaside sand dunes; to provide good fall color; to build soils in marshes and alluvial floodplains; to provide food and protection to wildlife; and to improve the appearance and attractiveness of the landscape. Fortunately, there are numerous ornamental grasses and grasslike relatives that are suitable for use in these unusual and difficult sites.

The relative acidity or alkalinity of the soil has a major influence on the choice of ornamental grasses used in landscape improvement. The unit commonly used to express the hydrogen ion concentration of a solution is pH, which is defined as the negative of the logarithm of the hydrogen ion concentration in grams per liter of solution. The results of testing soils for acidity or alkalinity are reported in pH values. By definition, a pH value of 7.0 is considered neutral, pH values less than 7.0 denote acidity, whereas those values greater than 7.0 indicate alkalinity. Soils in medium- or high-rainfall belts tend to be acid in nature, as opposed to alkaline soils in arid regions. Very often there is a gradual variation in acidity or alkalinity among soils, and in some instances there are wide ranges in the pH of different soils. Reputable nursery workers usually have this type of information available and will recommend certain grasses for certain soils and sites. State universities usually have soil-testing laboratories that will provide a test for soil pH for a nominal fee. Should a complete soil analysis be required, that service would be available also. Commercial soil-testing laboratories provide the same services; however, the cost is usually higher. Before investing much money and labor in landscaping, it is prudent to have the soil tested, at least for pH. One way of alleviating the alkalinity problem, in addition to using grasses with known tolerance to alkalinity, is to use acid-forming fertilizers, such as ammonium sulfate.

Some ornamental grasses have been identified that are best adapted to neutral soils, others that prefer slightly acid or alkaline conditions, and yet others that are adapted to either acid or alkaline soils. Side-oats grama (*Bouteloua curtipendula*) grows best on neutral soil with pH near 7.0. Species with a wider pH tolerance—that is, those types that grow equally well in slightly acid or alkaline soils—include *Bouteloua gracilis* and *Chloris distichophylla*. Some species useful in acid soils include *Andropogon stolonifer, Anthoxanthum odoratum, Arrhenatherum elatius, Briza maxima, Ctenium aromaticum, Deschampsia flexuosa, Distichlis spicata, Holcus mollis, Poa nemoralis, Setaria geniculata,* and *Stenotaphrum secundatum.* Species that thrive best on alkaline soils include *Andropogon barbinodis, Andropogon gerardi, Bouteloua briveseta, Bouteloua hirsuta, Chloris glauca, Milium effusum,* and *Spartina gracilis.* Additional species adapted to acid or alkaline soils are as follows:

Acid Soils

Andropogon stolonifer
Andropogon virginicus
Anthoxanthum odoratum
Arrhenatherum elatius
Bouteloua gracilis
Briza maxima
Bromus secalinus
Chloris cucullata
Chloris distichophylla
Chloris verticillata
Ctenium aromaticum
Cynodon dactylon
Deschampsia flexuosa
Distichlis spicata
Holcus mollis and cvs.
   Albevariegatus, Variegatus
Molinia caerulea
Oryza sativa
Pennisetum alopecuroides and cvs.
   and varieties
Phalaris arundinacea and cvs. and
   varieties
Phleum pratense
Poa nemoralis
Setaria geniculata
Stenotaphrum secundatum

Alkaline Soils

Andropogon barbinodis
Andropogon gerardi
Andropogon virginicus
Bouteloua breviseta
Bouteloua curtipendula
Bouteloua hirsuta
Bromus secalinus
Chloris glauca
Cynodon dactylon
Distichlis spicata
Koeleria cristata
Milium effusum
Phleum pratense
Spartina gracilis

Floodplains and marshlands near the sea are often overgrown with unattractive, useless plants. These areas are periodically frequented by migratory wildfowl and other wildlife. Establishing such areas with plants of ornamental and utilitarian value that provide food and shelter for wildlife, particularly migratory birds, may be a challenge that could be overcome through the use of proper plants. Grasses that are most beneficial for such difficult sites should be aquatics or semiaquatics capable of growing in mud and water; they should be perennials, preferably tolerant of acid conditions. These plants should be capable of preventing soil erosion, building soils, and providing food and shelter for wildlife. Some species may provide good fall color as an added attraction. Some grasses suitable for naturalizing brackish- and freshwater marshes, which also provide wildlife protection and a food source, include *Calamagrostis arundinaceae*, *Calamagrostis canadensis*, *Gynerium sagittatum*, and *Zizania aquatica*. Additional species suitable for these conditions include the following:

Alopecurus aequalis
Calamagrostis arundinacea
Calamagrostis canadensis
Calamagrostis canescens and cv. Variegata
Chloris glauca
Ctenium aromaticum
Glyceria canadensis
Glyceria fluitans
Glyceria maxima and cvs. Pallida, Variegata
Gynerium sagittatum
Hierochloa odorata
Leersia oryzoides
Oryza sativa and cv. Nigrescens
Paspalum dissectum
Phalaris arundinacea vars. *picta* and variegata
Phragmites australis
Spartina alterniflora
Spartina cynosuroides
Spartina pectinata and cv. Aureo-marginata
Spartina spartinae
Zizania aquatica

There are additional *Carex, Cyperus,* and *Typha* species of equal or greater importance that are useful for such difficult sites. Some of these aquatic species are best used alone in pure stands, whereas other species are compatible with each other and with other water-loving plants. Compatible forms are encouraged, as their use adds diversity in plant form, size, and color to the landscape of these otherwise uninteresting sites. The best balance and diversity of flora are usually achieved through the use of aquatic grasses with other water plants, such as water lilies, sedges, and cattails. The aquatic ornamental grasses in low, wet, boggy sites either dominate the area or supplement and complement existing vegetation; in either case, they perform a useful function. Ornamental aquatic grasses, when used in such locations, usually provide ground cover and feed, particularly for migratory wildfowl, in addition to arresting erosion, building soil, and, for some species, providing good autumnal color.

Saltwater marshes constitute a unique habitat requiring salt-tolerant plants. Some salt-tolerant species useful for such sites include *Agropyron pungens, Calamagrostis epigejos, Distichlis spicata, Phragmites australis, Puccinellia* species, *Setaria magna, Spartina alterniflora,* and *Spartina patens.* The need for wildlife food and protection in the lowlands and salt marshes near the sea is the same as that for similar sites of freshwater and brackish-water marshes inland. Some of the species recommended for these areas are more useful and attractive than those that occur there naturally. It should be pointed out that some of the aquatic grasses and grasslike plants recommended for brackish-water, freshwater, and saltwater marshes already occur in some sites naturally, but not in all of them, nor in sufficiently dense stands. Additional species useful in saltwater marshes include:

Agropyron pungens
Calamagrostis epigejos and cv. Hortorum
Distichlis spicata
Paspalum dissectum
Phragmites australis
Puccinellia fasciculata
Puccinellia maritima
Setaria geniculata
Spartina alterniflora
Spartina cynosuroides
Spartina patens
Spartina pectinata and cv. Aureo-marginata
Spartina spartinae
Sporobolus virginicus

Certain ornamental grasses are adapted to dry soils. Some information on drought tolerance, in addition to other environmental conditions for each species described, is included in the "Cultivation" section of each species description. Those species included in Appendix 1, column 5 are used primarily as ground-cover plants and in naturalized areas on dry soils. Grasses should never be allowed to fail because their drought tolerance is not known. General guidelines regarding drought tolerance should be obtained from plant nurseries and should be carefully considered in the choice of species for certain situations. The trial-and-error approach to ascertaining drought tolerance could be both expensive and disappointing.

Sandy soils are usually very dry, because of their poor water-holding capacity, unless they occur in high-rainfall belts, in which moist sandy soils are prevalent. Drought-tolerant grasses are required for dry, sandy soils with low moisture content. These grasses include deep-rooted forms, such as smooth brome, *Bromus inermis,* and strongly rhizomatous forms, such as bahiagrass, *Paspalum notatum,* and creeping softgrass, *Holcus mollis.* Certain ornamental grasses are adapted to hard, dry, rocky soils that are prevalent in some regions, especially at intermediate or high elevations. Soils of this type make root penetration difficult and usually drought tolerant, deep-rooted grasses are required for these conditions. Tufted hairgrass, *Deschampsia caepitosa,* and *Helictotrichon pubescens,* are useful in these difficult soils. Some species are better adapted to sunny sites in dry soils than others; fortunately, there are both tufted and stoloniferous forms that are suitable for such conditions. The following grasses are good examples for sunny, dry sites: big and little bluestem, *Andropogon gerardi* and *Schizachyrium scoparium,* respectively; buffelgrass, *Cenchrus ciliaris;* natal grass, *Rhynchelytrum repens;* squirreltail grass, *Sitanon hystrix;* and weeping lovegrass, *Eragrostis curvula.* Other species remarkably adapted to dry conditions include *Bouteloua gracilis, Briza maxima,* and *Stipa giganteus.* Additional species suitable for dry soils are included in Appendix 1, column 5.

Poor and impoverished soils often pose a problem in home gardens and adjacent areas. However, some grasses thrive on infertile soils. Among the grasses that thrive in such inhospitable habitats are *Andropogon virginicus, Eleusine coracana, Poa compressa, Rhynchelytrum repens,* and *Schizachyrium scoparium.* Although broomsedge does not qualify for use in the garden proper, it is ideal as a ground cover in naturalized areas, where it reduces erosion, affords cover for wildlife, and provides good fall color.

Rocky soils at low, middle, and high elevations are the most difficult sites on which to establish and maintain an attractive ground cover or ornamentals for other purposes. Cespitose, rhizomatous, and stoloniferous grasses are useful on rocky soils. Grasses useful on wet, rocky soils at high elevations include, among others, *Alopecurus alpinus* and *Fingerhuthia sesleriaeformis.* Ideal grasses for dry, rocky soils include such types as *Aristida purpurascens, Aristida wrightii,* and *Vetiveria zizanoides.*

Saline soils in southern California, for example, and in low tidelands along the coast present a special problem for crop plants in some areas and for other species used as ground cover and ornamentals. A few grasses of ornamental value have been evaluated for salt tolerance for such conditions. The tolerance of edaphic and atmospheric salinity is not the same. Some species that are tolerant of salt spray are not necessarily tolerant of soil salinity, and vice versa. The species in the following list are tolerant of saline soils:

High Salt Tolerance	**Medium Salt Tolerance**
Agropyron pungens	*Bromus inermis*
Bromus unioloides	*Oryza sativa*
Calamagrostis epigejos	*Phalaris arundinacea* var. *picta*
Chloris gayana	*Phragmites australis*
Cynodon dactylon	*Spartina spartinae*
Distichlis spicata	*Sporobolus virginicus*
Puccinellia fasciculata	*Triticum aestivum*
Puccinellia maritima	*Uniola paniculata*
Spartina alterniflora	
Spartina cynosuroides	
Spartina patens	

These species, among others, would be useful to establish on saline soils, where it is extremely difficult to achieve success with any form of ground cover or ornamental plantings. Rhizomatous species of *Bromus, Calamagrostis, Cynodon, Distichlis, Puccinellia,* and related forms of *Scirpus* and perhaps *Typha* are useful for such sites. Stoloniferous types, some of which include *Agrostis stolonifer, Cynodon dactylon, Glyceria maxima,* and *Paspalum dissectum,* are equally useful for ground cover on saline soils.

Certain ornamental grasses have the ability to thrive in wet soil, in mud, or directly in water (Appendix 1, column 13). These water plants are at home in bog and water gardens, in and around natural or other ponds, pools, and lakes, and in or near slow-moving streams. Rice and its purplish green cultivar, along with some variegated forms of reed canary grass, are attractive house-plants grown in water. Plant size and growth habit determine to some extent their usage as water-loving plants. Certain species form compatible combinations with other aquatics in producing contrasts in form, texture, and color. Some forms occur naturally in brackish- and freshwater bogs, marshes, and swamps; others tolerate saltwater marshes. Floating sweetgrass does well in shallow water and along sluggish streams; reedgrass and its variants thrive in wet, shaded sites of the water garden. Variegated cordgrass makes an excellent display in wet sites in the water garden and along canals, ditches, and streams. The cordgrasses (i.e., alkali, big, gulf, and saltmeadow) all have a place in brackish-water, freshwater, and saltwater swamps as ground-cover, soil-building, and erosion-control plants. Common reed, along with cattails, is used for the same purpose; these large, erect forms thrive in marshes, where their reflection on the water is an added attraction. Giant reed and its variegated variety, along with the variegated culti-var of *Spartina pectinata,* make excellent displays in freshwater marshes. Sand and sea couch and bushgrass and its cultivar are all adapted to saltwater marshes.

Many home gardens and other areas requiring landscaping or improvement are in low, wet areas. Such sites can be a real problem unless they are well drained. Adequate draining is not always possible, especially in urban areas. A partial or possible complete solution to the development or improvement of the landscape in low, wet areas is through the use of flowers and ornamentals that are tolerant of wet soils. Certain species are recommended for use as ground cover and naturalizing on wet soils; however, their intended use is not restricted to these categories (Appendix 1, column 6). Some forms are useful in other areas of the garden as accent or specimen plants, in mixed border plantings, and in water gardens. A few species, such as *Oplismenus hirtellus, Oryza sativa,* and *Phalaris arundinacea* var. *variegata,* are useful as houseplants.

Clay and clay loam soils occurring in low-lying areas in moderate-rainfall belts are usually moist or wet. At higher elevations, these soils retain moisture much better and longer than sandy soils. Certain ornamental grasses are adapted to soils of this type. A few such species include *Agrostis stolonifera, Axo-nopus compressus, Distichlis spicata,* and *Stipa splendens.* Some bamboo species are likewise suitable for heavy clay soils with a high water-retention capacity. Such soils usually do not dry out rapidly, thereby aiding plants in escaping drought periods. Ornamental grasses that are suitable for wet soils vary in size and growth habit from small, mat-forming types to large, erect forms, including some bamboo species. Some forms have attractive green or variegated foliage, whereas others are noted for their spectacular flowering panicles, and yet others for their flowers and foliage. Forms with variegated foliage include variants of *Alopecurus pratensis, Arundo donax, Miscanthus sinensis,* and *Spartina pectinata.* Some species with attractive flower heads include *Arundo donax, Miscanthus* species, and *Phragmites australis. Miscanthus* species and their variants exemplify attractive foliage and flowers when used in wet areas. Additional species suitable for wet acid soils are included in Appendix 1, column 6.

The seashore and sand dunes are subject to erosion from water and wind. The constant erosion of beaches is devastating. More land surface is lost each year to the pounding sea than is readily apparent. Ground-cover erosion-control plants are a high priority for this delicate habitat. Seaside sand dunes are considered a unique location requiring grasses to reduce the damage caused by blowing sand and to stabilize moving sand dunes. A combination of low-growing, mat-forming grasses and tall, tufted forms provides the best protection from damage caused by wind erosion and sand dune movement. Grasses that form extensive, impenetrable, tight colonies are ideally suited for this purpose. They serve a dual purpose of erosion control and wildlife protection and food. Among the grasses and grasslike relatives, both large, tufted forms and low-growing mat-forming types are useful in arresting blowing sand, reducing wind damage, and stabilizing sand dunes. Common reed and cattails are examples of tall forms that act somewhat as windbreaks. Rhizomatous species of *Elymus* and *Spartina*, along with *Distichlis spicata*, are valuable for sand stabilization in warm climates. Broad-leaved uniola, *Chasmanthium latifolium*, and sea oats, *Uniola paniculata*, occur naturally along the beaches in temperate zones. Excellent sand-binding, mat-forming grasses include such forms as *Agropyron pungens*, *Ammophila arenaria*, *Ammophila breviligulata*, *Distichlis spicata*, *Sporobolus virginicus*, and *Uniola paniculata*. Additional grasses that are useful for erosion control on seashore sand dunes and saline soils occur in Appendix 1, column 24.

It is usually difficult to maintain a good ground cover in shaded woodland sites. Ornamental grasses suitable for shaded locations vary greatly in form, size, color, growth habit, and shade tolerance. They range in size from minuscule forms that form miniature lawns or meadows to huge, tree-size bamboos commonly found in woods or along wooded borders, usually in wet soils. Species such as *Agropyron canium* and *Brachypodium sylvaticum* afford good ground cover in shaded locations. Certain bamboos exhibit shade tolerance in varying degrees; for example, dwarf species of *Sasa* and *Shibataea* afford good ground cover in partial shade in zones 7 and 8. Some woodland grasses adapted to shade are *Elymus virginicus*, *Hackonechloa macra*, and *Poa chaixii*. These grasses form good ground cover in the shade and require only minimal maintenance. Most ornamental, shade-tolerant grasses perform satisfactorily in partial or light shade, whereas fewer species are tolerant of medium shade, and hardly any will survive in deep shade.

Despite the paucity of shade-tolerant ornamental grasses, some forms do make a significant contribution to the flora in such difficult sites. Their most significant contribution in shaded, naturalized areas is along wooded borders and near buildings, where they receive direct sunlight for only a portion of the day, or when growing in semishade or light shade among other broad-leaved and usually larger ornamentals. Some small forms are useful in underplantings among shrubbery and under high-canopy trees, where they receive filtered light. The shallow root system is an asset to shade-loving grasses, especially those grown in the shade of deep-rooted trees whose roots do not compete with the grass for moisture and nutrients. Shade-tolerant ornamental grasses grown among ornamental shrubs provide an added dimension of color, form, and texture to the garden, unobtainable from any other ornamentals. This certainly is sufficient justification for their use in the formal garden or in any naturalized area or difficult site involving the need for shade-tolerant, attractive ornamentals. No green plant can thrive or survive in the absence of light, although some plants are tolerant of shade, since they occur in shaded sites in their native habitat. Additional grasses adapted to shade are listed in Appendix 1, column 15.

An important desirable attribute required of grasses used in ornamental horticulture includes their cold tolerance (i.e., winter hardiness). Rough estimates of winter hardiness are included as designated plant-hardiness zones in the following plant descriptions. Plant-hardiness zones are included in Appendix 5. Although plant-hardiness zones are not delineated accurately enough for some species, they do serve as a guideline for describing winter hardiness for most species. Winter hardiness of ornamental types should definitely be considered in the choice of grasses for different regions of the country. Topography, elevation, cities and other densely populated areas, and nearness to the sea or large bodies of water all have a significant impact on microclimates. Highly variable microclimates within each plant-hardiness zone are a common occurrence. Plant habitats such as full sun or shade, wet or dry soil, and exposure (i.e., northern or southern) all influence winter survival. Considering all of these variables, it is still prudent to consider the range in plant-hardiness zones for which each species is adapted. Even when this is done, certain plant-protection measures may become necessary on occasion.

USES

Ornamental

One way of describing the uses of ornamental grasses in the garden is to provide examples of species that may be used for specific purposes. The manner and purpose for which these plants are used in the home garden are outlined to some extent in Appendix 1. For example, onion couch, *Arrhenatherum elatius* var. *bulbosum* 'Variegatum,' is used as an accent plant in massed stands in foreground borders.

Houseplants are those that thrive in the home, providing pleasure to the occupants and decorating the rooms. They are grown either for their foliage, their flowers, or both. The majority of house plants are grown for their foliage. They are used as potted specimens, as cut flowers, and in dry floral arrangements, either dyed or in their natural color. Most house plants are more or less permanent acquisitions; however, others, such as certain holiday plants, including potted flowering bulbs, are only of ephemeral value and are maintained only temporarily. Basically, there are four growth forms of plants grown in the home: upright-open, upright-open to spreading, spreading, and mound-forming.

The home environment should be analyzed to ensure success in growing houseplants. The analysis should certainly include those rooms and locations in the home in which plant culture is intended. Four major environmental factors influencing plant growth indoors are light, temperature, humidity, and the growing medium. Plants grown indoors rely on ambient natural light, a combination of artificial and natural light, or artificial light alone. A cozy greenhouse with controlled heat, humidity, and light is the ultimate solution to the space problem of growing plants indoors. Much valuable information can be obtained by perusing the extensive literature available on houseplants and their culture. Much good information about house plants and their identities and cultural requirements is contained in home magazines, the garden section of large metropolitan newspapers, and scientific literature. Officers of the Federal Extension Service are also a valuable source of information. Houseplants may grow and be enjoyed in many locations within the home—in bedrooms, hallways, living rooms, porches, atriums, basements, and sun rooms. Any space is adequate that meets the specific requirements of the plants to be grown. Placing plants near windows is usually ideal. Many new homes have windows built especially for growing plants. Miniature greenhouse windows are available that permit better control of humidity, heat, and light and allow small ornamentals, including grasses, to be grown advantageously. Enclosed porches and sun rooms are especially good locations for houseplants. Solar-heated sun rooms are becoming increasingly popular as an ideal area for houseplants. The Indoor Light Gardening Society of America is devoted to followers of artificial-light gardening indoors. Some home magazines advertise homemade, do-it-yourself planters and lamps for growing plants indoors. These methods are exceedingly successful for growing certain houseplants, for carrying others over winter, and for providing seeding and propagating beds. This technique of house gardening is rapidly increasing among home owners, particularly in cold climates.

Selecting the kinds of house plants that are best suited for your own home environment usually ensures success. Each different type of dwelling provides a different environment. The optimal environment necessary to achieve maximum success with house plants requires a properly equipped conservatory; an indoor planter or growth chamber with adequate controls for artificial light, temperature, humidity, and other environmental factors; or terrariums, in which most growth requirements can be maintained. The average home usually does not have such elaborate facilities.

The essential requirements of houseplants include adequate light, temperature, moisture, and humidity, in that order. Some home gardeners depend entirely upon natural light in which to grow houseplants, others use a combination of artificial and natural light, while yet others use artificial light only. Each form of lighting has advantages and disadvantages. The light requirements of house plants vary among species; some forms require light of longer duration than others, while other forms require light of high, medium, or low intensity. The use of artificial light alone is a relatively new and easy method of house-plant propagation and maintenance. Space of any kind may be used, even the basement, which often receives no natural light.

Ornamental grasses and grasslike plants of variable growth habit and form may be grown successfully in artificial light. Examples of upright-open forms include *Cymbopogon* species, *Lagurus ovatus* and *Oryza sativa;* upright-open to spreading grasses include *Agrostis nebulosa, Arrhenatherum elatius* var. *bulbosum, Phalaris arundinacea* var. *variegata;* spreading forms include *Stenotaphrum secundatum* 'Variegatum'; mound-forming types include *Festuca ovina* var. *glauca* and *Molinia caerulea* and cultivars. Not all of these examples are small, compact species, but plants of this stature best lend themselves to this form of culture.

Planters equipped with artificial light are particularly useful for starting flowering bedding plants or vegetables for the vegetable garden and for propagating other ornamentals, such as ornamental grasses and grasslike plants. Various types of planters, some homemade, are used, together with specially designed, fluorescent growing lamps which, with the use of a timer, can automatically supply any photoperiod required. The same type of planter is also very useful in maintaining mature house plants through difficult periods, particularly during the dark winter months. These planters are often used to rejuvenate house plants that have been living in areas with poor light. Planters with artificial lighting are ideal for the maintenance of garden plants that have been brought indoors for overwintering. Most of the foliage of grasses, grasslike plants, and sedges is usually removed before they are brought indoors for winter maintenance. The growth rate of these plants is drastically reduced after partial defoliation, resulting in initially lowered requirements of light, water, and fertilizer. Such plants in pots placed on the floor beneath a planter can take full advantage of light and heat in a basement equipped with a planter with artificial light. A rectangular wood planter (2 ft/0.6 m × 8 ft/2.4 m) lined with plastic, whose bottom is suspended about 2 ft/0.6 m above the floor and is supplied with one 4 ft/1.3 m fluorescent growth bulb above the planter, will provide ample space for plant propagation by seeding, cuttings, or plant division and ample light for the maintenance of a limited number of mature plants placed on the floor immediately surrounding and below the planter. The light that extends beyond the planter and its contents is sufficient to overwinter many other plants in excellent condition. Taking advantage of the light, space, and heat in this manner should be considered an added bonus. The author has been successful with a planter of this type with a 12-hour light period per 24-hour day. Flowering plants normally require 12 to 16 hours of light per day, and foliage plants require only 4 to 6 hours.

Growing house plants under artificial light has numerous advantages. Plants grown under artificial light usually grow more symmetrically, and flowering plants usually produce more flowers than those grown in other spaces in the home. Furthermore, flowering plants can be induced to flower as desired by controlling the normal photoperiodic requirements, rather than depending upon slower seasonal changes of natural day length. The investment of a planter and a growth lamp will usually pay big dividends for the home gardener who admires plants throughout the year.

Certain ornamental grasses recommended as house plants have been grouped by light, temperature, humidity, and moisture requirements. Species requiring high light intensity (5,000–8,000 footcandles per day) include *Cymbopogon citratus* and *Cymbopogon nardus,* medium intensity (1,000–4,000 footcandles per day) *Agrostis nebulosa,* and low intensity (100–500 footcandles per day) *Arrhenatherum elatius* var. *bulbosum, Arrhenatherum elatius* var. *bulbosum* 'Variegatum,' *Phalaris arundinacea* and cultivars, *Phalaris arundinacea* var. *picta,* and *Phalaris arundinacea* var. *variegata.* Species requiring cool temperatures (average 60°F/6°C) include *Arrhenatherum elatius* var. *bulbosum* and *Arrhenatherum elatius* var. *bulbosum* 'Variegatum'; those requiring warm temperatures (average 75°F/24°C) include *Cymbopogon citratus* and *Cymbopogon nardus,* and those requiring hot temperatures (average 80°F/27°C) include *Lagurus ovatus.* One species, *Stenotaphrum secundatum,* and its cultivar Variegatum require high humidity (above 75%). The following species prefer wet soil and require frequent watering: *Arrhenatherum elatius* var. *bulbosum, Arrhenatherum elatius* var. *bulbosum* 'Variegatum,' *Oryza sativa* and its cultivar, *Phalaris arundinacea* and cultivars, and *Phalaris arundinacea* var. *variegata. Cymbopogon citratus, Cymbopogon nardus,* and *Miscanthus sacchariflorus* 'Dwarf' prefer dry soil.

Some house plants require cool night temperatures. Most ornamental grasses and grasslike plants will withstand minimum temperatures of 50 to 60°F/10 to 16°C without serious damage. This temperature range coincides fairly well with night temperatures maintained in most homes. Day temperatures will usually range 10° to 15°F higher during the winter months. Day temperatures will be higher on bright, sunny days than on cloudy, dark days during the winter. Plants of tropical or subtropical origin may not thrive well at these temperatures. Perhaps the best way of testing survival is by trial and error. Rice, *Oryza sativa,* for example, thrives in an extraordinarily wide range of temperatures, from high temperatures at low elevations in the tropics, to low temperatures at high elevations in temperate regions.

The ambient air in most homes is too dry for most house plants. This is especially true in homes that are heated by forced-air systems, even those that are equipped with a humidifier. One commonly used method of compensating for the lack of adequate humidity is to mist potted plants at frequent intervals. Small window greenhouses are useful in maintaining adequate humidity, as it can be controlled much easier in these small enclosures. Another method of increasing ambient humidity is that of growing plants in pots or planters in which watering is done from below. Aquatic and semiaquatic house plants, such as sedges and rice, easily lend themselves to such a culture. Trailing plants grown in hanging baskets require frequent watering and spraying for optimum growth.

The moisture requirements of ornamental grasses, similar to those of other house plants, are variable. Some forms thrive in dry soil and low humidity; others require watering at regular intervals to keep the soil moist or wet. Species of *Arrhenatherum* and *Phalaris,* among others, require frequent watering to prevent the containers from drying out. Species of *Cymbopogon,* by contrast, thrive in relatively dry soil and low humidity. Perhaps the best way of ascertaining the water requirements of house plants is through trial and error. House plants should be watered according to their need rather than on a fixed schedule. The time to water potted plants is when the soil is dry to the touch, and then watering should be sufficient to have it run out of the drainage hole. The bottom of some pots is designed to hold a small amount of excess water. The excess water should be drained from such pots within a very short time following watering, as the roots of most plants will not stand wet feet. All containers should have a drainage hole in the bottom, regardless of the type used. Any excess water left remaining on the surface following watering should also be drained off. Some house plants, such as ribbongrass, *Phalaris arundinacea* var. *picta,* and rice will thrive when grown directly in water. Growing certain house plants in water is accomplished by establishing them in ordinary garden soil. They usually require a soil medium that supports them by simultaneously providing the necessary moisture, nutrient, and oxygen requirements for optimum growth.

It is preferable to sterilize all soil and sand used for potted plants. This may be accomplished by baking the soil in an oven at 200°F/93°C for one hour. Most hardware stores, nurseries, garden shops, and some department stores have treated soil or soil-based mixtures for growing potted house plants. One soil mixture that has been found to be satisfactory for most house plants and is fairly universally used includes two parts peat moss and one part sand. The peat moss provides better water and nutrient retention, and the sand aids in drainage and aeration. Many other soil-based mixtures are available that may be used for specific needs. Most house plants should be repotted in clean, sterile containers, either annually or when the plants become potbound. Repotting potbound plants does not necessarily involve placing the plants in larger containers, as some plants thrive in a potbound condition. Repotting is usually best done in late spring or summer, when the newly potted plants may be placed outside to become readjusted during the summer season. Newly potted plants must be watered carefully and kept in the shade until they adjust. Foliage and roots may be pruned during the repotting operation.

Potted house plants normally require fertilizing less frequently than those grown outside, as their growth rate is usually slower and they do not attain the size of plants grown outdoors. Numerous commercial fertilizers are available that may be applied in either a solid or a liquid form; liquids are the most popular and commonly used. Solid fertilizer mixtures to which water is added according to directions are also popular, and they are easy to use. Perhaps more popular are concentrated liquid formulations that may be used in water solution according to directions. Fertilizers may be applied monthly during active growth. Preferably, a more dilute solution may be used weekly or fortnightly. Fertilizer mixtures high in nitrogen usually produce abundant vegetative growth, which is not very conducive to flowering. Fertilizer mixtures high in nitrogen content are most useful for larger house plants grown primarily for their foliage. Fertilizer mixtures high in phosphorus and potash are recommended for maximum flower production. One mixture that usually produces optimum growth and maximum flower production consists of 7-7-20 fertilizer, which is medium in nitrogen and phosphorus and high in potash. As with watering, the proper fertilizer and its timely application for specific house plants can best be discovered by experience. No two species are necessarily alike in their fertilizer and water requirements.

Natural plant pests, including diseases and insects, are usually a problem of lower magnitude on potted house plants grown indoors than on those grown outside in the garden. Indoor potted plants are usually isolated from their natural pests, whereas those grown outdoors are exposed to such pests. Plant pests are usually introduced on new plants. If possible, it is prudent to keep newly acquired plants isolated from established house plants until they are determined to be healthy and free of pests. Sanitation methods are the best insurance against the presence and damage that plant pests may cause. Diseased plants and those heavily infested with insects should be removed and destroyed immediately. Sucking insects are the most common insects pests of houseplants; they include aphids, mealybugs, red spiders, scale, and white fly. Nursery personnel, master gardeners, and Federal Extension Service agents are all helpful with advice and recommendations concerning houseplant problems, particularly those concerning plant pests.

Other concerns regarding maintenance of houseplants in a healthy and attractive state include plants becoming unmanageable by becoming too large and untidy or potbound, large diurnal changes in temperature, uneven exposure to natural or artificial light, foliage plants becoming leggy or lanky, or flowering plants that fail to flower. These problems are usually remedied with careful attention and care. Fortunately, ornamental grasses used as house plants can be trimmed back rather radically without the plants sustaining permanent injury; likewise, root trimming, when necessary, does not seriously damage the plants. Ornamental grasses that become unattractive and too large may be cut back, divided, or replaced by smaller specimens. Potbound plants may be divided or replanted in larger pots. Drastic temperature changes may result in foliage discoloration and, eventually, death of the plant. Foliage discoloration, particularly yellowing, usually results from insufficient natural light. This may be overcome by periodically changing the location of the plants within the house to sites that receive more natural light. Plants remaining in one position too long near an opening become asymmetrical and unattractive, as do plants grown under artificial light. This is easily overcome by rotating the plants at intervals or by placing them in different locations relative to the light source.

Foliage plants that become lanky, unattractive, or too large may result from receiving either too much fertilizer or the wrong kinds of nutrients. Similarly, failure of flowering species to flower may be caused by incorrect lighting and fertilizers. Foliage of house plants may require periodic cleaning to keep them attractive and free of dust. Grasses and other narrow-leaved plants may be syringed by being held over the bathtub or sink. Holding the pots on their sides during this operation prevents the danger of making the soil too wet. Houseplants should be syringed only on bright, sunny days so that they will dry quickly. Plants should not be left overnight with wet or soaking leaves, as this invites attack by leaf fungi.

The usual concept of the use of grasses in beautifying the garden is limited to their use in the lawn. This concept is gradually changing, however. Ornamental horticulturists, nursery personnel, and florists have been at the forefront in bringing the value and usefulness of ornamental grasses before the public. Ornamental grasses found in florist shops, in particular, but also in other outlets throughout the United States, have aided in popularizing their use in beautifying the landscape. Just as we have acquired ornamental grasses from Europe through introduction in the past, we are now benefiting by the impact that European gardeners, florists, and others have had on their American counterparts. Landscape architects, ornamental horticulturists, and nursery workers are knowledgeable in the use and value of ornamental grasses in supplementing other ornamentals in garden and landscape beautification. They are increasingly involved by assisting public and private park planners and those whose responsibility is that of landscaping public buildings, canals, and streets. The results of these activities are reflected in increased awareness, appreciation, and use of ornamental grasses in the home garden.

The lawn, which usually occupies the largest area of the garden, may be surrounded by border plantings and divided in various ways by flower beds. The design of the lawn can vary, depending on its overall size and shape. The presence of trees, and their size, kind, shape, location, and number may be a deciding factor in the location and extent of the lawn. Shade created by trees, shrubbery, buildings, or other objects during various intervals and intensity during daylight hours has a detrimental effect on the establishment, growth, and maintenance of lawn grasses. Columnar trees often used in landscape plantings do not cast a shadow over as large an area as do large trees with broad, spreading crowns, such as maples and oaks. Large shrubbery in border plantings, especially when used in abundance, also influences lawn grass development through the effect of shading, as does the presence of large, tall buildings. The detrimental effects of shade on the development of lawn grass must be considered in planning the lawn. The problem of attempting to establish and maintain lawns in shaded areas cannot be overemphasized.

Many lawn grasses are easily established in shaded sites, but difficulty is encountered in their maintenance for sustained periods. The lack of success with ordinary lawn grasses in shaded locations is overcome in part by the use of shade-tolerant types. The success of shade-tolerant lawn grasses depends upon the density and duration of shade. Shade-tolerant lawn grasses are quite easily established; however, maintaining them over sustained periods is usually a problem. Instead of attempting to grow shade-tolerant lawn grasses in shade, with limited success, gardeners might consider some other shade-tolerant grasslike plants as substitute lawns. Some grasslike plants thrive in light to medium dappled shade. Moreover, their maintenance requires less time and labor than that needed for lawn grasses. They usually do not require mowing, but only light trimming and tidying around the edges once or twice each growing season.

Most shade-loving grasses used in wooded sites are usually taller than regular lawn grasses; they do not withstand heavy traffic as do lawn grasses. This presents no problem, however, as wooded areas are usually not subjected to heavy traffic. The use of winding pathways through wooded areas permits better access to all of the shade-loving plants, including grasses, thus enhancing their effectiveness. Trees require tremendous amounts of water, and their deep roots dry out the soil, despite the fact that they are not in direct competition with the shallow-rooted grasses and ground-cover plants. Woodland soils tend to be acid and dry, particularly under coniferous trees. Another advantage of using woodland grasses and their close relatives as ground cover and substitute lawns in shaded sites is that some of them are usually quite tolerant of drought and soil acidity. Any grasses or other ground-cover plants grown under trees have to compete with them for soil fertility, moisture, and sunlight. There is considerable variation among shade-loving grasses and their close relatives in tolerance of acid soils, drought, shade, and ground-covering ability. Some forms are used primarily as ground cover on acid soils in deep shade, whereas other, variegated types are grown in light shade for their foliage and flower color. An ideal grass for ground cover or a lawn substitute in wooded areas is tolerant of acid soil, drought, and shade. Unfortunately, few grasses meet these requirements.

Alpine hairgrass, *Deschampsia alpina,* a small, tufted grass about 16 in./4 dm high with dark green, fine-textured foliage and purplish panicles, is ideal for alpine miniature shaded meadows or lawns. Other hardy species suitable for ground cover or as a lawn substitute in open woodland and naturalized areas with wet poorly drained soils include *Deschampsia caespitosa* and *Deschampsia flexuosa.* Although these graceful species are noted for their plant form, dark green foliage, and early, spectacular flowers, they are also valuable as substitute lawn grasses where ordinary lawn grasses fail and for specimen plantings in shaded locations. The range in height of these species is 10–48 in./0.3–1.2 m, with *Deschampsia flexuosa* being the smallest. Additional grasses suitable for shaded sites are included in Appendix 1, column 15.

Accent and specimen plants are used to emphasize and enhance other ornamentals in the garden by adding additional variety in texture and color to the landscape. Accent plants are used advantageously in several situations, including full sun or shaded locations that may vary in density of shade; on dry, steep slopes or mounds; in low wet locations; on soils varying in fertility, moisture content, pH, texture, and salinity; near or in ponds, pools, lakes, and streams. Specimen plants are used likewise in a similar manner for the same purposes. Accent plantings may be in the form of small clumps of small, low-growing plants, such as the variegated form of bulbous oatgrass planted in the front of foreground borders where the plants are shaded by surrounding larger plants. Both the green and variegated forms of bulbous oatgrass are useful in appropriate shaded locations in rock and water gardens, provided they are not overcome by competition for light and moisture by larger ornamentals. These two perennials are beneficial in these situations because they are small and low growing, shade tolerant, semievergreen, and adapted to a wide range of soils, and they provide a compact ground cover. They are grown primarily for their foliage, as their flowers are small and inconspicuous.

Accent plants are used in border plantings, on berms, and on the lawn. They are used in various combinations with other ornamentals to augment, emphasize, and complement them. They are not necessarily the center of attraction, as are specimen plants. An outstanding example is a planting of gardener's garters surrounding a clumped specimen of pampas grass in the lawn, in which the variegated foliage of low-growing gardener's garters complements the green foliage of pampas grass, in addition to that of the lawn. Other combinations are available to demonstrate the use and value of accent plants. Other species used as accent plants are included in Appendix 1, column 1.

A single plant or plant clump representative of the species or cultivar is known as a specimen plant. A specimen plant may be characterized as having some attractive, unique, and desirable attribute, such as foliage, stem, or inflorescence color, or a plant form that distinguishes the species or cultivar. Specimen plants are ordinarily used in conspicuous places in the garden or lawn to demonstrate their unique ornamental value; they are generally planted singly or together in groups. One of the primary uses for specimen plants is their visual appeal and impact. Specimen plants are useful in pebble, rock, or water gardens; in border plantings, particularly foreground borders; or in movable pots or tubs. They lend form, color, and attractiveness to the landscape, and they deserve special attention.

The most spectacular specimen plant, pampas grass, *Cortaderia selloana,* and its cultivars offer a spectacular sight anywhere they are placed in the landscape; pampas grass is often planted on the edge of the lawn in background borders or on the lawn itself, forming an island, usually surrounded by accent plants. The large, flowering, feathery, colorful plumes, borne high above most border plants, make a commanding display. Clumps of plumegrass, *Erianthus ravennae,* provide a similar effect, but perhaps not quite as striking. Smaller forms, such as *Miscanthus sinensis* var. *gracillimus,* with reddish, spreading panicles and dark green foliage, provide a pleasing effect as group specimens near wooded borders or in background borders, among shrubbery, or in water gardens, along with smaller aquatics. Yet smaller tufted forms with bluish green or silvery blue foliage, such as *Poa bulbosa* and *Festuca ovina* var. *glauca,* respectively, are effective as edging accent plants in foreground borders in front of larger plants with green foliage, providing a contrast in plant color and form. Similarly, both are effective as specimens in pebble and rock gardens. Other tufted perennials uniquely suited as specimen plants include small Japanese bloodgrass, *Imperata cylindrica* 'Rubra,' with shiny, reddish foliage, and that of black pampas grass, *Cortaderia richardii,* a tall specimen with blackish green foliage. Either of these specimens will draw the attention of the most casual observer.

Some species worthy as specimens are noted for their foliage, whereas others are unique for their flowering plumes. Yet others, such as zebragrass, *Miscanthus sinensis* var. *zebrinus,* provide a spectacular show of flowers and foliage. Many forms of *Miscanthus* species are worthy as specimens; most of them blossom in late summer or early fall, affording color and interest during a period in which a paucity of plants are flowering in the garden. Furthermore, their flowering period is rather long, their plumes remaining intact into winter, along with changing foliage color, which provides good autumnal color. Additional species useful as specimens are included in Appendix 1, column 2.

Garden border plantings are usually a combination of flowering plants and shrubs of various forms, sizes, and colors. Both broad-leaved dicotyledonous and narrow-leaved monocotyledonous plants are used in various combinations, varying in longevity from short-lived annuals to perennials capable of sustained growth for many years. Ornamental grasses and grasslike plants used in border plantings are also variable in plant form, size, color, and growth habit. Grasses grown among flowering plants and shrubs in beds and borders add color, form, and texture to the landscape. Interplanting and underplanting grasses in flower borders add diversity to the borders and usually result in a more attractive garden. The lawn may be partially or completely surrounded by flower beds and borders; some garden designs may consist of a series of beds. Ornamental grasses for use in garden borders range in size from a few inches to more than 5 ft/1.5 m high. For convenience, those forms up to 20 in./5 dm high are recommended for foreground borders, whether planted in a single border or in a series of two or more parallel borders. Similarly, plants 21–60 in./0.5–1.5 m high are considered for use in middleground borders, while those taller than 5 ft/1.5 m are included in background border plantings. Examples include big quaking grass, *Briza maxima* (15–20 in./4–5 dm high) for foreground borders, broad-leaved uniola, *Chasmanthium latifolium* (3–5 ft/0.9–1.5 m high) for middleground, and plumegrass, *Erianthus ravennae* (6–12 ft/1.8–3.7 m high) for background borders. Strong rhizomatous and stoloniferous grasses are undesirable and are not recommended for borders because of their invasiveness.

Tufted grasses neither spread nor create undue competition to surrounding plants. Tufted perennials, which are noted for their attractive foliage, whether it be unusual or variegated in color or of unusual plant form and foliage texture, such as pampas grass, *Cortaderia selloana,* and weeping lovegrass, *Eragrostis cur-*

vula, are useful in border plantings. Ornamental grasses are established singly, or in small groups as accent or specimen plants in borders, or perhaps underplanted in small, massed stands as additional ground cover. The grasses are usually interplanted among shrubs and other flowering plants. Those with unusual foliage color, such as bluish green, reddish green, greenish yellow, or yellowish golden, complement and act as a foil for surrounding ornamentals with green or dark green foliage. Representative of tufted grasses with these unusual foliage colors are *Festuca ovina* var. *glauca, Briza maxima* var. *rubra, Milium effusum,* and *Alopecurus pratensis* 'Aureus,' respectively. Forms with bright, multicolored foliage provide additional contrast in color when planted among shrubbery and flowers. Tufted forms with multicolored or variegated foliage useful in borders include *Arundo donax* var. *versicolor, Holcus lanatus* 'Variegatus,' and *Miscanthus sinensis* var. *zebrinus.*

Colorful flowering plumes and flower heads are an additional attraction provided by some forms used as border plants. A wide range in inflorescence form and color exists among tufted grasses suitable for border plantings. Examples of some of these, along with their inflorescence color, include *Anthoxanthum odoratum* (bronze-green), *Alopecurus pratensis* (purplish), *Eragrostis spectabilis* (reddish purple), *Koeleria cristata* (silvery white), *Milium effusum* 'Aureum' (yellowish), and *Cortaderia selloana* 'Violacea' (violet). Yet other tufted forms with attractive foliage and flowers may be employed advantageously in border plantings. Outstanding among these are *Chasmanthium latifolium, Cortaderia richardii, Cortaderia selloana* and cultivars, variegated cultivars of *Miscanthus sacchariflorus, Miscanthus sinensis* varieties *gracillimus, variegatus,* and *zebrinus, Pennisetum alopecuroides* and cultivars, and *Pennisetum setaceum* and cultivars. There is a wide choice in foliage and flower color among tufted grasses suitable for borders. These grasses could be used effectively as a foil for other ornamentals to blend colors with them or to produce drastic contrasts in color. Among small, tufted species suitable for foreground borders are *Poa colensoi,* with bluish green foliage; *Milium effusum* 'Aureum,' with greenish yellow foliage and yellowish flowering panicles; and variegated cultivars of *Dactylis glomerata* and *Holcus lanatus.* Some forms with colorful flowers include *Aristida wrightii* with purplish flowers, and *Lamarckia aurea,* with greenish yellow panicles. Similarly, grasses that grow 21–60 in / 0.5–1.5 m high are useful in middleground borders. Among these are *Elymus canadensis,* with glaucous foliage, and *Panicum virgatum* 'Rubrum' with reddish green foliage. Those with colorful flower heads or seedheads include *Cenchrus ciliaris,* with light purplish flowers, *Melica altissima* 'Atropurpurea,' with deep purple flowers, and *Chasmanthium latifolium,* with bronze seedheads. Some grasses taller than 5 ft / 1.5 m high for background borders include *Cortaderia richardii,* with blackish green foliage, *Miscanthus sinensis* 'Silberfeder,' with metallic, bluish green foliage, and *Arundo donax* var. *versicolor,* with variegated foliage. Two cultivars of *Cortaderia selloana,* 'Rosea' and 'Violacea,' have large pinkish and purplish flowering plumes, respectively.

Flowering ornamental grasses interplanted with other ornamentals in borders provide additional color, form, and texture, which usually results in interesting and attractive borders. Some gardeners prefer a harmony of color when using a large proportion of grasses in relation to other ornamentals in border plantings; others may settle for fewer grasses in colors that contrast with surrounding plants. The plant forms and colors of foliage and flowers are matters of choice. The prudent use of ornamental grasses provides additional interest and beauty to garden borders. Many additional species are adaptable for use in border plantings (see Appendix 1, column 7).

The use of small edging grasses is an integral part of foreground border plantings; larger forms are commonly used in other areas around the periphery of the garden. Small forms are used as edging plants in foreground borders, primarily to provide additional color, as a foil for the lawn and other larger ornamentals, and as ground cover. An outstanding example of a low-growing, variegated grass suitable for edging in foreground borders is onion couch, *Arrhenatherum elatius* var. *bulbosum* 'Variegatum.' This small cormose, hardy, semievergreen perennial adapted to zones 5–9 grows well in shade during the cool weather of spring and fall. It spreads very slowly and is not considered invasive; therefore, it is useful in foreground borders; its bright variegated foliage provides a perfect contrast for the adjacent lawn and for other large, green-leaved plants. Another example is that of striped St. Augustine grass, *Stenotaphrum secundatum* 'Variegatum.' This small, semievergreen, sod-forming species is adapted to zones 9 and 10; it does not perenniate in colder regions. Although it is stoloniferous and invasive, its growth rate is drastically reduced in colder climates, where it acts as a horticultural annual. For this reason, it is admirably suited as a foreground edging plant in zones 5, 6, and 7. Other species are also suitable for use as edging plants (Appendix 1, column 4). Edging plants are usually established in clumps, groups, or massed stands in small areas. Group plantings consist of a clump of plants grown together; the clump may be quite variable in size and shape. Many ornamentals are best exhibited when grown in clumps or groups, usually among other flowering plants in borders. A few of these include species of *Avena, Briza, Calamagrostis, Chloris,* and *Dactylis.* Massed plantings are usually pure stands of a single species established over a limited or extended area.

Most home gardens are designed to minimize the effects of soil erosion. Despite these precautionary measures, serious erosion may occur on occasion in the most well-designed garden. Erosion-control grasses in ornamental horticulture are usually used as ground cover in naturalized areas surrounding the garden, along streams, and on steep slopes or inaccessible sites that are subject to erosion. Both tufted and mat-forming species are used for erosion control; the latter are most commonly used. Some species that are useful primarily for erosion control are of more ornamental value than others. Species recommended for erosion control in the home garden, in naturalized areas, along highway banks, and in seashore plantings and other sites are included in Appendix 1, column 24. The fact that some erosion-control plants are of ornamental value is an added benefit.

Many home gardens or yards have variable amounts of shade in which shade-tolerant ornamentals are required. Most shade-tolerant species included in this work are either small or medium in size. They include both annuals, such as wild chess, and perennials, such as wood bluegrass. Bulbous, cespitose, rhizomatous, and stoloniferous forms are included; examples of each type are (bulbous) bulbous oatgrass, (cespitose) slender brome and orchardgrass, (rhizomatous) broad-leaved uniola and bushgrass, and (stoloniferous) striped St. Augustine grass. All variegated grasses prefer shaded sites, they are useful in dark, shaded nooks of the garden.

Shade-tolerant ornamental grasses play a major role in landscape improvement. They are useful in understory plantings of shrubbery, in open and closed woodland, in sites with partial or dappled shade, and in the shade of buildings, bridges, and other structures. Shade-tolerant forms are used as lawn substitutes (Appendix 1, column 14). Some shade-tolerant species that are useful as lawn substitutes include *Festuca rubra* var. *heterophylla, Hakonechloa macra* and cultivars, *Melica altissima* 'Atropurpurea,' and *Melica uniflora* and cultivars. Ornamental grasses vary in their shade tolerance; some are tolerant of deep shade, others of partial or dappled shade, and yet others of light shade. Full sunlight usually blisters the leaves of variegated forms; consequently, these are recommended for shaded locations. There are many niches in the garden in which shade-tolerant grasses are suitable.

Some tall, tufted grasses with relatively shallow root systems are more drought tolerant than rhizomatous types with more extensively invasive root systems. Job's tears, *Coix lacryma-jobi,* a warm-season, tufted, deciduous, annual or very weak perennial, requires moist or wet soil in light shade or full sun for maximum growth, in contrast to deertongue, *Panicum clandestinum,* a hardy, rhizomatous, semievergreen perennial requiring less moisture, while thriving in deep shade to full sun. These same two species provide excellent contrasts in shade tolerance and ground-covering ability. Job's tears, a tall-growing form, tolerates only light shade and provides no effective ground cover and little weed competition, in contrast to deertongue, which thrives equally well in deep shade to full sun, forming an impenetrable ground cover and providing excellent weed competition. A species such as deertongue competes with weeds in two ways: (1) by its rhizomatous invasive roots and (2) by the dense shade provided by its impenetrable ground cover. Another contrast in shade tolerance and ground-covering capacity is that between the hardy, small, mat-forming, low-growing cultivar Variegatum of bulbous oatgrass, *Arrhenatherum elatius* var. *bulbosum,* and large, tufted, warm-season, upright-open, variegated palmgrass, *Setaria palmifolia* f. *variegata.* The former does best in light shade, whereas the latter prefers deep shade when grown outside; both species require moist or wet soils. Variegated palmgrass, on the other hand, requires light of high intensity when grown indoors; it does not form an extensive, tight ground cover as does bulbous oatgrass.

A tall, tufted, warm-season perennial, *Pennisetum macrostachyum,* is adapted to open woodland, as is giant fescue, *Festuca gigantea.* Additional shade-loving tall forms (i.e., 2–6 ft/0.6–2.0 m high) include stoloniferous creeping bluestem, *Andropogon stolonifera,* and three rhizomatous grasses: bluejoint, *Calamagrostis canadensis,* broad-leaved uniola, *Chasmanthium latifolium,* and bushgrass, *Calamagrostis epigejos.* Other forms varying from 1–3 ft/3–9 dm high include *Deschampsia caespitosa* var. *parviflora*; bearded couch, *Agropyron caninum*; blue Junegrass, *Koeleria cristata*; milletgrass, *Milium effusum*; purple melic, *Melica altissima* 'Atropurpurea'; ribbongrass, *Phalaris arundinacea* var. *picta*; and smooth brome, *Bromus inermis,* all of which are tufted, except ribbongrass, which is weakly rhizomatous. Additional smaller species only about 1 ft/3 dm high include alpine hairgrass, *Deschampsia alpina*; blue fescue, *Festuca ovina* var. *glauca*; shade fescue, *Festuca rubra* var. *heterophylla*; Virginia wild rye, *Elymus virginicus*; and onion couch, *Arrhenatherum elatius* var. *bulbosum* 'Variegatum.' These shade-loving species are useful as specimen plantings in shaded locations around the periphery and in the garden; they are most spectacular when used in large, showy clumps. The smaller types do equally well in shaded areas of rock gardens. The variegated forms of these and other species are of particular value when used in the shade.

Grasses used in shaded sites should be chosen for their size, foliage color, and flower color. Grasses of the correct size are required to keep all the landscape plantings to scale; they also provide a texture that is emphasized when used with broad-leaved ornamentals. Grasses used in the shade should have bright, colorful foliage and startling, colorful flowers to be conspicuous. Their bright flowers, and particularly their bright variegated foliage, add color and diversity to the drabness and darkness commonly found under trees.

Shaded areas of the garden may include portions that are shaded only part of the day by tall, woody shrubs in border plantings, or the periphery, which may be shaded by adjacent buildings and trees. Shade of different intensity from adjacent buildings or wooded areas may be common in rock and water gardens. These are only some of the possibilities for shaded areas of the garden and landscape. Wooded areas may be wet, moist, or dry, requiring different grasses for each of these conditions. A stream, pool, lake, or pond may comprise part of the garden; water is usually associated with large shrubs and trees that provide shade.

Certain shade-loving grasses are needed to enhance the landscape for all the conditions that may be present in the garden. Some small types are needed in peripheral foreground border plantings that have colorful flowers and particularly colorful foliage comprised of colors other than the usual green, such as bluish green, bronze, golden, and particularly vividly variegated forms. Larger plants are useful in peripheral middleground borders, keeping in mind the scale of the entire landscape. Plants of 5 ft/1.5 m or more in height are useful in background borders adjacent to wooded areas; variegated types and those with any colorful foliage other than ordinary green are most conspicuous. Shade-tolerant substitute lawn grasses requiring minimum maintenance are needed for open woodland. Deep shade along streams requires water-loving, shade-tolerant species.

Shade-tolerant grasses are needed for many possible conditions in shaded gardens. Fortunately, a considerable choice of ornamental grasses is available for the specific conditions for almost any garden. Some of the shade-loving grasses are too large and coarse for use in the more formal portion of the garden; others are too invasive; yet others may become a nuisance because of their prolific reseeding ability. Nevertheless, with a little assistance from the local nursery or landscape artist, the problems of which grass to use and how to use it can be easily solved.

Certain shade-loving ornamental grasses are adapted for use in shaded areas of the garden proper and in adjacent areas that are less formal, such as miniature meadows, naturalized sites along streams, and other peripheral locations. They are useful from an aesthetic and a utilitarian viewpoint. Their utilitarian value lies in their use as substitute lawns in areas where conventional lawn grasses fail, as miniature meadows, as ground cover and erosion control on steep slopes, and a source of bird food and wildlife cover in naturalized areas. Their ornamental value is demonstrated by their luxuriant, usually dark green foliage, and beautiful flowering plumes. Additional use of ornamentals in formal areas of the garden include their use as bedding plants in border plantings, as windbreaks and screens of various heights, and particularly as specimen plantings in the lawn, or bog, rock, and water gardens. Small types are ideal in specimen plantings in foreground borders in the shade of larger plants, including broad-leaved, woody ornamentals. Grasses of intermediate size are likewise useful in the same manner in middleground borders, as are taller forms for background borders. Additional tufted grasses for use in the shade on drier soils include *Brachypodium sylvaticum, Festuca rubra* var. *heterophylla, Hystrix patula, Melica altissima, Milium effusum,* and *Poa nemoralis. Brachypodium sylvaticum* is a compactly tufted perennial with medium green foliage that is medium in texture. Its flower heads are light purplish, spikelike racemes; the plants average 1–3 ft/3–9 dm high. The densely tufted perennial, *Festuca rubra* var. *heterophylla,* which is 16–40 in./0.4–1.0 m high, forms a dense ground cover when left unattended. It is an excellent grass for ground cover in naturalized shaded sites and as a substitute lawn. Bottlebrush grass, *Hystrix patula,* with medium green, medium-textured foliage, is an upright-narrow perennial with unique flowers. The inflorescence is a sparse, erect, light green spike that resembles a brush used to clean bottles—hence, the vernacular name. It has a long flowering period, from July through October. Siberian melic, *Melica altissima,* a tufted perennial, 2.5–3.0 ft/8–9 dm high, with medium to dark green, fine-textured foliage, has a long flowering period, from June through August. The flower heads are tawny to purple, spikelike panicles. Milletgrass, *Milium effusum,* with light, shiny green, medium-textured foliage, is 18–36 in./5–9 dm high with a light green erect to nodding panicle. Wood bluegrass, *Poa nemoralis,* is a rather small, hardy perennial 1–2 ft/3–6 dm high, with medium green, fine-textured foliage; the inflorescence is a lax, light green erect to nodding panicle. Additional shade-tolerant species are listed in Appendix 1, column 15.

Some ornamental grasses are noted primarily for their attractive, colorful flowers (Appendix 1, column 17), others for their attractive foliage (Appendix 1, column 20), and yet others for their flowers and foliage (Appendix 1, column 21). Considerable variation exists among species in inflorescence shape, size, and color. The shape of inflorescences varies from dense spikes to open or loosely branched panicles with several intermediate forms. Flower heads of *Agropyron canium* consist of rather dense spikes, whereas those of *Bouteloua breviseta* are racemose spikes. Short-awned foxtail, *Alopecurus aequalis, Ammophila arenaria, Calamagrostis arundinacea,* and *Pennisetum alopecuroides* have less dense, spikelike, paniculate flower heads. Silver hairgrass flower heads are small, delicate, and loosely branched, in contrast to the erect, dense, cylindrical panicle of buffelgrass and the exserted spicate panicle of *Chloris ciliata.* The bristled spicate flower heads of *Setaria* species are quite different from the ovate, branched flower heads of *Panicum virgatum.* The large, feathery inflorescences of pampas grass are in sharp contrast to the cylindrical flower heads of *Fingerhuthia sesleriaeformis.* Switchgrass has attractive, long-exserted, ovate to pyramidal flower heads, whereas those of big quaking grass are pyramidal, and those of the cultivar Violacea are broadly pyramidal. Flower heads of the latter two species are light green and violet, respectively. Species with oblong inflorescences include *Agrostis nebulosa, Arundo donax, Eragrostis triticoides,* and *Erianthus giganteus.* The inserted panicles of *Bromus inermis* are ovate to oblong, whereas the inflorescences of *Aristida purpurea* and *Festuca rubra,* red fescue, are narrow. The inflorescences of red fescue remain erect, in contrast to the nodding flower heads of purple three-awn grass, *Aristida purpurea.* Flower heads of *Andropogon gerardi* are erect, conjugate racemes, in contrast to the elongate flower heads of *Pennisetum setaceum,* or the ovoid to narrow form of *Rhynchelytrum repens.* The lanceolate to oblong, nodding flower heads of *Calamagrostis canescens* provide quite a contrast to the radiating digitate or curled, exserted spikes of *Chloris cucullata.* The flower heads of many forms, such as *Arrhenatherum elatius* and *Stipa pennata,* are either erect or nodding, loosely branched panicles. Inflorescences of some paniculate grasses are more colorful than others. Additional diversity in the shape of inflorescences is found among species of *Coix, Ctenium, Erianthus,* and *Miscanthus.*

Some species are noted for the size of their flower heads; pampas grass and uvagrass both have very large heads. Aside from inflorescence size and shape is flower color, which is of paramount significance from an ornamental viewpoint. Colorful inflorescences add to the attractiveness of certain ornamental grasses (Appendix 1, column 17). Inflorescences of some species may be attractive but not necessarily colorful, such as those of big quaking grass, and weeping windmill grass. Inflorescence color is influenced to some extent by whether or not the plants are grown in full sun or shade, or in acid or alkaline soil. There is considerable variation in inflorescence color among ornamental grasses. The various colors may be described by many terms that indicate different hues and tones of the same color. Grasses with colorful inflorescences are more attractive than those with whitish or tawny flower heads. Inflorescence color should be used as one criterion in the selection of grasses for specific uses in the garden. Large, colorful inflorescences augment or act as a foil for the foliage, and vice versa. The choice and use of grasses with colorful flower heads provides additional variation in landscape improvement. Species with attractive and colorful flower heads are easily identified in Appendix 1, column 17. Variations in the color of flower heads among ornamental grasses range from bronze through copper, with various hues in between, to pinkish, purplish, and violet. Fountain grass has bronze to rose flower heads, while those of short-awn foxtail are light green, and those of *Miscanthus sinensis* 'Silberfeder' are silvery white. The cylindrical paniculate flower heads of *Cenchrus ciliaris, Setaria lutescens* and *Uniola paniculata* are interesting, as are the feathery, conical flower heads of *Phragmites australis,* which are purplish, becoming tawny at maturity. Outstanding species with colorful inflorescences include *Cortaderia* species and cultivars, *Deschampsia* species and cultivars, *Erianthus* species, *Miscanthus sacchariflorus* and its cultivar Giganteus, *Miscanthus sinensis* and variants, *Pennisetum alopecuroides, Pennisetum macrostachyum, Pennisetum setaceum* and cultivars, *Rhynchelytrum repens,* and *Sorghastrum nutans.* The crowning glory of pampas grass, the acknowledged ''queen of ornamental grasses,'' is its large, erect, colorful inflorescence. Grasses that are suitable as ornamentals offer a wide array of colors in their inflorescences while on the plants (Appendix 1, column 17). Some are suitable for almost any situation.

The mature seedheads of some grasses are attractive on the plants or when used in dried arrangements. A few grasses with particularly attractive seedheads include the silvery white and violet seedheads of Sunningdale Silver and Violacea cultivars of pampas grass, the bronze, flattened seedheads of broad-leaved uniola, and the tiny, hard, red, shiny seeds of switchgrass.

Grasses with unusual foliage color are exciting and interesting to use in landscape improvement. Certain ornamental grasses are grown primarily for their attractive foliage (Table 1.1; Appendix 1, column 20). Fortunately, as with inflorescence color, there is considerable variation in foliage color among ornamental types. This wide assortment of foliage color provides the gardener much choice in the use of grasses in mixed plantings with other ornamentals. The texture and foliage colors of grasses add interest and diversity to the garden and landscape, regardless of how they are used. Grasses with unusual foliage color are useful singly or in groups or massed stands. They serve as accent or specimen plants in borders and elsewhere in the landscape. Grasses with attractive foliage color are particularly striking when used as ground cover, in multicolored lawns, and in edging and specimen plantings. Numerous combinations of grasses provide a sharp contrast in color and other combinations that provide more subtle color changes. Both types are equally useful in ornamental horticulture. Species with attractive foliage color are arbitrarily divided for convenience into two

Table 1.1   Foliage Color of Ornamental Grasses

Unusual

Agropyron pungens
Agrostis stolonifera
Alopecurus aequalis
Alopecurus lanatus
Alopecurus pratensis cvs. Aureo-
    variegatus, Aureus, Glaucus
Ammophila arenaria
Ammophila breviligulata
Andropogon gerardi
Andropogon virginicus
Arrhenatherum elatius
Arundo donax
Briza maxima var. *rubra*
Festuca amethystina
Festuca gigantea
Festuca ovina var. *glauca*
Festuca rubra
Festuca spp. and cvs.
Hakonechloa macra
Helictotrichon sempervirens
Holcus lanatus
Holcus mollis
Hordeum jubatum
Imperata cylindrica cv. Rubra
Lagurus ovatus and cv. Nanus
Melica ciliata
Milium effusum and cv. Aureum
Miscanthus saccharoides cv. Dwarf

Miscanthus sinensis cvs. Purpurascens,
    Silberfeder
Oryza sativa cv. Nigrescens
Panicum miliaceum
Panicum virgatum and cvs.
    Rostrahlbusch, Rubrum, Strictum
Pennisetum alopecuroides cv.
    Weserbergland
Pennisetum alopecuroides var. *viridescens*
Pennisetum macrostachyum
Pennisetum setaceum and cvs. Astrosangui-
    neum, Cupreum, Rubrum
Pennisetum villosum
Poa bulbosa
Poa colensoi
Poa compressa
Poa glauca
Poa labillardieri
Poa pratensis
Puccinellia fasciculata
Puccinellia maritima
Rhynchelytrum repens
Schizachyrium scoparium
Spartina spartinae
Stipa arundinacea
Vetiveria zizanioides
Zea mays

Multicolored

Alopecurus pratensis cv. Aureo-variegatus
Arrhenatherum elatius var. *bulbosum*
    cv. Variegatum
Arundo donax var. *versicolor*
Calamagrostis canescens cv. Variegata
Coix lacryma-jobi cv. Aurea Zebrina
Cortaderia selloana cvs. Gold Band,
    Silver Stripe
Dactylis glomerata cvs. Elegantissima,
    Variegata

Glyceria maxima cvs. Pallida,
    Variegata
Hakonechloa macra cvs. Albo-aurea,
    Albo-variegata, Aureola
Holcus lanatus cv. Variegatus
Holcus mollis cvs. Albo-variegatus,
    Variegatus
Melica uniflora cv. Variegata
Miscanthus sacchariflorus cvs. Aureus,
    Variegatus

Table 1.1   *(continued)*

Multicolored *(continued)*

Miscanthus sinensis cvs. Strictus, Univittatus	*Phalaris arundinacea* var. *variegata*
	Phragmites australis
Miscanthus sinensis var. *variegatus*	*Setaria palmifolia* f. *variegata*
Miscanthus sinensis var. *zebrinus*	*Spartina pectinata* cv. Aureo-marginata
Molinia caerulea cv. Variegata	*Stenotaphrum secundatum* cv.
Oplismenus hirtellus cv. Vittatus	Variegatum
Phalaris arundinacea cvs. Dwarf's Garters, Feesey's Form	*Zea mays* cv. Harlequin
	Zea mays var. *japonica* cvs.
Phalaris arundinacea var. *picta*	Quadricolor, Variegata

categories: (1) those with unusual color and (2) multicolored or variegated forms (see Table 1.1). Among the unusual colors of foliage are bluish green, olive green, rose green, reddish green, blackish green, and purplish red. Grasses with multicolored or variegated foliage provide yet another dimension in color. Some forms have leaves with longitudinal stripes (e.g., *Miscanthus sinensis* var. *variegatus*). and others have leaves with horizontal stripes (e.g., *Miscanthus sinensis* var. *zebrinus*). There is nothing more striking than a large clump of 'Gold Bond' pampas grass or zebragrass in the middle of the lawn as a specimen. Variegated grasses are used advantageously in dark, shaded nooks of the garden; of course, shade-tolerant forms are required for such sites. Grasses with variegated foliage accentuate the normal green foliage of other ornamentals. Grasses of unusual foliage color, including multicolored forms, when used judiciously, add diversity and color to the landscape.

Ornamental grasses with unusual foliage color may be used in many ways in ornamental horticulture. The decisions are entirely those of the individual gardener or landscape artist. The possibilities in beautifying the garden and improving the landscape with ornamental grasses are numerous. Some species with attractive foliage are used in border plantings, especially those with bluish green, glaucous, reddish, or silvery blue foliage. Other types are also useful in mixed borders or any other site where they provide a contrast for each other and for other green-leaved plants. Grasses with unusual foliage color are used in producing multicolored lawns, as edging in foreground borders, in rock and water gardens, as specimens, and as houseplants.

Grasses with multicolored or variegated foliage provide yet another dimension of diversity and color to the landscape. Species of this type are most commonly used in shaded areas, as direct sunlight may blister or discolor the foliage. Some of these forms retain their attractive coloration throughout the growing season, whereas others lose their attractiveness toward the end of the season. Although some forms will tolerate full sun, they exhibit their maximum coloration in shade. Bright, variegated grasses are ideal for dark patches or niches in the garden. Smaller, mat-forming types are useful in naturalized areas and in water gardens. Multicolored grasses are often used to advantage with colorful grasslike relatives. Plantings of grasses with unusual or variegated foliage color are most impressive when established in large clumps. A large clump of pampas grass, *Cortaderia selloana* 'Silver Stripe,' or zebragrass, *Miscanthus sinensis* var. *zebrinus,* located in a prominent spot on the lawn, exemplifies the optimum use of variegated grasses in contrast to truly green forms. Variegated basketgrass, *Oplismenus hirtellus* 'Vittatus,' and striped St. Augustine grass are spectacular as houseplants in hanging baskets; the latter is often used as edging in water gardens. Variegated mannagrass, *Glyceria maxima* 'Variegata,' and *Spartina pectinata* 'Aureo-marginata' are likewise attractive and useful in water gardens and in low, wet sites.

The foliage and flowers of some grasses are attractive (Appendix 1, column 21). The large, colorful, flowering panicles of *Arundo donax, Cortaderia selloana* and cultivars, *Erianthus ravennae, Miscanthus sacchariflorus* and cultivars, *Miscanthus sinensis* and variants, and *Phragmites australis* serve as a perfect foil for their colorful foliage. Grasses with unusual or variegated foliage accentuate the normally green foliage of other ornamentals. Grasses of unusual foliage color, including multicolored forms, when used judiciously, add interest, diversity, and color to the garden and landscape. Many variations are possible in diversifying and improving the garden and landscape through the use of ornamental grasses with unusual foliage and inflorescence color. They form unusually spectacular sights when grown together, as well as with shrubbery and other flowering ornamentals.

Large, tufted grasses such as *Arundo donax, Cortaderia selloana, Erianthus ravennae,* and *Phragmites australis* are often used as shrubs. Similar use is made of some of the large bamboos (i.e., *Bambusa* and *Phyllostachys* species). These and other large forms are widely used as medium or tall hedges, screens, or windbreaks (Appendix 1, columns 8, 9, and 10). Hedges are often used to separate various areas of the garden; in a sense, hedges may be considered screens. Screens are often used to hide unsightly areas or to provide privacy from neighbors. Large bamboo species planted in lines or rows act as screens and windbreaks and also are effective as noise barriers. Garden-size screens normally are comprised of smaller forms 2–5 ft/0.6–1.5 m high, such as crimson fountain grass, fountain grass, lemongrass (zone 10), small cultivars of Japanese silvergrass, pampas grass, switchgrass, tall oatgrass, and weeping lovegrass. Tufted grasses are recommended for garden hedges and screens. Rhizomatous grasses are recommended if a "moving hedge" is desired. Moving hedges and screens usually grow out of control, however. Moving hedges, screens, or windbreaks are useful in the wild garden, or in wet, marshy areas, or along the coast. Medium hedges and screens for these areas would include such forms as bushgrass and American beachgrass and taller forms such as common reed, giant reed, reedgrass, *Calamagrostis arundinacea,* and uvagrass. Tall forms for garden use include grasses such as giant plumegrass, Japanese silvergrass, pampas grass, plumegrass, and silver plumegrass.

The color, size, and shape of inflorescences of many ornamental grasses makes them suitable for use as fresh, cut flowers (Appendix 1, column 18). Grasses from which cut flowers are taken may come from plants growing in different gardens (i.e., pebble or rock gardens, water gardens, or vegetable gardens). Cut flowers may come from plants growing in full sun or shade in wet or dry sites, from border or specimen plants, and from plants inhabiting almost any area of the garden. Fresh bouquets are made from groups of inflorescences of the same species, from mixtures of ornamental grasses, or from grass inflorescences mixed with flowers of the same species. As with dried floral arrangements, innumerable combinations of cut flowers may be used in making bouquets.

The sizes and shapes of inflorescences of grasses suitable for cut flowers are included in the description of each species. Species with colorful inflorescences are given in Appendix 1, column 17. The range in size, shape, and color of inflorescence affords much choice in their use as cut flowers. The ingenuity and imagination of the individual gardener are the only limitations in the use of cut flowers for decorative purposes. The ephemeral value of the decoration does influence their use under certain circumstances. This shortcoming is overcome to some extent by having a generous number of plants from which cut flowers may be gathered, by using those species that have long flowering periods, and possibly by having types that flower at different periods during the season.

The inflorescences of many ornamental grasses are adaptable for dried arrangements (Appendix 1, column 19). There is considerable variation in inflorescence size, shape, color, and texture among species used as dried specimens. They range in size from the small, delicate, open, oblong panicles of dense, silky bentgrass, *Agrostis nebulosa,* to the large, oblong, feathery, flowering panicles of pampas grass, or yet larger, rather dense, plumelike panicles of uvagrass. Inflorescence shapes vary from the dense panicles of *Fingerhuthia sesleriaeformis* to less dense paniculate spikelike flower heads of fountain grass and short-awn foxtail. Conical flower heads are exemplified by common reed, and cylindrical inflorescences by buffelgrass. Switchgrass has pyramidal panicles, whereas those of big quaking grass and pampas grass are broadly pyramidal. The oblong inflorescences of cloudgrass are quite different from the narrow flower heads of red fescue. The cylindrical oblong flower heads of buffelgrass provide quite a contrast to the radiating digitate exserted spikes of hooded windmill grass. Inflorescences of some forms remain erect throughout the growing season, whereas others are drooping, even before they mature. There is a wide range of inflorescence color among ornamental species. Inflorescences range from dense spikes to delicate, open, loosely branched panicles, with flower heads of intermediate forms between these extremes.

The major problem encountered in the use of flower heads as dried specimens is that of collecting them at the proper stage of maturity. It is most difficult to determine the precise time at which flower heads should be collected for drying. Considerable variation exists among species as to the stage of maturity. Panicles of big quaking grass should be collected early, to avoid their disintegration during the drying process. Plumegrass panicles, by contrast, may be collected when they are mature without incurring serious disintegration upon drying. Each species should be considered separately in gauging the stage at which its flower heads should be collected. A trial-and-error approach may be employed in ascertaining the best stage at which flower heads should be collected. As a general rule, flower heads should be cut for drying just prior to or during anthesis. This may be considered a base from which to explore further. Flower heads collected before their full development will usually continue their maturity and will become fluffed out during the drying process. Usually, only minimum damage occurs to flower heads during drying when they are collected before or during anthesis. Inflorescences that are collected too early are immature and do not truly represent the species, whereas those collected too late disintegrate upon drying, losing their flowers and immature seeds, thus becoming very unattractive. Partially dry flower heads collected too late tend to become discolored and unattractive and eventually disintegrate.

Various treatments have been employed in preserving the natural form, color, and sheen of collected flower heads. Inflorescences of certain species may not require any treatment whatever to prevent their disintegration upon drying, but others may require some sort of treatment to prevent such damage. Each species that is used in dried arrangements should be considered individually as to whether the seedheads require treatment to prevent disintegration. For example, the seedheads of Japanese silvergrass require treatment to prevent disintegration, whereas the seedheads of common reed do not require treatment. Glycerine, which is absorbed by the plant parts, has been used with some degree of success in preserving and retaining the color and sheen of some species. Inflorescences that disintegrate usually lose their original shape in addition to their mature blossoms or seeds. A technique with which the author has met with partial success involves spraying the entire inflorescence with hairspray when it is collected. This process minimizes other detrimental effects, in addition to reducing or preventing the loss of seeds.

Inflorescences of some ornamental grasses are suitable for drying, whereas others are not. Flower heads dry at different rates, depending somewhat upon their density and the stage of maturity at which they are collected. Green, immature, dense spikes are difficult to dry. Species with open, branched panicles usually respond best to drying. Different drying techniques produce different results, not all of which are satisfactory. Inflorescences should be dried in a cool, well-ventilated room, preferably of low humidity. Drying specimens in full sun is unsatisfactory. Drying techniques employed by the author include (1) drying in partial sun or shade for the entire period, or alternatively in the sun and shade, (2) suspending the inflorescence upside down, (3) placing the inflorescence in a bottle or other container in the manner in which it was growing on the plant, (4) laying the inflorescence on a flat board or table (but this tends to result in an unnatural shape), (5) drying treated specimens as well as untreated inflorescences.

Optimum results were obtained from drying treated specimens (those to which hairspray was applied) versus untreated specimens. Specimens that were placed in an upright position in bottles or jars and allowed to dry in the shade were satisfactory. Specimens dried in this manner retained their shape, color, and sheen best of all. Two precautionary measures are worth mentioning: (1) leave an extra-long stem on the inflorescence when it is collected; this may be shortened later if desired; and (2) do not attempt to dry too many specimens in the same container. The number of specimens that are dried in each container depends largely upon their size. Too many specimens in a single container become tangled and impossible to separate after drying. Species of the following genera make outstanding dried specimens: *Agrostis, Arundo, Avena, Briza, Chasmanthium, Chloris, Cortaderia, Erianthus, Gynerium, Hordeum, Oryza, Pennisetum, Phragmites,* and *Triticum* (Appendix 1, column 19).

Attractive specimens may be made of dry seedheads of certain species. The tiny, white seeds of teff, *Eragrostis tef,* are attractive, as are the small, shiny, red seeds of *Panicum virgatum,* switchgrass, and the bronze seedheads of *Chasmanthium latifolium,* broad-leaved uniola. Ears of corn containing multicolored seeds are standard among dried specimens.

Dried specimens of ornamental grasses and other plants are used universally for decoration both inside and outside the home, workplace, church, and elsewhere. They range from a single flower head to elaborate designs containing a mixture of grasses, or grasses with other broad-leaved plants. Simple specimens consisting of a single flowerhead or seedhead are usually placed in an upright position in a jar, bottle, vase, or other suitable container. More elaborate specimens may consist of a group of flower heads of the same species or a mixed group from different species. Often grasses are used in conjunction with other plants in preparing floral arrangements. There are innumerable floral designs possible, depending upon the ingenuity and imagination of the artist. Dried specimens may be used in all rooms of the house, including hallways, porches, basements and sun rooms. Parts of corn plants or entire plants are often made into outdoor designs for display at the entrance of the home, or even into self-supporting displays on the lawn. Most floral arrangements consist of dry flower heads or seedheads, although other plant parts, such as stems and leaves, may also be included. The foliage of some grasses remains green upon drying, which makes it valuable in dried arrangements. More spectacular is the mature, colorful foliage of species that exhibit good autumnal color. The mature, colorful seedheads of certain species are a favorite source of dried material with which to make floral designs. There is a wide range of color and shapes of flower heads among those species used for dried floral arrangements (Appendix 1, column 19). Most dried flower heads, especially the colorful ones, are used in their natural color; however, some people prefer dyed inflorescences.

Dyeing dried flower heads for display and floral arrangements is becoming popular again. This does not imply that it has not been in practice for many years, and perhaps for centuries. The flower heads of certain species are adaptable to dyeing (Appendix 1, column 26). The flower heads of some species respond to dyeing very readily, whereas those of other species cannot be dyed easily. Extremes in response to dyeing include the flower heads of canary grass, *Phalaris canariensis,* and those of *Spartina pectinata* 'Aureo-marginata,' which do not respond well, in contrast to those of pampas grass, *Cortaderia selloana,* and *Miscanthus* species, which can be dyed very well. The flower heads of *Miscanthus* species respond best of all, although they are among the most attractive in their natural color.

Certain ornamental grasses are grown primarily for their attractive foliage, whereas others are noted for their flowers and foliage (Appendix 1, column 21). Outstanding among species that have attractive flowers and foliage are broad-leaved uniola, eulaliagrass, fountain grass, Japanese silvergrass and its variants, and pampas grass and its variants. The flower heads are a perfect foil for the foliage of those grasses that have attractive flowers and foliage. Grasses with attractive flowers and foliage benefit from other ornamentals in mixed plantings; conversely, other ornamentals benefit from ornamental grasses in admixtures.

Spring, summer, and fall flora of the garden are enhanced by grasses that flower at different times during the growing season. Some ornamental grasses flower in the spring, others flower during the summer, and yet others flower and bear fruit from late July or August until frost (Table 1.2). Those that flower in the spring are augmented by other spring flowers, as are those that flower in June and July with summer flowers. Large grasses that flower late (i.e., August–October) are perhaps the most conspicuous and provide the most benefit and pleasure. A paucity of ornamentals and shrubs are in flower during late summer and early fall, which emphasizes the importance of having grasses in full flower at this time. Another significant attribute some grasses possess is their long flowering period, which extends their attractiveness.

Some interesting oddities in flowering occur among a few ornamental grasses. Canegrass and uvagrass, for example, flower during the winter months, whereas basketgrass, used as a house plant, flowers sporadically. Early sandgrass flowers in spring and fall, while sea oats flowers throughout the growing season. Several species flower sporadically throughout the growing season. One species, *Holcus lanatus,* flowers twice daily.

Among grasses that blossom early (i.e., April–May) are bluegrass, bromegrass, fescues, fingergrass, foxtails, hairgrasses, purple needlegrass, oats, orchardgrass, quaking grass, sweet vernalgrass, and wheat (see Table 1.2). Some forms that blossom early are annuals; others are perennials. Some of these come into blossom after the flowering spring bulbs but before the summer flowers reach their prime.

Most ornamental grasses blossom during the summer months, which coin-

Table 1.2   Blossoming Seasons of Ornamental Grasses

April and May

Alopecurus aequalis
Alopecurus lanatus
Anthoxanthum odoratum
Aristida purpurea
Avena sativa
Axonopus compressus
Bouteloua breviseta
Briza maxima
Briza media
Briza minor
Bromus unioloides
Chloris glauca
Ctenium aromaticum
Dactylis glomerata cvs. Elegantissima, Variegata
Deschampsia caespitosa and cvs.; exception cv. Tardiflora
Deschampsia flexuosa
Elymus condensatus
Elymus virginicus
Festuca ovina var. *glauca*
Fingerhuthia sesleriaeformis

Hierochloa odorata
Holcus lanatus cv. Variegatus
Hystrix patula
Imperata brasiliensis
Lamarckia aurea
Melica altissima
Melica uniflora and cv. Variegata
Milium effusum cv. Aureum
Panicum clandestinum
Paspalum notatum
Poa chaixii
Poa compressa
Poa pratensis
Polypogon monspeliensis
Puccinellia fasciculata
Puccinellia maritima
Setaria geniculata
Sitanion hystrix
Stipa rubens
Stipa spartea
Triticum aestivum

June and July

Agropyron canium
Agropyron pungens
Agrostis stolonifera and cvs. Emerald, Penncross, Penneagle
Alopecurus alpinus
Alopecurus pratensis and cvs. Aureo-variegatus, Aureus, Glaucus
Ammophila breviligulata
Andropogon barbinodis
Arrhenatherum elatius
Arrhenatherum elatius var. *bulbosum* cv. Variegatum
Bouteloua curtipendula
Bouteloua gracilis

Brachypodium sylvaticum
Bromus inermis
Calamagrostis arundinacea
Calamagrostis canadensis
Calamagrostis canescens and cv. Variegata
Calamagrostis epigejos cv. Hortorum
Cenchrus ciliaris
Chasmanthium latifolium
Chloris cucullata
Chloris gayana
Chloris verticillata
Coix lacryma-jobi and cv. Aurea Zebrina

Table 1.2   Blossoming Seasons of Ornamental Grasses (*continued*)

June and July (*continued*)

Cynodon dactylon
Cynosurus cristatus
Deschampsia caespitosa cv. Tardiflora
Elymus arenarius
Elymus canadensis
Elymus giganteus
Elymus glaucus
Elymus villosus
Eragrostis capillaris
Eragrostis tef
Eragrostis trichodes
Erianthus contortus
Festuca amethystina
Festua gigantea
Festuca tenuifolia
Glyceria canadensis
Glyceria fluitans
Glyceria maxima and cvs. Pallida,
   Variegata
Helictotrichon pubescens
Helictotrichon sempervirens
Hemarthria altissima
Holcus mollis and cvs. Albo-variegatus,
   Variegatus
Hordeum jubatum
Hordeum vulgare
Koeleria cristata
Lagurus ovatus and cv. Nanus
Oryza sativa and cv. Nigrescens

Oryzopsis miliaceae
Pennisetum alopecuroides and cvs.
   Hameln, Weserbergland
Pennisetum alopecurus
Phalaris arundinaceae and cvs. Dwarf's
   Garters, Feesey's Form
Phalaris arundinacea var. *picta*
Phalaris arundinacea var. *variegata*
Phalaris canariensis
Phalaris minor
Phleum pratense
Poa confinis
Poa glauca
Poa labillardieri
Poa macrantha
Poa nemoralis
Rhynchelytrum repens
Setaria italica
Spartina spartinae
Sporobolus virginicus
Stenotaphrum secundatum and cv.
   Variegatum
Stipa comata
Stipa gigantea
Stipa pennata
Stipa tenuissima
Trichloris crinita
Triticum turgidum

August through October

Agrostis nebulosa
Ammophila arenaria
Ampelodesmos mauritanicus
Andropogon gerardi and cvs. Champ,
   Kaw, Pawnee
Andropogon stolonifer
Andropogon virginicus

Aristida purpurascens
Aristida wrightii
Arundo donax
Bouteloua hirsuta
Chloris distichophylla
Cortaderia richardii
Cortaderia selloana and cvs.

Table 1.2 *(continued)*

August through October *(continued)*

Cymbopogon citratus	*Pennisetum nervosum*
Cymbopogon nardus	*Pennisetum orientale* var. *triflorum*
Deschampsia alpina	*Pennisetum setaceum* and cvs.
Distichlis spicata	Astrosanguineum, Cupreum, Rubrum
Erianthus giganteus	*Pennisetum villosum*
Erianthus ravennae and var.	*Phragmites australis*
purpurascens	*Schizachyrium scoparium*
Erianthus strictus	*Setaria palmifolia* f. *variegata*
Hakonechloa macra and cvs.	*Sorghastrum nutans*
Albo-aurea, Albo-variegata, Aureola	*Spartina alterniflora*
Leersia oryzoides	*Spartina cynosuroides*
Miscanthus sacchariflorus and cvs.	*Spartina gracilis*
Miscanthus sinensis and cvs. and	*Spartina patens*
varieties	*Spartina pectinata* and cv. Aureo-
Molinia caerulea and cvs.	marginata
Oplismenus setarius	*Sporobolus heterolepis*
Panicum miliaceum	*Stipa calamagrostis*
Panicum virgatum and cvs.	*Tripsacum dactyloides*
Paspalum dissectum	*Vetiveria zizanioides*
Pennisetum alopecuroides	*Zizania aquatica*
Pennisetum macrostachyum	

cides with summer flowers. They include a wide range in plant form, growth habit, inflorescence form and color, and foliage color (see Table 1.2).

Species with truly majestic inflorescences blossom in late summer and early fall. Some of the flower heads are large, delicate, and very colorful; others are small, less delicate and not as colorful. Species that blossom in late summer and early fall include a wide range in plant form, growth habit, inflorescence color and form, and foliage color. Some of the outstanding ornamental grasses that are in flower during late summer and early fall include citronella and lemongrass (zone 10); common reed, bristle grass, cordgrass, eulaliagrass and its variants, fountain grass, giant reed, Japanese silvergrass and its variants, pampas grass and its cultivars, and switchgrass (see Table 1.2). Not only are these flower heads ornamental and attractive on the plants, but many of them are useful in cut-flower and in dried floral arrangements. Many of the inflorescences provide excellent fall color and, just as importantly, persist into the winter. The following grasses are outstanding for maintaining their colorful flower heads intact into winter: common and giant reed, eulaliagrass and its variants, fountain grass, crimson fountain grass, Japanese silvergrass and its variants, lemongrass, plume-grass, silver plumegrass, and vetivergrass (see Appendix 1, column 22).

Another desirable characteristic of some ornamental grasses is their produc-tion of good autumnal colors (Appendix 1, column 22). The foliage of certain species changes color with the coming of cooler weather in the autumn. Various hues of green, tan, brown, yellow, and golden, among other colors, are pro-duced, all of which add to the beauty and attractiveness of the garden. The color changes that occur in the foliage and inflorescences further enhance the attractiveness of the plants. The longevity of attractiveness is increased, especially for those species that retain their foliage for a considerable period following the first killing frost. Several species are outstanding in the autumn color of their foliage and mature seedheads. The rich bronze foliage and seedheads of broad-leaved uniola produce a spectacular effect in early fall; fountain grass and its cultivars are among the most handsome of ornamental grasses, particularly when in full blossom in late summer and early fall. Massed plantings of fountain grass, with its yellowish green foliage and rose-colored, hairy panicles, produce a spec-tacular effect when in full blossom and fruit. The reddish green or bronze foliage of certain clones of limpograss in massed stands provides excellent fall color. Purple moorgrass and its cultivars produce beautiful fall colors, as do switchgrass and its cultivars. Species that produce particularly striking fall color of both foliage and mature seedheads include eulaliagrass and its variants, Japanese silver-grass and its variants, and pampas grass and its cultivars. Perhaps the mature seedheads of these species are more colorful than their foliage, although the foliage is always attractive into the fall. The mature seedheads, having reached their maximum coloration, become dry and fluffy after frost, exhibiting excel-lent fall color.

Although attractive foliage color is the center of attraction in the fall, the accompanying inflorescences and seedheads should also share the spotlight. Spe-cies that exhibit good coloration of the seedheads and foliage in the fall are unique and outstanding. Fall coloration of grasses is somewhat different from that of grasslike plants and other broad-leaved, deciduous ornamentals. Grasses can be used effectively in producing a harmonious range of autumn colors with other ornamentals, as well as among themselves. Some species with variegated foliage retain their coloration throughout the growing season and into autumn.

A few ornamental grasses produce pleasant fragrances (Table 1.3). Citro-nella, lemongrass, prairie dropseed, sweetgrass, sweet vernalgrass, and vetiver-grass each produce a distinct, pleasant fragrance. The fragrances of citronella grass, lemongrass, and sweetgrass or vanilla grass are easily detected when the green leaves are broken and crushed. Sweet vernalgrass becomes fragrant when dried; the aromatic fragrance is a result of the presence of coumarin. The roots of vetivergrass impart a pleasant fragrance when wet. The fragrant roots are dried and used in clothes closets in the home. They are most commonly used when incorporated in screens through which air is blown to perfume an entire

Table 1.3   Ornamental Grasses That Produce a Pleasant Fragrance

Species	Vernacular Name
Anthoxanthum odoratum	Sweet vernalgrass
Cymbopogon citratus	Lemongrass
Cymbopogon nardus	Citronella grass
Hierochloe odorata	Sweetgrass
Sporobolus heterolepis	Prairie dropseed
Vetiveria zizanioides	Vetivergrass

room. Calamus, *Acorus calamus,* a grasslike plant containing coumarin, also imparts a pleasant fragrance.

Miscellaneous Uses

Miscellaneous uses of ornamental grasses involve their use as ground-cover plants in naturalized areas and as attractive ground-cover and ornamental plants along streets and highways, in parks, sports fields, and zoos. Certain ornamental species are used for erosion control and to provide a wildlife sanctuary. The utilitarian and economic value of certain ornamental grasses overshadows their ornamental value.

Ground covers in the agronomic sense are usually considered to be annual or perennial pasture and range plants requiring some maintenance for sustained usage and persistence of stand. Ground covers in the horticultural sense are usually considered to be perennial plants that require minimal maintenance once established. Ground-cover plants are normally considered to be substitutes for lawn grasses on certain sites where lawn grasses are difficult, if not impossible, to grow successfully or where lawn maintenance becomes difficult, as on steep slopes or terraces, in dense shade, or on sandy, dry, rocky soils where little moisture is available. Ground covers are also needed for low, wet, soggy soils.

It is a usual practice to upgrade and improve areas adjacent to the formal garden or lawn. This is ordinarily done through the use of ground covers, including certain ornamental grasses. Their use in improving the landscape in such areas is considered by some to be naturalizing the area in a manner similar to planting spring bulbs haphazardly in a wooded site adjacent to the formal garden. Inasmuch as the same grasses may be used as ground cover and for naturalizing, it is difficult to consider the two means of landscape improvement separately. In some aspects, the two forms of improvement are clearly distinguishable, while in others they are inseparable, to the extent of being one and the same.

Lawn grasses are excellent ground covers, although they are also usually high-maintenance plants requiring repeated mowing, fertilizing, insect and disease-control measures, and watering. Lawns provide outdoor living and recreational space; ground covers, however, are not suited or planted for such usage. Some forms of *Liriope,* lily turf, and *Ophiopogon* species are used occasionally as lawns in the southeastern and western states. However, they are not mowed, nor do they withstand continued recreational traffic; consequently, they are usually considered to be ground covers. Ornamental grasses are not normally considered to be ground-cover plants in the strict sense, although in a broader context, in which they are used as lawn substitutes and as ground cover on difficult sites, they could be considered as ground-cover plants.

Numerous situations and sites located in vastly different climatic regions may be improved through the use of ground-cover plants. Such sites are often referred to as naturalized areas and are usually adjacent to the more formal portion of the garden or lawn area. These sites may be upgraded through the use of certain ornamental grasses used as ground cover. These improvements are brought about by using ornamental grasses to supplement any existing ground cover, by establishing simple or mixed grass stands, or by using grasses in mixed stands with other attractive ground-cover species. The grasses used in naturalizing sites in New England would necessarily be different from those used for the same purpose in other regions, such as the midwestern, northwestern, southeastern, or western states. The various difficult sites that require ground-cover plants in addition to those useful in naturalizing such areas include the following:

1. Dry, rocky sites in full sun that require xerophytes and drought- and heat-tolerant grasses, including both cespitose and sod-forming types
2. Low, wet, boggy, water-logged soils requiring bog plants, such as species of *Carex, Cyperus,* and *Typha* and certain water-loving aquatic grasses
3. Shaded woodlots or other shaded sites around lakes, pools, streams, and ponds, which require shade- and drought-tolerant plants for ground cover or naturalizing
4. Freshwater or saltwater marshes with water-logged saline soils posing another problem in certain situations, which require bog plants and certain salt-tolerant grasses
5. Steep slopes, ditch and stream banks, usually largely inaccessible, requiring sod-forming stoloniferous or rhizomatous grasses to arrest and prevent erosion
6. Sand dunes that require stabilization.

Blown sand and constant wind are usually problems encountered in coastal areas. Grasses required for coastal regions include erect, tall, strongly tufted forms that reduce wind damage, arrest blown sand, and stabilize moving sand dunes; and smaller stoloniferous or rhizomatous grasses with extensive root systems, which also perform the same functions.

Some of the desired attributes of ornamental grasses other than lawn grasses for use as ground cover in difficult sites are as follows:

1. Ease of establishment
2. Site adaptation, such as dry, rocky, sandy, soil in full sun versus saline salt marshes in partial or full shade
3. Compatibility with other species when grown in mixed stands
4. Minimum maintenance requirements
5. Maintenance of stand for sustained duration without crowding out other desired species
6. Possessing both aesthetic attractiveness and utilitarian value
7. Tolerance of drought, shade, and edaphic and atmospheric saline conditions.

One economic advantage of using ornamental grasses as ground cover and naturalizing plants on difficult sites is their minimum or no maintenance cost. An aesthetic advantage lies in the texture and diversity they give to the landscape, otherwise unobtainable from other ornamental species. There are also some useful side benefits resulting from the use of ornamental grasses in ground cover and naturalized plantings. Some large species such as *Arrhenatherum elatius,* tall oatgrass, *Arundo donax,* giant reed, and *Phragmites australis* provide good ground cover and food and protection for wildlife; their massive size acts as a windbreak and perhaps as shade for other species, in addition to reducing the impact of rain on the soil surface; their extensive root system stabilizes the soil and sand, thus reducing erosion. Some species are useful in soil building over extended periods; other forms provide good ground cover in freshwater and saltwater swamps or in brackish or saline marshes either inland or near the sea. Yet other species have attractive inflorescences that are useful in fresh and dried floral arrangements, and some forms provide excellent fall color. Ornamental grasses that are useful as ground cover and naturalizing plants may be considered to be ground-cover plants with considerable aesthetic and utilitarian value. Certain species provide supplemental ground cover in difficult sites, whereas other cespitose and stoloniferous species are compatible in forming a complete ground cover, in addition to improving the overall appearance of the landscape in what otherwise might consist of weedy unattractive plants or be bare soil.

Many grass species of lesser ornamental value but of considerable utilitarian value are useful as ground cover and naturalizing plants in locations adjoining the formal garden or in more difficult, sometimes inaccessible, sites. Some species are most useful in pure stands, while other compatible species are grown in mixed stands. Some ornamental grass species that are compatible with broadleaved or other ground-cover plants are useful in improving the landscape. Some aquatic grasses are compatible with cattails, rushes, and sedges in low, wet, marshy sites; some bamboo species make excellent ground-cover plants in densely shaded locations. Although some of these grasses are of lesser ornamental value, they make a significant contribution to any naturalized area in which they are used. Their use in difficult sites other than the formal garden provides added beauty, structure, texture, and balance to the landscape not achieved from other ornamentals.

There are many ornamental grasses, varying in form, size, growth habit, and persistence, from which to choose as ground-cover or naturalizing plants for dry, sandy, or rocky soils in sunny locations. Some of these include low-growing sod-forming types, such as *Cynodon dactylon,* and larger forms, such as *Andropogon stolonifer* and *Hemarthria altissima,* or tufted types, such as *Andropogon virginicus, Aristida purpurascens, Bouteloua hirsuta,* and certain *Bromus* species. These species, among others, are useful in minimizing the drastic change from the neat, formal garden or lawn to any adjacent area or otherwise wild, unkempt sites. Ornamental grasses used in this manner play a significant role in balancing and harmonizing the entire landscape. Such species may be advantageously employed as ground-cover plantings in naturalized areas as the particular situation and need dictate. Compatible combinations or mixtures of grasses and other broad-leaved plants are commonly used in naturalized areas on difficult and inaccessible sites where a permanent ground cover is needed. Low, wet, sunny sites around lakes and streams, bogs, marshes, and swamps in need of ground cover usually require perennials that are easily established and require no maintenance once they are planted. Plants that fill these requirements include bog plants, such as species of *Carex, Cyperus, Juncus,* and *Typha,* along with certain aquatic grasses such as *Arundo, Calamagrostis, Glyceria,* and *Spartina* species. Some aquatic species are best used alone in pure stands, whereas other species are compatible with each other and with other water-loving plants. Compatible forms are recommended, as their use adds diversity in plant form, texture, size, and color to the landscape. The best balance and diversity of flora is achieved through the use of aquatic grasses with other water plants, such as water lilies, sedges, and cattails. The aquatic ornamental grasses in low, wet, boggy sites either dominate the area or supplement and complement the existing vegetation; in either case, they perform a useful function. Ornamental aquatic grasses used in such locations provide a good wildlife sanctuary, in addition to arresting erosion, building soil, and, for some species, providing good fall color.

Ornamental grasses suitable for naturalized shaded locations vary greatly in form, size, color, growth habit, and shade tolerance. They range in size from very small types that form miniature lawns or meadows to huge, tree-size bamboo species commonly found either in woods or along wooded borders, usually in low, wet sites. Species such as *Agropyron caninum, Andropogon virginicus, Brachypodium sylvaticum,* and *Calamagrostis canescens,* among other species, including certain bamboos, exhibit varying degrees of shade tolerance. Types are available that provide a wide range of shade tolerance, from that of very deep shade to light, dappled shade; they include a wide range of annuals and perennials. Some forms, such as lawn substitutes, survive in lightly shaded woodland, whereas other species with more shade tolerance will thrive in medium shade. Most ornamental, shade-tolerant grasses perform satisfactorily in partial or light shade, whereas fewer species are tolerant of medium shade, and almost none will survive in deep shade. Despite the paucity of shade-tolerant ornamental grasses, some forms do make a significant contribution to the flora of such difficult sites. Perhaps their most significant contribution in shaded, naturalized areas is along wooded borders near buildings, where they receive direct sunlight for only a portion of the day, or when growing in semishade or light shade among other, broad-leaved, larger ornamentals. The shallow root system is an asset to shade-loving grasses, especially those grown in the shade of deep-rooted trees whose roots do not compete for moisture and nutrients with grasses grown under them. Shade-tolerant ornamental grasses provide an added dimension of color, form, and texture to the garden and its surroundings. This certainly is sufficient justification for their use in the formal garden or in any naturalized area or difficult site involving the need for shade-tolerant, attractive ornamentals. No green plant can survive in the absence of light, although some plants are tolerant of shade in that they occur in shaded sites in their natural habitat. Ornamental grasses are much used and in great demand in ornamental horticulture, including those used in naturalization. Many types, forms, and colors are available for use in naturalization (Appendix 1, column 11).

Certain ornamental grasses are used in upgrading and improving the appearance and attractiveness of city canals and streets. Similarly, city, state, and federal officials use these same species in beautifying parks, sports fields, and zoos. State and federal highway departments are in constant need of grasses possessing ornamental and utilitarian value for use along highway banks and median strips. Perennial rhizomatous or stoloniferous, low-growing, mat-forming types are required for ground cover and erosion control. Their utilitarian value lies in their ground-cover and erosion-control capacity; their ornamental value is chiefly that of their foliage. These forms are usually less than 40 in./1 m high. Taller, perennial, cespitose species (i.e., 3–5 ft/0.9–1.5 m high) are useful for their foliage and flowers. Yet larger perennial cespitose types are useful as specimen plants. Highway and street plantings are usually established as individual specimens, in groups, or in massed stands.

Particularly difficult sites on which mat-forming perennial grasses of ornamental and utilitarian value should be established include steep banks along highways from which the topsoil has been removed. These sites offer a challenge to highway departments to establish and maintain plants that are useful as well as attractive. Median strips along highways, where ground cover is needed that is attractive and also controls erosion, offer perhaps a less difficult challenge. Grasses recommended for these difficult sites are low-growing perennial forms, such as *Andropogon stolonifer* and certain species of *Cynodon, Digitaria, Hemarthria, Paspalum, Poa,* and *Rhynchelytrum repens.*

The same species employed in street and highway plantings are used to improve the landscape of parks, zoos, and sports fields, including golf courses. Low-growing, mat-forming perennials with attractive foliage are useful for such areas. Larger cespitose perennials noted for their foliage and towering plumes produce striking specimens wherever they are located. Some forms have unusual foliage color other than ordinary green, such as bluish green or variegated; other forms have large fluffy inflorescences of variable colors and hues. Those forms with both colorful foliage and inflorescences make outstanding specimens (Appendix 1, column 21). Bermuda grass, Indian grass, buffelgrass, pampas grass, and limpograss are but a few of the outstanding grasses for use in parks, sports fields, and zoos, and along streets and highways. Fountain grass, silvergrass, and eulaliagrass should be added to this list, along with cattails and pygmy forms of bamboo. Additional species are also valuable for use in parks, sports fields, zoos, and along highways:

Andropogon virginicus
Anthoxanthum odoratum
Arundo donax var. *versicolor*
Bromus inermis
Cenchrus ciliaris
Chasmanthium latifolium
Chloris gayana
Coix lacryma-jobi and cv. Aurea Zebrina
Cortaderia selloana and cvs.
Cymbopogon citratus
Cymbopogon nardus
Cynodon dactylon
Eragrostis curvula
Erianthus ravennae
Hemarthria altissima
Hordeum jubatum
Miscanthus sacchariflorus and cvs. Aureus, Variegatus
Miscanthus sinensis and cvs. and varieties
Panicum virgatum and cvs.
Pennisetum alopecuroides and cvs. Hameln, Weserbergland
Pennisetum setaceum and cvs. Astrosanguineum, Cupreum, Rubrum
Phalaris arundinacea var. *picta*
Phalaris arundinacea var. *variegata*
Phragmites australis
Rhynchelytrum repens
Schizachyrium scoparium
Sorghastrum nutans

Certain ornamental grasses existing naturally or planted in naturalized areas, marshes, swamps, floodplains, and in seaside plantings provide a good source of bird food and wildlife protection (Appendix 1, column 25). Many aquatic and semiaquatic grasses occurring naturally or planted in coastal wetlands provide prodigious amounts of bird feed, especially for migratory wildfowl. Large forms also provide an ideal wildlife sanctuary. Reed canary grass, *Phalaris canariensis* and *Phalaris minor,* are grown primarily as a commercial source of bird seed. Such grasses have both utilitarian and ornamental value, although the latter to a lesser degree.

The economic and utilitarian value of some ornamental grasses is demonstrated by certain forms serving as a source of food—bamboo sprouts (*Bambusa* and *Phyllostachys* species), barley (*Hordeum vulgare*), corn (*Zea mays*), popcorn (*Zea praecox*), rice (*Oryza sativa*), teff (*Eragrostis tef*), and wheat (*Triticum aestivum*). A plant patent has been issued for a particular cultivar of limpograss, *Hemarthria altissima,* as a source of tea, because of its coumarin content. Barley, corn, and rice also serve as sources of alcohol. Other forms, either planted or growing wild, serve primarily as a commercial source of bird seed and secondarily for wildlife feed and protection (e.g., *Arrhenatherum elatius, Puccinellia* species, *Sorghastrum nutans,* and certain species of *Setaria, Spartina, Sporobolus,* and *Zea*). Large, tufted species, such as common reed, *Phragmites australis,* provide excellent wildlife cover. Plant parts of *Cortaderia* and *Pennisetum* species, including bits of stems, leaves, awns, bristles, and silky seeds, have been found in bird nests. Some ornamental forms, including *Arundinaria gigantea* ssp. *tecta,* switchcane, when growing in the wild, are grazed by domestic livestock and wild animals. Giant tropical uvagrass, *Gynerium sagittatum,* provides good ground cover and erosion control in freshwater marshes and along streams in zone 10. Its large, silky plumes are in much demand for dried floral arrangements. The utilitarian value of this giant grass is that of its stems, which are used as arrow shafts and for indoor decorating purposes; hats and baskets are made from its large, long leaves. Fishing poles and walking canes are made from the stems and from those of the bamboo genera *Bambusa* and *Phyllostachys.* The canes of certain large species of *Bambusa* and *Phyllostachys* are excellent sources of building materials; smaller forms of *Sasa* species are good erosion-control plants, in addition to their having ornamental value.

Each ornamental grass species has some attribute not shared by any other species. A few species are of particular interest, based on their utilitarian value as well as their ornamental value: their obscure use, unique method of propagation, or other interesting characteristic. Densely tufted, bulbous bluegrass, *Poa bulbosa,* exemplifies an interesting method of propagation; its culms are bulbous at the base, and the upper portion of the spikelets are replaced by miniature plants. The weight of the miniature plants bend the panicle to the ground, thereby allowing them to come into contact with the soil, take root, and continue their development. Grasses usually blossom only once daily; however, one species, *Holcus lanatus,* is known to blossom twice daily, in the morning and in the afternoon. The foliage of some species (e.g., lemongrass and sweetgrass) has a pleasant fragrance. The roots of vetivergrass, *Vetiveria zizanioides,* impart a pleasant fragrance when wet. They are sold in some tropical regions for use in the home to freshen the air in clothes closets; they are particularly useful when woven into mats through which air is passed, thus producing a pleasant fragrance throughout an entire room. The curved, flowering spikes of toothache grass, *Ctenium aromaticum,* are interesting on the plants and as cut flowers or in dried arrangements. The plants have a pungent taste. Bruised spikes produce an orange-colored juice, and the enlarged base, when chewed, deadens the tongue and gums.

SELECTED SPECIES

The habitat, description, use and cultivation of selected species that follow are arranged in alphabetical order by genera and by species within genera (Hitchcock and Chase, 1951).

Agropyron **Gaertn. (Wheatgrass, Dog grass).** Name from Greek *agrios,* wild, and *puros,* wheat. Lectotype, *Agropyron cristatum* (L.) Gaertn. There are about 60 species, restricted to temperate regions of both hemispheres. Cespitose or usually rhizomatous and sod-forming, erect perennials with spicate inflorescences. Spikelets several-flowered, usually solitary, rarely in pairs, sessile, placed flatwise at each joint of a continuous rachis, rarely disarticulating, the rachilla disarticulating above the glumes and between the florets; glumes equal, firm, several-nerved, rarely two-nerved, one-nerved or nerveless, usually shorter than the first lemma, acute or awned, rarely obtuse or notched; lemmas convex on the back, rather firm, five-to-seven-nerved, acute or awned from the apex; palea about as long as the lemma.

> **Latin name:** *Agropyron caninum* (L.) Beauv.
> **Synonym:** *Triticum caninum* L.
> **Common names:** Bearded wheatgrass, Bearded couch, Awned wheatgrass
> **Habitat:** Open woods; along roads, canals, and streams
> **Hardiness:** Zones 3 through 5
> **Description:** A more or less cespitose, upright-narrow perennial, rarely rhizomatous. Culms simple, erect or bent, 1–4 ft/0.3–1.2 m high, glabrous or minutely hairy at the nodes. Foliage bright green, medium in texture. (The textures of foliage described in this book are fine, i.e., leaf width up to 0.4 in. / 10 mm; medium, i.e., leaf width 0.4–0.6 in./10–15 mm; and coarse, i.e., leaf width greater than 0.7 in./15 mm). Leaves evenly spaced along the culm, ascending, flat, long attenuate, 4–12 in./1–3 dm long, 0.25–0.50 in./6–13 mm wide, finely nerved, rough, glabrous or loosely hairy above, scabrous beneath, veins rather prominent above and scabrous, more or less pubescent, margins scabrous; sheaths round on the back, longer than the internodes, glabrous or the lower with short hairs; ligule membranous, up to 0.1 in./3 mm long, entire or erose-ciliate. Inflorescence a curved, long-exserted, cylindrical spike, 2–8 in./ 0.5–2.0 dm long, 0.2–0.4 in./5–10 mm in diameter, slender, dense, green or

light purple, slightly nodding at maturity; rachilla internodes pilose; spikelets sessile, adnate to the sides of the rachis with their broader side appressed to it, lanceolate to oblong, 0.4–0.8 in./10–20 mm long, two-to-five-flowered; glumes about equal, persistent, lanceolate, 0.3–0.4 in./8–10 mm long, rounded on the back, sharply pointed, sometimes short awned from the tip, the awns straight, up to 0.1 in./3 mm long, two-to-five-nerved, the nerves rough; lemmas imbricate, rounded on the back, rigid, five-to-seven-nerved, lanceolate-oblong, 0.4–0.5 in./10–13 mm long, minutely hairy at the base, usually with scattered hairs in the upper part or glabrous, narrowed at the tip into a flexuous straight awn or bent outward, 0.3–0.8 in./8–20 mm long; palea as long as the lemmas, very obtuse, scabrous on the keels; caryopsis with a tuft of hairs at the apex, adherent to the palea. Flowering and fruiting occur from June through July.

Uses: The bright green foliage of bearded couch makes it an attractive grass for naturalizing areas in open, shaded woodland and along wooded borders. Its shade tolerance makes bearded couch useful in any shaded area.

Cultivation: Propagation is by seeding. Bearded couch thrives best in shaded areas on a wide range of soil types when afforded sufficient moisture.

Latin name: *Agropyron junceum* (L.) Beauv.
Synonym: *Triticum junceum* L.
Common name: Sand couch
Origin: Eastern Mediterranean region
Habitat: Sand dunes, seaside shore areas
Hardiness: Zones 3 through 5
Description: An upright-narrow perennial with long, slender, wiry rhizomes. Culms solitary or in loose tufts, erect, hollow, spreading or drooping, slender or somewhat stout, brittle, simple, with few nodes above the base, glabrous, 1–2 ft/3–6 dm high. Foliage bluish green, tinged grayish, fine in texture; leaf blades 4–16 in./1–4 dm long, 0.15–0.25 in./4–6 mm wide, long attenuate, flat or often rolled, stiff to rather soft, glabrous below, prominently ribbed above, with the ribs densely and minutely hairy; sheaths longer than the internodes, imbricate, rounded on the back, bladeless, glabrous; ligule membranous, truncate, about 1 mm long. Inflorescence a dull green, straight or curved, stout, rather dense spike, axis glabrous, fragile, disarticulating above each spikelet; spikelets sessile, glabrous, adnate to the axis, alternating in two rows on opposite sides, with their sides appressed to it, oblong or elliptic, 0.5–1.0 in./13–25 mm long, three-to-eight flowered, their own length apart, breaking up at maturity beneath each lemma; glumes similar, narrowly oblong, about equal, keeled or round on the back, very tough and rigid, 0.50–0.75 in./13–19 mm long, glabrous, prominently seven-to-ten-nerved; lemmas imbricate, oblong or lanceolate-oblong, blunt or awnless, rounded on the back, keeled above, about as long as the glumes, five-nerved, glabrous; palea shorter than the lemma, two-keeled, minutely pubescent; caryopsis puberulent near the tip, enclosed. Flowering and fruiting occur from June through August.

Uses: Sand couch is tolerant of both edaphic and atmospheric salinity. The rhizomatous root system of sand couch makes it ideal for use as ground cover and for erosion control of shifting sand dunes in seashore plantings. It is also useful in stabilizing and reclaiming soil in salt marshes.

Cultivation: Propagation is by seeding and by plant division. Sand couch prefers full sun on sandy, acid soils.

Latin name: *Agropyron pungens* (Pers.) Roem. & Schult.
Synonym: *Triticum pungens* Pers.
Common name: Sea couch
Origin: Europe
Habitat: Maritime areas, salt marshes
Hardiness: Zones 3 through 5
Description: An erect, upright-narrow perennial, spreading extensively by rhizomes, forming large colonies. Culms glabrous, glaucous, 24–32 in./6.0–8.1 dm high, simple, erect or slightly geniculate at the base, rigid, slender to stout. Foliage glaucous, fine in texture; leaves spaced equidistant apart along the culm, leaf blades flat, or often enrolled, 4–14 in./1.0–3.5 dm long, 0.10–0.25 in./3–6 mm wide, stiff, prominently ribbed above, smooth below, rough on the margins and ribs, with sharp-pointed tips; sheaths longer than the internodes, round on the back, glabrous, with short auricles at the summit; ligule membranous, about 1 mm long. Inflorescence a stiff, erect, compact spike, 2–8 in./0.5–2.0 dm long, slender, axis rough and tough; spikelets imbricate, sessile, about half their length apart on the rachis, singly and alternating in two rows on opposite sides of the axis, three-to-nine-flowered, oblong, compressed, 0.50–0.75 in./13–19 mm long; glumes about equal, pointed, lanceolate-oblong, tough, and rigid, 0.3–0.5 in./8–13 mm long, keeled, rough on the keels, four-to-seven-nerved; lemmas closely imbricate, blunt or pointed, five-nerved, 0.25–0.40 in./6–10 mm long, keeled upwards; palea two-keeled, about as long as the lemmas, the keels rough; caryopsis puberulent at the tip, enclosed by the lemma and palea. Flowering and fruiting occur from June through August.

Uses: This stiff, wiry, rhizomatous, maritime grass is ideal as a ground cover in wet, saline areas, especially near the sea. The strong, extensive, rhizomatous root system, forming extensive patches, makes sea couch ideal as an erosion-control plant on sand dunes.

Cultivation: Propagation is by seeding or by division of the plant crowns. Sea couch thrives best in wet, saline soils in full sun.

Agrostis L. **(Bentgrass, Bent).** Name from Greek *agrostis,* a kind of grass, from *agros,* "field." Lectotype, *Agrostis alba* L. There are about 100 species native to temperate and cool regions. Annual or perennial (ours perennial) grasses with glabrous stems, flat or sometimes involute, scabrous leaf blades and open or contracted panicles or small spikelets. Spikelets one-flowered, disarticulating above the glumes, the rachilla usually not prolonged; glumes equal or nearly so, acute, acuminate, or sometimes awn-pointed, thin, the lower one-nerved, the upper one- or three-nerved, usually scabrous on the keel and sometimes on the back; lemmas obtuse, usually shorter and thinner than the glumes, mostly three-nerved, awnless or dorsally awned, often hairy on the callus; palea usually shorter than the lemma, two-nerved in only a few species, usually small and nerveless or obsolete.

Latin name: *Agrostis nebulosa* Boiss. & Reut.
Common name: Cloudgrass
Origin: Europe (Spain)
Habitat: Cultivated, escape from cultivation
Hardiness: Zones 3 through 7
Description: A loosely tufted upright-open to spreading annual. Culms very slender, branching, erect, purplish, 10–18 in./2.5–4.5 dm high, with swollen nodes. Foliage sparse, light to medium green, fine in texture; leaf blades flat, mostly glabrous, elongate, long attenuate, 4–6 in./1.0–1.5 dm long, 0.10–0.25 in./3–6 mm wide; sheaths longer than the internodes, rough; ligule membranous, about 1 mm long. Inflorescence a whitish or light green, delicate, oblong panicle, 4–6 in./1.0–1.5 dm long, about two-thirds as wide, branches profuse, verticillate; spikelets sessile, 1–2 mm long, one-flowered; flowers pale pink, whitish, or pale greenish; glumes about equal, acuminate, three-nerved; lemmas nearly as long as the glumes, obtuse, hyaline; palea almost as long as its lemma; caryopsis enclosed. Flowering and fruiting occur from July through August, with the spikelets persisting.
Uses: Flowers of cloudgrass are whitish to pale pink, and the plants are in full blossom during midsummer. Cloudgrass has been compared to a morning mist with the sun shining through the plants. The flowers resemble miniature baby's breath, *Gypsophila elegans* Bieb. Unfortunately, cloudgrass is short-lived, with the plants turning brown by late summer. Cloudgrass is useful in foreground plantings of annual borders and in clumps as ground cover in rock gardens and along walks and driveways. The flowering panicles of cloudgrass are excellent as cut flowers and in dried arrangements because the seedheads do not shatter. The delicate foliage and flowering panicles are conducive to its use outdoors and as a potted plant indoors. The flowering period of cloudgrass is of short to medium length (i.e., 6–8 weeks); for this reason, it is useful in annual borders. Cloudgrass is grown primarily for its flowers.
Cultivation: Propagation is by seeding; seeding may be done in the spring or autumn. Almost all soils are suitable for maximum growth, although poorly drained sites are undesirable locations. Cloudgrass thrives best in full sun but tolerates light shade. The early maturity of the seedheads results in the plants reseeding themselves, thus becoming a potential nuisance. Unwanted reseeding can be avoided by cutting the seedheads off before they mature. To be most effective in producing a cloudlike effect, cloudgrass should be planted in large clumps.

Latin name: *Agrostis stolonifera* L.
Synonym: *Agrostis alba* L.
Cultivars: Several in cultivation, including 'Emerald,' 'Penncross,' 'Penneagle'
Common names: Creeping bentgrass, Redtop
Origin: North America
Habitat: Cultivated, escape from cultivation
Hardiness: Zones 3 through 7
Description: A stoloniferous perennial, usually tufted. Culms ascending from a spreading base, 8–20 in./2.5 dm high, the lower nodes rooting from leafy stolons. Foliage slightly greenish yellow or bluish green, fine in texture; leaf blades minutely rough or smooth, 2–3 in./5.8 cm long, 0.1–0.3 in./3–8 mm wide, rolled when young, eventually flat, closely nerved; sheaths open, round on the back, longer than the internodes, mostly glabrous; ligule membranous, blunt, 0.1–0.2 in./3.5 mm long. Inflorescence a compound branched panicle somewhat open, oblong, 2–6 in./0.5–1.5 dm long, about 1 in./25 mm wide, pale purple, some of the branches spikelet-bearing from near the base, branches clustered, closely divided, pedicels rough, about 2 mm long; spikelets densely clustered, lanceolate to narrowly oblong, 2–3 mm long, one-flowered; glumes persistent, about as long as the spikelets, nearly equal, narrowly lanceolate to oblong-lanceolate, pointed, membranous, one-nerved, rough upwards on the keels; lemmas ovate to oblong, about three-fourths the length of the glumes, very blunt, thin, five-nerved, usually awnless or rarely with a short awn at or near the tip, minutely bearded on the callus; palea approximately two-thirds the length of the lemma. Flowering and fruiting occur from June through August.
Uses: Creeping bentgrass may be used as ground cover along walks and driveways and in corners of the garden. It is also useful as a lawn grass and in water gardens where an ample and constant moisture supply is available. Creeping bentgrass is a highly variable species represented by several cultivated cultivars.
Cultivation: Creeping bentgrass is usually propagated by planting the stolons in the spring in moist soil. The plants prefer full sun and high moisture-retaining soils. Creeping bentgrass does not withstand hot dry weather.
Cultivars: The cultivars Emerald, Penncross, and Penneagle are used in the same manner as creeping bentgrass.

Alopecurus L. (Foxtail, Vulpin). Name from Greek *alopex*, "fox," and *oura*, "tail," alluding to the cylindrical panicles. Lectotype, *Alopecurus pratensis* L. There are about 30 species inhabiting the Northern Hemisphere. Low or moderately tall perennials and some annuals with flat leaf blades and soft, dense, spikelike panicles. Spikelets one-flowered, disarticulating below the glumes, strongly compressed laterally; glumes equal, usually united at the base, ciliate on the keel; lemmas about as long as the glumes, five-nerved, obtuse, the margins united at the base, bearing from below the middle a slender dorsal awn, this included or exserted two or three times the length of the spikelet; palea wanting.

Latin name: *Alopecurus aequalis* Sobol.
Synonym: *Alopecurus aristulatus* Michx.
Common name: Short-awn foxtail
Origin: Eurasia
Habitat: In shallow water in ponds, ditches, lakes subject to desiccation
Hardiness: Zones 4 through 8
Description: A tufted annual, biennial, or short-lived perennial. Culms erect or spreading from a prostrate base, usually not rooting at the lower nodes unless the plants are growing in water, slender, whitish toward the panicle, glabrous, 1–2 ft/3–6 dm high. Foliage medium green or glaucous, fine in texture; leaf blades glabrous or rough above and beneath, flat, abruptly pointed, finely nerved, 2–4 in./0.5–1.0 dm long, 0.1–0.2 in./3–5 mm wide; lower sheaths shorter than the internodes, purplish, glabrous or rough, the upper whitish green, longer than the internodes, barely inflated; ligule membranous, blunt, 0.15–0.20 in./4–5 mm long. Inflorescence a branched, dense, spikelike, cylindrical panicle, 0.8–2.0 in./2–5 cm long, 0.2–0.3 in./5–8 mm in diameter, usually light green or sometimes light bluish, spikelets pedicellate, pedicels 1–2 mm long, one-flowered, elliptic or oblong, 2–3 mm long, 1 mm wide, flattened, very blunt; glumes about equal, 2–3 mm long, slightly connate at base, keeled, ciliate on the keels, appressed-pubescent on the sides, a lateral nerve in each glume; lemmas four-nerved, thinly membranous, slightly longer than the glumes, keeled, elliptic, very blunt, smooth, with margins united up to half their length, awned on the back below the middle, the awn included in the glumes or slightly protruding by as much as 1 mm; palea absent; caryopsis enclosed in the lemmas. Flowering and fruiting occur from May through June.

Uses: Short-awn foxtail is good for ground cover in wet sites in the water garden and naturalized areas. The plants are not attractive enough for use in the formal garden, although the compact, flowering panicles are attractive when in full blossom. This small perennial is attractive in pure or mixed stands.

Cultivation: Propagation is by seeding and by plant division, preferably the former. The plants thrive best in mud or shallow water in and around pools, ponds, and lakes in full sun or light shade.

Latin name: *Alopecurus alpinus* J. E. Smith
Synonym: *Alopecurus occidentalis* Scribn.
Common name: Alpine foxtail
Origin: North America, Asia
Habitat: Mountain meadows
Hardiness: Zones 2 through 4
Description: An upright-open, loosely tufted perennial with slender rhi-

zomes. Culms geniculate at the base, becoming erect, glabrous, slender, stiff, 4–30 in./1.0–7.6 dm high. Foliage medium green, fine in texture; leaf blades flat, lanceolate, 2–8 in./0.5–2.0 dm long, 0.1–0.2 in./3–5 mm wide, glabrous beneath, rough above, closely nerved, upper leaves much shorter than the lower; upper sheaths somewhat inflated, smooth; ligule membranous, 1–2 mm long, truncate, finely erose. Inflorescence a dense, woolly, spikelike panicle, cylindrical or most commonly ovate, 1–2 in./2.5–5.0 cm long, 0.25–0.50 in./6–13 mm in diameter, purplish or bluish green to greenish gray; spikelets pedicellate, pedicels 1–2 mm long, one-flowered, three-nerved, elliptic or ovate, flattened blunt, 0.10–0.15 in./3–4 mm long; glumes elliptic and pointed, 0.10–0.15 in./3–4 mm long, their margins united toward the base, three-nerved, the nerves green, membranous, woolly, with fine, spreading hairs; lemmas keeled, as long as the glumes or slightly shorter, broadly ovate, very blunt, with margins united toward the base, four-nerved, membranous, glabrous or slightly hairy toward the margins, awnless, or usually awned on the back from one-third above the base, with the awn sometimes projecting beyond the tip of the spikelet by as much as 0.2 in./5 mm; palea absent; caryopsis enclosed in the lemmas. Flowering and fruiting occur from June through July.

Uses: An ideal site for alpine foxtail is in alpine rock gardens in which the plants thrive in wet or damp crevices. The low-growing plants form miniature grass patches.

Cultivation: Propagation is by seeding and by plant division, preferably the latter. The plants grow equally well in full sun or light shade on wet rocky soils; they are not adapted to warm climates. The plants are easily contained despite their rhizomatous root system.

Latin name: *Alopecurus pratensis* L.
Cultivars: 'Aureo-variegatus,' 'Aureus' Golden foxtail, 'Glaucus'
Common names: Meadow foxtail, Foxtail grass
Origin: Eurasia
Habitat: Meadowlands, fields, waste grounds
Hardiness: Zones 4 through 6
Description: An upright-open, mound-forming, densely tufted perennial with weak rhizomes. Culms erect, or at first decumbent becoming erect, 1–3 ft/3–9 dm high, slender, glabrous, green or becoming whitish green near the panicle. Foliage medium green, fine in texture; leaf blades rough or nearly smooth, long attenuate, 2–4 in./0.5–1.0 dm long, 0.10–0.25 in./3–6 mm wide, flat, the upper blades shorter than the lower; sheaths cylindrical, smooth, split, the basal part turning brown, the upper light green, somewhat inflated; ligule membranous, 1–2 mm long. Inflorescence a very dense cylindrical spikelike panicle, 1–3 in./2.5–8.0 cm long, 0.2–0.4 in./5–10 mm thick, green or purplish, cylindrical, blunt, very soft, branches short, erect; these "foxtails" (inflorescences) may be green or purplish tinted with orange or russet conspicuous anthers; spikelets pedicellate, pedicels 1–2 mm long, one-flowered, cuneate or

Alopecurus pratensis.
**Habit, × 1/2; glumes and
floret, × 10.** *Source: Manual
of the Grasses of the United
States.* USDA Misc. Pub. 200.
1951.

lanceolate or elliptic, 0.15–0.25 in./4–6 mm long, flattened; glumes narrowly
lanceolate and pointed, 0.2 in./5 mm long, equaling the lemmas, their margins
united toward the base, firm, three-nerved, fringed with fine hairs on the keels
and sides, connate at base; lemmas ovate or elliptic, rather blunt, as long as the
glumes or slightly longer, keeled, with the margins united below the middle,
membranous, smooth, four-nerved, awned from the lower third on the back,

the straight awn exceeding the glumes by 0.1–0.2 in./3–5 mm; palea lacking; caryopsis enclosed in the lemmas. Flowering and fruiting occur from May through July.

Uses: Meadow foxtail, with its green foliage, is best suited as ground cover for extended naturalized areas in full sun or light shade on wet soils. Although the plants do best in wet sites, they are low in salt tolerance. The glaucous and variegated cultivars, particularly the latter, are outstanding among grasses with colored foliage. They are ideal accent plants in foreground and middleground perennial borders, depending on their size. The tufted glaucous and variegated cultivars are grown primarily for their foliage, which remains attractive throughout most of the growing season; they are attractive as specimen plants in water gardens or in middleground borders and in group or massed plantings.

Cultivation: Propagation of meadow foxtail and its cultivars is by seeding and by plant division, preferably the latter. The plants thrive best on wet but well-drained, fertile soils in full sun or light shade. The culms of plants grown in the shade become weak and lodge badly unless they are staked or supported by surrounding plants. Although the plants have a rhizomatous root system, they do not become invasive to the extent that precautionary measures are required. The colorful cultivars are adapted to the same sites and plant-hardiness zones as is the parent species; likewise, their soil and light requirements are the same as that of meadow foxtail. Meadow foxtail is slightly salt tolerant.

Cultivars: *Alopecurus pratensis* L. 'Aureo-variegatus' A truly unique grass grown for its beautiful golden foliage, which is fine in texture. The leaves have light yellow, longitudinal stripes with broad margins of gold, the golden color continuing the entire length of the leaf, with the tip entirely golden. The short, dense, spikelike flowering panicles are pale yellow. This hardy, mound-forming perennial is 1–2 ft/3–6 dm high. Flowering and fruiting occur from June through July.

Alopecurus pratensis L. 'Aureus' Golden foxtail An upright-open, tufted form of meadow foxtail. Plants are 12–18 in./3.0–4.5 dm high when in flower. The foliage is fine in texture; leaves have a light green midvein with indistinct, pale yellow margins, giving the appearance of an entire yellow or golden leaf. The dense, flowering spikes are pale green to greenish yellow, usually 1–3 in./2.5–8.0 cm long, and about 0.5 in./13 mm thick. Flowering and fruiting occur from June through July. It is useful in group or massed plantings and in water gardens.

Alopecurus pratensis L. 'Glaucus' The plants of this glaucous cultivar are usually 18–24 in./4.5–6.0 dm high. The foliage is fine in texture and glaucous. The glaucous foliage and stems with a bluish bloom make this cultivar superior to meadow foxtail from a garden or an ornamental viewpoint. Flowering and fruiting occur from June through July. Each of the cultivars of meadow foxtail is adapted to zones 6 through 9.

Other ornamental species: *Alopecurus lanatus* Sibth. & J. E. Smith, Woolly foxtail A densely tufted, dwarf perennial. Culms bluish green, stout, densely covered with white, woolly hairs, 6–12 in./1.5–3.0 dm high. Foliage fine in texture, bluish green, densely covered with woolly, whitish hairs; leaves extraordinarily thick, U-shaped, about 2 in./5 cm long and 0.25 in./6 mm wide, narrowing to an abrupt point; sheaths round on the back, covered with woolly hairs. Inflorescence a dense, spikelike, erect, ovoid panicle covered with silky, white hairs. Flowering and fruiting occur from March through May. A small, hairy perennial, unique for its combination of woolliness and blueness; perhaps best suited for a gravelly or pebbly soil in dry, sunny sites in the rock garden or in a miniature specimen planting in foreground borders. Propagation is by careful plant division; the plants are extremely slow growing. Woolly foxtail is adapted to plant-hardiness zones 7 and 8, although the plants may die during the winter unless the crown remains dry; they also require perfect drainage on dry or moist soil.

Ammophila **Host (Beachgrass, Sand reed, Marram, Psamma).** Name from Greek *ammos,* ''sand,'' and *philos,* ''loving,'' alluding to the habitat. Type species, *Ammophila arenaria* (L.) Link. There are four species, widely distributed in the Northern Hemisphere. Erect, tough, rather coarse, perennial grasses with hard, scaly rhizomes and long, involute, tough leaves and pale, dense, spikelike panicles. Spikelets one-flowered, compressed, the rachilla disarticulating above the glumes, produced beyond the palea as a short bristle, hairy above; glumes about equal, chartaceous; lemma similar to and a little shorter than the glumes, the callus bearded; palea nearly as long as the lemma.

> **Latin name:** *Ammophila arenaria* (L.) Link
> **Synonym:** *Arundo arenaria* L.
> **Common name:** European beachgrass
> **Origin:** Europe
> **Habitat:** Cultivated, escape from cultivation
> **Hardiness:** Zones 5 through 9
> **Description:** A sod-forming, glabrous perennial, spreading extensively by horizontally spreading or vertical rhizomes forming compact tufts. Culms erect or spreading, glabrous, moderately stout, 20–50 in./0.5–1.3 m high, rooting at the nodes under the sand, simple, smooth. Foliage greenish gray, fine in texture; leaf blades expanded at first, becoming tightly enrolled, rigid, long attenuate, 2–3 ft/6–9 dm long, 0.15–0.25 in./4–6 mm wide when open, closely ribbed above, the ribs minutely and densely hairy, glabrous beneath; sheaths imbricate, glabrous, longer than the internodes; ligule acute, firm, conspicuous, narrow, 0.4–1.2 in./1–3 cm long, margins entire. Inflorescence a pale, spikelike, narrowly oblong to lanceolate oblong, coarse, bristlelike panicle, 3–9 in./0.8–2.3 dm long, 0.3–0.8 in./8–20 mm in diameter, tapering upwards, branches erect, pedicels 1–3 mm long; spikelets sessile or short-pedicellate, pedicels 1–3 mm long, imbricate, or gaping, narrowly oblong, compressed, 0.5–0.7 in./13–18

mm long, one-flowered; glumes equal or slightly unequal, firm, narrow, pointed or blunt, 0.4–0.6 in./10–14 mm long, minutely rough on the sides and on the keels, lower mostly one-nerved, upper three-nerved; florets shorter than the glumes, with hard, knoblike, bearded callus; lemmas keeled, blunt, firm, 0.3–0.5 in./8.13 mm long, five-to-seven-nerved, the middle nerve excurrent into a short awn from the back just below the thin apex, minutely rough, surrounded at the base with fine white hairs, 0.1–0.2 in./3–5 mm long; palea nearly as long as the lemma, two-to-four nerved; caryopsis enclosed. Flowering and fruiting occur from June through September.

Uses: European beachgrass has no particular ornamental value but is most valuable for binding drifting sand and for controlling erosion caused by water and wind. The extensive mat of culms and leaves break the force of the wind causing the blown sand to be deposited and the extensive root system stabilizes the sand. European beachgrass and prairie cordgrass, *Spartina pectinata,* make a good combination of plants for windbreaks and erosion control in seaside plantings.

Cultivation: Propagation is by plant and rhizome division. Planting is most successful when done in the spring or fall. European beachgrass prefers sand or sandy soil in full sun; the plants are somewhat salt tolerant.

Latin name: *Ammophila breviligulata* Fern.
Synonym: *Ammophila champlainensis* Seymour
Common name: American beachgrass
Origin: North America
Habitat: Cultivated, escape from cultivation
Hardiness: Zones 4 through 9
Description: A rhizomatous, erect, tufted, sod-forming perennial. Culms erect to spreading, 24–42 in./0.6–1.1 m high, moderately stout, stiff, rooting at the nodes under the sand, simple, smooth. Foliage bluish green, fine in texture; leaf blades ascending or spreading, elongate, firm, soon involute, rigid, long attenuate, 1–3 ft/3–9 dm long, 0.1–0.2 in./3–5 mm wide, scabrous on the upper surface and the margins, more or less glabrous beneath, closely ribbed above; sheaths crowded toward the base, glabrous, broad, imbricate, longer than the internodes; ligule short, chartaceous, truncate, 1–3 mm long. Inflorescence a pale, dense, spikelike, cylindrical panicle, narrowly oblong, 6–12 in./1.5–3.0 dm long, 0.3–0.6 in./8–15 mm in diameter, the axis scabrous, branches erect or ascending; spikelets pedicellate, pedicels 1–2 mm long, one-flowered, compressed, imbricate, 0.4–0.5 in./10–13 mm long; glumes scabrous, firm, equal, or slightly unequal, the lower one-nerved, shorter than the upper, the upper three-nerved, minutely rough on the sides, about equaling the lemma; lemmas similar to the glumes, slightly shorter, 0.2–0.4 in./5–10 mm long, keeled, minutely rough, five-to-seven-nerved, obtuse or slightly bifid, the midrib usually slightly excurrent from about 1 mm back of the apex, the callus hairs fine, white, 0.1–0.2 in./3–5 mm long; palea two- or three-nerved, nearly as long

Ammophila breviligulata.
**Habit, × 1/2; spikelet and
floret, × 5.** *Source: Manual
of the Grasses of the United
States.* USDA Misc. Pub. 200.
1951.

as the lemma; caryopsis enclosed, oblong, about 0.10–0.15 in./3–4 mm long.
Flowering and fruiting occur from June through August.

Uses: American beachgrass is not of any great ornamental value. It is most
valuable in seaside plantings for ground cover, erosion control, and stabilization
of drifting sand. The extensive mat of plants breaks or reduces the force of the
wind causing blown sand to be deposited, which in turn is stabilized by the

extensive root system. American beachgrass makes a good combination with either bent-awn plumegrass, *Erianthus contortus,* or common reed, *Phragmites australis,* for windbreaks and erosion control in seaside plantings. Both American and European beachgrass withstand burial in drifting sand by producing new branches from higher nodes.

Cultivation: Propagation is by seeding and by plant division, preferably the latter, as the seeds are usually infertile. Plantings should be made in the early spring or in the autumn when the weather is cool. Plant spacing would be determined by the quantity of planting stocks available and the size of the area to be established. The spacing used in planting would determine the rapidity with which the plants form a ground cover. American beachgrass prefers sand dunes or sandy soils in full sun; the plants are somewhat salt tolerant.

Ampelodesmos **Link (Vine reed).** A monotypic genus, native to the Mediterranean region. A robust, tufted perennial.

> **Latin name:** *Ampelodesmos mauritanicus* (Poir.) Dur. & Schinz
> **Synonym:** *Arundo mauritanica* Poir.
> **Common names:** Vine reed, Mauritania vine reed
> **Origin:** Mediterranean region
> **Habitat:** Cultivated, escape from cultivation
> **Hardiness:** Zones 8 through 10
> **Description:** A robust, upright-open, semievergreen perennial that forms large clumps. Culms solid, erect, 5–9 ft / 1.5–2.8 m high or higher. Foliage dark green, medium in texture; leaf blades elongate, long attenuate, 12–18 in./3.0–4.5 dm long, 0.4–0.5 in./10–13 mm wide, wiry, curved at the base, bending forward across the culm, the upper surface downward. Inflorescence an erect, branched, many-flowered, plumose panicle, 8–20 in./2–5 dm long, about half as wide, the flexuous, slender, very scabrous branches glabrous at the base, drooping, spikelets crowded toward the ends of the branches; spikelets two-to-five flowered, 0.5–0.6 in./13–15 mm long; glumes somewhat unequal, keeled on the back, the lower part of the lemma and rachilla joints densely pilose with white hairs; palea nearly as long as the lemma. Flowering and fruiting occur from August through October.

Uses: The large, plumose flowering panicles of vine reed are attractive on the tall plants and as cut flowers. The tawny, dried panicles, usually dyed, are found in florist shops and novelty stores. The semievergreen plants are good as tall hedges, screens, or windbreaks and in background perennial borders in warm climates.

Cultivation: Propagation is by seeding and by plant division, preferably the latter. The plants cease flowering in the winter but remain semievergreen; they prefer full sun on moist, fertile soil. The plants form large clumps, and, because of their enormous size, may be damaged by strong wind if grown in a single line or in small clumps.

Andropogon L. (**Bluestem, Beardgrass, Barbon**). Name from Greek *aner* (*andr-*), "man," and *pogon,* "beard," referring to the villous pedicels of the spikelets. Type species, *Andropogon hirtum* L. There are about 200 species, widely distributed throughout both hemispheres. Rather coarse annuals or usually perennials with solid culms. The numerous spikelets arranged in racemes, these numerous, aggregate on an exserted peduncle or single, in pairs, or sometimes in threes or fours, the common peduncle usually enclosed in a spathaceous sheath, these sheaths often num rous, the whole forming a compound inflorescence, usually narrow, but som times in dense, subcorymbose masses. Spikelets in pairs at each node of an articulate rachis, one sessile and perfect, the other pedicellate and either staminate, neuter or reduced to the pedicel, the rachis and pedicels of the sterile spikelets often villous, sometimes conspicuously so; glumes of fertile spikelet coriaceous, narrow, the lower round, flat, or concave on the back, the median nerve weak or wanting, the upper laterally compressed; sterile lemma shorter than the glumes, empty, hyaline, fertile lemma hyaline, narrow, entire or bifid, usually bearing a bent and twisted awn from the apex or from between the lobes; palea hyaline, small or wanting; pedicellate spikelet awnless, sometimes staminate and about as large as the sessile spikelet, sometimes consisting of one or two reduced glumes, or sometimes wanting, only the pedicel present.

> **Latin name:** *Andropogon barbinodis* Lag.
> **Synonym:** *Andropogon leucopogon* Nees
> **Common names:** Cane bluestem, Beargrass
> **Origin:** North America
> **Habitat:** Open meadows, rangeland, and mesas
> **Hardiness:** Zones 8 through 10
> **Description:** A densely tufted, upright-open to spreading perennial. Culms numerous, simple or branched from the lower nodes, often glaucous, spreading to ascending, the nodes enlarged, barbed, and bearded with short spreading hairs, 2–4 ft/0.6–1.2 m high. Foliage medium green, nearly glabrous, fine in texture; leaf blades elongate, flat, the margins and upper surface toward the tip slightly scabrous or glabrous, nearly straight to geniculate, 4–8 in./1–2 dm long, 0.10–0.25 in./3–6 mm wide; sheaths shorter than the internodes, often sparsely villous at the throat; ligule membranous, 2–3 mm long. Inflorescence a subflabellate, long-exserted, linear-oblong panicle becoming ovate or obovate branched and bearing slender racemes near the base, often partly included in the dilated sheaths, silvery white, bearing paired spikelets, racemes several to many or sometimes few, usually compact, 1–2 in./2.5–5.0 cm long, the common axis usually

Andropogon barbinodis.
Habit, × 1/2; spikelet, ×
5. *Source: Manual of the
Grasses of the United States.*
USDA Misc. Pub. 200. 1951.

shorter than the racemes, rarely longer, rachis joints and pedicels copiously long-villous; sessile spikelets perfect, flattened, lanceolate, 0.2–0.3 in./5–8 mm long; glumes about equal, the lower glume minutely hispid toward the apex, pubescent at the base, the enrolled margins ciliate, the upper three-nerved, minutely hispid on the keels and at or near the apex; lemmas about equal, the fertile lemma bearing a scabrous awn, geniculate and twisted, 0.75–1.00 in./19–25 mm long, glabrous or sparingly pubescent; palea small or wanting; pedicellate spikelets reduced, about 2 mm long, a single, narrow scale, with pedicel about 0.1 in./3 mm long. Flowering and fruiting occur from June through August.

Uses: Cane bluestem makes an excellent ground cover in meadows or in naturalized areas adjoining the more formal portion of the garden. Although *Andropogon* species are of little horticultural importance, several species are useful in improving the landscape.

Cultivation: Propagation is by seeding and by plant division, preferably the former. Cane bluestem does best in full sun on well-drained, moist soils. Maximum growth is achieved on sandy loam to loam calcareous soils that overflow often, providing a constant moisture supply.

Latin name: *Andropogon gerardi* Vitman
Synonym: *Andropogon provincialis* Lam.
Cultivars: 'Champ,' 'Kaw,' 'Pawnee'
Common names: Big bluestem, Turkeyfoot
Origin: North America
Habitat: Prairies, woodlands, cultivated
Hardiness: Zones 4 through 9
Description: An upright-open to upright-arching, cespitose perennial; rhizomes short or absent. Culms robust, pinkish, forming large tufts, 4–7 ft/1.2–2.2 m high, usually sparingly branched toward the summit, grooved above the nodes. Foliage medium green or often glaucous, fine in texture; leaf blades somewhat villous, flat, elongate, 12–16 in./3–4 dm long, 0.1–0.4 in./3–10 mm wide, with very scabrous margins; sheaths glabrous or more or less villous, occasionally densely so, longer than the internodes; ligule membranous, 1–2 mm long, finely lacerate. Inflorescence a panicle of 2–5 erect conjugate racemes, 2–4 in./5–10 cm long, borne on long-exserted terminal peduncles bearing paired spikelets, usually purplish, sometimes yellowish, rachis straight, the joints and pedicels stiffly ciliate on one or both margins, the joints hispid at the base, sessile spikelets fertile, 0.25–0.40 in./6–10 mm long; glumes coriaceous, narrow, the lower usually scabrous, slightly sulcate, round, flat, or concave on the back, the median nerve weak or wanting, the awn geniculate and tightly twisted below, 0.4–0.8 in./10–20 mm long, the upper glume laterally compressed; lemmas about as long as or shorter than the glumes, sterile lemma shorter than the glumes, empty, hyaline, fertile lemma hyaline, narrow, entire, bifid, usually bearing a bent and twisted awn from near the apex or from between the lobes; palea hyaline, small or lacking; pedicellate spikelets staminate, similar to fertile spikelets but reduced in size and awnless, 0.2–0.3 in./5–8 mm long. Flowering and fruiting occur from August through September.

Uses: Big bluestem is tall enough for use in background plantings in borders or along the edges of woods and in massed plantings in naturalized areas. The dried colorful panicles make good additions to dried arrangements. They may be used as a tall screen or windbreak. Big bluestem is useful in specimen plantings

Andropogon gerardi. **Habit,** × **1/2; pair of spikelets,** × **5.** *Source: Manual of the Grasses of the United States.* USDA Misc. Pub. 200. 1951.

in water gardens, where the light bronze foliage exhibits good fall color and the plants persist in the landscape throughout the winter. It is useful along highways as ground cover and for erosion control.

Cultivation: Propagation is by seeding and by plant division, usually the former. Big bluestem is deep rooted and does well in rich, heavy clay, calcareous soils that are well drained. The deep root system of big bluestem makes the plants heat and drought tolerant; it thrives in hot, dry sites in full sun. Despite its drought tolerance, big bluestem plants are more luxuriant when grown on fertile, moist soil.

Cultivars: *Andropogon gerardi* Vitman 'Champ,' 'Kaw,' 'Pawnee' The cultivars Champ, Kaw, and Pawnee are used in the same manner as big bluestem; they are adapted to zones 4–9.

Latin name: *Andropogon stolonifer* (Nash) Hitchc.
Synonym: *Schizachyrium stoloniferum* Nash
Common name: Creeping bluestem
Origin: North America
Habitat: Open woods on sandy, acid soils
Hardiness: Zones 9 through 10
Description: An upright-open to spreading perennial with scaly, creeping rhizomes. Culms 2–5 ft/0.6–1.5 m high, solitary or few in a tuft. Foliage glabrous to villous, medium green, fine to medium in texture; leaf blades flat or slightly V-shaped, abruptly tapered at the tip, 6–18 in./1.5–4.5 dm long, 0.25–0.50 in./6–13 mm wide, very hairy toward the base; sheaths strongly flattened, often light purplish at the base, upper part very hairy, otherwise glabrous, longer than the internodes; ligule membranous, slightly rough, 1–3 mm long. Inflorescence a panicle of several pedunculate, terminal and axillary racemes, usually long-exserted, 1–2 in./2.5–5.0 cm long, the slender rachis joints and pedicels silky villous, the entire inflorescence 1–2 ft/3–6 dm long; spikelets in pairs, sessile spikelets fertile, 0.2–0.4 in./5–10 mm long, scabrous on the margins and toward the summit, glumes of fertile spikelets narrow, coriaceous, the lower slightly sulcate, scabrous, flat, round or concave on the back, the awn tightly twisted below, geniculate, 0.4–0.6 in./10–15 mm long, the upper laterally compressed; lemmas about as long as the glumes, fertile lemma narrow, entire or bifid, hyaline, usually bearing a bent and twisted awn, the sterile lemma shorter than the glumes, empty, hyaline; palea small, hyaline, or lacking; pedicellate spikelets smaller than the sessile spikelets, 0.2–0.3 in./5–8 mm long. Flowering and fruiting occur from August through September.

Uses: Creeping bluestem remains evergreen through most winters in areas where it is adapted. This sod-forming, semievergreen perennial is used as ground cover in extensive areas and for erosion control on sandy, acid soils. It may be employed effectively as medium screens or windbreaks.

Cultivation: Creeping bluestem grows best in open areas but tolerates light or partial shade. Seed production is very erratic. Propagation is by division

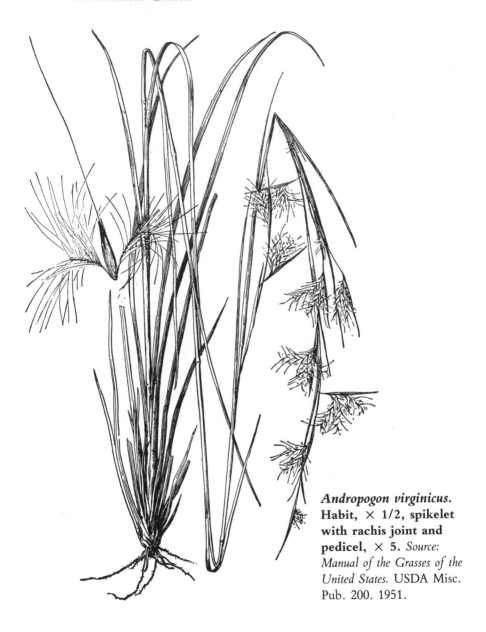

Andropogon virginicus.
Habit, × 1/2, spikelet
with rachis joint and
pedicel, × 5. *Source:*
Manual of the Grasses of the
United States. USDA Misc.
Pub. 200. 1951.

of the plant crowns, which is best done in early spring when new growth
appears.

Latin name: *Andropogon virginicus* L.
Synonym: *Anatherum virginicum* K. Spreng.
Common name: Broomsedge

Origin: North America
Habitat: Open ground, pastures, old fields, waste grounds, cultivated
Hardiness: Zones 3 through 10
Description: An upright-narrow, strongly tufted, vigorous perennial. Culms slender, simple at the base, many-branched above with short, sterile branches at the base, 2–5 ft/0.6–1.5 m high. Foliage light green when young, becoming dark green and eventually bronze at maturity, fine in texture; leaf blades flat or folded, 12–16 in./3–4 dm long, 0.1–0.2 in./3–5 mm wide, hirsute near the base on the upper surface, slightly rough on the margins; lower sheaths compressed, keeled, equitant, somewhat hirsute on the margins with long hairs, upper sheaths glabrous or more or less pilose, occasionally conspicuously pilose along the margins and at the throat, shorter than the internodes; ligule membranous, short, strongly minutely ciliate. Inflorescence a long, linear, terminal panicle bearing racemes mostly in pairs, 0.8–1.2 in./2–3 cm long, shorter than and included in the spathes, rachis flexuous, long villous, bearing paired spikelets at each node, one sessile and perfect, the other pedicellate and rudimentary, rachis internodes as long as the spikelets; sessile spikelets perfect, 0.10–0.15 in./3–4 mm long, narrow, glumes almost equal, the lower acute or minutely bifid at the apex, grooved on the back between the two sharp keels on the sides, the keels more or less scabrid, upper glume acute, round on the back, the keel scabrous, lower glume dorsally flattened with a strong nerve near each margin; sterile lemma hyaline, often pubescent on the margins, fertile lemma bifid about one-fourth its length, sometimes pubescent on the margins, with a scabrous, straight awn 0.4–0.8 in./10–20 mm long, sometimes curved but never coiled, always green, exserted part 0.4–0.6 in./10–15 mm long; palea lacking; pedicellate spikelets lacking or, if present, reduced to a small scale, the pedicel exceeding the sessile spikelet. Flowering and fruiting occur from July through September.

Uses: Broomsedge provides good ground cover over extensive areas; it is especially striking in clumps in rock gardens and for naturalizing along margins of woods; the stramineous to bronze foliage provides good fall color, with the plants persisting into the winter. The stems and leaves of broomsedge have been used to dye cloth.

Cultivation: Broomsedge is a heavy seeder; it thrives in full sun on poor, depleted soils varying from sandy loams to heavy clays. It is widely distributed in the eastern United States in rainfall belts above 25 in./6 dm per annum on both acid and alkaline soils. Propagation is by seeding and by plant division. It is advisable to cut back the old growth each spring, which may enhance the growth rate of the new growth in addition to adding to its uniformity and attractiveness.

Anthoxanthum L. (**Vernalgrass, Flouve, Foin d'odeuer**). Name from Greek *anthos,* "flower," and *xanthos,* "yellow," referring to the yellow inflorescence. Type species, *Anthoxanthum odoratum* L. There are five or six species, native to Eurasia and North America. Aromatic annuals or perennials, with flat leaf blades and spikelike panicles. Spikelets with one terminal perfect floret and two sterile lemmas, the rachilla disarticulating above the glumes, the sterile lemmas falling attached to the fertile floret; glumes unequal, acute or mucronate; sterile lemmas shorter than the glumes, empty, awned from the back; fertile lemmas shorter than the sterile ones, awnless; palea one-nerved, round on the back, enclosed in the lemma.

Latin name: *Anthoxanthum odoratum* L.
Synonym: *Xanthonanthos odoratum* St. Lag.
Common name: Sweet vernalgrass
Origin: Eurasia
Habitat: Pastures, waste grounds in acid soils, cultivated
Hardiness: Zones 5 through 10
Description: A densely tufted, upright-narrow, fragrant perennial. Culms erect, simple or branching, tufted, slender, with one to three nodes, 12–14 in./3.0–3.5 dm high. Foliage medium green, fine in texture; leaf blades erect, 4–6 in./10–15 cm long, 0.1–0.3 in./3–8 mm wide, long attenuate, flat, rough, glabrous or sparingly pubescent above, sometimes pubescent or glabrous beneath, but slightly scabrous, sheaths glabrous or sparingly pubescent, shorter than the internodes, round on the back, open, bearded at the apex; auricles well developed, about 1 mm long, pilose-ciliate; ligule acute, membranous, 0.10–0.15 in./3–4 mm long. Inflorescence a congested, narrow, spikelike, branched long-exserted panicle, 1–3 in./2.5–8.0 cm long, 1–2 in./2.5–5.0 cm wide when in flower, loosely cylindrical, the branches erect, ascending or spreading, tawny or bronze green; spikelets brownish green becoming yellowish, crowded, linear-oblong, 0.25–0.30 in./6–8 mm long, three-flowered, with one terminal, perfect floret and two sterile lemmas; glumes unequal, glabrous or sparingly hirsute, keeled, acute or acuminate, 0.3–0.4 in./8–10 mm long, the lower one-nerved, ovate, 0.15–0.20 in./4–5 mm long, thin, about half the length of the upper, the upper three-nerved, firmer than the lower, 0.25–0.30 in./6–8 mm long, about 0.1 in./3 mm wide; sterile lemmas unequal, brownish, appressed long-pubescent, emarginate at the apex, about 0.1 in./3 mm long, the lobes obtuse and minutely erose, nerves obscure, the lower slightly longer than the upper, about 2–3 mm long, bearing a straight, barbed awn on the back inserted about halfway between the base and apex, projecting beyond the lemma about half the length of the lemma, upper lemma bearing an awn from the back from near the base; this awn is generally longer than the upper glume, bending outward at maturity about 1 mm beyond the apex of the lemma; the part below the bend stout, dark, smooth, almost black and twisted; that part above the bend straight and barbed; lemma of fertile floret smooth, firm, suborbicular, 2–3 mm long, somewhat twisted, nerves obscure; palea subacute, round on the back, glabrous, one-nerved, enclosed in the lemma, caryopsis-free, smooth, compressed, enclosed, about 2 mm long and 1 mm wide. Flowering and fruiting occur from

Anthoxanthum odoratum. Habit, × 1/2; spikelet, sterile lemmas, and fertile floret, × 5. *Source: Manual of the Grasses of the West Indies.* USDA Misc. Pub. 243. 1936.

May through July, with the plants producing their maximum coumarin during flowering.

Uses: The pleasant coumarin fragrance of sweet vernalgrass makes it popular for foreground border plantings and as group or specimen plants along walks, in rock and water gardens, and in mixed flower beds. It is often planted as a curiosity along streets and highways, in parks, golf courses, and in zoos and is well suited for the wild garden.

Cultivation: Sweet vernalgrass prefers full sun and thrives equally well on a range of soil types varying from loamy sands to heavy clays; it prefers acid soils. This polymorphic grass does well in both damp and dry sites, particularly the latter. It is usually established by direct seeding. Sweet vernalgrass may also be propagated by division of the plant crowns or transplanted as seedlings from seeding boxes.

Aristida **L. (Three-awn grass, Triple-awned grass, Needlegrass, Wiregrass).** Name from Latin, *arista,* "awn." Type species, *Aristida adscensionis* L. There are about 300 species, inhabiting the warmer regions of the world. Slender, tufted, low, annual and perennial grasses with narrow, frequently convolute leaf blades and narrow, sometimes open, panicles. Spikelets one-flowered, the rachilla disarticulating obliquely above the glumes; glumes equal or unequal, narrow, acute, acuminate, or awn-tipped; lemma indurate, narrow, terete, convolute, with a hard, sharp-pointed, usually minutely bearded callus, terminating above in a usually trifid awn, the base sometimes undivided, forming a column.

> **Latin name:** *Aristida purpurascens* Poir.
> **Synonym:** *Aristida purpurascens* var. *minor* Vasey
> **Common names:** Arrowfeather three-awn grass, Arrowgrass, Broomsedge
> **Origin:** North America
> **Habitat:** Dry, sandy soils
> **Hardiness:** Zones 4 through 9
> **Description:** A weakly tufted, upright-narrow perennial. Culms erect, simple, or sparingly branched, slightly roughened below the panicle, tufted, sometimes from a decumbent base, the lower internodes short and sometimes zigzag, slender, 15–30 in./3.8–7.6 dm high. Foliage medium green, fine in texture; leaf blades flat or involute and slightly rough toward the tip with a few hairs on the upper surface near the base, elongate, long attenuate, usually 5–8 in./1.3–2.0 dm long, 1–2 mm wide; sheaths longer than the internodes, sometimes shorter above, the lower flattened and keeled, glabrous or with a few loose hairs; ligule a fringe of short hairs. Inflorescence a rather lax, nodding, narrow, branched panicle, fully exserted, 6–12 in./1.5–3.0 dm long, about 1 in./25 mm in diameter, purplish or brownish, the branches 0.8–1.0 in./20–25 mm long, the lower somewhat distant, the upper crowded, rather laxly ap-

pressed, bearing spikelets commonly two to four, nearly to the base, crowded on each branch, axillary panicles usually much shorter than the terminal; spikelets one-flowered, narrow, 0.3–0.5 in./8–13 mm long, exclusive of the awns; glumes about equal, 0.3–0.5 in./8–13 mm long, the lower slightly longer than the upper, awn-pointed, one-nerved, scabrous on the keel, the upper one-to-three-nerved, nearly glabrous; lemmas 0.25–0.30 in./6–8 mm long, slightly pubescent or glabrous, scabrous on the keels, margins, and at the barely beaked summit; callus very short, about 0.25 in./6 mm long; awns unequal, the central usually somewhat longer, divergent, spreading or somewhat reflexed, 0.8–1.2 in./2–3 cm long, the lateral 0.7–1.0 in./18–25 mm long; palea thin, included in the lemma. Flowering and fruiting occur from July through September.

Uses: Arrowfeather three-awn grass is an excellent ground-cover plant for naturalized areas. It is hardy and persistent and grows well in dry, hard, rocky or sandy soils on difficult sites. This perennial is of no particular ornamental value; its chief asset is its adaptation to a wide range of growing conditions.

Cultivation: Propagation is by seeding or by plant division, preferably the former. The plants prefer full sun on dry sites.

Latin name: *Aristida purpurea* Nutt.
Synonym: *Aristida purpurea* var. *laxiflora* Merr.
Common names: Purple needlegrass, Purple three-awn grass
Origin: North America
Habitat: Dry grassland, plains
Hardiness: Zones 5 through 10
Description: A densely tufted, upright-narrow perennial. Culms erect, 12–30 in./3.0–7.6 dm high, with numerous innovations, the outer culms somewhat decumbent at the base, often branched at the base and at the lower nodes, sometimes rough just below the panicle. Foliage medium green, fine in texture; leaf blades variable in length, 4–10 in./1.0–2.5 dm long, almost 0.1 in./3 mm wide, involute, sometimes flat, rough on the upper surface toward the apex; sheaths usually longer than the internodes, the lower usually very rough and villous at the throat; ligule a fringe or rim of short hairs. Inflorescence a narrow, nodding, lax, purplish panicle, becoming exserted, 4–8 in./1–2 dm long, about 1–2 in./2.5–5.0 cm in diameter, including the long awns, the branches rather distant, about 2 in./5 cm long, often in pairs, one short, the branches and long pedicels often curved or flexuous, capillary, the lower longer and naked at the base; spikelets narrow, one-flowered, 0.4–0.6 in./10–15 mm long; glumes unequal, acuminate, one-nerved, bearing short awns, 1–2 mm long, often between two slender, irregular teeth, the lower 0.25–0.30 in./6–8 mm long, scabrous on the keel, the upper glabrous, about 0.8 in./20 mm long; lemmas 0.3–0.4 in./8–10 mm long, the body tapering to a scarcely beaked summit, tuberculate-scabrous in lines from below the middle to the summit, the background usually purplish, the raised parts whitish, callus hirsute, less than 1 mm long, awns nearly equal, nearly glabrous on the outside of the slightly contorted base, scab-

Aristida purpurea. **Habit,** × **1.** *Source: Manual of the Grasses of the United States.* USDA Misc. Pub. 200. 1951.

rous above, finally spreading, 1.2–2.0 in./3–5 cm long; palea thin, included by the lemma. Flowering and fruiting occur from May through July.

Uses: The large, twisted or curved, purplish inflorescence is the main attraction of purple needlegrass. The flowers are borne high above the foliage and complement the latter. The feathery, flexuous inflorescence is colorful when in full flower. Clumps of this grass add diversity to rock gardens and to perennial borders.

Cultivation: Propagation is by direct seeding and by plant division, preferably the former. The plants prefer full sun in moist or dry soil as they are quite drought tolerant; they produce copious quantities of seeds.

Latin name: *Aristida wrightii* Nash
Common names: Wright's three-awn grass, Wright's triple-awned grass
Origin: North America
Habitat: Rangeland, pastures, dry plains
Hardiness: Zones 6 through 10
Description: An upright-narrow, weak, short-lived perennial. Culms densely tufted, erect, simple, glabrous to rough, 1–2 ft/3–6 dm high. Foliage medium green, fine in texture; leaf blades 3–9 in./0.8–2.3 dm long, 1–2 mm wide, those of the innovations longer, involute, glabrous or slightly rough below, filiform, twisting or curling, sheaths mostly basal, round on the back, open, usually villous with a hispid line across the collar, those of the innovations often rough; ligule a fringe or rim of short hairs. Inflorescence an erect, branched, narrow panicle, 6–8 in./1.5–2.0 dm long, about 1.0–1.6 in./2.5–4.0 cm in diameter, initially included, becoming erect, exserted, purplish becoming straw yellow at maturity, branches rather distant, straight, ascending or appressed, the lower sometimes flexuous, about 2 in./5 cm long, usually bearing two to five spikelets per branch; spikelets narrow, one-flowered, about 0.5 in./13 mm long; glumes unequal, one-nerved, acuminate, the lower scabrous on the keel, 0.20–0.25 in./5–6 mm long, the upper glabrous, about 0.5 in./13 mm long; lemmas 0.4–0.5 in./10–13 mm long, callus short, pubescent, about 1 mm long, triple-awned, the awns nearly equal, 0.8–1.2 in./2–3 cm long, somewhat contorted at the base, divergent, sometimes almost horizontally spreading; palea thin, enclosed within the lemma. Flowering and fruiting occur from June through September.

Uses: The flowering panicles of Wright's three-awn grass are attractive and interesting. The curled, needlelike leaves are especially attractive, as are the flowering panicles with long, divergent, curved awns. The delicate flower heads, with their long, divergent awns, excel when cut and dried for winter displays. The curled, long-awned inflorescence adds to the attractiveness of the grass when planted in clumps in foreground borders and in specimen plantings in rock gardens.

Cultivation: Propagation is by direct seeding. The plants prefer full sun on rocky, sandy, and clay soils. Wright's three-awn grass seeds itself copiously;

the plants are quite drought tolerant. New growth begins in early spring, with the plants becoming semidormant during the summer but resuming growth in the autumn. Flower heads appear a month after growth commences.

Arrhenatherum Beauv. (Oatgrass). Name for the Greek *arren,* "masculine," and *ather,* "awn," referring to the awned staminate floret. Lectotype, *Avena elatior* L. There are six species, native to the Mediterranean region. Rather tall perennials, with flat leaf blades and narrow panicles. Spikelets two-flowered, the lower floret staminate, the upper perfect, the rachilla disarticulating above the glumes and produced beyond the florets; glumes rather broad and chartaceous, the lower one-nerved, the upper a little longer than the lower and about as long as the spikelet, three-nerved; lemmas five-nerved, hairy on the callus, the lower bearing near the base a twisted, geniculate, exserted awn, the upper bearing a short, straight, slender awn just below the tip.

Latin name: *Arrhenatherum elatius* (L.) J. Presl
Synonym: *Avena elatior* L.
Cultivars: *Arrhenatherum elatius* var. *bulbosum* 'Variegatum' (Willd.) Spenner Onion couch
Varieties: *Arrhenatherum elatius* var. *bulbosum* (Willd.) Spenner Bulbous oatgrass, Tuber oatgrass
Common name: Tall oatgrass
Origin: Europe
Habitat: Cultivated, escape from cultivation
Hardiness: Zones 4 through 9
Description: A loosely tufted, upright-open perennial with slowly spreading, yellowish rhizomes. Culms stout, erect to somewhat spreading, 3–5 ft / 0.9–1.5 m high with a 3 ft/9 dm spread when in flower; the nodes are usually smooth but sometimes hairy. Foliage medium green, becoming slightly reddish or bronze toward the end of the growing season, fine in texture; leaf blades flat, 10–15 in./2.5–3.8 dm long, 0.2–0.4 in./5–10 mm wide, long attenuate, usually smooth beneath and slightly hairy above; sheaths round on the back, longer or shorter than the internodes; ligule membranous, 1–2 mm long. Inflorescence a loosely branched, erect or nodding, semicompact, oblong panicle, 6–12 in./1.5–3.0 dm long and almost as wide, becoming light beige with age, the short branches verticillate; spikelets two-flowered, approximate, oblong, 0.25–0.30 in./6–8 mm long, the lower staminate, the upper perfect, the rachilla prolonged behind the upper palea into a hirsute bristle; glumes chartaceous, finely pointed, persistent, minutely rough, lower lanceolate, one-nerved, shorter than the upper, the upper narrowly ovate, three-nerved, minutely scabrous, about as long as the spikelet; lemmas almost 0.5 in./13 mm long, five-to-seven-nerved, firm except for the thin tips, short-bearded or hairy on the callus, the upper or both loosely pubescent or glabrous on the back, minutely rough upwards, that

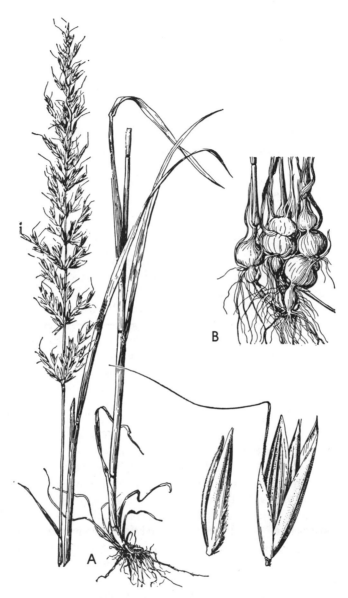

Arrhenatherum elatius. A, Habit, × 1/2; spikelet and floret, × 5. B, var. **bulbosum,** basal corms, × 1. *Source: Manual of the Grasses of the United States.* USDA Misc. Pub. 200. 1951.

of the staminate floret awned from the back, the geniculate twisted awn 0.5–0.6 in./13–15 mm long, that of the fertile floret awnless or both with a short bristle from near the tip; palea two-keeled, keels puberulent, hyaline, as long as its lemma, ciliate on the nerves; caryopsis sulcate. Flowering and fruiting occur from June through July; seeds are mature by late August or early September.

Uses: The principal utilitarian value of tall oatgrass is that of providing feed and wildlife protection in naturalized areas. Its ornamental value lies in its use in middleground plantings of perennial borders, or as a screen or windbreak of medium height when planted in rows. The colorful rustic foliage, particularly late in the growing season, and its shiny reddish seeds are an added attraction in the autumn. The flowering panicles are useful in dried floral arrangements. The shiny, hard, bright red seeds shatter and fall to the ground upon maturity.

Bulbous oatgrass, with its green foliage, and its cultivar Variegatum, with its bright, variegated foliage, are grown primarly for their foliage. They are used as ground cover in water gardens and as bedding plants in foreground perennial borders. The dark green foliage of bulbous oatgrass and the variegated foliage of its cultivar Variegatum are the chief assets of these curious ornamental grasses. Both forms may be grown with some success indoors if they have a high light intensity. The leaves of bulbous oatgrass and its cultivar retain their shape and color well into the winter. The plants are semievergreen or evergreen when grown indoors and outdoors in zones 7–9. Onion couch, *Arrhenatherum elatius* var. *bulbosum* 'Variegatum,' is often used in sink gardens.

Cultivation: Tall oatgrass is usually propagated by seeding or by plant division, preferably the former. It thrives best in full sun or fertile, well-drained, moderately acid to neutral soils. The foliage occasionally suffers severe damage from leaf fungi in the class Hyphomycete.

Bulbous oatgrass is propagated by plant division. The plants require frequent division to remain robust. These low-growing forms may become weedy in some situations, but they are easily controlled. The plants grow best in cool weather and remain semievergreen and colorful into the winter in warmer areas. Some of the leaves may turn brown and die during hot summer weather. Bulbous oatgrass and its cultivar Variegatum have compact hard corms near the base of the plant just below ground level, which aid the plants in surviving extended periods of drought and low temperatures. Bulbous oatgrass, with its green foliage, tolerates full sun, but it does best in light or partial shade. The variegated cultivar prefers light shade because the foliage usually becomes damaged and discolored by direct sunlight. Both forms require moist, fertile, well-drained soils.

Cultivars and varieties: *Arrhenatherum elatius* var. *bulbosum* (Willd.) Spenner 'Variegatum,' Onion couch   The cultivar Variegatum is the most exciting bulbous oatgrass, with its bright, variegated, soft foliage. A tufted, cormatose, low-growing, open to spreading, semievergreen perennial with hard, compact corms near the base. Culms 8–16 in./2–4 dm high with an equal spread. Foliage glabrous, soft, tufted near the base of the plant, fine in texture, variegated; leaves with longitudinal yellowish and green stripes, 2–3 in./ 5–8 cm long, about 0.25 in./6 mm wide, sharply tapering to a fine point. Inflorescence a loosely branched panicle bearing small, inconspicuous, greenish white flowers. The distinctly variegated colorful foliage retains its color throughout the growing season and into the autumn. Flowering and fruiting occur from July through August; flowering may occur earlier on plants grown indoors. Onion couch is adapted to zones 4 through 9; it grows best in partial shade during early spring and early fall in cool weather. The small, variegated, spreading plants are useful in accent groups or edging plantings in foreground borders and as houseplants. Onion couch is grown primarily for its multicolored foliage.

Arrhenatherum elatius var. *bulbosum* (Willd.) Spenner Bulbous oatgrass, Tuber oatgrass   A tufted, open to spreading, hardy, semievergreen perennial with hard, compact corms near the base of the plant. Culms 8–16 in./2–4 dm high with an equal spread. Foliage soft, dark green, fine in texture; leaves flat, smooth, glabrous, 2–3 in./5–8 cm long, about 0.25 in./6 mm wide, tapering to a fine point. Inflorescence a loosely branched panicle bearing small, inconspicuous, whitish flowers. Flowering occurs from July through August; flowering may be earlier in the year for plants grown indoors. Bulbous oatgrass is best adapted to partial shade in zones 4 through 9. The small, mound-forming to spreading plants are grown in groups or as edging plants in foreground borders, in rock gardens, and as houseplants. The small plants do not spread rapidly and may be used as edging plants.

Arundo L. The ancient Latin name. Lectotype, *Arundo donax* L. This genus consists of six species, native to the tropics and subtropics of the Old World. Usually tall perennial reeds, with broad, linear blades and large, plumelike, terminal panicles. Spikelets several-flowered, the florets successively smaller, the summits of all about equal, the rachilla glabrous, disarticulating above the glumes and between the florets; glumes somewhat unequal, membranous, three-nerved, narrow, tapering into a slender point, about as long as the spikelet; lemmas thin, three-nerved, densely and softly long-pilose, gradually narrowed at the summit, the nerves ending in slender teeth, the middle one extending into a straight awn.

Latin name: *Arundo donax* L.
Synonym: *Arundo sativa* Lam.
Varieties: *Arundo donax* var. *versicolor* (P. Mill) J. Stokes Striped giant reed

Common names: Giant reed, Carrizo, Cana brava
Origin: Southern Europe
Habitat: Cultivated, escape from cultivation
Hardiness: Zones 7 through 10
Description: A vigorous, upright-narrow to upright-arching, perennial reed with short, stout, woody rhizomes, the plants forming large colonies. Culms glabrous, woody, hollow, with few branches, 10–26 ft/3.1–8.0 m high, up to 1.6 in./4 cm in diameter at the base. Foliage conspicuously distichous, glaucous or light green, coarse in texture; leaves rather evenly spaced along the culm, arching, blades 18–24 in./4.5–6.0 dm long, 2–3 in./5–8 cm wide, the upper shorter and narrower, lanceolate-acuminate, clasping, margins slightly scabrous, otherwise glabrous except slightly rough toward the apex; sheaths shorter than the internodes, wide, imbricate, glabrous, persistent, collar light green; ligule membranous, fringed, about 1 mm long. Inflorescence a many-branched, semicompact, feathery, oblong panicle, 18–30 in./4.5–7.6 dm long, 6–10 in./1.5–2.5 dm wide, narrowing toward the top, usually tawny, finally copiously hairy, dense, plumelike, branches 12–18 in./3.0–4.5 dm long, ascending with numerous shorter branchlets, naked at the base, main axis glabrous, axis of branches and branchlets scabrous; spikelets numerous, crowded, three-to-several-flowered, narrowly lanceolate, 0.4–0.5 in./10–13 mm long, successively smaller, on slender, scabrous pedicels nearly as long as the spikelets; glumes somewhat unequal, membranous, three-nerved, 0.3–0.4 in./8–10 mm long, acute, about the length of the spikelets tapering into a slender point, purplish, the upper slightly longer than the lower, acute; lemmas densely long-pilose, thin, three-nerved, 0.3–0.4 in./8.10 mm long, the awns sometimes extending above the glumes, slender, acuminate, lower hairs as long as the lemmas, awn 1–2 mm long, borne between two teeth, longer than the teeth; palea one-half as long as its lemma, truncate, ciliate on the keels. Flowering and fruiting occur from September until frost with the panicles persisting into winter.

Uses: The foliage of giant reed and striped giant reed turns beige or light tan following the first killing frost in the fall, remaining on the plants throughout the winter; in addition, the terminal tawny panicles remain intact on the plants, thus extending their attractiveness into the fall and winter seasons. Both forms are particularly striking when grown in large clumps as specimens; they are noted for their architectural qualities, foliage color, and decorative, flowering panicles. These plants are used to protect other plants from damage by wind and wind-blown sand; they are useful as screens. Both forms are useful and attractive when grown as a tall or medium hedge if kept cut to the desired height. The plants also serve as tall screens and barriers along property lines or screens for buildings or unsightly areas and for shade. They are nearly unexcelled in specimen plantings in rock and water gardens or in the background of perennial borders. The large, plumelike panicles are excellent as cut flowers or in dried floral arrangements. The dried, flowering plumes of giant reed and its variety may be dyed. The tough, hollow canes of giant reed are a source of reeds for

Arundo donax. Habit, × 1/3; spikelet and floret, × 3. *Source: Manual of the Grasses of the United States.* USDA Misc. Pub. 200. 1951.

musical instruments. When used in water gardens or near pools and lakes and along streams, the plants should be located so that they are reflected in the water for some portion of the day, thus enhancing their attractiveness. Striped giant reed is grown primarily for its multicolored foliage; it is an excellent specimen plant when grown in clumps. Giant reed and striped giant reed are often used in landscape improvement of parks, golf courses, and zoos.

Cultivation: Fertile, well-drained soil with adequate moisture is essential for maximum growth of giant reed and its variety. Giant reed and its botanical variety thrive best in moist or wet soils. Both giant reed and its variety versicolor may be grown outside with success in zone 7 but less successfully in zone 6. The plants may not flower before frost when grown in the cooler regions. Clumps of giant reed may become too large over the years, thus requiring the removal of some plants to maintain the desired size. The location of giant reed in gardens, particularly small gardens, may become a problem on occasion; therefore, careful consideration should be given to its location. The tall, large, densely growing plants may shade other, smaller plants in close proximity. The plants are killed to ground level in colder climates, with the old culms, including their panicles, remaining erect throughout the winter. New plants arise from the plant crowns each spring. Old culms may or may not be removed as desired. The removal of old culms in the spring after regrowth has begun prevents them from remaining an eyesore for the remainder of the growing season. The plants are propagated by seeding and by vegetative propagation, most commonly the latter. Vegetative propagation is done by division of the plant crowns or rhizomes and by rooting cuttings of the culms. The lower portions of canes should be cut into three-node (three-eye) seed pieces and planted directly on the growing site. The seed pieces may be treated with a root-promoting substance if desired and planted directly in place, provided they are watered regularly enough to promote new growth. The cuttings should be planted with one or possibly two nodes below the soil surface, making certain that they are planted in the same way they were on the old culms. Division of plant crowns in early spring is a sure easy and fast method of propagation, as new growth is usually more rapid than that from cuttings.

Varieties: *Arundo donax* var. *versicolor* (P. Mill.) J. Stokes, Striped giant reed   The plants of this rhizomatous variety are identical in shape, growth habit, and texture to those of giant reed, except that the plants are shorter and have coarse, variegated foliage. Culms usually 6–10 ft / 1.8–3.1 m high, and very conspicuous by their broad, variegated foliage. Leaves are usually 12 in./3 dm long, 2 in./5 cm wide, with pale green and white longitudinal stripes that fade into each other. The relative amount of green and white stripes in the variegated leaves may vary throughout the growing season. The markings are most distinct on young, new growth in early spring. Plumelike white or light green, terminal panicles, 12–18 in./3.0–4.5 dm long, form in September and October. Giant reed and its variants remain upright throughout the winter, retaining their beige or tan foliage and portions of the flowering plumes, providing fair fall color. Striped giant reed thrives in frost-free greenhouses, where the plants are usually much smaller than those grown outside. It is a good accent and specimen plant on the edge of the lawn.

Other ornamental species include *Arundo conspicua* 'Toe-toe,' a tussock-forming, warm-season, upright-open perennial, and *Arundo fulvida* 'Kakaho' erect-plumed tussock grass (see Appendix 1).

Avena **L. (Oats, Avoine).** The old Latin name for oats. Lectotype, *Avena sativa* L. There are about 55 species, native to Europe, the Mediterranean region, and North Africa to Central Asia. The most important species of the genus is *Avena sativa* L., the familiar cultivated oat. Low or moderately tall annuals and perennials, mostly the former, with narrow or open, usually rather few-flowered panicles of large spikelets. Spikelets two- or three-flowered, the rachilla bearded, disarticulating above the glumes and between the florets; glumes about equal, membranous or chartaceous, seven-to-nine-nerved, longer than the lower floret, usually exceeding the upper floret; lemmas indurate, except toward the summit, five-to-nine-nerved, bidentate, bearing a dorsal bent and twisted awn, straight and reduced in *Avena sativa* L., the awn commonly breaks at the bend with age. Oats are one of the basic foods for human beings and for livestock.

Latin name: *Avena sativa* L.
Synonym: *Avena fatua* var. *sativa* Hausskn.
Cultivars: Many in cultivation
Common name: Oats (Cultivated oat)
Origin: Eurasia
Habitat: Cultivated, escape from cultivation
Hardiness: Zones 5 through 10
Description: An upright-open, short-lived annual. Culms solitary or occasionally tufted, thick, 20–40 in./0.5–1.0 m high, erect or slightly geniculate. Foliage light to medium green, medium to coarse in texture; leaves evenly distributed along the culm; blades flat, finely pointed, 10–18 in./2.5–4.5 dm long, 0.3–0.8 in./8–20 mm wide, more or less scabrous on upper surface and along the margins; sheaths slightly shorter than the internodes, round on the back, open; ligule membranous, toothed, round on the back, almost truncate, 0.15–0.20 in./4–5 mm long. Inflorescence a narrow, one-sided, open, erect or nodding, branched panicle, 8–10 in./2.0–2.5 dm long, its branches ascending with drooping spikelets; spikelets 0.7–1.0 in./18–25 mm long excluding the awns, two-flowered, pedicellate, pedicels thickened below the spikelet, rachilla of lower floret bearded; glumes about equal, persistent, broad, acute, membranous

and prominently many-veined, usually 7-to-11-nerved, 0.8–1.0 in./20–25 mm long; lemmas round on the back, the apex two-toothed, glabrous, awnless, or one or both with a straight, dorsal, long awn, 1.0–1.6 in./2.5–4.0 cm long, lower lemma 0.5–0.8 in./13–20 mm long, upper shorter, five-to-nine-nerved, the awn borne on the midvein near the middle of the back of the lemma; palea two-keeled, two-toothed, ciliate, nearly as long as its lemma; caryopsis enclosed, hardly sulcate. Flowering and fruiting occur from May through June, with the seedheads maturing by late July or early August.

Uses: Dry, mature seedheads of oats are useful in dried floral arrangements, which may be used in their natural color or dyed. The immature, green flower heads are attractive on the plants and are useful as cut flowers. Oats are grown occasionally in rock gardens.

Cultivation: Propagation is by seeding; the plants easily reseed themselves. Oats grow best in full sun in a wide range of soil types.

Latin name: *Avena sterilis* L.
Synonym: *Avena algeriensis* Trab.
Cultivars: Several in cultivation
Common name: Animated oats
Origin: Mediterranean region, Central Asia
Habitat: Cultivated, escape from cultivation
Hardiness: Zones 3 through 8
Description: An upright-open, short-lived annual. Culms solitary or in small tufts, erect or slightly bent near the base, glabrous, with three or four nodes, 2–4 ft/0.6–1.2 m high. Foliage light to medium green, fine in texture; leaf blades flat, rough, medium attenuate, 4–20 in./1–5 dm long, 0.15–0.30 in./4–8 mm wide; sheaths light green, about the length of the internodes or longer, round on the back; ligule membranous, blunt, 0.15–0.25 in./4–6 mm long. Inflorescence a loosely branched, pyramidal, nodding panicle, 4–18 in./1.0–4.5 dm long, 4–8 in./1–2 dm wide, branches mostly clustered, widely spread, loosely divided; spikelets scattered, pendulous, borne on nearly equal or unequal pedicels, two- or three-flowered, 1.6–2.0 in./4–5 cm long excluding the awns; glumes about equal, acuminate, 7-to-11 nerved, membranous; lemmas densely appressed pubescent, narrowly oblong-lanceolate, two-to-four-toothed at the apex, round on the back, five-to-nine-nerved, 0.5–0.8 in./13–20 mm long; a stout straight awn 2–3 in./5–8 cm long, borne from the middle of the back of the lemma; palea ciliate, keeled, about as long as the lemma; caryopsis sulcate, enclosed. Flowering and fruiting occur from May through mid-June.

Uses: Animated oats are ideal in middleground plantings of annual borders. The flowering panicles are attractive on the plants and as cut flowers when green and in dried floral arrangements when mature. The mature panicles are attractive in their natural color or when dyed. The plants of animated oats are unattractive at their best, but they are occasionally cultivated as a curiosity; the plants have a short flowering period. The movement of immature and mature spikelets on the plants is interesting in that they twist and turn according to changes in ambient humidity and temperature.

Cultivation: Propagation is by seeding; the plants readily reseed themselves. Animated oats thrive best in full sun in a wide range of soil types.

Axonopus **Beauv.** Name from Greek *axon,* "axis," and *pous,* "foot." Lectotype, *Axonopus compressus* (Sw.) Beauv. There are about 60 species; perennial or, rarely, annual grasses, mostly in the Western Hemisphere. Our species are cespitose or stoloniferous glabrous perennials; usually with flat, abruptly round or somewhat pointed leaf blades, and two to four slender, spikelike racemes, digitate or racemose along the main axis. Spikelets depressed-biconvex, not turgid, oblong, usually obtuse, solitary, subsessile, and alternate, in two rows on one side of a trigonous rachis, the back of the fertile lemma turned from the rachis; lower glume wanting; upper glume and sterile lemma equal, the lemma without a palea, fertile lemma and palea indurate, the lemma oblong-elliptic, usually obtuse, the margins slightly enrolled.

Latin name: *Axonopus compressus* (Sw.) Beauv.
Synonym: *Anastrophus compressus* Schlect. ex Doell
Common names: Carpet grass, Jointgrass
Origin: North and South America
Habitat: Cultivated, escape from cultivation
Hardiness: Zones 7 through 10
Description: A decumbent perennial with elongate, leafy stolons with short internodes. Culms stout, compressed, flattened, branching, 1–2 ft/3–6 dm high, the nodes usually densely pubescent, stolons numerous and creeping. Foliage dark green, medium in texture; cauline leaves 3–10 in./0.8–2.5 dm long, 0.3–0.5 in. mm wide, the uppermost greatly reduced, 2–4 in./5–10 cm long, flat or folded at the base, narrowly linear, obtuse, scabrous on the margins and toward the apex, sometimes the margins sparsely ciliate at the base, stolon leaves 1.0–1.6 in./2.5–4.0 cm long, 0.10–0.15 in./3–4 mm wide; sheaths crowded below, flattened, glabrous with few soft hairs, often sparsely ciliate at the throat; ligule short, membranous, short-ciliate. Inflorescence two to five terminal and axillary spikelike racemes on slender peduncles, long-exserted on the long filiform portion of the culm, in pairs, the upper two conjugate, or an additional one or two below, subdigitate, 1.6–4.0 in./4–10 cm long, slender, bearing spikelets to the base, spikelets equal to the internodes or slightly overlapping; spikelets appressed, somewhat flattened, oblong-elliptic, obtuse or subacute,

Axonopus compressus.
Habit, × 1/2. *Source:
Manual of the Grasses of the
West Indies.* USDA Misc.
Pub. 243. 1936.

2–3 mm long, solitary, sessile, and alternate in two rows on one side of a three-angled rachis; the lower glume wanting, upper glume and sterile lemma equal and slightly longer than the caryopsis, distinctly pointed, sparsely pubescent, five-nerved, or by suppression of the midnerve four-nerved, the two lateral nerves close together and near the margins; the sterile lemma depressed along the middle and without a palea, fertile lemma indurate, oblong-elliptic, obtuse, the margins slightly enrolled; caryopsis oblong-elliptic, minutely rugose, with few hairs at the obtuse apex. Flowering and fruiting occur from April through August; it usually occurs later in zone 10.

Uses: The ornamental value of carpet grass lies in its use as a lawn grass and as a ground-cover and erosion-control plant. Carpet grass is grown primarily as a ground cover in addition to being used in lawns. The plants form a dense mat and perform well in areas of heavy traffic. The plants remain evergreen in warmer climates except during long periods of extreme drought.

Cultivation: Propagation is by seeding and by plant division, usually the latter. The plants are easily propagated by planting sections of the strong stolons. Carpet grass thrives best in full sun or light shade in heavy clay soils with high moisture-retention capacity.

Bouteloua **Lag. (Grama, Grama grass, Gramma, Gramma grass, Mesquite grass).** Named for the brothers Bouteloua, Claudio, and Esteban. Type species, *Altheropogon agludoides* Hornemann ex Beauv. There are about 50 species, from the central United States southward to Argentina. Low or rather tall perennials or sometimes annuals with two to several racemose spikes on a common axis, or sometimes solitary, the spikelets few to many in each spike, rarely solitary, pectinate, or more loosely arranged and appressed, the rachis usually naked at the tip. The sterile florets forming the rudiment are variable in all the species and commonly in individual plants. The general pattern of rudiment is fairly constant for each species, the variability being in the reduction or increase in number and size of the sterile florets, the reduction from three awns to one, and in the amount of pubescence. Spikelets one-flowered, with the rudiments of one or more florets above, sessile, in two rows along one side of the rachis; glumes unequal, one-nerved, acuminate or awn-tipped, the lower shorter and narrower, lemmas as long as the upper glume or a little longer, three-nerved, the nerves extending into short awns or mucrones, the internerves usually extending into lobes or teeth; paleas sometimes two-awned; rudiment various, usually three-awned, the awns usually longer than those of the fertile lemma, a second rudimentary floret sometimes present.

Latin name: *Bouteloua breviseta* Vasey
Synonym: *Bouteloua ramosa* Scribn. ex Vasey
Common name: Chino grama
Habitat: Open grassland on gypsum soils and calcareous rocks
Hardiness: Zones 8 through 10
Description: A wiry, loosely tufted, hardy perennial with a woody base. Culms erect, rigid, 10–15 in./2.5–3.8 dm high, branching from short, scaly

rootstocks, internodes often covered with a thick, grayish bloom, slightly rough, nodes mostly pubescent. Foliage light green, fine in texture; leaf blades flat or slightly convolute, rigid, acuminate, ascending, 1–3 in./2.5–8.0 cm long, 1–2 mm wide, sparingly pubescent on upper surface, usually ciliate-papillose on the margins; sheaths round on the back, overlapping, rather close, ciliate on the margins, sometimes villous at the throat, usually as long as or shorter than the internodes; ligule a small, short ring of hairs. Inflorescence one to three straight or curled racemose spikes, 1.0–1.6 in./2.5–4.0 cm long, distant about their own length, erect or spreading, bearing many pectinately arranged spikelets; in two rows on one side of the rachis; spikelets sessile, one-flowered, 0.15–0.20 in./4–5 mm long including the awns; glumes unequal, one-nerved, acuminate, barely pubescent at the base, scabrous on the keel, the lower 2–3 mm long, the upper 0.10–0.15 in./3–4 mm long; lemma of fertile floret 0.15–0.20 in./4–5 mm long including the awns, pubescent, three-nerved, the nerves extending into three nearly equal hispid awns, 1–2 mm long, middle awn slightly longer and two-toothed; palea two-nerved, awnless, or sometimes two-awned; rudiment 0.10–0.15 in./3–4 mm long, densely bearded at the summit of the rachilla joint, about 0.15 in./4 mm long including the awns and stipe, stipe about 1 mm long, villous at the apex, the three hispid awns about equal, and a rudimentary scale; occasionally a second rudiment of a very small scale with short awns or teeth. The curled spikes resemble cockscomb. Flowering and fruiting occur from May through September, with the empty seedheads persisting.

Uses: The sparse foliage and small size of chino grama add little to the garden landscape. The individual, or sometimes two- or three-curved spikes make chino grama a curiosity in the flower or vegetable garden. The flower heads provide a good source of cut flowers and are used in dried arrangements.

Cultivation: Propagation is by direct seeding and by plant division. Chino grama thrives best in full sun in calcareous clay loam soils and in gypsum sands. The plants are quite drought tolerant and will thrive in difficult sites. The dry leaves will curl during prolonged droughts and at maturity.

Latin name: *Bouteloua curtipendula* (Michx.) Torr.
Synonym: *Chloris curtipendula* Michx.
Cultivars: Several in cultivation
Common names: Side-oats grama, Tall grama grass
Origin: North America
Habitat: Cultivated, escape from cultivation
Hardiness: Zones 3 through 10
Description: A loosely tufted, upright-narrow to upright-arching perennial with scaly rhizomes. Culms 1–3 ft/3–9 dm high, erect, smooth, simple, thin. Foliage mostly basal, light green, fine in texture; leaf blades numerous, flat or subinvolute, scabrous throughout, or occasionally more or less hairy and thinly papillose on the margins near the base, prolonged into a long, filiform,

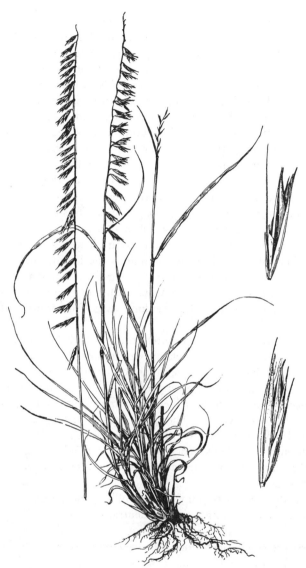

Bouteloua curtipendula. **Habit, × 1/2; spikelet and florets, × 5.** *Source: Manual of the Grasses of the United States.* USDA Misc. Pub. 200. 1951.

scabrous tip, 5–12 in./1.3–3.0 dm long, 0.10–0.15 in./3–4 mm wide; sheaths loose, striate, glabrous, or the lower densely papillose-hairy toward the summit, the throat pilose or papillose-hispid, usually shorter than the internodes; ligule a very short ciliate ring of hairs. Inflorescence a racemose panicle, included at the base or finally exserted, 5–15 in./1.3–3.8 dm long, slender, erect or slightly nodding, with 30 to 60 spikes, 0.3–0.6 in./6–15 mm long, spreading or reflexed, flattened, puberulent, peduncles purplish, approximate or distant, spreading or pendulous and mostly twisted to one side of the slender axis; spikelets sessile, in two rows along one side of the rachis, usually five to eight or more per spike, one-flowered, green, purplish, or brownish, bilateral on a flattened rachis, not pectinate, 0.2–0.3 in./5–8 mm long; glumes unequal, scabrous, one-nerved, keeled, scabrous on the keels and on the sides, the lower subulate, 0.15–0.20 in./4–5 mm long, the upper glabrous, broader, linear-lanceolate, longer than the lemma, acuminate, 0.25–0.30 in./6–8 mm long; lemma of fertile floret 0.15–0.25 in./4–6 mm long, more or less scabrous on the sides and keel, especially toward the apex, three-nerved, the nerves prolonged, the middle ones aristate to short-awned, up to 1 mm long, lemmas of sterile florets deeply bifid at the apex, the three nerves prolonged into awns, the middle usually up to 0.1 in./3 mm long, the lateral ones 1–2 mm long on well-developed florets; palea of fertile floret two-nerved, about as long as the lemma, minutely pubescent between the nerves, the nerves slightly prolonged; rudiment a minute scale with a delicate scabrous awn, and a rudimentary palea of two very delicate awns, or almost a full-formed lemma with rather long awns. Flowering and fruiting occur from June through September.

Uses: Specimen plantings are interesting, provided a few plants are maintained in small clumps and their relative size compared to the surrounding vegetation is kept in mind. The unique inflorescence of side-oats grama makes it an interesting component of the flower garden. The common name is derived from the inflorescence, in which the spikes are arranged lineally along one side of the slender straight or zigzig axis. The spikes do not shatter readily, making side-oats grama ideal for cut flowers. Although the seeds shatter upon maturity, the spikes with empty seedhulls intact are useful in dried arrangements. Side-oats grama is the largest of the grama grasses; it is useful in massed plantings in naturalized areas.

Cultivation: Side-oats grama prefers full sun and grows best on calcareous, moderately alkaline soils rather than on neutral or acid soils. The plants are quite drought tolerant. Propagation is by seeding and by division of the plant crowns or rhizomes, preferably the former. Side-oats grama is established by direct seeding more readily than blue grama, *Bouteloua gracilis,* probably because of differences in the vigor of the plants.

> **Latin name:** *Bouteloua gracilis* (H.B.K.) Lag. ex Steud.
> **Synonym:** *Chondrosium gracile* H.B.K.
> **Common names:** Blue grama, Mosquito grass, Mesquite grass
> **Origin:** North America
> **Habitat:** Cultivated, escape from cultivation
> **Hardiness:** Zones 3 through 10

Bouteloua gracilis. **Habit,**
× 1/2. *Source: Manual of the
Grasses of the United States.*
USDA Misc. Pub. 200. 1951.

Description: A densely tufted, upright-open, perennial with very slowly
spreading rhizomes. Culms erect, sometimes branching at the base, 8–24 in./
2–6 dm high; the plants form a rough sod. Foliage light green, fine in texture;
leaf blades linear, flat or involute when dry, 2–4 in./5–10 cm long, 1–2 mm
wide, slightly scabrous on margins and toward apex; sheaths striate, shorter

than the internodes; ligule very short with few ciliate hairs. Inflorescence usually two straight or occasionally slightly curved greenish spikes, with no projecting rachis, 0.8–2.0 in./2–5 cm long; spikelets many, sessile, in two rows along one side of the rachis, one-flowered, pectinate, about 0.20–0.25 in./5–6 mm long, on short, pubescent pedicels, densely crowded, often more than 60 per spike; glumes unequal, persistent, one-nerved, lanceolate, keeled, awn-tipped, minutely scabrous, the lower narrow, 0.10–0.15 in./3–4 mm long, persistent, the upper sometimes sparingly glandular on the keel and ciliate, 0.20–0.25 in./5–6 mm long; lemma of fertile floret pubescent, lanceolate, about 0.25 in./6 mm long including the awn, three-awned, the central awn longer, usually four-lobed, with lateral awns from the apex of the lobes, the central from between two teeth or lobes; palea about the length of the lemma; rudiment about 0.2 in./5 mm long and consisting of three scabrous awns with two or three scales at their base, on a short pedicel, with a tuft of white hairs at the base and apex; in addition, another rudiment comprised of one or two pale glumes. Flowering and fruiting occur from June through September, with the reddish to purplish seedheads persisting.

Uses: The overall form and small size of blue grama add little to the garden or landscape except perhaps as specimen plants in rock gardens, in foreground edging, and in naturalized areas. Blue grama may be seeded directly in meadows and open fields, where it serves as a substitute turf grass. Blue grama is short enough not to require any mowing when used as a turf grass in pure or mixed stands in naturalized areas. Blue grama is grown as a curiosity for its unique flower heads rather than for its contribution to the landscape. The common name, mosquito grass, is derived from the unique form of the inflorescence. The main axis of the inflorescence is at an oblique angle to the spike, with spikelets on the lower side of the axis subtended by florets resembling a fine-toothed comb or mosquitoes clinging to the flower. It is attractive in group plantings in foreground borders and in rock gardens or in massed plantings in naturalized areas. Its uniquely shaped flower heads are used as cut flowers and in dried arrangements.

Cultivation: Propagation is by direct seeding and by plant division. The plants are slow in becoming established by seeding. Division of plant crowns or rhizomes in early spring is a safe and fast method of propagation. Blue grama thrives best in full sun on loamy and sandy loam soils; the plants are moderately salt tolerant and will grow in slightly acid, light sandy, and dry soils.

>**Latin name:** *Bouteloua hirsuta* Lag.
>**Synonym:** *Bouteloua hirta* Lag.
>**Common names:** Hairy grama, Black grama
>**Origin:** North American great plains
>**Habitat:** Cultivated, escape from cultivation
>**Hardiness:** Zones 3 through 9

Description: A densely tufted, upright-open perennial. Culms rigid, erect or often geniculate, branched at the base, striate, sometimes slightly pubescent below, variable in height, usually 6–30 in./1.5–7.6 dm high. Foliage light green, fine in texture; basal leaf blades 3–8 in./0.8–2.0 dm long, upper only 1–4 in./ 2.5–10.0 cm long, 1–2 mm wide, long attenuate, sparsely papillose-hispid on the margins, hirsute on the upper surface near the base, rough except below, near the base; upper sheaths shorter than the internodes, glabrous, or the lower pubescent, sometimes pilose at the throat; ligule a short, small, thin ring of hairs. Inflorescence a racemose panicle, axis on the shorter form 1–2 in./2.5–5.0 cm long, on the longer up to 6 in./1.5 dm, bearing one to six spikes, rarely more than four spikes, 0.6–1.6 in./1.5–4.0 cm long, with a prominent rachis projecting about 0.2–0.3 in./5–8 mm beyond the last spikelet; spikelets numerous, sessile, crowded in two rows and forming 1–6 sessile, one-sided spikes, one-flowered, pectinate, usually 0.25–0.30 in./6–8 mm long, including the black awns; glumes unequal, persistent, the lower minutely hispid, narrow, acuminate, up to 2–3 mm long, the upper minutely hispid and conspicuously tuberculate, the tubercles black, hairy, acuminate, short-awned, 0.15–0.20 in./ 4–5 mm long; lemma of fertile floret 0.20–0.25 in./5–6 mm long including the awn, pubescent, three-nerved, three-toothed, deeply two-cleft, the lateral lobes acuminate or short-awned, the middle lobe with a hispid awn longer than the lateral teeth, the middle awn often having a tooth on one side of its base, lemmas of imperfect flowers three-awned, borne at the end of the rachilla; palea oval, broadly pointed, two-nerved, about as long as the lemma; rudiment comprised of three equal hispid awns about 0.25 in./6 mm long and two scales on a stipe about 2 mm long, the stipe short-pubescent above, the awns extending above the remaining balance of the spikelet. Flowering and fruiting occur from July through September, with the empty seedheads persisting.

Uses: The small size and abundant foliage of hairy grama add very little to the landscape. The most interesting characteristic of hairy grama is its blackish, hairy, flowering spikes. Hairy grama forms a good sod and ground cover in open, naturalized areas, whether in pure or mixed stands.

Cultivation: Propagation is by seeding. Hairy grama is adapted to sandy loam soils and to gravelly loams. The plants prefer full sun on neutral to slightly calcareous soils; they are more drought tolerant than blue grama, *Bouteloua gracilis.* Hairy grama is widely adapted; it is cultivated in zones 4 through 9.

Brachypodium **Beauv.** Name from *brachys,* "short," and *podion,* "foot," referring to the very short pedicels. Lectotype, *Brachypodium pinnatum* (L.) Beauv. There are 15 species, mostly in temperate regions of the world. Annual or perennial grasses with erect racemes of usually subsessile spikelets. Inflorescence sometimes reduced to a single, terminal spikelet. Spikelets rarely sessile, large, several-to-many-flowered, the rachilla disarticulating between the florets and above the glumes; glumes unequal, five-to-seven-nerved, sharp-pointed; lemmas firm, round, or flattened on the back, seven-nerved, awned or mucronate, the midvein extending into a short or long awn from an entire apex; palea two-keeled, as long as the body of the lemma, concave, often with stiff pectinate-ciliate hairs on the nerves.

Latin name: *Brachypodium sylvaticum* (Huds.) Beauv.
Synonym: *Festuca sylvatica* Huds.
Common names: Slender brome
Origin: Eurasia, Europe
Habitat: Cultivated, escape from cultivation
Hardiness: Zones 6 and 7
Description: A densely tufted, upright-narrow, rhizomatous perennial. Culms slender to moderately stout, erect, or spreading, with four or five nodes, simple, hairy at or near the nodes, otherwise glabrous, 1–3 ft /3–9 dm high. Foliage medium green, medium in texture; leaf blades narrowed toward the sheath, finely pointed, flat, 8–12 in./2–3 dm long, 0.25–0.50 in./6–13 mm wide, erect or finally drooping, soft, loosely hairy, rarely glabrous and rough; sheaths round on the back or keeled upwards, loosely hairy; ligule 1–3 mm long, more or less erose-ciliate, pubescent. Inflorescence a spikelike raceme, loose, erect, or nodding, 2–8 in./0.5–2.0 dm long, about 2 in./5 cm wide; spikelets cylindrical, lanceolate or narrowly oblong, alternating in two rows on opposite sides of the axis, 1.0–1.6 in./2.5–4.0 cm long, many-flowered, the lower distant, the upper imbricate; glumes unequal, persistent, round on the back, sharply pointed, firm, usually hairy, lower lanceolate, 0.25–0.30 in./6–8 mm long, five-to-seven-nerved, upper lanceolate to narrowly oblong, 0.30–0.45 in./8–11 mm long, seven-to-nine-nerved; lemmas round on the back, imbricate, oblong-lanceolate, pointed, 0.30–0.45 in./8–11 mm long tipped with a rough, fine, straight awn, 0.4–0.5 in./10–13 mm long, seven-nerved, shortly hairy, rarely rough or quite smooth; palea about as long as the lemma, narrowly oblong, with short-haired keels. Flowering and fruiting occur from June through July.
Uses: Slender brome is good in shaded, open woods in naturalized areas because it is somewhat shade tolerant. The dense, light purplish, spikelike racemes add an additional dimension to dried floral arrangements.
Cultivation: Propagation is by seeding and by plant division. Slender brome grows equally well in full sun and light to medium shade. The plants prefer loamy soils, well-drained but with adequate moisture available. The plants do not require any maintenance when planted in naturalized areas.

Briza L. (Quaking grass). Name from Greek *Briza*, a kind of grain, from *brizein*, "to nod." Lectotype, *Briza minor* L. This is one of the oldest genera of ornamental grasses; it occurs in the earliest herbals. There are about 20 species, in temperate regions throughout the world. Low annuals or perennials, with erect culms; leaf blades flat, and usually open, showy panicles, the pedicels of our species capillary, allowing the spikelets to vibrate in the wind. Spikelets several-flowered, broad, often cordate, the florets crowded and spreading horizontally, the rachilla disarticulating above the glumes and between the florets; glumes about equal, broad, with scarious spreading margins, cordate at base, several-nerved, the nerves often obscure, the apex in our species obtuse or acute; palea much shorter than the lemma.

Latin name: *Briza maxima* L.
Varieties: *Briza maxima* var. *rubra* L.
Common names: Big quaking grass, Large quaking grass
Origin: Europe
Habitat: Cultivated, escape from cultivation
Hardiness: Zones 5 through 10
Description: An upright-open, short-lived, glabrous annual. Culms erect, round, glabrous, with two nodes, 15–20 in./3.8–5.0 dm high. Foliage medium in texture, light green, becoming medium green to light beige at maturity; leaf blades glabrous, almost straight, 6–8 in./1.5–2.0 dm long, 0.10–0.25 in./3–6 mm wide, tapering to a blunt or fine point; sheaths round on the back, open, glabrous; ligule oblong, blunt. Inflorescence a somewhat pyramidal, sparingly branched, lax, many-flowered, drooping panicle, light green to mauve or cream with silvery sheen, 2–4 in./5–10 cm long, 1–4 in./2.5–10.0 cm wide; spikelets plump, light green, sometimes diffused reddish to purple, 0.4–0.5 in./10–13 mm long, up to 0.3–0.4 in./8–10 mm wide, many-flowered, glabrous or pubescent, the pedicels capillary, curved; glumes about equal, chartaceous, broad, with scarious margins, three-to-five-nerved; lemmas imbricate, orbicular, 0.25–0.30 in./6–8 mm long, glabrous, margins membranous, bright red to purplish, turning beige or light brown at maturity, several-nerved; palea about 2 mm long, much shorter than the lemma, two-nerved, two-keeled, the keels winged and sparsely hirsute; caryopsis brownish, enclosed. Flowering and fruiting occur from May through June, after which the plants die.
Uses: Big quaking grass is ideal for foreground annual borders and rock gardens. The flowers are attractive on the plants, as the spikelets vibrate or shiver in the slightest breeze, thus adding another dimension to their value. The panicles make interesting additions to fresh cut-flower arrangements when harvested before they mature. Usually very few, if any, seeds are retained in mature, dry panicles; despite this, the dry, empty panicles are useful in dried arrangements, either in their natural color or when dyed. The empty, dry, grayish spikelets, which remain on the plants throughout the summer, are an added attraction.
Cultivation: Propagation is by direct seeding. The plants are quite drought tolerant; they thrive on a wide range of soil types in full sun. Big quaking grass prefers light, sandy, acid to neutral soils, although they thrive on heavy clay

soils. Big quaking grass, like many ornamental grasses, is most conspicuous and effective when planted in medium to large clumps. Fungus diseases may cause damage to the leaves occasionally. Control could be achieved by the application of fungicides recommended for turfgrass diseases.

Varieties: *Briza maxima* var. *rubra* L.   This variety is distinguishable from the species by its foliage color (i.e., reddish green) and by its whitish glumes.

Latin name: *Briza media* L.

Common names: Perennial quaking grass, Quakers, Quaking grass, Pearl-grass, Rattle grass, Common quaking grass

Origin: Mediterranean area

Habitat: Cultivated, escape from cultivation

Hardiness: Zones 5 through 9

Description: A loosely tufted, upright-open perennial with short rhizomes. Culms erect, occasionally decumbent, becoming erect, slender, stiff, glabrous, 15–36 in./3.8–9.0 dm high, usually arched near the tip. Foliage medium green, becoming beige at maturity, fine in texture; leaf blades flat, minutely rough on the margins, 4–6 in./1.0–1.5 dm long, 0.10–0.15 in./3–4 mm wide, narrowing to a blunt tip; sheaths entire, glabrous; ligule of upper leaves about 1 mm long, truncate. Inflorescence a loosely branched, shiny, light green, pyramidal panicle, 4–6 in./1.0–1.5 dm long and almost as wide, with wide-spreading branches; spikelets 5-to-12-flowered, broad, often heart-shaped, about 0.2 in./5 mm long, loosely scattered, drooping, compressed, shining, light green becoming purplish to beige with age; glumes about equal, compressed, deeply concave, hooded, three-to-five-nerved, up to 0.15 in./4 mm long, firm, membranous, with broad, scarious margins, persistent; lemmas variegated with green and purple stripes, imbricate, cordate at base, round on the back, glabrous, about 0.15 in./4 mm long, five-to-many-nerved; palea keeled, the keels narrowly winged, slightly shorter than the lemma; caryopsis brownish, enclosed by the chartaceous lemma and palea. Flowering and fruiting occur from May through June, with the mature, dry spikelets persisting on the plants.

Uses: Perennial quaking grass and its cultivars are grown primarily for their decorative flowers. They are useful in foreground border plantings, in rock gardens, and as ground cover in massed plantings in naturalized areas. The plants require minimal maintenance when grown as ground cover in naturalized areas. The small spikelets vibrate in the slightest breeze, adding another dimension to their attractiveness. The flower heads remain quite firm and may be collected any time during flowering or later in the year; they make excellent cut flowers. The seedheads of perennial quaking grass do not shatter as readily as those of big quaking grass, *Briza maxima*, or of little quaking grass, *Briza minor*. They make excellent dried flower arrangements, either in their natural color or when dyed. Cutting the flower heads off when they are light green in the spring or in the summer after they are mature and grayish white results in dried flower heads of different colors. Usually the seeds shatter upon the plants reaching maturity, leaving the empty, grayish spikelets intact, which are attractive and useful in dried arrangements. The empty, dry, grayish spikelets, which remain on the plants throughout the summer, are an added attraction, especially when grown in massed, naturalized stands.

Cultivation: Propagation is usually by seeding. The plants thrive best in full sun or light shade on light or heavy soils that are well drained. Perennial quaking grass is quite drought tolerant, although it is susceptible to rust and leaf spot diseases. Fungus diseases may attack the plants occasionally; the best control is achieved through the use of fungicides that are recommended for turfgrass diseases. Perennial quaking grass has an advantage over big quaking grass, *Briza maxima,* and little quaking grass, *Briza minor,* in that it does not require establishment each year.

Latin name: *Briza minor* L.
Common names: Little quaking grass, Lesser quaking grass
Origin: Asia and Europe
Habitat: Cultivated, escape from cultivation
Hardiness: Zones 5 through 10
Description: An upright-open, loosely tufted, glabrous annual, a miniature version of big quaking grass. Culms several, round, glabrous, with few nodes, 6–16 in./1.5–4.0 dm high, very slender. Foliage light green, becoming the color of light straw at maturity, coarse in texture; leaf blades narrowly lanceolate, minutely rough above and on the margins, flat, slightly undulate, finely nerved, 2–10 in./0.5–2.5 dm long, 0.4–0.8 in./10–20 mm wide, tapering to a fine point; sheaths open, glabrous; ligule membranous, acute, up to 0.25 in./6 mm long. Inflorescence a very lax, open, branched pyramidal, erect to nodding panicle, 2–3 in./5–8 cm long, 1–4 in./2.5–10.0 cm wide, the branches stiffly ascending, finally spreading, bearing fascicled branchlets; spikelets pendulous, trigonous-ovate, three-to-six-flowered, plump, pinkish or reddish, up to 0.2 in./5 mm long; glumes about equal, compressed, membranous, three-to-five-nerved, at right angles to the rachilla, persistent; lemmas 2–3 mm long, compressed, round at the top, cordate at base, deeply concave, seven-to-nine-nerved, glabrous, with broad, whitish, membranous margins; palea with two winged keels, flat, shorter than the lemma; caryopsis enclosed. Flowering and fruiting occur from April through May, with the dry, empty spikelets remaining persistent. Little quaking grass is easily distinguished from big quaking grass by its wider leaves and more numerous and smaller spikelets.

Uses: Little quaking grass should be included in the vegetable or cut-flower garden, as the panicles are attractive on the plants, where they vibrate or quake in the slightest breeze. The panicles are useful in fresh cut-flower bouquets when harvested before they mature and the empty, dry panicles are used in dried arrangements, either in their natural color or dyed. The plants are attractive when

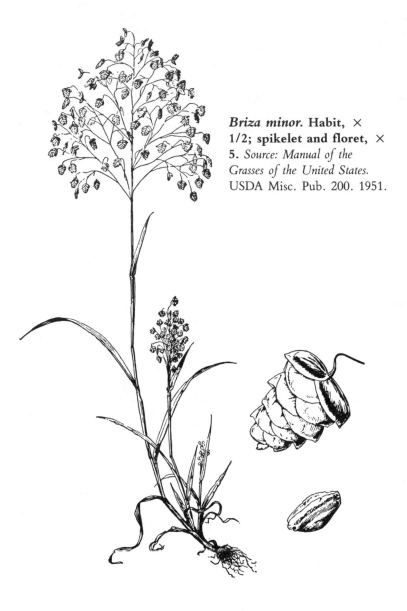

Briza minor. Habit, ×
1/2; spikelet and floret, ×
5. *Source: Manual of the
Grasses of the United States.*
USDA Misc. Pub. 200. 1951.

planted in clumps in foreground annual borders and in rock gardens. The dry, empty, grayish spikelets, which remain on the plants throughout the summer, are an added attraction.

Cultivation: Propagation is by direct seeding. The plants grow well on a wide range of soil types in full sun. Little quaking grass is not drought tolerant, and the plants are subject to damage from strong wind and heavy rain.

Bromus L. (**Bromegrass, Brome, Chess**). Name from ancient Greek *bromas,* the "oat," from *broma,* "food." Lectotype, *Bromus* secalinus L. There are about 100 species, native mostly to temperate regions of the Northern Hemisphere. The annual species, mostly introduced from Europe, are weedy forms, whereas the native perennial species are abundant in the western United States. Low or rather tall annuals or perennials with closed leaf sheaths, flat leaf blades, and open or contracted panicles of large spikelets. Spikelets several-to-many-flowered, the rachilla disarticulating above the glumes and between the florets; glumes unequal, acute, the lower one-to-three-nerved, the upper usually three-to-five-nerved; lemmas convex on the back or keeled, five-to-nine-nerved, two-toothed, awned from between the teeth or awnless; palea usually shorter than the lemma, ciliate on the keels.

Latin name: *Bromus brizaeformis* Fisch. & C. A. Mey.
Common names: Rattlesnake brome, Rattlesnake chess, Rattlesnake grass, Quakegrass
Origin: Caucasus, Europe
Habitat: Open waste grounds, sandy soils
Hardiness: Zones 2 through 8
Description: An upright-open annual or biennial. Culms tufted, rarely single, erect or decumbent at base becoming erect, round, glabrous, or slightly pubescent or hairy at the nodes, 1–2 ft /3–6 dm high. Foliage medium green, fine in texture; leaf blades flat, pilose-pubescent on both surfaces, 4–10 in./1.0–2.5 dm long, 0.1–0.2 in./3–5 mm wide, long attenuate; sheaths closed, pilose-pubescent, shorter than the internodes; ligule somewhat laciniate, 1–2 mm long, pubescent. Inflorescence a light green, lax, loosely branched panicle, 2–10 in./0.5–2.5 dm long, secund, drooping, the branches long, slender, and spreading, up to 2–3 in./5–8 cm long, the lowest in three to five fascicles, each branch usually bearing one spikelet; spikelets much compressed, oblong-ovate, 10-to-15-flowered, glabrous, 0.6–1.0 in./15–25 mm long, about 0.4 in./10 mm wide, acute, usually with a faint purplish tinge; glumes unequal, broad, subacute or obtuse, glabrous or minutely scabrous toward the apex, the lower 0.10–0.25 in./5–6 mm long, three-to-five-nerved, the upper 0.2–0.3 in./5–8 mm long, seven-to-nine-nerved; lemmas inflated, bifid, obtuse, very broad with scarious margins, about 0.4 in./10 mm long, glabrous or slightly scabrous toward the apex, five-to-nine-nerved, awnless, or the lower ones awnless and the upper with awns between the teeth, 1–2 mm long; palea obtuse, shorter than its lemma, ciliate on the keels; caryopsis hairy at the tip, adherent to the palea. Flowering and fruiting occur from June through July.
Uses: Rattlesnake brome is among the most spectacular *Bromus* species; it is grown primarily for its decorative flowers. The flowers, when cut before they mature, are superb in dried arrangements. It is commonly used in foreground mixed borders, depending upon the size of surrounding plants. Rattlesnake brome is attractive in clumps among broad-leaved perennials in foreground bor-

ders. This small annual is used in almost any area requiring an annual ground cover. The lightweight, flattish spikelets tend to wave in the slightest breeze, providing an interesting, intermittent movement unique among grasses and very rarely found among other ornamentals.

Cultivation: Propagation is by seeding. Direct seeding may be done where the plants are to grow, either in the spring or in the autumn. The plants grow best in full sun on almost any fertile, well-drained soil. The usual preventive measures necessary to keep it from becoming weedy should be taken, especially when it is grown in border plantings.

Latin name: *Bromus inermis* Leyss.
Synonym: *Festuca inermis* DC. & Lam.
Cultivars: Several in cultivation
Common names: Smooth brome, Awnless bromegrass, Hungarian bromegrass
Origin: Europe (Hungary), China
Habitat: Disturbed sites, abandoned fields, cultivated
Hardiness: Zones 3 through 7
Description: An upright-open to spreading, rhizomatous perennial. Culms erect, stout, tufted from creeping rhizomes, 30–40 in./0.8–1.0 m high and almost as wide at maturity, glabrous or minutely puberulent beneath the nodes and panicles. Foliage light to medium green, fine in texture; leaf blades 6–12 in./1.5–3.0 dm long, 0.2–0.4 in./5–10 mm wide, flat, glabrous above, glabrous or slightly pubescent beneath, margins scabrous; sheaths glabrous, closed, longer than the internodes, the lower imbricate; ligule membranous, 1–2 mm long. Inflorescence a terminal, inserted, greenish, branched panicle, 4–8 in./1.0–2.0 dm long, ovate to oblong, somewhat open, the axis scabrous above, the short branches erect, slightly spreading, or usually in five to eight fascicles, at first ascending, later more or less spreading; spikelets erect, purplish, 0.4–1.0 in./10–25 mm long, about 0.2 in./5 mm wide, oblong or nearly terete, round at the base, five-to-nine-flowered; glumes unequal, membranous, persistent, acute, persistent, the lower one-nerved, 0.25–0.30 in./6–8 mm long, the upper three-nerved, 0.25–0.40 in./6–10 mm long; lemmas obtuse, 0.4–0.5 in./10–13 mm long, round or keeled on the back, entire or emarginate, five-to-seven-nerved, glabrous or slightly scabrous on some of the nerves, especially on the midnerve toward the apex, awnless or, rarely, awn-pointed, round or keeled on the back; palea ciliate, two-keeled, almost as long as the lemma; caryopsis oblong, 0.25–0.30 in./6–8 mm long, furrowed, hairy at the tip, adherent to the palea. Flowering and fruiting occur from June through August.

Uses: The sod-forming growth habit of smooth brome makes it ideal for ground cover and erosion control along highways and in naturalized areas where mowing is not required; it is also planted as ground cover near the sea. The semicompact inflorescence of smooth brome dries to a golden brown, thus enhancing its value in dried arrangements.

***Bromus inermis.* Habit,** ×
1/2; spikelet, × **2 1/2.**
*Source: Manual of the Grasses
of the United States.* USDA
Misc. Pub. 200. 1951.

Cultivation: Propagation is usually by seeding, although new plants may be started by division of the plant crowns and rhizomes. The plants prefer full sun on well-drained soil; smooth brome is quite drought and salt tolerant.

Latin name: *Bromus secalinus* L.
Synonym: *Bromus mollis* var. *secalinus* Huds.
Common names: Wild chess, Cheat, Chess

Bromus secalinus. Habit, × 1/2; spikelet and floret, × 5. *Source: Manual of the Grasses of the United States.* USDA Misc. Pub. 200. 1951.

Origin: Europe
Habitat: Grain fields, waste grounds, pastures, cultivated
Hardiness: Zones 4 through 9
Description: An upright-narrow annual. Culms solitary or loosely tufted, 1–3 ft /3–9 dm high, simple, rigid, glabrous, with five to seven nodes, the swollen nodes minutely hispid. Foliage medium green, fine in texture; leaf blades pointed, flat, smooth or rough, often puberulent on the upper surface, 4–10

in./1.0–4.5 dm long, 0.1–0.3 in./3–8 mm wide, strongly nerved; sheaths as long as the internodes, strongly nerved, glabrous or the lower puberulent, tubular, round on the back, soon splitting; ligule toothed, membranous, 1–2 mm long, glabrous or sparsely pubescent on the outer surface. Inflorescence an exserted, branched, greenish panicle, 3–4 in./8–10 cm long, narrow, finally spreading and drooping, the branches fascicled, in whorls of four to six, one long, the remainder short, usually 1–3 in./2.5–8.0 cm long, the shorter bearing one spikelet and the longer three or four spikelets at their extremities; spikelets erect or slightly drooping, 5-to-12-flowered, somewhat flattened, ovoid-lanceolate, 0.4–0.7 in./10–18 mm long, 0.15–0.30 in./4–8 mm wide, glumes unequal, scabrous along the margins and toward the apex, the lower acute, three-to-five-nerved, 0.15–0.20 in./4–5 mm long, the upper obtuse, five-to-seven-nerved, 0.20–0.25 in./5–6 mm long; lemmas broad, 0.25–0.30 in./6–8 mm long, elliptic, turgid, emarginate or toothed, scabrous along the margins and rough toward the apex, becoming convex at maturity, with convolute margins, seven-nerved, the nerves obscure, bearing a straight, spreading, scabrous awn below the obtuse or emarginate apex, the awn usually 0.10–0.25 in./3–6 mm long; palea ciliate-hispid, about as long as its lemma, the keel fringed with short, stiff hairs; caryopsis adherent to the palea, oblong, about 2 mm wide, deeply grooved on the palea side. Flowering and fruiting occur from May through July.

Uses: Dried purplish panicles of wild chess are attractive on the plants and in dried floral arrangements. The turgid florets in fruit are somewhat distant, so that when the spikelet is viewed from the side, the light passes through small openings at the base of each floret. Like other *Bromus* species, wild chess is useful as ground cover in naturalized areas and along highways. The rich, golden-brown, dried panicles are the main reason for growing wild chess.

Cultivation: Propagation is by seeding. Wild chess is somewhat shade tolerant and grows best in fertile, moist soils. It occurs on both slightly acid and alkaline soils.

Latin name: *Bromus unioloides* H.B.K.

Synonym: *Bromus wildenowii* Kunth

Common names: Rescue brome, Prairie brome, Rescuegrass, Schrader's brome

Origin: South America

Habitat: Cultivated, escape from cultivation

Hardiness: Zones 6 through 8

Description: An upright-open to spreading annual or biennial. Culms erect or spreading, sometimes decumbent at the base, 1–5 ft/0.3–1.5 m high, the younger plants conspicuously pubescent or pilose, the older ones usually nearly or completely glabrous. Foliage medium green, fine in texture; leaf blades flat, usually rough, especially on the upper surface, from pilose or pubescent, or occasionally glabrous, 6–15 in./1.5–3.8 dm long, 0.3–0.4 in./8–10 mm wide; sheaths smooth to rough, pilose-pubescent, flattened, shorter than the internodes; ligule somewhat pubescent, membranous, 0.1–0.2 in./3–5 mm long. Inflorescence a narrow or pyramidal, branched, erect or nodding panicle, 5–15 in./1.3–3.8 dm long, 3–5 in./0.8–1.3 dm wide, the branches erect or spreading, those of larger plants diffusely spreading as much as 6 in./1.5 dm, with two to five spikelets near the tip of each branch, the main axis and pedicels scabrous; spikelets many, compact, often drooping, 6-to-12-flowered, flattened, green, tinged with purple, 0.8–1.6 in./2–4 cm long; glumes unequal, glabrous, acute, the lower 0.3–0.4 in./8–10 mm long, seven-to-nine-nerved, the upper 0.4–0.5 in./10–13 mm long, 7-to-11-nerved; lemmas glabrous, minutely scabrous or sometimes pubescent, broadly lanceolate, imbricate, concealing the short rachilla joints, 0.4–0.7 in./10–18 mm long including the awn, two-toothed, acute, 7-to-11-nerved, awn dorsal, inserted just below two-toothed apex; palea two-keeled, about two-thirds the length of its lemma; caryopsis adherent to the palea, oblong, 0.1–0.2 in./3–5 mm long, grooved on one side. Flowering and fruiting occur from April through July.

Uses: Rescue brome is useful as an annual or biennial ground cover and in erosion control in sunny sites. It is large enough, 2–5 ft/0.6–1.5 m high, for use in medium screens and windbreaks. Rescue brome is ideal in naturalized areas along the edges of woods and stream banks. Minimum seed shattering occurs in dried seedheads when used in dried arrangements.

Cultivation: Propagation is by direct seeding. Rescue brome thrives in full sun on well-drained, fertile soils, ranging in texture from sandy loams to heavy clays.

Calamagrostis **Adans. (Reedgrass).** Name compounded from Greek *kalamos,* "reed," and *agrostis,* a kind of grass. Type species, *Arundo calamagrostis* L. There are about 100 species, inhabiting the cool and temperate regions of both hemispheres. Usually moderately tall, perennial grasses, mostly with creeping rhizomes, with small spikelets in open or usually narrow, sometimes spikelike panicles. Spikelets one-flowered, the rachilla disarticulating above the glumes, prolonged behind the palea, in introduced and naturalized species except *Calamagrostis epigejos,* as a short, commonly hairy bristle; glumes about equal, acute, or acuminate; lemmas shorter and usually more delicate than the glumes, usually five-nerved, the midnerve exserted as an awn, the callus bearing a tuft of hairs, these often copious and as long as the lemma.

Latin name: *Calamagrostis arundinacea* Roth
Common name: Reedgrass
Origin: Eurasia, USSR
Habitat: Wet soils in shaded locations, marshes
Hardiness: Zones 5 through 9
Description: An upright-narrow to upright-open, rhizomatous perennial. Culms upright, tufted from rhizomes, somewhat hirsute, simple, 5–7 ft/1.5–

2.2 m high. Foliage medium green, medium in texture; leaf blades flat, becoming somewhat involute near the tips, erect or ascending, 8–16 in./2–4 dm long, 0.25–0.50 in./6–13 mm wide, long attenuate; sheaths glabrous or obscurely pubescent, somewhat shorter than the internodes, much compressed; ligule membranous, more or less scabrid, 1–3 mm long. Inflorescence a compact, spike-like panicle, loosely branched, whitish or light reddish, 4–8 in./1–2 dm long, about one-third as wide, fascicled branches 3–4 in./8–10 cm long, ascending or spreading; spikelets one-flowered, 0.15–0.20 in./4–5 mm long, the rachilla prolonged behind the palea as a short, hairy bristle, 0.10–0.15 in./3–4 mm long; glumes about equal, acute or acuminate, 0.25–0.30 in./6–8 mm long, scabrous, the lower one-nerved, usually longer than the upper, the upper three-nerved; lemmas shorter than the glumes, thin, with a tuft of hairs at the base, these usually copious and about three-fourths as long as or as long as the glumes, awned from the back, usually below the middle, the awn delicate and straight or geniculate, longer than the glumes, about 0.5 in./13 mm long; palea well developed, two-nerved, shorter than its lemma. Flowering and fruiting occur from June through July.

Uses: Reedgrass is useful in naturalized areas in freshwater bogs and swamps around lakes and ponds and in water gardens where adequate moisture is constantly available. The size of the plants depends largely upon the moisture supply. Reedgrass exhibits good fall and winter color; it is used on occasion in seashore plantings as tall screens and windbreaks and for erosion control. The seedheads, which shatter sparsely, are useful in dried floral arrangements.

Cultivation: Propagation is by seeding and by plant division. Reedgrass clumps increase in diameter slowly; therefore, caution should be used in spacing the plants when planting. Reedgrass may become invasive; the plants may be kept under control by digging out any excess plants. The plants prefer full sun or light shade in wet, brackish soils but will also thrive in heavy, clay soils with less moisture.

> **Latin name:** *Calamagrostis canadensis* (Michx.) Beauv.
> **Synonym:** *Arundo canadensis* Michx.
> **Common name:** Bluejoint, Reedgrass, Foin bleu
> **Origin:** North America
> **Habitat:** Marshes, wet grounds, open woods, wet meadows
> **Hardiness:** Zones 3 through 7
> **Description:** An upright-open to spreading rhizomatous perennial. Culms suberect to erect, densely tufted, simple or branched near the base, smooth, rarely pubescent, 4–7 ft /1.2–2.2 m high. Foliage dark green or glaucous, fine in texture; leaf blades elongate, flat, or becoming involute toward the apex, 10–12 in./2.5–3.0 dm long, 0.15–0.30 in./4–8 mm wide, scabrous above, nearly smooth beneath, the margins scabrous; sheaths glabrous on the collar, otherwise obscurely pubescent; ligule rather delicately membranous, 0.1–0.3 in./3–8 mm long. Inflorescence a nodding, rather dense or loose, branched panicle, 4–10 in./

Calamagrostis canadensis.
Habit, × 1/2. *Source:
Manual of the Grasses of the
United States.* USDA Misc.
Pub. 200. 1951.

1.0–2.5 dm long, 2–4 in./5–10 cm wide, the slender, fascicled branches ascending or spreading; spikelets one-flowered, 0.10–0.15 in./3–4 mm long, the rachilla prolonged behind the palea as a short, hairy bristle; glumes about equal, acute or acuminate, keeled, smooth, or scabrous on the keel, exceeding the erose-truncate lemma, the lower usually longer than the upper, one-nerved, the upper three-nerved; lemmas shorter than the glumes, usually more delicate, glabrous, or more or less sparsely scabrous, five-nerved, with a delicate, straight awn from the back below the middle, the awn usually about as long as the lemma or sometimes only half as long or up to slightly longer, the callus hairs copious, about three-fourths as long as the lemma; palea thin, hyaline, faintly two-nerved, shorter than its lemma. Flowering and fruiting occur from June through August.

Uses: Bluejoint is used in wet, shaded areas near wooded borders and for medium or tall screens and windbreaks. The plants provide good fall color, and the dried panicles are used in dried floral arrangements. Bluejoint is useful in naturalized areas along wooded streams and around lakes, in water gardens, and in seashore plantings.

Cultivation: Propagation is by direct seeding and by division of the plants or rhizomes. Mature plantings several years old may become invasive, thus requiring thinning or partial removal to keep them under control. Bluejoint prefers full sun on wet, marshy soils.

Latin name: *Calamagrostis canescens* (Weber) Roth
Synonym: *Calamagrostis lanceolata* Roth
Cultivars: 'Variegata'
Common name: Purple reed
Origin: Europe
Habitat: Cultivated, escape from cultivation
Hardiness: Zones 3 through 7
Description: An upright-open rhizomatous perennial. Multiple culms, loosely tufted, erect or slightly spreading, forming large clumps, moderately slender, glabrous, with three to five nodes, 2–4 ft /0.6–1.2 m high. Foliage medium green, fine in texture; leaf blades pubescent above, rough on both surfaces, flat, 16–24 in./4–6 dm long, 0.15–0.25 in./4–6 mm wide, long attenuate; sheaths glabrous, longer than the internodes; ligule membranous, scabrous, 1–3 mm long. Inflorescence an open, lanceolate to oblong, spreading panicle, becoming flexuous or finally nodding, 4–10 in./1.0–2.5 dm long, 1–4 in./2.5–10.0 cm wide, purplish or greenish, rarely yellowish, main axis rough, branches slightly spreading, very slender, the lower up to 3 in./8 cm long, pedicels up to 0.1 in./3 mm long; spikelets lanceolate, clustered, 0.15–0.25 in./4–6 mm long, one-flowered; glumes about equal, narrowly lanceolate, persistent, finely pointed, slightly rough, membranous, usually one-nerved or, occasionally, the upper three-nerved; lemmas thin, membranous about half the length of the glumes, ovate, smooth, three-to-five-nerved, with a short, fine awn from the narrow tip, surrounded and exceeded by long, fine, white callus hairs from the base; palea almost two-thirds the length of the lemma, finely two-nerved. Flowering and fruiting occur from June through July.

Uses: Purple reed is useful as middleground borders on wet sites. It is grown mainly for its open, flowering panicles, which are usually greenish or purplish and move gently in the slightest breeze; they are also useful as cut flowers and in dried arrangements. Purple reed and its cultivar Variegata are useful in shaded, wet, naturalized areas around wooded borders, lakes, and ponds and along streams, where constant ample moisture is available.

Cultivation: Propagation is by seeding and by plant division. Mature plantings may become invasive, thus requiring thinning and partial removal to be kept under control. Purple reed prefers moist or wet sites in full sun or light shade.

Cultivars: *Calamagrostis canescens* (Weber) Roth 'Variegata' This cultivar is somewhat similar to the species in size but differs from it in having variegated foliage; the green-yellow leaves are longitudinally striped. The variegation of the foliage fades as the growing season progresses, thus rendering it of little garden value. This cultivar is more decorative than purple reed. The flower heads are used as cut flowers, and the grass is used occasionally as an accent plant in middleground borders; it is adapted to zones 3 through 7.

Latin name: *Calamagrostis epigejos* (L.) Roth
Synonym: *Calamagrostis epigejos* var. *georgica* (K. Koch) Ledeb.
Cultivars: 'Hortorum'
Common names: Bushgrass, Reedgrass, Feathertop
Origin: Eurasia
Habitat: Cultivated, saltwater marshes
Hardiness: Zones 3 through 6
Description: A rhizomatous, upright-narrow to upright-open perennial. Culms 3–6 ft /0.9–1.8 m high, more or less glabrous, with extensive creeping rhizomes. Foliage medium to dull green, medium in texture; leaves rather widely spaced along the culm, leaf blades flat, scabrous, 10–12 in./2.5–3.0 dm long, about 0.4–0.5 in./10–13 mm wide, long attenuate; sheaths glabrous, longer than the internodes; ligule membranous, becoming erose. Inflorescence a rather dense, more or less contracted, narrow, branched panicle, erect, 10–14 in./2.5–3.5 dm long, about 3–4 in./8–10 cm wide, purplish, brownish, or green, the branches short; spikelets crowded, pedicellate, pedicels short, one-flowered, narrowly lanceolate, 0.25–0.30 in./6–8 mm long; rachilla obsolete; glumes unequal 0.20–0.25 in./5–6 mm long, very narrowly lanceolate, attenuate, lower one-nerved, the upper three-nerved, usually shorter than the lower, rough on the keels; lemmas membranous, three-nerved, about half as long as the glumes, two-toothed at the apex, the awn attached below the middle near the base, delicate, often obscure, slightly bent, about as long as the lemma; palea faintly two-lobed, shorter than the lemma; caryopsis enclosed. Flowering and fruiting occur from June through July.

Uses: Bushgrass is grown primarily for its decorative, colorful flowers. It is useful as background borders in shaded, wet, or moist sites, as a tall screen or windbreak, and in seaside plantings. Bushgrass is useful for soil reclamation in salt marshes, as it has a high salt tolerance. It is also useful in naturalized areas bordering on lakes and streams and in water gardens where sufficient moisture is

Calamagrostis epigejos. **Panicle,** × **1; glumes and floret,** × **10.** *Source: Manual of the Grasses of the United States.* USDA Misc. Pub. 200. 1951.

constantly available. The plant size and form are conducive for its use in perennial background borders and in specimen plantings. The plants exhibit good fall and winter color. The light-colored, compact panicles are excellent as cut flowers and in dried arrangements. The cultivar Hortorum, with its rich, foxy-red panicles, is useful for cut flowers and in specimen plantings in water gardens.

Cultivation: Propagation is by seeding and by plant division. Bushgrass is more drought tolerant than bluejoint, *Calamagrostis canadensis.* Bushgrass and its cultivar Hortorum thrive best in partial or light shade in low-lying, wet areas in water gardens and along streams, lakes, and wooded borders. Clumps should be divided every few years to keep it under control. The plants become quite invasive in light, sandy soils because of their creeping rhizomes; however, in heavy clay soils, this is usually not a problem.

Cultivars: *Calamagrostis epigejos* (L.) Roth 'Hortorum' Although this cultivar is slightly smaller (3–5 ft /0.9–1.5 m high) than the species, it is far superior to the type plant for garden decoration and flower arranging. The growth habit is upright narrow, and it spreads slower than the type plant. The foxy-red inflorescence remains more tightly erect than that of the type plant, which adds to its attractiveness as an excellent source of fresh, cut flowers and for dried floral arrangements. This colorful cultivar is also used as medium screens and windbreaks, in middleground borders, and in group and specimen plantings in shaded areas; it is adapted to zones 3 through 7.

Cenchrus L. (Sandbur, Burgrass). Name from Greek *kegchros,* a kind of millet. An ancient Greek name of *Setaria italica* (L.) Beauv., foxtail millet. Lectotype, *Cenchrus echinatus* L. There are about 25 species, in the warm regions of both hemispheres. Low, branching annuals or perennials, with flat leaf blades and terminal spikes of readily deciduous burs. Spikelets solitary or in groups of two or three, surrounded by an involucre of bristles, these united only at the very base, often plumose, falling attached to the spikelets; lower glume shorter than the spikelet, sometimes minute or wanting, upper glume shorter than or equaling the sterile lemma; fertile lemma chartaceous, glabrous, the thin margin enclosing the palea. The seed germinates within the old involucre, the spines usually retrorsely barbed.

> **Latin name:** *Cenchrus ciliaris* L.
> **Synonym:** *Pennisetum ciliare* (L.) Link
> **Cultivars:** Many in cultivation
> **Common name:** Buffelgrass
> **Origin:** Africa, India
> **Habitat:** Cultivated, escape from cultivation
> **Hardiness:** Zones 8 through 10
> **Description:** An upright-open, tufted perennial. Culms much branched and geniculate at the base from a knotted crown, erect or spreading, 1–5 ft / 0.3–1.5 m high; usually a small, very hard corm borne at the base of the culm. Some forms are rhizomatous. Foliage variable, light to medium green, sometimes yellowish green, fine in texture; leaf blades ascending and becoming arched, scabrous, slightly pilose, flat, or involute, 4–18 in./1.0–4.5 dm long, 0.25–0.30 in./6–8 mm wide, long attenuate; sheaths glabrous or sparingly pilose, laterally compressed, light green, longer than the internodes; ligule minute, ciliate. Inflorescence a dense, erect, or sometimes arching, cylindrical, purplish panicle, 2–6 in./0.5–1.5 dm long, 0.8–1.0 in./20–25 mm in diameter, including the bristles, rachis flexuous, internodes 1–3 mm long; spikelets surrounded and enclosed by a spiny involucre composed of numerous coalescing bristles, solitary or in groups of two to four per bur, two-flowered, persistent, 1–3 mm long, burs subglobular to elongate, 0.10–0.15 in./3–4 mm wide, the peduncle short and thick, articulate at base, falling with the spikelets, the spines usually retrorsely barbed; bristles variably colored, usually purplish, 0.15–0.40 in./4–10 mm long, barbed, united near the base, long-ciliate on the margins, the bristle conspicuously elongated beyond the bur, inner bristles plumose; the lower floret usually staminate, the upper fertile, the rachilla remaining intact; lower glume one-to-three-nerved, membranous, minute, upper glume similar in texture, three-to-seven-nerved, nearly the length of the remainder of the spikelet, lower

lemma membranous, three-to-seven-nerved, about the length of the spikelet, fertile lemma slightly hard, acuminate at the tip, convex dorsally, revolute along the margins, enclosing the palea; palea shorter than its lemma; caryopsis enclosed with numerous bristles attached. Flowering and fruiting occur from May through September.

Uses: The ornamental value of buffelgrass is short-lived, as the fluffy seeds shatter easily at maturity and are widely disseminated by the wind. The flowering panicles are attractive as long as they remain intact, but they soon disintegrate upon maturity. Buffelgrass is used primarily as a ground-cover plant in naturalized areas. The plants produce copious seed crops. The heavy seed production coupled with the rhizomatous root system and prolific branching of some forms results in its gregarious growth habit, producing dense stands over extended areas. There is considerable variation in size and vigor among the many cultivars in the trade. Buffelgrass is used to some extent in mixed stands along highways.

Cultivation: Propagation is by seeding and by plant division. The light, fluffy seeds are difficult to handle and plant, either by hand or by machine. Mixing the seeds with fine sand or dry, sandy soil, when planted by hand, usually results in better distribution of seeds over the planted area. Buffelgrass seeds require a dormant period, usually of six months or more before planting. New, freshly collected seeds will not germinate. The plants, particularly the rhizomatous forms, are quite drought tolerant; once established, they thrive in difficult dry sites. The rhizomatous forms are the most cold tolerant or winter hardy. Buffelgrass may be grown as an annual in zones 5 through 7, where it fails to perenniate; the plants prefer full sun and thrive on many different soil types in dry, difficult locations.

Chasmanthium **Link.** An ancient Latin name of a plant. Type species, *Holcus laxus* L. There are nine species, all of which are American. Rather tall, erect, perennial grasses, with flat or sometimes convolute leaf blades and narrow or open panicles of compressed, sometimes very broad and flat spikelets. Spikelets three-to-many-flowered, the lower lemmas empty, the rachilla disarticulating above the glumes and between the florets; glumes compressed-keeled, rigid, usually narrow, three-to-seven-nerved, acute or acuminate, rarely mucronate; lemmas compressed, sometimes conspicuously flattened, chartaceous, many-nerved, the nerves sometimes obscure, acute, or acuminate, the empty ones at the base and the uppermost usually reduced; palea rigid, strongly keeled, bowed out at the base.

Latin name: *Chasmanthium latifolium* (Michx.) Yates
Synonym: *Uniola latifolium* Michx.
Common names: Broad-leaved uniola, Northern sea oats, Wild oats
Origin: United States

Chasmanthium latifolium. **Habit,** × 1/2; **spikelet and floret,** × 3. *Source: Manual of the Grasses of the United States.* USDA Misc. Pub. 200. 1951.

Habitat: Cultivated, escape from cultivation

Hardiness: Zones 5 through 10

Description: An upright-narrow to upright-arching rhizomatous perennial forming small colonies. Culms glabrous, erect to arching, 3–5 ft /0.9–1.5 m high, tufted, with short, bronze, stout rhizomes. Foliage light green, becoming bronze at maturity, coarse in texture; leaves alternately and evenly spaced along the culm, leaf blades flat, somewhat stiff but slightly arching, narrowly lanceolate, 4–8 in./1–2 dm long, about 0.5–1.0 in./13–25 mm wide, tapering at both ends, rough on the margins, commonly a few hairs on the upper surface at the base; sheaths rather loose, round on the back, slightly inflated, especially the lower ones, usually shorter than the internodes; ligule membranous, short, about 2 mm long, truncate, fringed with very short hairs. Inflorescence an open, branched, drooping, lax panicle, axis and branches scabrous, the filiform branches bearing a few pendulous spikelets on long capillary pedicels; spikelets few, very flat, two-edged, 6-to-15-flowered, 0.8–1.2 in./2–3 cm long, ovate or oblong, green and finally tawny or bronze; glumes compressed keeled, acute or acuminate, equal, 0.2–0.3 in./5–8 mm long; lemmas lanceolate, acute, 0.3–0.5 in./8–13 mm long, strongly keeled, the keels winged and ciliate, many-nerved, the lower lemma empty; palea shorter than its lemma, keels winged, bowed out at base; caryopsis flat, oval, black, about 0.2 in./5 mm long. Flowering and fruiting occur from June through September; the seedheads, which mature and become rusty, tan, brown, or bronze before frost, persist.

Uses: Broad-leaved uniola ranks among the best of grasses for any garden. It is one of the few species that will survive the summer shade as well as thrive in full sun. The three seasons of interest for this striking perennial include summer, when it is in flower; fall, when the foliage and seedheads become rusty or rich bronze; and winter, when the seedheads persist on the plant and it remains an upright-arching specimen. Broad-leaved uniola is grown primarily for its unique, flattened spikelets, which persist on the panicle. The plants are attractive in accent and specimen plantings and in middleground borders. They are also effective in rock gardens and in mixed, massed, grass plantings in naturalized areas, even along the seashore. The green seedheads are excellent for cut flowers, and the mature beige or bronze seedheads make an attractive contribution in dried arrangements, as they very rarely shatter. The rich bronze foliage and drooping bronze seedheads provide excellent fall color. Broad-leaved uniola panicles are commonly found in florist shops, usually in their natural color, as they are difficult to dye. Broad-leaved uniola is one of the few native ornamental grasses of particular importance in the United States. Broad-leaved uniola is used in botanical gardens, parks, golf courses, and zoos.

Cultivation: Propagation is by seeding and by division of the plant crowns and rhizomes. The seeds may require two to three weeks to germinate; although the seeds may be difficult to germinate, the plants readily reseed themselves under most conditions. Broad-leaved uniola is both drought and shade tolerant. Plants grown in full sun are usually lighter green than those grown in partial shade. Broad-leaved uniola thrives on fertile, light to heavy, well-drained soils with ample moisture. The plants tend to lodge when grown in specimen plantings unless they are supported by staking or by other surrounding plants.

Chloris **Sw. (Fingergrass, Windmill grass).** Named for Greek *Chloris,* the goddess of flowers. Lectotype, *Chloris cruciata* (L.) Sw. There are about 70 species, cosmopolitan in tropical and subtropical regions of the world. Tufted perennials or sometimes annuals with flat or folded scabrous leaf blades and up to several, usually showy and feathery, spikes, aggregate at the summit of the culms. Spikelets with one perfect floret, sessile in two rows along one side of a continuous rachis, the rachilla disarticulating above the glumes, produced beyond the perfect floret and bearing one to several reduced florets consisting of empty lemmas, these often truncate, and, if more than one, the smaller ones usually enclosed in the lower, forming a somewhat club-shaped rudiment; glumes somewhat unequal, the lower shorter, narrow, acute; lemma keeled, usually broad, one-to-five-nerved, often villous on the callus and villous or long-ciliate on the keel or marginal nerves, awned between the short teeth of a bifid apex, the awn slender or sometimes reduced to a mucro, the sterile lemmas awned or awnless.

> **Latin name:** *Chloris cucullata* Bisch.
> **Common name:** Hooded windmill grass
> **Origin:** Southeastern United States
> **Habitat:** Open grassland
> **Hardiness:** Zones 7 through 10
> **Description:** An upright-open to somewhat spreading perennial. Culms

tufted, erect from a decumbent base, flattened, simple, rarely branched, 8–20 in./2–5 dm high. Foliage medium green, fine in texture; leaf blades lanceolate, rough, 2–6 in./0.5–1.5 dm long, 1–3 mm wide, the upper very short, flat, becoming folded, scabrous on the upper surface and margins, abruptly acute at the apex; sheaths flattened, with membranous margins, shorter than the internodes; ligule membranous, truncate, ciliate, about 1 mm long. Inflorescence 12–18 radiating, digitate, flexuous or curled, purplish spikes exserted in one or two whorls, ascending or slightly drooping, 1–2 in./2.5–5.0 cm long, bearing spikelets to the base, rachis scabrous; spikelets four-flowered, with one perfect floret, sessile or subsessile, in two rows along one side of a continued rachis, 2–3 mm long, exclusive of the awns, trigonous, about as broad as long; glumes unequal, lanceolate, acute, scabrous on the keel, the lower about half as long as the spikelet, the upper obtuse or abruptly acute, longer and broader than the lower; lemmas three-nerved, somewhat flattened, obtuse, 2 mm long, short-villous on the callus, the lateral nerves densely pubescent, the midrib sparsely so, awn very short, usually less than 1 mm long, sterile lemma five-to-seven-nerved, protruding, the lateral nerves branching, distant from the midrib, each half of the lemma truncate, as broad as long, the apex and margins involute, the awn about 1 mm long; palea shorter than its lemma; caryopsis free within the lemma and palea. Flowering and fruiting occur from July through August, with the empty seedheads remaining intact.

Uses: Hooded windmill grass may be interplanted with other ornamentals in foreground and middleground border plantings and in rock gardens. The plants do not shade other ornamentals when used in this manner, as the foliage is low. Green flower heads are used as cut flowers; the dry spikes, which are usually curled into peculiar shapes, and the empty, stramineous spikelets are attractive on the plants and in dried arrangements. The culms and dry seedheads provide good fall color. Hooded windmill grass is also useful as ground cover and in mixed grass plantings in naturalized areas.

Cultivation: Hooded windmill grass is usually propagated by seeding, although division of plant crowns is also successful. This tufted perennial may be grown as an annual by being seeded directly in the garden. The plants are quite drought tolerant and thrive best in full sun; they are adapted to acid or neutral soils, medium to coarse in texture. The plants may produce more than one seed crop each growing season; they reseed themselves readily.

Latin name: *Chloris distichophylla* Lag.
Synonym: *Eustachys distichophylla* Nees
Common name: Weeping windmill grass
Origin: South America
Habitat: Cultivated, escape from cultivation
Hardiness: Zones 7 through 9
Description: An upright-open perennial. Culms tufted, erect, or decumbent at the base, sometimes rooting at the lower nodes, glabrous, 24–30 in./6.0–7.6 dm high. Foliage dark green, fine in texture; leaf blades flat or folded, glabrous or slightly rough on the margins, 3–8 in./0.8–2.0 dm long, 0.10–0.25 in./3–6 mm wide, abruptly acute at the tip; upper sheaths usually shorter than the internodes, lower about as long as the internodes; ligule a dense ring of very short hairs, less than 1 mm long. Inflorescence of 10–15 compressed, radiating, digitate spikes, exserted, flexuous or curled, slender, 2–4 in./5–10 cm long, dark brownish, closely aggregate, erect, finally ascending or drooping, the subsessile spikelets crowded on a scabrous rachis; spikelets trigonous, 2–3 mm long, excluding the hairs, about as broad, two-flowered, stramineous, turning fuscous at maturity; glumes about equal, acute, 1–2 mm long, the upper longer than the lower, about 2 mm long, truncate, bearing a very short awn from the sinus or the round lobes, minutely scabrous; lemmas brown, awnless, the lower about 2 mm long, acute, lanceolate, acute, villous on the margins, the hairs about 1 mm long, sterile lemma obovate, five-nerved, mucronate, about 1 mm long; palea about as long as the lemma, minutely two-toothed, ciliate; caryopsis free. Flowering and fruiting occur from July through August, with the dry, empty seedheads persisting.

Uses: Weeping windmill grass is interesting when planted in clumps in accent and specimen plantings in rock gardens and in foreground and middle-ground borders. Green flower heads are interesting as cut flowers. The dry inflorescences of irregularly curled, empty, or partially empty spikes are attractive in dried arrangements; the unique, weeping inflorescences are attractive when remaining on the plants. Occasionally the leaves have reddish tips, which adds to their attractiveness in affording good, early, fall color.

Cultivation: This perennial may also be grown as an annual. The plants are somewhat drought tolerant; they thrive best in full sun, but they will tolerate light shade. Propagation is by seeding and by division of the plant crowns, preferably the former. The sticky, fuzzy seeds tend to cling together, thus making it difficult to obtain an even distribution of seeds over the planted area. Weeping windmill grass is adaptable to acid to neutral soils, medium to coarse in texture; it does equally well on loamy and clay soils.

Latin name: *Chloris gayana* Kunth
Common name: Rhodesgrass
Origin: Africa
Habitat: Cultivated, escape from cultivation
Hardiness: Zones 7 through 10
Description: A loosely tufted perennial with stout, leafy stolons. Culms erect or ascending, 3–5 ft /0.9–1.5 m high, stout, wiry, internodes compressed, nodes dark green, occasionally rooting at the lower nodes. Foliage medium green, fine in texture; leaf blades 4–18 in./1.0–4.5 dm long or longer, 0.1–0.2 in./3–5 mm wide, long attenuate, the upper shorter, scabrous, flat, becoming folded when dry; sheaths flattened, glabrous except toward the apex, long-villous at the throat, shorter than the internodes; ligule membranous, very short, less than 1 mm long, ciliate, the hairs 0.10–0.25 in./3–6 mm long. Inflorescence 10 to 20 sessile or subsessile, paired spikes gathered into a false, large, leafy spikelike panicle, spikes pale or purplish, digitate 2–5 in./0.5–1.3 dm long, usually slender, stout, erect or ascending, internodes and pedicels cuneate, ciliate, the pedicel more or less bilobed at the tip, pale or tawny; spikelets crowded, pale or tawny, sessile or subsessile, lanceolate, appressed to the rachis, 0.10–0.15 in./3–4 mm long, excluding the awns, consisting of two or more florets, lower floret glabrous on the keel, appressed-hispid along the margins, the hairs longer toward the summit, about 0.1 in./3 mm long, the awn 0.15–0.20 in./4–5 mm long, second floret smaller than the first, glabrous, the awn about 0.1 in./3 mm long, third floret about 2 mm long, truncate, mucronate, sometimes a rudimentary fourth floret present; glumes unequal, one-nerved, lanceolate, scabrous on the nerves, the lower narrowly oblong, 1–2 mm long, flat on the back, with many nerves between the lateral keels and a conspicuous median groove, glabrous, upper glume mucronate, 2–3 mm long exclusive of a short awn; upper lemma deeply bilobed with an awn 0.4–1.2 in./1–3 cm long, lower lemma 2–3 mm long, fertile or empty, glabrous on the keel, villous along the margins,

Chloris gayana. **Habit,** × 1/2; **florets,** × 5. *Source: Manual of the Grasses of the West Indies.* USDA Misc. Pub. 243. 1936.

three-nerved, midnerve prolonged between a bilobed apex into an awn about 0.2 in./5 mm long, sterile lemma included with the lower lemma, awnless or short-awned; palea two-keeled, acute, obovate, slightly shorter than the lemma; caryopsis free. Flowering and fruiting occur from June through August.

Uses: The invasiveness and competitiveness of rhodesgrass make it suitable as a ground-cover and erosion-control plant. It is ideal for steep slopes and highway banks and along stream banks in naturalized areas where erosion may be or may become a problem. Rhodesgrass remains semievergreen in warm climates. The green flower heads are attractive on the plants.

Cultivation: Propagation is by direct seeding and by plant division. Seeds should be sown broadcast in sunny, naturalized areas following seedbed preparation. Some forms are not stoloniferous; most forms are heavy seeders. Once a stand is established, the plants form a dense ground cover that almost completely excludes all weeds. Maintenance is minimal; should the plants get too high, mowing once a growing season will suffice. Ratoon growth is increased by mowing, thus increasing the density of ground cover. Rhodesgrass is highly salt tolerant.

Latin name: *Chloris verticillata* Nutt.
Common name: Windmill grass
Origin: South America
Habitat: Open grassland
Hardiness: Zones 6 through 10
Description: An upright-narrow, tufted perennial. Culms tufted, usually a few in a tuft, erect or decumbent, branching at the base, sometimes rooting at the lower nodes, flattened, commonly sterile, 6–18 in./1.5–4.5 dm high. Foliage medium to dark green, fine in texture; leaf blades crowded at the base, flat or folded, elongate or obtuse, 2–6 in./0.5–1.5 dm long, 0.10–0.15 in./3–4 mm wide, abruptly pointed, glabrous or rough, the upper shorter; sheaths loose, flattened, shorter than or about as long as the internodes; ligule very short, less than 1 mm long, membranous, fringed. Inflorescence many, slender, loose, radiating, digitate spikes, 3–7 in./0.8–1.8 dm long, borne in one to three whorls, ascending, finally wide-spreading, axis very short, villous, the slender rachis scabrous; spikelets subsessile, two-to-four-flowered, one perfect flower, cuneate-obovate, flattened, 0.15–0.20 in./4–5 mm long, excluding the awns, crowded in two rows in verticillate or approximate spikes; glumes acuminate, narrow, awn-pointed, one-nerved, scabrous on the nerves, the lower about 2 mm long, the upper about as long as the spikelet; lemmas obtuse, 2–3 mm long exclusive of the awns, three-nerved, the nerves ciliate, the lateral nerves near the margins sparsely hispid with appressed hairs above the middle, the internerves rough, the midnerve scabrous toward the apex with a scabrous, straight awn 0.2–0.4 in./5–10 mm long from the bifid apex, callus pubescent, sterile lemma three-nerved, truncate, 1–2 mm long, usually bearing a short awn just below the apex, usually shorter than that of the fertile lemma; palea folded, two-keeled,

usually shorter than its lemma; rudiment cuneate-oblong, rather turgid, about 1 mm wide, rarely fertile; caryopsis free within the lemma and palea. Flowering and fruiting occur from June through September. The inflorescence breaks away and forms a tumbleweed at maturity like that of *Amaranthus albus.*

Uses: Windmill grass is useful as an edging plant in foreground borders and in specimen plantings in rock gardens. The plants remain attractive throughout the growing season because the foliage remains green. The inflorescence is interesting and attractive before maturity.

Cultivation: Propagation is by seeding and by plant division, preferably the former. Seeding may be done directly on the site where the plants are to grow. This perennial is easily cultivated successfully as an annual because the plants will mature in one season from seeding. The plants are adapted to a wide range of soils and microclimates, including acid or neutral soils, medium to coarse in texture. Windmill grass is somewhat drought tolerant but requires full

Chloris glauca. **Habit,** × **1; florets,** × **5.** *Source: Manual of the Grasses of the United States.* USDA Misc. Pub. 200. 1951.

sun. The mature inflorescence breaks away at maturity and rolls before the wind as a tumbleweed.

Other ornamental species: *Chloris glauca* (Chapm.) A. Wood. Saltmarsh chloris An upright-open, tufted perennial. Culms 2–5 ft /0.6–1.5 m high, erect, compressed, stout. Foliage glaucous, medium in texture; leaf blades flat or folded, 2–4 in./5–10 cm long, 0.3–0.5 in./8–13 mm wide, with abruptly round tip; sheaths mostly basal, longer than the internodes, broad, compressed, keeled, overlapping; ligule membranous, about 1 mm long. Inflorescence numerous ascending spikes, 1–4 in./2.5–10.0 cm long, borne in a single whorl; spikelets about 2 mm long excluding the awns, borne on one side of the rachis, hairy, hairs appressed, brownish; glumes lanceolate, scabrous; lemmas glabrous or scaberulous on the nerves; palea about the length of the lemma. Saltmarsh chloris occurs in coastal flatwoods, swamp margins, and sloughs on calcareous soils. It is useful as ground cover and in land reclamation in brackish marshes, around lakes and ponds, and along streams. Flowering and fruiting occur from May through June. Propagation is by seeding or by plant division. Saltmarsh chloris is adapted to zones 7 through 10.

Coix L. (Job's tears). Name from Greek *koix,* a kind of palm. Lectotype, *Coix lacryma-jobi* L. There are four species, native to Asia. Tall, branched grasses with broad, flat, leaf blades, the monoecious inflorescences numerous on long, stout peduncles. Spikelets unisexual; staminate spikelets two-flowered, in twos or threes on a continuous rachis, the normal group consisting of a pair of sessile spikelets with a single pedicellate spikelet between, the latter sometimes reduced to a pedicel or wanting; glumes membranous, obscurely nerved; lemma and palea hyaline; stamens three; pistillate spikelets three together, one fertile and two sterile at the base of the inflorescence; glumes of fertile spikelet several-nerved, hyaline below, chartaceous in the upper narrow part, the lower very broad, infolding the spikelet, the margins infolded beyond the two lateral, stronger nerves, upper glume narrower than the lower, keeled, sterile lemma similar but a little narrower; fertile lemma and palea hyaline; sterile spikelets consisting of a single, narrow, tubular glume as long as the fertile spikelet, somewhat chartaceous.

>**Latin name:** *Coix lacryma-jobi* L.
>**Synonym:** *Coix lacryma* L.
>**Cultivars:** 'Aurea Zebrina' Striped Job's tears
>**Common names:** Job's tears, Adlay, Christ's tears, Teargrass
>**Origin:** East Asia
>**Habitat:** Cultivated, escape from cultivation
>**Hardiness:** Zones 5 through 10
>**Description:** An upright-narrow, loosely tufted, monoecious annual or

weak, short-lived perennial in warm climates. Culms usually several, freely

Coix lacryma-jobi.
Inflorescence, × 1. *Source: Manual of the Grasses of the West Indies.* USDA Misc. Pub. 243. 1936.

branching, 3–6 ft /0.9–1.8 m high, bright light green. Foliage bright, shiny, light green, coarse in texture; leaf blades 1–2 ft /3–6 dm long, usually less, about 0.6–1.6 in./1.5–4.0 cm wide, flat or U-shaped, somewhat undulate along the margins, arching, with a prominent midvein, especially on the lower side, flared near the sheath, then gradually tapering to a fine point; sheaths glabrous, light green, the lower longer than the internodes, the upper shorter; ligule membranous, about 1 mm long. Inflorescence numerous monoecious spikelets, borne on long, stout pedicels clustered in the leaf axils; each inflorescence consists of an ovate or oval, pearly white, beadlike, very hard, tardily deciduous involucre containing a pistillate lower portion, the points of the pistillate spikelets and the slender axis of the staminate portion of the inflorescence protruding through the orifice at the apex, the staminate upper portion about 0.8–1.6 in./2–4 cm long, becoming deciduous, consists of several clusters of staminate spikelets; spikelets unisexual, staminate spikelets two-flowered, in twos or threes on a continuous rachis, the group consisting of a pair of sessile spikelets with a single pedicellate spikelet between, the latter sometimes reduced; glumes membranous, unequal, about 0.25–0.30 in./6–8 mm long, obscurely many-nerved, the lower subacute, the upper acute; lemmas nearly as long as the glumes, hyaline, five-nerved, awnless; paleas hyaline, slightly shorter than the lemmas; pistillate spikelets three together, one fertile and two sterile, at the base of the inflorescence; fertile spikelets consist of two glumes, one sterile lemma, a fertile lemma and a palea; glumes several-nerved, hyaline below, chartaceous in the upper portion, the first broad, enfolding the spikelet, the margins enfolded beyond the two lateral stronger pair of nerves, the second glume keeled, narrower than the first; lemmas hyaline, sterile lemma about the length of the second glume, similar in shape, hyaline below, chartaceous above, fertile lemma narrow, somewhat shorter than the sterile lemma; palea narrow, hyaline, shorter than the lemma; sterile spikelets consist of a single, narrow, tubular glume as long as the fertile spikelet, somewhat chartaceous; caryopsis ovoid, smooth, about 0.5 in./13 mm long, 0.25 in./6 mm across, initially shiny, light greenish, becoming whitish to bluish gray and eventually dark gray or black at maturity, often streaked. Flowering and fruiting occur from July through September; the seeds fall to the ground at maturity.

Uses: Job's tears is valuable and useful as a curiosity rather than as an ornamental. The beadlike, teardrop, shiny, gray or mottled seeds are often used as beads. The plants are of little garden value, although they are often used in annual background borders, whereas the variegated cultivar Aurea Zebrina is useful in middleground borders and as specimen plants. Job's tears and its variegated cultivar are often grown as a curiosity in rock, water, and vegetable gardens and in parks and zoos. It is useful for food in some parts of Asia.

Cultivation: Propagation is by seeding. New plants may be started indoors in individual pots in colder climates. Seeding of this tender annual may be done in place in the garden in the spring as soon as the soil temperature is conducive to seed germination; allow two to four weeks for germination. Germination may be hastened by soaking the seeds in water for 12–24 hours prior to planting. Job's tears grows best in full sun but will tolerate light shade. The plants prefer a well-drained soil with a continuous moisture supply; they require a long growing season; some forms are only 2 ft/6 dm high. Job's tears is grown as an annual in zones 5–8, whereas it acts as a weak, short-lived perennial in zones 9 and 10.

Cultivars: *Coix lacryma-jobi* L. 'Aurea Zebrina' Striped Job's tears   The uncommon cultivar Aurea Zebrina is smaller in size than Job's tears, about 36–40 in./0.9–1.0 m high. The main attraction of this cultivar is its variegated foliage; the leaves have green and white longitudinal stripes merging together. Striped Job's tears is adapted to zones 5–10 and prefers light shade, where it serves as a specimen plant.

Cortaderia **Stapf (Pampas grass).** Lectotype, *Cortaderia selloana* (Schult.) Asch. & Graebn. There are 24 species, native to South America and New Zealand. Large, densely tufted, gynodioecious, perennial grasses. Spikelets several-flowered; rachilla internodes jointed, the lower part glabrous, the upper bearded, forming a stipe to the floret; glumes longer than the lower florets; lemmas of pistillate spikelets clothed with long hairs.

Latin name: *Cortaderia selloana* (Schult.) Asch. & Graebn.
Synonym: *Cortaderia dioica* Spreng.
Cultivars: More than a dozen recognized cultivars in cultivation, including 'Argenteum,' 'Bertini,' 'Carminea Rendadleri,' 'Carnea,' 'Elegans,' 'Gold Band,' 'Marabout,' 'Monstrosa,' 'Pumila,' 'Rosa Fedder,' 'Rosea,' 'Silver Stripe,' 'Sunningdale Silver,' 'Violacea'
Common name: Pampas grass
Origin: South America, Argentina
Habitat: Cultivated, escape from cultivation
Hardiness: Zones 8 through 10
Description: A gynodioecious, upright-open, weak perennial. Culms of staminate plants stout, erect, glabrous or nearly so, densely tufted, forming large clumps, 6–12 ft / 1.8–3.7 m high, lower internodes short, the upper very long. Culms of pistillate plants of equal size and vigor. Foliage medium to glaucous green, medium in texture, mostly crowded at the base of the culm; upper leaves 1–8 ft / 0.3–2.5 m long, 0.4–0.6 in. / 10–15 mm wide, extra-long attenuate, usually more or less arching, flat or slightly U-shaped with sharp scabrid margins, lower leaves usually shorter and wider than the upper; sheaths longer than the internodes, glabrous or pubescent toward the summit, villous at the throat; ligule a ring of dense hairs. Staminate inflorescence a branched, oblong, panicle 24–30 in. / 6.0–7.6 dm long, about 8–12 in. / 2–3 dm wide, the branches erect or ascending and spreading, bearing spikelets nearly to the base; spikelets approximate, pedicellate, on flexuous, slightly scabrous pedicels usually shorter than the spikelet, two-flowered, 0.4–0.5 in. / 10–13 mm long, rachilla about 1 mm long; glumes three-nerved, more or less equal, 0.3–0.5 in. / 8–13 mm long, the lower chartaceous, thin, narrow, slightly shorter than the upper, long attenuate, mostly two-toothed; lemmas 0.4–0.5 in. / 10–13 mm long including the awns, the awns narrow, glabrous, hyaline, 0.15–0.20 in. / 4–5 mm long; paleas hyaline, two-keeled, shorter than the lemmas, 0.10–0.15 in. / 3–4 mm long, downy at the apex; the branched, pistillate inflorescence broadly pyramidal, usually longer and broader than the staminate inflorescence, quite variable, hairy, silky, and more showy in color; lemmas villous, the hairs usually longer than the body of the lemmas and shorter than the awns; the flowering plumose inflorescence borne high above the cascading foliage is very fluffy, variable in color, usually silvery white, whitish, or with a light tinge of pink at maturity; the staminate

Cortaderia selloana.

inflorescence is usually white or off-white. Flowering and fruiting occur from early June until frost.

Considerable variation exists among cultivars of pampas grass as to plant size, vigor, winter hardiness, and foliage and flower color. Pampas grass is not an evergreen plant in the true sense. Although its range and winter hardiness have been delineated and described, many cultivars do not perform according to their descriptions. Plants are evergreen only in the milder climates, whereas in colder climates they perform as deciduous, rather weak perennials, or are killed by severe winters. Various cultivars of pampas grass have plumes of different colors: beige, carmine, pink, purple, rose, yellow, violet, off-white, silvery white, and white; cultivars with white, off-white, and silvery white are most common. Plumes of the pistillate plants are usually larger and brighter in color than those of the staminate plants. Panicles are usually a darker shade upon emergence, fading to white and becoming very fluffy when mature.

Uses: Pampas grass is adaptable for multifarious uses in any garden of sufficient size. Garden size may limit its use in some instances; however, dwarf or small cultivars are available for use in smaller gardens. Careful thought should be given to its location and use in the garden because of its height and spread. Its use in the central and northern United States is limited somewhat by its lack of winter hardiness. Clones from England have proven to be hardy in plant-hardiness zone 7, whereas other clones reputed to be winter hardy in this zone have repeatedly failed to survive. Careful searching for cold-hardy cultivars is recommended.

Pampas grass constitutes a stately addition to any garden regardless of whether or not it flowers and perenniates. Pampas grass is an imposing sight during all seasons. The large mound of gracefully arching leaves gives it a worthwhile architectural quality, even when it is not in flower. The variegated cultivars are grown primarily for their multicolored foliage. The flowering plumes are impressive, not only for their size but for their color, gracefulness, and longevity. Pampas grass flowers during summer or early fall and the flowering plumes remain more or less intact well into winter. The beige foliage and flowering panicles provide good fall color following killing frosts. The majestic structure and large inflorescence of pampas grass could form the focal point in specimen and accent plantings in lawns, in rock and water gardens, and around swimming pools and patios; it acts as a screen along driveways and property lines.

Pampas grass contrasts harmoniously with broad-leaved plants when used in background plantings of permanent borders and as tall screens and windbreaks. Pampas grass requires sufficient space to be fully appreciated as to form, size, and color. The flowering plumes are most effective when grown against a dark background. It is advisable to locate the plants so that the afternoon or evening sun shines through the flowers, unobstructed by a darker background. Cultivars of varying size and foliage and plume color make a spectacular sight when established in massed plantings. Pistillate plants are preferred to the staminate plants because the plumes are usually larger, more brightly colored, and longer lasting.

Pampas grass and its cultivars are excellent sources of cut flowers when the inflorescence has attained its maximum size and brilliance in color; the mature panicles are useful in dried arrangements, as they do not shatter readily. Although dyed plumes are commercially available, the natural colors are far superior. Pampas grass and its colorful cultivars are useful in decorative plantings along highways and streets and in parks, zoos, and golf courses.

Cultivation: Pampas grass may be grown as an annual in marginal areas of winter hardiness (i.e., zones 5–7) and as a weak perennial in zones 8–10. Plant crowns may be maintained indoors during the winter and replanted in the spring. Pampas grass should be considered a weak perennial; the plants are often mulched in marginal areas of winter hardiness. Leaving old growth on the plants in areas where they are deciduous is debatable; however, its timely removal either in the fall or spring will aid new growth. Propagation is by seeding and by plant division. Plant division is usually done in the spring as soon as new growth has begun. Division of pistillate plants is preferred, as the plumes are the largest, most colorful, and longer lasting. This method of propagation ensures the type and color of plants desired.

Pampas grass and its cultivars all grow best in full sun in fertile, well-drained soils. The plants are intolerant of cold, clay soils. Pampas grass requires an adequate supply of moisture; however, it does not grow well if its roots are actually in water. Best coloring of foliage is achieved from plants grown on sandy soils under rather dry conditions. Suggested opposing sites for its use in the garden include (1) brightening dark corners of the garden with white-flowered forms; (2) establishing cultivars with colorful plumes beside a pond, pool, or lake, where their reflection on the water will enhance their appearance and appeal. Unfortunately, very few of the cultivars and clones are available in the United States.

Cultivars: *Cortaderia selloana* (Schult.) Asch. & Graebn. 'Argenteum' Silvery pampas grass   Plants 9–12 ft /2.8–3.7 m high, with silvery panicles.

'Bertini'   A perfect miniature of the type; plants 2–3 ft /0.6–0.9 m high; leaf blades very narrow, up to 0.1 in./3 mm wide; panicles symmetrical, rather broader in proportion to their length than those of the type.

'Carminea Rendadleri'   Distinctive pinkish to purplish plumes borne high above the foliage on weak culms, 8–9 ft /2.5–2.8 m high.

'Carnea'   Very similar to the type but with delicate, pale pink plumes.

'Elegans'   Plants produce distinctly silvery white panicles.

'Gold Band'   Leaves are broadly margined with rich, golden yellow stripes, turning completely golden with age; plants are 4–5 ft /1.2–1.5 m high when in flower; plumes become ragged with age.

'Marabout'   Plants bear large, dense, white plumes.

'Monstrosa'   The largest of all cultivars; plants form a symmetrical mound of foliage up to 6 ft /1.8 m high, bearing enormous panicles to 2 ft /6 dm long high above the foliage on culms 11–12 ft /3.4–3.7 m high.

'Pumila' A dwarf form suitable for small gardens; plants attain 4–6 ft / 1.2–1.8 m high when in flower.

'Rosa Feder' Plants 9–12 ft /2.8–3.7 m high with pink panicles.

'Rosea' Plants are most effective when grown in combination with other cultivars; panicles tinged light pink.

'Silver Stripe' Plants 4–5 ft /1.2–1.5 m high when in flower; leaf blades with moderately wide, white margins, the whiteness persists throughout the growing season.

'Sunningdale Silver' An outstanding, large cultivar bearing symmetrical white-flowered panicles high above the foliage on strong culms 6–9 ft /1.8–2.8 m high.

'Violacea' Plants are very similar to the type; panicles are distinctly violet. The cultivars of pampas grass are adapted to the same plant-hardiness zones and used in the same manner as the type.

Other ornamental species: *Cortaderia fulvida* J. Buchan. 'Kakaho' A large, tufted, upright, mound-forming perennial. Culms erect, up to about 5– 6 ft /1.5–1.8 m high when in flower. Foliage mainly basal, light to medium green, fine in texture; leaves narrower than those of the type, leaf blades involute, sparsely covered with soft hairs, margins rough, toothed, leaf tips ending in a long, curling attenuation. Inflorescence a many-branched panicle, 12–16 in./3–4 dm long, about 4–5 in./1.0–1.3 dm wide. The large, heavy panicles cause the culms to bend over; the plumelike panicles are pale brown, tan, or beige at maturity. This cultivar makes an ideal specimen plant; it is adapted to zones 8–10. This exotic cultivar is native to New Zealand.

Cortaderia richardii (Endl.) Zotov Black pampas grass A tufted, upright-narrow to upright-open perennial. Culms are 5–9 ft /1.5–2.8 m high when in flower. Foliage dark to blackish green, medium in texture. Inflorescence a much-branched, plumelike panicle, 8–12 in./2–3 dm long, tawny when mature. It is grown for its conspicuous foliage and decorative flowering plumes, which are useful as cut flowers and in dried floral arrangements, sometimes dyed. Black pampas grass is useful as a screen, and it is especially conspicuous in accent, border, and specimen plantings. Flowering and fruiting occur from late June until frost. The plants grow best in full sun and are adapted to zones 8–10.

***Ctenium* Panzer (Toothache grass).** Name from Greek *ktenion,* "small comb," alluding to the pectinate arrangement of the spikelets. Type species, *Ctenium carolinianum* Panzer. There are 12 species, inhabiting the warmer regions of both hemispheres. Rather erect, tall, slender perennials, with usually solitary, often curved, spikes. Spikelets several-flowered but with one perfect floret, sessile and pectinately arranged on one side of a continuous rachis, the rachilla disarticulating above the glumes; lower glume small, hyaline, one-nerved, the upper about as long as the lemma, firm, three- or four-toothed, bearing a strong, divergent awn on the back; lemmas rather chartaceous, three-nerved, with long hairs on the lateral nerves and short, straight or curved awn on the back just below the apex, the first and second lemmas empty, the third enclosing a perfect flower, the upper one to three empty and successively smaller.

Latin name: *Ctenium aromaticum* (Walt.) A. Wood
Synonym: *Campulosus aromaticus* Scribn.
Common names: Orange grass, Toothache grass
Origin: Southern France
Habitat: On moist sandy soils, cultivated
Hardiness: Zones 8 through 10
Description: An upright-narrow, tufted perennial. Culms erect, simple, 3–5 ft /0.9–1.5 m high, glabrous or somewhat scabrous. Foliage dark green, fine in texture; leaf blades dark green above, light green beneath, the lower longer than the upper, 6–8 in./1.5–2.0 dm long, 0.2–0.3 in./5–8 mm wide, long attenuate, flat or involute; sheaths shorter than the internodes, rough, old sheaths persistent and fibrillose at base; ligule truncate, 1 mm long. Inflorescence usually a single, curved spike, 2–6 in./0.5–1.5 dm long, about 0.8–1.0 in./20–25 mm in diameter excluding the awns, the rachis extended into a point, spikelets arranged pectinately along one side of the continuous rachis, giving it a characteristic comblike appearance; spikelets feathery, several-flowered, but with only one perfect floret, sessile and closely imbricate, 0.20–0.25 in./5–6 mm long; glumes unequal, lower glume hyaline, one-nerved, about 2 mm long, the upper three- or four-nerved, firm, 0.15–0.20 in./4–5 mm long, with a row of warty glands on each side of the midnerve, bearing a stout, horizontal or recurved awn just about the middle, 0.10–0.15 in./3–4 mm long; lemmas chartaceous, 0.15–0.20 in./4–5 mm long or the upper shorter, three-nerved, scabrous, villous at the base and on the margins at the middle, bearing a straight awn from below the two-toothed apex, or the uppermost awnless and glabrous. Flowering and fruiting occur from May through June; seedheads are mature by late June or early July.
Uses: Toothache grass is useful in pure stands as ground cover in water gardens and in natural areas along streams and around lakes, pools, and ponds. The curved, flowering spikes are interesting in the garden and as cut flowers or in dried arrangements. The plants are pungent to the taste. The bruised spikes produce an orange-colored juice, and the enlarged base, when chewed, deadens the tongue and gums, which may account for the common names associated with the plant.
Cultivation: Propagation is by direct seeding and by plant division. The plants prefer full sun but will tolerate light shade. Toothache grass thrives best on wet, poorly drained, acid soils; it withstands stagnant water or slow-moving streams for short periods.

Ctenium aromaticum. **Habit, × 1/2; spikelet and fertile floret, × 5.**
Source: Manual of the Grasses of the United States. USDA Misc. Pub. 200. 1951.

Cymbopogon **K. Spreng. (Oilgrass).** Lectotype, *Cymbopogon schoenanthus* (L.) Spreng. There are about 30 species, native to the Old World tropics. Rather tall, tufted, aromatic, perennial grasses with flat leaf blades and terminal panicles with small spikelets. Inflorescence a panicle, often brightly colored, composed of few to many frequently densely clustered racemes in pairs at the ends of the slender branches, spreading or reflexed, one usually subsessile, the other pedunculate, each pair supported by a narrowly cymbiform, purplish spathe. Spikelets in pairs, one sessile, the other pedicellate, those of the lowest pair alike and awnless, all other pairs different in sex and structure, the sessile awned, the pedicellate awnless. Awned, sessile spikelet, two-flowered, with a ring of hairs at the base, lower floret reduced to a lemma, upper bisexual; lower glume flat, concave on the back, two-keeled near the margins in the upper half, the keels often winged; upper lemma narrow, two-lobed, awned from between the lobes, awn glabrous, bent and twisted; palea lacking; awnless spikelets all alike, one-flowered, usually staminate, rarely sterile, more or less like the awned spikelets in shape and size, but the lower glume never grooved and usually with more numerous nerves.

> **Latin name:** *Cymbopogon citratus* (DC.) Stapf
> **Synonym:** *Andropogon citratus* DC.
> **Common names:** Lemongrass, Fevergrass, West Indian lemongrass
> **Origin:** Old World tropics

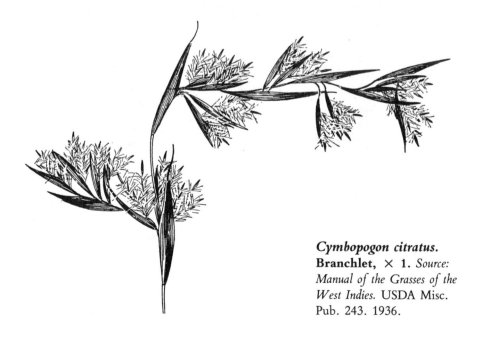

Cymbopogon citratus.
Branchlet, × **1.** *Source: Manual of the Grasses of the West Indies.* USDA Misc. Pub. 243. 1936.

Habitat: Cultivated, escape from cultivation

Hardiness: Zones 9 and 10

Description: A stout, upright-open, rhizomatous, evergreen, aromatic perennial. Culms densely tufted, branched, arching, with leafy, sterile shoots from short rhizomes, 3–6 ft /0.9–1.8 m high. Foliage light green to yellowish green, medium to coarse in texture; leaf blades flat, ascending, narrowly linear, 2–3 ft /6–9 dm long, 0.25–0.80 in./6–20 mm wide, long attenuate toward the base, tapering to a setaceous point, glabrous or scabrous on the margins and above toward the tip, midrib below rather stout and conspicuous, whitish on the upper side; sheaths rather long, as long as or longer than the internodes, round on the back, mostly glabrous with a pilose collar; ligule membranous, stiff, 2–3 mm long. Inflorescence a branched, pyramidal panicle, light purplish, composed of a few densely clustered, paired racemes, the branches elongated and somewhat pendulous, each pair supported by a narrow, cymbiform, purplish spathe, entire panicle 1–2 ft /3–6 dm long, 3–4 in./8–10 cm wide; spikelets in pairs, one sessile, the other pedicellate, 0.15–0.20 in./4–5 mm long excluding the awns, lower pair pedicellate, pedicels with prominent whitish hairs, awnless, one-flowered, similar in size and shape, sterile, staminate or neuter, sessile spikelets awned, fertile, linear-lanceolate, dorsally compressed, flat or dorsally grooved, sharply two-keeled on the edges, two-flowered, with a ring of hairs at the base, lower floret reduced to a lemma, upper bisexual; lower glume flat, concave on the back, two-keeled, the keels often winged; upper lemma narrow, two-lobed, awn from between the lobes, glabrous, bent and twisted, 0.25–0.30 in./6–8 mm long; palea absent. Flowering and fruiting occur from October through January in the tropics and subtropics and from August through September in colder climates.

Uses: Lemongrass is grown primarily for its foliage as an ornamental; it is also unique in that the leaves produce a pleasing lemon fragrance when crushed. This erect, stout perennial is used in group and specimen plantings along driveways and walkways, around swimming pools and patios, and in other areas. Lemongrass makes an excellent medium screen or windbreak and is used in background borders when grown outdoors and as a potted specimen indoors. Potted plants grown indoors usually are not as large as those grown outdoors. Lemongrass is the commercial source of lemon oil. It is also used in botanical gardens, parks, and zoos, along with its relative citronella grass, *Cymbopogon nardus.*

Cultivation: Propagation is by seeding and by plant division. Lemongrass is grown as an annual in zones 5–9 and as a perennial in zone 10. The plants prefer full sun on well-drained, fertile soil that is continuously supplied with ample moisture; when grown on light, sandy soils, lemongrass may require irrigation during extended droughty periods. Lemongrass may perenniate but not flower in zone 9; it does not spread very rapidly, despite its short rhizomes. Plants started indoors in early spring and transplanted to the garden will usually blossom the same year when grown in zones 7–9.

Latin name: *Cymbopogon nardus* (L.) Rendle
Synonym: *Andropogon nardus* L.
Common names: Citronella grass, Nard grass
Origin: Asia
Habitat: Cultivated, escape from cultivation
Hardiness: Zone 10
Description: An upright-open, stout, evergreen, aromatic perennial with fibrous roots and sterile shoots from short rhizomes. Culms much branched, densely tufted, erect, 3–5 ft /0.9–1.5 m high, rough. Foliage light green or glaucous, coarse in texture; leaves often distichous, leaf blades 24–30 in./6.0–7.6 dm long, 0.6–0.8 in./15–20 mm wide, long attenuate toward the base and tip, scabrous above toward the tip and on the margins, midrib conspicuous below, whitish and less conspicuous on the upper side; sheaths as long as or longer than the internodes, light green, round on the back, slightly setaceous; ligule stiff, membranous, about 1 mm long. Inflorescence paired racemes included in a narrow, cymbiform, light purplish spathe, the spathes comprising a large branched panicle, 12–18 in./3.0–4.5 dm long, 3–4 in./8–10 cm wide, branches rather long and somewhat pendulous; spikelets in pairs, the lower pair pedicellate, pedicels with prominent whitish hairs, awnless, one-flowered, similar in size and shape, sterile, staminate or neuter, sessile spikelets fertile, awned, linear-lanceolate, dorsally compressed, flat or dorsally grooved, sharply two-keeled, two-flowered, with a ring of hairs at the base, lower floret reduced, upper bisexual; lower glume flat on the back, two-keeled; upper lemma two-lobed, narrow, awn from between the lobes, glabrous, bent and twisted, 0.20–0.25 in./5–6 mm long; palea lacking. Flowering and fruiting occur from September through December in the tropics and subtropics and from August through September in colder climates.

Uses: Citronella grass is one of the oil grasses of commerce. Its ornamental value is in its foliage; the citronella odor is evident and pleasing, especially when the leaves are crushed. The fibrous, somewhat aromatic rootstocks are used occasionally as a toothbrush. Citronella grass, like lemongrass, is useful in specimen plantings, in middleground and background border plantings, and as screens and windbreaks. It is also useful as a potted plant indoors. Both citronella grass and lemongrass afford a continuous source of curiosity and joy to the gardener.

Cultivation: Propagation is by seeding and by plant division. Citronella grass prefers full sun on fertile, well-drained soil. Citronella grass, like lemongrass, may be grown as an annual in temperate climates. Plants started indoors in very early spring and transferred to the garden may or may not flower the same year. Both citronella grass and lemongrass should be considered as weak or very weak perennials.

Cynodon **L. C. Rich. (Bermuda grass, Scutchgrass, Baygrass).** Name from *kuon (kun-)* "dog," and *odous,* "tooth," referring to the sharp, hard scales of the rhizome. Type species, *Cynodon dactylon* (L.) Pers. There are 10 species, of Old World origin. Low-growing perennial grasses with creeping stolons or rhizomes with short leaf blades and several slender spikes digitate at the summit of the upright culms. Spikelets one-flowered, awnless, sessile, in two rows along one side of a slender, continuous rachis and appressed to it, the rachilla disarticulating above the glumes and prolonged behind the palea as a slender, naked bristle, sometimes bearing a rudimentary lemma; glumes narrow, acuminate, one-nerved, about equal, shorter than the floret; lemma firm, strongly compressed, pubescent on the keel, three-nerved, the lateral nerves close to the margins.

Latin name: *Cynodon dactylon* (L.) Pers.
Synonym: *Panicum dactylon* L.
Cultivars: Many in cultivation
Common names: Bermuda grass, Couch, Kweek, Scutchgrass, Wiregrass
Origin: Eurasia, Old World
Habitat: Cultivated, escape from cultivation
Hardiness: Zones 6 through 10
Description: A decumbent, spreading perennial. Plants extensively creeping by scaly rhizomes and by strong, flat stolons that root at the nodes. Flowering culms usually erect or ascending, 6–16 in./1.5–4.0 dm high, flattened, very slender, aerial stems decumbent, branched, freely rooting at the nodes; old, bladeless sheaths of the stolons and the lowest ones of the branches often forming conspicuous "dogs teeth." Foliage grayish green, light, medium, or dark green, fine in texture; leaf blades elongate, flat, rigid, auricled, scabrous above, smooth or scabrous below, villous at the base near the ligule, those of the innovations conspicuously distichous, 4–6 in./1.0–1.5 dm long, 0.10–0.25 in./3–6 mm wide, narrowed to a blunt tip, usually at 45-degree angle to the culm; sheaths crowded at the base of the culm and along stolons, round on the back, mostly glabrous, except pilose near the auricles, becoming pale on older culms; ligule a conspicuous ring of white hairs, ciliate. Inflorescence usually four or five digitate, radiating, dark purple spikes borne in a single whorl at the summit, 1–2 in./2.5–5.0 cm long, rachis flat; spikelets awnless, sessile, imbricate, laterally compressed, borne in two rows on one side of the very narrow rachis, ovate-oblong, 2–3 mm long, usually only one-flowered, light purple or green; glumes about equal, 1–2 mm long, lower slightly shorter than the upper, membranous, more or less persistent, narrow, acuminate, one-nerved, keeled, scabrous on the keels; lemmas acute, acuminate, firm, strongly compressed, cymbiform 1–2 mm long, three-nerved, keeled, usually densely and minutely hairy on the keel and near the margins, lateral nerves near the margins; palea two-keeled, ciliate on its prominent keels, about the length of its lemma; caryopsis free within the lemma and palea. Flowering and fruiting occur from May through August.

    Uses: Bermuda grass is ubiquitous in warm and cool regions of the world; its multifarious use is well known. The many cultivars and clones are primarily

Cynodon dactylon. Habit, × 1/2; spikelet and two views of floret, × 5.
Source: Manual of the Grasses of the West Indies. USDA Misc. Pub. 243. 1936.

useful in ground-cover and erosion-control plantings over extensive areas. The invasiveness of the plants precludes their use in flower beds, border plantings, and rock gardens. Some low-growing, fine cultivars are ideal lawn grasses, whereas other larger, coarser cultivars that withstand intensive footwear and trampling are useful in parks, playgrounds, and sports fields. Bermuda grass is used extensively by highway departments on median strips of highways and streets and on cuts and fills for ground cover and erosion control. The invasiveness and competitiveness of Bermuda grass are hardly surpassed when used in ground-cover plantings. The plants produce a meadowlike effect and require minimum maintenance, which could include mowing once or twice each growing season. Bermuda grass may be condemned on one hand as an aggressive invasive weed and lauded on the other as a valuable, sod-forming grass; some clones are somewhat salt tolerant.

Cultivation: Propagation is by seeding and by plant division. Some cultivars and clones produce viable seeds (i.e., the cultivar Common), whereas others are sterile, requiring vegetative propagation. Bermuda grass is very easy to establish, regardless of the propagation method employed. Vegetative propagation consists of planting plant crowns, rhizomes, or stolons. The plants survive drought, heat, and inundation for short periods. Bermuda grass grows well in full sun or light shade on a wide range of soil types, including both wet and dry sites; it is ubiquitous in its area of adaptation. Bermuda grass usually remains semievergreen in zone 9 and evergreen in zone 10. Propagating stocks in the form of seeds or vegetative stocks (stolons) are readily available in the plant trade.

Cynosurus **L. (Dog's-tail).** Name from Greek *kuon (kun-)* "dog," and *oura,* "tail." Lectotype, *Cynosurus cristatus* L. There are four species, of Old World origin. Annual or perennial grasses with very narrow, flat leaf blades and dense spikelets or subcapitate panicles. Sterile and fertile spikelets paired, the rachilla disarticulating above the glumes, the fertile glume sessile, nearly concealed by the pedicellate sterile one, these pairs imbricate in a dense, one-sided panicle. Sterile spikelets consisting of two glumes and several narrow, acuminate, one-nerved lemmas on a continuous rachilla, fertile spikelets two- or three-flowered, the glumes narrow, the lemmas broader, round on the back, awn-tipped.

Latin name: *Cynosurus cristatus* L.
Common name: Crested dog's-tail
Origin: Europe
Habitat: Fields, gardens, waste places, cultivated
Hardiness: Zones 4 through 7
Description: An upright-narrow, slender perennial. Culms tufted or singly, slightly geniculate at the base, becoming erect, 1–2 ft /3–6 dm high. Foliage sparse, mostly basal, light to medium green, fine in texture; lower leaves

arching, upper ascending, straight, leaf blades linear, flat or convolute, narrow, 3–5 in./0.8–1.3 dm long, 2–3 mm wide, glabrous, wiry, long attenuate; upper sheaths about as long as the internodes, round on the back, glabrous; ligule blunt, short, about 1 mm long. Inflorescence a linear, erect, spikelike, subcapitate, one-sided panicle, more or less curved, 1–3 in./2.5–8.0 cm long, about 0.5 in./13 mm in diameter; spikelets unisexual, usually borne in pairs, the fertile spikelets sessile, nearly covered by the short-pedicellate sterile one, the pairs imbricate in a dense, spikelike panicle, fertile spikelets sessile, two- or three-flowered, oblong, 0.15–0.20 in./4–5 mm long, the rachilla disarticulating above the glumes; glumes unequal, 2–3 mm long, narrow, strongly keeled, scabrous with broad, membranous, serrulate margins; the lemmas broader 0.10–0.15 in./3–4 mm long, round on the back, awn-tipped, awns very short, about 1 mm long; sterile spikelets ovate-obovate, flat, 0.15–0.20 in./4–5 mm long, with two glumes and several narrow, acuminate, one-nerved lemmas, about 0.20–0.25 in./5–6 mm long, on a continuous rachilla; caryopsis enclosed. Flowering and fruiting occur from July through August.

Uses: The slightly curved or straight, spikelike, compact panicles are the most interesting characteristic of ornamental value of this small perennial. The flowering panicles, which are usually far above the foliage, are interesting and useful as fresh cut flowers. The principle value of crested dog's-tail lies in its use in mixed stands in naturalized areas.

Cultivation: Propagation is by seeding; the plants are easily established. Crested dog's-tail is adapted to a wide range of soil types. The plants prefer moist soil in full sun.

Dactylis L. (**Orchardgrass**). Name from Greek *dactulos,* ''finger,'' referring to the stiff branches of the panicle. Lectotype, *Dactylis glomerata* L. There are two species, native to Eurasia. Orchardgrass is known as cock's-foot in Europe. Densely tufted, upright perennials with flat leaf blades and fascicled spikelets. Spikelets few-flowered, compressed, finally disarticulating between the florets, nearly sessile in dense, one-sided fascicles, these borne at the ends of the few branches of the panicle; glumes unequal, carinate, acute, hispid-ciliate on the keel; lemmas compressed-keeled, mucronate, five-nerved, ciliate on the keel.

> **Latin name:** *Dactylis glomerata* L.
> **Synonym:** *Bromus glomeratus* Scop.
> **Cultivars:** Several in cultivation, including 'Elegantissima,' Variegata'
> Striped orchardgrass
> > **Common names:** Orchardgrass, Cock's-foot
> > **Origin:** Eurasia
> > **Habitat:** Cultivated, escape from cultivation
> > **Hardiness:** Zones 4 through 9

Dactylis glomerata. **Habit,** × 1/2; **spikelet and floret,** × 5. *Source: Manual of the Grasses of the United States.* USDA Misc. Pub. 200. 1951.

Description: A densely tufted, upright-open, semievergreen perennial with compressed vegetative shoots. Culms tufted, simple, erect, or spreading, slender or stout, with three to five nodes, rough or smooth, 2–4 ft /0.6–1.2 m high. Foliage medium green or greenish gray, fine in texture; leaf blades stiff, flat, or more or less conduplicate, both surfaces and margins rough, long acuminate, 4–20 in./1–5 dm long, 0.1–0.4 in./3–10 mm wide; lower sheaths longer than the internodes, upper shorter, keeled, at first entirely rough, becoming glabrous or rarely short-hairy, flattened; ligule chartaceous, 0.1–0.2 in./3–5 mm long. Inflorescence a loosely branched panicle, 4–12 in./1–3 dm long, 2–4 in./5–10 cm wide, greenish, purplish, or yellowish, branches compact and spikelike, erect, spreading or occasionally reflexed, lower branches 1–4 in./2.5–10.0 cm long, stiff, glabrous; spikelets in dense, ovate or globose, one-sided fascicles, subsessile, flat, three-to-five-flowered; 0.10–0.15 in./3–4 mm long; glumes unequal, the upper longer than the lower, one-to-three-nerved, firm and glabrous or scabrous, the broad side hyaline and ciliate, the upper 0.20–0.25 in./5–6 mm long, 1–2 mm wide, one-nerved, sometimes three-nerved, more or less scabrous on the keel; lemmas acuminate and mucronate or short awned, 0.25–0.30 in./6–8 mm long, compressed keeled, ciliate on the keels, smooth or scabrous-pubescent, five-nerved; palea acute, shorter than the lemma, two-keeled, minutely ciliate on the keels; caryopsis enclosed. Flowering and fruiting occur from May through mid-August.

Uses: The glabrous green foliage of orchardgrass forms large, imperfect mounds as the leaves cascade to the ground. It is ideal in specimen plantings, in middleground borders, and as ground cover in naturalized areas. Orchardgrass is compatible with many other grasses as well as broad-leaved plants; its main attraction is its luxuriant, cascading, semievergreen foliage. The colorful foliage of the variegated cultivars is decorative during spring and summer, but the plants turn brown in early fall. The seedheads are useful in dried arrangements.

Cultivation: Propagation is by seeding and by plant division. The variegated cultivars rarely form seedheads, thereby requiring propagation by plant division. They prefer light shade, as do most other variegated grasses, although they may tolerate full sun. The cultivars prefer well-drained soils, whereas orchardgrass is tolerant of heavy clays with high moisture-retention capacity. Sufficient space should be allowed for expansion of the plants in size when they are initially established; otherwise, they will become too crowded for their full value to be appreciated. Orchardgrass is not difficult to keep under control by weeding out seedlings and by trimming back established stands.

Cultivars: *Dactylis glomerata* L. 'Elegantissima'   A slender, dwarf, mound-forming cultivar, with variegated green-white striped foliage; the plants form mounds about 8 in./2 dm high. It is excellent in accent plantings in foreground borders and in rock gardens and as ground cover for small areas. Propagation is by plant division, as the plants seldom flower. Flowering and fruiting occur from June through July. This cultivar is adapted to zones 4–9.

Dactylis glomerata L. 'Variegata' Striped orchardgrass   This tufted, upright-open, cultivar is slightly larger and more vigorous than the cultivar Elegantissima, attaining up to 2 ft /6 dm in height. It may be difficult to distinguish the cultivars Elegantissima and Variegata other than by their size, as they both have very similar variegated foliage. The leaves of striped orchardgrass have longitudinal stripes of green and creamy or silvery white; they are fine in texture. The uses of the two cultivars are very similar; they are grown for their multicolored foliage. Striped orchardgrass is adapted to zones 5–9 and grows best in full sun; it is useful in group plantings and as edging in foreground borders.

Deschampsia **Beauv. (Hairgrass).** Named for Deschamps (Loiseleur-Deslongchamps), a French botanist. Lectotype, *Deschampsia caespitosa* (L.) Beauv. There are more than 50 species, inhabiting temperate and cold regions, chiefly in the Northern Hemisphere. Some members of the genus are included in *Aira* by some authors. Low to moderately tall annuals or usually perennials, with leaf blades expanded, rolled, or folded, with shining pale or purplish spikelets in contracted or open panicles. Spikelets two-flowered, disarticulating above the glumes and between the florets, the hairy rachilla prolonged beyond the upper floret and sometimes bearing a reduced floret; glumes about equal, acute or acutish, membranous; lemmas thin, truncate and two-to-four-toothed at the summit, bearded at base, bearing a slender awn from below the middle, the awn straight, bent, or twisted.

Latin name: *Deschampsia alpina* (L.) Roem. & Schult.
Common name: Alpine hairgrass
Origin: Europe, USSR
Habitat: Mountainous areas, wet rocks, grassy slopes
Hardiness: Zones 2 through 4
Description: A densely tufted, upright-narrow, apomictic perennial. Culms erect or decumbent near the base, glabrous, with two to four nodes, 5–16 in./1.3–4.0 dm high. Foliage dark green, fine in texture; leaf blades glabrous beneath, rough on the ribs and margins and conspicuously ribbed above, flat or enrolled, 2–8 in./0.5–2.0 dm long, 0.10–0.15 in./3–4 mm wide, with blunt tips; ligule acute or obtuse, 2–3 mm long; sheaths glabrous, round on the back. Inflorescence a dense or rather loose, erect, branched panicle, 2–6 in./0.5–1.5 dm long, 2–3 in./5–8 cm wide, green or purplish, sexual or usually proliferous, branches fine, divided, glabrous or slightly rough, pedicels 0.1–0.2 in./3–5 mm long; spikelets pedicellate, oblong, two- or three-flowered, 0.15–0.20 in./4–5 mm long or longer with the upper flower replaced by a plantlet, breaking up beneath each lemma; glumes almost equal, 0.15–0.30 in./4–8 mm long, persistent, membranous, pointed, keeled, rough on the keels toward the tip, shining, variegated with green or white or purple and yellow, lower lanceolate, one-nerved, upper lanceolate to elliptic, three-nerved; upper lemma 0.10–0.25 in./3–6 mm long, lower 0.2–0.3 in./5–8 mm long in proliferating spikelets, ovate

or oblong, round on the back, toothed at the apex, membranous, five-nerved, short-bearded at the base, awned on the back from the middle upward or from the tip; awns 0.10–0.15 in./3–4 mm long; palea two-keeled, the keels rough; caryopsis enclosed. This apomictic perennial produces sexual panicles and proliferous panicles exhibiting varying degrees of viviparous reproduction. Flowering and fruiting occur from July through August.

Uses: This rare species is best adapted for use in shaded, alpine rock gardens. The small plants should be grown in clumps to be conspicuous; their small size and dark green foliage are conducive for its use in foreground border plantings.

Cultivation: Propagation is by seeding and by plant division. Alpine hairgrass thrives best in shaded sites on stony ground. This rare species may be difficult to locate in the plant trade.

Latin name: *Deschampsia caespitosa* (L.) Beauv.

Synonym: *Aira cespitosa* L.

Cultivars and varieties: 'Bronzeschleier,' 'Goldgehaenge,' 'Goldschleier,' 'Goldstaub,' 'Schottland,' 'Tardiflora' Late-blooming tufted hairgrass, 'Tautraeger'; *Deschampsia caespitosa* var. *vivipara* S. F. Gray, Viviparous hairgrass

Common name: Tufted hairgrass

Origin: Europe, North America

Habitat: Cultivated, escape from cultivation

Hardiness: Zones 4 through 9

Description: A densely tufted, upright-open, mound-forming, semievergreen perennial. Culms in dense tufts, erect, leafy at the base, 18–36 in./4.5–9.0 dm high. Foliage dark green, fine in texture; leaves matted at the base, acute or obtuse, leaf blades firm, flat or folded, elongate, 10–18 in./2.5–4.5 dm long, 0.1–0.2 in./3–5 mm wide, tapering to a fine, attenuate point or sometimes rather blunt at the tip, upper surface scabrous on the ribs and margins, lower surface glabrous; sheaths longer than the internodes, round on the back, usually smooth or somewhat rough; ligule 0.2–0.4 in./5–10 mm long. Inflorescence an open, loosely branched, erect or nodding panicle, 10–20 in./2.5–5.0 dm long, 6–8 in./1.5–2.0 dm wide, capillary branches scabrous, bearing spikelets toward the ends; spikelets 0.15–0.20 in./4–5 mm long, variable in color within the same panicle, usually pale or purplish, 0.10–0.15 in./3–4 mm long, two-flowered; the florets distant, the rachilla internodes one-half the length of the lower floret, upper floret slightly exceeding the glumes; glumes about equal, narrow, the upper acute, 0.1–0.2 in./3–5 mm long, obscurely three-nerved, somewhat erose, the lower one-nerved, about the size of the upper; lemmas smooth, awned, two-to-four-toothed, the callus hairs short, jagged at the apex, awned from near the base, the awn straight and inclined to weakly geniculate and twice as long as the spikelet, exceeding the body of the lemma; palea shorter than its lemma; caryopsis enclosed. Flowering and fruiting occur from May through August. It is among the earliest grasses to flower in the spring, and its flowering period is comparatively long. The inflorescences are colorful and graceful.

Deschampsia caespitosa. **Habit,** × 1/2; **glumes and floret,** × 10. *Source: Manual of the Grasses of the United States.* USDA Misc. Pub. 200. 1951.

Uses: Tufted hairgrass and the botanical variety vivipara are grown for their large, colorful, graceful, early-blooming flowers. The plants are outstanding in specimen and group plantings during all seasons. They make ideal specimen plants in water gardens and in shaded sites on moist soil. The dark green foliage and large, colorful panicles make tufted hairgrass ideal for open woods in naturalized areas and for middleground borders that are shaded for most of the day. The large, colorful panicles are used in a fresh or dried state for decorative purposes. The botanical variety *vivipara* is grown primarily for its unique method of reproduction. It is best demonstrated by plants grown on a raised bed; this variety is also quite shade tolerant. Tufted hairgrass is also useful in massed plantings of naturalized areas. The variety and cultivars of tufted hairgrass, with the exception of viviparous hairgrass and the cultivar Tardiflora, are used in more or less the same manner as that of the parent species; with the exception of the cultivar Tardiflora, they are noted for their early spring flowers.

Cultivation: Propagation is by seeding and by plant division. Tufted hairgrass prefers slightly acid or neutral soils. This species and its variants thrive in dry or moist soil in full sun or light shade.

Cultivars and varieties: *Deschampsia caespitosa* (L.) Beauv. 'Bronzeschleier'   The plants are 30–36 in./ 7.6–9.0 dm high, with bronze yellow inflorescence.

Deschampsia caespitosa (L.) Beauv. 'Goldgehaenge'   The plants are 2–3 ft / 6–9 dm high, with golden yellow inflorescence.

Deschampsia caespitosa (L.) Beauv. 'Goldschleier'   The plants are 2–3 ft /6–9 dm high, with bright yellow inflorescence; this cultivar is adapted to zones 6–9.

Deschampsia caespitosa (L.) Beauv. 'Goldstaub'   The plants are 2–3 ft /6–9 dm high, with yellow inflorescence; this cultivar is adapted to zones 6–9.

Deschampsia caespitosa (L.) Beauv. 'Schottland'   The plants are 4–6 ft /1.2–1.8 m high.

Deschampsia caespitosa (L.) Beauv. 'Tardiflora' Late-blooming, tufted hairgrass.   The plants are 3 ft /9 dm high.

Deschampsia caespitosa (L.) Beauv. 'Tautraeger'   The plants are about 3 ft / 9 dm high.

Deschampsia caespitosa var. *vivipara* S. F. Gray (see Appendix 1).

Latin name: *Deschampsia flexuosa* (L.) Trin.
Synonym: *Aira flexuosa* L.
Common names: Common hairgrass, Crinkled hairgrass, Wavy hairgrass
Origin: Eurasia, North America
Habitat: Cultivated, escape from cultivation
Hardiness: Zones 4 through 9
Description: A densely tufted to loosely tufted, upright-open, semievergreen perennial. Culms slender, wiry, erect, or bent at the base, glabrous, with

three or four nodes, 8–36 in./2–9 dm high. Foliage medium to dark green, fine in texture; leaf blades linear, glabrous, slender, flexuous, 6–12 in./1.5–3.0 dm long, almost 1 mm wide, tightly enrolled, rough toward the tip, rather blunt-tipped; sheaths chartaceous, round on the back, often somewhat roughened upwards; ligule membranous, blunt, up to 0.1 in./3 mm long. Inflorescence a branched panicle, 2–6 in./0.5–1.5 dm long, 2–3 in./5–8 cm wide, main axis rough, branches flexuous, filiform, rough, divided and spreading in the upper portion, bearing pedicellate spikelets toward the ends, pedicels 0.2–0.4 in./5–10 mm long; spikelets loosely scattered, oblong to cuneate, 0.15–0.25 in./4–6 mm long, pale or purple tinged, usually two-flowered, breaking up at maturity above shining, colorful glumes; glumes keeled upward, persistent, pointed, very minutely rough or glabrous, lower ovate, shorter than the upper, one-nerved, upper elliptic-ovate, one-to-three-nerved, as long as the spikelet; lemmas up to 0.25 in./6 mm long, round on the back, elliptic to oblong, blunt and toothed or two-lobed at the tip, membranous, slightly rough or smooth, short bearded at the base, four-nerved, awned from near the base with a twisted brown awn, 0.15–0.30 in./4–8 mm long; palea two-keeled, rough on the keels, about as long as the lemma; caryopsis enclosed. Flowering and fruiting occur from June through July.

Uses: Crinkled hairgrass is grown for its plant form and decorative flowers. It is ideal in clumps in foreground or middleground shaded borders and in rock gardens. The colorful, shiny inflorescence with its brown, gracefully twisted awns and dark green foliage make it a spectacular sepcimen plant. The beautiful flowers are often used in fresh arrangements as are the dried inflorescences in dried arrangements. Crinkled hairgrass is also used for ground cover in shaded, naturalized areas.

Cultivation: Propagation is by seeding and by plant division. Crinkled hairgrass prefers acid soils; the plants thrive best in dry or moist locations in full sun or light shade.

Distichlis **Raf. (Saltgrass, Alkaligrass).** Name from Greek *distichos,* "two-ranked," alluding to the distichous leaf arrangement. Lectotype, *Uniola spicata* L. There are about 6 to 10 species, inhabiting mostly the warmer regions of North America. Low dioecious perennials with extremely creeping, yellowish, scaly rhizomes; culms erect, rigid, with short, erect, dense, rather short-branched panicles. Spikelets several-to-many-flowered, the rachilla of the pistillate spikelets disarticulating above the glumes and between the florets; glumes unequal, broad, acute, keeled, three-to-seven nerved, the lateral nerves sometimes faint; lemmas closely imbricate, firm, the pistillate coriaceous, acute or subacute, with 9 to 11 mostly faint nerves; palea as long as the lemma or shorter, the margins bowed out near the base, the pistillate coriaceous, enclosing the caryopsis.

Latin name: *Distichlis spicata* (L.) Greene
Synonym: *Uniola spicata* L.
Common names: Seashore saltgrass, Saltgrass, Spikegrass, Marsh spike-grass, Alkaligrass
Habitat: Salt marshes and sand dunes along the coast, in alkaline soils in the interior
Hardiness: Zones 4 through 10
Description: A dioecious, mat-forming, evergreen perennial with extensive, scaly, thick rhizomes forming large, dense colonies. Culms decumbent, becoming erect, slender, glabrous, wiry, and rigid, 3–18 in./0.8–4.5 dm high, sometimes higher, internodes short. Foliage conspicuously distichous, glaucous, fine in texture; leaf blades stiff, usually stiffly ascending, flat or involute, rolled when dry, pungent, 2–4 in./5–10 cm long, 0.10–0.15 in./3–4 mm wide, long

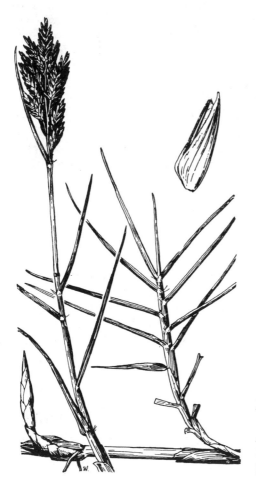

Distichlis spicata. **Habit, × 1; floret, × 5.** *Source: Manual of the Grasses of the United States.* USDA Misc. Pub. 200. 1951.

attenuate; sheaths overlapping, glabrous except for a few long hairs at the throat at each end of the ligule; ligule membranous, about 0.2 in./5 mm long. Staminate inflorescence an oblong or ovoid, greenish, branched panicle, 1–2 in./2.5–5.0 cm long, about 1 in./25 mm in diameter, dense, spikelike; pistillate inflorescence usually shorter than the staminate; staminate spikelets five-to-nine-flowered, imbricate, flat, subsessile or short-pedicellate, light green, 0.25–0.40 in./6–10 mm long, pistillate spikelets similar to the staminate except more coriaceous and more closely imbricate; glumes unequal, broad, acute, keeled, three-to-seven-nerved, the lateral nerves sometimes faint, unequal, the lower about three-fourths as long as the upper, up to 0.1 in./3 mm long, the upper 0.10–0.15 in./3–4 mm long, three-nerved; lemmas imbricate, firm, the coriaceous pistillate ones more closely imbricate than the staminate, 9-to-11-nerved or with three nerves and intermediate green streaks; palea coriaceous, as long as the lemma or shorter, two-keeled, the keels narrowly winged, soft, narrow, the margins bowed out at the base. Flowering and fruiting occur from July through October in zones 4–9 and from November through January in zone 10 and in the tropics and subtropics.

Uses: The natural habitat of saltgrass is salt marshes near the sea and brackish marshes along streams and around lakes and lagoons; saltgrass is commonly found on sand dunes. It is adapted to highly saline marsh soils of clay to sandy texture. The plants do best when the water level fluctuates between 2 in./5 cm above the soil surface and 6 in./1.5 dm below, or when growing in sand; saltgrass does not withstand extended periods of inundation. It is useful in low-lying, wet land for ground cover or along the seashore to stabilize sand dunes. The low-growing plants form an impenetrable ground cover, and their extensive rhizomatous root system aids in sand dune stabilization. Dense, extensive colonies of pistillate plants are common along the seashore, where they often produce several seed crops per year, especially in warmer regions. The plants provide wildlife cover and an excellent source of food for migratory wildfowl. Numerous stands of staminate barren plants are also common along beaches.

Cultivation: Propagation is by seeding and by plant division, preferably the latter. Saltgrass is easily propagated by dividing existing culms or by planting the rhizomes. The plants are quite salt tolerant, withstanding high levels of both atmospheric and edaphic salinity. Saltgrass prefers full sun in damp or wet sand.

Elymus L. (**Wild rye, Lymegrass**). Name from *Elumos,* an old Greek name for a kind of grain. Lectotype, *Elymus sibiricus* L. There are about 50 species, occurring in temperate regions of the Northern Hemisphere. Erect, rather tall perennial, one annual, grasses with flat or rarely convolute leaf blades and slender or bristly spikes, the spikelets usually crowded, sometimes somewhat distant. Spikelets usually in pairs, or more rarely in threes or fours at each node of a usually continuous rachis, two-to-six-flowered, the rachilla distorted at the base, bringing the florets more or less dorsiventral to the rachis; rachilla disarticulating above the glumes and between the florets; glumes equal, somewhat asymmetric, usually rigid, sometimes indurate below, narrow to subulate, one-to-several-nerved, acute to aristate; lemmas round on the back or nearly terete, obscurely five-nerved, acute, or usually awned from the tip.

Latin name: *Elymus arenarius* L.
Synonym: *Leymus arenarius* (L.) Hochst.
Common names: Blue lymegrass, Lymegrass, Sea lymegrass, Rancheria grass, European lymegrass
Origin: Europe, Eurasia
Habitat: Cultivated, escape from cultivation
Hardiness: Zones 2 through 6
Description: A robust, upright-narrow or irregular, densely tufted perennial with long, stout rhizomes. The culms form large tufts, stout, often geniculate at the base, glabrous, erect or spreading, 2–5 ft /0.6–1.5 m high, with numerous imbricate basal leaves. Foliage metallic bluish green or glaucous, coarse in texture; leaf blades flat or convolute, attenuate, rigid, 1–2 ft /3–6 dm long, 0.3–0.8 in./8–20 mm wide, minutely rough on the prominent nerves above, glabrous beneath; sheaths round on the back, glabrous, with two narrow, spreading auricles at the apex; ligule membranous, minutely hairy, truncate, about 1 mm long. Inflorescence a long-exserted, stout, stiff, compact spike, 3–10 in./0.8–2.5 dm long, 0.5–1.0 in./13–25 mm in diameter, metallic bluish green, becoming buff or brown at maturity; spikelets sessile, usually in pairs, 0.8–1.2 in./2–3 dm long, the pairs alternating on opposite sides of the axis, oblong or cuneate, three-to-six-flowered; glumes equal, awnless, narrowly lanceolate and finely pointed, about as long as the spikelet, keeled, three-to-five-nerved, rigid, hairy, especially on the keel; lemmas lanceolate, pointed, tough, seven-nerved, densely hirsute with stout, soft hairs, awnless, lemmas decrease in size upwards, the lowest 0.6–1.0 in./15–25 mm long; palea two-keeled, as long as the lemma; caryopsis hairy at the tip, enclosed. Flowering and fruiting occur from June through August, although sporadic flowering is common; sometimes the plants may not flower for several years.
Uses: Lymegrass is grown solely for its beautiful, metallic, bluish green foliage; it is one of the largest ornamental grasses with bluish green foliage. It is most conspicuous when grown in specimen plantings as a foil in contrast to dark green shrubbery or plants with bright flower colors. Lymegrass is often grown in specimen plantings along streams and around pools in water gardens, where the plants are reflected on the water. The rhizomatous growth habit of lymegrass is valued as a means of soil stabilization in seashore and conservation plantings. The plants form large colonies over extensive areas when left unconfined. Lymegrass is a highly desirable garden grass despite its invasiveness; the plants retain their attractiveness throughout the summer.
Cultivation: Propagation is by seeding and by plant division. Locations in

full sun in dry, moist, or wet soils are most suitable. The aggressiveness and invasiveness of blue lymegrass is a distinct disadvantage in its use in garden plantings unless necessary measures are taken to contain the plants. The plants may be contained by sinking edging barriers at least 5 in./1.3 dm into the ground surrounding the plants. When only a small number of plants are grown, they may be planted in a container of metal, wood, or other material that is sunken in the soil. If a wooden barrier or container is used, it will rot eventually and require replacement. Lymegrass may be hard to find in the trade, as it is a European species.

Latin name: *Elymus canadensis* L.
Synonym: *Hordeum patulum* Moench
Common names: Canada wild rye, Nodding wild rye
Origin: North America
Habitat: Cultivated, escape from cultivation
Hardiness: Zones 2 through 8
Description: A loosely tufted, upright-narrow perennial, forming small clumps. Culms slender, glabrous, simple, erect to slightly nodding, 2–5 ft /0.6–1.5 m high. Foliage medium green or glaucous, medium in texture; leaves mostly cauline, leaf blades linear, acuminate, thin, flat, slightly narrowed toward the base, 8–16 in./2–4 dm long, 0.4–0.6 in./10–15 mm wide, rough, sometimes sparsely hirsute on one or both surfaces near the base; auricled; upper sheaths glabrous, shorter than the internodes, the lower longer, appressed pubescent, the exposed margin more or less ciliate-pubescent; ligule truncate, membranous, about 1 mm long, ciliate. Inflorescence a dense, long-exserted, loosely flowered, stout spike, 5–8 in./1.3–2.0 dm long, about 1.0–1.2 in./2.5–3.0 cm in diameter, often interrupted below, erect, finally nodding at maturity, flat or sometimes cylindrical; spikelets slightly spreading, three-to-five-flowered, mostly in pairs; glumes equal, persistent, narrowly lanceolate, 0.6–1.2 in./1.5–3.0 cm long including the slender rough awns, about 1 mm wide, rigid, three-to-five-nerved, more or less round at the base, sometimes flat, generally green, but sometimes indurated and colorless at the base, glabrous except for scabrous margins and sometimes the nerves, the long, spreading awns as long as the body; lemmas round on the back, scabrous-hirsute to hirsute-pubescent, rarely glabrous, 0.3–0.5 in./8–13 mm long excluding the awns, about 2 mm wide, margins scabrous, gradually tapering into a scabrous, slender, divergent, awn, 0.4–2.0 in./1–5 cm long, usually curved outward when dry, strongly five-nerved above, often with short lateral awns, 1–2 mm long; palea two-keeled, 0.4–0.5 in./10–13 mm long, short appressed pubescent on the face and longer and coarsely pubescent on the keels; caryopsis about 0.25 in./6 mm long, 1 mm wide, the tuft of hairs at the summit about 1 mm long, adherent to the lemma and palea. Flowering and fruiting occur from June through September.
Uses: Canada wild rye is grown primarily for its metallic bluish green or

Elymus canadensis. **Habit,** × 1/2; **spikelet and floret,** × 5. *Source: Manual of the Grasses of the United States.* USDA Misc. Pub. 200. 1951.

glaucous foliage. Its foliage is best demonstrated as an accent plant in middle-ground border and rock garden plantings in contrast to plants with colorful flowers and dark green foliage.

Cultivation: Propagation is by direct seeding and by plant division. The widespread distribution of Canada wild rye is indicative of its winter hardiness and tolerance of a wide range of soils. The plants thrive best in full sun or light shade in moist, sandy soils.

Latin name: *Elymus condensatus* J. Presl
Synonym: *Aneurolepidium condensatum* Nevski
Common name: Giant wild rye
Origin: North America
Habitat: Sand dunes, sandy or rocky soil, cultivated
Hardiness: Zones 9 and 10
Description: A loosely tufted perennial with short, thick rhizomes. Culms in large tufts, 6–9 ft /1.8–2.8 m high, glabrous. Foliage medium green, coarse in texture; leaf blades flat, firm, glabrous, strongly nerved, 12–30 in./3.0–7.6 dm long, 1.0–1.2 in./2.5–3.0 cm wide; sheaths shorter or longer than the internodes; ligule membranous, 0.1–0.2 in./3–5 mm long. Inflorescence a dense, erect, spike, 6–19 in./1.5–4.8 dm long, about 1 in./25 mm in diameter, the branches erect, 1–3 in./2.5–8.0 cm long, usually more or less compound; spikelets often in threes or fives, four-to-six-flowered, commonly distorted, sometimes sparingly pubescent; glumes subulate, awn-pointed, usually one-nerved or nerveless, about as long as the lower lemma, sometimes longer; lemmas glabrous to sparsely strigose, with a hyaline margin, awnless or mucronate; palea nearly as long as the lemma; caryopsis hairy at tip, adherent to the lemma and palea. Flowering and fruiting occur from May through July.

Uses: The size of giant wild rye is conducive to its use as a tall screen or windbreak along the coast. It is useful in preventing wind and water erosion and as a sand dune stabilization plant.

Cultivation: Propagation is by seeding and by plant division. The plants prefer full sun in pure sand or sandy loam soil.

Latin name: *Elymus giganteus* Vahl
Synonym: *Leymus giganteus* Pilg.
Common name: Siberian wild rye
Origin: USSR
Habitat: Cultivated, escape from cultivation
Hardiness: Zones 4 through 7
Description: A coarse, robust, open to spreading or irregular perennial with short, stout, robust rhizomes. Culms semierect, spreading and irregular, glabrous, conspicuously glaucous, 3–5 ft /0.9–1.5 m high with numerous basal leaves. Foliage mostly basal, conspicuously glaucous, completely covered with a light gray bloom, medium in texture; leaf blades linear, thick, long attenuate,

broad near the base, stiff, 10–12 in./2.5–3.0 dm long, 0.4–0.5 in./10–13 mm wide; sheaths glabrous, round on the back, about as long as the internodes; ligule membranous, about 1–2 mm long. Inflorescence an erect, dense spike, 6–8 in./1.5–2.0 dm long, about 0.8–1.0 in./20–25 mm in diameter, initially light greenish white, gradually becoming lighter; spikelets two-to-six-flowered, awnless, 0.6–0.8 in./15–20 mm long, glabrous; glumes slightly longer than the spikelets, glabrous; lemmas shorter than the glumes, sparsely pubescent below, glabrous above; palea about the length of the lemma; caryopsis hairy at tip, adherent to the lemma and palea. Flowering and fruiting occur from June through July.

Uses: Siberian wild rye looks best when planted in clumps in inaccessible sites. The irregular shape and conspicuously glaucous foliage make Siberian wild rye a curiosity in rock garden plantings.

Cultivation: Propagation is by seeding and by plant division, preferably the latter. The plants grow best in full sun, often in drought conditions. Siberian wild rye is adapted to most soils; however, the plants require good drainage.

Latin name: *Elymus glaucus* Buckl.
Synonym: *Elymus sibiricus* var. *glaucus* Ramaley
Common name: Blue wild rye
Origin: North America
Habitat: Open woods, dry hills, cultivated
Hardiness: Zones 4 through 9
Description: An upright-narrow or irregular loosely tufted to densely tufted perennial, forming large clumps. Culms clustered, erect or often geniculate at the base, leafy, glabrous, 2–4 ft /0.6–1.2 m high. Foliage bluish green, medium in texture; leaf blades usually lax, 6–12 in./1.5–3.0 dm long, 0.3–0.6 in./8–15 mm wide, usually scabrous on both surfaces, flat or sometimes narrow and subinvolute, long attenuate; sheaths smooth or scabrous, usually longer than the internodes; auricles present and well developed on some leaves; ligule membranous, erose-ciliate, 1–2 mm long. Inflorescence a purplish, erect or somewhat nodding, long-exserted spike, slender, usually dense, 2–8 in./0.5–2.0 dm long, about 0.5 in./13 mm in diameter; spikelets usually in pairs, appressed to the rachis, two-to-six-flowered; glumes narrowly lanceolate, mostly about equaling the spikelet, erect, almost parallel, three-to-five-nerved, membranous except the flattened base sometimes indurate, acuminate or short-awned; florets, three to six; lemmas awned, glabrous to somewhat scabrous, 0.4–0.5 in./10–13 mm long, usually conspicuously nerved, usually with a straight or divergent awn mostly 0.4–0.8 in./10–20 mm long; palea slightly shorter than its lemma; caryopsis hairy at the summit, adherent to the lemma and palea. Flowering and fruiting occur from June through August.

Uses: Blue wild rye is grown for its bright bluish green foliage. The plants are not invasive and may be grown in various sites in the garden. As accent plants, the bluish green foliage of blue wild rye complements the bright, colorful flowers and foliage of other ornamentals in perennial middleground borders, as the plants are attractive throughout the growing season. The colorful foliage makes blue wild rye ideal in accent, group, and specimen plantings in rock gardens; its flowers are of no particular ornamental value or interest. It is also useful in massed ground-cover plantings near the sea.

Cultivation: Propagation is by direct seeding. Blue wild rye requires a moist, fertile, well-drained soil in full sun. It differs from blue lymegrass by not having rhizomes.

Latin name: *Elymus villosus* Muhl.
Synonym: *Elymus ciliatus* Muhl.
Common names: Slender wild rye, Wild rye
Origin: North America
Habitat: Moist or dry woods and shaded areas
Hardiness: Zones 3 through 8
Description: An upright-narrow, tufted perennial. Culms in small tufts, ascending, slender, 24–40 in./0.6–1.0 m high, more or less pubescent. Foliage dark green, fine in texture; leaf blades flat, linear, 5–10 in./1.3–2.5 dm long, 0.15–0.40 in./4–10 mm wide, lax, pubescent on upper surface, glabrous and glossy to scabrous beneath; sheaths round on the back, shorter or longer than the internodes, glabrous or usually sparsely to densely hirsute; ligule membranous, stiff, very short, less than 1 mm long. Inflorescence a long-exserted, stout, drooping spike, dense, stiff, 2–5 in./0.5–1.3 dm long, 1.0–1.6 in./2.5–4.0 cm in diameter including the awns; spikelets paired and solitary or somewhat divergent, one-to-three-flowered, the paired spikelets near the middle of a continuous rachis; glumes awl-shaped, 0.4–0.8 in./10–20 mm long excluding the capillary awns, spreading, distinctly one-to-three-nerved above the firm, nerveless divergent or somewhat bowed out base, hispid or hirsute, equal, placed on edge in front or toward the sides of the florets, which are dorsiventral to the rachis; lemmas oblong or lanceolate, round on the back, hispid, obscurely five-nerved, 0.25–0.30 in./5–8 mm long, usually awned, the straight, slender awn 0.4–1.2 in./1–3 cm long; palea shorter than the lemma; caryopsis hairy at the summit, adherent to the lemma and palea. Flowering and fruiting occur from June through August.

Uses: This perennial is useful as ground cover in open woods and lightly shaded sites. Although the plants are not necessarily ornamental, they do form a good permanent ground cover in naturalized areas. The compact, long-awned seedheads make ideal contributions to dried floral arrangements. The plants produce a meadow effect when left undisturbed.

Cultivation: Propagation is by seeding. Direct seeding in the spring should establish good stands. Maintenance would be minimal; the only requirement would involve occasionally cutting the plants back, if desired, should they become too tall. Slender wild rye prefers full sun but will tolerate light shade.

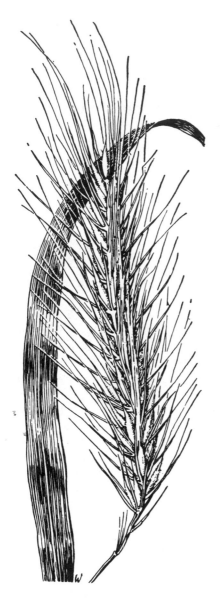

Elymus villosus.
Inflorescence, × **1.** *Source: Manual of the Grasses of the United States.* USDA Misc. Pub. 200. 1951.

Latin name: *Elymus virginicus* L.
Synonym: *Hordeum virginicum* Schenck
Common names: Virginia wild rye, Terrell grass
Origin: North America
Habitat: Open wet woodland, fields, waste grounds, cultivated
Hardiness: Zones 3 through 9

Description: An upright-narrow, tufted perennial. Culms erect, simple, rigid, often stout, 36–42 in./0.9–1.1 m high, glabrous or scabrous, the lower internodes 0.10–0.15 in./3–4 mm in diameter. Foliage glaucous or dark green, medium to coarse in texture; leaf blades flat, becoming involute on drying, auricled, 5–12 in./1.3–3.0 dm long, 0.4–0.7 in./10–18 mm wide, usually only 0.4–0.5 in./10–13 mm, glabrous, scabrous toward the tip; auricles well developed; sheaths usually slightly shorter than the internodes, usually ciliate-pubescent on the exposed margin, glabrous or sometimes the upper part sparsely pubescent, the lower imbricate, the upper often inflated and enclosing the base of the spike; ligule chartaceous, truncate, about 0.5 mm long, ciliolate. Inflorescence an erect, included or scarcely exserted, terminal spike, 2–8 in./0.5–2.0 dm long, about 0.8–1.0 in./20–25 mm in diameter, rigid, dense, the rachis internodes about 0.2 in./5 mm long, bluish green; spikelets sessile, two or three at each node, three-to-five-flowered; glumes stout, linear-lanceolate, indurate, 0.4–0.5 in./10–13 mm long, usually twisted, curved outward at the round nonstriate base, awn-pointed, with a needlelike awn 0.5–0.8 in./13–20 mm long, 1–2 mm wide, conspicuously five-to-seven-nerved, nerves scabrous toward the apex, glabrous on the margins; lemmas glabrous and nerveless below, rarely somewhat scabrous and nerved above, oblong or lanceolate, round on the back, the lower 0.25–0.30 in./6–8 mm long with a scabrous awn 0.3–0.7 in./8–18 mm long; palea shorter than the lemma, 0.25–0.40 in./6–10 mm long, elliptic, ciliate, caryopsis 0.15–0.20 in./4–5 mm long, 1–2 mm wide, the tuft of hairs at the summit about 1 mm long, adherent to the lemma and palea. Flowering and fruiting occur from May through September.

Uses: Virginia wild rye is grown for its beautiful, curled, flowering spikes and dark green foliage. The strong, flowering culms often bend or droop under the weight of the inflorescences, forming a moundlike clump of dark green foliage. The plants are ideal in accent and specimen plantings and as ground cover in open woods and other shaded areas, including middleground borders, where they may be partially shaded by larger ornamentals. The entire plant is an interesting brownish color when grown in full sun.

Cultivation: Propagation is by direct seeding and by plant division. The plants prefer shaded sites on fertile, moist soil, where their foliage remains dark green; in full sun they are brownish green.

Eragrostis **Wolf (Lovegrass).** Name from the Greek *eros*, "love," and *agrostis*, a kind of grass. Lectotype, *Eragrostis minor* Host. There are about 250 species, in the temperate and tropical regions of the world. Annuals or perennials of various habit, the inflorescence an open or contracted panicle. Spikelets few-to-many-flowered, the florets usually closely imbricate, the rachilla disarticulating above the glumes and between the florets, or continuous, the lemmas deciduous, the paleas persistent; glumes somewhat unequal, shorter than the first lemma, acute or acuminate, one-nerved, or the second rarely three-nerved, the lateral

Eragrostis curvula. Habit, greatly reduced; inflorescence, slightly reduced; spikelet, × 8. *Source: The Grasses and Pastures of South Africa. Central News Agency. 1955.*

nerves sometimes obscure; palea usually about as long as the lemma, the keels sometimes ciliate.

Latin name: *Eragrostis curvula* (Schrad.) Nees
Synonym: *Poa curvula* Schrad.
Cultivars: Several in cultivation
Common name: Weeping lovegrass
Origin: Africa
Habitat: Dry grassland, cultivated
Hardiness: Zones 8 and 9
Description: A densely tufted, mound-forming, upright, cascading perennial. Culms strictly erect to geniculately ascending, simple, or sometimes branching at the lower nodes, glabrous, slender to robust 3–5 ft /0.9–1.5 m high. Foliage medium to dark green, fine in texture; leaf blades narrow, filiform, long attenuate with a setaceous tip, or broad and flat, varying in length, usually 1–2 ft /3–6 dm long, 0.20–0.25 in./5–6 mm wide, strongly arcuate, spreading; sheaths crowded at the base, narrow, persistent, strongly striate with prominent nerves, glabrous or sparsely hispid, the lower densely hairy toward the base, dark green; ligule a ring of hairs 1–2 mm long. Inflorescence a lax, open, branched panicle, 8–12 in./2–3 dm long, 2–3 in./5–8 cm wide, branches appressed or spreading, approximate, ascending, usually solitary or in pairs or pseudowhorls, glabrous at the base, at least the lower densely pilose in the axils; spikelets approximate, appressed, or occasionally spreading, linear-oblong to oblong, 0.15–0.40 in./4–10 mm long, 1–2 mm wide, 3-to-12-flowered, usually dark, olive gray; rachilla tardily disarticulating between the florets; glumes unequal, one-nerved; lemmas obtuse to subobtuse, membranous, 2–3 mm long, lateral nerves distinct and prominent; palea about as long as the lemma; caryopsis subellipsoid, about 1 mm long. Flowering and fruiting occur from June through August. The geniculating culms and very long, pendulous, filiform leaves, which cascade to the ground, produce a large, symmetrical mound.

Uses: Weeping lovegrass is best known for its almost perfectly pyramidal plant form and its loosely branched, grayish green, flowering panicles. The plant size and form and colorful inflorescence make weeping lovegrass ideal in specimen plantings in lawns and rock gardens. The curious, grayish inflorescence is a perfect foil to the dark green, persistent, cascading foliage. A thick row of weeping lovegrass provides an excellent middleground border, screen, or windbreak; it is also useful as a perennial ground cover in naturalized areas and for erosion control. The colorful flowering panicles can be used as cut flowers and in dried arrangements. A most interesting aspect is its light green fine foliage, which cascades to the ground, forming a beautiful somewhat symmetrical mound. It is often found in parks and zoos in specimen plantings.

Cultivation: Propagation is by seeding and by plant division. Weeping lovegrass is widely adapted and prefers full sun in clay and sandy soils. A hot, dry location is perfect for this symmetrical perennial, as the plants are extremely drought tolerant. The old, untidy foliage may be removed in the spring, which may enhance regrowth and provide uniformly symmetrical plants. Weeping lovegrass may be grown as an annual in zones 5–7; it is winter hardy in the lower regions of zone 8. The plants produce copious quantities of seeds and reseed themselves quite easily.

Latin name: *Eragrostis spectabilis* (Pursh) Steud.
Synonym: *Eragrostis spectabilis* var. *sparsihirsuta* Farw.
Common names: Purple lovegrass, Petticoat climber, Tumble grass
Origin: North America
Habitat: Cultivated, escape from cultivation
Hardiness: Zones 5 through 9
Description: A loosely tufted, upright-open perennial with slowly spreading, slender or short rhizomes. Culms slender, stiff, erect or ascending, simple, 12–30 in./3.0–7.6 dm high. Foliage light green, fine in texture; leaf blades elongate, flat or folded, involute in drying, firm, stiffly ascending, long attenuate, 8–14 in./2.0–3.5 dm long, 0.1–0.3 in./3–8 mm wide, rough on the margins and both surfaces except below near the base, glabrous or hirsute at the base and pilose near the apex on the upper surface, pubescent below near the base, more or less papillose; sheaths longer than the internodes, imbricate, throat hirsute, glabrous or pubescent below to papillose-hirsute toward the summit; ligule a ring of hairs, 0.10–0.15 in./3–4 mm long. Inflorescence a bright reddish purple, rarely pale, branched panicle, 8–16 in./2–4 dm long, 6–8 in./1.5–2.0 dm wide, loosely flowered, included or finally exserted, ovate to pyramidal, the rigid branches up to 8–10 in./2.0–2.5 dm long, ascending, horizontal or even reflexed, branchlets mostly 2–3 in./5–8 cm long, main axis and branches scabrous or glabrous to pilose, the axils from pilose to copiously villous; the entire panicle breaks loose as a tumbleweed; spikelets numerous, purplish, 0.15–0.25 in./4–6 mm long, 1–2 mm wide, 4-to-10-flowered, linear-oblong, flat, the stiff scabrous pedicels slightly variable, slightly shorter, as long as, or twice as long as the spikelets, the terminal ones very long; glumes almost equal, 1–2 mm long, acute, ovate, more or less scabrous, especially on the keel; lemmas minutely scabrous, especially on the keel and toward the tip, acute, 1–2 mm long, prominently three-nerved; palea two-keeled, almost as long as the lemma, obtuse, incurved, ciliate on the nerves; caryopsis oval, dark brown, less than 1 mm long. Flowering and fruiting occur from June through August.

Uses: Purple lovegrass is grown for the size and beauty of its uniquely colored, flowering panicles, which are ideal as cut flowers or in dried arrangements. The overall size of the plants makes them useful in foreground border plantings among or in front of other dark green, broad-leaved ornamentals.

Cultivation: Propagation is by seeding and by plant division. The plants perform best in full sun on dry, sandy soils; they are somewhat drought tolerant.

Other ornamental species: *Eragrostis capillaris* (L.) Nees Tiny lacegrass An upright-open annual. Culms tufted, glabrous, erect, 8–20 in./2–5 dm high,

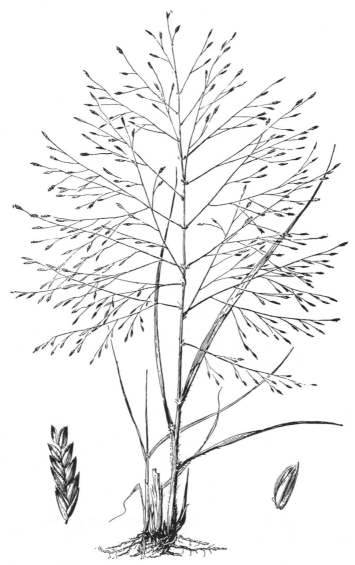

Eragrostis spectabilis. **Habit,** × 1/2; **spikelet,** × 5; **floret,** × 10. *Source: Manual of the Grasses of the United States.* USDA Misc. Pub. 200. 1951.

spreading and branching from a decumbent base, the branches erect. Foliage light green, fine in texture; leaf blades long attenuate, 3–9 in./0.8–2.3 dm long, up to 0.1 in./3 mm wide, flat or sometimes involute, filiform at the apex, scabrous above, glabrous or sparingly pilose on the upper surface and margins near the base, smooth or nearly so beneath; sheaths shorter than the internodes, imbricate and crowded near the base, the upper enclosing the base of the panicle, villous at the throat, ciliate or sparingly pilose; ligule a ring of hairs, very short less than 1 mm long. Inflorescence a branched, open, diffuse, exserted panicle, oblong-ovoid, nearly three-fourths the height of the plant, 4–15 in./1.0–3.8 dm long, the capillary branches ascending or spreading, 2–5 in./0.5–1.3 dm long, usually in ones or threes, glabrous in the axils, usually a few scattered spikelets at the end of the branches, the lateral on pedicels 0.2–0.6 in./5–15 mm long; spikelets only slightly flattened, ovate to oblong, up to 0.1 in./3 mm long, two-to-four-flowered, on long, divergent pedicels; glumes almost equal, about one-half as long as the spikelet, scabrous on the keels, narrow, lanceolate, acute; lemmas about 1–2 mm long, broadly ovate, subacute, the lateral nerves obscure, scabrous on the keel, the scabrous rachilla joint or node about 1 mm long; palea about two-thirds as long as the lemma, green, somewhat fringed at the obtuse apex, less than 1 mm long; caryopsis scabrous, less than 1 mm long. Flowering and fruiting occur from July through October. Tiny lacegrass is so named for its delicate and finely branched inflorescence, which makes an interesting contribution to dried arrangements. Because of its diminutive size, tiny lacegrass is usually grown as a curiosity in foreground borders and rock gardens. Propagation is by direct seeding; the plants grow best in full sun on sandy soils in hot, dry locations. Tiny lacegrass is adapted to zones 4–8.

Eragrostis tef (Zucc.) Trotter, Teff (Synonym: *Eragrostis abyssinica* Link) An upright-open to spreading annual forming small tufts. Culms erect, branching, and spreading, 24–40 in./0.6–1.0 m high. Foliage light to medium green, fine in texture; leaf blades pendulous, flat or subinvolute, 12–18 in./3.0–4.5 dm long, about 0.25 in./6 mm wide, glabrous, long attenuate to a sharp, bristlelike tip; sheaths glabrous, somewhat keeled; ligules distinct, often brownish. Inflorescence an erect to arching, feathery, open, loosely branched, grayish white panicle, large in relation to the size of the plant, 18–24 in./4.5–6.0 dm long and about one-half to three-fourths as wide, branching three to four times, capillary branches loosely ascending or arching, filiform and flexible; spikelets small, 0.25–0.30 in./6–8 mm long, five-to-nine-flowered, greenish white with long, flexible pedicels; glumes unequal, lower a little more than half the length of the upper, acute to acuminate; lemmas with prominent green nerves, lowest lemma up to 0.1 in./3 mm long, uppermost 1–2 mm long; caryopsis minute, about 1 mm long, smooth, whitish. Flowering and fruiting occur from July through August. Teff is propagated by direct seeding; it is adapted to hard, dry, heavy to light, well-drained soils and prefers full sun. Teff is somewhat drought tolerant. The delicately branched, grayish white, flowering panicles are attractive on the plant and are useful in both fresh and dried arrangements. Teff, an introduction from northern Africa, serves as a primary food source in that area, despite its minute seeds. The foliage turns a rustic light tan following frost, exhibiting an attractive fall color. Teff is large enough to be noticeable and attractive in accent and specimen plantings when grown in clumps. This large, spreading annual is useful in naturalized areas and in borders. Teff is adapted to zones 7–10.

Eragrostis trichodes (Nutt.) A. Wood, Sand, lovegrass A densely tufted, upright-open, weak perennial. Culms erect, simple, slender; all the internodes near the base are short, except the upper, which extends from near the base to the panicle, 24–50 in./0.6–1.3 m high. Foliage dark green, shiny, fine in texture; leaf blades flat, elongate, narrowed toward the base, attenuated into a long, sharp, slender point, 6–30 in./1.5–7.6 dm long, 0.10–0.25 in./3–6 mm wide, rough or hirsute on the upper surface near the base, or a few scattered hairs toward the apex, margins smooth or rough; sheaths mostly basal, longer than the internodes, hirsute at the throat, otherwise glabrous; ligule a dense ring of short hairs, almost 1 mm long. Inflorescence a comparatively narrow, oblong, branched panicle, purplish, 1–3 ft/3–9 dm long, over half the length of the culm, usually exserted, sometimes included at the base, interrupted below, finally nodding, axis rigid and scabrous, the lower axils sometimes pilose, capillary branches erect or ascending, scabrous, 3–4 in./8–10 cm long, naked below, often solitary below and whorled above, the scabrous branchlets 1–2 in./2.5–5.0 cm long, the flexuous, scabrous pedicels twice to several times as long as the spikelets; spikelets pale purplish, 0.1–0.3 in./3–8 mm long, 3-to-10-flowered; glumes unequal, 0.10–0.15 in./3–4 mm long, the upper acute, slightly longer than the lower, scabrous on the keel and sometimes on the body; lemmas up to 0.1 in./3 mm long, acute, three-nerved, scabrous on the midnerve, three-nerved, the lateral nerves faint; palea obtuse, ciliate, two-nerved, about as long as the lemma. Flowering and fruiting occur during the summer, from July through August. Sand lovegrass, native to the United States, is best suited for group or ground-cover plantings in mixed stands in naturalized areas. The plants are not particularly attractive as the flowering panicles are not borne distinctly above and separate from the foliage. Propagation is by seeding and by plant division, preferably the former. Sand lovegrass is quite drought tolerant; it grows best in hot, dry locations in full sun on sandy or sandy-clay soils. The plants are adapted to zones 5 through 9 and survive the winters in zones 8 and 9.

Erianthus Michx. (Plumegrass, Woolly beardgrass). Name from Greek *erion*, "wool," and *anthos*, "flower," referring to the woolly glumes. Lectotype, *Erianthus giganteus* (Walt.) Muhl. There are about 20 species, in temperate and tropical regions of both hemispheres. Usually large, erect, tufted, perennial grasses with elongate, flat leaf blades and terminal oblong, usually dense, silky panicles and small, hairy spikelets. Spikelets in pairs, one bisexual, sessile, the other pedicellate, along a rachis that disarticulates below the spikelets, the rachis joint and pedicel falling attached to the sessile spikelet; glumes coriaceous, equal, usually copiously clothed, at least at the base, with long, silky, spreading hairs; sterile lemma hyaline; fertile lemma hyaline, the midnerve extending into a slender awn; palea small, hyaline.

> **Latin name:** *Erianthus alopecuroides* (L.) Ell.
> **Synonym:** *Erianthus alopecuroides* var. *hirsutus* Nash
> **Common names:** Silver plumegrass, Woolly beardgrass
> **Origin:** Southern Europe

Habitat: Cultivated, escape from cultivation

Hardiness: Zones 5 through 10

Description: An upright-narrow, tufted perennial. Culms erect, robust, 3–10 ft/0.9–3.1 m high, appressed-villous below the panicle, nodes glabrous or appressed-villous. Foliage medium green, medium in texture; leaf blades elongate, somewhat tufted, evenly spaced along the culm, 4–24 in./1–6 dm long or longer, 0.2–0.6 in./5–15 mm wide, narrowed toward the base, scabrous, often papillose-hirsute on the upper surface near the base; sheaths shorter than the internodes, hirsute at the throat; ligule a short-ciliate membrane, about 1 mm long. Inflorescence a terminal, densely flowered, oblong, branched panicle, 6–12 in./1.5–3.0 dm long, 2–4 in./5–10 cm wide, axis very villous, cream-colored or pale, silky; spikelets in pairs, one sessile and bisexual, the other pedicellate, crowded, yellowish, 0.20–0.25 in./5–6 mm long, sparsely villous, usually concealed by the copious basal hairs, which are two to three times the length of the spikelet; glumes coriaceous, unequal, about two-thirds as long as the basal hairs, lanceolate, acuminate, long-pilose, scabrous toward the tip, the lower five-to-six nerved, two-toothed, the upper acute, three-nerved; sterile lemma slightly shorter than the glumes, thin, three-nerved, ciliate above on the margins, fertile lemma about 0.1 in./3 mm long, deeply two-cleft at the apex, the teeth about 2 mm long, acuminate, awned, the flat, scabrous awn 0.4–0.7 in./10–18 mm long, closely spiraled at the base, the remainder loosely spiraled, usually with three or four twists; palea thin, hyaline, about 1 mm long, long-ciliate for about half its length. Flowering and fruiting occur from mid-August through September, with the panicles remaining intact.

Uses: Silver plumegrass is ideal in background borders, tall screens, and windbreaks. It is also used in specimen plantings, although the plumelike panicles do not measure up to those of plumegrass. The terminal panicles are borne high above its foliage as well as that of most other garden plants; they are attractive on the plants and useful in their natural color as cut flowers and in dried arrangements.

Cultivation: Propagation is by seeding and by plant division. Silver plumegrass prefers damp areas along wooded borders, lake and pond banks, and streams; the plants prefer full sun but are somewhat shade tolerant, they may be grown in partial shade. The most expeditious way of propagating any species of *Erianthus* is by plant division. This is accomplished by dividing the old plant crowns in early spring after new growth has begun; plant division in this manner is usually quite successful until the new plants are about 1 ft/3 dm high. Another method of propagation involves rooting sections of mature stems containing at least three nodes in a good potting mixture. Care should be taken to plant the cuttings with the top end up, just as they were on the original stem. The cuttings should be planted deep enough so that at least two nodes are below the soil surface. Propagation by plant division or by cuttings ensures the maintenance of plant type and especially the panicle form and color desired. The removal of old canes or stems in the spring is usually a matter of choice; their removal usually improves overall appearance and probably ensures more uniformity in new growth.

Latin name: *Erianthus contortus* Baldw.
Synonym: *Saccharum contortum* Nutt.
Common names: Bent-awn plumegrass, Beardgrass
Origin: Southern Europe
Habitat: Cultivated, escape from cultivation
Hardiness: Zones 7 through 10
Description: An upright-narrow, tufted perennial. Culms 3–6 ft/0.9–1.8 m high, about 0.5–0.6 in./13–15 mm in diameter at the base, erect, somewhat contorted, stout, glabrous or sparsely appressed-pilose below the panicle, the nodes glabrous or pubescent with erect, deciduous hairs. Foliage mostly basal, medium green, medium to coarse in texture; leaf blades elongate, 1–3 ft/3–9 dm long, 0.25–1.00 in./6–25 mm wide, attenuate into a sharp tip, flat or folded at the narrow base, smooth or rough, densely hirsute on the upper surface at the base, often more or less papillose on both surfaces; sheaths smooth or scabrous, usually longer than the internodes, often sparsely hirsute at the throat; ligule firm, minutely ciliate, 1–2 mm long. Inflorescence an erect, terminal, exserted, branched panicle, 6–18 in./1.5–4.5 dm long, 2–4 in./5–10 cm in diameter, dark purplish, densely flowered, the main axis four-sided, stout, rigid, more or less ciliate on the edges, scabrous and somewhat flattened, zigzag branches in ones or twos, about 3–4 in./8–10 cm long, distant, appressed or slightly spreading, pubescent at the base, the branches with numerous racemes 1–3 in./2.5–8.0 cm long, the rachis joints and pedicels more or less ciliate, about half as long as the spikelets; spikelets in pairs, one sessile and perfect, the other pedicellate, brown, equaling or exceeding the basal hairs, about 0.25–0.30 in./6–8 mm long; glumes almost equal, dark brown, the lower slightly shorter than the upper, hirsute on the back and margins, the hairs often as long as the basal hairs surrounding the spikelet, scabrous toward the apex, often two-toothed, the upper more or less hirsute on the back and margins; sterile lemma more or less pubescent, shorter than the glumes, fertile lemma two-toothed, the midnerve extending into a scabrous awn, 0.4–0.8 in./10–20 mm long, flattened toward the base, loosely spiraled above; palea thin, hyaline, shorter than its lemma. Flowering and fruiting occur from late July until frost, with the silky panicles persisting.
Uses: Bent-awn plumegrass, like other *Erianthus* species, is useful in background borders along property lines and in specimen plantings, where its full value may be appreciated. The plumelike, silky panicles are attractive on the plants and are useful as cut flowers and in dried bouquets. The size and growth habit of bent-awn plumegrass make it ideal for naturalizing, even along the seashore.
Cultivation: Propagation is by seeding and by plant division. The plants prefer full sun but are somewhat shade tolerant in that they may be grown in light or partial shade. Fertile, moist, well-drained soil ensures maximum growth

and size. The removal of old stems in the spring is optional, although their removal increases the attractiveness of the garden.

Latin name: *Erianthus giganteus* (Walt.) Muhl.
Synonym: *Erianthus saccharoides* Michx.
Common names: Giant plumegrass, Sugarcane plumegrass
Origin: Southern Europe
Habitat: Cultivated, escape from cultivation
Hardiness: Zones 7 through 10
Description: An upright-narrow to upright-open, stout perennial. Culms solitary or tufted, 4–9 ft /1.2–2.8 m high, appressed-villous below the panicle, the nodes appressed-hispid with deciduous hairs. Foliage light to medium green, medium in texture; leaf blades elongate, the upper short, the basal 12–30 in./ 3.0–7.6 dm long, 0.3–0.6 in./8–15 mm wide, the long blades at the base folded and narrowed for about half their length, flat above, rough, glabrous or sparsely to densely hirsute toward the base, sometimes papillose near the base; sheaths longer or upper shorter than the internodes, smooth or scabrous, glabrous or sparsely to densely appressed hirsute, especially at the throat and collar; ligule membranous, 0.15–0.20 in./4–5 mm long. Inflorescence a terminal, exserted, purplish, broadly oblong panicle, compressed, 8–16 in./2–4 dm long, 5–8 in./ 1.3—2.0 dm wide, erect or slightly nodding, conspicuously woolly, the axis rather rigid, the branches 3–4 in./8–10 cm long, bearing spikelets to the base, rachis joints and pedicels more than half as long as the spikelets, pilose, the ring of hairs at the base of the spikelet about as long as or longer than the spikelet; spikelets in pairs, one sessile and perfect, the other pedicellate, lanceolate, 0.15– 0.25 in./4–6 mm long exclusive of the awns, sparsely villous on the upper part, shorter than the basal hairs; glumes about equal, naked or pilose above the base, the lower slightly longer, scabrous toward the apex, two-toothed, flattened or slightly two-keeled, the upper acuminate, sometimes awn-pointed; sterile lemma about three-fourths as long as the glumes, fertile lemma slightly shorter than the sterile lemma, ovate, with a straight awn 0.4–1.0 in./10–25 mm long, terete or flattened, scabrous, slightly twisted near the base; palea hyaline, shorter than the lemma. Flowering and fruiting occur from late August until frost, with the plumelike panicles persisting.

Uses: Giant plumegrass is used in perennial background border plantings, as the flowering panicles rise above most other ornamentals, "topping off" the entire border. The giant grass is often used in group and specimen plantings in open areas, in lawns and water gardens, or as tall screens and windbreaks. The flowering panicles are often used as cut flowers and in dried floral arrangements. The purplish panicles do not require dyeing, as they are beautiful and attractive in their natural color.

Cultivation: Propagation is by seeding and by plant division, preferably the latter. The stiff, upright culms seldom cause lodging problems. The plants should be either mulched or taken inside over winter in marginal areas of adapta-

Erianthus giganteus. **Habit,** × **1/2; spikelet with pedicel and rachis joint,** × **5.** *Source: Manual of the Grasses of the West Indies.* USDA Misc. Pub. 243. 1936.

tion. The removal of old growth in the spring usually improves the appearance of the garden; however, this is a matter of choice. Rootstocks should be planted in the spring as soon as new growth appears. The plants may not blossom in colder climates, although they reseed themselves very easily in warmer areas. Giant plumegrass prefers moist, well-drained soil in full sun for maximum growth; it is adapted to a wide range of soil types.

Latin name: *Erianthus ravennae* (L.) Beauv.
Synonym: *Andropogon ravennae* L.
Varieties: *Erianthus ravennae* var. *purpurascens* (Anderss.) Hack.
Common names: Plumegrass, Hardy pampas grass, Ravena grass
Origin: Southern Europe

Erianthus ravennae.

Habitat: Cultivated, escape from cultivation
Hardiness: Zones 5 through 10
Description: An upright-narrow, stout perennial. Culms robust, erect, tufted, growing in large clumps with erect sterile shoots, glabrous except a few hairs at or near the nodes and the lower internodes, 6–12 ft/1.8–3.7 m high, 0.4–0.6 in./10–15 mm thick at the base. Foliage medium green, medium in texture; cauline leaves 12–30 in./3.0–7.6 dm long, 0.2–0.5 in./5–13 mm wide, flat above the middle, narrowed, thick, folded or grooved toward the base, the upper often revolute toward the base, scabrous, densely long-villous at the base on both surfaces or those of the sterile shoots densely villous on the upper surface the entire length of the narrowed portion, more or less papillose toward the base; sheaths longer than the internodes, rough, the upper glabrous or sparsely hairy, the lower and those of the sterile shoots densely appressed hirsute, all more or less papillose; ligule minutely ciliate, about 1 mm long. Inflorescence an erect, terminal, branched, dense, silky panicle, usually silvery tawny or light purplish, densely flowered, exserted, finally nodding, 1–2 ft/3–6 dm long, 5–7 in./1.3–1.8 dm wide, lower branches closely appressed, ascending or spreading, 6–8 in./1.5–2.0 dm long, the numerous branchlets 1–2 in./2.5–5.0 cm long, each with several sessile racemes, rachis joints and pedicels villous and about half as long as the spikelets; spikelets in pairs, one sessile and perfect, the other pedicellate, 0.15–0.20 in./4–5 mm long, densely villous at the base, the hairs about the length of the spikelet; glumes about equal, three-nerved, lanceolate, awn-pointed, often two-toothed, usually pilose; sterile lemma hyaline, about three-fourths as long as the glumes, fertile lemma hyaline, about two-thirds as long as the spikelet, three-nerved, with a straight terete awn 0.1–0.2 in./3–5 mm long, or awnless; palea hyaline, acute ovate, two-toothed, shorter than the lemma. Flowering and fruiting occur from August until frost, with the fluffy, shiny, beige panicles remaining intact into winter.
Uses: Plumegrass and its botanical variety *purpurascens* are perhaps the largest of flowering ornamental grasses. They are noted for their architectural forms and dramatic autumnal coloring of both panicles and foliage. As cool weather approaches, the foliage changes from light green to shades of light brown or tan to beige, tinged with orange and purple, which persists into winter, thereby extending its attractiveness. The fluffy, beige panicles also remain intact on the plants into winter. The large silhouette of plumegrass on a snowy-white background is most striking. It is excellent as a specimen plant in rock and water gardens and in perennial borders. The value of majestic clumps of plumegrass in specimen plantings appropriately located along streams or around lakes and ponds is enhanced by the reflection of the plants on the water. Plumegrass is attractive as a screen and when integrated with broad-leaved, woody ornamentals in perennial borders. The beautiful, fluffy panicles are attractive while on the plant, as fresh cut flowers, and in dried arrangements; in addition, the attractive, large leaves are also useful in dried arrangements. The size of plumegrass and of its variety makes them ideal in background borders

and for tall screens and windbreaks. With its size and majestic appearance, plumegrass exhibits a lovely fountain effect that dominates almost any location in the garden. The potential multifarious use of plumegrass warrants its use in any garden. Plumegrass is used in parks and zoos and on golf courses.

Cultivation: Propagation is by seeding and by plant division; the latter is preferred, provided planting stocks are available. Propagating plumegrass by vegetative means ensures the inflorescence color and type, size, and color of plant desired. Plumegrass seldom causes any plant-lodging problems, because of its stout, robust culms. If old culms are left remaining from the previous year's growth, the new stems grow right through them; the removal of old culms probably expedites new growth, ensures its uniformity, and improves the appearance of the new growth. The plants may not blossom in colder climates, although they reseed themselves copiously in warmer climates. The plants should be mulched or maintained indoors in marginal areas of winter hardiness. Plumegrass prefers full sun on fertile, well-drained, moist or wet soil. The plants may be grown in light or partial shade; they are adaptable to a wide range of soil types. This is the most popular species of plumegrass found in the trade.

Varieties: *Erianthus ravennae* var. *purpurascens* (Anderss.) Hack. The plant size and form of this variety are similar to that of the type species. The erect plants are stately and produce good autumnal colors, including shades of brown, orange, and purple. The panicles of this variety are silver purplish and shiny initially, distinctly different from those of other plumegrass. This variety is adapted to zones 5–10.

Latin name: *Erianthus strictus* Baldw.
Synonym: *Saccharum strictum* Nutt.
Common name: Narrow plumegrass
Origin: Southern Europe
Habitat: Cultivated, escape from cultivation
Hardiness: Zones 5 through 9
Description: A tufted, upright-narrow perennial. Culms few to a tuft, erect, terete, slender, 3–6 ft/0.9–1.8 m high, glabrous or sparsely pubescent at the nodes, with erect, stiff, deciduous hairs. Foliage medium green, medium in texture, the entire plant reddish brown; leaf blades elongate, long attenuate, slender, 6–24 in./1.5–6.0 dm long, 0.2–0.5 in./5–13 mm wide, flat, or becoming conduplicate toward the base on drying, glabrous or sometimes short-pubescent or hirsute above near the base, margins scabrous; sheaths more or less glabrous, shorter than the internodes; ligule membranous, truncate, fringed, about 1–2 mm long. Inflorescence an erect, terminal, exserted, branched panicle, reddish purple or reddish brown, 8–20 in./2–5 dm long, 0.5–1.0 in./13–25 mm in diameter, the branches 2–4 in./5–10 cm long or sometimes longer, appressed, the main axis smooth and rigid, rachis joints about two-thirds as long as the spikelets, the pedicels about half as long as the spikelets, angled and scabrous; spikelets in pairs, one sessile and perfect, the other pedicellate, appressed to the

Erianthus strictus.
Inflorescence, × 1/2.
Source: Manual of the Grasses of the United States. USDA
Misc. Pub. 200. 1951.

rachis, linear-lanceolate, 0.3–0.4 in./8–10 mm long exclusive of the awns, basal hairs sparse and very short or wanting; glumes unequal, the upper slightly longer, keeled above, strongly appressed-hispid, the lower two-toothed, dorsally flattened or slightly two-keeled; sterile lemma dark purple, acute, 0.25–0.30 in./6–8 mm long, fertile lemma three-nerved, two-toothed, 0.20–0.25 in./5–6 mm long, with a scabrous straight awn, 0.4–0.8 in./10–20 mm long; palea shorter than the lemma, up to 0.1 in./3 mm long. Flowering and fruiting occur from late August until frost.

Uses: Narrow plumegrass is sufficiently large for use in middleground borders and for planting in rows to divide the garden into various areas. The colorful, long, narrow panicles emphasize its value in specimen plantings and for use as fresh cut flowers and in dried arrangements. It is also useful in group and massed plantings, especially on the seashore.

Cultivation: Propagation is by seeding and by plant division. Narrow plumegrass prefers moist, fertile, well-drained soil in full sun; the plants are adaptable to a wide range of soil types. The removal of old culms from the previous year's growth improves the appearance of the new growth in addition to that of the entire garden.

Festuca L. (**Fescue, Fescuegrass, Fetuque**). Name from *Festuca,* an old Latin name for a weedy grass. Lectotype, *Festuca ovina* L. There are over 100 species, worldwide in distribution but most abundant in temperate or cold regions. Low or rather tall annuals and perennials; leaf blades flat, occasionally auriculate; spikelets in narrow or open panicles. Spikelets two-to-several-flowered, the rachilla disarticulating above the glumes and between the florets, the uppermost floret reduced; glumes narrow, acute, unequal, the lower sometimes very small; lemmas round on the back, membranous or somewhat indurate, five-nerved, the nerves often obscure, acute or rarely obtuse, awned from the tip, or rarely from a minutely bifid apex, sometimes awnless.

Latin name: *Festuca amethystina* L.
Common name: Large blue fescue
Origin: Europe
Habitat: Cultivated, escape from cultivation
Hardiness: Zones 4 through 8
Description: A slender, upright-open, semievergreen perennial. Culms erect, simple, tufted, 12–18 in./3.0–4.5 dm high. Foliage bluish green, but less so than that of blue fescue, *Festuca ovina* var. *glauca,* fine in texture; leaf blades arching, glabrous, filiform, 6–10 in./1.5–2.5 dm long, 0.1–0.2 in./3–5 mm wide, involute and angular, long attenuate; sheaths rolled, with a distinct groove the greater part of their length; ligule hyaline, membranous. Inflorescence a glaucous or brownish green, thick, branched panicle, 2–4 in./5–10 cm long, 1–2 in./2.5–5.0 cm wide, branches in pairs except the apical one; spikelets lanceolate, 0.10–0.15 in./3–4 mm long, four-to-five-flowered, greenish to purple or violet; glumes slightly unequal, firm, acute, the lower 0.10–0.15 in./3–4 mm long, one-nerved, the upper three-nerved, about 0.15 in./4 mm long; lemmas obscurely five-nerved, acute, about as long as the upper glume, awned from the tip, the awn shorter than the body of the lemma; palea equaling or slightly exceeding its lemma; caryopsis brownish, enclosed. Flowering and fruiting occur from June through August.
Uses: Large blue fescue is grown for its glaucous or bluish green foliage, which makes it useful in accent and specimen plantings in foreground borders and rock gardens and as ground cover in naturalized areas. The slow invasiveness of large blue fescue does not preclude its use in rock and water gardens and in border plantings. The inflorescence is more spectacular and slightly larger than

that of blue fescue, *Festuca ovina* var. *glauca. Festuca amethystina* is useful as ground cover in full sun.

Cultivation: Propagation is by seeding and by plant division. The plants require constant moisture in well-drained soil in full sun or light shade to exhibit their maximum beauty. This species is more tolerant of wet soils than most other *Festuca* species. The foliage contrasts with that of other ornamentals with dark green foliage; specimen plantings should occupy a sunny spot in the garden for the sunlight to maximize the brilliance of the foliage.

Latin name: *Festuca ovina* var. *glauca* (Lam.) Koch
Synonym: *Bromus ovinus* Scop.
Cultivars: Many in cultivation (see Table 1–4)
Common name: Blue fescue
Origin: North America, Eurasia
Habitat: Cultivated, escape from cultivation
Hardiness: Zones 5 through 7
Description: A mound-forming, densely tufted, evergreen perennial. Culms erect, stiff, slender, bluish green, 6–12 in./1.5–3.0 dm high; the plants form symmetrical mounds 8–12 in./2–3 dm in diameter. Foliage silvery blue or glaucous, fine in texture; basal leaf blades elongate, glabrous, rigid, ascending to arching, tightly inrolled and sharply pointed, 3–8 in./0.8–2.0 dm long, 0.10–0.15 in./3–4 mm wide, cauline leaves shorter; sheaths bluish green, longer than the internodes; ligule membranous, hyaline, up to 0.1 in./3 mm long. Inflorescence a bluish green, narrow, almost spikelike, thick panicle, 2–3 in./5–8 cm long, about 0.8–1.0 in./20–25 mm in diameter, with few spikelets; spikelets lanceolate, appressed, mostly four- or five-flowered, 0.15–0.25 in./4–6 mm long; florets close, the flowers perfect or the upper ones staminate; glumes unequal, acute, narrow, keeled, scabrous, the lower 0.15–0.20 in./4–5 mm long, one-nerved, the upper slightly longer, three-nerved; lemmas round on the back below, smooth or slightly scabrous, three- to seven-nerved, 0.10–0.15 in./3–4 mm long, awned, the awn shorter than the body of the lemma, about 1–2 mm long; palea nearly as long as its lemma; caryopsis enclosed. Flowering and fruiting occur from May through June.

Uses: Blue fescue is noted for its mound-forming growth habit and its beautiful silver-blue foliage. It is popular as a house plant when used in hanging baskets, flower pots, and window boxes. It is usually used outdoors in accent, edging, and specimen plantings in flower borders and rock gardens in addition to massed, ground-cover plantings in naturalized areas. The blue-green foliage is attractive, with red or purple-leaved plants, other flowering plants, natural rocks or stones, or with ground-cover plants with dark red foliage, such as *Ajuga reptans* 'Atropurpurea.' Blue fescue is unsurpassed as an evergreen, small, blue garden grass for accent and edging in border plantings. It is also useful in multicolored lawns.

Cultivation: Propagation is by seeding and by plant division. Seedlings from indoor plantings may be transplanted into any desired location. Blue fescue thrives equally well in full sun or light shade in a well-drained, moist to dry soil. Blue fescue is definitely a cool-season, evergreen perennial; the plants become discolored and die back during hot, dry weather and require watering in summer to prevent browning. In warmer areas, the plants do best in partial shade, although the intensity of the blue cast may be lost. The bluest foliage is achieved by clipping the foliage in midsummer, thus producing new foliage. The inconspicuous flowers should be removed so that the plants can maintain their mound-forming habit and effect. Blue fescue has a tendency to die out in the center of the plant crown when grown in heavy, poorly drained soils in warm climates. The plants should be divided every other year to stay alive and vigorous. The foliage color of blue fescue often varies widely, from various shades of blue-green to yellowish green. Blue fescue grows more vigorously and looks best during early spring and fall, when the weather is cooler; the plants retain their color throughout the growing season and into the autumn in cooler climates. The plants may be somewhat short-lived and tend to die out in the center when grown on heavy, clay soils in flat terrain, thus requiring more frequent propagation.

Latin name: *Festuca rubra* L.
Synonym: *Festuca oregona* Vasey
Varieties: Several in cultivation   There is considerable intraspecific variation in *Festuca rubra,* red fescue. American authorities include no less than 28 synonyms associated with this species, whereas English botanists include 8; the former include botanical varieties and the latter involve subspecies. Some examples of synonymy follow: *Festuca rubra* var. *commutata* Gaud., *Festuca rubra* var. *heterophylla* (Lam.) Mutel, *Festuca rubra* var. *lanuginosa* Mert. & W. Koch, *Festuca rubra* var. *prolifera* Piper
Common name: Red fescue
Origin: Asia and Europe
Habitat: Cultivated, escape from cultivation
Hardiness: Zones 5 through 8
Description: An upright-open perennial with creeping rhizomes. Culms solitary or few in loose or occasionally dense tufts, decumbent at the reddish or purplish base, erect or ascending, 16–36 in./4–9 dm high; innovations extravaginal. Foliage russet or reddish green, fine in texture; leaf blades soft, glabrous, folded or involute, 8–20 in./2–5 dm long, 0.10–0.15 in./3–5 mm wide; sheaths tubular, round on the back, soon splitting, light purplish, lower sheaths entire, thin, brownish fibrillose; ligule hyaline, glabrous, membranous, very short, about 1–2 mm long. Inflorescence an erect, contracted and narrow, greenish panicle, 2–8 in./0.5–2.0 dm long, about 1.0–1.6 in./2.5–4.0 cm wide, usually congested, the branches mostly erect or ascending, not ciliate on the angles;

spikelets pale green or glaucous, often purple tinged, four-to-six-flowered, 0.25–0.30 in./6–8 mm long; glumes unequal, lanceolate, glabrous, the lower 0.10–0.15 in./3–4 mm long, the upper 0.15–0.30 in./4–8 mm long; lemmas 0.2–0.3 in./5–8 mm long, glabrous or scabrous toward the apex, bearing an awn about half as long. Flowering and fruiting occur from May through June.

Uses: Red fescue and its variety heterophylla are desirable and useful as ground cover in naturalized areas; the plants produce a rather thick ground cover in the form of a meadow when left unattended.

Cultivation: Propagation is by seeding and by plant division. Red fescue is adapted to a wide range of soils, and the plants prefer full sun but are somewhat shade tolerant. Red fescue requires only minimum maintenance once it is established.

Varieties: *Festuca rubra* var. *heterophylla* (Lam.) Mutel, Shade fescue   A densely tufted, perennial form, used as ground cover or lawn substitute in shaded locations.

Other ornamental species: *Festuca gigantea* (L.) Vill., Giant fescue   An upright-open to arching, semievergreen, loosely tufted perennial. Culms erect, simple, glabrous, 2–4 ft/0.6–1.2 m high, the nodes purple to deep purple. Foliage glaucous or light green, coarse in texture; leaf blades flat or shallowly V-shaped, 1–2 ft/3–6 dm long, 0.8–0.9 in./20–23 mm wide, long attenuate, glabrous and glossy beneath, rough and dull green on upper surface; sheaths glabrous, round on the back and with auricles at the apex. The contrast in color of the lower and upper leaf surfaces is conspicuous and accentuated by the leaves twisting in an unusual manner in which both surfaces may be seen simultaneously. Inflorescence a greenish, loosely branched, erect or nodding panicle, 12–18 in./3.0–4.5 dm long, 4–6 in./1.0–1.5 dm wide; the branches usually widely separated, spreading and flexuous, usually produced in pairs. Flowering and fruiting occur from July through August. Giant fescue is adapted to damp, open woodlands. It may be used in shaded niches, where it requires little or no maintenance, or in clumps in middleground borders. The unusual foliage color is the main attraction of giant fescue; it is the largest species of ornamental fescues. Propagation is by seeding and by plant division; the plants reseed themselves readily. Giant fescue, an introduction from Europe, is useful in naturalized areas; it is adapted to zones 6 through 9.

Festuca tenuifolia Sibth. Hair fescue, Bearskin grass (Synonym: *Festuca capillata* Lam.)   A densely tufted mound- or carpet-forming perennial with short rhizomes. Culms 4–6 in./1.0–1.5 dm high, erect, very slender. Foliage dark green, fine in texture; leaf blades enrolled, stiff, up to 6 in./1.5 dm long, 0.1–0.2 in./3–5 mm wide, terminating in a long, sharp point. Inflorescence an erect, branched, narrow panicle, 2–4 in./5–10 cm long, branches narrowly ascending; spikelets initially greenish, becoming beige or reddish brown. Flowering and fruiting occur from June through July. Its invasive growth habit prevents hair fescue from use in rock gardens; however, it forms attractive, low carpets in water gardens and in open woods in light to medium shade. The soft, dark, rich green foliage is the main attribute of hair fescue. Propagation is by plant division. Hair fescue is adapted to zones 4 through 7.

Festuca vivipara (L.) J. E. Smith   A densely tufted, viviparous perennial. Culms stiff, glabrous, becoming rough near the inflorescence, 10–14 in./ 2.5–3.5 dm high. Foliage medium green, fine in texture; leaf blades straight to slightly reflexed, involute, filiform, 6–8 in./1.5–2.0 dm long, up to 0.1 in./3 mm wide, long attenuate; sheaths smooth to slightly rough, round on the back, open to the base. Inflorescence an erect, contracted, branched panicle. The spikelets are abnormal in lacking usual sexual organs; they are replaced by vegetative growths (i.e., plantlets) that may form vestigial roots before falling to the ground. Their weight bends the flowering stem over to the ground, although the small viviparous plants seldom take root and continue growth. *Festuca vivipara* prefers moist or wet soil in sunny locations. Its curious growth habit is best demonstrated when it is planted on raised beds that are kept moist. This species is grown for its amusing, curious, viviparous growth habit, as very few grasses possess this unique method of reproduction. This viviparous species, an introduction from Europe, is adapted to zone 3.

Additional ornamental species and cultivars of *Festuca* are given in Table 1.4. The following species from Table 1.4 are useful in pebble or rock gardens: *Festuca alpestris, Festuca alpina, Festuca pallens, Festuca pseudoeskia, Festuca rupicaprina, Festuca scoparia,* and *Festuca varia*. The following are recommended for massing in full sun: *Festuca ovina* var. *glauca* 'Blaufink,' 'Blauglut,' 'Blausilber,' 'Daeumling,' 'Fruehlingsblau,' 'Harz,' Meerblau,' 'Platinat,' 'Sea Urchin,' 'Silberreiher,' 'Solling'; *Festuca elegans; Festuca mairei; Festuca muelleri*; and *Festuca scoparia*. These *Festuca* species and their cultivars are noted primarily for their foliage color. The cultivars Blausilber, Fruehlingsblau, and Meerblau of *Festuca ovina* var. *glauca* are outstanding for their colorful foliage, which makes them useful in accent plantings.

Fingerhuthia Nees. Type species, *Fingerhuthia africana* Nees. There are three or more species, native to eastern and southern Africa. Densely tufted, variable perennials with strong root systems; leaf blades flat, tapering to a long, fine point; inflorescence a dense, spikelike panicle; spikelets two-to-four-flowered, lowest floret bisexual, the others staminate or sterile and reduced; glumes equal, one-nerved, short-awned; lemmas glabrous or hairy, short-awned.

Latin name: *Fingerhuthia sesleriaeformis* Nees
Origin: Southern Africa
Habitat: Dry, open grassland
Hardiness: Zones 7 through 10
Description: An erect, upright-narrow, rhizomatous perennial. Culms rather robust, very densely tufted on a short oblique rhizome, erect, smooth,

Table 1.4   Additional Ornamental Species and Cultivars of *Festuca*

Species	Plant Height (in./dm)	Hardiness Zones
F. alp'estris	4/1.0	4–8
F. alpina	4/1.0	4–8
F. elegans	12/3.0	5–8
F. mairei	24/6.0	5–9
F. muelleri	8/2.0	5–9
F. ovina var. glauca 'Blaufink'	6/1.5	6–9
F. ovina var. glauca 'Blaufuchs'	6/1.5	6–9
F. ovina var. glauca 'Blauglut'	6/1.5	6–9
F. ovina var. glauca 'Blausilber'	6/1.5	6–9
F. ovina var. glauca 'Daeumling'	6/1.5	6–9
F. ovina var. glauca 'Fruehlingsblau'	6/1.5	6–9
F. ovina var. glauca 'Harz'	6/1.5	6–9
F. ovina var. glauca 'Meerblau'	6/1.5	6–9
F. ovina var. glauca 'Palatinat'	6/1.5	6–9
F. ovina var. glauca 'Sea Urchin'	6/1.5	6–9
F. ovina var. glauca 'Silberreiher'	6/1.5	6–9
F. ovina var. glauca 'Solling'	8/2.0	6–9
F. pallens	4/1.0	4–7
F. pseudeskia	6/1.5	4–8
F. pulchella	12/3.0	6–9
F. rupicaprina	4/1.0	5–7
F. scoparia 'Pic Carlit'	3/0.8	4–6
F. varia	5/1.3	4–8

glabrous, 1–3 ft/3–9 dm high, with two nodes and long internodes. Foliage medium green, fine in texture; leaf blades long attenuate, linear, 4–8 in./1–2 dm long, 0.10–0.25 in./3–6 mm wide when expanded, convolute, rather flat, rigid, glaucous, smooth below, finely scabrous above, margins rough; lower sheaths conspicuous, shining. Inflorescence a dense ellipsoid to cylindrical panicle, 1–2 in./2.5–5.0 cm long, 0.4–0.6 in./10–15 mm in diameter, dull greenish, sometimes light purplish; spikelets two-to-four-flowered, 0.10–0.25 in./3–6 mm long; lowest floret bisexual, the other staminate or sterile and reduced; glumes equal, lanceolate in profile, mucronate-acuminate, one-nerved, rigidly ciliate along the keels, up to 0.1 in./3 mm long, awned, awns fine, 1.0–1.6 in./ 2.5–4.0 cm long; lemmas oblong-lanceolate in profile, mucronate-acuminate, about 0.15 in./4 mm long, rather firm except at the narrow hyaline margins, glabrous or scantily and minutely hairy below and toward the margins, three-to-five-nerved, side nerves rather close, more or less prominent, joining the

Cm.

*Fingerhuthia
sesleriaeformis.* Source: *The
Grasses and Pastures of South
Africa.* Central News Agency.
1955.

middle nerve below the apex, fertile lemma short-awned from an acuminate apex; palea cuneate, 1–2 mm long. Flowering and fruiting occur from May through July.

Uses: This exotic perennial is grown primarily for its purplish green, dense seedheads or spikelike panicles, which are useful as cut flowers, and in dried arrangements, either in natural color or dyed. The panicles resist shattering when dry, provided they are cut before they mature.

Cultivation: Propagation is by seeding and by plant division, either of which should be done in the spring. This species could be grown in a container to prevent its spread. The plants spread very slowly despite their rhizomatous root system. The plants thrive on a wide range of soil types but usually occur naturally on rocky, clay soils in full sun.

***Glyceria* R. Br. (Mannagrass).** Name from the Greek *glukeros,* ''sweet,'' the seed of the type species being sweet, referring to the taste of the grain. Type species, *Glyceria fluitans* (L.) R. Br. There are 35 species, in temperate regions of both hemispheres. Usually, tall aquatic or marsh perennials, with creeping and rooting bases or with creeping rhizomes; culms simple; leaf blades flat; sheaths closed or partly closed; panicles open or contracted. Spikelets few-to-many-flowered, subterete, or slightly compressed, the rachilla disarticulating above the glumes and between the florets; glumes unequal, short, obtuse or acute, usually scarious, mostly one-nerved; lemmas broad, convex on the back, firm, usually obtuse, scarious at the apex, five-to-nine-nerved, the nerves parallel, usually prominent.

Latin name: *Glyceria canadensis* (Michx.) Trin.
Synonym: *Briza canadensis* Michx.
Common names: Rattlesnake mannagrass, Rattlesnake grass

***Glyceria canadensis.* Panicle, × 1; floret, × 10.** *Source: Manual of the Grasses of the United States.* USDA Misc. Pub. 200. 1951.

Origin: North America
Habitat: Bogs and wet places
Hardiness: Zones 3 through 7
Description: An aquatic, loosely tufted, semievergreen perennial. Culms solitary or a few in a loose tuft, erect, 2–5 ft/0.6–1.5 m high, glabrous or slightly scabrous. Foliage medium to light green, fine in texture; leaf blades ascending, scabrous, 5–10 in./1.3–2.5 dm long, 0.1–0.3 in./3–8 mm wide, acute, rough above, glabrous below; sheaths imbricate partly or entirely closed from below the summit, scabrous; ligule up to 0.1 in./3 mm long. Inflorescence a branched, lax, open panicle, 6–12 in./1.5–3.0 dm long and about as wide when expanded, drooping at maturity, the branches in groups of two, three or five, long and drooping, rather distant, glabrous below; spikelets ovate to oblong, 5-to-10-flowered, 0.15–0.30 in./4–8 mm long, 0.1–0.2 in./3–4 mm wide, the florets crowded, spreading; glumes acute, ovate, one-nerved, the lower 1–2 mm long, the upper almost 0.1 in./3 mm long; lemmas glabrous, oval, subacute or abruptly acute, 0.10–0.15 in./3–4 mm long, seven-nerved, the nerves obscured in the firm tissue of the lemma; palea broadly oval, glabrous, about 0.1 in./3 mm long, two-keeled, the keels indurated; caryopsis enclosed, brownish, oblong-oval, about 1 mm long. Flowering and fruiting occur from June through September.
Uses: Rattlesnake mannagrass is useful for planting in or around lakes, ponds, or ornamental pool margins, in water gardens, and along streams.
Propagation: Propagation is by plant division. The long culms may be cut into segments and rooted in water or planted directly in water or wet, marshy sites. It is one of the few grasses that may be grown either directly in water or in wet sites. The plants thrive equally well in full sun or light shade in acid soils.

Latin name: *Glyceria fluitans* (L.) R. Br.
Synonym: *Festuca fluitans* L.
Common names: Floating sweetgrass, Mannagrass, Floating mannagrass, Floatgrass
Origin: Eurasia
Habitat: Shallow water of lakes and ponds and along sluggish streams
Hardiness: Zones 4 and 5
Description: A semievergreen, spreading, aquatic perennial. Culms 36–40 in./0.9–1.0 m long, loosely tufted or forming loose masses in shallow water, few-noded, glabrous, slender or stout. Foliage medium to dark green, fine in texture; leaf blades pointed, 2–10 in./0.5–2.5 dm long, 0.25–0.40 in./6–10 mm wide. Flat or folded, glabrous except for the rough margins; sheaths tubular, glabrous; ligule membranous, blunt. Inflorescence a sparingly branched panicle, open in flower, afterwards contracted and narrow, erect or curved and nodding, 8–18 in./2.0–4.5 dm long, main axis glabrous, branches in pairs or solitary, the longer of a pair bearing one to four spikelets, the shorter with one spikelet,

Glyceria fluitans. **Panicle,**
× 1; **floret,** × 10. *Source:*
Manual of the Grasses of the
United States. USDA Misc.
Pub. 200. 1951.

appressed after flowering, pedicels 0.10–0.15 in./3–4 mm long; spikelets narrowly oblong, 0.6–1.6 in./1.5–4.0 cm long, up to 0.1 in./3 mm wide, 8-to-
16-flowered, green or light purplish; glumes persistent, unequal, elliptic-oblong
or oblong, blunt, thin, one-to-three-nerved; lower up to 0.1 in./3 mm long,
upper 0.1–0.2 in./3–5 mm long; lemmas scaberulous, round on the back, at
first imbricate, later with incurved margins, elliptic-oblong or oblong, some-

what pointed or blunt, entire, seven-nerved, the nerves distinct but not prominent, firm scabrous, slightly tinged with purple near the tip; palea about as long
as the lemma, sharply two-toothed, with the teeth reaching the top of the lemma
or usually shortly exserted; caryopsis brownish, enclosed, about 0.1 in./3 mm
long. Flowering and fruiting occur from June through August.

   Uses: Floating sweetgrass is useful in pools and ponds, along streams, and
in water gardens.

   Cultivation: Propagation is by seeding and by plant division. This succulent aquatic grass may dominate areas in which it is planted unless it is either
contained or partially removed, as necessary. Floating sweetgrass may be grown
in mud, marshy areas, or shallow water in full sun or light or partial shade.

   Latin name: *Glyceria maxima* (Hartm.) Holmb.
   Cultivars: 'Pallida,' 'Variegata' Variegated mannagrass
   Common names: Mannagrass, Reed mannagrass, Reed meadowgrass
   Origin: Eurasia
   Habitat: In shallow water of lakes and ponds, along canals and streams
   Hardiness: Zones 4 through 8
   Description: An aquatic, spreading or irregular, stoloniferous perennial.
Culms 3–8 ft/0.9–2.2 m high, erect, stout to robust, scabrous or smooth
toward the panicle. Foliage dark green, medium to coarse in texture; leaf blades
1–2 ft/3–6 dm long, 0.3–0.8 in./8–20 mm wide, abruptly pointed, rough beneath and on the margins; sheaths keeled upward, initially entire, later splitting,
smooth near the node, becoming hairy toward the ligule; ligule blunt, with
small point. Inflorescence a greenish, open, loosely branched panicle, becoming
contracted and dense, broadly ovate to oblong, 6–18 in./1.5–4.5 dm long, about
4–6 in./1.0–1.5 cm wide, branches clustered, very slender, rough, the lower up
to 8 in./2 dm long, pedicels 0.3–0.4 in./8–10 mm long; spikelets compressed,
narrowly oblong or oblong, 0.25–0.50 in./6–13 mm long, 1–2 mm wide,
closely 4-to-10-flowered, greenish yellow or tinged with purple; glumes unequal, persistent, broadly ovate to oblong or elliptic, membranous, one-nerved,
the lower up to 0.1 in./3 mm long, upper 0.10–0.15 in./3–4 mm long; lemmas
round on the back, imbricate, elliptic to ovate-elliptic, very blunt, 0.10–0.15
in./3–4 mm long, firm, prominently seven-nerved, scabrous on the nerves; palea
about as long as its lemma, oblong, with two rough keels; caryopsis brownish,
enclosed. Flowering and fruiting occur from July through August.

   Uses: Mannagrass is useful in water gardens. The variegated cultivars are
among the most desirable grasses for the garden. The brilliantly variegated foliage of these grasses contrasts sharply with that of other green-leaved plants and
enhances their value in specimen plantings. Other beneficial attributes these
grasses have in addition to their variegated foliage is their perenniality and ability
to grow directly in water and in wet, marshy areas.

   Cultivation: Propagation is by seeding and by plant division, preferably
the latter. These grasses are easy to propagate by cuttings. They may be grown

successfully in wet soil, in marshes, and directly in water in full sun or light shade. The plants are somewhat invasive and will eventually dominate areas in which they are planted unless they are contained by removing excessive growth as necessary. Their value as aquatic ornamentals more than compensates for the maintenance required to keep them under control.

Cultivars: *Glyceria maxima* (Hartm.) Holmb. 'Pallida' This cultivar is approximately the same size as the parent species, *Glyceria maxima,* and is also stoloniferous. Foliage is brilliantly variegated with pale, creamy white and green stripes. It is useful as an accent plant in zones 4–8.

Glyceria maxima (Hartm.) Holmb. 'Variegata' Variegated mannagrass An upright-open to spreading or irregular stoloniferous perennial. The plants are 30–36 in./7.6–9.0 dm high, irregular in shape. Leaves about 2 in./5 cm long, brilliantly variegated, with white or creamy yellow stripes, the amount of white or cream exceeding the amount of green in the leaf. The young leaves are pinkish in the spring before gradually changing color. The variegated coloring does not fade as the growing season progresses, as is so common with other variegated ornamental grasses. The foliage is suffused with rose-pink in the autumn. The plants remain attractive throughout the growing season and are capable of being grown directly in water. This cultivar is a tender perennial in zone 5, where it requires mulching to perenniate, whereas it perenniates in zones 6–8. It is grown for its multicolored foliage in group or massed plantings in water gardens or bogs and marshes as ground cover.

Gynerium **Humb. & Bonpl.** A monotypic genus. Name from Greek *gune,* ''female,'' and *erion,* ''wool,'' referring to the woolly, pistillate spikelets. A genus of tropical Old World origin that has become naturalized in the New World tropics. Tall, perennial reeds with plumelike panicles. Plants dioecious; spikelets several-flowered, the pistillate with long attenuate glumes and smaller, long, silky lemmas, the staminate with shorter glumes and glabrous lemmas.

Latin name: *Gynerium sagittatum* (Aubl.) Beauv.
Synonym: *Saccharum sagittatum* Aubl.
Common names: Uvagrass, Arrow cane, Wild cane
Origin: Old World tropics
Habitat: Stream banks, coastal marshes, wet sites
Hardiness: Zone 10
Description: An evergreen, dioecious, perennial reed. Culms cylindrical, stout, woody near the base, mostly unbranched but sometimes branched in the upper portion, up to 32 ft/9.8 m high, 0.5–1.0 in./13–25 mm or more in diameter at base. Foliage medium green, coarse in texture; leaf blades stiff, erect, becoming ascending to arching, deeply V-shaped near the base, becoming flat for most of their length, sharply serrulate, long attenuate, up to 6 ft/1.8 m long, 2–3 in./5–8 cm wide; those of the staminate culm approximate, forming

Gynerium sagittatum.
Habit, much reduced;
portion of culm with
imbricate sheaths, × 1/2;
staminate branch, × 1;
pistillate branch, × 1.
Source: *Manual of the Grasses
of the West Indies.* USDA
Misc. Pub. 243. 1936.

a fan-shaped summit beneath the panicle; sheaths rough, longer than the inter-nodes; old sheaths persistent on the lower portion of the culm, at first light to medium green, becoming light tan at maturity, U-shaped at the base, loosely surrounding the culm, giving it the appearance of being oval in outline. Inflores-cence a terminal, profusely branched, plumelike, rather dense panicle, pale, densely flowered, the main axis rough or scabrous, erect, the branches drooping, the staminate panicle glabrous, less silky than the pistillate, dull white, 10–20 in./2.5–5.0 dm long, 4–6 in./1.0–1.5 dm wide; spikelets several-flowered, very villous, dull white, the glumes and lemmas smaller than those of the pistillate spikelets, lemmas glabrous; pistillate panicle up to 39 in./1 m long or longer, 6–10 in./1.5–2.5 dm wide, whitish, very silky, spikelets many-flowered, glumes long attenuate, lemmas smaller, very villous with long hairs. Flowering and fruiting occur in the winter, from December through March or sporadically.

Uses: Uvagrass is an excellent erosion-control plant, as the plants form large, extensive, dense colonies. It is commonly used as a tall windbreak, although the plants are subject to wind damage themselves. It is particularly useful for difficult wet sites in and along streams and on ditch banks and steep, eroded areas. Uvagrass is too large and invasive for use in the formal garden; however, it forms a good ground cover in naturalized wet locations and in freshwater marshes near the sea. Uvagrass is noted for its large silky plumes, which are excellent in dried arrangements; the plumes are commonly found in florist shops, both dyed and undyed. Caribbean Indians used the stems for arrow shafts. The large stems are currently used for indoor decorative purposes.

Cultivation: Propagation is by plant division and by seeding, preferably the former. The plant crowns or three-eye seed pieces of the culms are easily established; best growth is attained when uvagrass is established in moist or wet soil, although the plants are quite drought tolerant. The plants prefer full sun but will tolerate light or partial shade.

Hakonechloa **Mak. ex Honda.** Type species, *Hakonechloa macra* (Munro) Mak. ex Honda Cespitose perennial grasses, native mostly to Japan. Culms elongate, not thickened at base; leaf blades linear, glaucous above; spikelets in loose panicles, 5-to-10-flowered, slightly flattened; glumes thinly chartaceous, one-to-three-nerved, acute, scarcely keeled, slightly distant; lemmas convolute when young, chartaceous, lustrous, narrowed into a slightly bidentate apex, the midnerve excurrent between minute teeth into an erect awn about 0.1 in./3 mm long, the internerves glabrous, the margins appressed-pilose; rachilla elongate, pilose, disarticulating at the base of each segment, forming a hairy stipe below the floret; palea slightly shorter than the lemma, sparsely long-pilose on the margins; stamens three; ovary glabrous; caryopsis oblong, scarcely flattened.

Latin name: *Hakonechloa macra* (Munro) Mak. ex Honda
Synonym: *Phragmites macra* Munro
Cultivars: 'Albo-aurea,' 'Albo-variegata,' 'Aureola'
Origin: Japan
Habitat: Cultivated, escape from cultivation
Hardiness: Zones 4 through 9
Description: A rhizomatous, upright-open, mound-forming perennial. Culms bright green, very slender, glabrous, wiry, erect, 1–2 ft/3–6 dm high.

Foliage bright or pale greenish yellow, fine in texture; leaf blades flat or with loosely involute margins, glabrous, gradually tapering at both ends, 8–10 in./ 2.0–2.5 dm long, about 0.3 in./8 mm wide; sheaths greenish or light purplish, round on the back, glabrous, with a fringe of hairs near the top. Inflorescence an erect, branched, open panicle, 6–10 in./1.5–2.5 dm long, about 2–3 in./ 5–8 cm wide; spikelets light green or pale. Flowering and fruiting occur from August through September.

Uses: This rhizomatous, slowly spreading, ornamental grass is noninvasive, despite its creeping growth habit. It is beautiful in group plantings in foreground borders, even more so when grown in massed stands as ground cover in naturalized areas or in clumps in rock or water gardens. The variegated cultivars are even more attractive, although less vigorous than the parent species. These perennials are shade tolerant and are grown primarily for the attractiveness and beauty of their foliage. This shade-tolerant perennial may be used as a lawn substitute in wooded sites; the variegated forms are useful in multicolored lawns.

Cultivation: Propagation is by seeding and by plant division. The less vigorous, variegated cultivars are best propagated by plant division; these cultivars should be grown in light shade, as full sun will discolor the leaves. The plants are more colorful when grown in light shade, although it may be grown in full sun; these grasses require fertile, moist, well-drained soil.

Cultivars: *Hakonechloa macra* (Munro) Mak. ex Honda 'Albo-aurea'   This cultivar is less vigorous than the parent species. The plants are 10–14 in./2.5–3.5 dm high; the arching, variegated leaves have longitudinal stripes of cream and yellow with very narrow bands of green or flushed bronze. The plant is excellent in group plantings as an accent plant in partial shade.

Hakonechloa macra (Munro) Mak. ex Honda 'Albo-Variegata'   This cultivar is about the same size as the parent species. The foliage color is very similar to that of the cultivar Albo-aurea, and it is used in the same manner in shaded locations.

Hakonechloa macra (Munro) Mak. ex Honda 'Aureola'   The plants are 12–14 in./3.0–3.5 dm high. The leaves are bright yellow with narrow, slender, green, longitudinal stripes. This cultivar is useful in group and massed plantings in partially shaded sites. The cultivars of *Hakonechloa macra* are adapted to zones 7–9. They are not as hardy as the parent species.

Helictotrichon **Besser ex Schult.** Name derived from *helictos,* "twisted," and *trichon,* apparently referring to the twisted awns. Type species, *Helictotrichon planiculmis* (Schrad.) Besser ex Schult. There are about 40 species, native to Eurasia and North America. Tufted perennials with low to moderately tall culms, rather narrow panicles of shining spikelets. Leaf blades flat or involute, usually contracted. Inflorescence a few-flowered panicle with large, erect, shiny spikelets; rachilla disarticulating between the florets and above the glumes. Spikelets three-to-several-flowered; glumes about equal, three-to-five-nerved, subhyaline except toward the base; lemmas convex, the lower half subindurate and several-nerved, the upper part subhyaline, awned from the middle, the awns twisted and geniculate, much exceeding the spikelets, usually toothed at the apex; palea two-keeled, well-developed.

Latin name: *Helictotrichon pubescens* (Huds.) Pilg.
Synonym: *Avena pubescens* Huds.
Common name: Hairy oatgrass
Habitat: Waste grounds, roadsides, cultivated
Hardiness: Zones 3 and 4
Description: A densely tufted, upright-narrow perennial. Culms geniculate at base, becoming erect, 20–30 in./5.0–7.6 dm high. Foliage medium green, fine in texture; leaf blades flat or rolled, pubescent, 6–12 in./1.5–3.0 dm long, 0.2–0.3 in./5–8 mm wide, long attenuate; sheaths pubescent, at least the lower. Inflorescence a narrow, open, branched, greenish panicle, 4–6 in./1.0–1.5 dm long, 2–3 in./5–8 cm wide, the flexuous branches paired or in whorls, ascending, bearing one to three spikelets, pedicels 0.25–0.80 in./6–20 mm long; spikelets mostly three-flowered, oblong, shiny, 0.4–0.6 in./10–15 mm long, breaking up at maturity beneath the lemmas; florets all bisexual, or the uppermost staminate or sterile and reduced; glumes about equal, three-to-five-nerved, thin, shiny, acuminate, 0.4–0.6 in./10–15 mm long, the lower lanceolate, three-nerved, 0.25–0.50 in./6–13 mm long, the rachilla and callus hairy; the upper longer than the lower, five-nerved; lemmas thin, shiny, 0.3–0.6 in./8–15 mm long, convex, round on the back, bearing a rough awn attached about the middle, awn sometimes bent and twisted, 0.5–0.8 in./13–20 mm long; palea about as long as its lemma, thin, two-keeled, the keels glabrous; caryopsis hairy at tip, enclosed. Flowering and fruiting occur from June through July.

Uses: Hairy oatgrass is useful in foreground borders and in specimen plantings of rock gardens; it is particularly attractive in clumps. The dried panicles, with their long awns, are useful in dried flower arrangements.

Cultivation: Propagation is by seeding and by plant division. The plants prefer rocky moist soil in full sun or light shade.

Latin name: *Helictotrichon sempervirens* (Vill.) Pilg.
Synonym: *Avena sempervirens* Host
Common name: Blue oatgrass
Origin: Eurasia, Europe
Habitat: Waste grounds, cultivated
Hardiness: Zones 4 through 8
Description: A densely tufted, semievergreen, upright-open, mound-forming perennial. Culms stiff, erect, becoming arching, 24–56 in./0.6–1.4 m high, bluish green. Foliage conspicuously glaucous, coarse in texture; leaf blades straight or slightly curved, 10–12 in./2.5–3.0 dm long, 0.6–0.8 in./15–20 mm wide, sparsely hairy, long attenuate; sheaths bluish green, mostly basal, slightly

hairy; ligule glabrous, 1–3 mm long. Inflorescence a whitish or light beige, drooping, branched, one-sided panicle, 4–6 in./1.0–1.5 dm long, about 3–4 in./ 8–10 cm wide, arching at the tips, branches in pairs or in whorls, main axis hairy, hairs 0.15–0.25 in./4–6 mm long; spikelets sparse, very pale, bluish, becoming light beige, 0.4–0.5 in./10–13 mm long, loosely three-to-five-flowered; glumes unequal, finely pointed, thin, one-to-three-nerved, lower narrowly lanceolate, about 0.25–0.50 in./6–13 mm long, upper wider, about 0.5 in./13 mm long; lemmas narrowly oblong-lanceolate, 0.5 in./13 mm long, round on the back, toothed at the tip, five-nerved, bearded at the base, awned from the back above the middle, the awn bent and twisted in the lower portion, 0.50–0.75 in./13–19 mm long; palea with short keels, nearly as long as its lemma; caryopsis hairy at tip, enclosed. Flowering and fruiting occur from June through August.

Uses: Blue oatgrass is grown primarily for its light bluish green or glaucous foliage. It is used in rock garden group plantings or in borders along wooded areas, as it is somewhat shade tolerant. The glaucous foliage provides an attractive contrast in middleground border plantings; it also provides beautiful fall and winter color. The fine-to-medium-textured foliage along with the flowers borne high above the foliage are attractive when blue oatgrass is grown in clumps in rock gardens. Sufficient space should be provided for the plants to expand and increase in size to fully show their form and beauty. Blue oatgrass is also attractive in massed stands.

Cultivation: Propagation is by plant division. Blue oatgrass grows best in fertile, moist soil in full sun or light shade. Plants grown in shade may become lanky and weak and subject to leaf diseases. Blue oatgrass thrives in a wide range of soils ranging from sandy loams to heavy clays.

Hemarthria **R. Br.** There are 12 species, native to tropical and subtropical regions of the New and Old worlds. Lectotype, *Hemarthria compressa* (L. f.) R. Br. Tufted or stoloniferous perennials; leaf blades elongate, flat. Inflorescence a single raceme enclosed below by the subtending sheath, borne in the upper axils of the culms; racemes dorsally compressed; internodes thickened, clavate, nearly always obliquely articulate, fused to the adjacent pedicel. Sessile spikelet dorsally compressed; glumes unequal, lower narrowly elliptic, rigidly herbaceous, broadly convex, two-keeled, smooth, indistinctly winged above, obtuse, caudate or bifid, upper glume obtuse to long attenuate; lower floret reduced to a hyaline lemma; upper lemma entire and awnless; caryopsis narrowly obovoid, slightly dorsally compressed; pedicellate and sessile spikelets similar, pedicels flattened, broadly linear.

Latin name: *Hemarthria altissima* (Poir.) Stapf & C. E. Hubb.
Synonym: *Manisuris altissima* (Poir.) Hitchc.
Cultivars: Several in cultivation

Hemarthria altissima.
Habit, × 1/2; spikelets,
× 2 1/2. *Source: The Grasses
and Pastures of South Africa.*
Central News Agency. 1955.

Common name: Limpograss
Origin: Southern Africa
Habitat: Cultivated, escape from cultivation
Hardiness: Zones 7 through 10
Description: A tufted or mat-forming, stoloniferous perennial. Culms branched, 2–8 ft/0.6–2.5 m long, 0.10–0.15 in./3–4 mm in diameter at the base, glabrous, internodes 1–3 in./2.5–8.0 cm long, prostrate or ascending; flowering culms erect, rooting at the lower nodes. Foliage light, medium, or dark green when young, usually becoming yellowish, russet, or reddish at maturity, fine in texture; leaf blades flat, 3–6 in./0.8–1.5 dm long, 0.2–0.3 in./5–8 mm wide, glabrous or with few long, white hairs, long attenuate; sheaths smooth, round on the back, as long as or longer than the internodes; ligule a very short, ciliate membrane, about 1 mm long. Inflorescence a single raceme, 2–6 in./0.5–1.5 dm long, sometimes branched, borne mostly singly in the upper

leaf axils and exserted from the axillary subtending sheath, tough, dorsally compressed, internodes thickened, clavate, nearly always obliquely articulate, fused to the adjacent pedicel; sessile spikelet elliptic-oblong with a trigonous callus, dorsally compressed; lower glume narrowly elliptic, rigidly herbaceous, broadly convex, 0.15–0.25 in./4–6 mm long, two-keeled, smooth, obtuse to emarginate, indistinctly winged above, with or without a constriction near the apex, upper glume obtuse to long acuminate; pedicellate spikelet narrowly trigonous, 0.15–0.25 in./4–6 mm long, truncate at the base without a callus, subacute to acute at the tip, pedicel flattened, broadly linear; lower floret reduced to a hyaline lemma; upper lemma entire and awnless; palea about one-half as long as the lemma; caryopsis embedded in the rachilla, narrowly obovoid, slightly dorsally compressed, yellowish white, smooth, about 1 mm long. Flowering and fruiting occur from June through September or usually until frost.

Uses: Limpograss has been repeatedly introduced from southern Africa for use primarily as a forage grass and as a ground-cover and erosion-control plant. There is considerable intraspecific variation within the species. The prostrate types form a complete, thick mat, producing a good ground cover. This characteristic coupled with that of rooting at the nodes make limpograss an excellent erosion-control plant. Limpograss is adaptable for use as ground cover and erosion control over extensive areas in different sites; the plants produce a meadow effect with good fall coloration.

Cultivation: The usual method of propagation is by planting stolons. Although the seeds are viable, they are difficult to harvest and are not available in the trade. Sections of stolons 2–3 ft/6–9 dm long taken in midsummer should be partially covered 2–3 in./5–8 cm deep in moist soil, leaving an occasional end or portion of the stolon aboveground. New plantings should be kept moist until they are well established. Limpograss prefers full sun and is adapted to soils varying from wet, sandy loams to heavy clays and peaty types.

Hierochloë R. Br. (**Sweetgrass, Holygrass, Foin d'odeur, Herbe sainte**). Name from Greek *hieros*, "sacred," and *chloë*, "grass,"—thus, "holy grass." Type species, *Hierochloë odorata* (L.) Wahlnb. There are 17 species, inhabiting the cool and arctic regions of the world. Perennial, fragrant grasses, with small panicles of broad, bronze-colored spikelets. Spikelets with one perfect floret and two staminate ones beneath it, the rachilla disarticulating above the glumes, the staminate florets falling attached to the fertile one; glumes equal, three-nerved, broad, thin and chartaceous, smooth, acute; staminate lemmas about as long as the glumes, cymbiform, hispidulous, hairy along the margin; fertile lemma somewhat indurate, about as long as the others, smooth or nearly so, awnless; paleas three-nerved, round on the back.

Latin name: *Hierochloa odorata* (L.) Wahlnb.
Synonym: *Hierochloa nashii* (Bickn.) Kaczmarek

Hierochloaë odorata. **Habit,** × **1/2; spikelet, florets, and fertile floret,** ×
5. *Source: Manual of the Grasses of the United States.* USDA Misc. Pub. 200. 1951.

Common names: Sweetgrass, Holygrass, Vanilla, Vanilla grass, Indian grass

Origin: North America

Habitat: Wet meadows, bogs, moist ground

Hardiness: Zones 2 through 6

Description: An apomictic, aromatic, upright-narrow, pseudoaquatic perennial with slender, creeping rhizomes. Culms few, smooth, erect, few-noded, slightly nodding at the tip, 1–2 ft/3–6 dm high. Foliage sparse, medium green, fine in texture; leaves erect, flat, the margins becoming somewhat involute on drying, the lower basal ones longest, 8–30 in./2.0–7.6 dm long, 0 .3–0.4 in./ 8–10 mm wide, the upper mostly 5–10 in./1.3–2.5 dm long, long attenuate and usually forming a blunt point, smooth above and below or occasionally the upper surface sparsely pubescent, the margins smooth or scabrous, the leaves aromatic when bruised; sheaths longer than the internodes, smooth or minutely scabrous, round on the back; ligule hyaline, variable, 0.1–0.2 in./3–5 mm long. Inflorescence an erect, pyramidal panicle, 2–3 in./5–8 cm long, about half as wide, with slender, drooping branches, naked below, the branches mostly 1–2 in./2.5–5.0 cm long, mostly in four to six pairs, spreading after anthesis; spikelets about 0.2 in./5 mm long, shining, green or purplish at the base, becoming bronze or brownish, three-flowered, one terminal and perfect and two staminate florets, short-pedicellate, pedicels glabrous, 0.10–0.15 in./3–4 mm long, glumes about equal, very thin, smooth, persistent, broad, blunt, lower usually as long as the florets or shorter, usually 0.15–0.20 in./4–5 mm long, up to 0.1 in./3 mm wide, three-nerved, upper always longer than the florets, about 0.15–0.20 in./ 4–5 mm long, up to 0.1 in./3 mm wide, three-nerved, long attenuate; florets staminate; lemmas obtuse or apiculate, three-to-five-nerved, scabrous and pubescent, lower lemma elliptic, 0.15–0.20 in./4–5 mm long, blunt, pubescent on the margins, firm, five-nerved, terminal lemma ovate, 0.10–0.15 in./3–4 mm long, pubescent, three-to-five-nerved; palea as long as its lemma, one-nerved, deeply bifid, with two ciliate keels, upper fertile floret about 0.1 in./3 mm long, the lemma smooth except the pubescent upper portion, five-nerved, acute, sometimes the outer nerves obscure, the palea shorter than its lemma, one-nerved, pubescent at the apex. Flowering and fruiting occur from May through July.

Uses: The pleasant fragrance of sweetgrass is its chief attraction; in addition, it is one of the earliest grasses to flower in the spring. The strong, rhizomatous root system of sweetgrass disqualifies it for use in rock gardens. It is best used in plantings along walks or driveways, where the leaves may be reached easily and crushed for their pleasant vanilla fragrance. Sweetgrass should be grown when possible as a novelty or curiosity; it is also adapted as a houseplant.

Cultivation: Propagation is by seeding and by plant division, and detached, rooted rhizomes. Propagation should be done in early spring as new growth emerges. Fertile soil enriched with humus in moist to wet sites is required for optimum growth. The plants may be grown in full sun or semishade, as new growth usually occurs before deciduous, broad-leaved shrubs and trees are in full leaf.

Holcus L. Name from Greek *olkos,* ''attractive,'' used by Pliny to describe a kind of grass. Type species, *Holcus lanatus* L. There are eight species, native to Africa and Europe. Perennials with flat leaf blades and terminal, contracted, densely flowered panicles. Spikelets two-flowered, articulate below the glumes; the lower floret perfect, raised on a curved stipe, awnless; the upper floret staminate, its lemma bearing a dorsal awn from below the apex; glumes thin, unequal, compressed, cymbiform, longer than the florets; lemmas somewhat indurated, boat-shaped; paleas thin, nearly as long as the lemmas.

> **Latin name:** *Holcus lanatus* L.
> **Synonym:** *Aira holcus-lanata* Vill.
> **Cultivars:** 'Variegatus' Variegated velvetgrass
> **Common names:** Velvetgrass, Yorkshire fog
> **Origin:** Europe
> **Habitat:** Cultivated, escape from cultivation
> **Hardiness:** Zones 4 through 10
> **Description:** An upright-open to upright-arching, semievergreen perennial, loosely or compactly tufted, velvety pubescent throughout. Culms slender to somewhat stout with two to five nodes, erect or ascending from a decumbent base, 12–40 in./0.3–1.0 m high. Foliage soft, hairy, greenish gray, fine in texture; leaf blades flat, lanceolate, 2–8 in./0.5–2.0 dm long, 0.15–0.30 in./4–8 mm wide, narrowing to a fine point, minutely hirsute on both surfaces and margins; sheaths shorter than the internodes, round on the back, usually with reflexed hairs; ligule membranous, 1–2 mm long, toothed, pubescent. Inflorescence a terminal, erect or nodding, soft, branched panicle, lanceolate to oblong or ovate, 2–8 in./0.5–2.0 dm long, about 2 in./5 cm wide, very dense to rather loose, whitish, light green, pinkish or purplish, branches closely divided, hairy, often interrupted below; spikelets pedicellate, oblong to elliptic or gaping, compressed, about 0.15–0.25 in./4–6 mm long, two-flowered, the lower bisexual and the upper usually staminate, rarely bisexual; glumes about equal, about as long as the spikelet, stiffly hairy on the keels and nerves, minutely hairy on the sides, chartaceous, lower narrowly lanceolate or oblong, one-nerved, upper broader, ovate to elliptic, three-nerved, usually tipped with an awn about 1 mm long; lemmas 2 mm long, enclosed in the glumes, keeled upward, obscurely three-to-five-nerved, firm, shining, glabrous except for the ciliate apex, the lower blunt, acute or obtuse, awnless with an equally long palea, the upper broader, two-toothed, awned on the back near the tip with a strongly hooked awn about 2 mm long, becoming curved when dry; palea two-keeled, thin,

***Holcus lanatus.* Habit, ×
1/2; spikelet, florets, and
fertile floret, × 5.** *Source:
Manual of the Grasses of the
United States.* USDA Misc.
Pub. 200. 1951.

shorter than the lemma. Flowering and fruiting occur from May through August. This is one of the few grasses that flower twice daily—for example, in the morning and in the late afternoon.

Uses: The green form of velvetgrass is good for ground cover over extended naturalized areas. The cultivar Variegata is ideal as edging in foreground borders, in multicolored lawns, and in specimen plantings. The plants remain attractive throughout the growing season; they are useful in dried arrangements.

Cultivation: Propagation is by seeding and by plant division. Velvetgrass prefers a fertile, well-drained, light, sandy soil. The plants are somewhat shade tolerant but grow best in full sun.

Cultivars: *Holcus lanatus* L. 'Variegatus' Variegated velvetgrass This open to spreading cultivar differs from the parent species in having variegated green and white foliage and in being smaller (e.g., 8–12 in./2–3 dm high). This is the form of velvetgrass that is used sometimes as an ornamental in the flower garden. Velvetgrass and the cultivar Variegatus are semievergreen when grown in plant-hardiness zones as far north as zone 5. It is useful in specimen plantings and as ground cover in shaded sites in zones 5–9.

Latin name: *Holcus mollis* L.
Synonym: *Aira mollis* Schreb.
Cultivars: 'Albo-variegatus,' 'Variegatus'
Common names: Creeping softgrass, Wood softgrass, Softgrass
Origin: Europe
Habitat: Cultivated, escape from cultivation
Hardiness: Zones 4 through 7
Description: An upright-open to spreading, pubescent, semievergreen perennial with tough, creeping rhizomes. Culms tufted, 12–40 in./0.3–1.0 m high, erect, or more often spreading, slender, with four to seven nodes, bearded at the nodes, otherwise glabrous. Foliage grayish green, medium in texture; leaf blades flat, linear, 2–8 in./0.5–2.0 dm long, 0.4–0.5 in./10–13 mm wide, long attenuate, villous or velvety, or nearly smooth; sheaths glabrous except the lower, which are occasionally softly hairy, round on the back; ligule membranous, blunt, 0.1–0.2 in./3–5 mm long. Inflorescence an upright, branched panicle, narrowly oblong to ovate, 2–5 in./0.5–1.3 dm long, 1–2 in./2.5–5.0 cm wide, compact to somewhat loose, whitish pale gray or purplish, branches hairy, pedicels 0.1–0.2 in./3–5 mm long; spikelets elliptic or oblong, flattened, 0.15–0.20 in./4–5 mm long, falling at maturity, two-flowered, the lower bisexual, the upper staminate or bisexual; glumes about equal, the upper elliptic or ovate, three-nerved, as long as the spikelets, pointed, chartaceous, glabrous or with short, stiff hairs on the keels and nerves, scaberulous on the sides, lower narrowly lanceolate, one-nerved; lemmas obliquely lanceolate, 2–3 mm long, enclosed in the glumes, five-nerved, bearded at the base, minutely hairy or glabrous above, firm, shining, lower awnless, upper awned just below the apex, the awn 0.1–0.2 in./3–4 mm long, slightly bent and protruding beyond the glumes; palea thin, about as long as the lemma, hairy on the nerves; caryopsis enclosed. Flowering and fruiting occur from June through August.

Uses: Creeping softgrass is useful as ground cover in open woodland, or over extended areas in full sun. The smaller, mat-forming, variegated cultivars

Holcus mollis. **A, Habit,** × 1/2; **B, inflorescence,** × 2 1/2. *Source: Selected Weeds of the United States.* USDA Agric. Handbook 366. 1970.

are useful in multicolored lawns and as specimen plants in water gardens and foreground borders despite their rhizomatous root system. Creeping softgrass and its cultivars make ideal miniature lawns; their variegated foliage provides good color in the garden during the summer and fall.

Cultivation: Propagation is by seeding and by plant division, preferably the latter. Creeping softgrass thrives on fertile, moist soil in full sun or light shade whereas the variegated cultivars require light or partial shade, as their foliage becomes discolored in full sun. The cultivars prefer fertile, moist, sandy, acid soils. The plants of these rhizomatous grasses will become invasive unless their rhizomatous roots are contained.

Cultivars: *Holcus mollis* L. 'Albo-variegatus'   The variegated foliage of this rhizomatous cultivar is quite similar to that of the cultivar Variegatus. It is smaller than the cultivar Variegatus and also less vigorous. The mat-forming plants are about 4 in./1 dm high. The leaves have broad margins of white, with a narrow green stripe up the middle. Although 'Albo-variegatus' does not flower freely, the flowers are variable in color (e.g., light green, slightly purplish, or bright red). Flowering and fruiting occur from June through July. This cultivar is adapted to the same plant-hardiness zones as the species (i.e., zones 4–7). It is worthy as a specimen plant in the water garden and in naturalized areas.

Holcus mollis L. 'Variegatus'   This semievergreen cultivar differs from the species in being smaller (i.e., 6–24 in./1.5–6.0 dm high) and in having variegated foliage (i.e., green and white, longitudinally striped leaves). It is popular for its semievergreen, variegated foliage and mat-forming growth habit; the variegated foliage makes it worthy as a specimen plant in water gardens and for naturalizing. Flowering and fruiting occur from June through July. This rhizomatous cultivar is adapted to zones 4–7.

Hordeum **L. (Barley, Orge).** The old Latin name for barley. Lectotype, *Hordeum vulgare* L. There are about 24 species, in temperate regions of the Northern and Southern hemispheres. Low or rather tall annual or perennial grasses with flat leaf blades and dense bristly spikes. Spikes disarticulating at the base of the rachis segment, this remaining as a stipe below the attached triad of spikelets. Spikelets usually one-flowered, rarely two-flowered, two or three together at each node of the articulate rachis, the back of the lemma turned from the rachis, the middle spikelet sessile, the lateral ones pedicellate, except in *Hordeum vulgare* and *Hordeum montanens;* rachilla disarticulating above the glumes and, in the central spikelet, prolonged behind the palea as a bristle and sometimes bearing a rudimentary floret; lateral spikelets usually imperfect, sometimes reduced to bristles; glumes narrow, often subulate and awned, standing in front of the spikelet; lemmas round on the back, five-nerved, usually obscurely so, usually tapering into a long awn.

Latin name: *Hordeum jubatum* L.
Synonym: *Critesion jubatum* Nevski
Common names: Foxtail barley, Squirreltail barley, Squirreltail grass, Queue d'ecureuil
Origin: North America
Habitat: Cultivated, escape from cultivation
Hardiness: Zones 4 through 9
Description: An erect, upright-open, annual, biennial, or perennial. Culms rarely solitary, usually tufted, erect, slender, geniculate at the base, greenish yellow, tufted, hardy, 1–2 ft /3–6 dm high. Foliage light green or light greenish yellow, fine in texture; leaf blades flat, becoming convolute at maturity, upright, slightly arching, scabrous, 5–8 in./0.8–2.0 dm long, 0.1 in./3 mm wide, long attenuate; auricles on some leaves; sheaths shorter than the internodes, loose, round on the back; ligule membranous, about 1 mm long. Inflorescence a dense, erect to nodding spike, 2–4 in./5–10 cm long, almost as wide, soft, green or purplish, turning pale beige with age, the numerous long awns soon spreading; spikelets three at each node of the articulate rachis, one-flowered, the middle sessile and fertile, 0.10–0.25 in./3–6 mm long, the lateral pedicellate and abortive; glumes of perfect spikelets setaceus, scabrous, 1–2 in./2.5–5.0 cm long, finally spreading; lemmas of fertile spikelets 0.25–0.30 in./6–8 mm long, lanceolate, scabrous toward the apex, with scabrous awns 1–2 in./2.5–5.0 cm long or longer, the corresponding parts of the lateral spikelets similar but reduced, the lemmas about 0.15–0.25 in./4–6 mm long including the pedicel, sometimes much reduced, short-awned; palea of the middle spikelet awn-pointed, about as long as its lemma, obtuse, two-keeled, with two strong nerves near the margin, glabrous; caryopsis with hairy tips, adherent to the palea at maturity. The overall appearance of the spike is very hairy and fluffy; it breaks into segments, becoming windborne at maturity. Flowering and fruiting occur from June through mid-July, after which the spikes disarticulate at the base of the rachis segment and the caryopses are disseminated by the wind.
Uses: Foxtail barley is grown for its beautiful, soft, feathery flower heads, which arch gracefully, with long, hairy spikelets, particularly on the upper side of the arch. The long, almost straight, awns curl and twist in an interesting manner, depending upon the ambient humidity. The fluffy, silky spikes are decorative on the plants, as they produce an undulating, wavelike movement with the slightest breeze. The spikes are very decorative as green cut flowers. Foxtail barley adds diversity and attractiveness to the garden when interplanted among broad-leaved ornamentals in foreground borders. It flowers in late spring or early summer, and the flowering period is rather long, at least six weeks. Foxtail barley occurs naturally along roads and highways, where it adds to their attractiveness.
Cultivation: Propagation is by direct seeding in early spring. Foxtail barley thrives best in full sun on moist or dry, fertile, well-drained soils. Foxtail barley

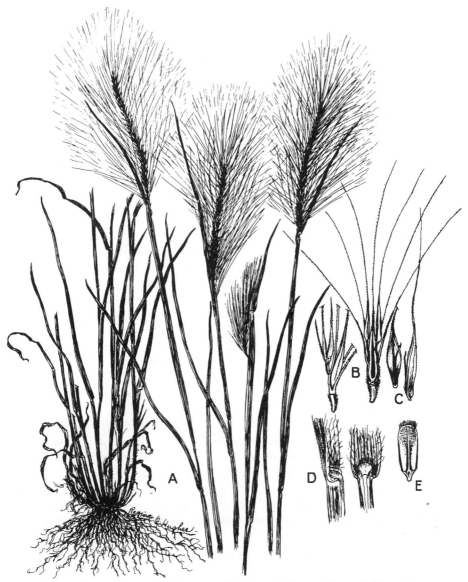

Hordeum jubatum. **A, Habit, × 1/2; B, spikelets, side and face views,
× 2 1/2; C, florets, × 2 1/2; D, ligules, × 2 1/2; E, caryopsis, × 5.**
Source: Selected Weeds of the United States. USDA Agric. Handbook 366. 1970.

will become weedy; the plants are subject to damage by strong wind and by heavy rain.

Latin name: *Hordeum vulgare* L.
Synonym: *Hordeum sativum* Pers.
Cultivars: Many in cultivation
Common names: Barley, Common barley, Nepal barley
Origin: Old World
Habitat: Cultivated, spontaneous from cultivation
Hardiness: Zones 4 through 9
Description: A short-lived, upright-narrow, tufted annual or winter annual. Culms erect, coarse, weak, smooth, 2–4 ft/0.6–1.2 m high. Foliage medium green, medium in texture; leaf blades flat, broad at the base, with prominent, long, glabrous auricles, pointed, 5–12 in./1.3–3.0 dm long, 0.3–0.5 in./8–13 mm wide, the lower surface scabrous; sheaths loose, round on the back, shorter than the internodes; ligule membranous, truncate, almost 1 mm long. Inflorescence an erect or arching, dense spike, 2–4 in./5–10 cm long, excluding the awns, about 1 in./25 mm in diameter, the rachis continuous, not disarticulating at maturity; spikelets alternately in threes at each node of the rachis, sessile, all perfect; glumes divergent at the base, narrow, nerveless, glabrous or pubescent, 0.2–0.3 in./5–8 mm long, with awns 0.3–0.4 in./8–10 mm long; lemmas fusiform, smooth, round on the back, five-nerved, narrowed into an erect, scabrous, straight awn 4–6 in./1.0–1.5 dm long, the rachilla extending into a short, hairy pedicel; palea about as long as its lemma; caryopsis hairy at the summit, usually adherent to the palea at maturity. Flowering and fruiting occur from June through July.

Uses: Barley is one of the oldest food crops of human civilization. Its ornamental value is its soft, hairy, erect or slightly arching, heavily awned seedheads. The long, erect, straight awns are the main attraction of the seedheads, which are useful as cut flowers, and particularly in dried arrangements. Barley lends attractiveness to middleground annual borders when established in clumps. The blunt, beardless spikes of beardless barley are particularly attractive when dry. The dried flower heads are useful in floral arrangements, either in their natural color or dyed.

Cultivation: Propagation is by direct seeding. Barley is widely adapted; it thrives on a wide range of soils, including slightly saline types. It thrives best on fertile, well-drained soils in full sun.

***Hystrix* Moench (Bottlebrush grass).** *Hustrix,* Greek name for "porcupine," referring to the bristly spikes. Type species, *Hystrix patula* Moench. There are four species, native to temperate regions of both hemispheres. Erect perennials, with flat leaf blades and bristly, loosely flowered spikes. Spikelets two-to-four-flowered, one to four at each node of a continuous, flattened rachis, horizontally

Hordeum vulgare. **Habit, × 1/2; group of spikelets and floret, × 3.**
Source: Manual of the Grasses of the United States. USDA Misc. Pub. 200. 1951.

spreading or ascending at maturity; glumes reduced to short or minute awns, the first usually obsolete, both often wanting in the upper spikelets; lemmas convex, rigid, tapering into long awns, five-nerved, the nerves obscure, except toward the tip; palea about as long as the body of the lemma.

Latin name: *Hystrix patula* Moench
Synonym: *Elymus hystrix* L.
Common name: Bottlebrush grass
Origin: North America
Habitat: Open woods, open grassland, cultivated
Hardiness: Zones 4 through 9
Description: A loosely tufted, upright-narrow to upright-open, rhizomatous perennial. Culms simple, slender, erect, rigid, 2–4 ft /0.6–1.2 m high, glabrous or scabrous or minutely retrorsely puberulent. Foliage medium green, fine to medium in texture; leaf blades flat, spreading, 4–8 in./1–2 dm long, 0.3–0.5 in./8–13mm wide, narrow at base becoming wider, scabrous or more or less pubescent above, the hairs inwardly appressed, scabrous beneath, rarely pubescent beneath, but the midrib frequently so; sheaths glabrous or scabrous, rarely retorsely pubescent; ligule membranous. Inflorescence a loosely flowered, barely exserted spike, 4–8 in./1–2 dm long, exclusive of the awns, 2–3 in./5–8 cm wide, erect at anthesis, often slightly nodding at maturity, rachis slender, flattened, internodes 0.2–0.4 in./5–10 mm long; spikelets bright pinkish, mostly borne in pairs on very short pedicels, 0.2–0.6 in./5–15 mm long, exclusive of the awns, two-to-four-flowered, easily detached, especially after maturity; glumes obsolete, usually reduced to short or minute awns, rarely as long as the spikelet, filiform, mostly glabrous; lemmas acuminate, lanceolate, rigid, 0.3–0.5 in./8–13 mm long, convolute, round on the back, five-nerved, the nerves obscure except toward the tip, usually pubescent at the summit or nearly glabrous, tapering into a long, slender, straight awn, 0.8–1.6 in./2–4 cm long; palea usually as long as the body of its lemma, indurate, deeply channeled, obtuse, usually glabrous, except toward the apex, sometimes more or less entirely scabrous; caryopsis oblong, pubescent at the summit, free within the lemma and palea. Flowering and fruiting occur from May through June.
Uses: Bottlebrush grass is considered attractive for its foliage and its flowering spikes. Its chief attraction is its unusual, stiff, long-awned, flowering spikes, which resemble a bottle brush. The flower heads, with their long-awned spikelets, are attractive and decorative in the garden and as cut flowers; they are also useful for drying, provided they are gathered early enough so as to prevent shattering. Bottlebrush grass is one of the best grasses for naturalizing shaded woodland sites, whether grown in groups or in massed stands on dry or moist soil.
Cultivation: Propagation is by seeding and by plant division. Direct seeding may be done where the plants are to grow; plant divisions should be made in the spring. The plants are adapted to a wide range of soils and prefer light,

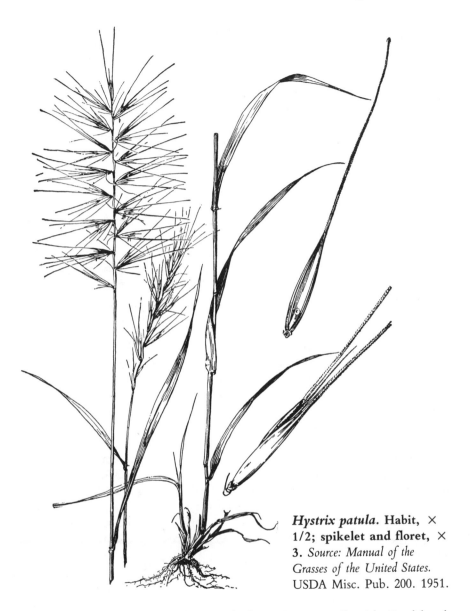

Hystrix patula. Habit, ×
1/2; **spikelet and floret,** ×
3. *Source: Manual of the
Grasses of the United States.*
USDA Misc. Pub. 200. 1951.

sunny sites; when grown in full sun the leaves become yellowish. Bottlebrush
grass, which reseeds itself readily, may be grown successfully in moist or dry
soil.

Imperata Cyrillo. Named for Ferrante Imperato, a Neapolitan apothecary and
naturalist of the sixteenth century. Type species, *Imperata arundinacea Cyrillo.*

There are five species, inhabiting nearly all tropical and subtropical regions. Slender, erect perennials from scaly rhizomes with narrow, woolly panicles. Spikelets all alike, awnless, in pairs, unequally pedicellate on a slender, continuous rachis, surrounded by long, silky hairs; glumes about equal, membranous; sterile lemma, fertile lemma, and palea thin and hyaline.

Latin name: *Imperata brasiliensis* Trin.
Synonym: *Imperata brasiliensis* var. *mexicana* Rupr.
Common name: Silver plume
Origin: Brazil
Habitat: Open grassland, pinelands, sand dunes
Hardiness: Zones 9 and 10
Description: A large, tufted perennial with long, scaly rhizomes. Culms simple, 2–4 ft/0.6–1.2 m high. Foliage medium green, fine in texture; leaves mostly basal, crowded below, leaf blades linear, flat, long attenuate, 4–8 in./ 1–2 dm long, 0.1–0.3 in./3–8 mm wide, the lower blades elongate, those of the culms shorter, the uppermost much reduced; sheaths usually glabrous; ligule membranous, about 2 mm long. Inflorescence a terminal, oblong, branched, rather lax panicle, pale or silvery, 4–6 in./1.0–1.5 dm long, 2–4 in./5–10 cm wide; spikelets awnless, all alike, 0.10–0.15 in./3–4 mm long with basal hairs twice as long, lanceolate at base, borne on a slender, continuous rachis; glumes about equal, membranous, about as long as the spikelets, lower glume five-to-nine-nerved, upper glume with three to six inconspicuous nerves; paleas usually scaly, nerveless; sterile lemma, fertile lemma and palea thin and hyaline; lodicules absent; caryopsis ellipsoidal, about 1 mm long, enclosed. Flowering and fruiting occur from May through August.

Uses: The ornamental value of silver plume is its terminal, silvery, plume-like panicles, which are attractive on the plants and suitable for dried arrangements. The terminal panicles are quite similar to those of *Miscanthus* species, differing in usually being somewhat smaller and narrower than those of *Miscanthus*. The economic value of silver plume is that of its use as an erosion-control plant and for stabilizing blowing sand and sand dunes. The plants are quite conspicuous by their silvery, plumelike inflorescences when grown in clumps as specimens.

Cultivation: Propagation is by seeding and by plant division, both of which should be done in the spring. Sections of rhizomes provide good planting rootstocks. The plants are not as invasive as those of cogongrass, *Imperata cylindrica,* and are often tufted. Despite their slow invasiveness, precautionary measures should be taken to contain the plants within their designated area. These measures usually include sunken barriers in the soil, similar to those used in containing other rhizomatous species. Silver plume grows well in soils varying from sands to heavy clays; it prefers full sun.

Latin name: *Imperata cylindrica* (L.) Beauv. 'Rubra'
Common name: Japanese bloodgrass

Imperata brasiliensis. **Habit,** × 1/2; **spikelet,** × 5. *Source: Manual of the Grasses of the United States.* USDA Misc. Pub. 200. 1951.

Origin: Japan
Habitat: Cultivated, escape from cultivation
Hardiness: Zones 7 through 9
Description and Uses: The upright-narrow culms of this exotic cultivar are 12–18 in./3.0–4.5 dm high; the foliage is shiny, medium red. Japanese blood-

grass prefers partial or light shade. The plants are most attractive when grown in groups, particularly when grown in large clumps or in pure, massed stands. The plants are ideal in foreground borders as accent plants, where their red foliage contrasts with the green foliage of other ornamentals.

***Koeleria* Pers.** Named for G. L. Koeler. Lectotype, *Koeleria nitida* Lam. There are 20 species, in temperate regions of the Northern and Southern Hemispheres. Slender, low or rather tall annuals or perennials, with narrow flat or rolled leaf blades and shining, usually contracted, dense, cylindrical, spikelike panicles. Spikelets two-to-four-flowered, compressed, the rachilla disarticulating above the glumes and between the florets, prolonged beyond the perfect florets as a slender bristle or bearing a reduced floret at the tip; glumes usually about equal in length, unlike in shape, the lower narrow, sometimes shorter, one-nerved, the upper wider than the lower, broadened above the middle, three-to-five-nerved; lemmas somewhat scarious, shining, the lowermost a little longer than the glume, obscurely five-nerved, acute or short-awned, the awn, if present, borne just below the apex.

Latin name: *Koeleria cristata* (L.) Pers.
Synonym: *Koeleria gracilis* Pers.
Common names: Junegrass, Koeler's grass, Prairie Junegrass
Origin: North America, Eurasia
Habitat: Cultivated, escape from cultivation
Hardiness: Zones 3 through 9
Description: A densely tufted, upright-narrow, semievergreen perennial, with numerous leafy sprouts at the base. Culms erect, slender, simple, densely short-pubescent below the panicle and usually below the nodes, leafy at the base, 1–2 ft /3–6 dm high, usually with a spread of 12–18 in./3.0–4.5 dm. Foliage light green, fine in texture; leaf blades flat or involute, setaceous, 2–8 in./0.5–2.0 dm long, 1–2 mm wide, long attenuate, the basal leaves somewhat longer, stiffly erect or ascending, usually scabrous and more or less puberulent, or nearly scabrous on the margins; sheaths much longer than the internodes, not overlapping above, pubescent or puberulent, at least the lower part with retrorse hairs; ligule membranous, fringed, about 1 mm long, truncate. Inflorescence an erect, subcylindric, spikelike, silvery white panicle, exserted, 2–6 in./0.5–1.5 dm long, 0.25–1.00 in./6–25 mm wide, branched, the branches ascending or spreading at anthesis, the lower branches 1–4 in./2.5–10.0 cm long, gradually shorter above, often interrupted at the base, the main axis and branches pubescent; spikelets 0.15–0.25 in./4–6 mm long, two-to-four-flowered, puberulent, pedicellate, densely clustered or compressed, glabrous or downy; glumes unequal, varying from shorter to longer than the florets, pointed or short-awned, scaberulous, at least on the keel, persistent, with membranous margins, lower shorter than the upper, narrowly oblong, one-nerved, upper oblong or elliptic-oblong, 0.15–0.20

Koeleria cristata. **Habit,** × 1/2; **glumes and floret,** × 10. *Source: Manual of the Grasses of the United States.* USDA Misc. Pub. 200. 1951.

in./4–5 mm long, three-to-five-nerved, scaberulous; lemmas pointed, 0.10–0.15 in./3–4 mm long, scabrous on the keel, a little longer than the glumes, obscurely three-to-five-nerved, acute, shining, short-awned just below the apex, margins scarious; palea two-keeled, hyaline, about as long as or shorter than its lemma; caryopsis about 0.1 in./3 mm long, closely enclosed within the lemma, free. Flowering and fruiting occur from June through September.

Uses: Junegrass and its cultivars are grown for their foliage. Large masses of flowers are attractive on the plants and as cut flowers, although they are of little value in dried arrangements. The plants are attractive and useful in foreground plantings in beds of mixed perennials and as specimen plants in rock gardens in shaded sites. The semievergreen foliage provides excellent fall color.

Cultivation: Propagation is by seeding and by plant division, preferably the latter. Junegrass grows best in full sun or light shade in many soil types varying from sands to heavy clays. The plants prefer neutral to slightly alkaline soils and will withstand some drought.

Lagurus **L. (Hare's-tail).** Name from Greek *lagos,* "hare," and *oura,* "tail," alluding to the woolly seedheads. A monotypic genus from the Mediterranean region.

> **Latin name:** *Lagurus ovatus* L.
> **Cultivars:** 'Nanus'
> **Common names:** Hare's-tail, Rabbit-tail grass
> **Origin:** Southern Europe
> **Habitat:** Cultivated, escape from cultivation
> **Hardiness:** Zones 3 through 8
> **Description:** A short-lived, upright-open, velvety annual. Culms solitary

or tufted, branching at the base, mostly erect or ascending, 8–24 in./2–6 dm high, long pubescent. Foliage greenish gray, fine in texture; leaves linear or narrowly lanceolate, arching, long attenuate, flat, densely hirsute; sheaths pubescent, round on the back, the hairy upper sheaths somewhat inflated; ligule membranous, blunt, puberulent, up to 0.1 in./3 mm long. Inflorescence a dense, blunt, short, spikelike panicle, 1–3 in./2.5–8.0 cm long, 0.5–1.0 in./13–25 mm in diameter, ovoid or oblong, feathery, woolly or softly hairy, bristly, with dark awns, erect, or at length nodding, ivory or whitish or occasionally tinged light purplish, branches very short, pedicels 2 mm long; spikelets densely imbricate, narrow, 0.25–0.50 in./6–13 mm long, one-flowered, breaking up at maturity above the glumes; glumes unequal, persistent, very narrow, about 0.5 in./13 mm long, each tapering into a fine bristle as long as the spikelet, membranous, one-nerved, hairy with fine, spreading, silky hairs; lemmas elliptic, round on the back, terminating in a straight bristle, awned from the back in the upper portion, the awn bent and twisted below the middle, 0.50–0.75 in./13–19 mm long, the awns of the lemmas much exceeding them; palea shorter than its

Lagurus ovatus. **Habit,** × 1/2; **spikelet and floret,** × 5. *Source: Manual of the Grasses of the United States.* USDA Misc. Pub. 200. 1951.

lemma, narrow, two-keeled; caryopsis enclosed. Flowering and fruiting occur from June through August.

Uses: The white, downy panicles of hare's-tail are strikingly beautiful and bristling, with long awns. The dense panicles are attractive on the plants and are most popular as cut flowers and in dried floral arrangements, either in their natural color or dyed. The flower heads are ideal in floral arrangements, as they are easily dyed and handled with minimum care. Hare's-tail is excellent in clumps as accent plants in foreground borders, in rock gardens, or as potted specimens; the inflorescence is unusual in size and shape. The plants thrive among taller plants in various densities of shade; its greatest drawback is its short life span.

Cultivation: Propagation is by seeding. Direct seeding may be done if the area is well marked. Hare's-tail prefers full sun or light shade on well-drained, fertile, moist or dry, sandy, or sandy-loam soils. The plants are most attractive when grown in small or large dense clumps.

Cultivars: *Lagurus ovatus* L. 'Nanus'   The cultivar Nanus is a very dwarf type of hare's-tail; the plants seldom exceed 6 in./1.5 dm in height. This small cultivar breeds true; its foliage is grayish green. It is best suited for foreground borders and rock gardens; its small size makes it suitable as a potted plant for the patio or indoors. This cultivar is adapted to zones 3–8.

Lamarckia **Moench.** Name in honor of Lamarck, the naturalist. A monotypic genus of the Mediterranean region and naturalized in the United States.

Latin name: *Lamarckia aurea* (L.) Moench
Synonym: *Cynosurus aureus* L.
Common names: Toothbrush grass, Goldentop
Origin: Mediterranean region
Habitat: Cultivated, escape from cultivation
Hardiness: Zones 8 through 10
Description: A loosely tufted, upright-open to spreading annual. Culms erect or decumbent at the base, 12–18 in./3.0–4.5 dm high. Foliage light to medium green, soft, fine in texture; leaf blades flat, 6 8 in./1.5–2.0 dm long, 0.1–0.3 in./3–8 mm wide, gradually tapering to a rather abrupt point, undulate, twisting, glabrous or sparsely pubescent on the upper surface; sheaths round on the back, glabrous, slightly inflated, about as long as the internodes. Inflorescence a densely branched, one-sided panicle, golden yellow to purple, shining, linear-oblong, 1–3 in./2.5–8.0 cm long, 0.4–0.8 in./10–20 mm wide, branches short, erect, capillary branchlets flexuous, silklike, pedicels fascicled, pubescent with a tuft of white hairs at the base; spikelets in fascicles, the terminal spikelet of each fascicle fertile, the others sterile, fertile spikelets up to 0.1 in./3 mm long exclusive of the awns, with one perfect floret, the rachilla prolonged beyond the floret, sterile spikelets linear, 0.2–0.3 in./5–8 mm long, one to three in each fascicle, consisting of two glumes similar to those of the fertile spikelets and

Lamarckia aurea. **Habit,** × 1/2, **fertile spikelet and floret,** × 5. *Source: Manual of the Grasses of the United States.* USDA Misc. Pub. 200. 1951.

numerous imbricate, obtuse, awnless, empty lemmas; the short-pedicellate spikelets are initially light greenish, becoming golden yellow or light purplish; they are usually oriented toward one side of the rachis, producing a unique pattern; glumes about equal, sparsely scabrous; fertile lemma up to 0.1 in./3 mm long, or 0.15 in./4 mm long, including the stipe about 1 mm long, the awn about twice the length of the lemma, the sterile lemma with an awn nearly as long as that of the fertile lemma. Flowering and fruiting occur from March through July.

Uses: Toothbrush grass is grown primarily for its yellowish green flowers, which become silvery with age, producing a beautiful, shimmering, golden effect. The erect silvery plumes are most effective in the garden and as fresh cut flowers. Shattering seedheads limit but do not prohibit its use in dried floral arrangements. Toothbrush grass is excellent in foreground annual borders.

Cultivation: Propagation is by seeding. Toothbrush grass is easily grown in full sun in any fertile, well-drained, moist soil. The possible presence of some sterile spikelets suggests that seeding be done heavier than usual to ensure good stands.

Lasiacis (Griseb.) Hitchc. Name from Greek *lasios*, "woolly," and *akis*, "point," referring to the tuft of wool at the tip of the caryopsis. Type species, *Lasiacis divaricata* (L.) Hitchc. There are about 30 species, native to the tropics and subtropics of the Western Hemisphere. Large, branching perennials with woolly culms, often clambering several meters high into shrubs and trees; mostly firm leaf blades narrowed into a minute petiole and open to slightly compact panicles. Spikelets subglobose, placed obliquely on their pedicels; lower glumes broad, somewhat inflated-ventricose, usually not more than one-third the length of the spikelet, several-nerved; upper glume and sterile lemma about equal, broad, abruptly apiculate, chartaceous, shining, many-nerved, glabrous, or lanose at the apex only, the lemma enclosing a membranous palea and sometimes a staminate flower; fertile lemma white, indurate, obovoid, obtuse, this and the palea of the same texture, bearing a tuft of woolly hairs in a slight depression at the apex, the palea concave below, gibbous above, the apex often free at maturity.

> **Latin name:** *Lasiacis divaricata* (L.) Hitchc.
> **Synonym:** *Panicum divaricatum* L.
> **Common names:** Canegrass, Tibisee
> **Origin:** North America
> **Habitat:** Along roadsides, around wooded borders
> **Hardiness:** Zone 10
> **Description:** A woolly, semievergreen, branched, climbing perennial.
Culms climbing, slender, much-branched, somewhat pendant, 3–4 ft /0.9–1.2 m long or longer, glabrous, the main culm strong, about 0.2 in./5 mm in

***Lasiacis divaricata.* Habit, × 1/2; spikelet and floret, × 10.** *Source: Manual of the Grasses of the United States.* USDA Misc. Pub. 200. 1951.

diameter at the base, the main branches often fascicled, the vigorous secondary sterile shoots usually strongly divaricate. Foliage medium green, medium in texture; leaf blades deciduous on the basal portion of the old, fertile branches, glabrous or slightly scabrous on the margins, narrowly lanceolate, 2–7 in./0.5–1.8 dm long, 0.2–0.6 in./5–15 mm wide, or much larger on the sterile shoots, narrowed at the base, long attenuate, scabrous on the margins and sometimes

y on both surfaces; sheaths at the basal portion of old fertile shoots persis-
hispid on the collar and margins; ligule inconspicuous. Inflorescence loosely
ched, terminal panicles on the main culm and fertile branches, ovate to
long, 2–8 in./0.5–2.0 dm long, loosely flowered, the branches distant, spread-
ng or often reflexed, the axis angled, scabrous, flexuous, the lower usually
1–2 in./2.5–5.0 cm long, or sometimes longer; spikelets pedicellate, ovoid,
0.15–0.20 in./4–5 mm long, green, becoming black at maturity; the lower
glume enclosing the spikelet; a tuft of woolly hairs at the apices of the glumes,
lemmas, and paleas. Flowering and fruiting occur from December through
February.

Uses: Canegrass is more of a curiosity than an ornamental. It is good in
naturalized areas along the edge of woods or in thickets, where the trailing
culms climb over brush and other obstacles. The uniqueness of the grass lies in
its fat, plump, more or less glabrous spikelets, with a tuft of wool at the tip of
the caryopsis, which resembles miniature Job's tears in shape. Canegrass is useful
as a sand- and soil-stabilization plant along the seacoast.

Cultivation: Propagation is by seeding and by plant division. The plants
grow in full sun or light shade in almost any soil with adequate moisture.

Leersia **Sw. (Cutgrass, Whitegrass).** Named for Johan Daniel Leers, a German botanist of the eighteenth century. Type species, *Leersia oryzoides* (L.) Sw.
There are about 10 species, native to the temperate and tropical regions of North
America and Eurasia. Usually perennials with creeping rhizomes, flat, scabrous
leaf blades, and mostly open panicles. Spikelets one-flowered, strongly compressed laterally, disarticulating from the pedicel; glumes wanting; lemmas chartaceous, broad, oblong to oval, boat-shaped, usually five-nerved, the lateral pair
of nerves close to the margins, these and the keel often hispid-ciliate, the intermediate nerves sometimes faint; palea as long as the lemma.

> **Latin name:** *Leersia oryzoides* (L.) Sw.
> **Synonym:** *Homalocenchrus oryzoides* (L.) Pollard
> **Common name:** Rice cutgrass
> **Origin:** Eurasia
> **Habitat:** In water and mud along streams, ponds, and ditches
> **Hardiness:** Zones 4 through 10
> **Description:** An aquatic, upright-narrow perennial with slender, creeping
rhizomes, branching at the base, forming colonies. Culms tufted, erect or ascending, mostly from a decumbent base, 2–5 ft /0.6–1.5 m high, terete, glabrous, the nodes pubescent, often rooting at the nodes; rhizomes narrow with
short internodes, about 1 in./25 mm long, barbed at the nodes, otherwise glabrous. Foliage medium green, medium in texture; leaf blades lanceolate, long
attenuate, 5–10 in./1.3–2.5 dm long, 0.3–0.6 in./8–15 mm wide, erect or ascending, strongly retrorsely scabrous; sheaths shorter than the internodes, round

Leersia oryzoides. Habit, × 1/2; spikelet, × 5. *Source: Manual of the Grasses of the United States.* USDA Misc. Pub. 200. 1951.

on the back, strongly retrorsely scabrous or hispid-pubescent between the nerves; ligule membranous, truncate, about 1 mm long. Inflorescence loosely branched, open terminal and axillary panicles, 5–8 in./1.3–2.0 dm long, 3–6 in./8–15 cm wide, pyramidal, axis scabrous, the lateral panicles included or slightly exserted, branches scabrous, single or whorled below, smooth at the base, 3–8 in./0.8–2.0 dm long, at first erect, finally spreading, the branchlets short, with stout, scabrous peduncles; spikelets dark green, one-flowered, flattened, 0.15–0.20 in./4–5 mm long, 1–2 mm wide, sparsely hispidulous, the keels bristly ciliate, those in open panicles perfect but usually sterile, those enclosed in sheaths cleistogamous; glumes absent; lemmas chartaceous, broad, awnless, oblong, about 0.2 in./5 mm long, usually five-nerved, the lateral pair of nerves close to the margins, these and the keel often ciliate, the intermediate nerves faint; palea slightly longer than the lemma, hispid-ciliate on the back, margins and keels with very small prickles toward the apex, one-nerved; caryopsis smooth, compressed, about 0.1 in./3 mm long, 1 mm wide. Flowering and fruiting occur from August until frost.

Uses: This swamp grass, along with other water plants, including many species of *Carex* and *Scirpus,* is useful in water gardens. Like cattails, rushes, and sedges, it is an excellent erosion-control plant and is useful in soil building. Rice cutgrass is compatible with other water plants in the swamp environment. Its gregarious growth habit and size render it favorably competitive with other water-loving plants. The carefully dried panicles are attractive in dried arrangements.

Cultivation: Propagation is by seeding and by plant division. The plants grow best in wet ground or in water in full sun or partial shade. No fertilization or maintenance is required once stands are established. Rice cutgrass is effective in large clumps or over extended areas either in mixed or pure stands.

Melica L. (Melic, Melicgrass). An Italian name for a kind of sorghum, probably from the sweet juice (*mel,* ''honey''). Lectotype, *Melica ciliata* L. There are about 60 species, native to temperate regions of the Northern and Southern Hemispheres. Rather tall perennials, the base of the culm often swollen into a corm, with closed sheaths, usually flat leaf blades, narrow or sometimes open, usually simple panicles of relatively large spikelets. Spikelets two-to-several-flowered, the rachilla disarticulating above the glumes and between the fertile florets, prolonged beyond the perfect florets and bearing two or three approximate, gradually smaller, empty lemmas, each enclosing the one above; glumes somewhat unequal, thin, chartaceous, scarious-margined, obtuse or acute, sometimes nearly as long as the lower floret, three-to-five-nerved, the nerves usually prominent; lemmas convex, several-nerved, membranous or rather firm, scarious-margined, awnless or sometimes awned from between the teeth of the bifid apex, the callus not bearded.

Latin name: *Melica altissima* L.
Cultivars: 'Atropurpurea' Purple melic
Common names: Siberian melic, Melicgrass, Melic
Origin: Eurasia
Habitat: Cultivated, escape from cultivation
Hardiness: Zones 5 through 7
Description: A loosely tufted, upright-open perennial. Culms stout, erect or sometimes decumbent, and swollen at the base, becoming erect, 30–36 in./ 7.6–9.0 dm high or more. Foliage medium green, fine in texture; leaf blades flat, glabrous on upper surface, hairy or pubescent beneath, the midvein prominent beneath, 6–12 in./1.5–3.0 cm long, 0.2–0.4 in./5–10 mm wide; sheaths tubular; ligule membranous. Inflorescence a branched, spikelike, loose panicle, narrow, dense, tawny to purplish, 6–8 in./1.5–2.0 dm long, 2–3 in./5–8 cm wide; spikelets two-to-five-flowered, 0.4–0.5 in./10–13 mm long, conspicuously creamy white to white, curled at first, later spreading, the rachilla disarticulating above the glumes and between the florets, prolonged beyond the perfect florets, bearing two or three empty lemmas; glumes unequal, thin, chartaceous, broad, obtuse or acute, sometimes nearly as long as the floret, three-to-five-nerved, nerves prominent; fertile lemma broad, chartaceous, convex, strongly several-nerved, margins scarious; palea shorter than its lemma; caryopsis free, smooth, 1–2 mm long. Flowering and fruiting occur from May through July.
Uses: Melicgrass is grown for its flowering panicles. This perennial adds diversity to mixed grass stands in naturalized areas. The tawny to purplish panicles are attractive in middleground perennial borders, provided a mass effect is achieved by growing the plants in clumps. The cultivar Atropurpurea is grown for its dark purple flowers; it is adapted to shaded sites in perennial middleground borders; the panicles of melicgrass and its cultivar are useful in dried flower arrangements. The attractive, dark purple flowers of 'Atropurpurea' are appealing when the plants are grown in massed stands in naturalized areas of open woodland or as a lawn substitute.
Cultivation: Propagation is by seeding and by plant division. The plants grow well in moist soil in full sun to medium shade. Melicgrass requires a constant supply of moisture to maximize its size and beauty. The stems are weak and may require the support of surrounding plants or by staking.
Cultivars: *Melica altissima* L. 'Atropurpurea' Purple melic   This cultivar is similar in size and growth habit to Siberian melic but with distinctive, deep purple flowers. It is grown primarily for its deep purple flowers and is adapted to zones 5–7.

Latin name: *Melica ciliata* L.
Common names: Hairy melic, Silky-spike melic
Origin: Europe
Habitat: Cultivated, escape from cultivation

Hardiness: Zones 6 through 8

Description: A loosely tufted, upright-open perennial. Culms erect, slender, 12–18 in./3.0–4.5 dm high. Foliage bluish green, fine in texture; leaf blades flat, folded or rolled, 8–12 in./2–3 dm long, 0.15–0.20 in./4–5 mm wide, pubescent, with a blunt tip; sheaths tubular, rolled; ligule usually lacerate. Inflorescence a branched, spikelike panicle, narrow, condensed, silky, tawny or bright brownish, branches narrowly erect at first, becoming spreading; spikelets pubescent or hairy, one- or two-flowered, about 0.15–0.20 in./4–5 mm long, whitish or purplish, usually the latter; glumes nearly equal, thin, chartaceous, broad, three-to-five-nerved; lemmas ovate-lanceolate, acute, with long, silky, whitish hairs in the lowest floret, convex, chartaceous, several-nerved; caryopsis smooth, 1–2 mm long, enclosed. Flowering and fruiting occur from May through June.

Uses: Hairy melic is grown primarily for its purplish flowers. It is useful in group plantings in foreground and middleground borders, as is Siberian melic, *Melica altissima.* Hairy melic thrives best in light shade.

Cultivation: Propagation is by seeding and by plant division. Fertile, moist soil with a high moisture-retention capacity is required, although the plants do grow in dry soil in full sun. The culms are weak and may require some kind of support.

Latin name: *Melica uniflora* Retz.
Cultivars: 'Variegata'
Common name: Wood melic
Habitat: Cultivated, escape from cultivation
Hardiness: Zones 5 through 7
Description: A loosely tufted, upright-arching perennial with creeping rhizomes, forming large clumps. Culms slender arching, erect to spreading, glabrous, 8–24 in./3–6 dm high. Foliage bright green, fine in texture; leaf blades flat, with pronounced midvein beneath, sparsely pubescent above, minutely rough beneath and on the margins, 4–8 in./1–2 dm long, 0.15–0.20 in./4–5 mm wide, long attenuate; sheaths tubular, glabrous or loosely hairy, with short, reflexed hairs, forming a slender bristle at the apex opposite the blade, the purplish basal sheaths imbricate; ligule membranous, short. Inflorescence a branched, loose panicle, erect or nodding, 4–8 in./1–2 dm long, 1–2 in./2.5–5.0 cm wide, branches glabrous below, spreading, bearing two to six pedicellate spikelets toward the tips, pedicels up to 0.15 in./4 mm long; spikelets oblong or gaping, 0.15–0.30 in./4–8 mm long, with one fertile floret and two or three sterile lemmas in a mass; florets brownish, falling together at maturity; glumes usually equal or nearly so, elliptic, five-nerved, round on the back, membranous, glabrous, purplish, the upper as long as the spikelet, lower elliptic, three-nerved; fertile lemma green, 0.15–0.25 in./4–6 mm long, round on the back, elliptic, blunt, glabrous, tough and rigid, seven-nerved; sterile lemma about 0.1 in./3 mm long; paleas with two tough keels, narrowly winged and sparsely pubes-

cent, about the length of the lemmas; caryopsis tightly enclosed, 0.10–0.15 in./ 3–4 mm long. Flowering and fruiting occur from May through July.

Uses: Wood melic produces a meadowlike effect when left unattended in open woodland, where it may be considered a lawn substitute. The cultivar Variegata is useful in brightening dark corners of the garden and is most effective when grown in clumps; it is used in much the same manner as wood melic.

Cultivation: Propagation is by seeding and by plant division. Wood melic and its cultivars are shade tolerant. The plants require fertile, moist, well-drained soil. The melic grasses reseed themselves readily and may require trimming and tidying once each growing season.

Cultivars: *Melica uniflora* Retz. 'Variegata' This cultivar has longitudinally striped green and cream leaves. This form is grown primarily for its variegated foliage, which makes it useful in accent and specimen plantings. The plants are about the size of wood melic.

Milium L. **(Milletgrass).** An old Latin name for millet, of uncertain significance. Lectotype, *Milium effusum* L. There are six species, native to Eurasia and North America. Moderately tall annual and perennial grasses, with flat leaf blades, open panicles, and usually pale spikelets. Spikelets one-flowered, disarticulating above the glumes; glumes equal, obtuse, membranous, round on the back; lemmas a little shorter than the glumes, obtuse, obscurely nerved, round on the back, dorsally compressed in fruit, becoming indurate, smooth and shining, the margins enclosing the palea.

Latin name: *Milium effusum* L.
Synonym: *Miliarium effusum* Moench
Cultivars: 'Aureum' Golden millet
Common names: Wood melic, Milletgrass
Origin: North America, Eurasia
Habitat: Cultivated, escape from cultivation
Hardiness: Zones 6 through 9
Description: A loosely tufted, upright-open perennial with rhizomes. Culms glabrous, somewhat succulent, slender, erect from a bent base, 18–36 in./4.5–9.0 dm high. Foliage bright, light, greenish yellow, medium in texture; leaf blades flat, lax, 10–12 in./2.5–3.0 dm long, 0.5–0.6 in./13–15 mm wide, long attenuate at base and tip, glabrous or slightly scabrous above, glabrous beneath, scabrous on the nerves and margins, somewhat undulate on the margins; sheaths glabrous, round on the back, shorter than the internodes; ligule membranous, erose, short, about 0.2 in./5 mm long. Inflorescence an erect to nodding, diffuse panicle, 8–15 in./2.0–3.8 dm long, 3–4 in./8–10 cm wide, somewhat drooping, the branches in pairs or fascicled, 2–4 in./5–10 cm long, widely spreading, remote; spikelets light green, elliptic to ovate, pointed or

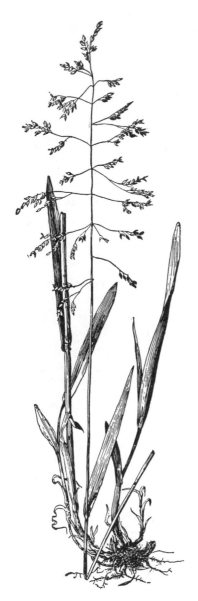

Milium effusum. **Habit,** ×
1/2. *Source: Manual of the
Grasses of the United States.*
USDA Misc. Pub. 200. 1951.

blunt, slightly compressed on the back, 0.10–0.15 in./3–4 mm long, three-nerved, one-flowered, scabrous; glumes ovate to elliptic, nearly equal, membranous, round on the back, persistent, greenish, up to 0.1 in./3 mm long, three-nerved, scaberulous throughout or only on the nerves, the upper narrower than the lower; lemmas and paleas glabrous, the lemmas imbricate, the paleas fertile lemma lanceolate to elliptic, pointed, as long as the glumes, shiny, indurated, the margins enrolled over a similar palea, obscurely nerved, round and compressed on the back, sterile lemma about 0.1 in./3 mm long, coriaceous; palea as long as the lemma and similar in texture; caryopsis acute, about 2 mm long, 1 mm wide, enclosed. Flowering and fruiting occur from May through June.

Uses: This shade-loving perennial and its cultivar are useful in many situations in the garden. Their light, shiny, greenish yellow leaves provide a good contrast to a darker background in shaded sites. These plants are useful in group plantings in less formal, wooded areas. Milletgrass and its cultivar Aureum also have a place in rock and water gardens. Like many ornamental grasses, they are most effective when grown in large clumps or in massed stands. The pale green flowers of milletgrass and the yellow flowers of golden millet contrast well with the darker green and variegated foliage of other ornamentals.

Cultivation: Propagation is by seeding and by plant division. The plants require a lightly shaded location in rich, moist soil high in humus. The plants reseed themselves readily. These are perennials, but they are most commonly grown as annuals. Although these grasses are rhizomatous, their invasiveness is negligible.

Cultivars: *Milium effusum* L. 'Aureum' Golden millet   Golden millet is noted for its yellow flowers and yellow foliage, which is occasionally greenish yellow. Foliage is medium in texture; the leaves are 0.4–0.5 in./10–15 mm wide. The plants are upright-open, about 2 ft /6 dm high, the branched, flowering panicles are 4–8 in./1–2 dm long, bright greenish yellow or yellow. Flowering and fruiting occur from June through July. Propagation is usually by plant division. The plants are quite shade tolerant and thrive best in fertile, moist soil. Their attractiveness is best exhibited in group plantings in foreground borders.

Miscanthus **Anderss.** Name from Greek *mischos,* "pedicel," and *anthos,* "flower," both spikelets of the pair pedicellate. Lectotype, *Miscanthus capensis* (Nees) Anderss. There are 20 species, native to eastern Asia. Robust, moderately tall perennials with long, flat leaf blades and terminal panicles of aggregate, spreading, slender racemes with fibrous or stout rhizomatous roots. Spikelets all alike, in pairs, unequally pedicellate along a slender, continuous rachis; glumes equal, membranous or somewhat coriaceous; sterile lemma a little shorter than the glumes, hyaline, fertile lemma hyaline, smaller than the sterile lemma, extending into a delicate, bent, and flexuous awn; palea small and hyaline.

Latin name: *Miscanthus sacchariflorus* (Maxim.) Hack.
Synonym: *Imperata sacchariflora* Maxim.
Cultivars: 'Aureus,' 'Dwarf,' 'Giganteus' Giant eulaliagrass, 'Robustus,' 'Variegatus'
Common names: Eulaliagrass, Amur silvergrass
Origin: China, Japan
Habitat: Cultivated

Hardiness: Zones 5 through 9

Description: A vigorous, densely tufted, upright-narrow to upright-open perennial with thick, horizontal rhizomes. Culms erect, stout, 4–7 ft /1.2–2.2 m high. Foliage olive green or medium green, coarse in texture; leaf blades 2–3 ft /6–9 dm long, 0.8–1.0 in./20–25 mm wide, arching, long attenuate, rough on both surfaces, with sharply appressed teeth along the margins, a markedly white midrib, especially conspicuous below; sheaths greenish to light brown, rigid, splitting early in the season, longer than the internodes; ligule membranous, short. Inflorescence a terminal, erect, more or less flabellate, branched, silky panicle, light green at first, becoming silvery white, 10–12 in./ 2.5–3.0 dm long, 3–4 in./8–10 cm wide when mature, racemes many, aggregate or more or less digitate; spikelets pedicellate, awnless, variable in color, whitish, purplish, reddish, or pinkish, surrounded at the base by copious soft hairs, about twice as long as the spikelet; glumes unequal, membranous, coriaceous; sterile lemmas hyaline, two-toothed, ciliate, shorter than the glumes, fertile lemmas smaller than the sterile lemmas, hyaline, awned with flexuous awn 0.2–0.3 in./ 5–8 mm long; palea hyaline, small. Flowering and fruiting occur from late August until frost.

Uses: This stately, tall ornamental and its cultivars are attractive throughout most of the year. The large, bold stature of the plants, with their arching foliage and late flowering, readily distinguishes them from many other ornamental grasses. Flowering occurs during late summer and early fall, which coincides with a paucity of flowers in the garden. Their colorful foliage persists and usually provides good fall color. Eulaliagrass remains erect throughout the winter, with its flowering plumes mostly intact. The flowering period of eulaliagrass and its cultivars usually coincides with that of silvergrass, *Miscanthus sinensis* var. *variegatus* and pampas grass, *Cortaderia selloana*. The flowering panicles are somewhat smaller in size and different in shape than those of silvergrass. Although they are conspicuously different in color, they also contrast with pampas grass in size, shape, and color. Eulaliagrass and pampas grass complement each other very effectively in plant form and size, especially when in full blossom. One acts as a perfect foil to the other—the large, mound-forming pampas grass with its large, whiter, flowering plumes forms an interesting contrast to the usually upright-narrow plant form of eulaliagrass, with its smaller, silky, light green to silvery, flowering panicles. Eulaliagrass and its cultivars Giganteus, Robustus, and Variegatus are used extensively as specimen plants in background perennial borders, rock and water gardens, lawns, and other appropriate sites, such as naturalized areas in addition to tall screens and windbreaks. Likewise, the smaller cultivar Aureus is used in a similar manner in middleground borders, rock and water gardens, medium screens and windbreaks.

Each cultivar provides good fall color, with the plants remaining erect and their flowering panicles intact into the winter. The basal leaves of these grasses become senescent during the summer and are unattractive. These forms are ideal for middleground and background borders for this reason. The upper portion of the plants usually towers above other ornamentals, with their elongated culms and large, flowering plumes. The large, towering plumes, especially in mixed stands, are often mistaken as arising from some other ornamental plants. The flower heads make excellent cut flowers and are also used in dried arrangements. The flower heads are excellent for drying and dyeing. The flower heads, which are used in their dried form, must be collected before they are mature because they tend to lose their individual flowers very rapidly upon drying.

Eulaliagrass may be used along with other grasses and ornamentals in naturalizing areas adjacent to the garden. The small cultivar Dwarf, with its slender, dark purple, trailing culms, makes an excellent pot plant for use either indoors or outdoors. The combination of attractive foliage and flowers of eulaliagrass and its variegated cultivars results in their use in botanical gardens, parks, and zoos.

Cultivation: Propagation is by seeding and by plant division, preferably the latter. Division of plants of known size, form, and color ensures the maintenance and use of desired types. The plants grow best in full sun but will tolerate light shade, although they may become weak and subject to wind damage. Almost any soil is adequate if it is moist and fertile; extra humus and moisture usually increases the vigor and size of the plants. The cultivars are adapted to the same plant-hardiness zones as that of the species. Eulaliagrass and its cultivars produce prodigious quantities of wind-blown seeds, thereby enabling the plants to profusely reseed themselves. The invasiveness of eulaliagrass is reduced by growing the plants in heavy, clay soils and by confining the roots in light, sandy soils. It is essential to provide sufficient space for these moderately large plants to fully show their maximum ornamental value. Considerable attention should be given to the location of these large plants in the garden, keeping in mind their form and size and how they fit into the landscape, as well as their compatibility with surrounding plants. Planting specimens near streams or pools in water gardens, where their image is reflected on the water at some time during the day, further enhances their beauty and value.

Cultivars: *Miscanthus sacchariflorus* (Maxim.) Hack. 'Aureus'   The plants of this cultivar are similar in all their parts to the species but differ from it in being less vigorous, smaller in size, and having different foliage color. The plants are 3–5 ft /0.9–1.5 m high; foliage is variegated, the leaves have longitudinal stripes of golden yellow and light green. This cultivar is adapted to zones 5–9.

Miscanthus sacchariflorus (Maxim.) Hack. 'Dwarf '   The culms of this cultivar are slender and trailing, becoming dark purple with age.

Miscanthus sacchariflorus (Maxim.) Hack. 'Giganteus' Giant eulaliagrass This giant cultivar is without rhizomes. The tufted plants are 9–12 ft /2.8–3.7 m high or higher; the foliage is medium green, coarse in texture. The upright, narrow plants are similar to the species in all their parts, although they are larger in size. Flowering and fruiting occur from September until frost. Giant eulaliagrass is adapted to zones 6–9.

Miscanthus sacchariflorus (Maxim.) Hack. 'Robustus'   The plants of this cultivar are 5–8 ft /1.5–2.5 m high; foliage is medium green, medium in texture. This cultivar is adapted to zones 5–9.

Miscanthus sacchariflorus (Maxim.) Hack. 'Variegatus' The plants are similar in all their parts to the species but slightly smaller (i.e., 3–6 ft /0.9–1.8 m high). The leaves are variegated longitudinally, with green-white stripes. This cultivar is adapted to zones 5–9.

Latin name: *Miscanthus sinensis* Anderss.

Synonym: *Saccharum japonicum* Thunb.

Cultivars: 'Autumn Light,' 'Herbstfeuer,' 'Natsubo,' 'November Sunset,' 'Purpurascens,' 'Silberfeder,' 'Strictus,' 'Univittatus,' 'Yaku Jima,' 'Yima Yuma'

Varieties: *Miscanthus sinensis* var. *condensatus* (Hack.) Mak.; *Miscanthus sinensis* var. *condensatus* (Hack.) Mak. 'Silberpfeil'; *Miscanthus sinensis* var. *gracillimus* Hitchc., Maidengrass; *Miscanthus sinensis* var. *variegatus* Beal, Silvergrass; *Miscanthus sinensis* var. *zebrinus* Beal, Zebragrass

Common names: Japanese silvergrass, Eulalia

Origin: China, Japan

Habitat: Cultivated, escape from cultivation

Hardiness: Zones 5 through 9

Description: A robust, upright-open, densely tufted perennial. Culms 5–8 ft /1.5–2.5 m or higher, glabrous, stout, with coarse, fibrous roots and numerous basal leaves. Foliage medium green, coarse in texture; leaf blades flat, arching, linear, 2–4 ft /0.6–1.2 m long, 0.8–1.0 in./20–25 mm wide, scabrous on the margins, hairy below, smooth above, margins almost parallel for most of the length of the leaf, long attenuate, with conspicuous, whitish midvein; sheaths longer than the internodes, bifid, rolled, splitting early in the season, somewhat flattened, ciliate; ligule long-haired, 1–2 mm long. Inflorescence a terminal flabellate, branched, pinkish, white or reddish panicle, wider at the top than at the bottom, 10–12 in./2.5–3.0 dm long, 4–8 in./1–2 dm wide, the racemes silky, aggregate, or more or less digitate in one whorl, many-flowered, 4–8 in./1–2 dm long, more or less ascending, becoming twisted, curled, and fluffy at maturity; spikelets in pairs, all alike, unequally pedicellate along a continuous rachis, 0.15–0.20 in./4–5 mm long, brownish yellow, shining, encircled at the base with white or purplish hairs, equaling or exceeding the spikelet; glumes equal, membranous or somewhat coriaceous, the lower flattened and obtuse, the upper keeled, acute, ciliate on the margins; sterile lemmas hyaline, two-toothed, ciliate, slightly shorter than the glumes, fertile lemmas hyaline, smaller than the sterile lemmas, extending into a bent and flexuous awn 0.3–0.4 in./8–10 mm long; palea small and hyaline. Flowering and fruiting occur from late August until frost.

Miscanthus sinensis Anderss common forms. There is considerable variation in plant size, shape, and foliage color among the various clones or forms of this species. Some forms are considerably larger than others and have broader leaves

Miscanthus sinensis. **Habit, much reduced; raceme,** × 1/2; **spikelet,** ×
5. *Source: Manual of the Grasses of the United States.* USDA Misc. Pub. 200. 1951.

and larger panicles. The culms of some forms are thin and tall, whereas those of other forms are short and stout. Another discernible difference among Japanese silvergrass forms is their flowering date and length of flowering period; some forms tend to flower earlier than others. The variation among forms of Japanese silvergrass provides the avid gardener a wide choice of materials with which to improve the landscape. Providing ample space around the planting reduces the frequency with which trimming becomes necessary to keep the plants under control. The culms near the center of the clump usually die out after the second or third year's growth. New plantings should be made every three to five years to avoid overcrowding or the loss of culms in established stands. The removal of the previous year's growth in the spring is a matter of choice. Old growth should be cut and removed before new growth begins in the spring, if for no other reason than to make the area more attractive. In marginal areas, where it is doubtful the plants will perenniate, the current year's growth should be removed in the fall and the plants heavily mulched. Another way of preserving rootstocks involves digging the rootstocks in the fall and storing them in pots inside during the winter in a cool, dark space or putting them in the greenhouse, to overwinter. All forms and varieties of Japanese silvergrass are heavy seeders; their wind-blown seeds enable the plants to reseed themselves readily, especially in warm climates. There is little difference, if any, in winter hardiness among varieties or forms of Japanese silvergrass. Some sources indicate that there are significant differences in winter hardiness among varieties and forms and classify *Miscanthus* as a weak perennial. All of the types included in this work have perenniated over a period of years in zones 6 and 7. Japanese silvergrass and its various forms are perhaps uncommon, but they are used as ornamentals in zones 5 and 6, where they may be maintained, provided ameliorating practices are followed. These practices include mulching the plants in the fall or moving them indoors during the winter; plants that are heavily mulched will usually survive. Also, during winter, a constant snow cover has a warming effect in protecting the plants. Japanese silvergrass and all its variants grow best in full sun in a wide range of soils in moist to wet sites. The plants are easy to propagate and grow. All types produce prodigious quantities of wind-blown seeds and easily reseed themselves.

Uses: The varieties and cultivars of Japanese silvergrass are very popular among gardeners, particularly those interested in ornamental grasses. Generally they are attractive throughout the growing season and their ornamental value extends into the fall and winter seasons. They are adaptable to multifarious use— for example, as fresh cut flowers, in dried arrangements, as specimens, accent plants, medium or tall screens, as windbreaks, and as middleground and background borders, providing good fall color, in rock and water gardens and naturalized areas. They provide good autumnal color, with their colorful foliage and flowering panicles. The cultivars are sufficiently distinctive from one another, and each has its special niche in the landscape design. They may be used separately in conjunction with other grasses and broad-leaved ornamentals, or they are perhaps even more dramatic when used collectively where they complement one another. Plant size and foliage and flower color are often used in selecting cultivars for use in specific situations. The same cultivar may be used in more than one way, in some instances. These grasses may be grown as potted plants on patios and porches, in atriums, around swimming pools, and in greenhouses; they are usually too large for indoor potted plants. The ragged panicles remain on the plants during the winter; the foliage turns variable colors following frost and provides good fall color, thus extending the attractiveness of the plants. The botanical variety *condensatus* and the cultivars Natsubo, Silberfeder, Strictus, and Univittatus are all used in specimen plantings. The flowering panicles of Japanese silvergrass and its various forms are useful in fresh and dried arrangements. Green, immature panicles remaining after the first killing frost may be cut and placed in a warm room, where they will continue to mature and fluff out for use in dried arrangements.

Cultivation: Propagation of Japanese silvergrass and its varieties is by seeding and by plant division. It is preferable to propagate these grasses by plant division, as this ensures continuity of the plant type desired. Propagation by seeding could result in a multitude of plant types, none of which may be desired. Japanese silvergrass is easy to propagate and grow successfully. The plants are adaptable to a wide range of soil types but require ample fertility and moisture for maximum growth; they prefer full sun but will tolerate light or partial shade in wet sites. Plants grown in shade tend to become weak and susceptible to wind damage, thus requiring some sort of staking for support or that provided by surrounding plants. These moderately large grasses tend to dominate the landscape in which they are located. For this reason, great consideration and care should be taken in choosing their location in the garden or landscape. The clumps increase in diameter when allowed to perenniate and may require trimming or thinning to be kept under control. Regardless of the planting site or situation, ample space should be provided around the plants so their total ornamental value may be realized and appreciated.

Cultivars: *Miscanthus sinensis* Anderss. 'Purpurascens' A tufted, upright-open perennial. Culms 3–4 ft /0.9–1.2 m high. Foliage medium in texture, reddish green. Inflorescence a terminal, tightly branched panicle. This cultivar prefers full sun on moist, fertile soil. It is useful in smaller gardens in group and specimen plantings. It is grown primarily for its unique foliage color and flowering panicles. This cultivar usually blossoms earlier than other forms and is adapted to zones 7–9.

Miscanthus sinensis Anderss. 'Silberfeder' An outstanding variation of the species. The erect, upright-narrow, closely tufted plants are 6–9 ft / 1.8–2.8 m high, with slender culms. Foliage is metallic bluish green and medium in texture; the leaves are gracefully arched with a conspicuous midvein. The loosely branched, terminal, many-flowered panicle is silvery shiny green at first, becoming dull whitish at maturity. This garden cultivar is distinctly different from other forms and in many ways is superior in ornamental value; it is grown primarily as a specimen plant but appears occasionally in background borders. This cultivar is adapted to zones 6–9.

Miscanthus sinensis Anderss. 'Strictus' This cultivar should be considered a miniature version of zebragrass. It is narrower and smaller than zebragrass but has the same variegated foliage. The plants are 4–8 ft /1.2–2.5 m high. This cultivar is useful in smaller gardens, where zebragrass is unsuited because of its excessive size. This cultivar makes an ideal specimen plant; it is adapted to zones 6–9.

Miscanthus sinensis Anderss. 'Univittatus' This cultivar is essentially a variegated form of Japanese silvergrass. Its size, growth habit, graceful, arching, filiform foliage, and flower color are quite similar to those of Japanese silvergrass. The foliage differs from that of maidengrass in that the leaves have a broad, yellow, median stripe; the plants are 5–6 ft /1.5–1.8 m high. The foliage produces good autumnal color.

Varieties: *Miscanthus sinensis* var. *condensatus* (Hack.) Mak. This variety differs from the species in having shorter culms and broader leaves than the species. The plants are 6–8 ft /1.8–2.5 m high, with purple flowers and leaves up to 3 in./8 cm wide. It is grown as a specimen plant in zones 6–9.

The botanical varieties *gracillimus, variegatus,* and *zebrinus* are most popular among gardeners; however, other new garden forms have been developed and are now available.

Miscanthus sinensis var. *gracillimus* Hitchc. Maidengrass A densely tufted, upright-open perennial. Culms erect, glabrous, stout, stiff, 5–7 ft /1.5–2.2 m high, with fibrous roots. Foliage dark green, fine in texture; leaf blades glabrous, scabrous on the margins, flat, arching, 2–3 ft /6–9 dm long, up to 0.1 in./3

Right, Miscanthus sinensis var. gracillimus; left, Miscanthus sinensis var. variegatus.

mm wide, long attenuate, with a conspicuous white midrib; sheaths longer than the internodes, rigid, rolled, splitting early in the season; ligule short, long-haired. Inflorescence an erect, bright, shiny, reddish, branched panicle 4–8 in./ 1–2 dm long, about two-thirds as wide, racemes many, aggregate or more or less digitate in one whorl, silky, becoming curled, twisted, and fluffy at maturity, 3–4 in./8–10 cm long; unequal pedicellate spikelets about 0.10–0.15 in./3–4 mm long, silky, with a tuft of reddish or light hairs at the base, the hairs about as long as the glumes; glumes equal, membranous or somewhat coriaceous, 2–3 mm long; sterile lemmas shorter than the glumes, hyaline, fertile lemmas hyaline, extending into a bent, flexuous awn about 0.3–0.4 in./8–10 mm long; palea small and hyaline. Flowering and fruiting usually occur from September until frost. Maidengrass is adapted to zones 6–9.

Maidengrass is unique among ornamental grasses in its outstanding stately appearance, architectural quality, and colorful foliage and flowers. Its overall attractiveness and beauty provide maidengrass a high priority for use in improving the landscape. The foliage is fine in texture; the rich, dark green foliage remains green down to ground level throughout the growing season. The crowning beauty of maidengrass is its large, graceful, curved, fluffy panicles bearing shiny, velvety spikelets that retain their color and sheen into fall. The filiform foliage usually turns beige following frost, and the plants provide a strikingly interesting spectacle throughout the fall season. The size of maidengrass makes it useful in middleground or background borders and in accent and specimen plantings.

Miscanthus sinensis and all of its variants, including maidengrass, are often used in parks and zoos, around public buildings, and along streets, canals, and highways, including median strips and around rest areas. It is useful in tall screens and windbreaks; the plants form an almost impenetrable dark green wall when planted close together in a row. The flower heads are used in both fresh and dried arrangements. The flowering racemes curl, twist, and become fluffy, forming interesting shapes and designs, and the flowers become lighter in color upon drying, thus providing additional interest in dried arrangements. The curled and twisted filiform leaves also make interesting dried arrangements or contributions to them. Specimen plantings in clumps in rock and water gardens or around patios and swimming pools are outstanding. Specimen plantings in water gardens should be located where the plant's beauty is enhanced by its reflection on the water for some period during the day. Maidengrass is an attractive addition to the landscape, even in areas where the short growing season prevents flowering. Maidengrass stands very high among large ornamental grasses and deserves to be used wherever possible.

Miscanthus sinensis var. *variegatus* Beal, Silvergrass A densely tufted, upright-open perennial. Culms erect, slender or stout, 5–8 ft /1.5–2.5 m high. Foliage variegated, coarse in texture; leaf blades flat, arching, long attenuate, 2–3 ft /6–9 dm long, 0.75–0.80 in./19–20 mm wide, more or less glabrous but scabrous on the margins, the margins parallel for most of the length of the leaf,

Miscanthus sinensis var. variegatus.

with a conspicuous whitish midvein on the lower surface and longitudinal green and yellow alternate stripes, the yellow median stripes usually broader; some forms have leaves with a narrow midrib, broad green stripes, and narrow yellow bands on the margins; sheaths longer than the internodes, stiff, rolled, splitting early in the season. Inflorescence an erect, flabellate, tightly branched panicle,

10–12 in./2.5–3.0 dm long, 4–8 in./1–2 dm wide, pinkish, tinged with yellow upon emergence, becoming lighter in color or more or less beige at maturity, the many-flowered, silky racemes are aggregate or more or less digitate in one whorl, 4–8 in./1–2 dm long, more or less ascending, becoming curled, twisted, and fluffy at maturity; spikelets unequal, pedicellate, with a dense tuft of whitish hairs surrounding the base, the hairs about as long as the glumes; glumes membranous or somewhat coriaceous, 0.15–0.20 in./4–5 mm long; sterile lemmas hyaline, shorter than the glumes, fertile lemmas hyaline, with a bent, flexuous awn about 0.3–0.5 in./8–13 mm long; palea small, hyaline. Flowering and fruiting occur from September until frost.

The variegated foliage, with longitudinal yellow or golden stripes, is the outstanding characteristic of silvergrass. The plants are usually slightly higher than maidengrass; they offer a contrast in color when planted in background borders behind other green-leaved ornamentals or when interplanted with them. Silvergrass is used in much the same manner as are the other varieties of Japanese silvergrass. Large clumps in specimen plantings in open spaces such as lawns are very distinctive, appealling, and impressive. Silvergrass is among the largest of variegated grasses. Although its variegated foliage is not as distinctive as that of some other variegated grasses, it retains its color throughout the growing season. The plant size, foliage, and flower color and longevity of attractiveness warrant serious consideration for using silvergrass in landscape improvement wherever possible.

Miscanthus sinensis var. *zebrinus* Beal Zebragrass   A densely tufted, upright-open perennial. Culms erect, stout, in large clumps, nodes barbed, 5–9 ft /1.5–2.8 m high. Foliage variegated, coarse in texture; leaves linear, crowded near the base, arching, long attenuate, the margins more or less parallel for most of the leaf length, 2–3 ft /6–9 dm long, 0.75–0.80 in./19–20 mm wide, flat, becoming revolute upon drying, margins very rough, papillose toward the base, the upper surface and sometimes the lower hirsute at the base with appressed hairs, leaf blades with a conspicuous midrib and broad, yellow, horizontal stripes or blotches 3–4 in./8–10 cm apart along the blade; sheaths longer than the internodes, sparsely hairy at the base, stiff, rolled, splitting early; ligules membranous, ciliate, about 1–2 mm long. Inflorescence a flabellate, tightly branched panicle, 10–15 in./2.5–3.8 dm long, 4–8 in./1–2 dm wide, pinkish upon emergence, becoming lighter or usually tawny at maturity, numerous silky racemes, commonly in whorls of three or four, distant, about 4–8 in./1–2 dm long, sometimes branching, the divergent spikelets alternate on a slender, scabrous, continuous rachis, one pedicel of the pair about 1–2 mm long, the other 0.15–0.20 in./4–5 mm long, the silky racemes become curled, twisted, and fluffy at maturity; spikelets all perfect, in pairs, pedicellate, with a dense tuft of hairs at the base about as long as the spikelet, narrowly lanceolate, 0.10–0.15 in./3–4 mm long; glumes almost equal, 2–3 mm long, the lower flattened, obtuse, slightly scabrous toward the apex, the upper keeled, acute, scabrous on the midnerve, ciliate on the margins; sterile lemmas shorter than the glumes, hya-

Miscanthus sinensis var. zebrinus.

line, two-toothed, ciliate, fertile lemmas hyaline, about equal to the sterile lemma, ciliate, deeply bifid with a twisted geniculate awn 0.25–0.30 in./6–8 mm long; palea hyaline, small. Flowering and fruiting occur from September until frost, with the twisted panicles persisting. Zebragrass is adapted to zones 6–9.

Table 1.5 Additional Ornamental Species, Varieties, and Cultivars of *Miscanthus*

Species	Plant Height (ft/m)	Hardiness Zones
M. floridulus	6–9/1.8–2.8	6–9
M. oliogstachys	3–4/0.9–1.2	6–9
M. sinensis 'Autumn Light'	6–9/1.8–2.8	4–9
M. sinensis 'Herbstfeuer'	3–4/0.9–1.2	6–9
M. sinensis 'November Sunset'	6–8/1.8–2.5	4–9
M. sinensis 'Univittatus'	5–6/1.5–1.8	6–9
M. sinensis 'Yaku Jima'	3–4/0.9–1.2	6–9
M. sinensis 'Yima Yuma'	3–4/0.9–1.2	6–9
M. sinensis var. condensatus 'Silberfeil'	5–7/1.5–2.2	7–9
M. transmoorisonensis	3–4/0.9–1.2	7–9

The horizontal-striped foliage makes zebragrass unique among ornamental grasses. The golden, horizontal stripes on a medium or light yellowish green background are a curiosity. This variety is slightly higher than silvergrass, although in some situations there may be no discernible size difference between it and other varieties of Japanese silvergrass. This cultivar is used in the same manner as maidengrass and silvergrass.

The additional *Miscanthus* species, varieties, and cultivars in Table 1.5 are all best adapted to full sun in moist or wet soil. They are used as screens or windbreaks, but primarily as specimen plants in borders, in open spaces, and in rock and water gardens. They are noted primarily for their flowering plumes, which are used in fresh and dried arrangements. The foliage of some forms is attractive, and some types produce good autumnal color (e.g., *Miscanthus sinensis* 'Herbstfeuer').

Molinia C. Gay. **(Moorgrass).** Named for J. I. Molina, an early student of the Chilean flora. Type species, *Molinia chilensis* C. Gay. There are five species, native to Eurasia. Slender, tufted perennials, with flat leaf blades and narrow, rather open panicles. Spikelets two-to-four-flowered, the florets distant, the rachilla disarticulating above the glumes, slender, prolonged beyond the upper floret and bearing a rudimentary floret; glumes somewhat unequal, acute, shorter than the first lemma, one-nerved; lemmas membranous narrowed to an obtuse point, three-nerved; palea bowed out below, equaling or slightly exceeding the lemma.

Latin name: *Molinia caerulea* (L.) Moench
Synonym: *Aira caerulea* L.

***Molinia caerulea*. Habit, × 1/2; spikelet and floret, × 5.** *Source: Manual of the Grasses of the United States.* USDA Misc. Pub. 200. 1951.

Cultivars and varieties: Several in cultivation (Table 1.6)
Common names: Purple moorgrass, Moorgrass
Habitat: Cultivated, escape from cultivation
Hardiness: Zones 4 through 8
Description: A densely tufted, upright-arching, mound-forming perennial. Culms 20–36 in./5–9 dm high, slender, sometimes stout, stiff and wiry, glabrous, the basal internode somewhat swollen. Foliage medium green, fine in texture; leaf blades erect, long attenuate, 4–18 in./1.0–4.5 dm long, 0.2–0.4 in./5–10 mm wide, slightly pubescent on upper surface and on the margins, rarely glabrous, falling from sheaths in early winter; sheaths glabrous, hairy at the summit, round on the back, longer than the internodes; ligule a fringe of short, white hairs. Inflorescence a variable dense or loose, branched panicle, variable in color, tawny, brownish, yellowish, but usually light to dark purple, 4–8 in./1–2 dm long, about one-half as wide, branches mostly floriferous or bare, glabrous or minutely rough; spikelets short-pedicellate, loosely one-to-four-flowered, lanceolate to oblong, 0.15–0.30 in./4–8 mm long, breaking beneath each lemma at maturity; glumes somewhat unequal, membranous, lanceolate or oblong, shorter than the lemmas; lower sometimes one-nerved, up to 0.1 in./3 mm long, upper one-to-three-nerved, 0.10–0.15 in./3–4 mm long; lemmas membranous, widely spaced, pointed or blunt, lanceolate or oblong, round on the back, three-nerved, firm, glabrous, about 0.1 in./3 mm long; palea with rough keels, about as long as the lemma, caryopsis enclosed. Flowering and fruiting occur from July through September.

Uses: Purple moorgrass is useful as a ground cover in low moist or wet sites, in middleground borders, and in specimen plantings, where it forms a distinctive addition to the landscape. It is grown primarily for its graceful plant form and purple-flowering panicles. The cultivar Variegata, with its variegated leaves striped green and cream, is grown for its variegated foliage and its flowering panicles. It is useful when planted in groups in conjunction with spring-flowering bulbs, as the plants come into flower after the spring bulbs have flowered. Purple moorgrass and some of its variants, including the cultivar Variegata are occasionally grown as potted specimens indoors. These grasses are popular among gardeners and are widely used; they provide good autumnal color.

Cultivation: Propagation is by seeding and by plant division, preferably the latter. Propagation may be done in the fall or spring. The plants prefer fertile acid to neutral soil in sunny moist or wet areas; they will not tolerate alkaline soils.

Cultivars: *Molinia caerulea* (L.) Moench 'Variegata' An upright to arching, variegated perennial. The plants are generally smaller than those of the type species (i.e., 18–24 in./4.5–6.0 dm high). The leaves are longitudinally variably striped greenish white or creamy white; the degree of variegation is somewhat

Table 1.6   Additional Cultivars of *Molinia caerulea*

Cultivar	Plant Height (ft/m)
M. caerulea 'Bergfreund'	5–6/1.5–1.8
M. caerulea 'Heidebraut'	2–3/0.6–0.9
M. caerulea 'Karl Foerster'	6–7/1.8–2.1
M. caerulea 'Moorhexe'	2–3/0.6–0.9
M. caerulea 'Strahlenquelle'	2–3/0.6–0.9
M. caerulea 'Skyracer'	7–8/2.1–2.4
M. caerulea 'Staefa'	5–6/1.5–1.8
M. caerulea 'Transparent'	5–6/1.5–1.8
M. caerulea 'Windspiel'	7–8/2.1–2.4

variable among individual plants. The flowering panicles are purple tinted. Flowering and fruiting occur from August through September, as for purple moorgrass and its other cultivars. This cultivar is adapted to shaded sites in zones 5 through 8.

***Oplismenus* Beauv.** Name from Greek *hoplismenos,* ''armed,'' alluding to the armed spikelets. Type species, *Oplismenus africans* Beauv. There are 20 species, native to the tropics and subtropics of both hemispheres. Creeping, freely branching, shade-loving annuals and perennials, with erect, flowering shoots, flat, thin, lanceolate or ovate leaf blades, and several one-sided, thick, short racemes rather distant on a slender axis. Spikelets terete or laterally compressed, subsessile, solitary or in pairs, in two rows crowded or approximate on one side of a narrow scabrous or hairy rachis; glumes about equal, entire or emarginate, awned from the apex or from between the lobes; sterile lemma exceeding the glumes and caryopsis, notched or entire, mucronate or short-awned, enclosing a hyaline palea; fertile lemma elliptic, acute, convex or cymbiform, the firm margins clasping the palea, not enrolled.

Latin name: *Oplismenus hirtellus* (L.) Beauv.
Synonym: *Panicum hirtellum* L.
Cultivars: 'Vittatus'
Common name: Basketgrass
Origin: Tropical America
Habitat: Cultivated, escape from cultivation
Hardiness: Zone 10
Description: An open, spreading, slender, stoloniferous, evergreen perennial. Culms slender, prostrate, creeping, rooting and freely branching from the

nodes, sometimes producing long, aerial roots from the nodes, highly variable in length, 0.2–0.3 in./5–8 mm in diameter, the flowering branches usually erect, simple, 12–18 in./3.0–4.5 dm long. Foliage medium to dark green, medium to coarse in texture; leaves sessile, borne on alternate sides of the stem; leaf blades usually inconspicuously hairy, rarely glabrous, thin, soft, lanceolate, 1–3 in./2.5–8.0 cm long, 0.4–0.8 in./0–20 mm wide, usually narrower, with small auricles; sheaths rather loose, round on the back, imbricate, slightly purplish at the base, glabrous to papillose-hispid; ligule a fringed scale. Inflorescence three to seven rather distant, one-sided racemes comprising a spikelike, short-branched panicle, 2–5 in./0.5–1.3 dm long, about 1–2 in./2.5–5.0 cm wide; racemes divergent, usually ascending and distant on a slender, central axis, dense, spike-like, the rachis fringed with tubular-based hairs; spikelets 0.10–0.15 in./3–4 mm long excluding the awns, more or less sessile or short-pedicellate, two-flowered, with a ring of short hairs at the base, green or purplish; glumes about equal, both shorter than the spikelet, hairy near the margins, the lower glume five-nerved, middle nerve excurrent into a stiff, viscid, purplish awn, 0.4–0.6 in./10–15 mm long, upper glume five-to-seven-nerved, middle nerve extended into an awn 0.10–0.25 in./3–6 mm long; sterile lemma hispiduous, several-nerved, about as long as the spikelet, mucronate or short-awned, fertile lemma thin, acute, lanceolate, the lateral margin revolute, enclosing the palea; palea membranous, shorter than the lemma; lower floret usually sterile, rarely staminate, with a narrow, reduced palea, the lemma 7-to-11-nerved, middle nerve excurrent into a short awn from the minutely two-lobed apex, upper floret bisexual, acute or minutely awned, indurate, glossy, glabrous. Flowering and fruiting occur sporadically throughout the year.

Uses: The variegated cultivar Vittatus or basketgrass is popular as a house-plant. It is usually grown in hanging baskets, where the stems, with their variegated colorful foliage, are allowed to cascade over the edges, producing a colorful, pleasing effect. Both basketgrass and its variegated cultivar are used in wet, shaded sites in the garden, where they form a complete ground cover; both forms thrive in wet sites in medium to deep shade. These trailing plants are also grown in pots, although they are most colorful and attractive when grown in hanging baskets. Basketgrass and its cultivar require high humidity and a temperature above 60°F/15°C for best results when grown indoors. They are ideal plants for shaded locations under greenhouse benches, where the humidity is relatively high and the temperature remains above 60°F/15°C.

Cultivation: Propagation is by planting portions of the prostrate culms and by rooted cuttings. When grown indoors, the plants require a constant moisture supply in the growing medium, warmth, and very high humidity; outdoor plantings in warm climates should be established in wet, shaded sites. Basketgrass and its cultivar may be grown outdoors in the warmer parts of zone 10. A water-soluble or slow-release fertilizer should be used on indoor plantings; moderate light intensity is adequate, although high-intensity light will probably result in better growth and more attractive plants. Normal room temperatures are suitable, although the plants will tolerate temperatures down to about 55°F/ 13°C. Water plentifully to keep the potting mixture thoroughly moist during periods of active growth; when the plants are in a rest period, water them only enough to prevent the mixture from drying out completely.

Cultivars: *Oplismenus hirtellus* (L.) Beauv. 'Vittatus'   This stoloniferous, semievergreen, variegated cultivar has leaves with longitudinal stripes of green and pink, dull white, or light purplish. The foliage is medium in texture. The plants are about the same size as basketgrass; they are low, open, and spreading.

Latin name: *Oplismenus setarius* (Lam.) Roem. & Schult.
Common name: Woodgrass
Origin: Tropical America
Habitat: Cultivated, escape from cultivation
Hardiness: Zones 8 through 10
Description: An open, spreading perennial. Culms ascending from a prostrate base, rooting at the nodes, nodes pubescent, otherwise glabrous, fertile culms erect, 4–12 in./1–3 dm high. Foliage soft, medium green, fine in texture; leaf blades glabrous, ovate to ovate-lanceolate, flat, abruptly narrowed at the base, thin, rough, sparsely pilose or glabrous, 1.0–1.6 in./2.5–4.0 cm long, 0.15–0.40 in./4–10 mm wide, margins conspicuously undulated; sheaths about as long as the internodes, villous along the margins, pubescent near the collar; ligule a very short, ciliate membrane about 1 mm long. Inflorescence racemose, a long-exserted panicle, 1–3 in./2.5–8.0 cm long, scabrous or puberulent, the racemes usually three to five, the rachis short, 0.1–0.2 in./3–5 mm long, pubescent or villous at the base; spikelets solitary or in pairs, pedicellate, pedicels short, usually three to nine per raceme, lower spikelet often abortive, rachis 2–3 mm long, bearing three to five spikelets; spikelets pubescent at the base, up to 0.1 in./3 mm long; glumes about equal, about two-thirds as long as the spikelets, each bearing a short, blunt awn, the upper only slightly longer, pubescent or glabrous, scabrous on the midnerve, ovate, five-nerved, the awn slightly shorter than the glume, the lower lanceolate, one-to-three-nerved, the awn 0.2– 0.4 in./5–10 mm long; sterile lemma broadly oval, up to 0.1 in./3 mm long, pubescent, the awn similar to those of the glumes, about 1 mm long, usually ascending; palea membranous, shorter than the lemma; caryopsis more or less ovate, shining, 1–2 mm long, less than 1 mm wide. Flowering and fruiting occur from July through September.

Uses: Woodgrass is usually grown in pots or hanging baskets in colder climates; the soil should be kept moist at all times, with high humidity and moderate to high light intensity for best growth. The culms cascade over the sides of the containers, producing a pleasing, attractive, vine appearance. Woodgrass makes a good ground cover in medium to dark shade in moist areas; it is grown for its pleasing, attractive foliage.

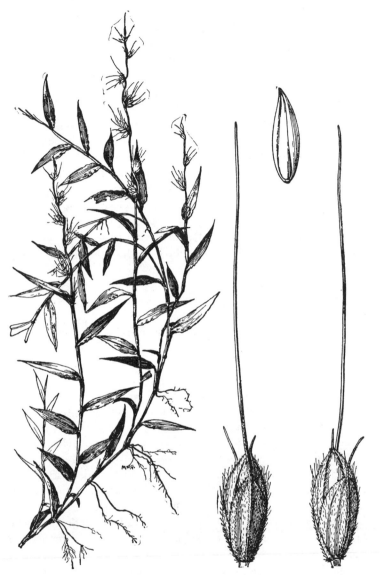

Oplismenus setarius. Habit, × 1/2; two views of spikelet and floret, ×
10. *Source: Manual of the Grasses of the West Indies.* USDA Misc. Pub. 243. 1936.

Cultivation: Propagation is by planting portions of the prostrate culms and by rooted cuttings. The plants require a moist or wet growing medium, warmth, and high humidity when grown indoors.

Oryza **L.** There are about 20 species, widely distributed in moist tropical and subtropical parts of the New and Old Worlds. Type species, *Oryza sativa* L. Annual and perennial swamp grasses with herbaceous culms; leaf blades lanceolate, flat; ligules membranous. Inflorescence an open or somewhat contracted panicle bearing large one-flowered spikelets; rachilla disarticulating below the glumes. Spikelets laterally flattened; glumes two, much shorter than the lemmas, narrow; lemmas awned or awnless, rigid, keeled, three-nerved; palea narrower but somewhat similar to the lemma, two-nerved close to the margins, keeled but without midnerve on the back, tightly enclosing the caryopsis; androecium usually of six stamens; lodicules two. *Oryza sativa* has two short, pointed bracts, these superficially resembling glumes, which are interpreted as being reduced lemmas or rudimentary florets.

> **Latin name:** *Oryza sativa* L.
> **Synonym:** *Oryza sativa* var. *rubribarbis* Desv.
> **Cultivars:** 'Nigrescens' (Many edible cultivars in cultivation)
> **Common name:** Rice
> **Origin:** Southeast Asia
> **Habitat:** Cultivated, escape from cultivation
> **Hardiness:** Zones 3 through 10
> **Description:** A loosely tufted, upright-open annual in temperate regions and a short-lived perennial in the tropics and subtropics. Culms simple, stout, glabrous, erect to arching, 3–6 ft /0.9–1.8 m, usually about 40 in./1 m high. Foliage medium green to yellowish green, medium in texture; leaf blades flat, elongate, 1–3 ft /3–9 dm long, 0.3–0.5 in./8–13 mm wide, narrowed toward the base, long attenuate, scabrous, especially on the upper surface and the margins, glabrous below; sheaths longer than the internodes, glabrous or rough; ligule membranous, smooth 0.2–0.4 in./5–10 mm long. Inflorescence a rather dense, branched panicle, exserted or included at the base, the branches initially ascending, spreading, and becoming one-sided at maturity, 5–10 in./1.3–2.5 dm long, 2–4 in./5–10 cm wide, the branches mostly 1–4 in./2.5–10.0 cm long, commonly single, naked at the base, the axis, branches, and pedicels slightly scabrous; spikelets oblong, laterally compressed, 0.3–0.4 in./8–10 mm long, about 0.1 in./3 mm wide, single or in pairs, one-flowered, rather loosely arranged, stout-pedicellate; glumes narrow, about equal, acute, one-nerved, linear-lanceolate, up to 0.1 in./3 mm long; lemmas keeled, rigid, five-nerved, the outer nerves near the margin, the apex sometimes awned; palea similar to the lemma, keeled, narrower, with a median bundle but with no strong midnerve

Oryza sativa. **Habit,** × 1/2; **spikelet,** × 5. *Source: Manual of the Grasses of the United States.* USDA Misc. Pub. 200. 1951.

on the back, two-nerved close to the margins; caryopsis brownish, rough, 1–3 mm long, enclosed. Flowering and fruiting usually occur from June through August.

Uses: The ornamental value of the garden cultivar 'Nigrescens' is its colorful foliage. The brownish purple foliage is most attractive when the plants are grown in a pool or pond during the summer. The dry seedheads are useful in dried arrangements. The ornamental value of rice lies in its dried seedheads, which are useful in dried floral arrangements. The panicle should be cut when the rice (caryopsises) are well swollen to prevent shattering as they mature and dry. The plants may be grown as a curiosity indoors in containers located in well-lighted areas. The economic value of rice is demonstrated by the fact that it is the principal diet of more than three-fifths of the world's population.

Cultivation: Propagation is by seeding. Seeding can be made directly in the mud in water gardens. Rice grows best with its feet in water. It may be grown in ordinary soil, but the plants may be smaller in stature. Rice plants may be started by seeding in a container and later transplanted to the garden or pond. Seeding should be done in good-quality potting soil. First, soak the soil thoroughly in the container until it is mud; plant seeds about 1–2 in./2.5–5.0 cm deep; then add water until it is even with the top of the soil. Additional water should be added when the plants are 1–2 in./2.5–5.0 cm high, and water should continue to be added as necessary to keep the soil covered, but the plants should not be inundated. The container need not have drainage for the short growth period of the plants. After the plants have attained 2–6 in./0.5–1.5 dm in height, they may be transplanted, either into a marsh, bog, or shallow water in the water garden. It is important that the roots be in mud or water at all times for maximum growth. Rice grows best in full sun; it requires light of high intensity when grown indoors. Some rice cultivars are moderately salt tolerant.

Cultivars: *Oryza sativa* L. 'Nigrescens'   This garden cultivar has rich, dark purple or brownish purple foliage. The plants are not quite as large as an average rice plant; culms are 30–36 in./7.6–9.0 dm high. Its colorful foliage makes it useful in specimen plantings in slow-moving streams and in freshwater pools and ponds.

Oryzopsis **Michx. (Ricegrass, Mountain rice).** Name from Greek *oruza,* "rice," and *opsis,* "appearance," referring to the resemblance to rice. Type species, *Oryzopsis asperifolia* Michx. There are 20 species, native to north, temperate regions of Eurasia and North America. Mostly slender, perennial grasses with flat or often involute leaf blades and terminal, narrow or open panicles. Spikelets one-flowered, disarticulating above the glumes; glumes about equal, obtuse to acuminate; lemma indurate, usually about as long as the glumes, broad, oval or oblong, nearly terete, usually pubescent, with a short, blunt, oblique callus, and

a short, deciduous, sometimes bent and twisted awn; palea enclosed by the edges
of the lemma.

> **Latin name:** *Oryzopsis miliacea* (L.) Benth. & Hook. f.
> **Synonym:** *Agrostis miliacea* L.
> **Origin:** Southeast Asia
> **Common names:** Ricegrass, Smilograss
> **Origin:** Mediterranean region
> **Habitat:** Cultivated, escape from cultivation
> **Hardiness:** Zones 6 through 9
> **Description:** A densely tufted, upright-open, perennial with short rhizomes. Culms stout, sometimes branching, erect from a decumbent base, 2–5 ft /0.6–1.5 m high. Foliage glabrous, medium to dark green, fine in texture; leaf blades flat, rough on the upper surface, glabrous below, leaf margins parallel for over one-half the length of the blade, then tapering to a point, 12–18 in./ 3.0–4.5 dm long, about 0.3–0.4 in./8–10 mm wide; sheaths dark green, glabrous or slightly rough, shorter than the internodes; ligules membranous about 2 mm long. Inflorescence a loosely branched panicle, 6–12 in./1.5–3.0 dm long, the branches spreading, bearing numerous spikelets beyond the middle; spikelets short-pedicellate, one-flowered, about 0.1 in./3 mm long, green, with a distinct green stripe on the glumes; glumes about equal, 0.1 in./3 mm long with a distinct green stripe, obtuse to acuminate; lemmas indurate, smooth, less than

Oryzopsis miliacea.
Inflorescence, × 3/5.
Source: An Illustrated Flora of the Pacific States. Stanford Univ. Press. 1923.

1 mm long, oval to oblong, with a short blunt callus, awned from the tip, awn straight, 0.10–0.15 in./3–4 mm long; palea enclosed by the lemma; caryopsis cylindrical, hard, enclosed by the lemma and palea. Flowering and fruiting occur from May through September.

Uses: Ricegrass culms often arch out gracefully, forming an imposing plant in middleground perennial borders. The culms are too weak to remain erect in specimen plantings. Ricegrass closely resembles tufted hairgrass, *Deschampsia caespitosa,* in growth habit and appearance; it is a good sand-binding plant.

Cultivation: Propagation is by seeding and by plant division. Ricegrass does well in any ordinary soil; good drainage and full sun are essential for maximum growth. The plants are quite heat tolerant.

Panicum **L.** An ancient name of Indian millet, *Setaria italica* (L.) Beauv., of uncertain origin and significance. Lectotype, *Panicum miliaceum* L. There are about 600 species, distributed throughout the world but mostly confined to the warmer regions. Annuals or perennials of various habits, usually with flat leaf blades and compact, open panicles. Spikelets more or less compressed dorsiventrally, in open or compact panicles, rarely racemes; glumes two, herbaceous, nerved, usually very unequal, the lower often minute, the upper typically equaling the sterile lemma, the latter of the same texture and simulating a third glume, bearing in its axil a membranous or hyaline palea and sometimes a staminate flower, the palea rarely wanting; fertile lemma chartaceous, indurate, usually obtuse, the nerves obsolete, the margins enrolled over an enclosed palea of the same texture.

Latin name: *Panicum clandestinum* L.
Synonym: *Milium clandestinum* Moench
Common name: Deertongue
Origin: North America
Habitat: Cultivated, escape from cultivation
Hardiness: Zones 4 through 9
Description: An upright-open, densely tufted, semievergreen, rhizomatous perennial. The vernal form in large, dense clumps with strong rhizomes, 2–4 ft /0.6–1.2 m long. Culms ascending or erect, scabrous to papillose-hispid below the nodes, 20–30 in./5.0–7.6 dm high, at least the lowest internode papillose-hispid below the node, the remaining internodes glabrous or more or less papillose-hispid. Foliage light grayish green to dark green, dense, coarse in texture; leaf blades spreading or finally reflexed, widest below the middle, slightly tapering to the cordate base, acuminate, 4–8 in./1–2 dm long, 0.6–1.2 in./1.5–3.0 cm wide, usually glabrous above and beneath but scabrous toward the apex, the margins scabrous and papillose-ciliate toward the base; sheaths up to the branches generally shorter than the internodes, strongly overlapping on the branches, papillose-hispid, at least the lower ones, the remaining sheaths the

same or glabrous, except the ciliate margins, a pubescent ring of short hairs at the summit; ligule almost obsolete. Inflorescence a long-exserted, branched panicle, broadly oval, 3–7 in./0.8–1.8 cm long, about three-fourths as wide, many-flowered, the flexuous branches in distant fascicles, ascending short branchlets in axils bearing spikelets; spikelets obovate-oblong, 2–3 mm long, 1–2 mm wide, 7-to-11-nerved, sparsely pubescent with weak hairs; glumes unequal, lower glume about one-third the length of the spikelet, subacute or obtuse, upper glume slightly shorter, seven-to-nine-nerved; sterile lemma less than 1 mm long, seven-to-nine-nerved; caryopsis elliptic, 2–3 mm long, 1–2 mm wide, free within the firmly closed lemma and palea. Autumnal culms erect or ascending, sparingly branched from the middle and upper nodes, the branches leafy, becoming top-heavy, sheaths imbricate, swollen and bristly on the shortened internodes, partially enclosing the secondary panicles, the latter ones entirely included; spikelets more turgid than those of the primary panicles. Flowering and fruiting occur from May through September.

Uses: Deertongue is an excellent ground-cover plant in open, moist, shaded woodland, where the plants produce dense extensive stands. The rhizomatous root system aids the plants in preventing erosion. Clump plantings are attractive in water gardens. The semievergreen foliage is another attractive attribute of deertongue. It is an ideal plant for inaccessible sites where it does not interfere with other plants. Deertongue is not suitable for the formal portion of the garden, but it does have value when used as ground cover or as a lawn substitute in correct locations. The panicles are used in dried arrangements.

Cultivation: Propagation is by plant division and by seeding, preferably the former. The plants prefer medium to light shade in moist soil, although they will grow in full sun. Plants grown in full sun are usually smaller than those grown in shade.

Latin name: *Panicum miliaceum* L.
Synonym: *Milium panicum* Mill.
Common names: Broomcorn millet, Broomcorn, Millet, Hog millet, Indian millet, Proso, Proso millet
Habitat: Cultivated, escape from cultivation
Hardiness: Zones 4 through 9
Description: A loosely tufted annual. Culms stout, erect or decumbent at the base, usually branching from the basal nodes, hispid or glabrous below the pubescent nodes, 12–40 in./0.3–1.0 m high. Foliage light greenish yellow, soft, coarse in texture; leaf blades linear, 12–18 in./3.0–4.5 dm long, 0.5–1.0 in./13–25 mm wide, round at the base, long attenuate, more or less pilose or glabrate on both surfaces, margins glabrous or scabrous; sheaths papillose-hispid, shorter than the internodes; ligule a ring of short hairs about 1 mm long. Inflorescence a nodding, rather compact, profusely branched panicle, more or less included at the base, 6–12 in./1.5–3.0 dm long, about 4–6 in./1.0–1.5 dm wide, the very scabrous branches ascending, 6–8 in./1.5–2.0 dm long, bearing spikelets toward

the summit; spikelets light green, ovate, acuminate, 0.15–0.20 in./4–5 mm long, strongly many-nerved; glumes unequal, lower glume about one-half the length of the spikelet or longer, acuminate, the upper and sterile lemma sub-equal; the sterile lemma subtending a small palea; caryopsis elliptic, yellowish or reddish brown, 0.1 in./3 mm long, about 2 mm wide. Flowering and fruiting occur from July through September.

Uses: The commercial value of broomcorn millet is in its use as a food crop for human beings and as feed for domestic livestock. The ornamental value of this widespread annual is its flowering panicles; the plants flower and fruit over a long period during the hot, summer months. The reddish brown seeds, which persist after flowering, add to the longevity and attractiveness of the plants. Clumps of plants are attractive in middleground borders.

Cultivation: Propagation is by direct seeding. Broomcorn millet prefers full sun on fertile, well-drained soil; the plants are somewhat drought tolerant and reseed themselves readily.

Latin name: *Panicum virgatum* L.
Synonym: *Panicum coloratum* Walt.
Cultivars: *Panicum virgatum* L. 'Haense Herms,' 'Rehbraun,' 'Rostrahl-busch,' 'Rubrum' Red switchgrass, 'Strictum'
Common name: Switchgrass
Origin: North America
Habitat: Prairies, cultivated
Hardiness: Zones 5 through 9
Description: An upright-open, vigorous perennial with numerous scaly rhizomes. Culms solitary or tufted in small or large clumps, simple, glabrous, or often glaucous, purple tinged, 3–7 ft /0.9–2.2 m high. Foliage medium green, becoming bronze at maturity, medium in texture; leaf blades linear, ascending, 1–2 ft /3–6 dm long, 0.2–0.6 in./5–15 mm wide, flat, long attenuate, scabrous or sometimes pilose or sparsely pubescent above near the base, smooth beneath or somewhat pilose toward the base, the margins hispid or scabrous; sheaths usually shorter than the internodes, often ciliate sometimes villous at the throat; ligule a dense fringe of hairs, 0.15–0.20 in./3–4 mm long. Inflorescence a long-exserted, branched panicle, 6–12 in./1.5–3.0 dm long, about one-half as wide near the base, ovate to pyramidal, sometimes contracted, many-flowered, the slender, scabrous, single or fascicled branches glabrous at the base, ascending or widely spreading; spikelets short-pedicellate, glabrous, elliptic-ovate, accumi-nate, 0.10–0.15 in./3–4 mm long, prominently nerved, turgid, lower floret usually staminate; glumes unequal, the lower glume clasping about two-thirds the length of the spikelet, rarely equaling the sterile lemma, the keel scabrous, 0.1–0.2 in./3–5 mm long, five-nerved, acuminate to cuspidate, the upper longer than the sterile lemma, five-to-seven-nerved, both exceeding the caryopsis, shorter than the upper glume; sterile palea as long as the spikelet, smooth elliptic-ovate, 2–3 mm long; caryopsis smooth, narrowly ovate, the margins of

Panicum virgatum. **Habit, × 1/2; two views of spikelet and floret, ×
10.** *Source: Manual of the Grasses of the United States.* USDA Misc. Pub. 200.
1951.

the lemma enrolled only at the base, about 1 mm long, shiny, light reddish. Flowering and fruiting occur from July through September.

Uses: Switchgrass is useful in background plantings in perennial borders and in medium or tall screens and windbreaks, depending upon the size of the plants. The large, many-branched, delicate panicles produce an attractive, purplish, hazy effect and hover over the foliage like a cloud, which makes clumps of the grass ideal for specimen plantings in water gardens. The late-flowering panicles produce hard, shiny, reddish seeds; these, along with the bronze foliage, remain attractive into fall. The foliage is usually a golden yellow or bronze following frost, providing good fall color. The panicles are useful as cut flowers and in dried arrangements. Switchgrass and its cultivars provide wildlife cover and bird feed when grown in naturalized areas around lakes and ponds and along the seashore in moist or wet soil, as the plants remain upright through the winter. These plants should be considered for plantings in transitional zones between the formal garden and wooded or unsightly areas. The reddish foliage of red switchgrass makes it ideal as a specimen plant. It is particularly attractive in group or in massed plantings along canals and highways.

Cultivation: Propagation is by direct seeding and by plant division, preferably the former. There is considerable variation among cultivars in plant size and foliage color. Switchgrass is adapted to a wide range of soils. The creeping rhizomes may spread slowly in light, sandy soils but less so in heavy, clay types. The plants grow best in full sun or light shade in moist, wet, or dry soils; they withstand poor drainage and occasional flooding. The tall plants occasionally may require staking because of their size; their maximum ornamental value is achieved in clump plantings.

Cultivars: *Panicum virgatum* L. 'Haense Herms'   This cultivar is 3–4 ft / 0.9–1.2 m high; it provides good fall color. The plants are large enough to provide medium screens and windbreaks.

Panicum virgatum L. 'Rehbraun' Red switchgrass   This cultivar is 3–4 ft / 0.9–1.2 m high; the plants provide good fall color.

Panicum virgatum L. 'Rostrahlbusch'   This cultivar is 3–4 ft /0.9–1.2 m high; the foliage is reddish in the fall, providing good fall color.

Panicum virgatum L. 'Rubrum' Red switchgrass   This cultivar is smaller and less vigorous than the species, attaining only about 3 ft /9 dm in height. The foliage is tinged reddish, mainly toward the tips of the leaves. Its color and size easily differentiate red switchgrass from the species. The reddish foliage provides good fall color. It is best demonstrated when planted in clumps in water gardens.

Panicum virgatum L. 'Strictum'   This cultivar, with bluish green foliage, is narrower and smaller than the species (i.e., 3–6 ft /0.9–1.8 m high). It is usually intermediate in size between switchgrass and the cultivar Rubrum. It usually flowers earlier than the species and the flowers are somewhat smaller than those of switchgrass. It prefers full sun on moist soil and is best demonstrated in group plantings.

***Paspalum* L.** Name from Greek *paspalos,* a kind of millet made into meal. Lectotype, *Paspalum dissectum* (L.) L. There are about 400 species, distributed throughout the world. Annual or mostly perennial grasses, with one to many spikelike racemes, solitary, paired, or several or many on a common axis. Spikelets plano-convex, usually obtuse, subsessile, solitary or in pairs, in two rows on one side of a narrow or dilated rachis, the back of the fertile lemma toward it; lower glume usually wanting; upper glume and sterile lemma commonly about equal; fertile lemma usually obtuse, chartaceous-indurate, the margins enrolled.

Latin name: *Paspalum dissectum* (L.) L.
Synonym: *Panicum dissectum* L.
Common name: Seashore paspalum
Origin: South America
Habitat: Marshes along the seacoast, lakes, ponds
Hardiness: Zones 6 through 10
Description: A stoloniferous, subaquatic perennial. Culms ascending, compressed, the nodes usually swollen, 8–20 in./2–5 dm high, stolons creeping, freely branching, rooting at the nodes. Foliage dull green, fine in texture; leaves distichous, leaf blades glabrous, thin, flat, 1–2 ft /3–6 dm long, 0.15–0.20 in. / 4–5 mm wide, scarcely narrowed at the base, rather abruptly acute; sheaths flat and bladderlike, often divergent, longer than the internodes; ligule hyaline, lacerate, extending down the sheath margins, about 2 mm long. Inflorescence usually two to four erect, terminal, and axillary short-exserted, racemes, persistent, one-half to three-fourths their own length distant on a slender, narrowly winged axis, racemes 0.8–1.0 in./20–25 mm long, 0.10–0.15 in./3–4 mm wide, the membranous rachis is 2–3 mm wide, abruptly pointed and terminating at the base of the uppermost spikelet, the minutely scabrous margins inflexed, covering the base of the spikelet; spikelets pale, solitary, obovate-oval, subacute, 2–3 mm long; the lower glume absent, the upper and sterile lemma thin, three-to-five-nerved, slightly exceeding the caryopsis in the terminal spikelet, forming a short point; caryopsis obtuse, minutely papillose-roughened, about 2 mm long, 1 mm wide. Flowering and fruiting occur from July through September.

Uses: Seashore paspalum is a good indicator of moderate salinity, usually to the extent that it is unsuitable for crops. The primary value of seashore paspalum is in its erosion control by forming an impenetrable ground cover, often in pure sand. This low-growing perennial produces several seed crops each growing season; the foliage turns brown and deteriorates after frost. This perennial is useful for ground cover and erosion control in wet, saline marshes.

Cultivation: Propagation is by seeding and by plant division, preferably the latter. The plants thrive in muddy, wet sites and do best when the water level fluctuates from 6 in./15 cm below the soil surface to 2 in./5 cm above; during the winter the plants tolerate deeper water. It is adapted primarily to firm, mineral, marsh soils of moderate salinity. Seashore paspalum is among the few grasses that grow directly in water; the plants prefer full sun but will tolerate light shade.

Latin name: *Paspalum notatum* Flugge
Synonym: *Paspalum taphrophyllum* Steud.
Cultivars: Several in cultivation
Common name: Bahiagrass
Origin: South America
Habitat: Cultivated, escape from cultivation
Hardiness: Zones 8 through 10
Description: A mat-forming, rhizomatous, spreading perennial. Culms arising from stout, woody, horizontal rhizomes, leafy at the base, 6–24 in./ 1.5–6.0 dm high. Rhizomatous roots numerous, rather coarse, the rhizomes covered with persistent bases of old sheaths, simple, flattened. Foliage medium

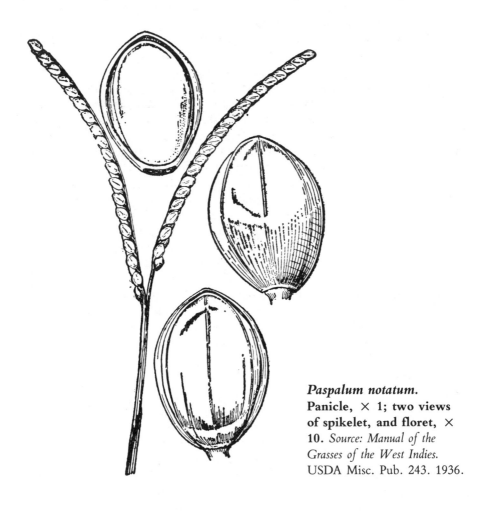

Paspalum notatum.
**Panicle, × 1; two views of spikelet, and floret, ×
10.** *Source: Manual of the Grasses of the West Indies.* USDA Misc. Pub. 243. 1936.

to dark green, usually the latter, fine in texture; leaves crowded at the base, leaf blades 3–9 in./0.8–2.3 dm long, 0.1–0.3 in./3–8 mm wide, glabrous, the upper reduced in size, flat or folded at the base, commonly ciliate toward the base; sheaths crowded at the base, overlapping, short, but longer than the internodes, flattened, keeled and ciliate toward the summit or occasionally pubescent throughout; ligule very short, membranous, with a row of hairs about 1 mm long on the back of it. Inflorescence two, rarely three subconjugate racemes, retrorse-ascending, about 2–4 in./5–10 cm long; rachis flat, about 1 mm wide, flexuous toward the summit; spikelets shiny green, plano-convex, ovate to obovate, solitary, 0.10–0.15 in./3–4 mm long, 2–3 mm wide; the lower glume absent, the upper and sterile lemma equal, smooth, shiny, thin, firm, five-nerved, the intermediate nerves often obscure; caryopsis oval, margins thick, the back convex, about 0.1 in./3 mm long, 2 mm wide. Flowering and fruiting occur from May through September.

Uses: Bahiagrass is valuable as a ground-cover and erosion-control plant. The plants make an impenetrable, thick sod in pure stands which successfully eliminates weed competition. The strong, extensive root system binds the soil and aids in preventing erosion. Bahiagrass is very useful in naturalized areas bordering the formal garden. The plants are highly competitive and invasive.

Cultivation: Propagation is by seeding and by plant division. Bahiagrass is adapted to a wide range of soils from sands to heavy clays, provided they are acid or neutral. The plants prefer full sun but will tolerate some light shade. Fertile soil with adequate moisture produces maximum growth, although established stands are quite drought tolerant. Bahiagrass withstands wet conditions and even inundation for short periods.

Pennisetum **L. Rich. ex Pers.** Name from Latin *penna,* "feather," and *seta,* "bristle," referring to the plumose bristles of some species. Lectotype, *Holcus spicatus* L. There are about 80 species, native to the tropics of both hemispheres. Annual or perennial grasses, often branched, usually with flat leaf blades and spikelike panicles. Spikelets solitary or in groups of two or three, surrounded by an involucre of bristles, sterile branchlets, these not united except at the very base, often plumose, falling attached to the spikelets; lower glume shorter than the spikelet, sometimes minute or wanting; upper glume shorter than or equaling the sterile lemma; fertile lemma chartaceous, smooth, the margin thin, enclosing the palea.

    Latin name: *Pennisetum alopecuroides* (L.) Spreng.
    Synonym: *Panicum alopecuroides* L.
    Cultivars and varieties: 'Hameln' Dwarf fountain grass, 'Weserbergland'; *Pennisetum alopecuroides* (L.) Spreng. var. *viridescens* (Miq.) Ohwi
    Common name: Fountain grass
    Origin: China

Habitat: Cultivated, escape from cultivation

Hardiness: Zones 6 through 9

Description: An upright-open, mound-forming, densely tufted, perennial with extensive, fibrous roots. Culms erect, compressed, becoming arched toward the tip, 2–4 ft /0.6–1.2 m high, pubescent below the panicles. Foliage medium to dark green, turning yellowish, medium in texture; leaf blades elongate, scabrous, 6–8 in./1.5–2.0 cm long, 0.3–0.4 in./8–10 mm wide, long attenuate; sheaths round on the back, inflated, slightly hairy; ligule a ring of short hairs. Inflorescence a bristly, spikelike panicle, erect with ascending branches, arching at the top, seemingly hairy, rustic brown or bronze, becoming bright reddish, 4–10 in./1.0–2.5 dm long, 2–3 in./5–8 cm wide, the fascicles about 1 in./25 mm long; bristles far longer than the spikelets, giving the panicles a bristly or feathery appearance. Flowering and fruiting occur from July through September, with the flower color persisting well beyond maturity.

Uses: Fountain grass is among the very best of ornamental grasses used in landscaping, whether it includes the home garden, parks, highways, golf courses, or any other areas. This medium-size, mound-forming perennial is attractive in late summer and early fall, when the plants are covered with many coppery-purple, bristly, flowering panicles. The slightest breeze causes a slow, soft, pleasing, rippling motion among the panicles. The foliage and flowering panicles gradually change through various hues of color with the advent of cool weather. The yellow or golden foliage produces excellent fall color, and the plant form and inflorescences persist into winter. There is considerable variation among clones of fountain grass in plant size and shape, blooming date and duration, and foliage and flower color and tone. It is commonly used in accent specimen plantings in open lawns, in middleground borders, and in rock and water gardens. The plants form middle-size, symmetrical mounds when grown in well-spaced group and specimen plantings. The reflection of the plants on water enhances their effectiveness and attractiveness when they are planted around ponds or pools or along streams. The size, color and form of fountain grass are conducive to its use in pure and mixed stands in naturalized areas. The plants form an attractive screen of medium height when planted in rows, with the foliage and seedheads producing attractive fall color. The flowering panicles are used as cut flowers and in dried arrangements. Fountain grass and its cultivars are among the most handsome of ornamental grasses. Massed plantings of fountain grass in full sun produce a spectacularly colorful effect in the fall when in full blossom. Fountain grass and its cultivars rank extremely high among perennial ornamental grasses because both their foliage and inflorescences are particularly attractive in late summer and early fall.

Cultivation: Propagation is by seeding and by plant division. Propagation by plant division ensures the form, size, and color of plants desired. Fountain grass grows well on almost any fertile, moist or wet, well-drained soil in full sun or light shade. Sufficient space should be allowed in planting for the plant mounds to develop to 40 in./1 m in diameter. Plant division is required every several years to prevent the center of the plant crown from dying. Fountain grass may become a nuisance if the seedheads are allowed to mature; however, their natural beauty overshadows their nuisance value. Cutting the seedheads before they mature destroys the beauty and value of fountain grass; therefore, weeding out young seedlings each spring prevents it from becoming a nuisance. Fountain grass and its cultivars are grown as annuals in zone 5, as weak perennials in zones 7 and 8, and as perennials in zones 9 and 10; they prefer slightly acid to neutral soils.

Cultivars: *Pennisetum alopecuroides* (L.) Spreng. 'Hameln' Dwarf fountain grass   A densely tufted, mound-forming perennial, 18–24 in./4.5–6.0 dm high; the plants form mounds about 12–14 in./3.0–3.5 dm wide. Foliage medium green, fine in texture. Inflorescence of pink flowers. Flowering and fruiting occur from July through September, with the flower color persisting beyond maturity. This cultivar is a handsome specimen when grown singly or in clump plantings in full sun. It is a weak perennial in zone 6.

Pennisetum alopecuroides (L.) Spreng. 'Weserbergland'   The plants are 2–4 ft /0.6–1.2 m high; they make excellent specimens in groups in full sun.

Pennisetum alopecuroides (L.) Spreng var. *viridescens* (Miq.) Ohwi   The plants are about 2 ft /6 dm high; foliage is greenish yellow. They make decorative specimens and provide fall color in group plantings in full sun. This variety and the cultivars of fountain grass are adapted to the same plant-hardiness zones as the type species.

Latin name: *Pennisetum nervosum* (Nees) Trin.
Synonym: *Cenchrus nervosus* Kuntze
Origin: Brazil, South America
Habitat: Open, moist grassland
Hardiness: Zones 9 and 10
Description: A tufted, upright-narrow perennial. Culms solitary or tufted, erect or ascending from a decumbent base, sometimes rooting at the lower nodes, strongly flattened, branching, 3–6 ft /0.9–1.8 m high. Foliage medium green, fine in texture; leaf blades flat, narrow, becoming folded toward the base, 4–15 in./1.0–3.8 dm long, 0.15–0.40 in./4–10 mm wide, upper surface and margins rough, more or less smooth below; sheaths flattened, loose, sometimes ciliate on the margins, shorter than the internodes; ligule about 1 mm long, membranous ciliate. Inflorescence a bristly, cylindrical, spikelike, nodding panicle, 4–6 in./1.0–1.5 dm long, 0.4–0.6 in./10–15 mm wide, initially pinkish or purplish, finally tawny, the spikelets solitary or sometimes two, enclosed in an involucre of about 20 to 30 unequal, scabrous bristles, the outer about as long as the spikelet, the inner 0.3–0.4 in./8–10 mm long; spikelets pale, lanceolate, 0.20–0.25 in./5–6 mm long; glumes unequal, lower glume one-nerved, lanceolate, acute or awn-pointed, 2–3 mm long, the upper and sterile lemma subequal, strongly nine-nerved, lanceolate, acuminate, 0.15–0.20 in./4–5 mm long; lemmas as long as the spikelets, minutely papillose, five-nerved, acuminate; palea

two-nerved, as long as the lemmas. Flowering and fruiting occur from August through September.

Uses: This tufted perennial is ideally suited for specimen plantings near shrubbery in middleground borders; its height may qualify it for background borders and tall screens. The plants provide a good medium screen when planted in rows. The dense, purplish, flowering panicles are used in both fresh and dried arrangements. The purplish panicles do not require dyeing when used in dried arrangements.

Cultivation: Propagation is by plant division, either in the spring or the fall. Propagation in the fall is successful in zones 8 and 9. Young plants up to 1 ft /3 dm high can be divided successfully in the spring. The plants prefer full sun on moist, fertile soil. This species, like other species of this genus, is easy to propagate by plant division.

Latin name: *Pennisetum setaceum* (Forsk.) Chiov.
Synonym: *Phalaris setacea* Forsk.
Common names: Crimson fountain grass, Fountain grass
Cultivars: 'Astrosanguineum,' 'Cupreum,' 'Rubrum'
Origin: Africa
Habitat: Cultivated, escape from cultivation
Hardiness: Zones 7 through 10
Description: An upright-arching, mound-forming perennial. Culms simple, tufted, 2–4 ft /0.6–1.2 m high, slender, weak. Foliage rusty green, fine in texture; leaf blades elongate, narrow, scabrous, almost straight to arching, 10–18 in./2.5–4.5 dm long, 0.1–0.2 in./3–5 mm wide, long attenuate. Inflorescence a bristly, villous, upright to nodding, branched panicle, elongate, 6–12 in./1.5–3.0 dm long, 2–4 in./5–10 cm wide including the bristles, pink, rose-colored or light to medium purple; branches in fascicles, fascicles pedunculate, rather loosely arranged, each fascicle containing two to five spikelets; spikelets 0.1–0.2 in./3–5 mm long, bristles plumose toward the base, unequal, the outer 1.0–1.6 in./2.5–4.0 cm long, the inner shorter. Flowering and fruiting occur from July through mid-September.

Uses: Crimson fountain grass is among the most beautiful ornamental grasses. It is grown for its long, narrow, purple flower heads and attractive symmetrical mounds. The reddish to dark purple flower heads are very attractive while they remain on the plants and are also decorative in fresh arrangements. The flowers tend to fade and become discolored with age. A slight breeze causes a slow rippling motion of the leaves and colorful arched flowering panicles, which lends additional interest to the plant. When crimson fountain grass is used in specimen plantings around pools and lakes or along streams, the reflection of the plants on the water enhances the attractiveness of the plants. The plants form middle-sized, symmetrical mounds topped by colorful, delicate flowers when grown in well-spaced specimen plantings in rock and water gardens and in border plantings. The plants form an attractive screen of medium height when

Pennisetum setaceum.

planted in rows. Crimson fountain grass flowers over a long period during mid- and late-summer, when many other ornamentals are not in flower or are otherwise unattractive. The foliage gradually changes color in the fall, providing good fall color, and the plants remain upright and attractive into winter; crimson fountain grass and its cultivars produce a prodigious amount of flowers and deserve serious consideration for inclusion in any flower garden for their longevity of flowering and their elegant beauty. Crimson fountain grass is used in specimen plantings on golf courses, along streets and highways, and in parks and zoos.

Cultivation: Propagation is by seeding and by plant division. The latter method of propagation ensures the form and blossom color desired, as there is considerable variation in plant form and flower color among clones of crimson fountain grass. Crimson fountain grass is adapted to a wide range of soils and moisture conditions. The plants are somewhat weak and subject to wind damage; they are quite drought tolerant and thrive on dry or moist soils in full sun. Shade-grown plants may become weak, lanky, and less colorful than those grown in full sun. Crimson fountain grass and its cultivars are grown as annuals in zones 5–6 and as perennials in zones 7–10. The plants readily reseed themselves; they should be divided every few years to prevent the culms from dying out in the middle of the clump or plant crown. Crimson fountain grass may be sold under the name *Pennisetum rupelii.*

Cultivars: *Pennisetum setaceum* (Forsk.) Chiov. 'Astrosanguineum'   The plants have purplish green foliage and purple spikes that provide good fall color.

Pennisetum setaceum (Forsk.) Chiov. 'Cupreum'   The plants have reddish green leaves and copper-colored spikes, which provide good fall color.

Pennisetum setaceum (Forsk.) Chiov. 'Rubrum'   The plants are 2–3 ft /6–9 dm high with rose-colored foliage and spikes. The cultivars of crimson fountain grass are adapted to the same plant-hardiness zones as the parent species and are used in the same manner.

Latin name: *Pennisetum villosum* R. Br.
Synonym: *Cenchrus villosus* Kuntze
Common name: Feathertop
Origin: Africa
Habitat: Cultivated, escape from cultivation
Hardiness: Zones 5 through 10
Description: An upright-open to irregular, short-lived, rhizomatous perennial. Culms loosely tufted in large clumps, erect or decumbent at the base, branched below, somewhat flattened, glabrous or villous, pubescent below the panicle, 1–3 ft /3–9 dm high. Foliage light to yellowish green, fine in texture; leaf blades flat or conduplicate, long attenuate, 12–20 in./3–5 dm long, 0.1–0.2 in./3–5 mm wide, glabrous, but rough on the margins and toward the tip, sometimes sparsely pubescent at the base and papillose-ciliate on the margins near the base; sheaths compressed and keeled, lower sheaths crowded and imbri-

Pennisetum villosum.
Panicle, × 1/2. *Source: Manual of the Grasses of the United States.* USDA Misc. Pub. 200. 1951.

cate, the upper shorter than the internodes, loose, ciliate toward the summit and villous at the throat, otherwise glabrous or sparsely pubescent; ligulea ring of hairs about 1 mm long. Inflorescence an ovoid or oblong, bristly, tawny, or whitish panicle, 2–5 in./0.5–1.3 dm long about 2–4 in./5–10 cm wide including the bristles, finally exserted, dense, the axis trigonous, puberulent, pilose on the margins; spikelets 0.3–0.4 in./8–10 mm long, solitary or two or three in a cluster in an involucre of many bristles; involucres short-pedunculate, bristles spreading, the inner very plumose below, the longer 1–2 in./2.5–5.0 cm long; glumes unequal, lower glume minute, about 1 mm long, trigonous or truncate, the upper lanceolate, acute, one-to-three-nerved, 0.10–0.15 in./3–4 mm long; sterile and fertile lemmas lanceolate and acuminate, seven-to-nine-nerved, minutely scabrous toward the apex, the sterile lemma shorter; palea of fertile lemma nearly as long as its lemma. Flowering and fruiting occur from July through August.

Uses: Feathertop is grown for its colorful, flowery, nodding panicles. It is ideal in specimen plantings when grown in clumps in foreground or middle-ground borders and in rock gardens. The delicate colorful flowering panicles and fine-textured foliage give the plants a delightful, unique appearance in the cut-flower garden. The slightest breeze causes a soft, slow, rippling effect among the plants, resulting in constant changes in hues. The light green foliage and pink or purplish flowers provide a pleasing contrast to other grasses and broad-leaved plants with dark green foliage. The delicate ivory or pink flower heads are much used in cut-flower arrangements. Although the flowers tend to shatter easily, the flower heads are occasionally used in dried bouquets. Feathertop can be grown as an annual in northern climates.

Cultivation: Propagation is by seeding and by plant division, preferably the former. The plants require well-drained, moist or dry soil in full sun. Plants grown in light shade become weak, and the flowers are not as richly colored as those grown in full sun. Sufficient space in planting should be allowed for the plants to spread, as is their tendency. The flowering culms are weak, thus making the plants subject to wind damage. There is considerable variation among clones of feathertop in flower color. For this reason, it is desirable to propagate the plants by division to ensure color, form, and size of plant desired. The plants should be divided on occasion to prevent those culms in the middle of the crown from dying; the plants reseed themselves readily. Feathertop is grown as an annual in zones 5–8 and a short-lived perennial in zones 9 and 10.

Other ornamental species: *Pennisetum alopecuros* Nees ex Steud.   An upright-open, mound-forming, densely tufted perennial. Culms 2–3 ft /6–9 dm high, erect becoming arched toward the tip. Foliage medium green, fine in texture; leaf blades elongate, 6–8 in./1.5–2.0 dm long, 2–3 mm wide, attenuated, slightly scabrous; sheaths round on the back, slightly hairy. Inflorescence a bristly, spikelike, dense panicle with ascending branches, narrow at the tip, 4–5 in./1.0–1.3 dm long, up to 2 in./5 cm wide including the bristles; bristles plumose, longer than the spikelets, 1.0–1.6 in./2.5–4.0 cm long, giving the panicles a feathery appearance. This densely tufted perennial resembles fountain grass in general form and appearance, but the plants are usually smaller. This species is grown for its colorful flowering panicles, which are attractive on the plants and as both cut and dried flowers. The plants make ideal specimens in rock and water gardens and in middleground borders. Flowering and fruiting occur from June through August. It is adapted to the same environment as that of fountain grass; it is grown as an annual in zones 5–7 and as a perennial in zones 8–10. Propagation is by seeding and by plant division. Its soil, water, and light requirements are similar to those of fountain grass.

Pennisetum latifolium Spreng.   A large, robust, tufted perennial; it is hardy in mild climates. Culms 42–60 in./1.1–1.5 m high, the nodes appressed-pubescent. Foliage medium green, coarse in texture; leaf blades linear, long attenuate, 18–36 in./4.5–9.0 dm long, 0.8–1.2 in./2–3 cm wide. Inflorescence of terminal and axillary nodding spikes, 2–3 in./5–8 cm long, with prominent bristles. This robust perennial is native to South America, where it is cultivated occasionally as an ornamental. It should be taken inside during the winter in colder climates. The dry panicles are used in dried floral arrangements.

Pennisetum macrostachyum (Brongn.) Trin. An upright-open to irregular, robust perennial. Culms glabrous, 3–7 ft /0.9–2.2 m high, 1.0–1.6 in./2.5–4.0 cm thick at the base, semidecumbent to erect. Foliage color varies among clones from dark green to dull, reddish green, coarse in texture; leaf blades glabrous, 8–16 in./2–4 dm long, 1.0–1.2 in./2.5–3.0 cm wide, bluntly pointed, conspicuously veined, with a particularly large midvein. Inflorescence a dense, compact, oblong, cylindrical, spikelike panicle, 4–6 in./1.0–1.5 dm long, 2–3 in./5–8 cm wide, greenish white to pinkish white, becoming brownish purple at maturity; spikelets appressed, awnless; bristles not plumose. Flowering and fruiting occur from August through September. Plants grown indoors are much smaller than those grown outside. This species is adapted to shade in its natural environment; therefore, it is useful as a house-plant. The most interesting forms include those with colorful foliage. The plants require a constant moisture supply when grown indoors and can hardly be overwatered. These perennials may be grown as specimen plants in the garden during the summer and transferred indoors during the winter.

Pennisetum orientale L. An upright-open perennial; the plants are 2–3 ft / 6–9 dm high. Flowering and fruiting occur from late July until frost. The plants thrive best in fertile soil in full sun. Propagation is usually by seeding.

Pennisetum orientale var. *triflorum* (Nees) Stapf A densely tufted, rhizomatous perennial. Culms erect or partially decumbent, 2–3 ft /6–9 dm high, slightly hairy. Foliage dark green, fine in texture; leaf blades straight to arching, 18–24 in./4.5–6.0 dm long, 0.25 in./6 mm wide, flat, slightly hairy above; sheaths slightly hairy, round on the back. Inflorescence an erect, elongate, bristly, lax, spikelike panicle 12–16 in./3–4 dm long, 2–3 in./5–8 cm wide. The bristles longer than the spikelets, very fine, feathery, pink to purplish. Flowering and fruiting occur from July through September. This variety is noted for its beautiful flowers; it is best used and appreciated in specimen plantings. Propagation is by seeding and by plant division, preferably the latter. The plants prefer fertile, well-drained soil in full sun. This ornamental, native to India, is adapted to zones 4–9.

Phalaris L. (Canary grass). The ancient Greek name, *phalaris;* probably alluding to the crestlike inflorescence. Lectotype, *Phalaris canariensis* L. There are about 20 species, native to North America, Europe, Asia, and North Africa. Annual or perennial grasses, with numerous flat leaf blades and narrow, spikelike panicles. Spikelets laterally compressed, with one terminal floret and two sterile lemmas below, the rachilla disarticulating above the glumes, the usually inconspicuous sterile lemmas falling closely appressed to the fertile floret; glumes equal, cymbiform, often winged on the keel; sterile lemmas reduced to two small, usually minute scales; fertile lemma coriaceous, shorter than the glumes, enclosing the faintly two-nerved palea.

Latin name: *Phalaris arundinacea* L.
Synonym: *Arundo colorata* Ait
Cultivars and varieties: 'Dwarf's Garters,' 'Feesey's Form'; *Phalaris arundinacea* var. *picta* L., Ribbongrass; *Phalaris arundinacea* var. *variegata* Parnell Gardener's garters
Common names: Reed canary grass, Roseau
Origin: North America, Eurasia
Habitat: Cultivated, escape from cultivation
Hardiness: Zones 4 through 8
Description: An upright-open, semievergreen, glabrous perennial with creeping rhizomes. Culms erect, 3–5 ft /0.9–1.5 m high, glaucous, smooth. Foliage medium green, coarse in texture; leaf blades flat, acuminate, arched, glabrous or more or less scabrous, 4–12 in./1–3 dm long, 0.25–0.75 in./6–19 mm wide; sheaths longer than the internodes, round on the back, the upper shorter, usually glabrous, the lower longer, scaberulous; ligule hyaline, 0.1–0.2 in./3–5 mm long. Inflorescence a dense, branched, spikelike panicle, greenish or sometimes purplish, 3–6 in./0.8–1.5 dm long, up to 1 in./25 mm wide, branches erect or later spreading during anthesis, contracted later, 1.0–1.6 in./2.5–4.0 cm long, somewhat crowded to one side of the axis, the lower up to 2 in./5 cm long; spikelets laterally compressed, three-flowered, with one terminal floret and two sterile lemmas below, 0.15–0.20 in./4–5 mm long; glumes about equal, greatly compressed, boat-shaped, narrow, acute, about 0.2 in./5 mm long, strongly keeled, the keel scabrous or very narrowly winged, the lower shorter than the upper, 0.10–0.15 in./3–4 mm long, three-nerved, the nerves and body more or less scabrous, rarely glabrous, the upper as long as the spikelet, about 2 mm wide; fertile lemma indurated, glossy, lanceolate, 0.10–0.15 in./3–4 mm long, about 2 mm wide, slightly bifid at the acute apex, awnless, three-to-five-nerved, more or less pubescent, enclosing the palea; palea almost as long as its lemma; sterile lemmas on opposite sides of the fertile lemma and at its base, reduced to minute hairy scales about 1 mm long; palea as long as its lemma; caryopsis enclosed. Flowering and fruiting occur from June through August.

Uses: Ribbongrass and gardener's garters, *Phalaris arundinacea* var. *variegata,* form a complete mat and are useful as ground cover in full sun in medium to large areas. Ribbongrass and gardener's garters both provide interesting variations in foliage color in the garden throughout the summer until frost. They also provide an interesting foil for other flowering plants, whether planted among them, or in the background, but particularly in groups or rows in the foreground. These grasses make ideal specimens when grown in clumps in perennial borders or in water gardens. The small cultivars (i.e., 'Dwarf's Garters' and 'Feesey's Form') and the varieties *picta* and *variegata* of reed canary grass are

Phalaris arundinacea.
Habit, × **1/2.** *Source:*
Selected Weeds of the United
States. USDA Agric.
Handbook 366. 1970.

all useful as bedding plants, specimens, and houseplants. The variety *variegata* is particularly striking as a bedding plant, especially when planted in front of other plants with dark green foliage; it is strongly invasive, however, and not conducive for use in rock gardens. Ribbongrass and gardener's garters are grown for their foliage, which is attractive on the plants and is used on occasion in fresh flower arrangements; the compact seedheads turn brown in late summer and are of little interest. The basal leaves of these variegated forms, particularly those of ribbongrass, begin to fade and discolor by midsummer, although their variegated coloration is maintained to some degree, even after frost, providing good fall color. The plants remain upright into winter, and their beige, greenish pink, or light tan foliage provides attractive autumnal color. Despite their invasiveness, these variegated forms are very popular among gardeners and provide an added dimension in beautifying the landscape. The small cultivars—'Dwarf's Garters' and 'Feesey's Form'—and the botanical variety *variegata* could be used with green grasses in producing a multicolored lawn. They are also valuable as houseplants, although they require light of high intensity. Ribbongrass is also useful in seaside plantings; along with the botanical variety *variegata,* it is used in parks and zoos.

Cultivation: Propagation is by seeding and by plant division. Propagation by plant division ensures obtaining the type of plant desired. The plants are easily divided for planting in early spring once new growth has begun. The botanical variety *variegata* is much smaller in size and far more invasive than ribbongrass, which may limit its use in the flower garden. These grasses are adapted to a wide range of soils, from sandy to clay types; they are quite drought tolerant and thrive in dry, moist, or wet soils and directly in water, performing best in moist or wet, slightly acid or neutral soils in full sun or medium to light shade. Reed canary grass and its variants thrive in pots submerged a few inches (i.e., 2–3 in./5–8 cm) under water in the water garden, greenhouse, or atrium. They are not as invasive when grown in heavy clay soils. These plants require some form of containment, especially when grown on sandy soils. Heavy clay soils may retard their encroachment somewhat, although it is best to provide some form of containment for the plants prior to planting. Clumps of plants may be contained by planting in flower pots or cans without bottoms or by sinking plastic or metal strips into the soil 6–8 in./1.5–2.0 dm deep.

Cultivars: *Phalaris arundinacea* L. 'Dwarf's Garters' This semievergreen garden cultivar is a diminutive form of ribbongrass; the plants seldom exceed 12–15 in./3.0–3.8 dm in height. Dwarf's Garters is conspicuously less invasive than ribbongrass, which may be advantageous. The plants are rather inconspicuous, although persistent. This cultivar is adapted to zones 4–10.

Phalaris arundinacea L. 'Feesey's Form' This semievergreen, variegated perennial is about 10–12 in./2.5–3.0 dm high. This cultivar is less invasive than ribbongrass, and consequently it is more easily controlled. It is far superior to ribbongrass as an ornamental, although its variegated foliage is not as conspicuously distinctive as that of the latter. Both cultivars, Dwarf's Garters and Feesey's Form, are useful in bedding and accent plantings in foreground borders and in water gardens. This cultivar is adapted to zones 4–10.

Phalaris arundinacea var. *picta* L. Ribbongrass A densely tufted, upright-narrow, semievergreen perennial with long, strong rhizomes. Culms bent at the base, becoming erect, flattened, glabrous, with few noticeably swollen nodes, 2–4 ft /0.6–1.2 m high, usually about 15–30 in./3.8–7.6 dm. Foliage soft, variegated, fine in texture; leaf blades 4–10 in./1.0–2.5 dm long, 0.2–0.3 in./5–8 mm wide, acuminate, long attenuate, narrowed toward the base, longitudinally striped green-white or green-pink, usually smooth or sometimes rough; sheaths glabrous, longer than the internodes, or the upper shorter, light greenish white, round on the back; ligule 0.10–0.25 in./3–6 mm long. Inflorescence an erect, dense, spikelike panicle, 2–8 in. / 0.5–2.0 dm long, 0.4–0.8 in./10–20 mm wide, tawny, more dense in upper portion, densely flowered, the axis, branches and pedicels scabrous, the branches appressed or spreading, commonly in twos, 0.5–1.6 in./1.3–4.0 cm long, the pedicels short, 1–2 mm long; spikelets lanceolate, pale, 0.15–0.25 in./4–6 mm long; glumes acuminate, equal, scabrous, one-nerved, not winged; lemmas about two-thirds as long as the glumes, chartaceous, pubescent with long, appressed hairs, sterile lemmas about half as long as the glumes, subulate, hairy; palea faintly two-nerved. Flowering and fruiting occur from June through July. Ribbongrass is among the oldest grasses grown as an ornamental; it is somewhat salt tolerant and adapted to zones 4–10.

Phalaris arundinacea var. *variegata* Parnell Gardener's garters A loosely tufted, upright-open to spreading, semievergreen perennial with rhizomes. Culms erect from a more or less decumbent base, geniculate at the base, growing in a more or less zigzag manner, smooth, glabrous, 12–18 in./3.0–4.5 dm high. Foliage very soft, variegated, fine to medium in texture; leaf blades flat, glabrous, mostly straight or occasionally slightly arching, smooth, 6–8 in./1.5–2.0 cm long, 0.3–0.5 in./8–13 mm wide, gradually tapering to a somewhat blunt point, longitudinally striped green-white with approximately equal portions of each color; sheaths glabrous, round on the back, greenish white. Flowering and fruiting occur from June through July. This form is adapted to zones 4–10.

Latin name: *Phalaris canariensis* L.
Synonym: *Phalaris avicularis* Salisb.
Common names: Canary grass, Birdseed grass, Graines d'oiseaux
Origin: Canary Islands, Mediterranean region
Habitat: Cultivated, escape from cultivation
Hardiness: Zones 4 through 9
Description: A tufted, upright-open, glabrous annual. Culms slender to stout, simple or branching at the base and sometimes at the nodes, erect or decumbent becoming erect, scabrous, nodes swollen, 2–4 ft /0.6–1.2 m high. Foliage medium green, fine in texture; leaf blades erect or ascending, flat, base of blade round, elongate, attenuate, 6–16 in./1.5–4.0 dm long, 0.15–0.25 in./4–6 mm wide, strongly scabrous; sheaths more or less inflated and rough, shorter than the internodes; ligule membranous, hyaline, 0.10–0.15 in./3–4 mm long. Inflorescence an ovoid to oblong, soft, dense, spikelike panicle, 0.8–1.6 in./2–4 cm long, 0.5–0.6 in./13–15 mm wide, greenish white, branches crowded, very short; spikelets imbricate, laterally compressed, three-flowered, with a terminal perfect floret and two sterile lemmas below; broadly ovate, 0.25–0.30 in./6–8 mm long, very flat, faintly striped; glumes almost equal,

Phalaris canariensis.
Habit, × 1/2; **spikelet and floret,** × 5. *Source: Manual of the Grasses of the West Indies.* USDA Misc. Pub. 243. 1936.

about as long as the spikelet, whitish with three prominent green nerves or stripes, strongly keeled, the keel minutely toothed and winged above, glabrous or sparingly pubescent; fertile lemma coriaceous, 0.15–0.20 in./4–5 mm long, elliptic, acute, densely appressed pubescent, brown, indurated, nerves obscure, sterile lemma about one-half as long as the fertile one, usually glabrous or appressed pubescent on the back, appearing as hairy scales; palea two-nerved, almost as long as its lemma, ciliate on the back and at the apex; caryopsis enclosed, slightly compressed, brown, about 0.15 in./4 mm long, 2 mm wide. Flowering and fruiting occur from June through July.

Uses: The ornamental value of canary grass is in its seedheads. The green, immature seedheads are used in fresh floral arrangements; although most, if not all, of the seeds shatter at maturity, the empty seedheads are useful in dried floral arrangements, which are sometimes dyed. Canary grass is useful in naturalized areas as ground cover for wildlife, and as a source of wildlife feed, especially wildfowl. The economic value of canary grass lies in its use as a commercial source of birdfeed.

Cultivation: Propagation is by seeding. Locations in full sun in moist soil produce the maximum flowering. The overall view of canary grass is not particularly attractive, so it should not occupy a choice location in the garden. The plants have a relatively short flowering period; after the seeds mature, the plants rapidly turn beige or light tan. A related species, *Phalaris minor,* is sold occasionally in the trade as canary grass; the flowers are slightly smaller than those of canary grass; otherwise, they are almost identical.

Latin name: *Phalaris minor* Retz.
Origin: Mediterranean region
Habitat: Cultivated, escape from cultivation
Hardiness: Zones 4 through 10
Description: A tufted, upright-narrow to upright-open annual. Culms erect thin, slender, glabrous, 8–24 in./2–6 dm high. Foliage light green, fine in texture; leaf blades erect or more often ascending, straight, flat, rough on upper surface, long attenuate, 4–8 in./1–2 dm long, about 0.25–0.30 in./6–8 mm wide; sheaths shorter than the internodes, round on the back, glabrous or scabrous, ligule membranous, 0.1–0.2 in./3–4 mm long. Inflorescence a dense, soft, ovate-oblong, spikelike panicle, light green, 0.8–2.0 in./2–5 cm long, about one-third as wide; spikelets densely arranged on the rachis, narrow, 0.15–0.20 in./4–5 mm long, 2–3 mm wide, not conspicuously striped, two-flowered, with a sterile lemma below; glumes about equal, narrowly oblong, 0.20–0.25 in./5–6 mm long, the wing of the keel narrowly three-nerved; fertile lemma lanceolate-ovate, acute, about 3 mm long, appressed pubescent, sterile lemma solitary, about one-half as long as the fertile lemma; palea almost as long as its lemma. Flowering and fruiting occur from June through August.

Uses: The compact, soft seedheads constitute the main ornamental value of small canary grass. The dense, immature seedheads are often used as cut flowers; although the seeds shatter at maturity the dry, empty, beige seedheads are used in dried floral arrangements. Small canary grass, like canary grass, is used in naturalized areas for wildlife protection and as a source of bird feed; mixtures of these two grasses are often grown together for this purpose. The economic value of small canary grass lies in its use as bird feed.

Cultivation: Propagation is by seeding. The plants prefer full sun and are adapted to a wide range of soils.

Phalaris minor. **Habit,** ×
1/2; inflorescence, × **1;**
spikelet, × **5.** *Source: The*
Grasses and Pastures of South
Africa. Central News Agency.
1955.

***Phleum* L. (Timothy, Fleole, Phleole).** From *phleos,* a Greek name for a
kind of reed. Lectotype, *Phleum pratense* L. There are about 10 species, native
to the temperate regions of both hemispheres. Annual or perennial grasses with
erect culms, flat leaf blades, and dense cylindrical panicles. Spikelets one-
flowered, laterally compressed, disarticulating above the glumes; glumes equal,
membranous, keeled, abruptly mucronate or awned or gradually acute; lemmas

shorter than the glumes, hyaline, broadly truncate, three-to-five-nerved; palea narrow, nearly as long as the lemma.

Latin name: *Phleum pratense* L.
Synonym: *Phleum nodosum* var. *pratense* St. Amanas
Common names: Common timothy, Timothy, Mountain timothy, Herd's grass

***Phleum pratense.* Habit,** ×
1/2; glumes and floret, ×
10. *Source: Manual of the Grasses of the United States.* USDA Misc. Pub. 200. 1951.

Origin: Europe
Habitat: Cultivated, escape from cultivation
Hardiness: Zones 4 through 8
Description: An upright-narrow, tufted, short-lived perennial. Culms erect, with a bulbous base, tightly tufted, forming large clumps, simple 20–40 in./0.5–1.0 m high, smooth or nearly so. Foliage medium green, fine in texture; leaf blades erect to arching, flat, elongate, 4–12 in./1–3 dm long, 0.3–0.4 in./8–10 mm wide, glabrous above and beneath, margins scabrous; sheaths longer than the internodes, scabrous; ligule membranous, more or less round, 2–3 mm long. Inflorescence a densely flowered, dull green, cylindrical, spikelike panicle, narrow, dense, obtuse, 2–6 in./0.5–1.5 dm long, 0.2–0.3 in./5–8 mm wide; spikelets numerous, sessile or nearly so, crowded on a dense spike, 0.10–0.15 in./3–4 mm long, one-flowered; glumes equal, 0.10–0.15 in./3–4 mm long, membranous, three-nerved, ciliate on the keel, truncate, the sides minutely pubescent, abruptly awn-pointed, the awns usually about 1–3 mm long; lemmas membranous, hyaline, truncate, narrow, about one-half as long as the glumes; palea narrow, almost as long as its lemma; caryopsis enclosed, longitudinally striate, elongate, about 2 mm long, 1 mm wide. Flowering and fruiting occur from June through August.

Uses: Timothy makes a good ground cover in naturalized areas, producing a meadowlike effect. The chief ornamental value of timothy is its dried flower heads. These are quite attractive in their natural color; however, in florist shops they are usually dyed bright colors. The purplish anthers are an added attraction to the flowers.

Cultivation: Propagation is by seeding. Large areas may be seeded in pure stands, which usually result in a good ground cover. Once a stand is established, the only maintenance that may be required is tidying the edges. Cutting the plants back produces more ratoon growth, thereby resulting in thicker ground cover. Timothy grows best in full sun on a wide range of soils varying in pH from slightly acid to slightly alkaline.

Phragmites **Adans. (Reed, Roseau).** Name from Greek, *phragma*, "fence," apparently from its hedgelike growth habit along streams and ditches. Type species, *Phragmites communis* Trin. There are four species, widely distributed on all continents. Perennial reeds with broad, flat, linear leaf blades and large, terminal, compound panicles. Spikelets several-flowered, the rachilla clothed with long, silky hairs, disarticulating above the glumes and at the base of each segment between the florets, the lowest floret staminate or neuter; glumes three-nerved, or the upper five-nerved, lanceolate, acute, unequal, the lower about half as long as the upper, the upper shorter than the florets; lemmas long attenuate, glabrous, three-nerved, the florets successively smaller, the summits of all about equal; palea much shorter than the lemma.

Latin name: *Phragmites australis* (Cav.) Trin. ex Steud.
Synonym: *Phragmites communis* Trin.
Common names: Common reed, Carrizo
Origin: Mediterranean region
Habitat: Cultivated, escape from cultivation
Hardiness: Zones 5 through 10
Description: A robust, upright-narrow perennial, spreading by leafy stolons or rhizomes or both. Culms erect, hollow, stout, usually simple, rigid, glabrous, usually 8–16 ft /2.5–4.9 m high. Foliage medium green or greenish yellow, coarse in texture; leaf blades straight, flat, contracted, and round at base, expanding and then attenuating into a long, fine-pointed tip, blades of lower leaves very short, 1–3 in./2.5–8.0 cm long, upper leaf blades usually 6–20 in./ 1.5–5.0 dm long, 0.8–2.0 in./2–5 cm wide, glabrous except the occasionally ciliate-serrate margins; sheaths round on the back, smooth, imbricate, loosely clasping the culm; ligules a fringe of short, white hairs. Inflorescence a loosely branched terminal, conical panicle, often purplish becoming tawny, short-exserted at first, finally long-exserted, the branches erect, compound, in five to seven fascicles, usually 6–10 in./1.5–2.5 dm long, 2–4 in./5–10 cm wide, woolly at the nodes, glabrous about half the distance from the base, scabrous, branchlets numerous, long, scabrous, spikelets numerous, borne on short, scabrous pedicels much shorter than the spikelets, 0.5–0.7 in./13–18 mm long, three-to-seven-flowered, the lower floret staminate, the others perfect; the silky hairs on the rachilla about as long as the lemmas, the rachilla disarticulates at the base, with the long, copious hairs remaining with the next florets above; glumes unequal, lanceolate, acute, glabrous, the lower about 0.2 in./5 mm long, 1–2 mm wide, three-nerved, the upper 0.25–0.30 in./6–8 mm long, 1–2 mm wide, five-nerved, the nerves of both often confluent with the midnerve toward the apex; lemmas long attenuate, that of the lowest spikelet longest, about 0.4–0.5 in./10–13 mm long, those above progressively shorter, three-nerved, about as long as the hairs of the rachilla; palea two-keeled, hyaline, about 0.1 in./3 mm long; caryopsis enclosed, obovate-oblong, light brown, about 1 mm long and 0.5 mm wide. Flowering and fruiting occur from August until frost.

Uses: These large, colonizing reeds form extensive, pure stands over vast areas of wetlands, providing wildlife protection in low-lying coastal areas and along streams and ditches. Their ornamental value is demonstrated by stands in and along streams or lakes, where the massive plants and their flowering panicles are reflected in the water. This value becomes more impressive when the variegated cultivar Variegatus is used in specimen plantings in water gardens. Common reed and its variegated variant are compatible with other plants in mixed, perennial background borders. An added special charm of the large, colorful panicles is their one-sided shape and the fact that they persist throughout most, if not all, of the winter. Before the foliage drops in the winter, it provides good fall color, usually beige or russet. These large reeds are not intended for the

Phragmites australis. **A, Habit, × 1/4; B, ligule, × 1/2; C, spikelet, ×
5.** *Source: Selected Weeds of the United States.* USDA Agric. Handbook 366. 1970.

small, formal garden but are useful in larger areas such as seaside plantings,
where they are beneficial as windbreaks, as medium or tall screens, and for
erosion control. Large colonies of common reed aid in soil deposition over long
periods. The flowering panicles are useful in either fresh or dried floral arrangements, the latter either in their natural color or dyed. The value of common

reed and its variants as wildlife cover in naturalized areas is unequaled. Common reed occurs spontaneously in low-lying floodplains and barpits along highways in which rainwater accumulates, where it provides wildlife protection and improves the landscape. It is used along with its variegated forms in specimen plantings in parks and zoos.

Cultivation: Propagation is by seeding and by plant division, preferably the latter. Careful long-term planning as to the location and utilization of common reed is necessary to prevent the plants from dominating the landscape. Common reed and its cultivars grow best in low, wet areas, including marshes, bogs, swamps, around springs, and in shallow water of lakes and streams. The plants tolerate moderate salinity and grow best in full sun in firm, mineral, clay soils, where the water level fluctuates from 6 in./1.5 dm below the soil to the same distance above. Common reed is somewhat salt tolerant.

Poa L. (**Bluegrass, Meadow grass, Speargrass, Paturin**). Name from Greek *poa,* "grass." Lectotype, *Poa pratensis* L. There are about 250 species, inhabiting the temperate and cool regions of the world. Low or rather tall, slender annuals or usually perennials with spikelets in open or contracted panicles, leaf blades relatively narrow, flat, folded or involute, terminating in a cymbiform, tip. Spikelets two-to-several-flowered, the rachilla disarticulating above the glumes and between the florets; the uppermost floret reduced or rudimentary; glumes subequal or the upper longer than the lower, shorter than the first floret, lanceolate, acute, the lower one-nerved and the upper three-nerved; lemmas somewhat keeled, acute, or acuminate, rarely obtuse, awnless, membranous, five-nerved, the nerves sometimes pubescent, the callus or the base of the lemmas in many species with scant or copious, cottony hairs; palea as long as the lemma, scabrous-ciliate on the keels; stigmas small, long and slender; caryopsis beaked.

Latin name: *Poa alpina* L.
Synonym: *Poa alpina* var. *minor* Scribn.
Common name: Alpine bluegrass
Origin: Europe
Habitat: Open grassland at high elevations
Hardiness: Zones 5 through 7
Description: An upright-narrow, tufted perennial. Culms simple, slender, spreading from a bent base or erect, glabrous, 6–16 in./1.5–4.0 dm high. Foliage mostly basal, medium green, fine in texture; upper leaf blades about the middle of the culm flat or folded about the middle nerve, abruptly pointed, 2–4 in./5–10 cm long, 0.10–0.15 in./3–4 mm wide, glabrous or minutely hirsute on the margins; lower sheaths with membranous margins, open, glabrous, longer than the internodes; ligule membranous, blunt, 0.15–0.20 in./4–6 mm long. Inflorescence a purplish, branched, rather compact panicle, 2–3 in./5–8 cm long, almost as wide, ovate, erect or nodding, branches mostly in pairs, spreading, minutely

scabrous, axis glabrous, pedicels 1–2 mm long; spikelets broad, subcordate, compressed, two-to-five-flowered, 0.15–0.30 in./4–8 mm long; glumes slightly unequal or pointed, keeled, scabrous on the keels with broad membranous margins, lower glume one-to-three-nerved, 0.10–0.15 in./3–4 mm long, upper three-nerved, 0.1–0.2 in./3–5 mm long; lemmas imbricate, pointed, oblong or elliptic-oblong, 0.1–0.2 in./3–5 mm long, keeled, five-nerved with a fringe of fine hairs along the keel and marginal nerves and with shorter hairs on the inner nerves; palea with minutely hirsute keels, about as long as the lemma. Flowering and fruiting occur from June through August.

Uses: Alpine bluegrass makes an excellent alpine meadow, as it is a hardy perennial particularly adapted to low temperatures at higher elevations. This small perennial has a place in the rock garden and in sunny, dry sites.

Cultivation: Propagation is by direct seeding. The plants prefer full sun on poor, rocky, shallow soils.

Latin name: *Poa bulbosa* L.
Synonym: *Poa bulbosa* var. *vivipara* Koel.
Common name: Bulbous bluegrass
Habitat: Cultivated, escape from cultivation
Hardiness: Zones 5 through 7
Description: An upright-open perennial. Culms erect or spreading, densely tufted, more or less bulbous at base, simple, slender, glabrous, 1–2 ft /3–6 dm high. Foliage bluish green, fine in texture; leaf blades flat, folded or loosely involute. 1–4 in./2.5–10.0 cm long, 2–3 mm wide, firm, minutely hirsute on the margins, otherwise glabrous; sheaths glabrous, purplish or green, the inner basal sheaths form a bulbous thickening at the base of the vegetative shoot, the outer sheaths membranous, open almost to base; ligule membranous, 0.10–0.15 in./3–4 mm long, blunt or acuminate. Inflorescence an erect, branched, contracted, or moderately dense panicle, 1–3 in./2.5–8.0 cm long, 0.5–1.0 in./13–25 mm wide, ovate or oblong, fine hairlike branches ascending, minutely hirsute, lower panicle branches usually more than two; spikelets pedicellate, pedicels 1–3 mm long, mostly proliferous, the florets converted into bulblets about 0.8 in./20 mm long with a dark purple base about 2 mm long, the bracts extending into slender green tips 0.15–0.60 in./4–15 mm long, unaltered spikelets about five-flowered, not forming seeds; glumes finely pointed, equal, 2–3 mm long, keeled, scabrous, on the keels with membranous margins, lower glume one-to-three-nerved, upper three-nerved; normal lemmas lanceolate or lanceolate-oblong, pointed, 2–3 mm long, imbricate, keeled, five-nerved with a fringe of short hairs at the base; palea minutely hirsute on the keels, about as long as the lemma; caryopsis enclosed; viviparous spikelets modified usually into a single bulbil, enclosed by leaflike lemmas 0.2–0.8 in./5–20 mm long. Flowering and fruiting occur from April through July.

Uses: The attractive bluish green foliage of bulbous bluegrass makes it useful as an accent plant in foreground borders. The reproductive method of bulbous bluegrass is the center of interest of this ornamental. The flowers are proliferous; that is, small bulblets or miniature plants are borne in dense clusters instead of seeds. Sometimes the flowers, i.e., bulblets, are used in dried arrangements. It is grown occasionally in small clumps in the rock garden as a curiosity rather than as an ornamental.

Cultivation: Propagation is by plant division and by planting bulblets. The weight of the dense clusters of bulblets bends the culms toward the ground; the bulblets that come into contact with the soil and those which fall to the ground begin to grow under favorable conditions. The plants exhibit their unique reproduction best when grown on raised beds; they require full sun on fertile garden soil with ample moisture.

Latin name: *Poa chaixii* Vill.
Origin: North America, Northern Europe
Habitat: Rich soil in wooded areas
Hardiness: Zones 4 through 7
Description: An upright-open, densely tufted perennial. Culms erect or bent at the base, terete, stout, 2–4 ft /0.6–1.2 m high, vegetative shoots strongly flattened, glabrous, and shining. Foliage shiny green, fine in texture; leaf blades initially folded, becoming flat and hooded at the tip, firm, abruptly pointed, 12–20 in./3–5 dm long, 0.3–0.4 in./8–10 mm wide, rough below on the midrib and margins, finely nerved; sheaths sharply keeled and compressed, prominently nerved, minutely hirsute on the nerves; ligule membranous, 1–2 mm long. Inflorescence an erect lax or nodding panicle, ovate to ovate-oblong, 4–10 in./1.0–2.5 dm long, 2–5 in./0.5–1.3 dm wide, greenish, axis minutely hirsute or glabrous below, branches very fine, in clusters, or whorls of five, bearing spikelets above the middle, the lower branches occasionally drooping, flexuous, glabrous and undivided toward the base; spikelets short-pedicellate, pedicels 1–3 mm long, ovate to oblong, imbricate, 0.10–0.15 in./4–6 mm long, two-to-four-flowered; glumes unequal, firm, pointed, rough on the keels, lower glume lanceolate, 2–3 mm long, upper three-nerved; lemmas lanceolate-oblong, imbricate, 0.10–0.15 in./3–4 mm long, keeled, abruptly pointed, finely five-nerved, minutely hirsute; paleas about as long as the lemmas, with two rough keels. Flowering and fruiting occur from May through June.

Uses: This hardy perennial provides a good ground cover in shaded, wooded sites. It may be considered as a lawn substitute in a broad sense, and it is ideal for incorporation in naturalized areas.

Cultivation: Propagation is by direct seeding. The plants prefer shaded locations and are tolerant of a wide range of soils.

Latin name: *Poa compressa* L.
Synonym: *Paneion compressum* Lunell
Common names: Canada bluegrass, Wiregrass
Origin: Eurasia, Europe

Habitat: Cultivated, escape from cultivation
Hardiness: Zones 4 through 9
Description: An upright-narrow perennial with horizontal rhizomes. Culms glabrous, solitary or in small tufts, often gregarious, much compressed, flattened, two-edged, wiry, erect from a decumbent base, 6–24 in./1.5–6.0 dm high, bluish green. Foliage bluish green, fine in texture; leaf blades 2–4 in./5–10 cm long, 0.10–0.15 in./3–4 mm wide, flat or conduplicate, usually stiff, erect or spreading, smooth beneath, rough above, scabrous on the margins, abruptly acute; sheaths shorter than the internodes, smooth, somewhat keeled on the back; ligule membranous, truncate or round, pubescent, 1–2 mm long. Inflorescence a terminal contracted, open, branched, rather oblong panicle, 2–4 in./5–10 cm long, about 0.5 in./13 mm wide, branches ascending or erect, 1–2 in./2.5–5.0 cm long, the middle branches mostly in threes or fours, bearing spikelets near the base on short pedicels about 2 mm long; spikelets crowded, subsessile, 0.10–0.25 in./3–6 mm long, three-to-seven-flowered, the uppermost floret imperfect or rudimentary, usually purplish, varying from the margins and tip of the glumes and upper portion of the lemma to only the tip of the lemma, fading out to a tan or light brown; glumes nearly equal, ovate, oblong or elliptic, 2–3 mm long, margins membranous, three-nerved, keeled, rough on the keels; lemmas firm, awnless, small or wanting, 2–3 mm long, obtuse, or subacute, scabrous on the keels below the middle and also on the lateral veins toward the base, sparingly cottony at the base, obscurely five-nerved or the intermediate nerves wanting or obscure, subacute, the marginal nerves glabrous or pubescent below; palea two-nerved, two-keeled, keels scabrous, nearly as long as the lemma. Flowering and fruiting occur from June through September.

Uses: Canada bluegrass is an excellent ground cover, producing a meadow effect. The plants form a dense sod, abetted by their strong, horizontal root systems. Canada bluegrass is useful in naturalized areas and in rock gardens, where its bluish green foliage is attractive.

Cultivation: Propagation is by direct seeding; seeding may be done in the fall or in the spring. The plants prefer full sun and will thrive on poor soils; they require practically no maintenance once established.

Latin name: *Poa confinis* Vasey
Origin: North America
Habitat: Sand dunes, sandy meadows
Hardiness: Zones 7 through 9
Description: An upright-open to spreading dioecious, rhizomatous perennial. Culms often geniculate at the base, usually 6–12 in./1.5–3.0 dm high, often rooting at the lower nodes, terete or slightly flattened. Foliage medium green, fine in texture; leaf blades involute, 2–4 in./5–10 cm long, 1–2 mm wide their entire length; leaves of the innovations numerous; sheaths chartaceous, open, tawny, longer than the internodes, persistent; ligule membranous, pubescent, acute, 1–3 mm long. Inflorescence a narrow, branched, compact to some-

what open, tawny panicle, 1–2 in./2.5–5.0 cm long, 0.25–0.50 in./6–13 mm wide, the short branches approximate and appressed or ascending, bearing spikelets to their tips, the two sexes similar; spikelets 0.15–0.20 in./4–5 mm long, mostly three-to-four-flowered; glumes about equal, 0.10–0.15 in./3–4 mm long, the upper slightly shorter than the lower, margins membranous, three-nerved, rough or smooth on the keels; lemmas 0.10–0.15 in./3–4 mm long, strongly keeled, scabrous, sparsely webbed at the base, obscurely four-nerved, palea with scabrous keels, about as long as the lemma; pistillate florets with minute, abortive anthers, staminate florets often with rudimentary pistils. Flowering and fruiting occur from June through July.

Uses: This native sand-binding grass occurs on sand dunes, where its chief value is in its ability to form a good ground cover, thus arresting blowing and moving sand or reducing erosion in naturalized seaside areas.

Cultivation: Propagation is by direct seeding and by plant division, preferably the former. The plants prefer full sun and grow best on pure sand or sandy clay soils; they are moderately salt tolerant and will withstand windy sites.

Latin name: *Poa glauca* Vahl
Synonym: *Poa caesia* J. E. Smith
Common name: Greenland bluegrass
Origin: Europe
Habitat: Rocky slopes in alpine regions
Hardiness: Zones 2 through 7
Description: A tufted, upright-open to spreading perennial. Culms compressed, flattened, stiff, slender, glabrous, simple, 4–12 in./1–3 dm high. Foliage mostly basal, glaucous or bluish green, fine in texture; leaf blades flat or usually folded, 1–3 in./2.5–8.0 cm long, 1–2 mm wide, stiff, spreading, abruptly pointed, almost glabrous; sheaths glabrous, overlapping, slightly keeled, round on the back; ligule blunt, membranous, 1–3 mm long. Inflorescence a rather compact, erect, branched panicle, 1–3 in./2.5–8.0 cm long, 1.0–1.5 in./2.5–4.0 cm wide, lanceolate to ovate, open or contracted, variegated with purple, scabrous branches erect or ascending, mostly in pairs or threes, angular, glabrous on the lower part, few-flowered, pedicels 0.15–0.20 in./4–5 mm long; spikelets mostly two-flowered, sometimes three-to-six-flowered, compressed, ovate to oblong, 0.15–0.25 in./4–6 mm long; glumes about equal, pointed, ovate to elliptic, 0.10–0.15 in./3–4 mm long, keeled, three-nerved, minutely hirsute on the keels in the upper portion; lemmas overlapping, oblong, 0.10–0.15 in./3–4 mm long, keeled, strongly pubescent on the lower half of the keel and marginal nerves and often slightly hairy on the faint, intermediate nerves, finely five-nerved, firm with broad, membranous tip and margins; palea minutely hairy or rough on the keels, about as long as the lemma. Flowering and fruiting occur from June through August.

Uses: Greenland bluegrass makes an excellent meadow at high elevations. It is grown for its foliage and ground-covering ability in cold climates. This small, glaucous, bluish green perennial is ideal in dry sunny locations in the rock garden.

Cultivation: Propagation is by direct seeding. The plants prefer full sun in dry, rocky soils.

Latin name: *Poa macrantha* Vasey
Synonym: *Melica macrantha* Beal
Origin: North America
Habitat: Sand dunes, sandy meadows
Hardiness: Zones 7 through 9
Description: An upright-open to spreading, dioecious perennial with creeping rhizomes and stolons. Culms glabrous, terete, erect from a decumbent base of extensively creeping rhizomes 6–18 in./1.5–4.5 dm high. Foliage medium green, fine in texture; leaves in dense basal tufts, leaf blades involute, puberulent, subflexuous, 3–6 in./0.8–1.5 dm long, about 2–3 mm wide their entire length; sheaths glabrous, shorter than the internodes, round on the back, open, chartaceous, tawny, glabrous; ligule membranous, 1–3 mm long, strongly pubescent, thick, truncate. Inflorescence a branched oblong or ovoid panicle, more or less contracted, pale or tawny, sometimes dense and spikelike, 2–5 in./0.5–1.3 dm long, about 0.8–1.0 in./20–25 mm wide, branches approximate, short; spikelets subsessile, keeled, the two sexes similar, about 0.4–0.5 in./10–13 mm long, five-flowered, occasionally proliferous; glumes more or less equal, 0.25–0.30 in./6–8 mm long, the upper indistinctly five-nerved, about 0.3–0.4 in./8–10 mm long, the lower about 0.3 in./8 mm long, three-nerved; lemmas about 0.25–0.30 in./6–8 mm long, short-webbed at the base, 7-to-11-nerved, pubescent on the keels and marginal nerves below, slightly scabrous on the keels above; palea rough, about the length of the lemma; pistillate florets with abortive stamens, staminate florets often with rudimentary pistils. Flowering and fruiting occur from June through July.

Uses: The chief ornamental value of this rhizomatous perennial is in its use as a ground-cover and sand-binding plant in naturalized coastal areas. The extensive, strong, rhizomatous root system coupled with its gregarious growth and size, enables the plants to stabilize blowing sand and moving sand. It is compatible with other seaside erosion-control species with a different growth habit (e.g., *Arundo donax* and *Phragmites australis*).

Cultivation: Propagation is by seeding and by plant division, preferably the latter. The plants prefer full sun in sand dunes or in very sandy soils.

Latin name: *Poa nemoralis* L.
Synonym: *Paneion nemorale* Lunell
Common names: Wood bluegrass, Foin à vaches
Origin: Europe
Habitat: Open woodland, occasionally in meadows, cultivated
Hardiness: Zones 3 through 9

Description: An upright-narrow, loosely tufted perennial. Culms erect or spreading, slender, thin, glabrous, 12–28 in./3.0–7.1 dm high. Foliage medium green, fine in texture; leaf blades straight, elongate, ascending, 2–5 in./0.5–1.3 dm long, 1–3 mm wide, usually weak, minutely pubescent or glabrous, long attenuate; sheaths slightly closed, keeled, about as long as the internodes; ligules membranous, truncate, less than 1 mm long. Inflorescence an erect or nodding, lanceolate to ovate or oblong, very lax panicle, sometimes contracted, finally exserted, 2–5 in./0.5–1.3 dm long, about two-thirds as wide, greenish or purplish, branches clustered, hairlike, flexuous, spreading, bare and undivided in the lower part, puberulent, pedicels 0.20–0.25 in./5–6 mm long; spikelets lanceolate to ovate or oblong, 0.10–0.25 in./3–6 mm long, compressed, two-to-five-flowered, florets normal; glumes equal or slightly unequal, narrow, acuminate, membranous, three-nerved, rough on the keels, lower glume lanceolate, 2–3 mm long, upper 0.10–0.15 in./3–4 mm long, lanceolate to ovate; lemmas imbricate, blunt or slightly pointed, 0.10–0.15 in./3–4 mm long, sparsely webbed at base, finally five-nerved, keeled, the keel and marginal nerves fringed with fine hairs, occasionally a few long hairs at the base; palea two-toothed, with minutely rough keels, about as long as the lemma; caryopsis enclosed. Flowering and fruiting occur from June through August.

Uses: Wood bluegrass, as the vernacular name implies, is particularly adapted for ground cover and as a lawn substitute in shaded woodlands. It is an ideal plant for naturalizing extended areas. Once established, it requires practically no maintenance unless it is used as a substitute lawn. The flower heads are elegant on the plants; however, they are of little value in dried bouquets.

Cultivation: Propagation is by direct seeding. The plants reseed themselves very readily. This perennial prefers slightly acid soils in light shade, although the plants will grow in a wide range of soils in full sun.

Latin name: *Poa pratensis* L.
Synonym: *Poa angustifolia* L.
Cultivars: Several in cultivation
Common names: Kentucky bluegrass, Junegrass, Speargrass
Origin: Europe
Habitat: Cultivated, escape from cultivation
Hardiness: Zones 3 through 9
Description: A rhizomatous, semievergreen, spreading, glabrous perennial. Culms compressed, simple, densely tufted, slightly compressed, 1–4 ft/0.3–1.2 m high but usually 1–2 ft /3–6 dm. Foliage greenish gray or medium to dark green, soft, fine in texture; cauline leaf blades 2–6 in./0.5–1.5 dm long, basal, leaf blades soft, flat or folded, often much longer, about 20–25 in./5.0–6.3 dm long, 0.10–0.25 in./3–6 mm wide, usually glabrous or pubescent on the upper surface, slightly rough beneath; lower sheaths imbricate, flattened, longer or shorter than the internodes, glabrous or sometimes scabrous; ligule truncate, entire or erose, finely ciliolate, about 1–2 mm long, those of the innovations

Poa pratensis. **Habit,** × 1/2; **spikelet,** × 5; **floret,** × 10. *Source: Manual of the Grasses of the West Indies.* USDA Misc. Pub. 243. 1936.

usually less than 1 mm long and those of the upper culm leaves up to 0.1 in./ 3 mm long and more coarsely erose. Inflorescence an open, branched, pyramidal or oblong-pyramidal panicle, 2–6 in./0.5–1.5 dm long, long-exserted on a long, slender peduncle, bearing spikelets above the middle, branches ascending, spreading or horizontal in whorls of three to five, lower longer and in half whorls of four or five, subdivided into branchlets; spikelets crowded at the end of the branches, ovate to lanceolate, 0.1–0.2 in./3–5 mm long, flattened, three-to-six-flowered, purplish; glumes slightly unequal, persistent, acute, scabrous on the keel, otherwise glabrous, the lower glume one-nerved, about 2 mm long, the upper three-nerved, about 2–3 mm long; lemmas copiously webbed or cottony at the base, about 0.1 in./3 mm long acute, five-nerved, keeled, the keels pubescent, the marginal and midnerves scabrous or silky pubescent below, the intermediate nerves glabrous and prominent; palea shorter than its lemma, two-nerved, two-keeled, scabrous on the keels; caryopsis smooth, enclosed. Flowering and fruiting occur from May through July.

Uses: Kentucky bluegrass and its many cultivars are widely used as lawn grasses. Some forms are more cold and shade tolerant than others. These grasses have many uses in addition to that of lawns. Kentucky bluegrass and its sod-forming variants form attractive ground covers and are useful in preventing soil erosion. They may be successfully grown in inaccessible and difficult locations adjacent to the lawn, where they require practically no maintenance, as they are usually low enough not to require mowing. Shade-tolerant forms are useful as ground cover in shaded locations. The wide range of adaptation and usefulness contribute to the popularity and widespread use of Kentucky bluegrass and its variants in landscape improvement.

Cultivation: Propagation is by seeding and by plant division. These grasses should be seeded in the fall (i.e., September or October) on a well-prepared seedbed. Seed stocks are readily available, and seeding should be done at prescribed rates. Kentucky bluegrass is usually propagated by seeding, although the rhizomatous plants may be divided successfully when they are in active growth during spring, summer, or early fall.

Other ornamental species include *Poa colensoi,* Blue tussock, and *Poa labillardieri,* Australian poa (see Appendix 1).

***Polypogon* Desf. (Beardgrass).** Name from Greek *polus,* ''much,'' and *pogon,* ''beard,'' referring to the bristly inflorescence. Type species, *Polypogon monspeliensis* (L.) Desf. There are 10 species, inhabiting temperate regions. Decumbent annual or perennial grasses with flat, scabrous leaf blades and dense, bristly, spikelike panicles. Spikelets one-flowered, the pedicel disarticulating a short distance below the glumes, leaving a short-pointed callus attached; glumes equal, entire or two-lobed, awned from the tip or from between the lobes, the awn slender, straight; lemma much shorter than the glumes, hyaline, usually bearing a slender, straight awn shorter than the awns of the glumes.

Latin name: *Polypogon monspeliensis* (L.) Desf.
Synonym: *Alopecurus monspeliensis* L.
Common names: Rabbit-foot grass, Rabbit's-foot, Annual beardgrass
Origin: Europe
Habitat: Wet or dry sites, often in brackish water
Hardiness: Zones 2 through 9
Description: An upright-narrow to upright-open, loosely tufted, aquatic annual. Culms erect from a decumbent base, sparingly branched, slender to somewhat stout, 18–30 in./4.5–7.6 dm high, scabrous or smooth beneath the panicle. Foliage medium green, fine in texture; leaf blades ascending, flat, narrowed at the base, acuminate, 4–6 in./1.0–1.5 dm long, 0.1–0.3 in./3–8 mm wide, puberulent on the nerves, scabrous above; sheaths smooth or scabrous upward, the uppermost inflated, sometimes slightly scabrous, about as long as the internodes; ligule membranous, 0.2–0.4 in./5–10 mm long, with truncate tip. Inflorescence a dense, spikelike, short-branched panicle, 2–6 in./0.5–1.5 dm long, 0.5–1.5 in./1.3–4.0 cm wide, sometimes interrupted below, oval or cylindrical, soft, silky, usually yellowish, shiny, light green when mature; spikelets numerous, narrowly oblong, about 2 mm long, one-flowered, flower perfect, subsessile, approximate, spikelets almost concealed by the long awns, which are four to six times as long as the spikelets; glumes unequal, one-nerved, slightly lobed, about 1–2 mm long, hispidulous, round on the back below, hispid, both with straight awns 0.15–0.30 in./4–8 mm long from an obtuse, slightly bifid or entire apex; lemmas about 1 mm long, truncate, erose, very smooth, hyaline, broad, shining, broadly elliptic, blunt, five-nerved, minutely toothed tip, awnless or with an awn 0.10–0.15 in./3–4 mm long from below the tip; palea slightly shorter than the lemma; caryopsis enclosed. Flowering and fruiting from May through September.

Uses: Rabbit-foot grass is grown for its massive flower production, which reaches its peak in midsummer. The greenish yellow or tawny flowers are attractive on the plants and in fresh and dried arrangements. The dense mass of abundant flowers produces a delightful, light, silky appearance when the plants are grown in clumps in foreground annual borders.

Cultivation: Propagation is by direct seeding. The plants prefer full sun or very light shade and grow well in fertile, moist, well-drained soil. Rabbit-foot grass is often confused with hare's-tail, *Lagurus ovatus;* the former has longer and narrower flower heads, which are greenish yellow rather than ivory or white, like those of hare's-tail. Rabbit-foot grass is weak and subject to damage by strong wind and heavy rain. This potential damage can be minimized by growing the plants in protected locations.

Puccinellia **Parl. (Alkali-grass, Goosegrass).** Named for Professor Benedetto Puccinelli, an Italian botanist. Type species, *Puccinellia distans* (L.) Parl. Low-growing, usually light green, smooth, tufted annual or perennial grasses

Polypogon monspeliensis. **Habit,** × **1/2; glumes and floret,** × **10.** *Source: Manual of the Grasses of the West Indies.* USDA Misc. Pub. 243. 1936.

with narrow to open panicles. Spikelets several-flowered, usually terete or subterete, the rachilla disarticulating above the glumes and between the florets;
glumes unequal, shorter than the first lemma, obtuse or acute, rather firm, often
scarious at the tip, the lower one-nerved or sometimes three-nerved, the upper
three-nerved; lemmas usually firm, round on the back, obtuse or acute, rarely
acuminate, usually scarious and often erose at the tip, glabrous or puberulent
toward the base, rarely pubescent on the nerves, five-nerved, the nerves parallel,
indistinct, rarely rather prominent; palea about as long as the lemma or somewhat shorter.

Latin name: *Puccinellia fasciculata* (Torr.) Bickn.
Synonym: *Puccinellia borreri* (Bab.) Hitchc.
Common name: Borrer's saltmarsh grass
Origin: Europe
Habitat: Salt marshes, brackish areas
Hardiness: Zones 5 through 7
Description: A loosely tufted to densely tufted, upright-open perennial.
Culms erect or spreading, rather stout, glabrous, 8–20 in./2–5 dm high. Foliage
light or grayish green, glaucous, fine in texture; leaf blades flat, folded or subinvolute, hooded at the blunt tip, 2–6 in./0.5–1.5 dm long, 0.10–0.15 in./3–4
mm wide, firm, rough above, smooth beneath; sheaths longer than the internodes, round on the back, glabrous; ligule membranous, truncate, acute or obtuse, very blunt, 1–3 mm long. Inflorescence an erect, branched, densely flowered, elipsoid panicle, 2–6 in./0.5–1.5 dm long, unilateral, contracted and dense
or loose and open, grayish green tinged with purple, branches fascicled, scabrous, rather stiffly ascending, whorled, spreading horizontally, densely flowered, spikelets approximate to the base, or the longer branches rarely bare there,
pedicels very short; spikelets approximate, 0.10–0.15 in./3–4 mm long, three-
to-eight-flowered, awnless; glumes unequal ovate or elliptic, mostly blunt, 1–2
mm long, round on the back, green and firm except for white, membranous
margins and tips, three-nerved; lemmas coriaceous, imbricate, elliptic, blunt,
obtuse, about 2–3 mm long, green and firm except for the white, membranous
margins and tips, minutely hairy at base, five-nerved, the middle nerve usually
projecting at the tip, middle and outer nerves often minutely hairy toward the
base; paleas oblong, as long as the lemmas, two-keeled, keels minutely hairy;
caryopsis usually adherent to the palea. Flowering and fruiting occur from June
through August.

Uses: This salt-tolerant, saltmarsh grass provides good ground cover, as
well as food and protection for migratory wildfowl in coastal regions. The salt
tolerance of Borrer's saltmarsh grass makes it useful in naturalizing difficult areas
of salt marshes. It is useful in saline areas inland and near the sea.

Cultivation: Propagation is by seeding and by plant division. The plants
prefer full sun in saline conditions.

Latin name: *Puccinellia maritima* (Huds.) Parl.
Synonym: *Poa maritima* Huds.
Common name: Saltmarsh grass
Origin: Europe
Habitat: Salt marshes
Hardiness: Zones 5 and 6
Description: An upright-open to spreading perennial with slender rhizomes. Culms erect, rather coarse, smooth, stout, 6–30 in./1.5–7.6 dm high. Foliage light to yellowish green, fine in texture; leaves distributed along the culm, not in basal tufts, leaf blades 3–8 in./0.8–2.0 dm long, 1–3 mm wide, folded or involute, with an abruptly pointed, slender, hooded tip, smooth beneath, rough on the nerves above; sheaths longer than the internodes, round on

Puccinellia maritima.
Habit, × 1; floret, × 10.
Source: Manual of the Grasses of the United States. USDA Misc. Pub. 200. 1951.

the back, glabrous; ligule membranous, obtuse or acute, 1–3 mm long. Inflorescence a stiff, erect, branched, pyramidal panicle, 3–8 in./0.8–2.0 dm long, 1–2 in./2.5–5.0 cm wide, rather dense, usually contracted, branches scabrous, stiff, ascending or appressed, or finally spreading, more or less whorled, lower branches longer than the upper; spikelets oblong or more or less terete or subterete, 0.2–0.5 in./5–13 mm long, 4-to-10-flowered; glumes unequal, lanceolate to ovate, lower glume 2–3 mm long, one-nerved, sometimes three-nerved, upper 0.10–0.15 in./3–4 mm long, three-to-five-nerved; lemmas obscurely five-nerved, round on the back, imbricate, elliptic or broadly oblong, rather blunt or slightly pointed, 0.1–0.2 in./3–5 mm long, tapered gradually to an acute tip, pubescent at the base of the lateral nerves and sometimes between the nerves; palea shorter than its lemma, the keels minutely hairy; caryopsis adherent to the palea. Flowering and fruiting occur from May through August.

Uses: Saltmarsh grass is not a true ornamental; however, it fills a niche that is unsuitable for many other species. Its salt tolerance permits its use in naturalizing coastal salt marshes and brackish areas along the coast. It provides feed and protection, particularly for migratory wildfowl. It is used in much the same way as Borrer's saltmarsh grass.

Cultivation: Propagation is by seeding and by plant division. The plants prefer full sun in saline marshes and brackish areas.

Rhynchelytrum Nees. Name from Greek *rhychos,* "beak," and *elytron,* "scale," alluding to the beaked upper glume and sterile lemma. Type species, *Rhynchelytrum dregeanum* Nees. There are about 40 species, mostly of African origin. Annual or perennial grasses with expanded or rolled leaf blades and open or contracted panicles of silky spikelets, the caryopsis not falling from the spikelet at maturity. Spikelets on short capillary pedicels; lower glume minute, villous; upper glume and sterile lemma equal, gibbous below, raised on a stipe above the lower glume, emarginate or slightly lobed, short-awned, covered, except toward the slightly spreading apex, with long silky hairs, the palea of the sterile lemma well developed; fertile lemma shorter than the spikelet, cartilanginous, smooth, cymbiform, obtuse, the margin thin, not enrolled, enclosing the margins of the palea.

> **Latin name:** *Rhynchelytrum repens* (Willd.) C.E. Hubb.
> **Synonym:** *Rhynchelytrum roseum* (Nees) Stapf & C.E. Hubb.
> **Common name:** Natal grass
> **Origin:** Southern Africa
> **Habitat:** Cultivated, escape from cultivation
> **Hardiness:** Zones 7 through 10
> **Description:** A loosely tufted, upright-open to spreading, short-lived perennial. Culms slender, rather thin, weak, simple or branched, often decumbent at base or ascending, rooting at the lower nodes; otherwise erect, 24–30 in./

Rhynchelytrum repens. **Habit,** × **1/2; spikelet and floret,** × **10.** *Source: Manual of the Grasses of the West Indies.* USDA Misc. Pub. 243. 1936.

6.0–7.6 dm high, the nodes conspicuously villous. Foliage light green, the upper leaves often tinged pinkish or purple, fine in texture; leaf blades flat, arching, glabrous or hairy, 5–10 in./1.3–2.5 dm long, up to 0.25 in./6 mm wide, long attenuate, often tinged with purple; sheaths sparsely hirsute or glabrous, round on the back. Inflorescence a branched, ovoid or narrow, erect to drooping panicle, silky, rosy purple or sometimes pale pink, 4–10 in./1.0–2.5 dm long, about two-thirds as wide, open and loose or contracted and fairly dense, branches slender, ascending with capillary branchlets; spikelets two-flowered, the upper floret perfect, the lower usually staminate, about 0.10–0.25 in./3–6 mm long, borne on short capillary pedicels, shiny, with dense, silky, rosy-red hairs extending 0.15–0.20 in./4–5 mm beyond the tip of the spikelet; the lower floret staminate; glumes unequal, lower glume about one-third the length of the spikelet, usually smaller, silky villous, linear-subulate, hidden among the hairs at the base of the spikelet, upper glume about as long as the spikelet, finely five-to-seven-nerved, usually convex on the back in the lower part projecting into a strongly compressed beak, sometimes tuberculate on the back, two-lobed, awned from between the lobes, awn straight filiform; upper floret bisexual, smaller than the lower, awnless, glabrous, membranous; lower lemma like the upper glume, enclosing the palea, fertile lemma much shorter than the sterile one, glabrous, chartaceous, the margins clasping the palea; palea about as long as the lemma, two-keeled, keels hairy. Flowering and fruiting occur from June through August. The delicate, branched panicles bear flowering spikelets with long, silky hairs varying in color and shades of white, silver, cream, mauve, pink, rose or purple, fading into pinkish silver at maturity.

Uses: The delicate, light, fluffy, flowering panicles of natal grass are beautiful when the plants are established in massed stands. The plants produce an abundance of pretty flowers in varying shades of color throughout the summer; unfortunately, they are easily dispersed by the slightest breeze at maturity. The delicate, massed, shining panicles are the crowning glory of natal grass. Natal grass is useful in middleground borders, in rock and water gardens, and in specimen plantings. This short-lived perennial is particularly attractive in full sunlight, with its light, fluffy, glossy panicles shining, undulating, and waving in the slightest breeze. The immature, colorful, flower heads are useful in fresh flower arrangements, although they will shatter badly upon drying.

Cultivation: Propagation is by direct seeding and by plant division. Prolific seed production enables the plants to reseed themselves readily. Natal grass thrives best in full sun on a wide range of well-drained soils that are low to average in fertility. Weak, lanky plants usually result when plants are grown in shade. The delicate, flowering panicles are easily damaged by wind and rain; the plants may be damaged by early frost in colder regions. The species is highly variable, there are perceptible differences in flower color among strains of natal grass. Natal grass may be found in the trade as *Tricholaena rosea,* or possibly *Rhynchelytrum roseum.* This short-lived perennial is grown as an annual in zones 5–9 and as a perennial in zones 9 and 10. The plants require a rather long growing season and should be started indoors in early spring when grown as an annual.

Schizachyrium Nees. Lectotype, *Schizachyrium brevifolium* (Sw.) Nees   Annual or perennial grasses, tufted or from rootstocks, with flat or involute leaf blades and spikelike racemes, singly disposed, terminating the stem or its branches. Internodes of the articulate rachis cup-shaped or crowned at the apex with a toothed or bifid appendage, the callus at the back barbed. Spikelets in pairs at each node of the hairy rachis, one sessile, the other pedicellate. Sessile spikelet dorsally compressed, one-flowered, the flower perfect; first scale enfolded on the margins, two-keeled, second scale awnless or rarely with a short bristle, one-nerved or sometimes awnless, keeled; third scale with enfolded margins, two-nerved or nerveless, fourth scale usually two-cleft at the apex, often almost to the base, bearing a perfect usually geniculate awn, rarely awnless. Pedicellate spikelet without flowers, of one or two scales, rarely of four scales and bearing a staminate flower, or wanting. Stamens usually three, very rarely one or two; style distinct, stigmas plumose, sometimes double the length of the styles, exserted below the middle of the spikelet.

Latin name: *Schizachyrium scoparium* (Michx.) Nash
Synonym: *Andropogon scoparius* Michx.
Common names: Little bluestem, Bluestem, Broom beard grass, Bunchgrass, Prairie bluegrass, Broom, Wiregrass
Origin: North America
Habitat: Cultivated, escape from cultivation
Hardiness: Zones 4 through 9
Description: An upright-open to spreading perennial. Culms densely tufted, erect, slender, 2–4 ft /0.6–1.2 m high, branching above, green or purplish, rarely glaucous. Foliage dark green or purplish, fine in texture; leaf blades flat, 4–8 in./1–2 dm long, 0.1–0.3 in./3–8 mm wide, usually rough, sparsely hirsute above near the base; sheaths flattened, shorter than the internodes, scabrous, glabrous to sparsely hairy; ligule membranous, truncate, about 1 mm long. Inflorescence numerous, long-exserted, solitary racemes, 1–3 in./2.5–8.0 cm long, usually curved, borne on slender peduncles, one to four from a single sheath, the entire inflorescence is 10–15 in./2.5–3.8 dm long and narrow, about 3–5 in./0.8–1.3 dm wide, rachis slender, flexuous, mostly zigzag, rachis joints and pedicels ciliate with hairs 1–3 mm long; sessile spikelets 0.2–0.3 in./5–8 mm long, somewhat longer than the pedicels, scabrous; glumes almost equal, acuminate, awn-pointed, the lower glume flattened below, scabrous, obscurely nerved, the upper keeled, scabrous on the keels, ciliate on the margins; sterile lemma nearly as long as the glumes, acuminate, fertile lemma shorter than the sterile lemma, with deeply bifid apex terminated by an awn 0.3–0.6 in./8–15 mm long, the awn twisted, scabrous, geniculate about 0.1 in./3 mm from the

Schizachyrium scoparium.
**Habit, × 1/2; pair of
spikelets, × 5.** *Source:
Manual of the Grasses of the
United States.* USDA Misc.
Pub. 200. 1951.

base; pedicellate spikelets divergent, usually 1–3 mm long, reduced to a single glume, pedicels pilose. Flowering and fruiting occur from July through September.

Uses: The ornamental value of little bluestem is primarily in its variable colored foliage—bluish green, glaucous or light purplish—and secondarily in its purplish flower heads, which persist on the plant throughout most of the winter. Little bluestem is a very good ground-cover plant in naturalized areas in that it produces a thick turf when allowed to perenniate. The small, purplish flower heads are used as cut flowers and in dried arrangements. An additional bonus is that the plants remain upright throughout the winter, with their flower heads intact; the foliage turns dark red or purplish, producing good fall color. Little bluestem is an attractive and handsome plant throughout the year, which enhances its value and usage as an ornamental. It is particularly valuable along highways as ground cover and for erosion control.

Cultivation: Propagation is by seeding and by plant division. Little bluestem is widely distributed on many soil types over wide climatic ranges. The plants are quite drought tolerant and winter hardy. Little bluestem thrives best in full sun on a wide range of soils of low moisture content.

Setaria **Beauv. (Bristle grass, Bristly foxtail).** Name from Latin *seta*, "bristle," alluding to the numerous bristles of the inflorescence. Type species, *Setaria viridis* (L.) Beauv. There are about 125 species, inhabiting warm regions. Annual or perennial grasses with narrow, terminal panicles, these dense and spikelike or somewhat loose and open. Spikelets subtended by one to several bristles, sterile branchlets, falling free from the bristles, awnless; lower glume broad, usually less than one-half the length of the spikelet, three-to-five-nerved; upper glume and sterile lemma equal, or the glume shorter, several-nerved; fertile lemma coriaceous-indurate, transversely rugose or smooth.

Latin name: *Setaria geniculata* (Lam.) Beauv.
Synonym: *Chaetochloa geniculata* Millsp. & Chase
Cultivars: Many in cultivation
Common name: Rootknot bristlegrass
Origin: North America
Habitat: Cultivated, escape from cultivation
Hardiness: Zones 4 through 9
Description: An upright-narrow, weak perennial with short knotty rhizomes. Culms wiry, weak, erect or geniculate at the base, often tufted, arising from rhizomes, 1–3 ft /3–9 dm high. Foliage mostly basal, light green, fine in texture; leaf blades long acuminate, flat, usually not twisted but narrow, 3–10 in./0.8–2.5 dm long, 0.1–0.3 in./3–8 mm wide, with prominent midrib, glabrous, except sometimes villous at the base, more or less scabrous; sheaths shorter than the internodes or the lower longer, flattened, smooth or sometimes scabrous toward the summit, often purple tinged; ligule membranous, ciliate, about 1 mm long. Inflorescence a terminal, branched, long-exserted, cylindrical, spikelike panicle, yellowish or purple, 1–4 in./2.5–10.0 cm long, 0.4–0.5 in./10–13 mm wide including the bristles, sometimes slightly interrupted at the base, axis densely pubescent, branches usually about 0.20–0.25 in./5–6 mm long, densely pubescent, each branch bearing one well-developed spikelet and below this a cluster of short branchlets ending in bristles, sometimes a second,

small, undeveloped spikelet borne in one of these secondary clusters, branchlets usually about 1 mm long but various in length, bearing one or two bristles, bristles yellowish, purplish, or tawny, upwardly barbed, usually two or three times the length of the spikelets; spikelets two-flowered, plano-convex, ovoid, 2–3 mm long, slightly narrowed toward the apex; glumes unequal, the lower about one-half as long as the spikelet, three-nerved, the upper about two-thirds as long as the spikelet, five-nerved; sterile lemma five-to-seven-nerved, staminate or neuter with well-developed palea, fertile lemma coriaceous and indurate, smooth or rugose; caryopsis enclosed, subacute, about equal to the sterile lemma, strongly marked with numerous transverse ridges, undulate. Flowering and fruiting occur from April through August. The plants reseed themselves copiously and produce up to three seed crops per year, the first during May or June.

Uses: Rootknot bristlegrass is ideal for ground-cover plantings in naturalized areas of saline marshes. Although the plants are not large enough to provide effective wildlife cover, their seeds provide a ready source of wildlife feed.

Cultivation: Propagation is by seeding and by plant division. The prolific seed production of rootknot bristlegrass enhances its value as a ground-cover plant and as a feed source for birds. The plants require no maintenance once they are established. Rootknot bristlegrass grows best in full sun or light shade. The plants thrive in salt marshes if the water level is relatively low and on salty prairie sites, in addition to wet, sandy, acid soils.

Latin name: *Setaria italica* (L.) Beauv.
Synonym: *Chaetochloa italica* (L.) Scribn.
Cultivars: Many in cultivation
Common names: Foxtail millet, Foxtail, Italian millet, Japanese millet, Hungarian grass, Bengal grass, German millet, Millet des oiseaux
Origin: Eurasia
Habitat: Cultivated, escape from cultivation
Hardiness: Zones 4 through 9
Description: A loosely tufted, upright-narrow, short-lived annual. Culms in small, loose tufts, robust, erect, simple or branched, scabrous below the panicles, 2–3 ft /6–9 dm high. Foliage light to medium green, coarse in texture; leaf blades lanceolate, 6 16 in./1.5–4.0 dm long, 0.5–1.0 in./13–25 mm wide, flat, narrowed at both ends, glabrous or scabrid on both surfaces; sheaths imbricate, shorter than the internodes, pubescent at the collar, ciliate on the margins; ligule a ring of stiff hairs, 1–2 mm long. Inflorescence an erect or nodding, compound, cylindrical, dense panicle, or with some of the branches elongated and the false spike irregular and rather open, 2–9 in./0.5–2.3 dm long, 0.5–1.0 in./13–25 mm thick, often many-lobed, yellow, green, or purple, compactly flowered, the rachis densely villous; spikelets 2–3 mm long, two-flowered, in clusters on the central axis or panicle branches, subtended by one to three slightly scabrous bristles, upwardly barbed, one to three times as long as the spikelet; glumes unequal, the lower ovate, three-nerved, about one-third as long as the spikelet,

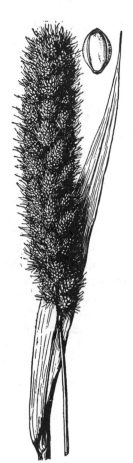

Setaria italica. **Panicle,** ×
1; floret, × **5.** *Source:*
Manual of the Grasses of the
United States. USDA Misc.
Pub. 200. 1951.

upper and sterile lemma more than half as long as the spikelet, five-to-seven-nerved; fertile lemma finely rugose or nearly smooth, sterile lemma five-to-seven-nerved, longer than the caryopsis; spikelets breaking up at maturity, the glumes and lower floret persistent, upper floret deciduous, lower floret sterile, usually reduced to a lemma, rarely with a minute palea; caryopsis plano-convex, finely transversely wrinkled or ridged, free. Flowering and fruiting occur from June through September.

Uses: Foxtail millet has been grown for almost five millenia. The seeds are extensively used as bird feed; perhaps at one time the seeds were used for human food. The plants provide an abundant source of bird feed and some protection for wildlife. Foxtail millet attracts birds from far and wide. The immature flower heads are useful as fresh cut flowers, and the empty, golden flower heads remain intact long enough for use in dried floral arrangements.

Cultivation: Propagation is by seeding. Foxtail millet is a prolific seeder, and the plants reseed themselves readily. The plants are rather short-lived; flowering begins in May, and the panicles are mature by midsummer. The plants thrive best in fertile, well-drained soil in full sun.

Another ornamental species is *Setaria palmifolia* f. *variegata,* variegated palmgrass (see Appendix 1).

Sitanion Raf. (Squirreltail). Name from Greek *sitos,* ''grain.'' Type species, *Sitanion elymoides* Raf. There are six or more species, native to the western United States. Low or rather tall, cespitose perennials with bristly spikes. Spikelets two-to-several-flowered, the uppermost floret reduced, usually two at each node of a disarticulating rachis, the rachis breaking at the base of each joint, remaining attached as a pointed stipe to the spikelets above; glumes narrow or setaceous, one-to-three-nerved, the nerves prominent, extending into one-to-several awns, these, when more than one, irregular in size, sometimes mere lateral appendages of the long, central awn, sometimes equal, the glume being bifid; lemmas firm, convex on the back, nearly terete, five-nerved, the nerves obscure, the apex slightly two-toothed, the central nerve extending into a long, slender, finally spreading awn, sometimes one or more of the lateral nerves also extending into short awns; palea firm, nearly as long as the body of the lemma, the two keels serrulate.

> **Latin name:** *Sitanion hystrix* (Nutt.) J. G. Smith
> **Synonym:** *Aegilops hystrix* Nutt.
> **Common names:** Squirreltail grass, Squirreltail
> **Origin:** North America
> **Habitat:** Open grassland
> **Hardiness:** Zones 4 through 10
> **Description:** A loosely tufted, upright-narrow to upright-open perennial.
Culms erect to spreading, rather stiff, wiry, simple, scabrous above, 6–18 in./
1.5–4.5 dm high. Foliage medium green, fine in texture; leaf blades flat, becoming involute, somewhat stiffly ascending, 2–8 in./0.5–2.0 dm long, 0.1–0.3 in./
3–8 mm wide, softly and densely pubescent, auricled, long attenuate; sheaths imbricate, keeled, round on the back, scabrous, the upper inflated and enclosing the base of the spike, sometimes scabrous, longer than the internodes; ligule membranous, about 1 mm long. Inflorescence an erect, cylindrical, rather compact spike, mostly short-exserted or partially included, green or tinged with purple, 3–8 in./0.8–2.0 dm long, 1–2 in./2.5–5.0 cm wide including the awns, usually two spikelets at each node; spikelets sessile, two-to-six-flowered, the upper floret reduced; glumes very narrow, one-to-two-nerved, the nerves extending into scabrous awns, 2–4 in./5–10 cm long, sometimes bifid to the middle or bearing a bristle or awn along one margin, lemmas convex, 0.3–0.4 in./
8–10 mm long, obscurely nerved, scabrous, smooth or strigose, occasionally glaucous with a long scabrous awn about 2–3 in./5–8 cm long at maturity, the

Sitanion hystrix. **Habit,** × 1/2; **spikelet and floret,** × **3.** *Source: Manual of the Grasses of the United States.* USDA Misc. Pub. 200. 1951.

apex sometimes two-toothed, the upper lemma usually short-awned; palea firm, nearly as long as the body of the lemma, two-keeled, the keels serrulate. Flowering and fruiting occur from April through August.

Uses: The flowering spikes of squirreltail grass and bottlebrush grass, *Hystrix patula,* are somewhat similar in appearance, with the exception of flower color; those of bottlebrush grass are bright pinkish green, whereas those of squirreltail grass are greenish white or white. Unlike those of bottlebrush grass, the flower heads of squirreltail grass shatter early and are not useful for drying. Squirreltail grass is useful in mixed grass stands in naturalizing dry sites. The greenish white spikes, with their conspicuously long awns, are attractive on the plants and as cut flowers; the plants provide good fall color following frost.

Cultivation: Propagation is by direct seeding and by plant division. The plants grow best in full sun or light shade on well-drained, dry soils; they reseed themselves readily.

Sorghastrum **Nash.** Name from *Sorghum* and the Latin suffix *-astrum,* "a poor imitation of," alluding to the resemblance to *Sorghum.* Type species, *Sorghastrum avenaceum* (Benth.) Nash. There are about 15 species, inhabiting tropical and temperate regions of the Western Hemisphere and Africa. Perennial erect, rather tall grasses, with auricled sheaths, narrow, flat leaf blades, and narrow terminal panicles of one-to-few-jointed racemes. Spikelets in pairs, one nearly terete, sessile, and perfect, the other wanting, only the hairy pedicel being present; glumes coriaceous, brown or yellowish, the lower hirsute, the edges inflexed over the upper; sterile and fertile lemmas thin and hyaline, the latter extending into a usually well-developed bent and twisted awn.

> **Latin name:** *Sorghastrum nutans* (L.) Nash
> **Synonym:** *Andropogon nutans* L.
> **Common names:** Indian grass, Woodgrass
> **Origin:** North America
> **Habitat:** Dry or moist sites
> **Hardiness:** Zones 6 through 10
> **Description:** An upright-open perennial with creeping, short, scaly rhizomes. Culms simple, with few sterile shoots at the base, 3–8 ft /0.9–2.5 m high, glabrous except the appressed pubescent or bearded nodes. Foliage medium green, often glaucous, medium in texture; leaf blades elongate, flat above and conduplicate below, 8–16 in./2–4 dm long, 0.3–0.5 in./8–13 mm wide, scabrous or puberulent, the margins hispid-ciliate, more or less upright, tapering to a narrow base and an attenuate tip; upper sheaths shorter than the internodes, glabrous or the lower sometimes pubescent; ligule cartilaginous, 0.1–0.3 in./3–8 mm long. Inflorescence a branched, bronze-yellow panicle, 8–12 in./2–3 dm long, 3–4 in./8–10 cm wide, exserted, nodding at the tip, branches in fascicles, erect or nearly so, exceeding the internodes, the panicle axis, branches, branch-

Sorghastrum nutans.
**Habit, greatly reduced;
spikelet, × 5.** *Source:
Manual of the Grasses of the
United States.* USDA Misc.
Pub. 200. 1951.

lets and pedicels appressed hirsute, the branchlets not flexuous; spikelets solitary
or rarely in pairs, one nearly terete, sessile, and perfect, the other usually wanting, sessile spikelet slightly flattened, brownish green, lanceolate, 0.25–0.30 in./
6–8 mm long, pedicellate spikelet usually wanting, the pedicel about half as long
as the spikelet, spikelets disarticulating at the base, callus hairs about 1 mm long;
glumes about equal, coriaceous, lanceolate, yellowish or golden brown, the

lower glume flat or convex, hirsute and scabrous toward the apex, nine-nerved, the upper ciliate on the margins above and at the apex, five-nerved; sterile lemma usually pubescent above, thin, hyaline, 0.15–0.25 in./4–6 mm long, fertile lemma about as long as the sterile lemma, 0.15–0.20 in./4–5 mm long, hyaline, the geniculate awn 0.4–0.6 in./10–15 mm long from the sinus of bifid apex, once bent, twisted to the bend, loosely so above; caryopsis 0.1–0.2 in./3–4 mm long, about 1 mm wide. Flowering and fruiting occur from July until frost.

Uses: Indian grass is used in simple and mixed stands in sunny locations of naturalized areas bordering the garden. The dark orange or purplish foliage following frost provides good fall color. The plants are grown for their attractive flowers; they are most attractive when in full flower during late summer, when few other ornamentals are in blossom. The flowers are shiny brown with light yellow anthers when in full flower, becoming darker with age; they are suitable for cut flowers and dried arrangements. The plants make good tall screens and background borders when planted in rows. Indian grass is very decorative when grown in groups or massed plantings (e.g., along canals and highways).

Cultivation: Propagation is by direct seeding and by plant division. Indian grass thrives best in full sun on a wide range of soils, usually in dry sites. The plants reseed themselves readily.

Spartina **Schreb. (Cordgrass, Marshgrass).** Name from Greek *spartine,* ''a cord made from *spartes,*'' *Spartium junceum* L. (Spanish broom), probably applied to *Spartina* because of the tough leaves. Type species, *Spartina schreberi* Gmel. There are 16 species, some native to the Western Hemisphere, Europe, and North Africa. Often tall, erect, stout, perennial grasses with usually extensively creeping firm, scaly rhizomes, wanting in some species, long tough leaf blades and two-to-many-appressed or sometimes spreading spikes, racemose on the main axis, the slender tips of the rachis naked, often prolonged. Spikelets one-flowered, much flattened laterally, sessile and usually closely imbricate on one side of a continuous rachis, disarticulating below the glumes, the rachilla not produced beyond the floret; glumes keeled, one-nerved, or the upper with a second nerve on one side, acute or short-awned, the lower shorter, the upper often exceeding the lemma; lemmas firm, keeled, the lateral nerves obscure, narrowed to a rather obtuse point; palea two-nerved, keeled and flattened, the keel between or on one side of the nerves.

> **Latin name:** *Spartina alterniflora* Loisel.
> **Synonym:** *Dactylis maritima* Walt.
> **Common names:** Saltwater cordgrass, Smooth cordgrass, Herbe salea
> **Origin:** North America
> **Habitat:** Salt marshes, often growing in water, tidal waters
> **Hardiness:** Zones 4 through 9

Description: An upright-narrow perennial with firm, stout, scaly rhizomes. Culms robust, simple, erect, soft or spongy or succulent at base, smooth, 2–8 ft /0.6–2.5 m high, 0.3–0.4 in./8–10 mm thick at base. Foliage light green, medium in texture; leaf blades flat at base when young, the tip involute, glabrous throughout or minutely scabrous on the margins, long attenuate to an involute tip, 10–18 in./2.5–4.5 dm long, 0.5–0.6 in./13–15 mm wide; sheaths longer than the internodes, glabrous, except slightly ciliate on the margins near the summit; ligule a ring of fine, dense hairs 1–2 mm long. Inflorescence few to several racemose spikes borne on the main axis, forming a narrow, oblong, straight panicle, 12–14 in./3.0–3.5 dm long; spikes few to several, erect, remote, appressed, 2–6 in./0.5–1.5 dm long, 0.8–1.0 in./20–25 mm thick; spikelets one-flowered, somewhat remote or crowded along the rachis, barely overlapping or sometimes more imbricate, 0.4–0.5 in./10–13 mm long, sparingly pilose or glabrous; glumes glabrous or sparingly pilose on the keel, the lower about two-thirds as long as the upper, narrow, the upper obtuse, a little longer than the lemma; lemmas glabrous or sparingly pilose, 0.3–0.4 in./8–10 mm long, firm, keeled, the lateral nerves obscure; palea two-nerved, keeled and flattened; caryopsis enclosed. Flowering and fruiting occur from July through September.

Uses: Cordgrass is useful in naturalizing saltwater and brackish-water marshes. The plants are important soil builders in coastal and interior marshes. Smooth cordgrass is usually a pioneer plant in such areas, where it affords some protection for wildlife, particularly migratory birds. The long-term value of spartinas as soil-building, soil-binding, and erosion-control plants cannot be overemphasized. The wide range of winter hardiness and salt tolerance encourages their widespread use in habitats in which few other plants are suited.

Cultivation: Propagation is by plant division. The culms or particularly the rhizomes may be used as propagating material to establish new stands. Cordgrass thrives best in full sun.

Latin name: *Spartina cynosuroides* (L.) Roth
Synonym: *Spartina cynosuroides* var. *polystachya* (Michx.) Beal ex Fern.
Common names: Big cordgrass, Salt reedgrass
Origin: North America
Habitat: Brackish-water and saltwater marshes
Hardiness: Zones 5 through 10
Description: An upright-narrow perennial with short, stout rhizomes. Culms stout, 3–10 ft /0.9–3.1 m high, sometimes 0.8–1.0 in./20–25 mm thick at base. Foliage medium green, coarse in texture; leaf blades erect, flat or nearly so, stiff, elongate, arching, rough below, very scabrous on the margins, 18–24 in./4.5–6.0 dm long, 0.5–1.0 in./13–25 mm wide; sheaths imbricate, round on the back, longer than the internodes, crowded toward the base; ligule a short densely ciliate membrane, the whitish hairs 1–2 mm long. Inflorescence 20 to 50 ascending spikes forming a rather loose, oblong, purplish panicle, 6–15 in./

1.5–3.8 dm long, about 2–4 in./5–10 cm wide; spikes pedunculate, approximate, usually appressed, narrowly ascending or spreading, 1–4 in./2.5–10.0 cm long, the rachis rough on the margins, peduncles dark-colored, short; spikelets one-flowered, 0.3–0.6 in./8–15 mm long including the awns, sessile, flattened, closely imbricate on one side of a continuous rachis; glumes keeled, one-nerved, acute or barely mucronate, strongly scabrous-hispid on the keels, the lower acute, about one-half as long as the upper but shorter than the lemma, the upper longer than the palea, awnless, acute or mucronate; lemmas nearly as long as the paleas, the lateral nerves obscure or wanting, scabrous on the upper part of the keel, ciliate on the margins, not toothed at the apex; palea two-nerved, slightly longer than the lemma; caryopsis enclosed. Flowering and fruiting occur from July through September.

Uses: Big cordgrass is most useful in naturalizing brackish and salt marshes. The plants are ideal as soil binders and soil builders in coastal areas, in inland marshes, and along tidal streams. Geese and ducks eat the young, tender shoots.

Cultivation: Propagation is by direct seeding and by plant division. The plants prefer full sun in wet, brackish marshes.

> **Latin name:** *Spartina gracilis* Trin.
> **Common name:** Alkali cordgrass
> **Origin:** North America
> **Habitat:** Alkaline meadows and plains
> **Hardiness:** Zones 4 through 6
> **Description:** An upright-narrow perennial with creeping, scaly, stout rhizomes. Culms erect, slender, 2–3 ft /6–9 dm high, firm, wiry. Foliage medium green, fine in texture; leaf blades ascending, flat near the base, becoming involute, 6–8 in./1.5–2.0 dm long, 0.1–0.2 in./3–5 mm wide, long attenuate to an involute tip, very scabrous above; sheaths crowded, imbricate; ligule membranous, ciliate. Inflorescence a loose, narrow, oblong panicle, 4–6 in./1.0–1.5 dm long, 0.3–0.5 in./8–13 mm wide, comprised of 4 to 9 ascending to spreading spikes, 0.8–1.6 in./2–4 cm long, closely appressed, racemose on the main axis; spikelets sessile, flattened laterally, imbricate in two rows in one-sided spikes, the rachis extending beyond the spikelets, 0.25–0.30 in./6–8 mm long; glumes unequal, keeled, ciliate on the keel, acute, the lower glume about half as long as the upper, one-nerved, upper glume 0.2–0.3 in./5–8 mm long; firm, the lateral nerves obscure; lemmas nearly as long as the upper glume, keeled, ciliate on the keel, palea almost hyaline, two-nerved, obtuse, about as long as the lemma; caryopsis enclosed. Flowering and fruiting occur from July through September.

Uses: Alkali cordgrass forms large, dense, extensive colonies to the exclusion of other plants. It is best used as a ground cover on dry sites.

Cultivation: Propagation is by plant division, rarely by seeding. The plants are quite drought tolerant; they prefer full sun in a wide range of soils but perform best in alkaline, dry, rocky soils.

Latin name: *Spartina patens* (Ait.) Muhl.
Synonym: *Spartina patens* var. *juncea* Hitchc.
Common names: Saltmeadow cordgrass, Saltmeadow grass, Highwater grass, Muscotte
Origin: North America
Habitat: Saltwater marshes, sandy meadows, low dunes
Hardiness: Zones 2 through 10
Description: An upright-narrow, deciduous perennial with long, slender rhizomes or sometimes without rhizomes. Culms slender, 2–3 ft /6–9 dm high, tough and wiry. Foliage medium green, fine in texture; leaf blades mostly involute but sometimes flat, spreading, tough, 2–10 in./0.5–2.5 dm long, 2–3 mm wide, long attenuate, smooth beneath; sheaths imbricate, ligule a ring of short, whitish hairs. Inflorescence a short-exserted panicle of 2 to 10 spikes, racemose and rather remote on the main axis, mostly ascending, appressed to somewhat spreading, more or less pedunculate, about 1–2 in./2.5–5.0 cm long; spikelets few to several, borne in two rows on a slightly scabrous rachis, 0.4–0.5 in./10–13 mm long, one-flowered, ascending or spreading; glumes keeled, scabrous on the keel, one-nerved, lower glume linear, mucronate, about one-half as long as the lanceolate acuminate upper glume, upper glume longer than the lemma; lemmas 0.2–0.3 in./5–8 mm long, firm, keeled, the lateral veins obscure, narrowed to a rather obtuse point, emarginate at the apex; palea two-nerved, flattened, a little longer than the lemma, keeled, the keel usually at the side of the nerves; caryopsis enclosed. Flowering and fruiting occur from July through September.
Uses: Saltmeadow cordgrass, like other *Spartina* species, is most useful in naturalizing low, wet, saline, and brackish-water marshes. The plants afford protection for wildlife, and their stout, rhizomatous roots aid in reducing soil erosion. The plants form extensive colonies, to the exclusion of many other plants. They are important soil builders and soil binders in coastal and interior marshes. The marsh hay of the Atlantic coast, much used in packing, often consists largely of saltmeadow cordgrass.
Cultivation: Propagation is by plant division. New plantings may be established by dividing the culms or by planting the rhizomes. The plants are invasive, and this should be considered in the choice of locating this water grass. Saltmeadow cordgrass should be established in wet, marshy areas in full sun.

Latin name: *Spartina pectinata* Link
Synonym: *Spartina michauxiana* Hitchc.
Cultivars: 'Aureo-marginata' Variegated cordgrass
Common names: Prairie cordgrass, Marsh grass, Freshwater cordgrass, Herbe à liens
Origin: North America
Habitat: Wet soils, brackish water and freshwater marshes

Spartina pectinata. **Habit,** × 1/2; **spikelet and floret,** × 5. *Source: Manual of the Grasses of the United States.* USDA Misc. Pub. 200. 1951.

Hardiness: Zones 5 through 9

Description: An upright-open perennial with fine, scaly rhizomes. Culms simple, erect to arching, robust, wiry, firm, thin, glabrous, 3–6 ft /0.9–1.8 m high. Foliage medium green, medium in texture; leaf blades ascending, gracefully arched, flat when young, becoming involute upon drying, 8–30 in./2.0–7.6 dm long, 0.25–0.60 in./6–15 mm wide, long attenuate to an involute point, margins scabrous, slightly rough above; sheaths longer than the internodes, imbricate, crowded below, scabrous, prominently veined; ligule membranous, ciliate with soft, slender hairs 1–2 mm long. Inflorescence 10 to 20 spikes borne on a spikelike panicle, spikes 2–3 in./5–8 cm long, narrowly ascending to spreading, somewhat distant, sometimes appressed, upper almost sessile, peduncles of lower spikes 0.8–1.0 in./20–25 mm long, rachis scabrous on the margins; spikelets one-flowered, sessile, flattened, imbricate in two rows on one side of a continuous rachis, 0.4–0.6 in./10–15 mm long including the awns; glumes unequal, awn-pointed or awned, keeled, strongly scabrous-hispid on the keel, the lower slender, acuminate, about as long as the lemma, awn-pointed or sometimes short-awned, about 0.3–0.4 in./8–10 mm long including the awn 1–3 mm long, the upper about 0.5–0.6 in./13–15 mm long including an awn 0.1–0.3 in./3–8 mm long, with five approximate nerves; lemmas firm, 0.3–0.4 in./8–10 mm long, strongly keeled, glabrous except hispid-scabrous on the keel, the midnerve terminating just below the bifid apex; palea keeled, two-nerved, hyaline, about as long as or longer than the lemma; caryopsis enclosed. Flowering and fruiting occur from August until frost.

Uses: The chief attraction of marsh grass is its attractive and colorful flowers. Marsh grass provides good ground cover in either freshwater marshes or in brackish or saltwater marshes. It is useful on difficult sites of naturalized areas where other plants are less well adapted. It has a niche along the seashore and around pools, ponds, and lakes, and in water gardens, where it is compatible with other aquatic grasses that occur and are used in similar environments. The extensive strong rhizomatous root system stabilizes the soil, which aids in soil conservation on steep slopes and along highway banks. Prairie cordgrass is particularly useful in group and massed plantings, or as a screen.

Cultivation: Propagation is by seeding and by plant division. The plants may be increased by dividing the culms or by planting its strong, rhizomatous roots; propagation is most successful in the spring. Although spartinas naturally occur in low, wet, marshy places, they may be grown successfully in ordinary garden soil provided with ample moisture; the plants do best in full sun or light shade in wet, heavy soil.

Cultivars: *Spartina pectinata* Link 'Aureo-marginata' Variegated cordgrass   An upright-open, tufted perennial, 4–6 ft /1.2–1.8 m high. Foliage variegated, fine in texture; leaf blades ascending, arching, 18–24 in./4.5–6.0 dm long, 0.1–0.2 in./3–5 mm wide, long attenuate; the leaves have either broad green stripes with yellow margins or narrow green margins interrupted with very narrow, yellow stripes; the green portion is either dull green or yellowish green. The chief attraction of this variant is its decorative flowers and gracefully arched variegated foliage borne on long, wiry stems, which afford good autumnal color when the leaves become golden or bright yellow in the fall. It is excellent in accent and specimen plantings, where its variegated foliage contrasts with other ornamentals with dark green foliage; the colorful flower heads and seedheads are useful as cut flowers and as dried specimens, respectively. This form is commonly used in groups in middleground borders and around pools and ponds. Propagation is by seeding and by plant division, preferably the latter. The plants prefer freshwater or brackish-water marshes and are ideal near the coast, where they form dense, extensive colonies along the edge of the water. They thrive in ordinary garden soil that is rich in humus and adequately supplied with a constant moisture supply; the plants thrive equally well in full sun or light shade; their invasiveness requires containment when planted in the water garden. The variegated foliage makes it particularly attractive along ditches, canals, and highways or as a medium screen. Variegated cordgrass is adapted to zones 5–9.

Latin name: *Spartina spartinae* (Trin.) Merr.
Synonym: *Spartina junciformis* Engelm. & A. Gray
Common name: Gulf cordgrass
Origin: North America
Habitat: Marshes, swamps, coastal marsh prairies
Hardiness: Zone 10
Description: An upright-narrow, tufted perennial. Culms densely tufted, forming large clumps, stout, rigid, simple, 2–4 ft /0.6–1.2 m high, glabrous, green but often turning purplish except just below the panicle. Foliage medium green with light tinge of purple, fine in texture; leaf blades folded, stiff, ascending, conduplicate, sharply pointed, 18–36 in./4.5–9.0 dm long, about 2 mm wide when folded, lower much longer than upper; sheaths slightly longer than the internodes, flattened, often tinged with purple; ligule a ciliate ring of short, whitish hairs. Inflorescence a dense, cylindrical, spikelike panicle, 5–10 in./1.3–2.5 dm long, about 0.3–0.5 in./8–13 mm thick, with 25 to 50 crowded, closely appressed, imbricate spikes, 1–2 in./2.5–5.0 cm long below, shorter above, upper often sessile, 0.5–0.6 in./13–15 mm long; spikelets one-flowered, green or purplish, 0.25–0.30 in./6–8 mm long, the stigmas with long styles maturing first, later covering the spikes with yellow stamens; glumes keeled, one-nerved, scabrous-hispid on the keel, acute, the lower narrow, 0.15–0.25 in./4–6 mm long, shorter than the lemma, the upper 0.25–0.30 in./6–8 mm long, acute, awnless; lemmas abruptly acute, 0.15–0.25 in./4–6 mm long, three-nerved, scabrous on the keel; palea two-nerved, hyaline, variable in length, 0.15–0.30 in./4–8 mm long, usually about as long as the lemma; caryopsis enclosed. Flowering and fruiting occur from May through September.
Uses: Gulf cordgrass is an excellent grass for naturalizing freshwater to

brackish to saline swamps and marshes. The plants provide good ground cover and wildlife protection; in addition, they are useful in reclaiming marshland.

Cultivation: Propagation is by seeding and by plant division. The plants thrive in full sun and light shade in mud and water in freshwater, brackish-water, and saltwater lagoons and on wet prairies near the sea.

Sporobolus **R. Br. (Dropseed, Rushgrass).** Name from Greek *spora,* "seed," and *ballein,* "to throw," alluding to the free seeds. Lectotype, *Sporobolus indicus* (L.) R. Br. There are about 100 species, inhabiting the Western Hemisphere, Africa, and Asia. Annual or perennial grasses with small spikelets in open or contracted panicles. Spikelets one-flowered, the rachilla disarticulating above the glumes; glumes one-nerved, usually unequal, the upper often as long as the spikelet; lemma membranous, one-nerved, awnless; palea usually prominent and as long as the lemma or longer; caryopsis free from the lemma and palea, falling readily from the spikelet at maturity, the pericarp free from the seed, usually thin and closely enveloping it, but readily slipping away when moist.

Latin name: *Sporobolus heterolepis* (A. Gray) A. Gray
Synonym: *Vilfa heterolepis* A. Gray
Common names: Prairie dropseed, Northern dropseed
Origin: North America
Habitat: Prairies, open grassland
Hardiness: Zones 3 through 9
Description: A densely tufted, upright-narrow perennial. Culms erect, simple, glabrous, slender, 12–30 in./3.0–7.6 dm high. Foliage medium green, fine in texture; leaves mostly basal, about half as long as the culm; leaf blades 8–24 in./2–6 dm long, about 2 mm wide, the basal about eight-tenths as long as the culm, the upper shorter, involute-setaceous, the upper surface, midrib and margins rough or sparsely pilose; sheaths glabrous with some hairs at the summit, longer than the internodes, the lower short, sparsely pilose on the back, the upper clasping the culm, somewhat pilose at the throat; ligule a ring of short hairs. Inflorescence a branched, long-exserted, grayish green panicle, narrowly pyramidal, 3–12 in./0.8–3.0 dm long, the branches distant, alternate or fascicled, 1–4 in./2.5–10.0 cm long, erect or ascending, finally spreading, naked below, bearing dark green spikelets toward their tips; spikelets short-pedicellate, 0.15–0.25 in./4–6 mm long, awnless, one-flowered; glumes unequal, one-flowered, acuminate or aristate, keels of some scabrous, lower glume awl-shaped, 2–3 mm long or about one-half as long as the upper, the upper lanceolate, about 0.15–0.20 in./4–5 mm long, slightly longer than the lemma, often awn-pointed; lemmas one-nerved, glabrous, obtuse or acute, about as long as or shorter than the upper glume; palea two-nerved, about as long as its lemma; caryopsis orbicular, smooth, roundish, about 2 mm long and of equal width,

pericarp nutlike, splitting the palea, caryopsis free. Flowering and fruiting occur from August until frost; the plants are strong scented.

Uses: Prairie dropseed has more economic value than ornamental value. Its chief ornamental value is its use as ground cover in dry, hot areas. It is useful in mixed grass stands in meadows and naturalized areas, where it provides bird-feed and wildlife protection.

Cultivation: Propagation is by direct seeding. The plants prefer dry, rocky soils in full sun.

Latin name: *Sporobolus virginicus* (L.) Kunth
Synonym: *Agrostis virginica* L.
Common names: Seashore rushgrass, Seashore dropseed
Origin: North America

Sporobolus virginicus.
Habit, × 1; glumes and floret, × 10. *Source: Manual of the Grasses of the West Indies.* USDA Misc. Pub. 243. 1936.

Habitat: Sandy, saline soils along coast, and salt flats

Hardiness: Zones 8 through 10

Description: An upright-open to spreading, semievergreen perennial with extensively creeping rhizomes. Culms from long rhizomes, mostly decumbent at the base, simple or freely branching, 6–24 in./1.5–6.0 dm high. Foliage light green, fine in texture; leaves conspicuously distichous, ascending, long attenuate, involute on the margins, convolute upon drying, stiff, wiry, mostly straight, leaf blades of the innovations numerous, crowded, 1–4 in./5–10 cm long, 0.10–0.15 in./3–4 mm wide at the base, scabrous above or sparingly hairy; upper sheaths shorter than the internodes, lower overlapping, short, sometimes pilose on the margins and at throat; ligule ring of very short hairs. Inflorescence a dense, spikelike panicle, 1–3 in./2.5–8.0 cm long, 0.15–0.40 in./4–10 mm thick, light colored or purplish, the branches short, more or less appressed; spikelets ellipsoidal, 2–3 mm long; glumes acute, unequal, the lower about 2 mm long, the upper about 0.1 in./3 mm long; lemmas acute, slightly shorter than the upper glume; palea obtuse, about as long as the lemma. Flowering and fruiting occur from May until frost; the plants usually produce several seed crops during the growing season.

Uses: Seashore dropseed and seashore saltgrass, *Distichlis spicata,* inhabit the same environment (i.e., saline marsh soils along the coast). Seashore dropseed is useful as ground cover in such areas, where it serves as winter food for wildfowl, particularly geese. The plants provide some ground cover for small wildlife, especially small wildfowl. Seashore dropseed serves a very useful purpose as ground cover and wildlife feed in naturalized marshes along streams and in coastal flatlands.

Cultivation: Propagation is by direct seeding and by plant division, preferably the latter. The plants grow best in full sun in highly saline marsh soils where the water level fluctuates from about 2 in./5 cm above soil level to 6 in./1.5 dm below; they are evergreen in zone 10 and semievergreen in zones 8 and 9. Seashore dropseed and seashore saltgrass, which cohabit the same environment, are very similar, although they are easily distinguished by differences in their seedheads.

Stenotaphrum **Trin.** Name from Greek *stenos,* "narrow," and *taphros,* "trench," referring to the cavities of the rachis. Type species, *Panicum dimidiatum* L. There are six species, of tropical and subtropical origin in the New and Old worlds. Creeping, stoloniferous, perennial grasses with short, flowering culms, rather short, broad, obtuse leaf blades, and terminal axillary racemes. Spikelets embedded in one side of the enlarged and flattened corky rachis, tardily disarticulating toward the tip at maturity, the spikelets remaining attached to the joints; lower glume small; upper glume and sterile lemma about equal, the latter with a palea or staminate flower; fertile lemma chartaceous.

Latin name: *Stenotaphrum secundatum* (Walt.) Kuntze
Synonym: *Ischaemum secundatum* Walt.
Cultivars: Several in cultivation, including 'Variegatum' Striped St. Augustine grass
Common names: St. Augustine grass, Buffalo grass
Origin: Caribbean region, Southeastern United States
Habitat: Cultivated, escape from cultivation
Hardiness: Zones 9 and 10
Description: A stoloniferous, sod-forming perennial. Flowering culms glabrous, erect or ascending from creeping, freely branching stolons, stolons glabrous with short internodes, 2–3 ft /6–9 dm long or longer, rooting at the nodes, each node branched or with a fascicle of leaves, branches 1–2 ft /3–6 dm long, flowering shoots 4–12 in./1–3 dm high. Foliage medium to dark green, fine in texture, although the shortness of the leaves makes them appear to be medium in texture; leaf blades 3–6 in./0.8–1.5 dm long, 0.15–0.40 in./4–10 mm wide on the upright culms, but only about 1–2 in./2.5–5.0 cm long on the stolons, glabrous, round at the apex; sheaths loose, flattened, ciliate on the margins toward the apex; ligule a ciliate ring of short hairs. Inflorescence terminal and axillary racemes, 2–4 in./5–10 cm long, about 0.15–0.20 in./4–5 mm wide, usually sheathed, the spikelets embedded in one side of the enlarged, flattened, corky rachis; spikelets lanceolate-ovate, about 0.10–0.15 in./3–4 mm long, acute, sessile, awnless, glabrous, solitary or in pairs, rarely in threes, persistent, dorsally compressed, with a single, fertile floret, light green; glumes membranous, dissimilar, the lower abaxil, small, obtuse, nerveless, about one-half as long as the spikelet, the upper ovate, acute, five-to-seven-nerved, about 0.10–0.15 in./3–4 mm long; sterile lemma and upper glume about equal, the former with a staminate flower, fertile lemma chartaceous; lower floret staminate, upper floret bisexual, more or less like the lower; caryopsis slightly shorter and more coriaceous than the sterile lemma. Flowering and fruiting occur from June through September.
Uses: St. Augustine grass is a common lawn grass in the extreme southern United States and in portions of the southwestern states; it is also useful as ground cover in naturalized areas. The variegated cultivar Variegatum is the more interesting form, with its colorful variegated foliage. Striped St. Augustine grass is an excellent bedding and accent plant in foreground annual borders and water gardens in warm climates, where its variegated foliage serves as a perfect foil for other plants with green foliage. It is commonly grown indoors in colder climates in flower pots and hanging baskets; it produces a colorful hanging basket plant, especially when the stolons are allowed to cascade over the outside of the basket.
Cultivation: Propagation is by plant division. The easiest and most expeditious way of propagating St. Augustine grass is by dividing the plant crowns and by taking cuttings. This is best done in late spring or summer, after the stolons have attained sufficient length. The stolons are usually rooted at the

Stenotaphrum secundatum. *Source: The Grasses and Pastures of South Africa.*
Central News Agency. 1955.

nodes; sections of these may be planted directly. They should be covered about 2 in./5 cm deep, leaving portions, about one-fourth to one-third, of each stolon above ground. Firm the soil over the planted cuttings, and water thoroughly. Unrooted cuttings may be rooted in water or a mixture of peat moss and sand before planting, or they may be planted directly without prior rooting. Plant crowns may be divided in early spring and planted. When rooting cuttings indoors, the containers should be maintained in bright, filtered light at about 55°F/13°C. The cuttings should be transferred to larger pots or hanging baskets or into the garden after they are well rooted and growing. St. Augustine grass should not be planted outside before the danger of frost has passed in the spring. Plants grown or maintained indoors are easily transferred outside in the spring, and vice versa in the fall. Another propagation method includes planting plugs from established sod. Both St. Augustine grass and its cultivar are invasive in growth habit. They may be easily controlled by cutting back and trimming the plants as necessary, as their aggressiveness is minimal. These grasses grow best in full sun on moist, fertile, well-drained soil. They respond to a constant moisture supply and fertilizer applied at rates recommended for sod grasses. The foliage color and luster of St. Augustine grass and its variegated cultivar are maintained throughout the growing season if an adequate moisture supply is maintained. The creeping stolons of the cultivar Variegatum have a tendency to become discolored when grown indoors; repeated, frequent trimming keeps the plants under control and maximizes their appearance by removing old, discolored foliage. Striped St. Augustine grass requires bright light when grown indoors, equivalent to three or four hours of direct sunlight daily. The foliage becomes green and loses much of its luster when the plants receive inadequate light. Some clumps become tinged with pale mauve, particularly near the base of the plants when grown in bright light.

Potted plants thrive at normal room temperature; however, they cannot tolerate temperatures below about 55°F/13°C. Humidity is usually low in homes heated by forced hot air, unless a humidifier is used. Premature yellowing of foliage occurs in low humidity; this can be prevented somewhat by standing the pots in trays or planters containing damp pebbles. Plants in hanging baskets should be sprayed daily. Potted plants should be watered enough to keep the potting mixture thoroughly moist, but the pots should never be allowed to stand in water. During rest periods, when the plants are not actively growing, they should be watered just enough to keep the potting mixture from drying out completely. Apply standard liquid fertilizer once per month when the plants are actively growing; overfertilizing often causes the leaves to become unduly large and limp, thereby reducing the attractiveness of the plants. St. Augustine grass prefers full sun in moist or wet locations on acid soils.

Cultivars: *Stenotaphrum secundatum* (Walt.) Kuntze 'Variegatum' Striped St. Augustine grass Striped St. Augustine grass is a variegated form of St. Augustine grass. It is similar in size and all its plant parts to the species; it is dissimilar only in foliage color. The leaf blades have longitudinal, merging stripes of green and white or green and pinkish white. Flowering and fruiting occur from July through September. This form is native to tropical America. It prefers light shade on moist soil when grown outdoors, usually in foreground borders for accent or as a specimen. This variegated form makes an ideal houseplant, especially when grown in hanging baskets.

Stipa L. (Needlegrass, Feathergrass, Speargrass). Name from Greek *stupe,* "tow," alluding to the feathery awns of the type species. Lectotype, *Stipa pennata* L. There are about 150 species, mostly in temperate regions of both hemispheres. Tufted annual or perennial grasses with usually convolute leaf blades and mostly narrow panicles. Spikelets one-flowered, disarticulating above the glumes, the articulation oblique, leaving a bearded, sharp-pointed callus attached to the base of the floret; glumes membranous, often chartaceous, acute, acuminate, or even aristate, usually long and narrow, terete, firm or indurate, strongly convolute, rarely the margins only meeting, terminating in a prominent awn, the junction of body and awn evident, the awn twisted below, geniculate, usually persistent; palea enclosed in the convolute lemma.

Latin name: *Stipa comata* Trin. & Rupr.
Synonym: *Stipa juncea* Pursh
Common name: Needle-and-thread
Origin: North America
Habitat: Prairies, plains, dry rangeland
Hardiness: Zones 4 through 9
Description: A densely tufted, upright-narrow perennial. Culms single or tufted, glabrous or sometimes pubescent at the nodes, sparingly branched, thin, 1–3 ft /3–9 dm high. Foliage light green, fine in texture; basal leaves filiform, 4–12 in./1–3 dm long, 1–3 mm wide, flat or involute, long attenuate, cauline leaves shorter, puberulent or more or less minutely scabrous above, glabrous beneath; sheaths about the length of the internodes, or either slightly shorter or longer, loose, smooth at the throat, the uppermost inflated and usually enclosing the base of the panicle, smooth or slightly scabrous; ligule membranous, decurrent, 0.10–0.15 in./3–4 mm long, those of sterile shoots shorter. Inflorescence a narrow, upright panicle, partially enclosed by the uppermost sheath, 4–12 in./ 1–3 dm long exclusive of the awns, branches ascending or appressed, slender, 3–4 in./8–10 cm long, scabrous, bearing few spikelets; spikelets one-flowered, narrow, 0.6–0.8 in./15–20 mm long exclusive of the awns; glumes about equal, 0.6–0.8 in./15–25 mm long, narrowed into a slender awn, thin, very light green or purplish, five-nerved, chartaceous; lemmas persistent, pale, mostly colorless, finally brownish, 0.3–0.5 in./8–13 mm long including the callus, the callus slender, about 0.1 in./3 mm long, the callus and body of lemma appressed pubescent with colorless hairs, or the hairs becoming tawny, especially on the callus, or glabrate toward the summit, the joint with the awn distinct, awn divided

***Stipa spartea*. Habit,** ×
1/2; glumes and floret, ×
2. *Source: Manual of the
Grasses of the United States.*
USDA Misc. Pub. 200. 1951.

into three parts, the basal straight with the lemma, 0.8–1.6 in./2–4 cm long,
twisted appressed pubescent, second part 0.4–0.8 in./10–20 mm long, the third
part 0.3–0.5 in./8–13 mm long, capillary, flexuous; palea about as long as the
lemma, enclosed within the lemma; caryopsis cylindrical, tightly enclosed in the
lemma. Flowering and fruiting occur from June through July.

Uses: Needle-and-thread is grown primarily for its flowering panicles, with their long, twisted, flexuous, tangled awns; the flower heads are attractive as cut flowers. The plants are useful in middleground borders and as ground cover in naturalized areas. Needle-and-thread should be planted in clumps when grown in borders or rock gardens for it to be most conspicuous.

Cultivation: Propagation is by seeding and by plant division. Naturalized stands are usually established by seeding. The plants are quite drought tolerant, prefer full sun, and thrive on a wide range of dry soils.

Latin name: *Stipa pennata* L.
Common names: European feathergrass, Speargrass
Origin: Europe
Habitat: Open grassland
Hardiness: Zones 5 through 9
Description: An upright-narrow to upright-open perennial. Culms densely tufted, erect to arching, slender to moderately stout, 3–4 ft /0.9–1.2 m high, glabrous or slightly rough toward the panicle. Foliage medium green, fine in texture; leaf blades elongate, involute, long and finely attenuate, 1–2 ft /3–6 dm long, about 0.20–0.25 in./5–6 mm wide; sheaths shorter than the internodes; ligule very short, ciliate, less than 1 mm long. Inflorescence a loosely branched, slightly drooping panicle with few branches, light green, becoming beige at maturity; spikelets one-flowered, large, 0.8–1.0 in./20–25 mm long excluding the awns, pale or yellow, more or less shining, glumes lanceolate, narrowed into a slender awned point about as long as the body, 1–2 in./2.5–5.0 cm long, the lower a little longer; lemmas narrow, terete, firm, 0.5–0.6 in./13–15 mm long, five-nerved, tuberculate at the short neck terminating in a deciduous geniculate awn 4–12 in./1–3 dm long, the lower one-third twisted, straight, more or less glabrous, the upper two-thirds almost straight, densely feathery villous, the hairs pale or tawny, 2–3 mm long; callus densely villous, 0.15–0.20 in./4–5 mm long, sparsely pilose; palea slightly shorter than the lemma; caryopsis 0.5–0.6 in./13–15 mm long. Flowering and fruiting occur from June through August.

Uses: Feathergrass is aptly named, for it is a beautiful, graceful grass. The sparse foliage is produced in an upright, rather tight tuft, opening near the top and giving the plants a graceful appearance. The few-flowered, slightly drooping panicle, with its spikelets of exceptionally long, curling awns, adds to the gracefulness and attractiveness of the plants. Feathergrass is attractive in the cut-flower garden, in middleground borders, and as specimen plants in rock gardens. The sparse foliage and drooping panicles produce a gentle, waving action with the slightest breeze, which accentuates their attractiveness. The feathery panicles are useful in dried floral arrangements.

Cultivation: Propagation is by plant division, as the seeds are difficult to germinate. Plant division may be done in the spring or fall. It is best to purchase plants, provided they are available. The plants thrive best in dry, well-drained, fertile soil in full sun or light shade.

Other ornamental species: *Stipa arundinacea* (Hook. f.) Benth., New Zealand windgrass A loosely tufted, upright-open, evergreen perennial with scaly rhizomes. Culms erect to arching, very slender, glabrous, 4–5 ft /1.2–1.5 m high. Foliage initially dark green becoming orange, bright beige, or purplish, fine in texture; leaf blades shiny, somewhat involute, coriaceous, rough, with well-marked nerves, 10–12 in./2.5–3.0 dm long, about 0.20–0.25 in./5–6 mm wide, long attenuate; sheaths round on the back, somewhat rough. Inflorescence an open, drooping panicle, greenish or with a light purplish tinge, the slender branches borne in whorls about the main axis, rarely divided, bearing few spikelets; spikelets one-flowered and purplish. Flowering and fruiting occur from July through September. New Zealand windgrass is a valuable ornamental for all seasons. The plants make an unusual ground cover in naturalized areas and are eye-catching in accent and specimen plantings in middleground borders and in rock gardens. The shiny, purplish foliage and spikelets become streaked with orange and beige or light, bright tan or brown as summer progresses, becoming orange-brown into winter. The plants produce a lasting flash in the fall and early winter. They are grown primarily for their ever-changing foliage color. Propagation is by seeding and by plant division. The plants thrive in hot, dry situations in dry soils in full sun. They are considered to be tender perennials adapted to zones 8–10.

Stipa calamagrostis (L.) Wahlenb. An upright-open, densely tufted, mound-forming perennial. Culms erect to arching, 2–3 ft /6–9 dm high, glabrous. Foliage medium green, fine in texture; leaf blades flat, elongate, arching, long attenuate, 1–2 ft /3–6 dm long, about 0.20–0.25 in./5–6 mm wide, glabrous below, pubescent above; sheaths round on the back, slightly rough or more or less glabrous, turning tan early in the season. Inflorescence a loosely branched, spreading, arching panicle, 8–12 in./2–3 dm long, 4–6 in./1.0–1.5 dm wide, white or lightly tinged purplish, lower branches clustered, bristly, and feathery. Flowering and fruiting occur from June through September. This hardy perennial is grown for its magnificent, feathery, colorful flowering panicles, which produce a light, feathery, light-colored appearance when fully mature; they are useful in both fresh and dried arrangements. This colorful perennial blooms early in the season, and the plants remain attractive throughout the entire growing season. It is useful as a specimen planting in rock gardens and middleground borders. The plants prefer sandy soils in hot, dry, sunny locations. Propagation is by direct seeding and by plant division, preferably the latter, because seed viability is usually low. This hardy perennial is adapted to zones 3 and 4.

Stipa capillata L. Feathergrass A tufted, upright-narrow perennial; the plants are 3–4 ft /0.9–1.2 m high. Flowering and fruiting occur from July through August. Feathergrass is best demonstrated in group plantings on dry sites in full sun. It is adapted to zones 7–9.

Stipa elegantissima Labill. Australian feathergrass An upright-open, tufted perennial. Culms erect, stout, glabrous, 16–32 in./4.0–8.0 dm high. Foliage scant, light green, fine in texture; leaf blades flat, 8–12 in./2–3 dm long, 0.1–0.2 in./3–5 mm wide. Inflorescence a loosely branched, large panicle, 8–16 in./ 2–4 dm long, 4–6 in./1.0–1.5 dm wide; the filiform, spreading branches are conspicuously feathery, bearing purplish, long-awned, one-flowered spikelets. This perennial is useful in group plantings in rock gardens and foreground borders. The plants are adapted to a wide range of dry soils and prefer full sun. Propagation is by direct seeding and by plant division. This species is adapted to zones 6–9; it is less hardy than *Stipa pennata*.

Stipa extremoirentalis Hara Eastern feathergrass A tufted, upright-narrow perennial; the plants are 2–3 ft /6–9 dm high. It is best demonstrated in group plantings on dry sites in full sun. Eastern feathergrass is adapted to zones 6–9. Propagation is usually by seeding.

Stipa gigantea Link Golden oats, Giant feathergrass A densely tufted, upright-open, semievergreen perennial. Culms erect, stout, leafy, rigid, 4–6 ft / 1.2–1.8 m high, glabrous. Foliage medium to dark green, fine in texture; leaf blades rolled or somewhat U-shaped, elongate, arching, 12–18 in./3.0–4.5 dm long, 0.20–0.25 in./5–6 mm wide, long attenuate; sheaths round on the back, slightly rough. Inflorescence an extremely loose, open, broad, yellowish panicle, 12–18 in./3.0–4.5 dm long, about 8–12 in./2–3 dm wide, the many branches dividing at least once; spikelets large, 0.8–1.0 in./20–25 mm long, one-flowered, yellowish or purplish, glistening with long awns, 4–6 in./1.0–1.5 dm long; glumes nearly equal, three-nerved, 1.0–1.2 in./2.5–3.0 cm long, lemmas 0.4–0.6 in./10–15 mm long, hairy on the back. Flowering and fruiting occur from June through July. The primary ornamental value of golden oats is its large, open, persistent, flowering panicles; these remain attractive throughout the summer. The large, long-awned, golden, two-pronged spikelets glisten in the sun when blown by the slightest breeze. Golden oats is most useful in specimen plantings where it is given sufficient space to demonstrate its full ornamental value. The plants thrive best in sandy, well-drained soils in full sun. Propagation is by direct seeding and by plant division. Golden oats is adapted to zones 7–9.

Stipa rubens Smirn. A tufted, upright-narrow perennial; the plants are about 12–15 in./3.0–3.8 dm high. This small perennial is best demonstrated in group plantings on dry sites in full sun; it is adapted to zones 7–9. Propagation is usually by seeding.

Stipa spartea Trin. Porcupine grass (Synonym, *Stipa robusta* Nutt.) A tufted perennial. Culms erect, simple, rather stout, 2–4 ft /0.6–1.2 m high. Foliage light green, fine in texture; leaf blades are grooved or flat, becoming involute on drying, short pubescent in addition to being somewhat scabrous, with some long, scattered hairs, glabrous beneath, basal leaves about two-thirds the length of the culm, those of the culm 4–12 in./1–3 dm long, long and evenly attenuate; sheaths mostly imbricate, glabrous or with a few hairs on their margins. Inflorescence a narrow, nodding, lax panicle, finally exserted, 6–8 in./1.5–2.0 dm long, about 1.0–1.3 in./2.5–3.0 cm wide, the branches few, distant, slender, erect, naked below, bearing one or two spikelets; spikelets one-flowered; glumes about equal, 1.0–1.4 in./2.5–3.5 cm long, long-awned, pale green or almost colorless, strongly five-nerved, long attenuate, exceeding the brownish lemma; lemmas 0.6–0.8 in./15–20 mm long, brownish, appressed pubescent below, almost glabrous above except for a line of pubescence on one side, three-nerved, the callus about 0.25 in./6 mm long, upwardly barbed with brown hairs, the body decreasingly pubescent to the ciliate crown except the back of the upper half, which is roughened; awn stout, twice-geniculate, 4–8 in./1–2 dm long, divided into three parts, the basal part 2–3 in./5–8 cm long, straight with lemma, tightly twisted, second part 0.8–1.2 in./2–3 cm long, loosely twisted, scabrous, bent almost to a right angle, third part straight and glabrous or scabrous; paleas completely enclosed. Flowering and fruiting occur from May through July. The flowering panicles with long, twice-geniculate, stout awns are the main attraction of porcupine grass. It is attractive in grass mixtures, as ground-cover plantings, and as specimen plantings in rock gardens and middle-ground borders. Propagation is by direct seeding and by plant division. The plants thrive in dry locations in full sun in zones 5 and 6.

Stipa tenacissima L. Esparto An upright-open, tufted perennial with a tough, branching base. Culms erect, slender, 1–3 ft /3–9 dm high. Foliage light green, fine in texture; leaf blades involute, elongate, tomentose at base, with erect auricles 0.1–0.4 in./3–10 mm long. Inflorescence a narrow, dense, branched panicle; awns 1.6–2.4 in./4–6 cm long, geniculate, feathery below the bend. The commercial value of esparto is its use as a source of paper and cordage. Its ornamental value is its flower heads, with long, obscurely geniculate, feathery awns that make it attractive in specimen plantings. Flowering and fruiting occur from June through August. Propagation is by direct seeding and by plant division. It may be somewhat difficult to plant the seeds if the long flexuous awns are not broken off the spikelets. The plants prefer sunny, dry locations and are adapted to a wide range of soils. Esparto is adapted to zones 7–9.

Trichloris **Fourn. ex Benth.** Name from Latin *tri,* "three," and *Chloris,* a genus of grass, the lemma being three-awned. Lectotype, *Trichloris pluriflora* Fourn. *Trichloris* inhabits arid and semiarid regions of South, Central, and North America. Erect, tufted, slender, perennial grasses, with flat, scabrous leaf blades and numerous erect or ascending spikes, aggregate but scarcely digitate at the summit of the culms. Spikelets two-to-five-flowered, nearly sessile, in two to five rows along one side of a continuous, slender rachis, the rachilla disarticulating above the glumes and prolonged behind the uppermost, perfect floret, bearing a reduced, usually awned, floret; glumes unequal, acuminate or short awned, the body shorter than the lower lemma; lemmas narrow, three-nerved, the midnerve and usually the lateral nerves extending into slender awns.

Latin name: *Trichloris crinita* (Lag.) Parodi
Synonym: *Chloris crinita* Lag.

Trichloris crinita. **A, Habit,** × 1/2; **B, glumes and florets,** × 5. *Source: Manual of the Grasses of the United States.* USDA Misc. Pub. 200. 1951.

Origin: Mediterranean region
Habitat: Plains, dry, sandy, rocky soils
Hardiness: Zones 3 through 8
Description: A tufted, upright-narrow perennial. Culms erect, single or tufted, 24–40 in./0.6–1.0 m high. Foliage light green, fine in texture; leaf blades hairy, 8–12 in./2–3 dm long, 0.10–0.15 in./3–4 mm wide, long attenuate. Inflorescence a dense, greenish white, aggregate spike, 4–6 in./1.0–1.5 cm long,

about 2–3 in./5–8 cm wide, becoming fluffy and wider at maturity; spikelets crowded, two-flowered, light greenish; fertile lemma three-awned, about 0.1 in./3 mm long, the second lemma much reduced, both with delicate, brownish awns about 0.4 in./10 mm long. Flowering and fruiting occur from June through July.

Uses: The ornamental value of this perennial grass is its flowering spikes, which appear feathery because of its long, brownish awns. It is valuable in middleground perennial borders and in naturalized areas.

Cultivation: Propagation is by direct seeding. This species is quite drought tolerant and prefers dry sites in full sun.

Tripsacum **L. (Gamagrass, Sesamegrass).** Name of unknown origin; possible from Greek *tribein,* "to rub," alluding to the smooth joints. Lectotype, *Tripsacum dactyloides* (L.) L. There are about 10 species, in temperate and tropical America. Robust perennial grasses, usually with broad, flat leaf blades and monoecious terminal and axillary inflorescences of one to three racemes, the pistillate part below, breaking up into bony, seedlike joints, the staminate above on the same rachis, deciduous as a whole. Spikelets unisexual; staminate spikelets two-flowered, in pairs on one side of a continuous rachis, one sessile, the other sessile or pedicellate, similar to those of *Zea,* the glumes firmer; pistillate spikelets solitary on opposite sides of each joint of the thick, hard, articulate lower part of the same rachis, sunken in hollows in the joints, consisting of one perfect floret and a sterile lemma; lower glume coriaceous, nearly enfolding the spikelet, fitting into and closing the hollow of the rachis; upper glume similar to the lower but smaller, enfolding the remainder of the spikelet; sterile lemma, fertile lemma and palea very thin and hyaline, these progressively smaller.

> **Latin name:** *Tripsacum dactyloides* (L.) L.
> **Synonym:** *Coix dactyloides* L.
> **Common name:** Eastern gamagrass
> **Origin:** North America
> **Habitat:** Wet grounds, along ditches and streams
> **Hardiness:** Zones 5 through 10
> **Description:** A densely tufted, upright-open, semievergreen perennial with thick, knotty rhizomes. Culms in large clumps, stout at base, erect, with few nodes, glabrous, narrower in the upper portions, 6–9 ft /1.8–2.8 m high. Foliage rich, medium to dark green, coarse in texture; leaf blades flat, more or less auricled at base, long attenuate, midrib large, entirely scabrous on the margins, sparsely hispid on the upper surface and especially so below, 6–15 in./1.5–3.8 dm long, those of the sterile shoots 20–30 in./5.0–7.6 dm long, 0.4–1.0 in./ 10–25 mm wide, broad for most of their length, usually terminating in a blunt point or splitting toward the tip; sheaths tightly surrounding the culms, flattened, shorter than the internodes; ligule a ring of short, ciliate hairs. Inflores-

Tripsacum dactyloides. Habit, × 1/2; pistillate spikelets with rachis joint and pair of staminate spikelets with rachis joint, × 5. *Source: Manual of the Grasses of the West Indies.* USDA Misc. Pub. 243. 1936.

cence terminal and axillary spikes, 6–10 in./1.5–2.5 dm long, the pistillate part about one-fourth the entire length, terminal spikes usually in twos or threes together, the contiguous sides flattened, those of the branches usually solitary, cylindrical; a rigid lower fourth pistillate, the upper portion staminate; spikelets unisexual, staminate spikelets 0.3–0.4 in./8–10 mm long, two-flowered, in pairs on a continuous rachis, one sessile the other sessile or pedicellate, on one side of the rachis, pistillate spikelets 0.25–40 in./6–10 mm long, narrowly ovate, single at each joint of the thick, hard, articulate part of the same rachis, sunken in hollows of the joints, consisting of one perfect floret and a sterile lemma, the joints rhomboid; glumes about equal, lower glume coriaceous or rather chartaceous, two-keeled, scabrous on the keels, ovate, about nine-nerved, infolding the spikelet by fitting into and closing the hollow of the rachis, upper glume similar but smaller than the lower, about five-nerved, enfolding the remainder of the spikelet; sterile and fertile lemma and palea hyaline. Flowering and fruiting occur from July until frost.

Uses: Eastern gamagrass is often grown as a curiosity, as it is an interesting plant throughout the year. The terminal flowering racemes, far above the foliage, with their bright red, exserted anthers and brownish pistils are a perfect foil for the medium green foliage. The plants and flowers are dramatized by their reflection on the water in specimen plantings in water gardens. Eastern gamagrass is ideal when grown in clumps for filling otherwise unused or inaccessible niches in the garden in addition to its use in perennial background borders.

Cultivation: Propagation is by direct seeding and by plant division, preferably the latter. The plants grow equally well in full sun or light shade in rich, moist soil. They also thrive in low, wet sites along streams or around lakes and ponds.

Triticum **L. (Wheat).** The old Latin name for wheat. Standard species, *Triticum aestivum* L. There are about 30 species, native to the Mediterranean region and southwest Asia. Low or rather tall annual grasses with flat leaf blades and thick spikes. Spikelets two-to-five-flowered, solitary, placed flatwise at each joint of a continuous or articulate rachis, the rachilla disarticulating above the glumes and between the florets or continuous; glumes rigid, keeled, three-to-several-nerved, the apex abruptly mucronate or toothed or with one or several awns; lemmas broad, keeled, very asymmetric, many-nerved, abruptly pointed or awned.

> **Latin name:** *Triticum aestivum* L.
> **Synonym:** *Triticum sativum* Lam.
> **Cultivars:** Many in cultivation
> **Common name:** Wheat
> **Origin:** Asia, Mediterranean region
> **Habitat:** Cultivated, escape from cultivation

Triticum aestivum. **Habit with awned spikes (bearded wheat),** × 1/2;
spikelet and floret, × **3.** *Source: Manual of the Grasses of the United States.*
USDA Misc. Pub. 200. 1951.

Hardiness: Zones 3 through 10

Description: A short-lived, upright-narrow annual. Culms erect, tufted, freely branching at the base, 2–3 ft /6–9 dm high, glabrous or pubescent at the nodes, usually hollow. Foliage medium to dark green, medium in texture; leaf blades ascending, more or less straight, upper arching, flat, 6–12 in./1.5–3 dm long, 0.4–0.6 in./10–15 mm wide, smooth or slightly scabrous on upper surface, young leaves auricled at the base, ciliate; sheaths usually longer than the internodes, pubescent, upper smooth to slightly scabrous; ligule membranous, about 1 mm long. Inflorescence an erect, dense spike, usually exserted, more or less four-sided, 2–6 in./0.5–1.5 dm long, about 0.8–1.0 in./20–25 mm wide; spikelets singly at the nodes in two rows, imbricate, alternating on a zigzag, continuous rachis, usually three-to-five-flowered, somewhat flattened, sessile, ovate; glumes rigid, three-to-several-nerved, shorter than the spikelets, strongly keeled to one side, the outer side broader, the sharp keel terminating in a short awn or point; lemmas keeled or round on the back, many-nerved, more or less three-toothed, the middle tooth sometimes extending into a long awn, awns appressed, straight, erect, 2–5 in./5–13 cm long, palea two-keeled, shorter than the lemma; caryopsis puberulent at the apex, furrowed, free. Flowering and fruiting occur from May through July.

Uses: The ornamental value of wheat is its decorative, flowering spikes, usually with long awns. The mature seedheads of wheat are used by florists either in their natural color or dyed. The decorative spikes may be picked green or after they mature, as the seeds and awns are not lost following maturity. Wheat is quite often grown in the vegetable garden; the immature flower heads are attractive as cut flowers. Wheat is one of the major grain crops of the world; perhaps it was grown as a food crop prior to historical records.

Cultivation: Propagation is by direct seeding. Wheat does best in full sun; it is adapted to a wide range of soils, including slightly saline types. The plants have a short flowering period and are short-lived.

Poulard wheat, *Triticum turgidum,* is another ornamental species (Appendix 1).

Uniola L. (**Sprangle grass, Spikegrass**). An ancient Latin name of a plant. Lectotype *Uniola paniculata* L. There are nine species, inhabiting North, Central and South America. Erect, rather tall perennials with flat or sometimes convolute leaf blades and narrow or open panicles of compressed, or sometimes very broad, flat spikelets. Spikelets three-to-many-flowered, the lower one to six lemmas empty, the rachilla disarticulating above the glumes and between the florets; glumes compressed-keeled, rigid, usually narrow, three-to-seven-nerved, acute or acuminate, rarely mucronate; lemmas compressed, sometimes conspicuously flattened, chartaceous, many-nerved, the nerves sometimes obscure, acute or acuminate, the empty ones at the base and the uppermost usually reduced; palea rigid, strongly keeled, bowed out at the base, weakly so in *Uniola paniculata* L.

Latin name: *Uniola paniculata* L.
Synonym: *Briza caroliniana* Lam.
Common names: Sea oats, Spikegrass
Origin: United States
Habitat: Cultivated, escape from cultivation
Hardiness: Zones 7 through 10
Description: An upright-open to upright-arching, densely tufted perennial with extensive creeping rhizomes. Stout culms arise from the rhizomes, 3–8 ft / 0.9–2.5 m high, erect becoming arched. Foliage medium green, fine to medium in texture; leaf blades ascending becoming arched, firm, elongate, flat, becoming involute toward the acuminate tip, 8–24 in./2–6 dm long, 0.4–0.5 in./10–13 mm wide; sheaths tightly clasping the culm with tufts of hairs at the collar, usually longer than the internodes; ligule with a tuft of short, whitish hairs.

Uniola paniculata. **Habit,** × 1/10; **spikelets,** × 1. *Source: Manual of the Grasses of the West Indies.* USDA Misc. Pub. 243. 1936.

Inflorescence an erect, exserted, many-branched, panicle, cylindrical, compact, 8–16 in./2–4 dm long, 2–3 in./5–8 cm wide, the branches ascending except the lower ones, which are arched and drooping, about 2–3 in./5–8 cm long, densely flowered, the pedicels short; spikelets 10-to-20-flowered, laterally compressed, ovate to ovate-lanceolate, 0.5–1.0 in./13–25 mm long, light green or pale, the lower florets sterile; glumes one-nerved or the upper three-nerved, compressed-keeled, rigid, narrow, acute or acuminate, 0.20–0.25 in./5–6 mm long, shorter than the lowest lemma; lemmas 0.3–0.4 in./8–10 mm long, strongly keeled, seven-to-nine-nerved, the midnerve often slightly excurrent, obtuse, scabrous on the keel, the lower lemmas shorter, acute, sterile; palea nearly as long as the lemma, lanceolate, two-keeled, the keels scabrous, ciliate, broadly winged; caryopsis flat, oval, black, about 0.2 in./5 mm long. Flowering and fruiting occur throughout the growing season.

Uses: This native perennial occurs along the Atlantic coast from New York southward and along the Gulf of Mexico. Sea oats is an excellent plant for naturalizing coastal areas and for sand dune stabilization and erosion control; it is somewhat salt tolerant. Sea oats is on the list of endangered species in the United States and is protected by law in most areas. The plants provide some protection and food for wildlife. The plants are attractive throughout the growing season and remain upright into winter. The rich bronze, nodding panicles are attractive on the plants and provide good autumnal color; they are used in dried arrangements.

Cultivation: Sea oats cannot be propagated by seeding because the seeds are usually inviable. Plants are rarely if ever available in the trade, as they are prohibited from being removed from natural coastal areas. Usually sea-grant officials can advise property owners about other conservation plants for use along the seacoast. They may be contacted usually through land-grant colleges or universities of each coastal state. The plants prefer sand dunes or sandy soil in full sun or light shade.

Vetiveria **Bory.** Name for *vettiver,* the native Tamil name. Type species, *Andropogon squarrosum* L. f. There are two species, native to the Old World tropics. Robust perennial grasses with simple stems and thick rhizomes. Terminal branched panicles disposed usually in thick whorls, the branches with many internodes. Spikelets in pairs, one sessile, the other pedicellate, those of each pair similar in shape and size, different in sex, two-flowered, the lower floret reduced to a lemma, upper bisexual in the sessile spikelet and staminate in the pedicellate spikelet; glumes armed with stout, tubercle-based spines; lemmas awnless or the upper of the sessile spikelet awned; palea minute. Sessile spikelet laterally compressed; first scale coriaceous, the margins inflexed or involute, second scale awned or awnless; third and fourth scales hyaline, the latter entire or shortly two-toothed, muticous, mucronate, or short-awned from between the teeth;

pedicellate spikelet usually awnless, rarely awned. Stigmas three, plumose, linear, up to four times the length of the style; ovary glabrous.

Latin name: *Vetiveria zizanioides* (L.) Nash
Synonym: *Phalaris zizanioides* L.
Common names: Vetivergrass, Khas-khas, Khus-khus, Vetiver

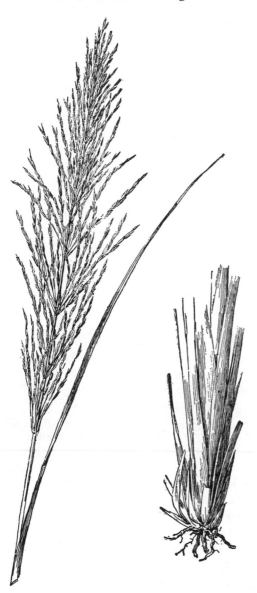

Vetiveria zizanioides.
Habit, × 1/2. *Source: Manual of the Grasses of the West Indies.* USDA Misc. Pub. 243. 1936.

Origin: Asia
Habitat: Cultivated, escape from cultivation
Hardiness: Zones 7 through 10
Description: An upright-open, densely cespitose, semievergreen perennial with rhizomatous, aromatic roots. Culms in large tufts, erect, rigid, simple, 4–7 ft /1.2–2.2 m high with numerous basal leaves. Foliage medium green to greenish yellow, medium in texture; leaf blades rather rigid, elongate, 15–36 in./3.9–9.0 dm long, 0.25–0.50 in./6–13 mm wide, conduplicate below and flat above, slightly rough toward the tip, papillose-pubescent above toward the base; sheaths compressed-keeled, longer than the internodes; ligule a very minutely pubescent line. Inflorescence a loose, branched, elongate-pyramidal panicle, light greenish yellow to purplish, 8–16 in./2–4 dm long, 3–4 in./8–10 cm wide, the primary branches commonly 8 to 20 per whorl, the whorls 1–2 in./2.5–5.0 cm distant, naked at the base, sometimes with one to three short branchlets or racemes, 1–2 in./2.5–5.0 cm long, slender, erect or ascending or somewhat spreading, the rachis joints flattened, scabrous on the margins; spikelets in pairs, pedicellate and sessile, pedicellate spikelets staminate, 0.15–0.20 in./4–5 mm long with scabrous pedicels about 2–3 mm long, awnless, muricate, the glumes sparingly muricate; sessile spikelets perfect, laterally compressed, 0.15–0.20 in./4–5 mm long, narrow, acute, about as long as the rachis joints or 0.15–0.25 in./4–6 mm long; glumes unequal, the lower minutely scabrous, two-keeled, the keels muricate, the upper keeled, the keel muricate, the margins membranous, ciliate; lemmas hyaline, about equal, margins of the sterile lemma ciliate, fertile lemma nearly as long as the glumes, with a short awn from the bifid apex, palea short and hyaline. Flowering and fruiting occur from October through January in the tropics and from August through September in colder climates when grown as an annual.
Uses: Vetivergrass is used as a hedge, tall screen, or windbreak in warm climates. The hedges are useful in controlling wind and water erosion. The culms are very stiff and robust; they are rarely damaged by wind. The plants deserve a place in landscape plantings, in rock gardens, and in background borders. The flower heads are attractive on the plants and are used in fresh and dried floral arrangements, either in their natural color or dyed. The aromatic roots are dug, washed, dried and packed with clothing for protection from moths and to add a pleasant scent to the clothing. Sometimes the aromatic roots are woven into screens which, when wet, are used to add perfume to living quarters. Vetivergrass has a niche in landscape plantings for its foliage and especially its aromatic roots, which are a beneficial and useful curiosity.
Cultivation: Propagation is by seeding and by plant division. Vetivergrass grows well in full sun on well-drained soil, it is adapted to a wide range of soils, including rocky types. The clumps gradually increase in size when the plants are allowed to perenniate in warm climates. Plants started by seeding indoors in early spring and transferred to the garden will usually blossom the same year.

Zea L. (**Maize**). Name from Greek *zea,* or *zeia,* a kind of grain. Type species, *Zea mays* L. There are two or possibly three species, native to the New World tropics. Robust, tall, annual grasses with terminal panicles (tassels) of staminate racemes, and short pedunculate, pistillate, eight-to-many-rowed spikes (ears) enclosed in numerous spathes (husks). Spikelets unisexual; staminate spikelets two-flowered, in pairs, on one side of a continuous rachis, one nearly sessile, the other pedicellate; glumes membranous, acute; lemma and palea hyaline; pistillate spikelets sessile, in pairs, consisting of one fertile floret and one sterile floret, the latter sometimes developed as a second fertile floret; glumes broad, round, or emarginate at apex; sterile and fertile lemmas hyaline, the palea developed; style very long and slender, stigmatic along both sides well toward the base.

Latin name: *Zea mays* L.
Synonym: *Zea americana* Mill.
Cultivars: Many in cultivation, including 'Harlequin,' 'Indian Corn,' 'Multicolored,' 'Strawberry Corn'
Varieties: *Zea mays* var. *japonica* (Van Houtte) A. Wood 'Quadricolor,' 'Variegata'; *Zea mays* var. *praecox* Bonaf., Popcorn; *Zea mays* var. *tunicata* Larr. ex St. Hil., Podcorn
Common names: Corn, maize
Origin: Central America
Habitat: Cultivated, escape from cultivation
Hardiness: Zones 5 through 10
Description: A tall, robust, upright-narrow annual. Culms erect, tufted, glabrous pithy, usually solitary or sometimes branching and producing short shoots near the base, 2–8 ft /0.6–2.5 m high, sometimes higher, about 1 in./25 mm in diameter at the base. Foliage conspicuously distichous, coarse in texture, variable in color, usually light to dark green, sometimes light shades of purple, red, or yellow; leaf blades with conspicuous, thick, whitish midvein, hairy on upper surface, glabrous beneath, margins ciliate, elongate, narrowly elliptic, undulate, becoming U-shaped near the base, 12–40 in./0.3–1.0 m long, 2–4 in./5–10 cm wide; sheaths chartaceous, light green, many veined, usually almost as long or longer than the internodes, tightly clasping the culm, occasionally a few long hairs near the throat; ligules usually a few long hairs. Inflorescence monoecious; staminate inflorescence a conical, branched, open, spreading terminal panicle (tassel), 2–12 in./0.5–3.0 dm long, about 6–8 in./1.5–2.0 dm wide, racemes spikelike, 6–10 in./1.5–2.5 dm long, staminate spikelets two-flowered, in pairs on one side of a continuous rachis, one almost sessile, the other pedicellate; glumes membranous, acute; lemma and palea hyaline; pistillate inflorescence borne in one or more leaf axils, spikelets sessile, in pairs consisting of one fertile floret and one sterile floret, the latter sometimes developed as a second fertile floret; glumes broad, round at the apex, sterile and fertile lemmas hyaline, the palea developed, borne in an even number of rows, usually 8 to 30, on a thick-

ened, woody axis (cob) 6–12 in./1.5–3.0 dm long, about 2.0–3.5 in./5–9 cm thick, the whole enclosed in numerous, large, foliaceous bracts (husks), the styles up to 10–12 in./2.5–3.0 dm long, protruding from the top of a sessile, silky mass. The ovules develop into kernels (seeds) of various sizes, shapes, and colors following fertilization. The floral bracts of common corn are much shorter than the kernel and remain on the cob when the kernels are shelled. Flowering and fruiting usually depend on the time of planting; flowering usually occurs within 60–90 days from date of planting.

There are several races of corn, the most important being dent, common (commercial field corn), flint, sweet, and popcorn. There are numerous cultivars and hybrids of commercial corn differing in size and height of culms (stalks), ear size, and tassels, in addition to cob color and length and tightness of husks.

Uses: The variegated cultivars of ornamental corn are grown primarily for their colorful foliage, whereas those cultivars with colorful ears are used in dried floral arrangements. The usual foliage color of corn is green, which varies in shades and hues; one form has dull purplish leaves. Variegated forms have foliage that has white, pink, yellow, bronze, and green stripes. Other cultivars have attractive, multicolored ears. The individual kernels (seeds) are of many colors and hues, arranged in a random manner on the cob. The cultivars with colorful multicolored ears are used along with portions of the dry brown or beige foliage in dried floral arrangements in both inside and outside decorations. The variegated cultivars are used as specimen plants in annual middleground borders and in rock, water, and vegetable gardens. Corn grows and matures rather rapidly, thus permitting two or more plantings during the same season. Planting corn at two-to-four-week intervals in the spring and early summer will result in colorful and interesting plants throughout the entire growing season.

Cultivation: Ornamental corn is easy to propagate and grow. Propagation is by direct seeding. Almost all soils are suitable, provided they are moist and fertile; the plants prefer full sun or light shade. Corn is a heavy feeder, particularly of nitrogen. The plants respond to fertilization and irrigation when it becomes necessary. Corn is a cross-pollinated plant, and therefore many plant forms, foliage, cob, and kernel colors may result when the various cultivars and varieties are grown in proximity to one another.

Cultivars and varieties: *Zea mays* L. 'Harlequin'   The plants are 3–4 ft / 0.9–1.2 m high. Foliage is coarse and variegated. Leaves have broad, longitudinal stripes of green and dull red or purple. The kernels (seeds) are dark red, as is the cob.

Zea mays L. 'Indian Corn'   The plants are 4–6 ft /1.2–1.8 m high. Foliage is coarse and green. The kernels are of many colors (i.e., various shades of red, yellow, and white), and some are bicolored. The variously colored kernels are interspersed at random on the cob, producing a truly uniquely colored ear. This cultivar, along with others, is easily dried for use in floral arrangements. The partially exposed multicolored ears are ideal as dried specimens.

Zea mays L. 'Multicolored' The plants of this cultivar and the multicolored ears are very similar to those of 'Indian Corn.' The similarities of plant size and kernel color of this cultivar make it difficult to distinguish it from 'Indian corn.'

Zea mays L. 'Strawberry Corn' The plants are 4–6 ft /1.2–1.8 m high. The foliage is medium green; ears are 2–8 in./0.5–2.0 dm long, about 2 in./5 cm thick. Small kernels are variable in shape and color, resulting in a multicolored ear.

Zea mays var. *japonica* (Van Houtte) A. Wood (Synonym, *Zea japonica* Van Houtte). 'Quadricolor,' 'Variegata' These small, variegated forms are usually 18–30 in./4.5–7.5 dm high. The variegated leaves are longitudinally striped green, white, and yellow and sometimes pink. They are grown for their interesting variegated foliage, which is used primarily in dried arrangements for both indoor and outdoor decorations. Various parts of the plant are used, including the entire plant with tassel and ear attached, portions of the stem with attached leaves, ears, and tassel, and detached leaves, tassels, and ears, including the attached husks.

Zea mays var. *praecox* Bonaf. Popcorn The plants of popcorn are 3–5 ft / 0.9–1.5 m high. The small ears are 2–6 in./0.5–1.5 dm long, about 2 in./5 cm thick, including the kernels; small kernels are somewhat variable in shape and color but usually reddish mahogany; the husks are beige or light tan when mature. The ears, husked and unhusked, and the kernels, popped and unpopped, are used in decorations; the popped kernels are also popular as food.

Zea mays var. *tunicata* Larr. ex St. Hil. Podcorn Podcorn has kernels borne on short ears, 4–6 in./1.0–1.5 dm long, about 2 in./5 cm thick, including the kernels, which develop into elongated, floral bracts. Podcorn is cultivated occasionally as a curiosity. The plants and plant parts are used for decorative purposes in the same manner as are those of other ornamental types.

Zizania L. (Wildrice, Water oats, Folle Avione). Name form *Zizanion*, an old Greek name for a weed growing in grain, the tares of the Scripture parable. Lectotype, *Zizania aquatica* L. There are three species, native to East Asia. Tall, aquatic, annual grasses, with flat leaf blades and large, terminal panicles, the lower branches ascending or spreading, bearing pendulous, staminate spikelets, the upper branches ascending, erect at maturity, bearing appressed pistillate spikelets, the staminate spikelets early deciduous, the pistillate spikelets tardily deciduous. Spikelets unisexual, one-flowered, disarticulating from the pedicel; glumes obsolete, represented by a small, collarlike ridge; pistillate spikelet terete, angled at maturity; lemmas chartaceous, three-nerved, tapering into a long, slender awn; palea two-nerved, closely clasped by the lemma; caryopsis cylindrical, 0.4–0.8 in./10–20 mm long; staminate spikelet soft; lemmas five-nerved, membranous, linear, acuminate or awn-pointed; palea three-nerved, about as long as the lemma; androecium six-merous.

Latin name: *Zizania aquatica* L.
Synonym: *Zizania clavulosa* Michx.
Common names: Indian rice, Eastern wildrice, Annual wildrice
Origin: United States
Habitat: Freshwater marshes, borders of streams
Hardiness: Zones 4 through 9
Description: A robust, upright-open, clump-forming annual. Culms 6–9 ft /1.8–2.8 m high, mostly simple, sometimes branching, erect but sometimes decumbent at the base, glabrous, the nodes shrunken, densely appressed pubescent. Foliage medium to dark green, coarse in texture; leaf blades elongate, 3–4 ft /0.9–1.2 m long, 0.5–0.8 in./13–20 mm wide, scabrous above and beneath, scabrous or hispid on the margins; densely appressed pubescent above at the sheath junction; sheaths longer than the internodes, glabrous or sparsely ciliate on the imbricate margin, densely appressed pubescent on the collar, except the posterior side, more or less scabrous between the nerves; ligule membranous, ovate, 0.4–0.6 in./10–15 mm long, usually lacerate. Inflorescence terminal and axillary branched panicles usually 1–2 in./2.5–5.0 cm long, smooth except the spikelets, axis compressed and more or less grooved, lower branches terete, ascending or spreading, bearing pendulous staminate spikelets, smooth, pedicels of staminate branches filiform but slightly clavate below the spikelets, the upper branches ascending, at maturity erect, bearing appressed pistillate spikelets; spikelets unisexual, one-flowered, the pistillate terete, linear, awned, angled at maturity, articulate, and tardily deciduous, on clavate pedicels of the appressed upper branches, the staminate lanceolate, early deciduous on the expanded lower branches of the same panicle; glumes absent; lemmas and paleas of pistillate spikelets chartaceous, three-nerved, tapering into a long, filiform awn closely clasping the two-nerved lemma; of staminate spikelets five-nerved, membranous, linear acuminate or awn-pointed, hairy at the apex, palea three-nerved, about as long; awns 0.8–1.0 in./20–25 mm long, short hairy, more densely hairy with longer hairs at the base; caryopsis cylindric, 0.6–0.8 in./15–20 mm long, enclosed in the membranous lemma and palea. Flowering and fruiting occur from May through September.

Uses: The luxuriant medium to dark green foliage complements the large, lax, flowering panicles of Indian rice. It is unsurpassed for sheer attractiveness and beauty in water gardens, marshes, or shallow water of streams and lakes. The large, lax, flowering panicles are decorative and useful in cut-flower arrangements; they often shatter badly with age and are useless in dried bouquets.

Cultivation: Propagation is by direct seeding. The seeds should be soaked thoroughly in water before planting. Place the pots in standing water or in mud where the plants are to grow. The growth rate of Indian rice is very slow, although the plants have a rather long flowering period. Indian rice is among the few ornamental grasses that can be grown directly in full sun in shallow but not stagnant water.

REFERENCE

Hitchcock, A. S., and Agnes Chase. 1951. *Manual of the Grasses of the United States.* USDA Misc. Pub. 200. Washington, DC: Govt. Printing Office.

2

Bamboo

Approximately 800 to 1,000 bamboo species constitute the tribe Bambuseae of the Gramineae, or grass, family. Bamboo is the largest member of the grass family, usually consisting of large, woody perennials. Bamboo occurs naturally in every continent except Antarctica and Europe, but it is most prevalent in southeast Asia, China, and Japan. A few species are indigenous in the Western Hemisphere. Natural stands occur from near sea level in the tropics to mountain slopes up to two and one-half miles high in temperate zones.

The culture of bamboo is older than historical records. Messages, including love notes, were scratched on bamboo culms long before paper was invented. Bamboo culture has been practiced in China and Japan for aeons. The culture of bamboo in the Americas is relatively new in comparison to that in China, Japan, and Southeast Asia.

ORIGIN, TYPES, PROPAGATION, AND GROWTH HABITS

Many species of bamboo are cultivated in the United States, although most of them are exotic. The oriental bamboos of China and Japan play an important and prominent role in American ornamental horticulture. Many species of hardy running types distributed among several genera have been introduced into the United States during the past century. The largest portion of this exotic germ plasm consists of hardy running bamboo in the genus *Phyllostachys*. Other hardy running types that are less common but are important in American horticulture include *Arundinaria*, *Chimonobambusa*, *Olmeca*, *Otatea*, *Pseudosasa*, *Sasa*, *Sasaella*, *Semiarundinaria*, *Sinobambusa*, and *Shibataea*. Similarly, many warm-season, clump-forming types of tropical and subtropical origin have been introduced successfully and are now in cultivation in the contiguous United States, American Samoa, Guam, Hawaii, the Panama Canal Zone, Puerto Rico, and the U.S. Virgin Islands. They include representatives in the genera *Bambusa*, *Dendrocalamus*, *Gigantochloa*, *Olmeca*, *Rhipidocladum*, *Sinarundinaria*, and *Thamnocalamus*. The origin of exotic bamboo now in cultivation in the United States is from such diverse regions as Burma, China, East Asia, the Himalayas, India, Japan, and Nepal. Exotic bamboo species and their origin now in cultivation in the United States include common bamboo from tropical Asia, *Bambusa* species from Burma, beechey and tonkin bamboo from China, black bamboo from southern China, meyer bamboo from central China, *Chimonobambusa* species from East Asia, calcutta and giant, thorny bamboo from India, and arrow and dwarf bamboo from Japan. In addition to those included in Appendix 2, bamboo genera currently being incorporated in American horticulture include *Gigantochloa*, *Olmeca*, *Otatea*, *Rhipidocladium*, *Sasaella*, *Sinarundinaria*, *Sinobambusa*, and *Thamnocalamus*. The American Bamboo Society has introduced more than 40 new species into the United States during the past decade. Considerable variation in plant size, form, color, and winter hardiness exists in this exotic germ plasm. This wide array of plant material provides gardeners and horticulturists great latitude in its use in landscape improvement. The introduction and evaluation of bamboo for horticultural purposes is a continuous process, usually requiring an extended period to obtain definitive and usable results. These plant materials are under continuous evaluation by scientists and others in a wide range of habitats. The results of this effort and of further evaluation and experience with this exotic germ plasm will reveal its value and contribution to American ornamental horticulture.

Arundinaria gigantea and *Arundinaria gigantea* ssp. *tecta* are bamboo species indigenous to the southeastern United States; *Olmeca*, *Otatea*, and *Rhipidocladium* are of tropical American origin.

The wide variation among and within endemic and exotic bamboo species in the United States is being exploited in their use as ornamentals. Although American ornamental horticulturists, landscape architects, and gardeners have not mastered the finer techniques and artistry of the Chinese and Japanese in the use of bamboo as an ornamental, they are following in their footsteps in the appreciation and use of bamboo in landscape design and improvement. These large, majestic, perennial grasses provide added diversity in size, color, texture, and form to the landscape that is otherwise unobtainable from other ornamentals.

Bamboo as an ornamental has a place in the home, greenhouse, home garden, and landscape. Bamboo may be used in many ways in ornamental horticulture—as a substitute for shrubs, for example. The typical overall form of a large, majestic, bamboo clump is unmistakable and unique among ornamentals. It is difficult to surpass the beauty in form and color of a large clump of the "queen" of bamboos, black bamboo, *Phyllostachys nigra*, with its bright green foliage and black culms. Equally striking as a specimen but smaller in size is semidwarf *Sasa palmata*, with its bright green foliage. Small pygmy bamboo, *Arundinaria pygmaea*, with its variegated foliage, produces a colorful ground cover in open shade; in addition, it is a spectacular houseplant. Square-stem bamboo, *Chimonobambusa quadrangularis*, is a unique curiosity among bamboos, with its almost square culms; large clump specimens make an excellent focal point in large gardens.

Bamboos are characterized by two groups, according to growth habit: monopodial, or running types; and sympodial, or clump types. Hardy running bamboos are native to temperate regions; warm-season clump bamboos are of tropical or subtropical origin. Monopodial running bamboo is characterized by its horizontal rhizomes, which continue their lateral growth and development, forming new culms from lateral buds at intervals from the parent plant. Not all buds produce new culms, which usually results in culms arising at various intervals from the parent plant. This growth habit, if not controlled, gradually fills in to form a dense thicket. The distinguishing characteristic of sympodial clump bamboo is its short, thick, woody rhizome, which grows upward, forming a new culm near the parent plant. This growth habit usually results in a tight or loose clump of culms.

Bamboo is propagated by asexual and sexual means. Asexual propagation is by branching of its rhizomes; sexual propagation is by seeds. Propagation of species that flower and produce viable seeds may be sexual or asexual or both. One school holds that bamboo does not flower with any precise flowering pattern or regularity. Old literature on bamboo reports a cyclical flowering pattern. Some species reportedly flower but fail to produce viable seeds. More flowering data is becoming available that will help to clarify bamboo flowering habits.

Shoot initiation of bamboos varies from early spring (March) through midsummer to late summer, depending upon the species and the region in which it is grown. Bamboo shoots that arise directly from underground rhizomes grow very rapidly in the spring, usually attaining their maximum height in about six to eight weeks. The new shoots are heavily covered with culm sheaths, some of which are deciduous early in the growth stage, whereas others are either tardily deciduous or persistent. Most of the young leaves have unfolded by the time the culm has completed its growth. Two to six leaves are formed on each twig or branch. The first leaves that form in the spring remain on the plant until autumn, whereas those that form later in the season remain on the plants over winter and are dropped after new leaves unfold the following spring. The evergreen culms remain alive for several years if they are not winter-killed; they produce a new set of leaves each year. The development of new leaves and twigs on old culms coincides with the formation of new culms from the lateral buds on the previous year's rhizomes. Monopodial running bamboo changes its foliage in the spring, whereas sympodial clump types shed theirs in winter.

Perennial bamboos may be long-lived plants. Bamboos are quite subject to winter injury and winterkill, despite their ability to perenniate for sustained periods in their zones of adaptation. When all the buds of a culm are killed by severe winter temperatures, its growth will cease, although it may remain alive for some time. The clump-forming bamboos of tropical origin will withstand little frost, if any; thus, their outdoor cultivation is restricted to the warmer parts of plant-hardiness zones 9 and 10. The hardy running bamboos remain evergreen until the temperature falls to about 3 to 5°F/ − 16 to − 15°C but exhibit symptoms of winter injury as the temperature drops below this point. Severe low winter temperatures may kill the culms to ground level, although the roots may remain alive. When culms are killed to ground level, it becomes necessary to cut them back to the base. It is prudent to delay any pruning until late spring, after it is obvious that all the buds are dead. Culms of both clump and running bamboo may be killed to ground level, although the underground rhizomes may remain alive, these giving rise to new shoots in the spring. Winter hardiness of bamboo may depend on the survival of its underground rhizomes and rootstocks, thereby distinguishing stem hardiness from that of rootstocks.

Many low-growing running bamboos produce a dense ground cover and prodigious quantities of rhizomes, usually just below ground level. This growth habit is in contrast to that of the large, clump-forming types that produce dense clumps and attain massive size. The culms of some species are erect, simple, and straight, in contrast to the arched, branched, curved culms of other species. Culm color and shape vary among species and cultivars; for example, some culms are shiny green, others are yellowish green or somewhat variegated, and yet others are almost black at maturity. The culms of some species are solid, while those of other species are either partially or completely fistulose. The culms of most species are spherical and more or less straight, in contrast to the more or less square culms and zigzag growth habit of other species. The size and number of branches varies from one to a few at each node among species, and among clones within species. Some species form branches fairly close to ground level, whereas others form branches only near the tip of the culms.

ECONOMIC AND HORTICULTURAL IMPORTANCE

The economic importance of bamboo overshadows its ornamental significance in many parts of the world, especially in tropical regions such as Southeast Asia. The economy of that region is based largely on bamboo and bamboo products. Throughout the Philippines, for example, bamboo is the only building material that is adequate in supply and sufficiently inexpensive to fill the overwhelming need for economic housing. Bamboo shoots, as a source of food, are of paramount economic importance in vast regions of the world; they constitute an export crop from Taiwan, for example. The use of bamboo as a source of food and housing materials lends emphasis to its economic importance in the human economy of some regions. Bamboo is cultivated primarily as a source of paper and paper products in Yugoslavia, where it provides a significant contribution to the economy. The economic value that bamboo and bamboo products contribute to the economy of many regions of the world is perhaps either not understood or misunderstood. It is difficult, if not impossible, to access the value of bamboo in economic terms when used in watersheds as erosion control and wildlife feed and protection. Bamboo is an excellent erosion-control plant, and it provides food and protection for wildlife wherever it occurs.

The horticultural importance of bamboo has not attained the economic level it has achieved when used for other purposes. In spite of this disparity, its horticultural importance is of considerable significance in the United States and elsewhere. With increased knowledge and significance of the role that bamboo plays in ornamental horticulture come increased appreciation and demand for its use as an ornamental. The many ways in which bamboo is used in landscape improvement all contribute to its aesthetic value. The major horticultural importance of bamboo lies in its use as an ornamental in garden and landscape plantings; of secondary significance is its use as a house or greenhouse plant and as a dried plant in dried floral arrangements. In the past, the horticultural importance of bamboo as an ornamental has probably been underemphasized rather than overemphasized, especially in the United States. Currently the horticultural importance of bamboo is gaining rapidly, especially in the United States, and it has become of significant economic value.

ESTABLISHMENT, MAINTENANCE, AND ERADICATION

Bamboo is usually easily established. Spring is generally the best time of year for planting bamboo, although fall and early winter plantings may be equally successful. The plants thrive on a wide range of soil types, either in full sun or partial shade. Bamboos are heavy feeders and prefer fertile, moist, well-drained, slightly acid soils. Propagation is by plant division, cuttings of culms and underground stems (i.e., rhizomes), layering culms (aboveground stems), and seeding. The least likely method of propagation is seeding.

Various species have interesting, long cycles of flowering and fruiting—for example, 7, 30, 60, or even more than 100 years apart—after which the plants of some of the species reportedly die. The death of some of these long-lived plants after flowering is producing a serious detrimental effect on the environment of northern China, the home of the world-famous, rare, giant panda. The replenishment of bamboo stands in the area in which the panda feeds depends upon seeds and the live rhizomes remaining in the soil. Several years of growth are required for the plants to attain full size and provide a dependable source of food. Meanwhile, the entire panda population may perish from the lack of food.

Seeds are not available for propagation of species that flower infrequently or fail to flower at all.

Plant divisions of clump bamboo are made by separating the young shoots from the parent plants before or soon after they emerge in the spring. New shoots, which usually arise near the parent plants, are simply dug out and replanted in the desired location. The small, new shoots, with attached rootstocks, should be planted slightly deeper than they were in the original planting. They should be kept well watered, at least during the first year's growth. When young, small shoots are transplanted after they emerge; they should be handled very carefully, as they are very tender and break easily. In relocating clump bamboo, the old culms should be cut back below about 12 in./3 dm in height in the spring before new growth is apparent. The entire clump should be dug out and separated into divisions containing one or more plants. After dividing the clump, replant the divisions. Plant divisions of running bamboo are made in a similar manner—that is, by digging out rhizomes or young shoots and replanting them where desired.

Propagation by rhizome cuttings is usually done in late winter or very early spring. The cuttings should be made while the plants are dormant. The cuttings should be planted in well-prepared soil at about the same depth at which they occurred naturally. As with plant divisions, the soil should be well packed following planting and be kept well watered for at least a year.

Propagation by stem cuttings involves stripping the culms of their branches, then cutting the lower section of the culm, which is comprised of several nodes, into segments about 2–3 ft/0.6–0.9 dm long. The sections are then planted at an oblique angle in the soil at least 12 in./3 dm deep, with the remainder left above ground. It is preferable to have two or more nodes buried to ensure good root formation. Care should be taken in propagation by stem cuttings to take the cuttings from the lower portion of the culm and to place the culm sections in an upright position; that is, the lower portion should be in the ground; otherwise, the new plants may not survive or may be initially distorted in shape. Make sure to keep the new cuttings well watered, particularly during the first year's growth.

Propagation by layering involves bending the culm over to a horizontal position and covering a portion (about 12 in./3 dm of it) with soil at least 4–6 in./1.0–1.5 dm deep. The portion of the culm that is buried should be somewhat below the growing tip (i.e., several nodes). The soil should be firmed and kept moist or wet until new roots appear and growth is apparent. After this, the old culm should be severed, and the new plant is then ready for transplanting. Occasionally, propagation by air layering has been attempted, but with only limited success.

All bamboo plants should be established in well-prepared, fertile, moist soil. Prepare the soil as soon as it is workable in the spring. Heavy soils may require some amelioration to improve their tilth and drainage. Bamboo thrives best in slightly acid soils (pH 6.0–7.0). Quite often, potential mature plant size is overlooked in establishing clump bamboo as specimens. Specimen plantings should be sufficiently spaced to demonstrate their maximum ornamental value at their maximum size. The distance between plants for specimens should be at least one-half the height that the plants are expected to be when mature; plants should be at least 5 ft/1.5 m apart for a species 10 ft/3.1 m high when mature; similarly, for a species that is 50 ft/15.4 m high at maturity, the plants should be at least 25 ft/7.7 m apart. It is advisable to use clump bamboo for specimens, as running types are usually too invasive. Set the plants in individual holes 6–12 in./1.5–3.0 dm deep, then fill the hole with loose soil and firm it around the roots. Finally, water the soil until it is completely soaked.

Low hedges of semidwarf running bamboo may be started by planting rhizomes in a trench about 12 in./3 dm deep and of equal width. Dig around young plants to locate the rhizomes. Cut the rhizomes into sections about 12 in./3 dm long from the end of the rhizome, as planting stocks from older portions seldom sprout. Do not allow the rhizomes to dry out before replanting. Arrange the rhizomes in a more or less upright position about 12 in./3 dm apart along the sides of the trench. (This spacing is recommended for a 40 in./1 m hedge.) Fill the trench with loose soil, press it firmly around the rhizomes, and water the new plantings thoroughly. When young plants are used to start the hedge, they should be at least one year old. Plant them in a trench about 6 in./1.5 dm deep and 18 in./4.5 dm wide. The plants should be spaced about 12 in./3 dm apart for a 40 in./1 m hedge. Fill the trench with loose soil, firm the soil around the plants, and water thoroughly.

For clump bamboo hedges, the plants should be spaced according to the desired height of the hedge. For a 3 ft/9 dm hedge, space the plants about 12 in./3 dm apart; similarly, for a 10 ft/3.1 m hedge, the plants should be spaced about 2 ft/6 dm apart. Choose a bamboo with a potential height of 10–20 ft/3.1–6.2 m for low hedges (i.e., below 10 ft/3.1 m). For taller hedges, use a species that has a potential height somewhat greater than the desired height of the hedge. Hedges may be started either from rhizomes or from plants, usually the latter. Plants or rhizomes should be planted in a trench that is about 6 in./1.5 dm deep and 12 in./3 dm wide. Follow the same procedure in planting and watering as described for running bamboo hedges.

Bamboo is considered a low-maintenance plant. Cultural needs of bamboo grown outdoors include the use of water, fertilizers, and weeding. Bamboo is a heavy feeder requiring ample fertility and moisture. Plants in an active growth state require at least 1 in./25 mm of water at 10–day intervals. Soak the soil around the base of the culms thoroughly every 10 to 14 days from spring to late fall to ensure that the plants have sufficient moisture. The watering cycle should be altered or omitted following heavy or prolonged rains.

The vigor, size, and color of bamboo are usually improved by fertilization, although many species grow vigorously in the wild without fertilization. Plants in an active growth state should be fertilized in early spring and again in early or late summer. A general fertilizer recommendation includes a slow-release complete fertilizer in the ratio of 20-5-10 applied at the rate of 2.2 lb/1 kg per 100 sq ft/10 centare. Silica should be added at the rate of five parts per 100 lb/ 41.6 kg to ensure maximum growth. Leaves that are lost from indoor plantings should remain in the containers, as they recycle needed silica and enhance the attractiveness of the specimen plants. Fertilization improves the vigor, increases the size, and enhances the color of bamboo, although natural stands thrive without fertilization.

Any weeding that is necessary should be done by pulling the weeds and grass from around the plants. Do not use hand or cultivating tools around bamboo, as the shallow-growing rhizomes near the surface of the soil may be injured.

Additional cultural requirements of bamboo grown indoors or outdoors include occasional pruning and thinning. Bamboo responds very well to trimming. This is especially important when it is grown as ground cover, hedges, or specimens, either indoors or outdoors. Low-growing types as ground cover are maintained attractive and manageable in size by periodic mowing. Hedges and specimens are easily kept manageable in size and attractive in form by repeated trimming. Bamboo hedges should be trimmed once or twice a year, depending on their growth rate. Established stands of small bamboo should not be cut until they are three to four years old, whereas larger types should not be trimmed for several years. The purpose is to encourage the formation of new shoots each year. In hedge plantings, allow the plants to attain their maximum size, then cut them back to the desired height. Cut the culms just above a joint or node by making an oblique cut rather than a right-angle cut; this allows the water to drain from that portion of the internode just above the node, thus preventing possible decay of the culm. Bamboo responds to top pruning very well; however, severe pruning is not recommended.

Established stands of bamboo require thinning as old culms die. The appearance and attractiveness of established stands is enhanced by selectively removing old culms each year, preferably in the autumn. The entire culm should be removed to below ground level, as they harbor insects, including termites, and hinder the formation of new shoots. Bamboo grown outdoors goes into dormancy during the winter, although the plants usually remain alive; the duration of dormancy is variable among species and their cultivars and is partially dependent upon the region in which they are grown. Indoor plants usually exhibit no perceptible dormancy; if they do, it is of short duration.

Outdoor plantings of bamboos with variegated foliage should always be located in shaded sites to prevent blistering and discoloration of the leaves. Considerable variation exists among species in shade tolerance; some types thrive in intermittent shade, others in partial shade, and yet others in full sun. Shade tolerance should be considered in the selection of species and their location in the landscape.

Mulching the soil around bamboo plantings reduces weed competition, conserves moisture, adds organic matter to the soil, and eventually improves its tilth. Grass clippings, Spanish moss, or any other vegetative material that is readily available is suitable as mulch. Heavy layers of mulch are useful in reducing and preventing winter injury to bamboo. Such treatments are most useful for weak perennials and for hardy running bamboos grown in marginal areas of adaptation.

Certain protective measures are required to successfully maintain tender, weak perennials and hardy types grown in marginal areas of adaptation. Although root hardiness usually exceeds that of stem hardiness, some stands are injured or occasionally lost from extremely low winter temperatures. Mulching the plants heavily is usually sufficient to protect them from detrimental low temperatures. Small species used as potted specimens may be transferred indoors to coincide with seasonal changes.

Small, erect or decumbent, low-growing bamboos are attractive and useful as house and greenhouse plants. Cultural needs of bamboo grown indoors include soil, water, and fertilizer, along with adequate light. Indoor plantings thrive in a slightly acid soil (pH 6.0–7.0), sandy loam, or loamy, well-drained soils that are high in organic matter. It is necessary to keep the soil continually well drained to prevent the buildup of harmful salts. Bamboo should be watered frequently to keep the soil moist but not wet or soggy; water should never be allowed to stand in the bottom of plant containers. Potted plants should never be left outdoors over winter, as they will freeze and die. As for outdoor plantings, a slow-release, complete fertilizer is recommended, applied once or twice annually and supplemented with liquid fertilizer about every two months. The analysis and application rate are the same as those recommended for outdoor plantings.

There is a strong tendency to overfertilize potted plants. Potted plants should be fertilized only when they are in an active growth state, keeping in mind their size and that of the plant container. Bamboo thrives best indoors in a cool room that is well ventilated and lighted. The light requirements for bamboo are in line with those of other houseplants. Bamboo is tolerant of low light levels (i.e., about 100 footcandles), although it thrives best at higher levels (e.g., about 1,000 footcandles). Bamboo will remain healthy and attractive for sustained periods indoors, provided it is maintained properly. Variegated forms are usually more attractive and more popular than those with ordinary green foliage.

Bamboo is easily established and maintained; contrarily, its control and eradication are usually difficult and expensive. Clump bamboos are easier to control than running types, due to their growth habit. Running types, on the other hand, are more difficult to control, as new plants continually arise from wide-spreading, far-reaching rhizomes. Running bamboo is very invasive, becoming weedy and a nuisance in certain situations. Unless running bamboo is restricted, it will soon form a thick jungle that extends far beyond the original planting, thus becoming an undesirable weed.

One of the most common oversights in the use of bamboo in landscape improvement is the choice of species (i.e., clump or running types) and their location in the landscape. Quite often, too little attention is given to the potential spread and ultimate size of the plants, resulting in complete dissatisfaction later. The potential invasiveness and weediness of running bamboo, in particular, cannot be overemphasized in its use as an ornamental. One method of preventing the spread of running bamboos is to establish them in open 55-gallon steel drums that are completely embedded. Other means include curbs of sheet metal or concrete sunk into the ground at least 40 in./1 m deep. Sidewalks, roads, wide driveways, and buildings also restrict the spread of bamboo. If you grow bamboo without curbs, make certain to choose a planting site that ensures that you and your neighbors will be protected from unwanted bamboo in lawns, flower beds, hedges, and shrubbery plantings. The site should be away from buildings to avoid culms growing into overhanging eaves, shading windows, and creating other problems.

Running bamboo usually spreads into unwanted sites, unless sustained control measures are employed. Running types may be controlled by repeatedly cutting the young shoots or culms to ground level before they attain full size; this usually requires repeated cuttings for one or more growing seasons. Repeated mowing of small, soft shoots will usually destroy unwanted culms in turf areas. The spread of running bamboo may also be curtailed by digging out and destroying rhizomes and unwanted plants. Considerable labor and expense are usually involved in this type of control. Digging out unwanted plants permits their removal without disturbing surrounding plants. Large running bamboo with rhizomes deep in the soil is difficult to control by digging it out, as some of the rhizomes may escape removal; any rhizomes remaining in the soil will eventually form new plants. Small running bamboo is perhaps the most difficult to control, as it produces copious quantities of rhizomes near the surface of the soil. Its spread may be controlled by digging out and destroying unwanted plants and their rhizomes or by repeated mowing.

Clump bamboo grown in hedges, windbreaks, noise-abatement plantings, or specimen plantings sometimes spreads beyond its designated sites, requiring some form of control or containment. Its spread may be controlled by digging out and destroying unwanted plants, leaving the remaining plants undamaged.

An easier and perhaps less expensive method of control or eradication of bamboo involves the use of chemical herbicides. Nonselective contact herbicides and systemic herbicides are most useful in the control or eradication of bamboo. It is necessary to kill the underground rhizomes as well as the aboveground culms. Bamboo culms may be killed with nonselective contact herbicides such as glyphosate and paraquat, without leaving any residual toxicity in the soil. The underground rhizomes require the use of systemic herbicides such as glyphosate which is translocated throughout the plant, eventually killing it. Species which are difficult to kill may require more than a single application. Caution should be exercised in the use of herbicides; directions pertaining to the use of the herbicide should be followed carefully. Where herbicidal control or eradication measures are employed, the lack of toxic residues remaining in the soil permits the early and safe establishment of other plants. Regardless of the techniques used, it usually requires much labor and expense to control or eradicate bamboo. The prudent use of bamboo as an ornamental cannot be overemphasized, although this should not be construed as a detriment to its use.

SHADE TOLERANCE
AND WINTER HARDINESS

Most bamboo species thrive best in full sun, although some ornamental types are somewhat shade tolerant. Shade tolerance of individual species, where known, is included with the species descriptions that follow.

Considerable variation in winter hardiness exists among and within bamboo species. This attribute should be given serious consideration in the choice of species for certain plant-hardiness zones and locations within the zone. A knowledge of winter hardiness is useful in the selection of species adapted to specific plant-hardiness zones. The plant-hardiness zones are also included with the species descriptions and in Appendix 2. Although they are necessarily rather broad in scope and therefore cannot define every situation, they do provide a general guideline to adaptation. Hardy running bamboos are cultivated in plant-hardiness zones 5 through 8, which encompass a large portion of the contiguous United States. Bamboos are subject to injury and winterkill, despite their ability to perenniate in their zones of adaptation. When all the buds of a culm are killed by severe winter temperatures, its growth will cease, although it may remain alive for some time. Hardy running bamboo remains evergreen until the temperature falls to about 3–5°F/ − 16 to − 15°C. As the temperature drops, the initial symptoms are leaf scorching followed by complete loss of leaves, buds, and culms of some species. Severe low winter temperatures may kill the culms to ground level, although the rootstocks may remain alive. Thus the root tolerance of certain species exceeds that of their stem tolerance. For this reason, it is possible to maintain bamboo in marginal areas of adaptation, although the plants may be killed to ground level each winter. Bamboo does not produce any adventitious buds; thus, all new shoots (culms) arise from buds on the underground rhizomes (stems). Winter hardiness of many species of running bamboo is dependent upon the cold tolerance of the rhizomes and rootstocks. Clump-forming species of tropical origin will withstand little frost, if any; thus, their outdoor cultivation is restricted to the warmer parts of plant-hardiness zones 9 and 10 only.

USES

Ornamental

We use bamboo in multitudinous and multifarious ways, including as an ornamental. Bamboo, the largest member of the grass family, is probably used in more ways than any other grass species. About a thousand species of bamboo have been reported, and innumerable uses have been made of this invaluable, giant member of the grass family.

Bamboos serve as ornamentals through their use as ground cover, hedges, house and greenhouse plants, screens, shade, sound barriers, specimens, and windbreaks (see Appendix 2). Certain species of *Chimonobambusa*, *Pseudosasa*, and *Sasa* are also being used in bonsai culture. Bamboo adds a new and different dimension in architecture, color, size, and texture to indoor plantings, the garden, and the landscape. Despite its drawbacks, bamboo is interesting, attractive, and colorful throughout the year. It makes a significant contribution to the landscape when established in well-designed plantings in conjunction with other ornamentals. Bamboo should be neither overused nor neglected altogether in landscape improvement. The prudent use of bamboo can result in a well-balanced, improved, attractive garden or landscape. Fortunately, hardy types are adapted for outdoor plantings in most of the contiguous United States, and warm-season, weak perennials are useful in plant-hardiness zones 9 and 10. The maximum effectiveness of bamboo as an ornamental outdoors is achieved in compatible stands with other ornamentals, and indoors as potted specimens or in dried arrangements.

Considerable variation exists among bamboo species in growth habit, form, size, texture, and color of the plants and plant parts. Variation in growth habit and form includes running types such as *Arundinaria pygmaea*, which forms ground cover; large, erect, clump types, such as *Arundinaria simoni*, which forms a typical arching clump; and giant forms such as *Bambusa polymorpha*, which forms veritable forests. Variations in size and texture (i.e., culm diameter and leaf width) are exemplified by dwarf *Arundinaria disticha*, with slender culms and narrow leaves, and by giant common bamboo, *Bambusa vulgaris*, with wide leaves and thick culms. Bamboo is grown primarily for its colorful foliage, culms, and culm sheaths. Variations in color are most apparent in the foliage, culms, and culm sheaths. Species with outstanding foliage color include *Sasa palmata* (bright green), *Phyllostachys dulcis* (medium green), *Chimonobambusa quadrangularis* (dark brown), and variegated types such as *Arundinaria viridistriata*. One species, *Arundinaria graminea*, has leaves that are bright green above and dull green beneath. Those species with variegated foliage are usually more attractive and desirable than green-leaved forms.

As with foliage color, considerable variation in culm color exists among species and cultivars. Species of variable culm color include *Bambusa tulda* (green), *Phyllostachys meyeri* (dull green), *Arundinaria viridistriata* (purplish green), *Arundinaria graminea* (yellowish green), *Arundinaria pumila* (dull purple), *Phyllostachys aurea* (golden), *Bambusa arundinacea* (golden yellow), *Phyllostachys bambusoides* (yellow), *Arundinaria simoni* (yellowish brown), *Phyllostachys bambusoides* 'Castillon' (variegated, bright yellow with green grooves), and *Phyllostachys nigra* (black). Additional tones and hues of culm color are found among other species. The color patterns of variegated culms are another characteristic that adds to the attractiveness of bamboo. Unique among these are the bright yellow, green-grooved culms of *Phyllostachys bambusoides* 'Castillon,' the golden green-striped culms of *Bambusa vulgaris* var. *striata*, and the spotted or mottled culms of *Ochlandra stridula* var. *maculata*. The presence or absence of bloom, a whitish mealy or granular coating on the culm, affects its color. A dense farinose coating produces an overall grayish or whitish appearance, whereas in its absence the culms are their normal color.

Colorful culm sheaths add to the attractiveness of the culms, particularly young culms less than two years old. Culm sheaths are deciduous in some forms (such as *Chimonobambusa falcata*), tardily deciduous in others (such as *Semiarundinaria fastuosa*), and persistent in others (such as *Arundinaria pygmaea*). Young culms less than one year old are usually thickly covered with layers of sheaths that may or may not remain on the plants until the new leaves unfold. Some species with variably colored sheaths include *Arundinaria pygmaea* (dull green, becoming brown), *Arundinaria disticha* (purple-tinged), *Dendrocalamus strictus* (brownish or blackish), *Bambusa tulda* (brownish), *Arundinaria variegata* (stramineous), and *Sasa veitchii* (dull purple, becoming tan). Other species, such as *Phyllostachys meyeri*, have blotched sheaths, and yet others are spotted (e.g., *Phyllostachys viridis*), while some are more or less variegated (i.e., *Phyllostachys aureosulcata*). Differences in culm sheath coloration act as an aid in species identification among certain species in the absence of inflorescences.

Other culm characteristics of ornamental value, in addition to those of color, include orientation, shape, and whether the culms are simple or branched. Culms of most species are erect and straight, such as *Arundinaria amabilis*, in contrast to the suberect culms of *Phyllostachys viridis* and the bent and drooping culms of *Bambusa multiplex* 'Willowy.' Culms of *Phyllostachys nigra* are arched and noticeably different from those of *Phyllostachys pubescens*, which are broadly arched near the tip.

Most species have straight, smooth, cylindrical culms that are more or less round in cross-section (e.g., *Phyllostachys aureosulcata*), in contrast to the zigzag, flattened, grooved culms of *Shibataea kumasaca*, which are roughly trigonous or slightly oval in cross-section. The square culms of *Chimonobambusa quadrangularis* and the zigzag culms of *Phyllostachys pubescens* var. *heterocycla* are interesting oddities; the internodes of the latter strongly resemble cowering terrapins. Some bamboo fanciers have produced triangular culms by forcing them to elongate in an upright, triangular box.

Most bamboo species have branched culms (e.g., *Phyllostachys nigra*), although those of *Sasa bicolor* are either simple or branched; the first year culms of *Arundinaria nitida* are simple, with few branches occurring in subsequent years. Another interesting characteristic of culms, not readily apparent, is whether or not they are hollow or solid. Variation of this characteristic is demonstrated by the fistulose culms of *Phyllostachys nuda*, the narrowly fistulose culms of *Bambusa multiplex*, and the solid culms of *Bambusa multiplex* var. *rivierorum*. Although this characteristic is of no visible ornamental value, it may be of indirect value in preventing possible wind damage to weaker fistulose culms.

The use of bamboo as an ornamental is presented in the order shown in Appendix 2.

Dwarf, semidwarf, and intermediate forms are most useful as ornamentals (Appendix 2). Dwarf and semidwarf forms (1–15 ft / 0.3–4.6 m high) are used primarily as ground cover, low hedges, and screens, and as specimens both indoors and outdoors. The primary use of intermediate forms (15–35 ft / 4.6–10.8 m high) includes tall hedges and screens and large specimens. Large and giant forms (over 35 ft / 10.8 m high) are used as sound barriers and windbreaks and to provide shade; they usually have more economic value than ornamental value.

Dwarf, low-growing, spreading bamboo is most useful as ground cover (e.g., *Arundinaria* and *Sasa* species); fortunately, some species of these genera are adapted to full sun or shaded sites (Appendix 2). As they are running bamboos, they require careful planning in their placement in the landscape so as not to become weedy. Some semidwarf forms, such as *Sasa chrysantha* and *Shibataea kumasaca*, are used in the same manner, as they are easily maintained in proper form and size by repeated trimming. Both green-leaved and variegated forms are commonly used as ground cover; pygmy bamboo, *Arundinaria pygmaea*, and its cultivar Variegata, exemplify the use of bamboo as ground cover.

Hedges constitute a significant ornamental use of bamboo. Semidwarf forms are suitable for hedges 5–10 ft / 1.5–3.1 m high, and intermediate forms are suitable for tall hedges (over 10 ft / 3.1 m high). Clump bamboo is more desirable as a hedge than running bamboo, because the latter type spreads more rapidly. Running hedges may be appropriate in some situations, however. Because bamboo responds very readily to trimming, the size and shape of the hedge is easily maintained. Hedge bamboo, *Bambusa multiplex*, and its cultivar 'Fernleaf' are both admirably suited and widely used in hedge plantings. The cultivar 'Fernleaf,' with its dense foliage, is a particularly attractive, thick hedge. The fernleaf character of the foliage results from an increase in the number and reduction in size of leaves compared to those of the type form. The number of leaves doubles or triples on the branches and twigs, with the leaves crowded toward the end of the branches and twigs, producing a plant with thick foliage that is an ideal hedge. Additional variegated cultivars of *Bambusa multiplex*, such as 'Silverstripe Fernleaf' and 'Silverstem Fernleaf,' are widely used as hedges whenever a variegated hedge is desired.

Dwarf, semidwarf, and even giant forms of bamboo are commonly used indoors as house and greenhouse plants. Many bamboo species are much reduced in size when grown indoors. The reduced size of plants grown indoors may be attributed in part to the environment—that is, the lack of sunlight and the reduced root system of potted plants. The indoor environment, which usually results in reduced growth rate, is beneficial in maintaining the plants at a manageable size. Potted specimens grown indoors are easily maintained, as the roots are contained and the plants are kept in proper form and at a manageable size by periodic trimming. Giant *Bambusa ventricosa* best exemplifies a reduction in size when grown indoors; it attains a height of about 60 ft / 18.5 m outdoors but only one-twelfth that height when grown indoors. Green-leaved and variegated species are available in the trade as houseplants. Variegated forms appear to be more popular than green-leaved forms.

Bamboo screens and hedges are useful as partitions in dividing the garden into appropriate areas or sections. Thick bamboo screens are quite often used to obstruct the view into unsightly areas or to isolate buildings, tanks, or other objects from view. As with hedges, screens may be grown to almost any desired height. Any number of species is adaptable for use as screens. Bamboo screens are established and maintained in the same manner as hedges.

Large and giant bamboo species usually provide ample shade for the lawn and smaller ornamentals, whether grown as specimens in large clumps, or as hedges and screens. Clump types are recommended where bamboo is grown primarily for shade, as they are less invasive and easier to control. Bamboo plantings whose purpose is to provide shade should be properly located in the landscape to maximize their effectiveness as shade and to minimize their interference with other plantings. Large forms properly located usually provide sufficient shade without interfering with other ornamentals or upsetting the balance of the landscape. Larger giant forms provide shade over more extended areas than smaller forms. Those species most commonly used for shade are included in Appendix 2.

Sound barriers are a common sight in urban areas along main arteries and highways. These usually are composed of high fences made of wood, concrete, or other materials that, at best, are not ornamental. Thick rows of tall perennial bamboo, which is far more attractive, would serve the same purpose. Bamboo sound barriers are equally useful in other urban areas, such as airports, public parks, zoos, playgrounds, and amphitheaters. Bamboo, when properly situated in such locations, serves the dual purpose of screen and sound barrier, in addition to improving the landscape.

Specimen plantings constitute a major ornamental use of bamboo. There are many kinds of bamboo useful as specimens, whether grown indoors or outdoors. Clump bamboo is most commonly used in outdoor plantings, primarily because it is less competitive and invasive than running types. Running bamboo may be safely used as potted specimens, since its roots are contained. Species varying in form, color, and size are commonly used as specimen plants. Plants varying from dwarf to giant size are in common use as outdoor specimens, whereas similar use is made of dwarf to large-sized plants when grown indoors.

The proper kinds of specimen plants and their correct location in the garden and landscape maximize their effectiveness. Specimens located where they are conspicuous but in harmony with other ornamentals usually result in an attractive, well-balanced landscape. There are innumerable ways in which specimen plants may be used in outdoor plantings, perhaps limited only by the imagination of the gardener. Specimens used in the formal garden, the water garden, the so-called wild garden, or in areas contiguous to the garden consist of clump and running types, but more commonly the former. The stiff, upright, golden-yellow culms of *Phyllostachys aurea* provide a spectacular large specimen, as do the mature black culms of *Phyllostachys nigra*. Similarly outstanding as specimens are the characteristically distorted culms of Buddha's-belly bamboo, *Bambusa ventricosa*, with shortened internodes and enlarged nodes, and the dark green culms of square-stem bamboo, *Chimonobambusa quadrangularis*. The culms of most species, such as *Sasa palmata*, are smooth, in contrast to the usually deeply grooved culms of *Phyllostachys aurea*; both are ideal specimens. Variegated bamboos make excellent specimens in semishaded locations; these include *Arundinaria viridistriata* and the striped cultivars of hedge bamboo, *Bambusa multiplex*. Most bamboo specimens respond very well to periodic trimming, making it possible to maintain them in a desirable form and at a manageable size.

The use of specimens in the home or greenhouse is limited somewhat by the kinds of bamboo adapted for indoor use. Nevertheless, bamboos enjoy a unique and prestigious place as indoor specimens. Potted specimens are widely used on decks and patios, around swimming pools, along driveways and walks, and in other areas of the garden during the summer. Movable potted specimens are usually transferred indoors during the winter and outdoors in the summer to coincide with seasonal changes. Specimens handled in this manner may be appreciated and enjoyed throughout the year. Potted bamboo specimens will remain attractive for sustained periods when properly maintained. Three outstanding species that exemplify the use of bamboos as indoor specimens include a dwarf form, *Sasa veitchii*, with purplish green to dull purple culms and bright dark green foliage; a semidwarf form, *Arundinaria nitida*, with bluish gray to purplish culms and purplish green foliage; and an intermediate form, *Phyllostachys nigra*, with green culms becoming purplish to blackish at maturity and bright, light green to medium green foliage. Bamboo specimens are unique in the home, in the greenhouse, and in the garden.

Windbreaks are necessary and used in many areas to protect ornamental plantings and to make outdoor living space more attractive and enjoyable. Windbreaks of various heights may be comprised of bamboo, trees, or woody vines trained on a trellis or wall. Large or giant forms of clump bamboo (i.e., more than 35 ft/10.8 m high), make ideal windbreaks. Clump-forming bamboo is preferred unless a running windbreak is desired. Bamboo windbreaks are established in the same manner as hedges and screens. Windbreaks usually consist of a single row of plants located at an approximate right angle to the prevailing wind. Two or more rows of plants may be more effective in certain situations, however. The plants should be established in parallel rows about 10–30 ft/3.1–9.2 m apart where two or more rows are used. Windbreaks established in this manner provide maximum effectiveness, in addition to acting as a screen and providing shade. The thick stand of culms and foliage that almost reaches ground level is usually more effective than some other ornamentals used for the same purpose.

Commercial, Industrial, and Miscellaneous Uses

The utilitarian value of bamboo overshadows its ornamental value in many parts of the world, especially in tropical regions. Multifarious use is made of bamboo in tropical regions. Bamboo is the only cheap source of building materials in vast areas of the tropics and subtropics; giant forms provide a renewable source of building materials and of paper and paper products. Bamboo is an important food source in many parts of the world. The young shoots of many species are edible and widely used in Oriental cookery. The shoots of some species, such as *Phyllostachys aurea*, are very palatable and free from acridity, even in the raw state. The astringent shoots of other species usually require some sort of amelioration before they are palatable.

Bamboo plays an important role in watershed preservation and in erosion control. Bamboo prefers damp or wet soil in low-lying areas subject to irregular inundation. The plants are useful along with rushes, sedges, and other semiaquatic and aquatic plants. Bamboo, with its voluminous rhizomatous root system, makes an excellent erosion-control plant. Its perenniality and invasive growth habit are all in its favor in the prevention and reduction of erosion by water. Bamboo is especially useful for erosion control in ravines and gullies, on steep slopes along highways and streams, or in any site where erosion control is needed. The hardy running bamboos are usually more effective than the clump-forming types for this purpose.

Many bamboo species growing in the wild provide feed and protection for wildlife. Switchcane, *Arundinaria gigantea* ssp. *tecta,* for example, is browsed by both domestic livestock and wild animals; in addition, it serves as shelter for the latter, particularly deer. Other species found in the wild serve the same purpose as switchcane. It is difficult to assess the value of bamboo in economic terms in its use in watershed preservation, wildlife feed and protection, and erosion control. The use of bamboo in these ways should be widely expanded.

Innumerable products and useful objects are made from bamboo. Some of these include bean, punting, and ski poles; birdhouses; fishing canes and rods; furniture; garden stakes; lamps; musical instruments; mats and floor coverings; ornaments; pen and pencil holders; picture frames; walking canes; window shades; and umbrella handles. Bamboo is used to make many other useful products in addition to those few mentioned. The canes are used in many ways for decorative purposes. The inflorescences and foliage are used on occasion in dried floral arrangements. Bamboo, the largest member of the grass family, is highly prized as an ornamental and valuable for commercial, industrial, and miscellaneous purposes.

SELECTED SPECIES

The habitat, description, uses, and cultivation of the following selected species are arranged in alphabetical order by genera and by species within genera.

***Arundinaria* Michx. (Bamboo).** Name from Latin *arundo*, ''reed.'' Type species, *Arundinaria macrosperma* Raddi. There are more than 30 species, some native to North America, others occurring in East and South Asia. Hardy grasses of rhizomatous growth habit; quite variable in size; Culms erect to arching, fistulose, branched, sheathed; branches variable in size and number at each node; leaves petiolate or sessile; leaves on basal portion of culm sessile, rudimentary or reduced to mere sheaths, upper leaves larger, petiolate, leaf blades usually tessellate; sheaths loose, chartaceous, imbricate. Inflorescence paniculate or racemose; flowering branchlets with nearly or quite bladeless sheaths borne in fascicles on the main stem or primary branches; bladeless, flowering shoots also arise from the rhizomes, the flowering stems apparently die after setting seeds; spikelets 6-to-12-flowered, large, compressed; rachilla joints rather thick, appressed-hirsute; glumes unequal, shorter than the lemma, the lower sometimes lacking; lemma chartaceous, thin, 10-to-12-nerved, acute to awn-tipped; palea two-keeled; androecium three-merous (Young, 1945, 1946).

Latin name: *Arundinaria amabilis* McClure
Common names: Tonkin bamboo, Teastick bamboo, Lovely bamboo, Tonkin cane, Tsingli
Origin: China, Vietnam
Habitat: Cultivated
Hardiness: Zone 8
Description: A semihardy, large running bamboo. Culms stiffly erect, straight, fistulose, branched, 30–40 ft /9.2–12.3 m high, 2.0–2.5 in./5–6 cm in diameter at the base. Inflorescence a terminal, lax panicle, 5-to-12-flowered, spikelets 2–3 in./5–8 cm long, 5-to-14-flowered, distinctly flattened; borders of all glumes, lemmas, and paleas bearing a fringe of hairs of variable length.
Uses: Tonkin bamboo is good in very large gardens as a windbreak, screen, or sound barrier, or for providing shade; it is also an excellent erosion-control plant. In addition to its ornamental value, the canes are preferred for the finest split-bamboo fishing rods.
Cultivation: Propagation is by plant division. The plants may require containment.

Latin name: *Arundinaria argenteostriata* (Regel) Ohwi
Synonym: *Bambusa argenteostriata* Regel
Origin: Japan
Habitat: Cultivated
Hardiness: Zones 7 and 8
Description: A hardy, semidwarf, running bamboo. Culms erect, cylindrical, branched, fistulose, 2–3 ft /6–9 dm high, 0.4–0.6 in./10–15 mm in diameter at the base, nodes initially densely hairy, becoming glabrous; culm sheaths ciliate; branches usually borne singly, occasionally in pairs at each node, bearing 6 to 12 leaves near the tip of the culms and main branches. Foliage medium green or sometimes variegated, coarse in texture; leaves petiolate; leaf blades round to acute at base, acuminate at apex, 10–12 in./2.5–3.0 dm long, 1.0–1.6 in./2.5–

4.0 cm wide, smooth, usually medium green on both surfaces. Inflorescence paniculate; spikelets 2.4–3.0 in./6–8 cm long, five-to-eight-flowered.

Uses: Useful as a hedge or in clump plantings as specimens. This species is attractive as a potted specimen.

Cultivation: Propagation is by plant division. The plants may require containment.

Latin name: *Arundinaria disticha* Pfitz.
Synonym: *Bambusa disticha* Mitf.
Common name: Dwarf fernleaf bamboo
Origin: Japan
Habitat: Cultivated
Hardiness: Zones 7 and 8
Description: A hardy, dwarf, running bamboo. Culms erect, straight, slender, cylindrical, fistulose, branched, 20–30 in./5.0–7.6 dm high, 0.3–0.5 in./8–13 mm in diameter at the base, bright green, shaded purple; culm sheaths tessellate, the upper ones tinged with purple; branches normally single, sometimes in pairs at each node, bearing many leaves near the tips. Foliage bright medium green, fine in texture; leaves numerous, arranged in pairs in opposite rows, blades 4–6 in./1.0–1.5 dm long, 0.3–0.4 in./8–10 mm wide, four-to-six-nerved, narrowed into a short petiole, acuminate, setose, margins serrulate, bright green on both surfaces. Inflorescence of flowering branchlets with nearly or quite bladeless sheaths borne in fascicles on the main culm or primary branches; bladeless, flowering shoots also arise directly from the rhizomes; flowering stems usually die after setting seeds; spikelets compressed, 6-to-12-flowered, large; rachilla joints thick, hirsute, suppressed; glumes unequal, shorter than the lemmas, the lower occasionally lacking; lemma chartaceous, thin, 10-to-12-nerved, acute to awn-tipped; palea prominently two-keeled; androecium three-merous.

Uses: This dwarf bamboo is best suited for ground cover in sunny sites of the water garden, or perhaps it is better used as a plant indoors, where its gregarious growth is kept under control. It is an excellent houseplant that is grown for its bright green foliage.

Cultivation: Propagation is by plant division, either by separating young shoots, which appear in middle or late spring, from the mother plants, or by planting rhizome cuttings taken when the plants are dormant before the new shoots appear. Necessary retaining measures should be taken to prevent the plants from spreading into areas beyond their designated site.

Latin name: *Arundinaria falconeri* (Hook. f.) Benth. & Hook. f.
Origin: Nepal
Habitat: Cultivated
Hardiness: Zone 8

Description: A hardy, large, running bamboo with woody rhizomes. Culms erect, cylindrical, fistulose, branched, 30–40 ft/9.2–12.3 m high, 2–3 in./5–8 cm in diameter at the base, olive green, maturing to dull yellow; internodes 6–8 in./1.5–2.0 dm long. The culms, which form dense clumps, are erect in the center but outward arching around the periphery; sheaths glabrous, with elongate ligule, but not fringed. Foliage light to medium green, medium in texture; leaves very thin, blades 3–4 in./8–10 cm long, 0.4–0.5 in./10–13 mm wide, striate above, inconspicuously tessellate. Inflorescence a large, terminal, branched panicle, branches 10–15 in./2.5–3.8 dm long; spikelets in simple racemes with one bisexual and a sterile floret; spathes sheathed and long. The flowering cycle of this species is reportedly approximately 30 years.

Uses: This intermediate to large bamboo is useful only in large gardens, where it provides a good screen, windbreak, or sound barrier. The mature, dull yellow culms are attractive in specimen plantings.

Cultivation: Propagation is usually by plant division, although natural seeding does occur. The plants may require containment.

Latin name: *Arundinaria gigantea* (Walt.) Muhl.
Synonym: *Arundinaria macrosperma* Raddi
Common names: Canebrake bamboo, Southern cane, Southern cane bamboo
Origin: Southeastern United States
Habitat: Cultivated
Hardiness: Zones 6 and 7
Description: A semihardy, semidwarf to intermediate running bamboo with extensive creeping rhizomes, 0.2–0.4 in./5–10 mm thick. Culms erect, branched, smooth, cylindrical, fistulose, 7–23 ft/2.2–7.1 m high, 0.8–1.0 in./20–25 mm in diameter at the base; sterile branches numerous and repeatedly branching, flowering branchlets crowded toward the ends of branches borne in fascicles on the main culm or primary branches; lower culm sheaths about half as long as the internodes, tardily deciduous, the upper 6 to 10 sheaths striate, usually hirsute, canescent at base, 10 to 12 bristles at summit, 0.2–0.3 in./5–8 mm long, these borne from the margin of a rather firm auricle, this sometimes prominent but often wanting, a dense band of hairs across the collar; ligule firm, scarcely 1 mm long. Foliage medium green, coarse in texture; leaf blades of main culm and primary branches 6–11 in./1.5–2.8 dm long, 1.0–1.6 in./2.5–4.0 cm wide, round at the base, petiolate, petioles 1–2 mm long, strongly finely tessellate, acuminate, glabrous on upper surface, margins finely serrulate; sheaths round on the back, imbricate; ligule a row of short hairs; blades of ultimate branchlets much smaller, often crowded in flabellate clusters, usually nearly glabrous. Inflorescence a panicle with few, simple, unequal racemes with few to several spikelets borne on angled, slender pedicels, 0.1–1.0 in./3–25 mm long, hirsute to glabrous; spikelets 1.6–3.0 in./4–8 cm long, about 0.3 in./8 mm

wide, 8-to-12-flowered, loose; glumes distant, acuminate pubescent, the lower very small, sometimes lacking; lemmas keeled, broadly lanceolate, 0.6–0.8 in./ 15–20 mm long, appressed-hirsute to canescent, rarely glabrous except toward the base and margins, tessellate; rachilla segments densely hirsute; palea scabrous on the keels; androecium three-merous; caryopsis narrowly elliptic, terete, 0.4– 0.5 in./10–13 mm long. Flowering and fruiting occur at infrequent intervals; flowering continuously for about a year, the flowering culms turn yellow and die after seeds form.

Uses: Canebrake bamboo, which forms extensive, dense, impenetrable stands, makes a good, tall hedge or screen when planted in rows. It is useful in improving unsightly areas and in screening buildings and other unsightly objects. The plants furnish feed and protection for wildlife; in addition, canebrake bamboo serves as an excellent erosion-control plant. The culms and leaves of canebrake bamboo have been used to dye cloth.

Cultivation: Propagation is by plant division. The plants require containment where necessary. The size of the culms of this species varies widely, partly because of the amount of moisture it receives. The species epithet indicates a large size, although this may be somewhat misleading, especially when its size is compared with that of other larger species.

Latin name: *Arundinaria gigantea* ssp. *tecta* (Walt.) McClure
Synonym: *Arundinaria tecta* (Walt.) Muhl.
Common names: Switchcane, Small cane
Origin: Southeastern United States
Habitat: Cultivated
Hardiness: Zones 6 through 9
Description: A semihardy, semidwarf, running, evergreen bamboo. The rhizomes are extensive, branched, fistulose, with air canals extending through the nodes, which adapts the plants to waterlogged soils, where they form large colonies. Culms erect, branched, cylindrical, fistulose, 4–7 ft/1.2–2.2 m high, 0.3–0.5 in./8–13 mm in diameter at the base, green when young, remaining mostly green to maturity; internodes 2–4 in./5–10 cm long; primary branches ascending, the individual culm with its branches broadly lanceolate in outline; culm sheaths usually as long as the internodes, those near the middle of the culm longer than the internodes and persistent; auricle at summit of sheath rarely developed; ligule a ring of short, stiff bristles across the collar, 0.1–0.2 in./3–5 mm long. Foliage medium to dark green, coarse in texture; leaves petiolate, flat, with petioles articulate with the sheaths, drooping, leaf blades of main culm and primary branches 8–12 in./2–3 dm long, 0.8–1.2 in./2–3 cm wide, round at the base, strongly tessellate, acuminate, pubescent to glabrous, finely serrulate, blades of branchlets much smaller, nearly glabrous. Inflorescence few aggregate spikelets in terminal, fascicled racemes, 6–8 in./1.5–2.0 dm long, borne on flowering shoots with loose sheaths, arising from rhizomes; spikelets pedicellate, 1.2–2.0 in./3–5 cm long, compressed, hirsute to glabrous, relatively compact,

Arundinaria gigantea ssp. tecta. **Flowering and leafy shoot, × 1/2; floret and spikelet, × 2; summit of culm sheath, outer and inner face, × 2.** *Source: Manual of the Grasses of the United States.* USDA Misc. Pub. 200. 1951.

6-to-12-flowered; glumes obtuse to acuminate, often nearly glabrous, unequal, shorter than the lemmas, the lower sometimes wanting; lemmas glabrous or minutely canescent at the base, rarely very faintly tessellate toward the summit, scarcely keeled, 0.5–0.6 in./13–15 mm long, faintly many-nerved, usually medium to dark purple; palea about as long as the lemma, prominently two-keeled; the rachilla strigose; androecium three-merous; caryopsis terete, narrowly elliptic, 0.3–0.4 in./8–10 mm long. Flowering and fruiting occur from June through August. There are numerous geographical forms of this species.

Uses: The ornamental value of switchcane is its use as hedges and screens. It has a definite place in large water gardens where sufficient moisture is available. The economic value of switchcane is its use as feed for domestic livestock and wildlife (deer) and for protection of the latter. It is ideal for low, wet, unsightly areas, as the plants form dense colonies that aid in erosion control. The foliage remains green throughout the winter in warmer climates, thus aiding in the protection of wildlife, in addition to serving as a feed source.

Cultivation: Propagation is by plant division; stem and rhizome cuttings may be used as propagating stocks in addition to new shoots separated from existing plants. Switchcane performs equally well in full sun or open shade. The plants may require containment.

Latin name: *Arundinaria graminea* (Mitf.) Mak.
Common name: Taiminchiku (Japanese)
Origin: Japan
Habitat: Cultivated
Hardiness: Zone 8
Description: A hardy, semidwarf, running bamboo. Culms erect, branched, fistulose, 3–16 ft/0.9–4.9 m high, 0.5–1.0 in./13–25 mm in diameter at the base, green, maturing to yellowish green; branches in twos or threes at each node near the bottom of the culm, numerous at each node on upper portion; four to six leaves on each branchlet. Foliage bright green, fine in texture; leaves distinctly grasslike, 4–10 in./1.0–2.5 dm long, 0.2–0.4 in./5–10 mm wide, acuminate, bright green above, dull green beneath.

Uses: This species is an attractive, decorative bamboo, although it is extremely invasive. Unless sufficient space is available for its spread, it probably should not be used; instead, another species of similar size that is far less invasive should be used. It is attractive and decorative enough for use as a potted specimen both indoors and outdoors, where its invasiveness is contained.

Cultivation: Propagation is by plant division.

Latin name: *Arundinaria humilis* Mitf.
Synonym: *Sasa humilis* (Mitf.) E. Camus
Origin: Japan
Habitat: Cultivated
Hardiness: Zone 7

Description: A hardy, dwarf, running bamboo. Culms erect, branched, very slender, narrowly fistulose, 2–3 ft / 6–9 dm high, 0.3–0.5 in. / 8–13 mm in diameter at the base; sheaths purplish at first, becoming greenish; usually two or three branches at each node, each branch bearing several leaves near the tip. Foliage medium green, coarse in texture; leaf blades 4–6 in. / 1.0–1.5 dm long, 0.6–0.8 in. / 15–20 mm wide, 6-to-10-nerved, round at the base, acuminate at the apex, sparsely hairy; leaf sheaths with clusters of bristles at the apex.

Uses: This dwarf form produces an excellent ground cover and is useful as a greenhouse and houseplant.

Cultivation: Propagation is by plant division. The plants may require containment.

Latin name: *Arundinaria nitida* Mitf.
Synonym: *Sinarundinaria nitida* (Mitf.) Nakai
Origin: China
Habitat: Cultivated
Hardiness: Zones 5 and 6
Description: A hardy, semidwarf, running bamboo. Culms erect, cylindrical, fistulose, 10–15 ft / 3.1–4.6 m high, 0.5–0.8 in. / 13–20 mm in diameter at the base; first-season culms are branchless and whiplike, bluish gray and deep purple by the third season; culm coloring varies among clones but is mostly purplish; second-year culms usually produce two to four branches at each node, usually purplish; then numerous, twiggy branches form. Foliage medium to purplish green, medium in texture; leaves elongate, 2–4 in. / 5–10 cm long, 0.4–0.6 in. / 10–15 mm wide, margins with fine bristles near the tip.

Uses: This semidwarf bamboo is dainty, graceful, highly ornamental, very winter hardy, not invasive, and somewhat shade tolerant. This small, attractive, and decorative bamboo is unique in having purple culms. It is useful in small and middle-sized gardens and as a specimen indoors.

Cultivation: Propagation is by plant division. This species grows slowly, although the plants may require containment. This small, graceful species thrives in partial or light shade and in full sun.

Latin name: *Arundinaria pumila* Mitf.
Synonym: *Sasa pumila* (Mitf.) E. Camus
Common name: Dwarf bamboo
Origin: Japan
Habitat: Cultivated
Hardiness: Zone 8
Description: A semihardy, dwarf, running bamboo. Culms semierect, branched, cylindrical, fistulose, 18–24 in. / 4.5–6.0 dm high, 0.3–0.8 in. / 8–20 mm in diameter at the base, dull purple, bearing a thick, white bloom under each node; branching freely, usually singly or rarely in pairs from the upper nodes of the culm, each branch bearing four to seven leaves; sheaths tessellate,

the upper ones tinged purple. Foliage bright green, coarse in texture; leaves petiolate, leaf blades 5–6 in./1.3–1.5 dm long, 0.6–0.8 in./15–20 mm wide, 8-to-10-nerved, margins serrulate, slightly hairy on both surfaces, abruptly acuminate or pinched toward the tip, round at the base, bright green above, dull silvery white below, tending to wither on the tips, margins, and midrib.

Uses: Dwarf bamboo makes a good ground cover in open or lightly shaded areas. The small plants are easily grown as potted specimens where their invasiveness is not a problem.

Cultivation: Propagation is by plant division. Dwarf bamboo is highly invasive, and particular consideration should be given to its location in the garden in addition to its use. Necessary retaining measures must be taken to prevent its rampant spread once it is established. It is not advisable to establish dwarf bamboo near the lawn or anywhere in the formal garden.

Latin name: *Arundinaria pygmaea* (Miq.) Asch. & Graebn.
Synonym: *Bambusa pygmaea* Miq.
Cultivars: 'Variegata'
Common names: Pygmy bamboo, Keroshimachiku (Japanese)
Origin: Japan
Habitat: Cultivated
Hardiness: Zone 8
Description: A hardy, dwarf, running bamboo. Culms erect, branched, flattened at top, 1–3 ft/3–6 dm high, 0.2–0.4 in./5–10 mm in diameter at the base, very slightly fistulose and seemingly solid, bright green, becoming purplish at the top, very slender, internodes zigzag, 0.8–1.0 in./20–25 mm long, nodes prominent, large for the size of the culms, purple with a protective band of waxy bloom and minute bristles around the base; branches usually solitary, occasionally produced in pairs at each node, long in comparison to the length of the culms; sheaths very persistent, dull green, becoming brown, pubescent, round on the back, longer than the internodes. Foliage bright green, coarse in texture; leaves petiolate, leaf blades tessellate, acuminate, 3–5 in./0.8–1.3 dm long, 0.7–0.8 in./18–20 mm wide, round at the base, terminating in a short, sharp point, upper surface covered with coarse hairs, lower surface with finer hairs, brilliant green above, dull silvery green below, tending to wither on the margins and midrib and at the tips. Inflorescence fascicled flowers borne on branchlets with nearly or quite bladeless sheaths on the main stem or primary branches; spikelets large, compressed, 6-to-12-flowered; rachilla joints rather thick, appressed-hirsute; glumes unequal, shorter than the lemma, the lower sometimes lacking; lemma thin, chartaceous, 10-to-12-nerved, acute to awn-tipped; palea prominently two-keeled; androecium three-merous.

Uses: Pygmy bamboo makes an excellent ground cover; it is equally at home as a houseplant. The strong invasiveness of pygmy bamboo renders it undesirable for the small garden unless it is confined. It is an excellent plant for erosion control, especially on steep slopes and along streams.

Cultivation: The plants rarely flower; if so, they do so at very irregular and infrequent intervals. Propagation is usually by plant division, either by separating young shoots that occur each spring from existing plants, or by planting cuttings or rhizomes taken when the plants are dormant before new shoots appear. When grown as ground cover, the plants may be left unattended or be mowed periodically. Mowing drastically changes the shape of the plants, as they respond by becoming rather prostrate, forming a perfect ground cover. The plants may require containment.

Cultivars: *Arundinaria pygmaea* (Miq.) Asch. & Graebn. 'Variegata'   The variegated foliage of this dwarf variant makes it a most desirable house plant. The leaves have longitudinal stripes of cream, white, and green. Like the species, it makes an ideal ground cover in open shade, as opposed to the parent species, which thrives best in full sun. The plants and all their parts are similar in size to the type form.

Latin name: *Arundinaria simoni* (Carr.,) A. & C. Riv.
Varieties: *Arundinaria simoni* var. *variegata* Hook. f.
Common names: Simon bamboo, Medake (Japanese)
Origin: Japan
Habitat: Cultivated
Hardiness: Zone 7
Description: A hardy, intermediate, running bamboo. Culms erect, outer ones arching outward, branched, cylindrical, fistulose, initially dark olive green, edged with purple and with white bloom, maturing to yellowish brown, 20–25 ft/6.2–7.7 m high, 1.0–1.3 in./2.5–3.3 cm in diameter at the base; branches increase from one at each node on first-year culms to two in the second year, then 8 to 15 the third year; sheaths 6–10 in./1.5–2.5 dm long, purplish when young, rather persistent. Foliage medium bright green, coarse in texture; leaf blades 4–12 in./1–3 dm long, 0.3–1.3 in./0.8–3.3 cm wide, 8-to-14-nerved, attenuate, broadly cuneate at the base, bright green above, glaucescent beneath on one side of the midrib, margins variably edged with fine bristles.

Uses: Simon bamboo is useful as a tall hedge, screen, or specimen in very large gardens. Simon bamboo resembles arrow bamboo, although it is larger, more decorative, and more elegant than the latter. There is a niche somewhere in large gardens for both simon bamboo and its variegated variety.

Cultivation: Propagation is by plant division. The plants may require containment.

Varieties: *Arundinaria simoni* var. *variegata* Hook. f.   This variety is 10–20 ft/3.1–6.2 m high and slightly more cold tolerant than the species; it is hardy in protected sites in the warmest parts of zone 6. This semidwarf to intermediate variety has leaves with longitudinal stripes of green and white and uniformly green leaves on the same plant; the variegated leaves are usually a little narrower than the green leaves. This variable variety is attractive as a hedge or as a specimen plant. The plants may require containment.

Latin name: *Arundinaria variegata* (Sieb. ex Miq.) Mak.
Synonym: *Arundinaria fortunei* (Van Houtte ex Munro) A. & C. Riv.
Common name: Dwarf white-stripe bamboo
Origin: Japan
Habitat: Cultivated
Hardiness: Zones 6 and 7
Description: A hardy, dwarf, running bamboo. Culms erect, very slender, branched, cylindrical, 2–3 ft/6–9 dm high, 0.20–0.25 in./5–6 mm in diameter at the base, nodes not prominent, internodes 1.0–1.3 in./2.5–3.3 cm long; branches arise somewhat irregularly from one or two nodes of the culm the first year, and others come later, usually singly, occasionally in pairs at each node; sheaths thick, stramineous, persistent. Foliage variegated, with longitudinal white and green stripes, coarse in texture; leaves borne near the culm tip and the tips of the branches, usually 5 to 10, leaf blades 2–6 in./0.5–1.5 dm long, 0.8–1.0 in./20–25 mm wide, bluntly round at the base, tapering to an attenuate, somewhat folded, tip, hirsute, one margin with thick bristles, the other less bristly. The variegation of the foliage is somewhat persistent, although occasionally some leaves on the same plant are either entirely white or dominantly green.
Uses: This dwarf bamboo is useful both as a potted house plant and in the garden as ground cover.
Cultivation: Propagation is by plant division. Special attention should be given to its use in the garden because of its invasive growth habit. The plants may require containment.

Latin name: *Arundinaria viridistriata* (Regel) Mak.
Synonym: *Bambusa viridistriata* Regel
Common name: Kamurozasa bamboo (Japanese)
Origin: Japan
Habitat: Cultivated
Hardiness: Zone 7
Description: A hardy, dwarf, running bamboo. Culms erect, slender, fistulose, dark purplish green, 18–30 in./4.5–7.6 dm high, 0.4–0.8 in./10–20 mm in diameter at the base; long ascending branches arise singly or in pairs at each node from near the base of the culm; sheaths persistent, hairy at the base, less so near the tip. Foliage coarse in texture, variegated, the leaves are longitudinally striped green and yellow in spring and early summer; later the striping disappears and the leaves become entirely green; leaves on basal portion of the culm and primary branches 6 to 10, sessile; leaf blades narrow, rudimentary, 0.5–0.8 in./13–20 mm long; sheaths loose, chartaceous; upper leaves petiolate, 2–5 in./0.5–1.3 dm long, 0.5–1.0 in./13–25 mm wide, mostly clustered near the apex, acuminate, abruptly attenuate, 10-to-12-nerved, round at the base, margins serrulate initially, sparingly pubescent or glabrous above, softly pubescent beneath, upper surface striped with golden longitudinal stripes, lower surface is a pale imitation of the upper surface; sheaths imbricate, round on the back, minutely

and irregularly ciliate, sparsely fimbriate or naked at the apex. The plants are killed to ground level in zone 7, although they are root hardy.

Uses: This variegated bamboo adds beauty to the home and garden. It is grown for its attractive, variegated, bright yellowish foliage, which is velvety in appearance when new, and the variegated tones meld together well, especially from a distance. It should not be used in rock garden plantings under any circumstances, as it is highly invasive. It is ideal in pots indoors or in planters located on patios or decks or around swimming pools. This variegated bamboo makes an attractive, unusual ground cover in mild climates.

Cultivation: Propagation is usually by plant division. Like almost all variegated grasses the plants require light or partial shade when grown outdoors.

Bambusa **Schreb. (Bamboo).** Type species, *Bambusa arundinacea* Retz. There are over 100 species, native to tropical and subtropical Africa and Asia, with some in Mexico and Central and South America. Tall, stout, perennial grasses. Stems erect or climbing, sometimes spiny, woody; leaves short-petiolate, the blades articulate with the sheath. Inflorescence a terminal, branched panicle, spikes combined in glomerules on the branches of the panicles; spikelets two-to-many-flowered, bisexual or unisexual, three or four lower glumes empty, gynoecium six-merous, rachilla jointed below the florets; fruit a caryopsis (McClure, 1946; Young, 1945, 1946).

> **Latin name:** *Bambusa arundinacea* (Retz.) Willd.
> **Synonym:** *Bambusa spinosa* Nees
> **Common name:** Giant thorny bamboo
> **Origin:** India
> **Habitat:** Along wooded borders and streams
> **Hardiness:** Zone 10
> **Description:** A warm-season, giant, evergreen, clump, thorny bamboo; the plants form dense colonies. Culms erect, branched, cylindrical, fistulose with thick walls, 80–100 ft/24.6–30.8 m high, 5–6 in./1.3–1.5 dm in diameter at the base, glossy green and zigzag when young, becoming straight and golden yellow at maturity; branches ascending, graceful, bearing spines on lower branchlets, the primary branch at each of several lower nodes is elongated, with the secondary pair at the base of the primary branch modified into sharp thorns; the branchlets at the nodes of the primary branches are modified into similar thorns, the branches and branchlets occurring higher on the culm are decreasingly changed to thorns or spines until finally only normal, leafy ones are found; sheaths deciduous, densely covered with appressed hairs, blackish on the inside of the sheath blade, the blade is short and very broad on lower sheaths and articulate with them. Foliage medium green, medium in texture; leaves short-petiolate, five or six per branch, leaf blades linear-lanceolate, acuminate, 3–8 in./0.8–2.0 dm long, 0.4–0.6 in./10–15 mm wide, nearly glabrous. Inflorescence a

large, terminal panicle. Flowering and fruiting occur sporadically, usually only after several years' growth; the plants die following fruiting.

Uses: Giant thorny bamboo develops rapidly from small, vegetative propagations. Its giant size makes it suitable as a source of wood and paper pulp, and the young shoots, which appear in the autumn, are edible. From an ornamental viewpoint, it serves as an ideal tall windbreak or screen in addition to providing erosion control in many areas. The plants provide a good sound barrier when planted in rows. Its giant size limits its usefulness to only very large, expansive areas. Giant thorny bamboo is the largest clump-forming bamboo grown in the United States.

Cultivation: Propagation is usually by plant division, by stem cuttings, or by stem layering, all of which should be done in the spring. Giant thorny bamboo is widely distributed in subtropical United States in the warmer parts of zone 10. Mature plants have been killed at temperatures below 27°F/−3°C.

Latin name: *Bambusa beecheyana* Munro
Synonym: *Sinocalamus beecheyana* (Munro) McClure
Common name: Beechey bamboo
Origin: China
Habitat: Cultivated
Hardiness: Zones 9 and 10
Description: A warm-season, large, clump bamboo. Culms erect, bright green, fistulose, cylindrical, or more often elliptic in cross-section, forming a somewhat open clump, 30–40 ft /9.2–12.3 m high, 3–4 in./8–10 cm in diameter at the base; sheaths glabrous except for fine pubescence at the base, drying to a grayish brown, with the veins becoming prominent and producing a striate appearance, the sheath narrows toward the apex, which is truncate and surrounded by a small trigonous, entire blade, a little narrower at the base than the apex; the ligule of the lowest sheaths is 0.10–0.25 in./3–6 mm long, the margins erose. Foliage medium green, coarse in texture; leaves occur 6 to 10 on a branch or twig, leaf blades lanceolate, acuminate, subsessile, slightly cordate, 3–5 in./0.8–1.3 dm long, 0.8–1.0 in./20–25 mm wide, 12–nerved, smooth, not tessellate. Inflorescence a terminal panicle, not rigid; spikelets in glomerules, hidden by the bracts, ovate to oblong, 7-to-11-flowered; lemma 18-to-20-nerved, mucronate; palea long-fimbriate. The plants seldom flower; if they do, it is usually only after a few to several years of growth.

Uses: Beechey bamboo, like other large bamboos, is suitable for tall screens and windbreaks; in addition, it serves as a good sound barrier. The mature dry canes have many miscellaneous uses. The young shoots are highly prized as food.

Cultivation: Propagation is usually by plant division. Beechey bamboo is cultivated in zones 9 and 10, where it survives temperatures down to 20°F/−7°C, with comparatively little injury.

Latin name: *Bambusa longispiculata* Gamble ex Brandis
Origin: Burma

Habitat: Cultivated

Hardiness: Zones 9 and 10

Description: A warm-season, evergreen, intermediate to large, clump bamboo. Culms clustered, erect, fistulose, 30–40 ft/9.2–12.3 m high, 2–3 in./ 5–8 cm in diameter at the base, shiny green when young, becoming dull green at maturity; sheaths slightly wavy or crinkled, auricles are more or less equal. Foliage medium to dark green, coarse in texture; leaves petiolate, flat, 4–10 in./ 1.0–2.5 dm long, 1–2 in./2.5–5.0 cm wide, 24-to-30-nerved. Inflorescence an erect, terminal, branched panicle, 10–15 in./2.5–3.8 dm long; spikelets 6-to-12-flowered; glumes 0.8–1.0 in./20–25 mm long.

Uses: This species is useful primarily as a screen, sound barrier, or windbreak. Like other *Bambusa* species, it is somewhat shade tolerant and is useful in arresting soil erosion.

Cultivation: Propagation is usually by plant division. This warm-season species is adapted to zone 10; its critical temperature is about 27°F/ −3°C.

Latin name: *Bambusa multiplex* (Lour.) Rausch.

Synonym: *Bambusa nana* Roxb.

Cultivars and varieties: *Bambusa multiplex* (Lour.) Rausch. 'Alphonse Karr' Young, Alphonse Karr bamboo, Suschiku (Japanese); *Bambusa multiplex* (Lour.) Rausch. 'Fernleaf ' Young, Fern-leaf hedge, Ho-o-chiku (Japanese); *Bambusa multiplex* (Lour.) Rausch. 'Silverstripe Fernleaf,' Silver-stripe fern-leaf hedge, Furi-ho-o-chiku (Japanese); *Bambusa multiplex* (Lour.) Rausch. 'Silverstripe' Young, Silver-stripe hedge, Hoshochiku (Japanese); *Bambusa multiplex* (Lour.) Rausch. 'Silverstem Fernleaf ' Young, Stripestem fern-leaf bamboo, Beni-ho-o-chiku (Japanese); *Bambusa multiplex* (Lour.) Rausch. 'Willowy' Young; *Bambusa multiplex* var. *riviereorum* Marie, Chinese-goddess bamboo, Koon yam chuk (Chinese)

Common names: Hedge bamboo, Oriental hedge

Origin: China

Habitat: Cultivated

Hardiness: Zones 9 and 10

Description: A warm-season, semidwarf to large, clump bamboo. Various forms of hedge bamboo range in height from 8 to 10 ft/2.5–3.1 m to over 40 ft/12.3 m. Culms of the typical form are erect, cylindrical, branched, green throughout, glabrous, narrowly fistulose, 30–40 ft/9.2–12.3 m high, 1.0–1.6 in./2.5–4.0 cm in diameter at the base, shrubby; branches range in number from several at the lowest branching nodes to 30 or more at some of the higher nodes; there is a primary branch of considerable length at each node, along with a pair of unequal smaller branches, one on each side, arising from two of the extremely crowded basal nodes of the primary branch; a number of small to diminutive branches and twigs develop successively within a year, along with the growth of these three branches, producing a bushy effect; this growth habit is common to all forms of the species, the primary branch and sometimes the two succeeding ones also give rise to branchlets at some distance from the base; sheaths green, devoid of any special color; auricles at the base of the rather long sheath blade are usually either poorly developed or absent, the sheaths of the type and all its forms are tardily deciduous. Foliage is vivid green, fine in texture; leaves sessile, leaf blades linear-lanceolate, 2–5 in./0.5–1.3 dm long, 0.2–0.3 in./5–8 mm wide, vivid green above and strikingly bluish glaucous or silvery beneath. Inflorescence a terminal panicle with few spikelets; spikelets three-to-five-flowered. Flowering and fruiting occur only after a few to several years of growth. Temperature and moisture conditions influence the appearance of new shoots; new shoots usually appear during May through July in the various latitudes in which the species is grown in the contiguous United States. Local weather conditions also influence the time of sprouting. Late-sprouting culms usually do not extend their branches until the following spring but remain bare during the ensuing winter.

Uses: The young shoots are not generally considered to be edible, although the very young ones, before they emerge from the ground, are reportedly eaten in the Dutch East Indies. Hedge bamboo and its variants are valuable chiefly for ornamental plantings. The smaller forms respond very well to pruning and make excellent hedges and screens. The type form is useful as tall screens, hedges, windbreaks, and sound barriers. The smaller variants are commonly grown both indoors and outdoors as specimens or hedges.

Cultivation: Propagation is usually by plant division. Hedge bamboo and its variants are the most common clump-forming bamboos grown in the South Atlantic, in the Gulf region, and in the middle parts of California. The species as a whole is probably the hardiest of all clump-forming bamboos. The foliage of the type and all its variants withstand temperatures down to about 16°F/ −9°C with little injury. It is a highly variable species in both botanical and horticultural characteristics, there being several cultivars of ornamental value in the trade.

Cultivars and varieties: *Bambusa multiplex* (Lour.) Rausch. 'Alphonse Karr' Young, Alphonse Karr bamboo, Suschiku (Japanese)   This large, warm-season cultivar is occasionally referred to as golden-striped bamboo hedge. The plants and all their parts are about the size of the type form. This cultivar differs from the type mainly in culm and foliage color. The culms are initially bright golden yellow, with conspicuous longitudinal green stripes of different widths irregularly spaced on the internodes; new culm sheaths are yellowish with green stripes; they dry to pale brownish or beige, with the stripes becoming stramineous. This colorful cultivar makes an ideal specimen.

Bambusa multiplex (Lour.) Rausch. 'Fernleaf' Young, Fernleaf hedge, Ho-o-chiku (Japanese) (Synonym, *Bambusa nana* var. *disticha* Hort.) The conspicuous characteristic of this intermediate cultivar is its fernlike foliage; the plants are usually smaller than those of the type (i.e., 10–20 ft/3.1–6.2 m high) when left untrimmed. The fernleaf character of the foliage results from the increase in the number and reduction in size of leaves from normal numbers and size of the type form. The number of leaves doubles or trebles on the branches and twigs, and the size of the individual leaf may be reduced with the leaves crowded toward the end of the branch or twig, producing a conspicuous, two-ranked or distichous effect. The culm sheaths dry to a dull straw color. This cultivar is unstable in that it frequently reverts to the type in respect to stature and character of the foliage. Reversion occurs more frequently when the soil fertility is increased or when small plants are established in richer soil than that in which they previously were growing. Although this cultivar is native to China, it is cultivated as an ornamental in Japan under the name Ho-o-chicku, meaning "phoenix" bamboo. This cultivar makes an ideal specimen, hedge, or screen.

Bambusa multiplex (Lour.) Rausch. 'Silverstripe Fernleaf' Young, Silverstripe fern-leaf hedge, Furi-ho-o-chiku (Japanese) (Synonym, *Bambusa argentostriata* Hort.) The cultivar Silverstripe Fernleaf apparently arose from the cultivar Silverstripe, as fern-leaved branches have been observed on the cultivar Silverstripe. This cultivar is similar in size to the cultivar Fernleaf but differs from it in color, with its white-striped leaves, which make it ideal as a specimen.

Bambusa multiplex (Lour.) Rausch. 'Silverstripe' Young, Silver-stripe hedge, Hoshochiku (Japanese) (Synonym, *Bambusa argentostriata* Hort.) This large cultivar is 30–40 ft/9.2–12.3 m high and slightly more vigorous than the type. It reacts to different environments by changes in growth habit. It is a low, spreading plant when grown in full sun in sandy soil, in contrast to an erect, much larger plant when grown on rich, heavy, clay soil. Silver-stripe hedge provides good ground cover in full sun in sandy soils. Larger forms on heavy clay soils produce excellent specimens. The cultivar differs from the type in the yellowish to white longitudinal striping on the lower, fernlike leaves on most of the branches and twigs and the thread stripes of the same yellowish color on other culms. Considerable variation is found in striping; some forms have striping that is much more conspicuous than other forms. The culm sheaths, green initially and with numerous yellowish stripes, dry to a dull straw color with the stripes becoming brownish.

Bambusa multiplex (Lour.) Rausch. 'Silverstem Fernleaf' Young, Stripestem fern-leaf bamboo, Beni-ho-o-chiku (Japanese) The vernacular name of this semidwarf cultivar indicates that it has striped fernleaf foliage and striped culms. Culms are 8–10 ft/2.5–3.1 m high; the basal portion of the slender culms is yellow and the green stripes are irregular in number and in width on the internodes. The culm sheaths dry to a dull stramineous color. This cultivar resembles the entire green cultivar Fernleaf except in the color markings of the culms and in its more dwarf stature. The culms and branches tend to be erect. The masses of small leaves form a perfect screen when grown as a hedge or screen. It responds to trimming very well. This cultivar, like that of 'Fernleaf,' also develops culms that bear larger, normal leaves of the type form. The fernlike character of the foliage and the dwarfness of the plants are probably best retained when the plants are grown in soil of low fertility. This variegated cultivar makes an attractive specimen indoors.

Bambusa multiplex (Lour.) Rausch. 'Willowy' Young The mature culms of this intermediate cultivar tend strongly to bend or droop, thus the cultivar name. The culms are 10–20 ft/3.1–6.2 m high, 0.5–0.8 in./13–20 mm thick at the base, very slender, bending or drooping when mature, the culms of young clumps up to 10 ft/3.1 m high remain erect, and the drooping tendency is not apparent even though the stems are slender; the lowest internodes are solid and the higher ones thick-walled. The culm sheaths dry to a dull stramineous color. The entire plant is green; foliage is bright green, fine to coarse in texture; leaves slender, 1–4 in./2.5–10.0 cm long, 0.2–0.3 in./5–8 mm wide, bright green above, silvery glaucous below. This cultivar is used primarily as a specimen.

Bambusa multiplex (Lour.) Rausch. var. *rivierorum* Marie, Chinese-goddess bamboo, Koon yam chuk (Chinese)   This bamboo was introduced directly from China by the U.S. Department of Agriculture and originally assigned Plant Introduction No. 77014 in 1927; subsequently it has achieved variety status under the name Chinese-goddess bamboo. It is a semidwarf, warm-season plant. Culms 10–12 ft/1–3.7 m high with solid internodes and slender branches. Foliage is fernlike, green; leaves thickly clustered on the branches and twigs, usually 12 to 24 on each twig; leaf blades slender 0.6–2.0 in./1.5–5.0 cm long. The culm sheath characters and foliage strongly resemble the fernleaf cultivars. The solid culms, fernlike foliage, and slight advantage in hardiness differentiate Chinese-goddess bamboo from the type form. The fernlike foliage is stable, in contrast to that of the type form. It also is consistently somewhat drooping and more graceful in all growth stages than the type form. Chinese-goddess bamboo merits attention in zones 9 and 10, where temperatures rarely fall below about 15°F/−9°C. It is ideal as a potted specimen in colder climates, where it requires fully lighted locations when grown indoors; some direct sunlight is necessary for indoor plantings. Chinese-goddess bamboo makes an attractive hedge in zones 9 and 10.

Latin name: *Bambusa oldhamii* Munro
Synonym: *Sinocalamus oldhamii* (Munro) McClure
Common names: Oldham bamboo, Giant timber bamboo
Origin: China
Habitat: Cultivated
Hardiness: Zones 9 and 10
Description: A warm-season, giant, clump bamboo, forming moderately open colonies. Culms almost herbaceous, very fistulose, erect, light green, unarmed, with numerous branches, 50–60 ft/15.4–18.5 m high, 3–4 in./8–10 cm in diameter at the base; sheaths are initially covered with short-appressed brown hairs that fall off as the sheath matures and dries; it dries to a somewhat dull stramineous color, and the veins do not become prominent; the sheaths are eventually glabrous, rather wide at the apex, with the base of the blade greatly extended, equaling the apex of the sheath in width, blades lanceolate, very acute, 10-to-12-nerved, not tessellate, rudimentary auricles sometimes present. Inflores-

cence a terminal panicle; spikelets ovate-lanceolate, 6-to-12-flowered, palea hyaline, fimbriate, membranous.

Uses: This oriental, handsome bamboo is one of six species that commonly attain giant proportions, along with *Bambusa arundinacea*, *Bambusa polymorpha*, *Bambusa tulda*, *Bambusa ventricosa*, and *Bambusa vulgaris*. It provides excellent windbreaks, sound barriers, and shades, and aids in erosion control. It is worthy of establishing stands around ponds and lakes, where ample space is available.

Cultivation: Propagation is by plant division.

Latin name: *Bambusa polymorpha* Munro
Origin: Burma
Habitat: Wet sites along streams
Hardiness: Zone 10
Description: A warm-season, giant, clump, woody, evergreen bamboo. The plants usually form huge, dense clumps. Culms erect, cylindrical, green, 60–90 ft/18.5–27.7 m high, 4–5 in./1.0–1.3 dm in diameter at the base, fistulose, with bluish waxy bloom, branched but the lower portion free of branches in mature clumps, the branches and twigs are long and slender; sheaths with very prominent auricles profusely margined with long, stiff bristles; the sheaths are exceedingly stiff and densely covered with fine appressed hairs, which when rubbed off give a silvery gray appearance when dry. Foliage is green, fine to medium in texture; leaf blades slender, 2–8 in./0.5–2.0 dm long, 0.3–0.5 in./8–13 mm wide.

Uses: This giant species is used primarily as a screen, windbreak, or sound barrier; the plants provide good shade. The large canes are made into useful utensils and furniture.

Cultivation: Propagation is by plant division.

Latin name: *Bambusa textilis* McClure
Origin: China
Common name: Wong chuk (Chinese)
Habitat: Cultivated
Hardiness: Zones 9 and 10
Description: A warm-season, large, clump, evergreen bamboo; the plants form large, compact clumps. Culms straight, branched, cylindrical, fistulose, erect but the tips arcuate or slightly pendulous, 40–50 ft/12.3–15.4 m high, 2.0–2.5 in./5.0–6.3 cm in diameter at the base, nodes not prominent, internodes elongate, slightly farinose; the 6 to 10 branches at each node differ very little in size; sheaths stiff and somewhat brittle, glabrous, drying to a brownish tan, the apex of the sheath proper is wide and forms a nearly symmetrical arch from both edges, the arch extending a little lower on one edge; the ligule is small, the blade very broadly lanceolate, nearly as wide as the apex of the sheath and somewhat broadly subcordate at the base; the base is extended on each side as

two small, unequal, delicately fringed auricles. Foliage bright green; leaves on primary branches 6–8 in./1.5–2.0 dm long, 0.5–0.6 in./13–15 mm wide, smaller elsewhere, leaf blades erect, narrowly trigonous.

Uses: The culms of this species are free of branches to a greater proportional height than are most other species. The straight, split, light, tough canes, with nonprominent nodes, are used extensively for handicrafts. The plant size makes this species suitable for sound barriers, windbreaks, and specimens in large, expansive areas.

Cultivation: Propagation is by plant division. This species is among the hardiest of the genus; it has withstood temperatures as low as 17°F/−8°C.

Latin name: *Bambusa tulda* Roxb.
Origin: India
Habitat: Cultivated
Hardiness: Zones 9 and 10
Description: A warm-season, giant, clump, evergreen bamboo. Culms erect, straight, branched, cylindrical, green, fistulose, woody, 60–70 ft/18.5–21.5 m high, 2–4 in./5–10 cm in diameter at the base, smooth, with very thick walls; usually three large branches at each node along with several smaller ones with 6 to 10 leaves on each branch; sheaths broad at apex, with sheath blade broadly trigonous, nearly equaling the width of the sheath apex and broader than high; densely covered with brownish hairs on the outside; the lower sheaths have a broad short blade, with a pair of prominent auricles, one of which is usually prolonged over and adherent to the sheath and is distinctly wavy or crinkled. Foliage medium green, coarse in texture; leaves flat, 3–10 in./0.8–2.5 dm long, 0.5–1.0 in./13–25 mm wide.

Uses: This species, like that of Chinese-goddess bamboo, was introduced directly from India by the U.S. Department of Agriculture and assigned Plant Introduction No. 21002. The stout, hard canes are outstanding for their use in construction and in the manufacture of furniture and other articles requiring split bamboo. The large plants are good for controlling erosion on steep slopes and for arresting erosion in gullies and ravines and along streams. This giant species, like that of other giant forms, makes an ideal windbreak or sound barrier and provides shade. Other introductions of this species propagated by seeding are smaller in size, less vigorous, and less attractive than the type form.

Cultivation: Propagation is by plant division. This species is cultivated extensively in the tropics and in zone 10 in the United States, where it withstands temperatures slightly lower than 27°F/−3°C.

Latin name: *Bambusa tuldoides* Munro
Synonym: *Bambusa pallescens* (Doll) Hack.
Common names: Punting-pole bamboo, Chang ko chuk, Nai chuk (Chinese)
Origin: China

Habitat: Cultivated

Hardiness: Zones 9 and 10

Description: A warm-season, large, clump bamboo. Culms slender, straight, branched, cylindrical, fistulose, but with fairly thick walls, 30–50 ft/9.2–15.4 m high, 2.0–2.5 in/5.0–6.3 cm in diameter at base; branches from few to several at each node, each branch or twig bearing 5 to 12 leaves; sheaths with broad apex, the base of the sheath blade nearly equaling the width of the sheath apex. Foliage dark green, coarse in texture; leaves oblong, variable in size, 2–10 in./0.5–2.5 dm long, 0.3–1.0 in./8–25 mm wide on older culms and somewhat smaller on new, young culms, dark green above, pale and hirsute on the lower surface; sheaths glabrous. Inflorescence a terminal, branched panicle; branchlets near the top, alternate and leafy, nearly whorled below; spikelets in more or less distant to densely aggregate glomerules, pale, not glossy; lower palea somewhat obtuse, abruptly mucronate. Flowering and fruiting occur after a few years of growth.

Uses: Punting-pole bamboo is used for erosion control and land stabilization. The large plants make excellent screens, windbreaks, and sound barriers. The mature culms are used in many ways. Its vernacular name is derived from the use of the canes for propelling small boats and punts along rivers and streams and fishing boats in shallow coastal waters. It has become naturalized in the United States, and it is an important economic species in southern China.

Cultivation: Propagation is by plant division. This species is cultivated in many mild-wintered locations in the southern and southwestern United States in zones 9 and 10. It withstands temperatures to about 20°F/−7°C.

Latin name: *Bambusa ventricosa* McClure

Common names: Buddha's-belly bamboo, Fu Du chu (Chinese)

Origin: China

Habitat: Cultivated

Hardiness: Zones 9 and 10

Description: A warm-season, giant, clump, semievergreen bamboo. Culms erect, branched, cylindrical, green, fistulose. Culms of plants grown outside are 40–60 ft/12.3–18.5 m high, 2–3 in./5–8 cm in diameter at base; the culms are much shorter when grown as a potted plant, usually 5–8 ft/1.5–2.5 m high and 0.5–0.6 in./13–15 mm in diameter at base; usually three branches at each node on normal culms in young clumps; the branches are usually unequal in size, but occasionally there may be two or more additional smaller ones; branches on dwarfed plants are sometimes borne singly at the nodes and have 6 to 8 leaves on each branch or twig, which are 3–5 in./0.8–1.3 dm long, 0.3–0.6 in./8–15 mm wide; sheaths on culms of adult plants are long and broad, noticeably asymmetrical, coriaceous, glabrous, with the veins of dry sheaths prominent, producing a striate effect; the apex of the sheath is rather wide, gently arched near the center; the ligule is short, sheath blades are distinctly asymmetrical and as wide as the apex but somewhat constricted near the base, which is extended to form two diminutive and unequal auricles. Foliage is medium green, coarse in texture. The leaves of adult plants are 5–7 in./1.3–1.8 dm long, 0.4–0.8 in./10–20 mm wide; the leaves of potted plants are much smaller than those on larger plants grown outside.

Uses: This species provides an excellent demonstration of the effect of environment on the size of the plants. When grown indoors, the culms grow only 5–8 ft/1.5–2.5 m high, in contrast to culms to 60 ft/18.5 m high when grown outdoors. Only the dwarf form is commonly grown in China, its place of origin. The culms and branches of plants grown in pot culture are often drastically shortened. The internodes likewise are usually shortened and enlarged, resulting in characteristically distorted culms with swollen internodes, to which the vernacular name buddha's-belly bamboo has been applied. The dwarf form is most commonly found in the trade. Potted plants respond to trimming, resulting in a handsome bamboo grown primarily as a curiosity and for its unique shape and foliage. Buddha's-belly bamboo is useful as screens, windbreaks, sound barriers, and specimens and is also grown to provide shade.

Cultivation: Propagation is by plant division. Buddha's-belly bamboo and punting-pole bamboo originated from the same general area of southern China. The two species are quite similar in appearance, size, and winter hardiness.

Latin name: *Bambusa vulgaris* Schrad. ex J.C. Wendl.
Synonym: *Bambusa siberi* Griseb.
Common names: Common bamboo, Feathery bamboo
Origin: Tropical Asia
Habitat: Cultivated
Hardiness: Zone 10
Description: A warm-season, giant, clump bamboo that forms large, open colonies. Culms fistulose, branched, cylindrical, erect, but when mature are arched outward near the periphery of the colony, 60–80 ft/18.5–24.6 m high, 2–3 in./5–8 cm in diameter at base; culm color varies among forms, some forms are bright green, others are yellow, whereas some are green with longitudinal yellow stripes and yet others are green blotched with black; usually three unequal branches at each node, each branch or twig bearing three to seven leaves; sheaths are variable, the lower sheaths are much shorter than broad, the apex is very wide, with the center arching gently; ligule with finely notched, shortly ciliate margin, sheaths are initially covered with short, appressed, stiff, brown hairs on the outside, most of which gradually fall off, the blades of lower sheaths are short and broad and much narrower at the apex, but a pair of fringed auricles extends to the edges of the sheath, the inside of the sheath blade is initially densely hirsute with brown hairs, but much is lost in drying, the sheaths dry to a pale brown. Foliage medium to dark green, coarse in texture; leaves oblong-linear or lanceolate-acuminate, round at the base, scabrous on the margins and beneath, leaf blades 6–10 in./1.5–2.5 dm long, 1.0–1.3 in./2.5–3.3 cm wide, not tessellate; sheaths striate to the base. Inflorescence a large, terminal panicle

borne on fascicled, flowering branches, elongate, leafless or slightly leafy, with large clusters of spikelets at the nodes; spikelets sessile, two-to-many-flowered, radiate in clusters, oblong-lanceolate, acuminate; glumes distichous, two or more, the inferior ones sterile, several imperfect, ciliate and many-nerved, chiefly striate above, superior, oblong-lanceolate, passing into inferior sterile ones; glumes and sterile lemma persistent after the florets fall; lemmas firm, sharp-pointed or awn-tipped; palea keeled, keels projecting but not winged; caryopsis lanceolate. Flowering and fruiting occur very erratically, usually not until the culms are a few years old. Common bamboo is a highly variable species.

Uses: Common bamboo is naturalized and widely cultivated throughout the tropics of both hemispheres. The ease of establishment and culture and the strength of its canes, of which multifarious use is made, is why this species is so popular. The giant size of the plants provides wood from which paper pulp is derived. The variation among the many different forms in culm color make it desirable for use in very large, expansive areas. The horticultural value and ornamental use of common bamboo is similar to that of other species of similar size. The size of common bamboo makes it useful for specimens, sound barriers, and windbreaks, and as a shade plant.

Cultivation: Propagation is by plant division. Common bamboo is adapted only in the tropics and the warmer parts of zone 10; the plants have been killed at 28°F/ − 2°C. Common bamboo is adapted to a wide range of soils on difficult sites. The plants thrive best in full sun.

Chimonobambusa **Mak.** From Greek *cheimon*, ''winter,'' and *Bambusa*, referring to the season of the innovation of the shoots. Lectotype, *Chimonobambusa marmorea* (Mitf.) Mak. There are 12 species, native to East and South Asia. A hardy, deciduous, shrubby bamboo with strong rhizomes. Culm terete, nearly solid; culm sheaths with conspicuous appendages, tardily deciduous; several branches at each node; leaf sheaths with smooth bristles at apex. Inflorescence a terminal panicle; spikelets racemose; lemma not tessellate, with prominent nerves; androecium three-merous; gynoecium two-merous (Young and Haun, 1961).

> **Latin name:** *Chimonobambusa falcata* (Nees) Nakai
> **Synonym:** *Arundinaria falcata* Nees
> **Common name:** Sickle bamboo
> **Origin:** Himalayas
> **Habitat:** Mountainous areas
> **Hardiness:** Zone 6
> **Description:** A hardy, intermediate, running bamboo that forms loose colonies. Culms erect, slender, slightly fistulose, cylindrical, branched, 15–20 ft / 4.6–6.2 m high, 0.3–0.5 in./8–13 mm in diameter at the base, covered with a bluish white, waxy coating when young, becoming yellowish green; branches,

several at each node, each bearing three to five leaves; culm sheaths with conspicuous appendages, deciduous. Foliage light green, fine in texture; leaf blades 4–6 in./1.0–1.5 dm long, 0.2–0.3 in./5–8 mm wide, striate-veined; sheaths glabrous, striate, ciliate at the ligule. Inflorescence racemose; spikelets with prominently nerved lemmas, not tessellate; androecium three-merous; gynoecium two-merous.

Uses: Sickle bamboo is useful as a tall hedge or screen. Although sickle bamboo is much smaller than *Arundinaria falconeri*, it is often confused with it because of the similarities in appearance of the two species. This species makes striking specimens because of the color of the mature culms.

Cultivation: Propagation is by plant division, made well before new shoots appear. The plants should be contained where necessary.

Latin name: *Chimonobambusa marmorea* (Mitf.) Mak.
Common name: Marbled bamboo
Origin: East Asia
Habitat: Cultivated
Hardiness: Zone 8
Description: A hardy, semidwarf, running, shrubby bamboo with strong rhizomes; the plants form rather dense clumps. Culms erect, cylindrical, smooth, slightly fistulose, branched, 6–10 ft/1.8–3.1 m high, 0.5–0.6 in./13–15 mm in diameter at the base, lower nodes lacking prominent air roots; new culms are light green, mottled brown, and silvery white, with pink stripes and tips, maturing to purplish when grown in full sun; branches usually occur in threes, one short and two longer, at each node; branches of new culms are arranged in herringbone fashion; later branching becomes tufted, giving the plant its attractive, shrubby appearance; sheaths membranous, spotted brownish purple, with conspicuous appendages, deciduous. Foliage rich medium green, medium in texture; leaves petiolate, blades smooth, lanceolate, 4–6 in./1.0–1.5 dm long, 0.4–0.5 in./10–13 mm wide; sheaths with smooth bristles at the apex, promptly deciduous. Inflorescence racemose; spikelets with prominently nerved lemmas, not tessellate; androecium three-merous; gynoecium compound, with two styles.

Uses: This hardy, shrubby species is most useful as a hedge. Although the plants are highly invasive, their shrubby appearance makes an attractive hedge. The plants respond very well to trimming, which keeps them manageable in size either as a hedge or as potted specimens. Despite its invasiveness, this species is widely used as a hedge.

Cultivation: Propagation is by plant division. The plants should be contained where necessary.

Latin name: *Chimonobambusa quadrangularis* (Fenzi) Mak.
Common names: Square-stem bamboo, Square bamboo
Origin: China

Habitat: Cultivated
Hardiness: Zone 8
Description: A hardy, intermediate, running bamboo with extensive rhizomes, forming colonies of medium density. Culms erect, branched, cylindrical when young, becoming squarelike when mature, slightly fistulose, slender, roughened, 20–30 ft /6.2–9.2 m high, 0.8–1.0 in./20–25 mm in diameter at the base, dark green, becoming brown, lower nodes with prominent air roots, nodes swollen and conspicuous, 4–5 in./1.0–1.3 dm apart, square, but round at the corners, very prominent, with a deep purple band on the lower side, densely fringed with yellowish brown bristles; branches three to seven at each node, bearing two to four leaves on each branch, breaking off easily when dry, leaving a little, raised scar, often depressed in the center; sheaths loosely tessellate, thin, and delicate, greenish at first, shading to purple, deciduous. Foliage dark green to dark brown, coarse in texture; leaf blades 6–8 in./1.5–2.0 dm long, 0.8–1.0 in./20–25 mm wide, sharply cuneate at the base, serrated on the margins, dark olive green above, dull green beneath. Inflorescence racemose; lemmas prominently nerved, not tessellate; androecium three-merous; gynoecium compound, three-merous.

Uses: Square-stem bamboo is truly unique among bamboos. It is popular as an ornamental bamboo for its attractive dark green foliage and particularly for its unique square culms. It is grown chiefly as a curiosity or specimen plant in large gardens.

Cultivation: Propagation is usually by plant division. Square-stem bamboo does best in well-manured soil in a moist, sheltered situation. The plants prefer full sun, where the color of the culm streaks develop best; they should be contained where necessary.

Dendrocalamus Nees (Giant bamboo). Type species, *Dendrocalamus strictus* (Roxb.) Nees There are about 20 species, native to south and southeast Asia. These are arboreal, clump-forming, tropical grasses that are tender perennials, and they will not withstand any frost. Inflorescence spikelets in globose heads in long panicles. Spikelets elliptic to oblong, few-to-many-flowered, lower florets imperfect, upper pistillate or bisexual; glumes two or three, upper glume keeled, lemma often mucronate, stamens six, filaments separate; fruit small, with thick, hard wall; seeds free (Young, 1945, 1946).

Latin name: *Dendrocalamus strictus* (Roxb.) Nees
Synonym: *Bambusa stricta* Roxb.
Common names: Male bamboo, Calcutta bamboo
Origin: India
Habitat: Cultivated
Hardiness: Zone 10

Description: A warm-season, large, clump, evergreen bamboo forming dense colonies. Culms erect, branched, cylindrical, slightly fistulose, 30–50 ft / 9.2–15.4 m high, or higher, 4–5 in./1.0–1.2 dm in diameter at base, glaucous green when young, becoming yellowish green at maturity; several branches at each node, the branches are long and slender; the primary branch is usually much larger than any of the three to six smaller ones; the number of leaves on each branch or twig is quite variable, usually from 5 to 13; sheaths more or less densely brown or blackish hairy or bristly, gradually or abruptly narrowing toward the apex, usually pliable but occasionally somewhat rigid and with a narrow, inseparable blade, or the same throughout. Foliage medium to light green, coarse in texture; leaves petiolate, blades 4–12 in./1.0–3.0 dm long, 0.8–1.0 in./20–25 mm wide with prominent midrib and strong nerves on each side, pubescent on both surfaces. Inflorescence spikelets borne in dense, globose heads, 1–2 in./2.5–5.0 cm across, in large, open panicles; spikelets few-to-many-flowered, elliptic to oblong, usually hairy; lower florets imperfect, upper pistillate or bisexual; glumes two or three, upper glume keeled; lemma usually mucronate; androecium six-merous, filaments separate; caryopsis small, with a thick, hard wall and free seed. Flowering and fruiting occur very irregularly, usually not until the plants are several years old.

Uses: Calcutta bamboo is cultivated in plant-hardiness zone 10 as a tender perennial. It forms an excellent windbreak and sound barrier. When grown in large colonies, it affords food and protection for wildlife. Calcutta bamboo serves as a source of paper pulp, which is its chief economic value. The strong canes are used in construction. The split canes are held in high esteem by rod makers as material for split-bamboo fishing rods.

Cultivation: Propagation is by seeding and by plant division. New annual shoots of Calcutta bamboo, which usually occur in late summer or early autumn, should be dug out a month or two before they emerge for replanting.

Phyllostachys **Sieb. & Zucc. (Bamboo).** Type species, *Phyllostachys bambusoides* Sieb. and Zucc. There are about 30 species, native to East Asia and the Himalayas. Evergreen, perennial grasses with wide-spreading rhizomes and woody stems, rhizomes slender, extensive. Culms erect, more or less cylindrical, 10–70 ft /3.1–21.5 m high, 2–6 in./0.5–1.5 dm in diameter at the base, fistulose, simple or branched, smooth or striate, with comparatively short, hollow internodes, internodes flattened or grooved on one or both sides; nodes prominent; sheaths variable in color, promptly deciduous; branches usually two at each node, quite unequal, with a smaller, third branch occasionally developing between the larger two. Leaves petiolate, small to moderately large, tessellate, articulate, with a patch of antrorse hairs on each side of the midrib at the base. Inflorescence a terminal, leafy panicle, appearing usually only after many years' growth; spikelets two or three, one-to-four-flowered, subtended by imbricate bracts; glumes usually unequal, many-nerved, glabrous; lemma ovate-lanceolate, acuminate; palea two-keeled, often with two short points; caryopsis small (McClure, 1957).

Latin name: *Phyllostachys aurea* Carr. ex A. & C. Riv.
Synonym: *Bambusa aurea* Hort.
Common names: Golden bamboo, Fishpole bamboo, Hotei-chiku (Japanese)
Origin: China
Habitat: Cultivated
Hardiness: Zones 7 and 8
Description: A hardy, intermediate, running, evergreen bamboo. Culms stiffly erect, straight, branched, 15–30 ft/4.6–9.2 m high, 1.0–1.6 in./2.5–4.0 cm in diameter at the base and gradually tapering toward the top, fistulose, bright green initially to strongly glaucous after sheaths fall, becoming gray to golden, glabrous and smooth; upper internodes deeply grooved, 4–6 in./1.0–1.5 dm long, with a swollen band below each node fringed with short, white hairs; nodes usually crowded near the base of the culm and variously inclined, giving the culms a unique, characteristic shape; new shoots slightly flattened, heavily covered with very dense layers of sheaths; branches borne in pairs at each node, stiffly upright, one long and one short at each node; sheaths pinkish or olive green with light green veins, sparsely strewn with small, brown spots, persistent, with very short, smooth, convex ciliate ligule; auricles lacking. Foliage dark green, coarse in texture; leaves petiolate, leaf blades glabrous or glabrescent, 2–7 in./0.5–1.8 dm long, 0.5–0.8 in./13–20 mm wide, cuneate at the base, denticulate on one side, dark green above, glaucous below; leaf sheaths with very short ligules; auricles well developed or often lacking. Shoot initiation begins about midseason.

Uses: The golden yellow culms and their stiff, upright habit, along with its narrow slender leaves, make this bamboo ideal for specimen plantings and house plants. The unique culms, particularly the lower portions, are highly valued for use as walking canes.

Cultivation: Propagation is by plant division. The plants should be contained where necessary.

Latin name: *Phyllostachys aureosulcata* McClure
Common names: Yellow-groove bamboo, Forage bamboo, Stake bamboo
Origin: China
Habitat: Cultivated
Hardiness: Zones 6 and 7
Description: A hardy, intermediate, running, evergreen bamboo. Culms erect or nearly so, more or less flexuous or nearly straight, branched, cylindrical, fistulose, 15–25 ft/4.6–7.7 m high, 1.0–1.6 in./2.5–4.0 cm in diameter at the base; internodes short, 1.0–1.6 in./2.5–4.0 cm long, more or less farinose, retrorsely scabrous initially, dull green with a panel above the insertion of the buds and branches, striped green and yellow, especially during the first year; nodes

FOUR INCHES

FOUR INCHES

Phyllostachys aureosulcata. **Left, small culm; center, culm showing characteristic zigzag growth; right, young shoots.** *Source: Bamboos of the Genus Phyllostachys.* USDA Agric. Handbook 114. 1957.

glabrous, a rather prominent farinose zone extending both above and below the sheath scar; new shoots more or less cylindrical, heavily covered with dense layers of sheaths; branches borne in pairs at each node, bearing three to five leaves; sheaths light green with white, yellow, and green stripes, never spotted; ligules well developed, broadly convex, margin irregular, toothed; sheath blades reflexed in lower sheaths to narrowly spreading, trigonous, not elongate; auricles lacking in lowermost and uppermost several sheaths, rather broad, variable, sparsely fringed with crinkly bristles. Foliage medium green, coarse in texture; leaves petiolate, leaf blades flat, densely pilose near the base, otherwise glabrous or glabrescent on the lower surface, 4–6 in./1.0–1.5 dm long, 0.5–0.8 in./13–20 mm wide; sheaths with weakly exserted ligules; auricles usually lacking. Shoot initiation begins about midseason. Two unmistakable characteristics of the culms are the pale golden or yellowish color of the sulcus during the first year's growth. The green color of the round part of the culm becomes paler, losing some of the yellow color of the sulcus, and by the third year it is usually indistinguishable from the faded green of the round portion of the culm. The second identifiable characteristic is the roughness of the new culms; this also becomes less perceptible as the culms mature.

Uses: Yellow-groove bamboo is perhaps the most winter hardy in the genus. It is suitable for medium-sized and large gardens, where it is used as hedges, screens, and specimens. The young shoots are edible.

Cultivation: Propagation is by plant division and by rhizome cuttings. The plants should be contained where necessary. Yellow-groove bamboo is among the most winter-hardy bamboos in cultivation in the United States.

Latin name: *Phyllostachys bambusoides* Sieb. & Zucc.
Synonym: *Phyllostachys reticulata* C. Koch
Cultivars: 'Allgold' McClure, Allgold bamboo, 'Castillon' McClure, Castillon bamboo
Common names: Giant timber bamboo, Hardy timber bamboo, Japanese timber bamboo, Madake (Japanese)
Origin: China
Habitat: Cultivated
Hardiness: Zones 7 and 8
Description: A hardy, giant, running, evergreen bamboo with strong rhizomes. Culms nearly erect to erect, cylindrical, branched, fistulose, glossy dark green becoming yellow, not farinose, 60–70 ft/18.5–21.5 m high, 5–6 in./1.3–1.5 dm in diameter at the base; internodes variable, 4–15 in./1.0–3.8 dm long, silicate, green or golden yellow, or variegated in some horticultural forms; nodal ridges variable among cultivars, usually more prominent than the sheath scars in the typical form; new shoots straight or slightly wavy, heavily covered with dense layers of sheaths; branches usually in pairs, rather long; sheaths greenish to buff, spotted throughout with dark brown spots; ligules moderately well developed with ciliolate margins on small culms and fringed with coarse bristles on larger culms; basal sheaths without auricles, others bearing two narrow to broadly ovate or falcate auricles fringed with greenish, crinkled bristles; sheath blades lanceolate, short, reflexed and crinkled in lower sheaths to long lorate and retrorse in upper ones, green or with pastel shades, or weakly variegated with alternate green, buff, and cream stripes. Foliage medium green, coarse in texture; leaf blades flat, 6–8 in./1.5–2.0 dm long, 1.0–1.2 in./1.5–3.0 cm wide,

Phyllostachys bambusoides. **View in grove at the United States Plant Introduction Garden, Savannah, Georgia.** *Source: Economic Botany 8(4):381. 1954.*

puberulent to subglabrous except at the base on the lower surface; sheaths with well-developed ligules and usually well-developed auricles. Shoot initiation begins late in the season.

Uses: Timber bamboo is the most versatile species in the genus; it is an important timber bamboo in the Orient. This species and its variants are widely cultivated in the United States. The golden yellow culms of the cultivars, with their sulcate internodes of various colors, are the main ornamental features of these bamboos. Giant timber bamboo is useful as a sound barrier, as a windbreak, and to provide shade.

Cultivation: Propagation is by plant division. The plants may require containment where necessary.

Cultivars: *Phyllostachys bambusoides* Sieb. & Zucc. 'Allgold' McClure, Allgold bamboo   Allgold bamboo is distinguished from the typical form by its size and overall color. This intermediate form is usually 25–40 ft/7.7–12.3 m high. The culms and branches are bright yellow in the lower portion of the culm, becoming rich golden yellow; the sulcate internodes are usually yellow; the groove is not green. Occasionally leaf blades are white or cream-striped, and the lower internodes show a longitudinal stripe of green. This variegated cultivar is useful as a tall screen, sound barrier, or specimen.

Phyllostachys bambusoides Sieb. and Zucc. 'Castillon' McClure, Castillon bamboo. Castillon bamboo is distinguishable from the typical form by its reduced size and overall color pattern. The plants of this intermediate form are 20–30 ft/6.2–9.2 m high but do not differ from the type form in any morphological characters. The lower internodes and branches of mature culms are bright yellow; the internodes of the culms and branches have a green groove above each bud or branch insertion. Foliage is mostly green, but occasionally a few leaves have one or two narrow, creamy-white stripes; leaves are borne three to five on each twig, commonly wavy, 2–6 in./0.5–1.5 dm long. Castillon bamboo is used in the same manner as allgold bamboo.

Latin name: *Phyllostachys dulcis* McClure
Common names: Sweetshoot bamboo, Chinese bamboo, Pah koh poo chi (Chinese)
    Origin: China
    Habitat: Cultivated
    Hardiness: Zones 7 and 8
    Description: A hardy, large, running, evergreen bamboo. Young culms more or less strongly curved and tapered, usually becoming erect prior to maturity, fistulose, branched, 30–40 ft/9.2–12.3 m high, 2.0–2.4 in./5–6 cm in diameter at the base; internodes 4–13 in./1.0–3.3 dm long, dull green, often striped with paler green or cream, more or less ribbed, copiously farinose; lower nodes thickened, asymmetrical, glabrous, strongly striate-ribbed, nodal ridges fairly prominent, thickened on the convex side of the culms; branches usually two but sometimes three at each node, short, nearly equal, with two or three

FOUR INCHES

Phyllostachys dulcis. **Left, culm; right, three young shoots.** *Source: Bamboos of the Genus Phyllostachys. USDA Agric. Handbook 114. 1957.*

leaves near the tips; sheaths glabrous, somewhat glaucous or with scattered, stiff, greenish hairs, with sparse, small, brown spots and usually more or less striped when young and thin, stramineous, or nearly white when dry; ligules strongly convex, ciliolate on the undulate margin, decurrent in the lower sheaths; auricles well developed, falcate, narrow with fringed margins, sheath blades lorate or lanceolate toward the tip, appressed or slightly spreading away from the culm in the lower sheaths, drooping or arched in the upper sheaths. Foliage medium green, coarse in texture; leaves petiolate, leaf blades flat, 4–5 in./1.0–1.3 dm long, 0.6–0.9 in./15–23 mm wide, usually densely pilose toward the base, sometimes throughout on the lower surface; sheaths with strongly exserted ligules, ciliolate on the margin; auricles either strongly developed or lacking entirely. Shoot initiation begins very early in the season.

Uses: The young shoots are particularly palatable; this is the most important species in China for its edible shoots. Its vernacular name is associated with the sweetness of the young shoots. Sweetshoot bamboo is good as an erosion-control plant; it is also good as a tall screen, windbreak, sound barrier, and to provide shade.

Cultivation: Propagation is by plant division. The plants may require containment.

Latin name: *Phyllostachys flexuosa* (Carr.) A. & C. Riv.
Common name: Zigzag bamboo
Origin: China
Habitat: Cultivated
Hardiness: Zone 7
Description: A semihardy, intermediate, running, evergreen bamboo. Culms usually erect or nearly so, branched, straight or often zigzag, with up to several geniculate nodes, outer culms flexuous and arching, 15–30 ft/4.6–9.2 m high, 2.5–3.0 in./6.3–8.0 cm in diameter at the base, fistulose; internodes 3–12 in./0.8–3.0 dm long, green but somewhat glaucous, especially below the nodes, striate-ribbed, glabrous, nodal ridges glabrous, thin; branches in pairs at each node, rather long and flexuous; leaf sheaths on branches without bristles, ligules not maroon; culm sheaths greenish to beige with purplish veins, somewhat maculate with small brownish areas, glabrous, lustrous; ligules strongly developed, dark maroon, apex usually truncate to convex, asymmetrical with ciliolate to fimbriate margin; auricles lacking; sheath blades narrow, lanceolate to lorate, mostly retrorse or strongly arched. Foliage dark green, coarse in texture; leaves petiolate, leaf blades more or less flat, of variable vesture, more or less densely tomentose to subglabrous, except on the lower surface, 4–6 in./1.0–1.5 dm long, 0.5–0.8 in./13–20 mm wide, 8-to-12-nerved, abruptly narrowed at the base, attenuate at the tip, serrulate on one margin, dark green above, glaucous beneath; leaf sheaths with moderately developed ligules but without auricles. Shoot initiation begins in early midseason.

Uses: The ornamental value and uses of this species are quite similar to

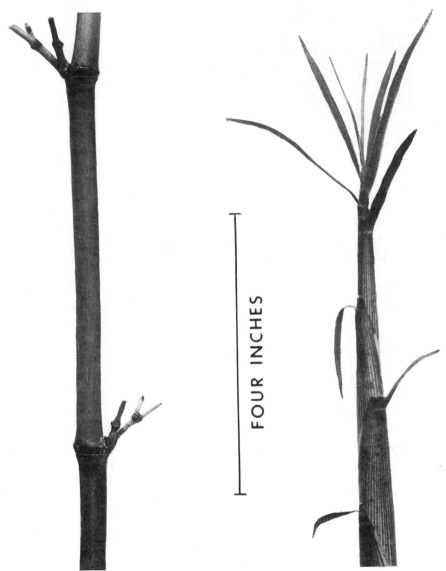

FOUR INCHES

Phyllostachys flexuosa. **Left, young culm; right, young shoot.** *Source: Bamboos of the Genus Phyllostachys.* USDA Agric. Handbook 114. 1957.

those of other *Phyllostachys* species of similar size. The young, small shoots, which appear in the spring, are edible and relatively free from acridity, even in the raw state.

Cultivation: Propagation is by plant division. The plants should be contained where necessary.

Latin name: *Phyllostachys meyeri* McClure
Common name: Meyer bamboo
Origin: Central China
Habitat: Cultivated
Hardiness: Zone 7
Description: A hardy, intermediate, running, evergreen bamboo. Culms erect, straight or rarely somewhat flexuous near the base, branched, 25–35 ft / 7.7–10.8 m high, 1.6–2.0 in./4–5 cm in diameter at the base, fistulose, green, maturing to dull green; internodes 6–14 in./1.5–3.5 dm long, glabrous, smooth, nodal ridges fairly prominent; branches borne in pairs at each node; sheaths greenish, spotted or more or less blotched with small brown areas, glaucous, glabrous except fringed along the base with a band of small, white hairs; ligules exserted, the apex convex, often slightly asymmetrical, the margin ciliate initially, becoming glabrate; auricles lacking; sheath blades lanceolate to narrowly lorate, very long near the middle of the culm, more or less wavy to slightly crinkled, broadly arched. Foliage medium green, coarse in texture; leaves petiolate, leaf blades densely pilose at the base becoming less dense toward the apex on the lower surface, 4–6 in./1.0–1.5 dm long, 1.0–1.6 in./2.5–4.0 cm wide; leaf sheaths with prominently exserted ligules, the apex strongly convex, the margin ciliolate or glabrous; auricles usually weak or lacking. Shoot initiation begins during midseason.
Uses: The extra-strong culms and in particular the strong root system make meyer bamboo less subject to damage from strong wind, thereby rendering it ideal for use as a tall hedge or screen. The young shoots, which occur in midspring, are edible.
Cultivation: Propagation is by plant division. The plants should be contained where necessary. The plants should be cut periodically to maintain a hedge of desired height.

Latin name: *Phyllostachys nigra* (Lodd. ex Lindl.) Munro
Synonym: *Bambusa nigra* Lodd. ex Lindl.
Cultivars: 'Henon' Henon bamboo
Common names: Black bamboo, Hachiku, Kurochiku (Japanese)
Origin: South China
Habitat: Cultivated
Hardiness: Zones 7 and 8
Description: A hardy, intermediate, running, evergreen bamboo with slender, wide-ranging rhizomes. Culms erect, becoming arched, cylindrical, branched, fistulose, 15–25 ft /4.6–7.7 m high, 1.0–1.6 in./2.5–4.0 cm in diameter at the base, green initially, gradually becoming speckled, then becoming purplish to brownish to black at maturity; internodes loosely farinose of variable vesture, initially setulose, becoming glabrescent to smooth but sometimes noticeably striate-ribbed, 4–12 in./1–3 dm long, with a pair of deep grooves above each node, nodes or nodal ridges moderately prominent, conspicuously edged

with white below; new shoots more or less cylindrical, heavily covered with dense layers of sheaths; branches usually in pairs at each node, quite unequal, occasionally with a third, smaller branch developing between the two, usually spotted; sheaths greenish to pale buff, not maculate, usually sparsely pubescent with erect hairs; ligules and auricles absent, sheath blades cymbiform, either broadly or narrowly trigonous, more or less wavy in larger culms, appressed in the lower sheaths, spreading away from the culm in the upper ones, abruptly deciduous. Foliage bright light green to medium green, medium in texture; leaves numerous, petiolate, leaf blades lanceolate, flat, base bluntly round, tips attenuate, 3–5 in./0.8–1.2 dm long, 0.5–0.7 in./13–18 mm wide, 6-to-12-nerved, denticulate, usually smooth throughout or sparsely to densely pilose on the lower surface; leaf sheaths with scarcely exserted, very short ligules; the auricles are either weak or lacking. Shoot initiation begins late in the season.

Uses: Black bamboo is the so-called queen of bamboos, with its bright green foliage and black culms when mature. The coloration of the foliage and particularly of the culms makes this a favorite ornamental bamboo, especially when grown in full sun. The young shoots, which appear in the spring, are edible. The plants are suitable for growing in pots or containers, as they attain only 9–10 ft/2.8–3.1 m in height when grown indoors. Black bamboo, with its mature black culms, is unique among ornamental bamboos.

Cultivation: Black bamboo thrives in zones 8 and 9 but may require some protection, inasmuch as the plants will not survive freezing temperatures, 32°F/0°C. Propagation is by plant division in midspring, when the young shoots develop around the periphery of the older culms, or by planting cuttings of young rhizomes made in very early spring during dormancy well before the young new shoots appear. New plants require more than six years to attain maturity. The plants perform best in light or partial shade when grown outdoors; however, they require good lighting when grown indoors.

Cultivars: *Phyllostachys nigra* (Lodd. ex Lindl.) Munro 'Henon' McClure, Henon bamboo   This large cultivar is distinguished from the typical black-stemmed form by its larger size and coloration of its culms and branches. It is larger in ultimate stature; that is, the culms are 40–50 ft/12.3–15.4 m high, 2–3 in./5–8 cm in diameter at the base; it does not differ morphologically from the typical form. The color markings on the green internodes and branches are lacking. Young culms are quite distinctive and infinitely more colorful and spectacular in appearance than mature culms, derived principally from the enveloping sheaths. The culm sheaths are light bluish, not spotted, and softened by a coat of brownish hairs; the sheath blade is terminal, subtended at the base, with a pair of well-developed auricles fringed with lavender bristles. The sheaths become light tan as they mature; at maturity, they fall to the ground, revealing spotless, bright green internodes of the young culm, perceptibly dimmed by a thin film of farinose coating. This cultivar is a favorite ornamental bamboo both in the United States and in the Orient. Other variants of black bamboo have been introduced and cultivated, but they have not received widespread acceptance. This cultivar is noted as a large specimen plant, or, when planted in rows, as a tall screen, sound barrier, or windbreak.

Latin Name:*Phyllostachys nuda* McClure
Origin: China
Habitat: Cultivated
Hardiness: Zones 5 and 6
Description: A hardy, intermediate, running, evergreen bamboo. Culms erect, more or less straight, fistulose, branched, 20–30 ft/6.2–9.2 m high, 1.0–1.6 in./2.5–4.0 cm in diameter at the base, smooth; internodes 6–8 in./1.5–2.0 dm long, green, perceptibly striate-ribbed, entirely glabrous and loosely covered with a farinose film, nodal ridges rather prominent; new shoots cylindrical, heavily enveloped with sheaths; branches usually two, sometimes three at each node, rather long; sheaths grayish, farinose, scabrous with glabrous margins, basal ones with blotches, the upper ones not blotched; ligules strongly exserted, with truncate apex, the margin ciliate; auricles lacking, sheath blades relatively short, lanceolate to narrowly trigonous, crinkled, spreading from the culm. Foliage medium to dark green, coarse in texture; leaves numerous, leaf blades 4–6 in./1.0–1.5 dm long, 0.6–0.8 in./15–20 mm wide, sparsely hirsute near the base on the lower surface, antrorsely scabrous throughout; sheaths with prominently exserted ligules, the apex strongly convex, the margin initially ciliolate; auricles lacking.
Uses: This intermediate, running bamboo is best suited as a houseplant, as it is much reduced in size when grown indoors; occasionally it is used as a garden specimen.
Cultivation: Propagation is by plant division. The plants should be contained where necessary. This species is the most cold tolerant in the genus.

Latin name: *Phyllostachys pubescens* Mazel ex Houx. de Leh.
Synonym: *Phyllostachys edulis* Houx. de Leh.
Common names: Moso bamboo, Mao Chu (Chinese), Moso-chiku (Japanese)
Origin: China
Habitat: Cultivated
Hardiness: Zone 8
Description: A hardy, giant, running, evergreen bamboo. Culms erect or, more commonly, more or less curved, suberect and broadly arched at the tip, often emerging at an angle from the ground, then curving upward and becoming more or less erect, branched, strongly tapered, 60–75 ft/18.5–23.1 m high, 4–5 in./1.0–1.3 dm in diameter at the base; internodes 4–12 in./1–3 dm long, light green, initially densely velvety throughout, becoming glabrescent, sometimes perceptibly ribbed, sometimes farinose initially and gray at length, nodal ridges nearly obsolete at unbranched nodes; short, new shoots appear pyramidal, eventually becoming strongly tapered, completely clothed with dense layers of

sheaths, branches two or three at each node, short, each branch or twig bearing two or three leaves; sheaths greenish buff, densely maculate with dark brown, completely glaucous, densely covered throughout with brown, erect hairs, densely ciliate on the margins; ligules long-exserted, narrowly convex at the apex, laciniate and fringed on the margin with long, coarse, brownish bristles; auricles strongly developed, dark purplish to brown, falcate; sheath blades narrowly lanceolate to nearly lorate, stiff, green, the lower ones often somewhat wavy, appressed to the culm, the upper ones strongly spreading away from the culm. Foliage medium green, medium in texture; leaves petiolate, unusually small, leaf blades more or less flat, 3–5 in./0.8–1.2 cm long, 0.4–0.6 in./10–15 mm wide, glabrous or nearly so, except at the base of the lower surface; sheaths with very short, scarcely exserted ligules; auricles usually lacking. Shoot initiation begins in early midseason.

Uses: Moso bamboo is perhaps the most majestic of all large bamboos. The canes have many uses in the Orient, such as heavy construction, tiles, toys, tobacco pipes; the rhizomes are used to make walking canes and umbrella handles. Moso bamboo is a major source of edible shoots in Japan. Edible shoots usually appear in early spring and continue until midseason. Dormant "winter shoots," which are dug before they emerge in early spring, are considered a delicacy when they are the only shoots available. Although they contain a considerable degree of acridity, they are very popular and much desired. This giant bamboo provides shade over extended areas and is an excellent windbreak.

Cultivation: Moso bamboo is difficult to propagate and establish. Propagation is by plant division. The plants should be contained where necessary. Moso bamboo is the largest and most handsome of the woody bamboos.

Latin name: *Phyllostachys viridi-glaucescens* (Carr.) A. & C. Riv.
Synonym: *Bambusa viridi-glaucescens* Carr.
Origin: China
Habitat: Cultivated
Hardiness: Zone 7
Description: A semihardy, intermediate, running bamboo. Culms erect and straight, the outer culms arching, fistulose, 20–35 ft/6.2–10.8 m high, 1–2 in./2.5–5.0 cm in diameter at the base; internodes farinose, smooth, not ribbed, initially dark green, becoming bright green and maturing to yellowish green, nodal ridges prominent, the upper portion of the nodes usually violet-colored; branches usually in pairs at each node, with an occasional weaker, smaller, third branch; sheaths pale buff, strewn with brown spots and blotches throughout, tinged with green, scabrous, loosely farinose, often sparsely setose; ligules often asymmetrical, rather long and narrow, more or less strongly convex at the apex, the margin more or less regular to laciniate, finely to coarsely ciliate, ultimately smooth; auricles usually two, sometimes one, falcate, long, narrow, dark purple, delicate, very breakable when dry, sheath blades ribbon-shaped, narrow, reflexed, usually more or less strongly crinkled. Foliage brilliant medium

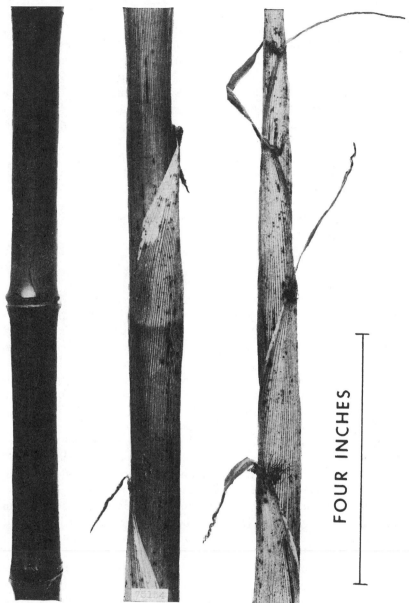

FOUR INCHES

Phyllostachys viridi-glaucescens. **Left, young culm; right, two shoots.**
Source: Bamboos of the Genus Phyllostachys. USDA Agric. Handbook 114. 1957.

green, coarse in texture; leaves borne two to five on each twig or branch, leaf blades flat, 2–6 in./0.5–1.5 dm long, 0.5–0.8 in./13–20 mm wide, smooth and bright green above, downy and bluish green below; leaf sheaths with exserted ligules that soon split and become mutilated; auricles fugacious, usually well developed. Shoot initiation begins early in the season.

Uses: This cold-tolerant, extremely graceful bamboo, like other species of its size, makes ideal tall screens and sound barriers. It is useful only in the largest gardens. Specimen plantings are useful in sites surrounding ponds and lakes.

Cultivation: Propagation is by plant division. The plants should be contained where necessary. Minimum winter temperatures of about 20°F/ − 7°C damage the leaves and top growth, although the plants will perenniate if the roots are adequately protected.

Latin name: *Phyllostachys viridis* (Young) McClure
Synonym: *Phyllostachys mitis* A. & C. Riv.
Origin: China
Habitat: Cultivated
Hardiness: Zones 7 and 8
Description: A semihardy, intermediate to large, running bamboo. Culms suberect, usually somewhat curved but not zigzag, branched, fistulose, 30–50 ft/9.2–15.4 m high, 3.0–3.5 in./8–9 cm in diameter at the base; internodes 3–12 in./0.8–3.0 dm long, glabrous, perceptibly glaucous, especially below the nodes, the surface marked by minute indentations in a pigskinlike pattern, not all striate-ribbed, nodal ridges, bright green when young, maturing to dull yellow, nodal ridges hardly perceptible or nearly so at nodes, the nodes marked by a broad band of farinose coating; branches short, usually borne in pairs at each node, branchlets numerous; sheaths glabrous, often noticeably glaucous, light rosy buff, the veins green, often darker than the background, which is conspicuously spotted with distinct brown spots; ligules truncate on small young culms to strongly convex on larger, older culms, the margin fringed with scabrous bristles in small culms, ciliolate to scabrous in larger ones; sheath blades narrowly lanceolate to ribbon-shaped, more or less wavy, sometimes slightly crinkled, usually spreading away from the culm, the lower ones completely reflexed; ligules exserted, well-developed; auricles well-developed on young culms, often obsolete in older culms. Foliage bright light to medium green, coarse in texture; leaves petiolate, leaf blades 2–5 in./0.5–1.3 dm long, 0.7–1.0 in./18–25 mm wide, sometimes pilose or scabrous on one side, otherwise glabrous or nearly so, except at the base of the lower surface, bright light green above, dull green beneath; sheaths with exserted, well-developed ligules; auricles usually well-developed on young culms, often lacking on older culms. Shoot initiation begins at midseason and continues longer than most species in this genus.

Uses: The new shoots, which appear in midspring, are edible; they are free of bitterness and widely used as food. The wood of this species is of good technical quality. Its ornamental value involves its use as tall screens, windbreaks, and sound barriers.

Cultivation: Propagation is by plant division. The plants should be contained where necessary.

Latin name: *Phyllostachys vivax* McClure
Common name: Elegant bamboo
Origin: China
Habitat: Cultivated
Hardiness: Zones 7 and 8
Description: A hardy, large, running, evergreen bamboo. Culms more or less zigzag or nearly erect, often somewhat curved, fistulose, branched, 40–45 ft/12.3–13.8 m high, 3–4 in./8–10 cm in diameter at the base; internodes 7–12 in./1.8–3.0 dm long, green, visibly glaucous just below the nodes, entirely glabrous, strongly and irregularly striate-ribbed; nodes noticeably asymmetrical, nodal ridges slightly prominent or usually a little more prominent on one side; branches are borne two or three at each node, each bearing three or four leaves; sheaths creamy buff, maculate with brown, the lowest spots sometimes almost completely black; ligules relatively short, decurrent, convex at the apex, the margin ciliolate to setose; auricles obsolete, sheath blades narrowly lanceolate to ribbon-shaped, strongly reflexed, very crinkly; branches are borne two or three at each node, each bearing three or four leaves. Foliage medium green, medium in texture; leaves petiolate, pendulous, leaf blades usually 4–6 in./1.0–1.5 dm long, 0.5–0.7 in./13–18 mm wide, bluntly round at the base, glabrous or nearly so on the lower surface; sheathes with weak exserted ligules, and with or without auricles. Shoot initiation begins in early midseason.

Uses: The new young shoots, which appear in midspring, are edible; they are entirely free from any unpleasant taste, even when uncooked. The use of this bamboo as an ornamental is similar to that of other *Phyllostachys* species of similar size. This is the most vigorous of the hardy "timber" bamboos.

Cultivation: Propagation is by plant division. The plants should be contained where necessary.

Pseudosasa **Mak. ex Nakai (Bamboo).** Lectotype, *Pseudosasa japonica* (Sieb. & Zucc. ex Steud.) Mak. There are three species, native to East Asia, particularly Japan. Woody, rhizomatous, perennial, evergreen grasses. Culms erect, cylindrical, fistulose, 10–20 ft/3.1–6.2 m high, 0.5–1.0 in./13–25 mm in diameter at base; branched, with one branch at each node; culm sheaths persistent, hispid outside. Foliage green or variegated; leaves large, petiolate; sheaths with or without flexuous, smooth bristles. Inflorescence a terminal lax panicle; spikelets two-to-eight-flowered; lemma curving, nearly awned; palea bifid at apex; androecium three-merous, rarely four-merous; style short, with three stigmas.

Pseudosasa japonica. *Source: Growing Ornamental Bamboo.* USDA Home and Garden Bulletin 76. 1961.

Latin name: *Pseudosasa japonica* (Sieb. & Zucc.) Mak.
Synonym: *Arundinaria japonica* Sieb. & Zucc. ex Steud.
Common names: Arrow bamboo, Hardy bamboo, Metake (Japanese)
Origin: China, Japan
Habitat: Cultivated
Hardiness: Zones 6 and 7

Description: A hardy, intermediate, running bamboo with wide-spreading rhizomes. Culms erect when young, becoming arched at maturity, branched, fistulose, 10–20 ft/3.1–6.2 m high, 0.6–1.0 in./15–25 mm in diameter at the base, hairy, initially dark glossy green, edged with purple, maturing to dull green; semierect branches are borne singly from some of the upper nodes, and these, with the apical section of the culm, bear clusters of leaves containing 4 to 11 leaves; sheaths coarse in texture, very persistent, equaling or longer than the internodes, covered initially with short hairs, later becoming smooth and turning light brown, terminated by a persistent, awl-shaped tongue 2–3 in./ 5–8 cm long, the upper sheaths often develop into true leaves. Foliage dark green and glossy, coarse in texture; leaves petiolate, leaf blades 4–12 in./1–3 dm long, 1–2 in./2.5–5.0 cm wide, narrowly oblong, the base cuneate with an attenuated tip, 10-to-20-nerved, tessellation quite marked, midrib yellow, conspicuous, the leaves edged with fine hairs on one margin only, dark green above, about one-half of the lower surface the same color as the upper; the other half silvery gray; sheaths with or without flexuous, smooth bristles. Inflorescence a lax, terminal panicle; spikelets two-to-eight-flowered; lemma nearly awned, curved, palea two-lobed at the apex.

Uses: Arrow bamboo is perhaps the most popular hardy bamboo cultivated in the United States. This species is particularly desirable as an ornamental bamboo because it has handsome foliage, it is quite winter hardy, and, despite its rhizomatous roots, spreads very slowly and does not become invasive or weedy. Arrow bamboo is useful as screens and hedges. Although it is not the most decorative bamboo, it is ideal in the wild or wooded garden and beside streams, pools, and lakes. Arrow bamboo may be used in pot culture, which usually reduces the size of the plants.

Cultivation: Propagation is usually by plant division. The plants should be contained where necessary. The plants require partial or light shade and rich, moist soil. This oriental bamboo is cultivated in the more northern areas in which bamboos thrive; its foliage remains evergreen at temperatures down to about 7°F/−14°C and the rootstocks perhaps survive slightly lower temperatures. Arrow bamboo is adapted to zone 7 and to the mild parts of zone 6. The popularity of arrow bamboo should make it readily accessible from most nurseries.

Sasa **Mak. & Shib. (Bamboo).** Lectotype, *Sasa veitchii* Carr. There are about 150 species, native to East Asia, especially Japan. Usually small, rhizomatous, perennial grasses. Culms erect, simple or branched, cylindrical, fistulose, not spotted, with one or two branches at each node; culm sheaths appendaged, persistent. Foliage variable in color; leaf blades petiolate, crowded at the ends of branchlets; sheaths with or without rigid scabrid bristles. Inflorescence a terminal, lax panicle; spikelets two-to-nine-flowered; glumes two, small; lemma acuminate; palea shorter than the lemma, keeled, bifid; androecium six-merous (Young, 1945, 1946).

Latin name: *Sasa bicolor* G. Koidz.
Origin: Japan
Habitat: Cultivated
Hardiness: Zone 8
Description: A hardy, dwarf, running bamboo. Culms erect, cylindrical, fistulose, simple or branched, light green, not spotted, 18–24 in./4.5–6.0 dm high, 0.4–0.6 in./10–15 mm in diameter at the base, nodes pilose, swollen; usually only one branch or, rarely, two branches at each node; leaves crowded near the ends of the branches and branchlets; sheaths appendaged, gray, striate-ribbed, persistent. Foliage variegated, coarse in texture; leaves petiolate, petiole 0.8–1.0 in./20–25 mm long, leaf blades linear-lanceolate, 5–7 in./1.3–1.8 dm long, 0.8–1.0 in./20–25 mm wide, abruptly acuminate, lower blades more ovate and smaller, margins with minute bristles, with white and yellowish stripes or zones; sheaths with or without rigid scabrid bristles; ligule very short, truncate. Inflorescence a terminal, lax panicle; spikelets two-to-nine-flowered; glumes two; lemma acuminate; palea shorter than the lemma, bifid, keeled; androecium six-merous; caryopsis small.

Uses: This miniature, variegated bamboo is popular as a ground cover and as a potted specimen. Its hardiness makes it useful in zone 8 in outdoor plantings in open, shaded sites; it also performs well as an attractive, variegated house-plant. No variegated ornamental, including this bamboo, achieves its maximum brilliance and color when grown in full sun; indeed, full sunlight may, and quite often does, discolor the foliage. This species may be easily confused with *Arundinaria pygmaea* 'Variegata,' inasmuch as they are quite similar in size but different in foliage color; the latter has leaves with cream-white-green longitudinal stripes, whereas the stripes of *Sasa bicolor* are white-yellow-green.

Cultivation: Propagation is usually by plant division; layering and cuttings are occasionally employed in propagation. The plants should be contained where necessary.

Latin name: *Sasa chrysantha* (Bean) E. Camus
Origin: Japan
Habitat: Cultivated
Hardiness: Zone 8
Description: A hardy, semidwarf, running bamboo. Culms erect, cylindrical, fistulose, medium green, branched, 5–7 ft/1.5–2.2 m high, 0.6–0.8 in./15–20 mm in diameter at the base, internodes 4–5 in./1.0–1.3 dm long; branches one or two at each node from the upper nodes, each bearing five to seven leaves; sheaths ciliate on one margin only, persistent. Foliage bright green or more or less variegated with yellow, longitudinal stripes, coarse in texture; leaves crowded near the tips of the branches and branchlets, leaf blades linear oblong,

4–5 in./1.0–1.3 cm long, 0.5–0.8 in./15–20 mm wide, oblique at the base, more or less acuminate at the tip, glabrous, 8-to-12-nerved, bright green above or often variegated. Inflorescence a lax, terminal panicle; spikelets three-to-nine-flowered; glumes two; lemma acuminate; palea shorter than the lemma, bifid; androecium six-merous; caryopsis small, 1–2 mm long.

Uses: This variegated species makes an excellent ground cover in open shade. Like other rhizomatous grasses, it is invasive and is perhaps best used in naturalizing rather extensive areas adjoining the more formal portion of the garden. When it is used in the water garden, be sure to allow sufficient space for expansion but not at the expense of other ornamentals. It is also very attractive as a potted specimen, either indoors or outdoors.

Cultivation: Propagation is usually by plant division. The plants should be contained where necessary.

Latin name: *Sasa palmata* (Bean) E. Camus
Synonym: *Arundinaria palmata* Bean
Origin: Japan
Habitat: Cultivated
Hardiness: Zone 6
Description: A hardy, semidwarf, running bamboo with strong rhizomes. Culms erect, somewhat curved, branched, cylindrical, brilliant green, maturing to dull green with a waxy bloom below the nodes, 6–8 ft/1.8–2.5 m high, 0.5–1.0 in./13–25 mm in diameter at the base, fistulose, smooth, internodes 5–7 in./1.3–1.8 dm long; culm sheaths usually much shorter than the internodes, appendaged, terminated by a deciduous, lanceolate, strongly tessellate, ciliate tongue. Foliage bright green, coarse in texture; leaves bright green above, pale silvery beneath, borne in palmate clusters of three to nine at the apex of the culm and tips of the branches, many-nerved, minutely tessellate, leaf blades 10–13 in./2.5–3.3 dm long, 3–4 in./8–10 cm wide, oblong to oblong-lanceolate, tapering broadly at the base, bright light green above, silvery green beneath, the secondary veins, 8 to 12 on each side of the midvein, are very prominent, especially when viewed with transmitted light; they enhance the beauty of the leaves. With the exception of *Sasa tessellata*, the leaves of this species are the largest among large-leaved, hardy bamboos.

Uses: This species is good in specimen plantings around pools and lakes. It is also adaptable as a potted plant, as the plants are usually apparently reduced in size when their roots are constricted.

Cultivation: Propagation is usually by plant division. The plants prefer full sun in deep, fertile, moist soil. This species is quite invasive, requiring preventive measures to control its spread. The leaf margins and tips usually wither in winter; the plants are only slightly injured at temperatures above 5°F/−15°C.

Latin name: *Sasa tessellata* (Munro) Mak. & Shib.
Origin: India

Habitat: Cultivated

Hardiness: Zone 6

Description: A hardy, dwarf, running, vigorous bamboo. Culms erect initially but soon arching, branched, narrowly fistulose, 2–4 ft /0.6–1.2 m high, 0.4–0.6 in./10–15 mm in diameter at the base, bright green, covered with a heavy wax bloom, new culms usually curved at the base, lower internodes about 3–4 in./8–10 cm long near the base with the higher ones becoming gradually shorter; branches few, usually singly or rarely in pairs at each node; sheaths smooth, one to three times the length of the internodes, initially light green, becoming dull yellow or stramineous, very persistent. Foliage medium green, coarse in texture; leaves petiolate, petioles very short and thick, yellow or blotched, oblong, tapering broadly at the base and rather narrowly tapering to an acuminate apex, medium green above, glaucous beneath, borne in pairs at the tip of the culm, there being no branches the first year; midrib very prominent for most of its length, and conspicuously yellow, with a line of fine hairs on one side of the lower surface; tessellation is clearly distinctive, with 16 to 18 pairs of secondary veins, leaf blades are 10–15 in./2.5–3.8 dm long, 1.6–4.0 in./ 4–10 cm wide, the largest leaves of the hardy dwarf bamboos.

Uses: The luxuriant foliage, which often bends the culms to an ascending position, drastically reduces the height of the plants. This small plant, but large-leaved bamboo, is attractive with other broad-leaved ornamental shrubs and with other bamboos with small, narrow leaves. It should be contained when grown in the garden as a specimen. The small size of this species makes it useful as ground cover and as a houseplant.

Cultivation: Propagation is usually by plant division. The plants should be contained where necessary. The winter hardiness of this dwarf, large-leaved bamboo is superior to that of other hardy species, which permits its use in the northern fringes of bamboo cultivation in the United States.

Latin name: *Sasa veitchii* Carr.

Synonym: *Arundinaria veitchii* Carr.

Common names: Kuma bamboo, Kuma bamboo grass, Kuma-zasa (Japanese)

Origin: Japan

Habitat: Cultivated

Hardiness: Zone 7

Description: A semihardy, dwarf, running, broad-leaved bamboo. Culms erect, cylindrical, narrowly fistulose, branched, 1–3 ft/3–9 dm high, 0.2–0.3 in./5–8 mm in diameter at the base, deep purplish green when young, becoming dull purple; new shoots light green, very densely covered with white thick bloom; branches solitary, often as long as the culms, bearing four to seven leaves clustered near the tips; sheaths initially densely white-hairy, dull purple, becoming tan, usually with a tuft of hairs at the tip when young. Foliage bright dark green, coarse in texture; leaf blades bright dark green above, glaucous beneath, usually oblong, 2–7 in./0.5–1.8 dm long, 0.6–1.6 in./1.5–4.0 cm wide, with prominent midrib, broadly tapering or round at base, apex acuminate, broadly oval in outline, with five to eight pairs of secondary veins, margins with fine bristles. The tendency of the leaves to wither and decay, turning whitish or brown in late autumn, gives the appearance of variegated foliage; this is conspicuous and striking in certain situations. Inflorescence a terminal, long, lax panicle; spikelets two-to-nine-flowered; glumes two, very small; lemma acuminate; palea shorter than the lemma, keeled, bifid; caryopsis small, 1–2 mm long.

Uses: Kuma bamboo is useful as ground cover. The leaf margins become stramineous-colored in the autumn, and the bicolored leaves provide interest for the winter garden. This small species makes a good house plant and thrives as a potted specimen either indoors or outdoors.

Cultivation: Propagation is by plant division. The plants should be contained where necessary.

Semiarundinaria **Mak. ex Nakai (Bamboo).** Lectotype, *Semiarundinaria fastuosa* (Marl.) Mak. ex Nakai   There are three species, native to Japan and East Asia. Perennial, rhizomatous, woody grasses. Culms erect, branched, with few branches at each node; stem sheaths deciduous, bearing a small blade. Leaf sheaths with rigid, smooth bristles. Spikelets one to three, in spicate fascicles on branchlets, three-to-four-flowered; lemmas 9-or-10-nerved; androecium and gynoecium each three-merous.

Latin name: *Semiarundinaria fastuosa* (Marl.) Mak. ex Nakai
Synonym: *Phyllostachys fastuosa* (Marl. ex Mitf.) Mak. ex Nakai
Common names: Narihira bamboo, Nirihiradake (Japanese)
Origin: Japan
Habitat: Cultivated
Hardiness: Zone 6
Description: A hardy, intermediate, running bamboo; the plants usually form a rather erect, straight clump. Culms erect and straight, branched, fistulose, thin-walled, cylindrical but the upper internodes flattened, 20–25 ft/6.2–7.7 m high, 1.0–1.6 in./2.5–4.0 cm in diameter at the base, dark green, marked with purplish brown, maturing to yellowish brown; branches short, stiff, and erect, usually in pairs or occasionally in threes at each node; sheaths 6–9 in./1.5–2.3 dm long, thick, initially green, becoming purplish, glossy, and stramineous inside and outside, many tardily deciduous. Foliage shiny, dark green, coarse in texture; leaf blades oblong to oblong–lanceolate, 5–7 in./1.2–1.8 dm long, 0.8–1.0 in./20–25 mm wide, 10-to-12-nerved, attenuate, gradually narrowed into a rather long, petiole, shiny dark green above, glaucous or dull green below, puberulent; sheaths with rigid smooth bristles. Inflorescence one to three

Semiarundinaria fastuosa. *Source: Growing Ornamental Bamboo.* USDA Home and Garden Bulletin 76. 1961.

spikelets in spicate fascicles on branchlets; spikelets three-or-four-flowered; lemma 9-to-12-nerved; androecium and gynoecium each three-merous, style short.

Uses: This species is far less rampant than many other running, gregarious bamboos. It is useful as a garden ornamental. The culms are loosely clothed for almost their entire length by rich, dark green foliage, which augments the attractiveness of this hardy bamboo. This species is popular because it is moderately decorative as a specimen or as a house plant.

Cultivation: Propagation is usually by plant division. Precautionary measures should be taken to contain it in its allocated area, despite its slow spread. One way this is done with variable success is by repeatedly cutting back all new shoots that appear outside its designated area.

Shibataea **Mak. ex Nakai (Bamboo).** Lectotype, *Shibataea kumasaca* (Zoll. ex Steud.) Mak. There are two species, one native to China, the other to Japan. The plants are small with elongate rhizomes. Culms erect, zigzag, much flattened, narrowly fistulose, grooved on one side; culm sheaths chartaceous, with short blades, branches three to five at each node, very short. Leaves terminal on branches, short petiolate; sheaths without bristles; flowering branches leafless, indeterminate; spikelets one-or-two-flowered; androecium and gynoecium each three-merous, styles long.

Latin name: *Shibataea kumasaca* (Zoll. ex Steud.) Mak.
Synonym: *Bambusa ruscifolia* Sieb. ex Munro
Common names: Bungozasa, Okamezasa (Japanese)
Origin: Japan
Habitat: Cultivated
Hardiness: Zones 6 and 7
Description: A hardy, semidwarf, running bamboo with elongate rhizomes. Culms slender, branched, narrowly fistulose, 3–6 ft /0.9–1.8 m high, 0.2–0.3 in./5–8 mm in diameter at the base, much flattened, grooved on one side, roughly trigonous to slightly oval in cross-section, pronounced zigzagging from node to node, nodes prominent, smooth, light green when young, becoming dull brown near maturity; internodes 3–4 in./8–10 cm long, sulcate on one side; branches short, 0.3–0.5 in./8–13 mm long, but rarely considerably longer, borne in pairs or in threes at each of the upper nodes, bearing three to five leaves near their tips; sheaths purple initially, rapidly fading to straw yellow, chartaceous, with short blades, persistent. Foliage medium green, coarse in texture; leaves ovate-lanceolate, 1–4 in./2.5–10.0 cm long, 0.8–1.0 in./20–25 mm wide, broadly pointed at the base, gradually tapering two-thirds of the way from the base into an attenuate tip, margins with fine bristles, markedly and prominently tessellate, dark green above, dull grayish beneath, 12-to-14-nerved; petioles relatively long for leaf size; sheaths without bristles. Flowering

branchlets leafless, indeterminate; spikelets one-or-two-flowered; androecium and gynoecium three-merous.

Uses: This is the most attractive and elegant of the small, hardy bamboos; it has unique qualities unlike those of other gregarious species, one of which is its very slow rate of spread, which enhances its value somewhat as an ornamental. It is useful as ground cover and as a potted specimen.

Cultivation: Propagation is usually by plant division. This species grows in full sun or light shade and prefers acid soils; alkaline soils will cause leaf burn. The foliage is injured at temperatures below 10°F/ − 12°C, but if the rhizomes have been adequately protected by mulch, the plants will perenniate successfully. The plants are root hardy in zone 6 if the roots are well protected; the culms are hardy in the warmer parts of zone 7. Although it is a rhizomatous bamboo, it seldom becomes invasive, as the plants usually form a dense clump. It is not as invasive in cold climates as it is in warmer climates.

REFERENCES

McClure, F. A. 1946. *The genus Bambusa and some of its first-known species. Blumea, Suppl.* 3:90–116.

———. 1957. *Bamboos of the genus Phyllostachys under cultivation in the United States with a key for their identification.* USDA Handbook No. 114. Washington, D.C.: Govt. Printing Office.

Young, Robert A. 1945. Bamboos for American Horticulture. I, II. *Natl. Hort. Mag.* 24(3):171–196, 24(4):274–291.

———. 1946. Bamboos for American Horticulture. III, IV, V. *Natl. Hort. Mag.* 25(1):40–64, 25(3):257–283, 25(4):352–365.

Young, Robert A., and J. R. Haun. 1961. *Bamboos in the United States: Description, Culture, Utilization.* USDA Handbook No. 193. Washington, D.C.: Govt. Printing Office.

3

Grasslike Plants

Several groups of grasslike plants are in common usage with ornamental grasses, rushes, and sedges in landscape development and improvement. Although these particular plants range from small, aquatic herbs to woody shrub forms, they all possess some grasslike characteristics. Some forms are readily distinguished from grasses, whereas others resemble grasses very closely and are often difficult to distinguish from them. The attribute most grasslike plants have in common with true grasses is their foliage or leaves. The filiform stems of certain grasslike species resemble grasses very closely and give them a grasslike appearance. Other species closely related to the grass family possess grasslike attributes, but they are less obvious. Very often, small, aquatic herbs occupy the same habitat as do aquatic grasses; they are commonly found growing in mixed stands in damp or wet areas in full sun or light shade. Many grasslike plants and true grasses share the same plant-hardiness zones. This is mutually advantageous when both types are used in the same area in landscape improvement.

Representatives of 65 species in 18 genera distributed among 10 plant families were arbitrarily chosen to demonstrate their value as ornamentals in landscape improvement. All of these plants possess some grasslike characteristics to varying degrees, although the ornamental value of some species may be questionable. Undoubtedly, there are many other grasslike plants of equal value for use in ornamental horticulture. The species included represent only a very small number of those that deserve consideration.

VARIATION AMONG GRASSLIKE PLANTS

Considerable variation exists among grasslike species in plant form, color, size, and growth habit. Grasslike species include small aquatic and semiaquatic herbs and large, woody, terrestrial types with little resemblance to grasses except their foliage. The following criteria deserve consideration in the choice of grasslike plants for use in ornamental horticulture. Relative winter hardiness is of paramount importance among perennial species. Tolerance of acid soils is important among aquatic and semiaquatic herbs. Likewise, tolerance of alkaline soils is important among other grasslike plants used as ornamentals. Both shade and drought tolerance are important considerations in the choice of grasslike species in ornamental horticulture. The compatibility of grasslike plants among themselves and with other ornamentals is an all-important consideration in their use with other ornamentals, including ornamental grasses, rushes, and sedges. The optimum value of grasslike plants is derived from their prudent use with other ornamentals in producing a pleasing effect. Grasslike plants should be used in compatible mixed stands, where they and other ornamentals complement each other. As with other ornamentals they should neither be overused nor neglected altogether.

The range in plant form among grasslike species includes wandering Jew, *Tradescantia* and *Zebrina* species, trailing, decumbent, succulent herbs of more or less irregular form, and erect, rushlike, common horsetail, *Equisetum hyemale.* Cespitose, low-growing, mat-forming herbs such as lily-of-the-valley, *Convallaria majalis,* represent a plant form that is totally different from erect *Yucca* species, with short simple or branched caudexes and copious leaves arising from a running rootstock.

Many grasslike plants are grown primarily for their colorful foliage. A wide range of color and color patterns is exhibited among grasslike plants. Leaves of various shades of green are common among many species. Species whose foliage is of a color other than green are usually more desirable and highly esteemed than ordinary green-leaved species. The foliage of black mondo grass, *Ophiopogon plansicapus,* is uniformly bluish black or almost black. Many species have cultivars with variegated foliage; the variegation may be in the form of horizontal or longitudinal stripes or spots on the leaves. The stripes and spots are of various colors and hues; they appear in numerous combinations, forming different color patterns. Many species and cultivars have variegated foliage whose leaves have longitudinal stripes of various colors and hues. Species with outstanding foliage of this type include certain cultivars of the following species: *Acorus gramineus, Chlorophytum* species, *Tradescantia albiflora, Yucca aloifolia,* and *Zebrina pendula.* The stems of variegated horsetail, *Equisetum variegatum,* have alternate green and light yellow stripes. The diversity in the coloration of grasslike plants is not lacking. This diversity should be exploited to the maximum extent in the use of grasslike plants in landscape improvement.

The grasslike species herein included range in height from about 6 in./1.5 dm to over 10 ft/3.1 m. For convenience, the genera are grouped according to size in Table 3.1.

Yucca species, which range from 1 to 9 ft/0.3 to 2.8 m high, are occasionally grown indoors as potted specimens. The smaller forms (i.e., 6–24 in./1.5–6.0 dm high) are often used as house plants, and the larger types are usually grown in the garden. Yuccas, as well as many other ornamentals that attain considerable size when grown outdoors, are much reduced in size when grown indoors.

The growth habit of grasslike plants influences the manner in which they are used in the garden or in landscape improvement. Grasslike plants included herein range from aquatic to semiaquatic to terrestrial forms. The sprawling growth habit of wandering Jew, *Zebrina pendula,* is quite different from that of the erect, rushlike perennial common horsetail. Other terrestrial forms with a sprawling growth habit include succulent herbs such as *Chlorophytum, Liriope,* and *Tradescantia.* Additional variation in growth habit is evident in larger, erect herbs such as *Acorus, Equisetum, Typha,* and *Yucca* species. Acaulescent, sod-forming herb mondo grass, *Ophiopogon jaburan* and scapose densely tufted lily turf, *Liriope muscari,* form good ground cover. Cespitose forms such as fangrass, *Reineckia carnea,* form clumps. The succulent herbs of *Tradescantia* species, with their sprawling growth habit, are ideal as house plants in hanging baskets.

PLANT TOLERANCE

The tolerance of highly acid or alkaline soils has some influence on the selection and use of grasslike plants in ornamental horticulture. Acid-tolerant aquatic and semiaquatic plants are usually required for low, wet sites in or near pools and ponds or along slow-moving streams. Calamus, *Acorus calamus,* cattails, *Typha* species, lily-of-the-valley, *Convallaria majalis,* stargrass, *Hypoxis hirsuta,* and St.

Table 3.1   Height of Grasslike Plants by Genus

0.5–1.0 ft (0.2–0.3 m)	1–2 ft (0.3–0.6 m)	2–4 ft (0.6–1.2 m)	4–10 ft (1.2–3.1 m)
Convallaria	Chlorophytum	Acorus	Phormium
Ophiopogon	Hypoxis	Butomus	Typha
Reineckia	Liriope	Commelina	Yucca
Tradescantia	Sisyrinchium	Equisetum	
Zebrina		Xerophyllum	
		Xyris	

Mary's grass, *Xyris baldwiniana,* are among grasslike herbs that thrive in acid soils, the last one being perhaps the most acid tolerant. These are the type plants that are best suited for the bog or water garden. Other situations in dry, rocky, alkaline-tolerant soils in low-rainfall belts require alkaline-tolerant ornamentals such as *Yucca* species.

Drought tolerance may not be as important as shade tolerance in the selection and use of grasslike plants. Most terrestrial forms possess some degree of drought tolerance; in other words, they are adaptable to a rather wide range of soil-moisture conditions. The aquatic and semiaquatic species are used in wet locations to which they are adapted. *Yucca* species exemplify drought-tolerant types that are useful in dry soils in arid regions.

Shade-tolerant grasslike plants are needed in the home and in many locations in the garden and landscape, such as in wooded sites and in understory plantings. Some amount of shade tolerance is required of species that are used as home and greenhouse plants. Some grasslike plants thrive in full sun, whereas others perform equally well in full sun or semishade, and some are best suited for shaded locations. Many forms may be maintained outside in full sun or semishade during the summer and indoors during the winter. Small, succulent, cespitose, mat-forming herbs, especially their variegated forms, are commonly used as edging or ground-cover plants in shaded, understory stands among flowers and shrubbery. Small, succulent, aquatic herbs prefer shaded, wet sites, particularly variegated forms whose foliage is subject to leaf scald when grown in full sun. Certain of these terrestrial and aquatic herbs are equally useful as house plants. The variegated forms of grasslike plants are widely used in several ways in shaded, dark nooks of the garden. Their light, colorful foliage usually brightens such sites, making them more attractive. The light variegated foliage of those herbs, which are subject to damage in full sun, renders them ideally suited for shaded sites. One example of a shade-tolerant, grasslike plant is lily-of-the-valley, which exemplifies a herbaceous ground-cover plant admirably adapted to shaded sites. Certain species of *Reineckia, Sisyrinchium, Tradescantia,* and *Zebrina* are likewise useful in shaded locations; some of these are commonly used as house plants.

WINTER HARDINESS

A knowledge of winter hardiness is helpful in the selection of grasslike plants for use in the various plant-hardiness zones and in their sustained maintenance. The winter hardiness of the species described herein is given where known. Species are available that will survive in a major portion of the contiguous United States. Species of the following genera possess a wide range of winter hardiness (i.e., zones 2–10): *Acorus, Hypoxis, Liriope, Ophiopogon, Sisyrinchium, Typha, Xerophyllum, Xyris,* and *Yucca.* Specimen plantings of *Yucca filamentosa*—Adam's needle, for example—are a perfect foil for some other ornamentals in zone 6; lily turf, *Liriope* species, adapted as far north as zone 6, provides a pleasing ground cover. Weak perennial herbs of tropical origin such as *Chlorophytum* and *Zebrina* are useful in the warmer parts of zones 9 and 10. Many of these herbs are commonly used as houseplants in colder regions. As potted specimens, their longevity is increased by their being transferred indoors and outdoors to coincide with seasonal changes.

USES

Ornamental

The various ways in which grasslike plants are used as ornamentals are given in tabular form in Appendix 3. Some of these species possess utilitarian value in addition to ornamental value. The use of these plants in the home and in improving the garden and landscape is presented in Appendix 3.

Accent plants are used to emphasize the boldness and attractiveness of other ornamentals in the garden. Small acaulescent and caulescent cespitose or sod-forming herbs are in common usage as accent plants in foreground borders, in understory plantings among shrubbery, and in flower beds. Almost all grasslike plants are grown for their colorful foliage. Leaves of various shapes, sizes, and color comprise the paramount attractive attribute of grasslike plants. Plants of unusual foliage color are best suited as accent plants, because their foliage produces various contrasts in color to green-leaved ornamentals; such forms include *Liriope, Ophiopogon,* and *Zebrina* species (Appendix 3, column 1). The blackish green foliage of the cultivars of black mondo grass, *Ophiopogon plansicapus,* certainly offers a sharp contrast to ordinary green-leaved ornamentals in border plantings. Examples of more subtle contrasts in color to other green-leaved ornamentals include the variegated foliage of lily-of-the-valley cultivars and the variably colored foliage of wandering Jew, *Zebrina pendula.* More colors are displayed in the leaves of wandering Jew cultivars than in those of black mondo grass, although they are more subtle in contrast. These and other accent plants provide a contrast in plant form and color to other green-leaved ornamentals, thus accentuating the latter. Other species, in addition to those cited, are equally valuable as accent plants. Many other combinations in plant size, color, and form are possible by using various species as accent plants.

Outstanding specimen plants are much needed and used in ornamental horticulture, including those grown indoors in movable containers and those grown outside in the garden. Small, cespitose, green and variegated forms are used as house plants indoors and in foreground borders or shaded corners of the garden. The spider plant, *Chlorophytum comosum,* best exemplifies this type of use (Appendix 3, column 2). The succulent, variegated forms of spider plant are useful as clumped specimens in foreground borders in shaded nooks of the garden in zone 10 or as house plants in hanging baskets in colder climates. The ornamental value of chlorophytums lies in their foliage, since the flowers are usually small and rather inconspicuous. Small, low-growing, black mondo grass is an excellent specimen plant when grown in clumps in foreground borders. Tropical forms such as New Zealand flax, *Phormium tenax,* and *Yucca filamentosa,* are widely used as house plants and as clumped specimens in the garden in the warmer parts of zones 9 and 10. Larger, tropical, woody plants with grasslike foliage are universally used as specimens both indoors and outdoors in zone 10. Hardy *Yucca* species are used in specimen plantings in middleground and background borders, in rock gardens, and in other sites in zones 6 through 8; weaker perennial forms of tropical origin are used in a similar manner in zones 8 through 10.

The appearance of foreground borders is improved through the use of edging plants, as is that of flower beds, walkways, trails, driveways, patios, and areas around pools, ponds, and swimming pools. Edging plants are needed for dry, sunny sites, such as the rock garden, and for shaded, wet locations, such as the water garden. Edging plants surrounding flower beds or in foreground borders are usually shaded for a portion of the day or grow in light shade, and must therefore be shade tolerant. Edging plants are usually small in stature, outstanding in color, and capable of producing an attractive ground cover. Small cespitose types are useful and attractive in small clumps in foreground borders, whereas other types are used in massed stands, usually covering small areas. Lily turf is probably the best-known small succulent herb universally used for edging. The small, mat-forming plants are admirably adapted to wet and dry sites, either in full sun or in shaded areas. The dark green leaves of lily turf and the variegated leaves of its variants are attractive during spring, summer, and fall. The plants are deciduous, however, and are killed to ground level in zones 5, 6, and 7. The variegated cultivars of Japanese sweetflag, *Acorus gramineus,* produce colorful edgings around ponds and pools in the water garden; their small size does not detract from the horizontal impression of the water (Appendix 3, columns 4, 6, 10). Blue-eyed grass, *Sisyrinchium angustifolium,* is particularly valuable as an edging plant, partly because of its small size, ground-covering ability, colorful foliage, and long flowering period (Appendix 3, column 4). Lily-of-the-valley is valuable as an edging plant in foreground borders because of its shade tolerance. Larger water-loving species, such as flowering rush, *Butomus umbellatus,* and yellow-eyed grasses, *Xyris* species, are useful along the edges of naturalized wet areas and bogs surrounding the formal garden or adjacent to it. Plants of different sizes, colors, and growth habit are useful in different situations for edging.

Some grasslike species have multiple uses as ornamentals; for example, lily turf is an excellent edging plant and is equally useful as ground cover in full sun or shade in wet or dry sites. Species capable of producing good ground cover are required for various locations and situations in landscaping. Ground-cover plants are needed for wet and dry locations, either in full sun or shade in tropical, subtropical, and temperate regions. Those species used in temperate regions must be cold tolerant. A basic requirement of ground-cover plants is that they form a thick, complete cover capable of being sustained for extended periods. Ground covers are needed for various situations in landscape improvement, such as along streams, walks, trails, and driveways, in open areas, in shaded woodlands and on earthen dams. Plants of various types and growth habit are required to fill these diverse needs. Mat-forming, stoloniferous types are usually best suited as ground cover; however, many cespitose forms whose foliage forms a complete cover are admirably suited for this purpose. Species with some ornamental value, such as attractive foliage in addition to ground-covering capability, are most desired and sought. Hardy, cespitose, mat-forming stargrass in simple culture in full sun on impoverished, acid, dry soils exemplifies one use of ground covers. Similarly, hardy, shade-tolerant lily-of-the-valley is an excellent ground cover in shaded woods. The large rhizomatous herbs, cattails, *Typha* species, form an excellent ground cover in full sun on low, wet, acid soils, as do smaller yellow-eyed grasses, *Xyris* species (Appendix 3, column 6). Wandering Jew, *Tradescantia bracteata,* is a colorful ground cover for understory plantings, in flower beds, and among shrubbery. Fortunately, grasslike, ground-cover plants are available to suit the needs of most situations in landscape improvement.

Grasslike herbs are used successfully in border plantings in compatible stands with flowers, ornamental grasses, shrubs, and other ornamentals. Grasslike plants used in border plantings are arbitrarily characterized by size in their use in foreground, middleground, and background borders (Appendix 3, column 7). Other important considerations in the choice of species for border plantings are winter hardiness and compatibility with other ornamentals in mixed stands. According to the definition of borders, small, low-growing species are recommended for foreground borders, middle-sized plants for middleground borders, and large forms (i.e., 5 ft / 1.5 m high or higher) for background borders. Border plantings usually consist of accent, edging, or specimen plants established singly or in small groups. Grasslike plants are best used in mixed stands in borders containing other ornamentals. Their presence adds diversity in plant form and color to the landscape. Species used in border plantings are chosen mainly for the purpose for which they are grown—that is, as accent, edging, or specimen plants. An understory of low-growing, shade-tolerant, green-leaved lily turf provides a perfect foil for large, erect, variegated zebragrass, *Miscanthus sinensis* var. *zebrinus,* in background borders. Such a combination vividly demonstrates a striking contrast in plant form, size, growth habit, and color. A clump of variegated wandering Jew, *Tradescantia albiflora,* established in mixed stands of green-leaved grasses such as weeping windmill grass, *Chloris distichophylla,* provides a more subtle contrast in color, size, and form in middleground borders. Beargrass, *Xerophyllum asphodeloides,* with its small, showy, creamy-white flowers, exemplifies the use of grasslike herbs as specimen plants in middleground borders; hardy beargrass is adapted to zones 5 through 9. Large *Yucca* species are used as specimen plants in background borders in zones 6 through 10. Other similarities, and dissimilarities, if contrast is desired, are available in the choice and use of grasslike plants with other ornamentals in border plantings.

Naturalized areas of the garden or wild garden and immediate surroundings provide an excellent opportunity for the use of grasslike plants, especially perennial herbs, in landscape improvement. Aquatic grasslike plants, along with rushes, sedges, and water-loving grasses, are most useful in bogs, the water garden, or any low, constantly wet area. Any number of rushlike perennials, such as common horsetail, *Equisetum hyemale,* and herbs, including *Acorus, Butomus, Convallaria, Hypoxis, Sisyrinchium, Typha,* and *Xyris,* are useful as ground cover in naturalized areas of temperate regions (Appendix 3, column 8). Species of *Acorus, Hypoxis,* and *Typha* are used for the same purpose in warmer climates. Types adapted to dry sites include *Convallaria, Hypoxis, Sisyrinchium,* and *Xerophyllum,* and those adapted to wet sites include *Acorus, Butomus, Convallaria, Equisetum, Typha,* and *Xyris.* For dry sites, lily-of-the-valley provides an excellent ground cover for naturalizing shaded woodlots. Different species are required for naturalizing other areas. Beargrass, for example, is useful in naturalizing the wild garden, while so-called blue-eyed grasses provide excellent ground cover in simple culture in naturalized areas. Stargrass is useful as ground cover in naturalizing impoverished acid soils. Cattails and flowering rush are excellent plants for naturalizing the margins of lakes and ponds or the area along streams, as both species grow in wet soil, mud, or directly in shallow water. Blue-eyed grasses, *Sisyrinchium* species, and common horsetail are useful in naturalizing wet meadows or the area along streams in temperate regions. Smaller, yellow-eyed grasses, especially *Xyris baldwiniana* and *Xyris platylepis,* are especially useful for naturalizing wet in warmer climates (i.e., zones 8 through 10).

Some of the same grasslike species useful as ground cover in dry, sunny sites are also useful in pebble and rock gardens. Xerophytic species that thrive in full sun are usually best suited for these sites. Lily turf, fangrass, *Reineckia carnea,* and mondo grass are excellent species as ground-cover, accent, and edging plants in rock gardens (Appendix 3, column 9). Decorative *Yucca* species are commonly used as specimens in rock and pebble gardens in zones 6 through 10. These species, along with other grasslike plants, when used in combination with other fleshy xerophytic plants, usually result in a well-balanced, attractive pebble or rock garden.

Bog and water gardens require aquatic and semiaquatic species, including those that thrive in full sun or partial shade, usually in acid soils. Some of the same species used in naturalizing wet sites are also useful in bog and water gardens, for example, cattails and flowering rush, *Butomus umbellatus* (Appendix 3, columns 8 and 10). Tall cattails exemplify the use of large, attractive, aquatic herbs as specimen plants in the water garden. Small blue-eyed grass, Japanese sweetflag, fangrass, and wandering Jew (i.e., *Tradescantia* and *Zebrina* species) are used as edging plants in shaded areas of the water garden. Larger forms, such as common horsetail, and yellow-eyed grasses, both of which thrive in full sun, are commonly found useful in water gardens. Maximum effectiveness in the use of grasslike herbs in the water garden is achieved from their use with rushes, sedges, and other aquatic and semiaquatic ornamentals, including ornamental grasses.

Ornamental shade-tolerant, grasslike plants are much used and in great demand in ornamental horticulture. They are commonly used in the home, the formal or wild garden in wooded areas, and elsewhere in shaded areas. Species of tropical origin are grown indoors as potted plants in colder climates and outdoors in shaded areas in the warmer parts of zone 10, where diluted sunlight prevails. Potted specimens are easily transferred indoors and outdoors to coincide with seasonal changes. Low-growing, sod-forming, shade-tolerant, winter-hardy species, such as lily-of-the-valley and lily turf provide excellent ground cover in wooded sites, as does the small colorful cultivar of black mondo grass, Ebony Night. For ground cover in shaded sites in warmer climates, wandering Jew (i.e., *Tradescantia* and *Zebrina* species) are commonly used. Other low-growing species are needed as understory ground cover in flower beds and among shrubbery, whereas yet other forms are required as edging plants in borders. Shade density and duration are quite variable in such locations, requiring species of variable shade tolerance. Japanese sweetflag and its cultivars are excellent edging plants around pools in shaded areas of the water garden and along borders where they are partially shaded. Species of St. Bernard's lily, *Chlorophytum* species, of tropical origin, serve the same purpose in zones 9 and 10. Lily turf, in its many forms, is very popular and commonly used as edging in shaded and semishaded sites in zones 6 through 10. Spiderwort, *Tradescantia* species, provides good ground cover in simple culture in light shade in warm climates. Common horsetail provides good ground cover in massed stands in light shade in cool climates (i.e., zones 6 through 9).

Grasslike species commonly used in the home, necessarily in shade, include small, succulent, erect or trailing herbs such as *Tradescantia* and *Zebrina* species. Most trailing herbs usually found in the home are grown in hanging baskets.

Many of the herbaceous, grasslike species discussed herein are adaptable to shaded conditions, where they serve as accent, edging, ground-cover, and specimen plants in the garden and as potted house plants. Their ornamental value and usefulness are enhanced by their use in simple and mixed stands with other ornamentals in the garden.

Some grasslike plants have attractive flowers, although most are grown primarily for their colorful foliage. The many small white or pink flowers of lily-of-the-valley, which usually form in April or May, and the bright golden yellow, star-shaped flowers of stargrass are attractive on these small, grasslike species. On larger forms, the umbellate showy flowers of flowering rush and the copious creamy-white showy flowers of beargrass are quite conspicuous and interesting while remaining on the plants. The uniquely shaped and colorful flower heads of cattails, borne high above its yellowish green, distichous foliage, are conspicuous and attractive on the plants throughout late summer and early fall. The dark green or brownish green flower heads terminating this large, interesting herb gradually change color as they mature (Appendix 3, column 13). Although cattails are ubiquitous, they remain the center of interest in the water garden and other wet sites. White or violet flowers borne in large, terminal panicles of *Yucca* species, with their stiff, dark green, gladiate or spatulate leaves, comprise a magnificent specimen in dry regions. Beargrass, a hardy middle-sized herb, is a popular specimen in the rock garden, borders, or elsewhere, with its light green foliage and many-flowered oval panicles consisting of showy, creamy-white flowers.

Lily-of-the-valley is foremost among grasslike herbs whose inflorescences are commonly used as cut flowers (Appendix 3, column 14). The plants are commonly forced into bloom to provide cut flowers for both the home and the market. The small, light yellow flowers of *Sisyrinchium micranthum* are useful in fresh cut-flower arrangements, although they are rather short-lived.

Very few grasslike plants have flower heads that are adaptable for use in dried floral arrangements; large, colorful, cattail flower heads are an exception. When cut at the proper stage and handled properly, the flower heads will remain intact and attractive for a long time.

Attractive foliage is the outstanding attribute of many grasslike plants. The overall appearance of the foliage is comprised of the arrangement, color, shape, size, and texture of the leaves. The arrangement of leaves on grasslike plants is variable among species. Some examples include (1) the basal, tufted leaves of acaulescent, low-growing herbs, such as calamus, lily-of-the-valley, and lily turf; and (2) the cauline, coriaceous, gladiate leaves of Spanish dagger, *Yucca aloifolia*, borne near the top of the stems. The color, shape, size, and texture (leaf width) of leaves of grasslike plants are also variable. Color is the most visible striking and appealing characteristic of the foliage, with leaf arrangement, shape, and size becoming more apparent upon closer observation and examination. Leaf color ranges among various hues and shades of green, from light green to blackish green, including shades of blue, gray, purple, red, and yellow-green. Other foliage colors include reddish, purplish, and glaucous types. The blackish green foliage of black mondo grass provides an excellent example of unusual foliage color among grasslike plants. Species with variegated foliage add a new and interesting dimension in color. The pattern and color of variegated forms vary among species. The leaves of variegated forms usually have alternate longitudinal stripes of various shades of green, white, golden, pink, yellow, or purple in variable patterns. Other patterns of variation include transverse cross bands, mottled and flecked markings, and spots. The various colors are arranged in different patterns on the variegated forms. Leaf shapes of grasslike plants include the lanceolate-ovate to elliptic leaves of lily-of-the-valley, the oblanceolate, almost filiform, leaves of the spider plant, the spirally twisted leaves of yellow-eyed grass, *Xyris arenicola*, the narrowly linear leaves of lily turf, the gladiate leaves of blue yucca, *Yucca baccata*, and the spatulate leaves of Adam's needle, *Yucca filamentosa*. Leaf size varies from the small, filiform leaves of mondo grass to the long, gladiate, stiff leaves of blue yucca. These two species also demonstrate the wide variation in leaf texture, such as leaf width, among grasslike plants.

Some outstanding examples used to demonstrate the variation in foliage of grasslike plants include the following: the alternate, coriaceous, gladiate, dark green leaves of Spanish dagger, with denticulate margins; the dark green, stiff, coriaceous, spatulate leaves of Adam's needle, with filiferous margins; dark green foliage of blue-eyed grass and blackish green foliage of 'Ebony Knight,' black mondo grass; the variously colored foliage of wandering Jew (i.e., *Tradescantia* and *Zebrina* species); the glaucous or yellowish green, distichous leaves of cattails; the tufted, equitant, dark green leaves of calamus; and the basal, narrowly linear, dark green or variegated leaves of lily turf.

Although most grasslike plants are noteworthy for their foliage, some species are conspicuous for their flowers and foliage. Lily-of-the-valley is widely acclaimed for its flowers and foliage (Appendix 3, column 17). The plants are commonly forced into flower and widely used as houseplants.

Many grasslike plants are used as houseplants, including small, acaulescent herbs and larger, woody types. These plants are used along with other decorative species in greenhouses and various locations within and around the home. These decorative plants are grown in pots, hanging baskets, or other containers. Weak perennials of tropical origin are suitable for this form of culture, as they can be transferred both indoors and outdoors to coincide with seasonal changes. Potted specimens are commonly placed on porches, decks, and patios, around pools, or along paths, sidewalks, and driveways. Other cultural practices include placing the potted specimens in selected locations in the garden without embedding the pot, or in some cases, embedding the pot while it remains in the garden during the summer. The potted house plants may be enjoyed throughout the year in this form of culture; an added benefit is that the plants are usually revitalized by this procedure.

Foremost among succulent trailing herbs cultivated in hanging baskets are common spiderwort *(Tradescantia)* and wandering Jew *(Zebrina)* species, respectively (Appendix 3, column 18). The variously colored foliage of *Tradescantia albiflora* cascading from hanging baskets is a colorful, attractive ornamental. Wandering Jew, *Zebrina pendula,* is used in the same manner. Another way in which their foliage is exhibited to maximum effectiveness is by training the trailing stems on an upright trellis. The leaves of the typical form of *Zebrina pendula,* for example, have longitudinal white stripes above and are purplish beneath, thereby exhibiting various color patterns. The variously colored common spiderwort is widely acclaimed and universally used as a house plant. The different plant forms and foliage color of common spiderwort provide considerable choice in their use in the home. Certain small, acaulescent, succulent herbs such as Japanese sweetflag, lily-of-the-valley, lily turf, and mondo grass are widely acclaimed and commonly used as house plants. These small herbs, usually grown in pots, are used in conjunction with and to augment other ornamentals in the home.

Certain species of yellow-eyed grass are admirably adapted to low, wet, highly acid soils, where they are compatible with other aquatic herbs, rushes, sedges, and other water-loving plants. These acaulescent, rushlike herbs are ideal for naturalizing low, wet areas, including the water garden, the so-called wild garden, and peat bogs. The larger species of yellow-eyed grass are used on sandy, saline soils along the seashore. Outstanding among species used for this purpose are *Xyris fimbriata* and *Xyris platylepis.*

Two erect, aquatic, perennial grasslike herbs—cattails and flowering rush—are useful additions to naturalized stands in and around lake and pond margins. Their size and dense foliage provide excellent ground cover and wildlife protection in low, wet, coastal areas. The uniquely shaped flower heads of cattails and the rose-colored flowers of flowering rush are added attractions of these species.

Other Uses

Several grasslike plants have some economic value, in addition to their ornamental value. Lily-of-the-valley is useful as a perfume plant, and its rhizomes contain medicinal properties. The drug calamus is made from the perennial herb *Acorus calamus.* Ropes, strings, and similar products are made from the fibrous leaves of *Yucca* species. The silica stems of common horsetail are used occasionally in polishing. The rootstocks of cattail are used for aboriginal food; the leaves are used for making mats; and the fluff of the seedheads is used in stuffing pillows, while birds use it in building nests.

SELECTED SPECIES

The habitat, description, uses, and cultivation of the following selected species are arranged in alphabetical order by genera and by species within genera.

***Acorus* L. (Calamus, Flagroot, Redote, Sweetflag).** Name derived from the Greek *akoras,* the classical name for the plant. Type species, *Acorus calamus* L. There are two species native to Eurasia but introduced early and naturalized in the United States. Acaulescent, aromatic, rhizomatous, perennial herbs of marshy places, 1.5–6.0 ft/0.5–1.8 m high. Leaves tufted, ensiform, arising directly from horizontal rhizomes, equitant, grasslike. Peduncle and spathe a continuous unit, bearing a green spadix above the middle; perianth of six concave sepals. Flowers bisexual; stamens six, filaments linear, anthers one-locular, opening transversely, reniform; ovary superior, two- or three-locular, ovules orthotropus, several in each locule; fruit baccate, dry at maturity (Buell, 1935; Robinson and Fernald, 1908).

> **Latin name:** *Acorus calamus* L.
> **Synonym:** *Acorus calamus* var. *americanus* (Raf.) H. D. Wulff.
> **Cultivars:** 'Variegatus'
> **Common names:** Calamus, Sweetflag, Myrtle flag, Flagroot
> **Origin:** Central and East Asia (Egypt)
> **Habitat:** Marshes and ponds, cultivated
> **Hardiness:** Zones 2 through 9

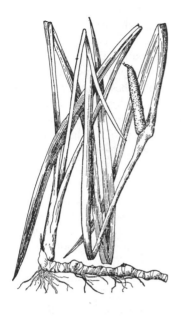

Acorus calamus. *Source:*
Wild Flowers in Kansas.
Kansas State Printing Plant.
1934.

Description: An acaulescent, cespitose, perennial herb, upright-open to spreading, with aromatic foliage and pinkish horizontal rhizomes about 0.6–0.8 in./15–20 mm thick with short joints and large brownish leaf scars. Scape and spathe in a continuous, leaflike unit bearing a greenish spadix. Scape simple, leaflike, trigonous, glabrous, 20–48 in./0.5–1.2 m high, bearing an apparently lateral blunt, tapering spikelike spadix of densely packed, very small flowers. A long, leaflike spathe borne immediately below the spadix forms an apparent continuation of the scape, but it is actually a lateral outgrowth from it, the spadix being terminal. Foliage dark green, medium in texture; leaves tufted, two-ranked, grasslike, equitant, erect, linear, and more or less ensiform, 18–40 in./0.5–1.0 m long, 0.3–0.8 in./8–20 mm wide, with a prominent midrib. Inflorescence a spadix, subtended by a spathe diverging laterally from the trigonous scape, brownish green, elongate-conic, 2–4 in./5–10 cm long, 0.2–0.4 in./5–10 mm thick; spathe linear, 6–20 in./1.5–5.0 dm long; flowers bisexual, yellowish brown; perianth of six rather narrow, concave sepals; ovary superior, two-or-three-locular; fruit baccate, crowded, obpyramidal, 0.10–0.15 in./3–4 mm; long, dry, hard, and gelatinous inside when mature. Flowering and fruiting occur from May through June, during which time the plants produce a sweet fragrance.

Uses: The ornamental value of calamus, like that of Japanese sweetflag, *Acorus gramineus,* lies in its use as ground cover in full sun in bog and water gardens. The plants resemble irises in appearance and growth habit. Calamus acts as a good backdrop for other foliaceous plants when grown outdoors. The economic value of calamus is its aromatic leaves and thick, creeping rootstocks, which are the source of the drug calamus. The variegated cultivar Variegatus is usually grown along with calamus as an ornamental. Calamus also has a niche in indoor and outdoor plantings, if for no other reason than its sweet fragrance.

Cultivation: Propagation is by plant or root division. The plants may be propagated at any time for indoor plantings; for outdoor plantings the divisions should be made in early spring or fall. The plants thrive best in full sun in bog and water gardens. When calamus is grown indoors, the planters should be kept moist at all times; they should be placed in a pan of water or in an indoor pool; periodically, the water should be drained from the pan or pool. Ordinary potting soil is a satisfactory medium for plants grown indoors; light of medium or, preferably, high intensity is required for optimum growth. Calamus thrives in ordinary garden soil; however, it prefers acid soils. The plants are easy to propagate and grow; outdoor plantings should be made in ordinary garden soil in water about 8–10 in./2.0–2.5 dm deep. The plants spread quickly, and care must be taken to prevent their spreading into unwanted areas by reducing the size of the clumps in the spring. Calamus remains green throughout the year when grown indoors. It is possible to grow calamus outdoors in containers or large pots; however, it is easier to establish it in a permanent location where it receives full sun, preferably in bogs or water gardens.

Cultivars: *Acorus calamus* L. 'Variegatus' The leaves of this cultivar are variegated, with longitudinal, alternate stripes of green and yellow. The plants and plant parts are similar in size to those of calamus. This cultivar is much more attractive than the species, and it produces the same sweet fragrance as calamus.

Latin name: *Acorus gramineus* Ait.
Cultivars: 'Albovariegatus,' 'Ogon' Golden variegated sweetflag, 'Pusillus' Dwarf sweetflag, 'Variegatus' Japanese whitestripe sweetflag
Common names: Japanese sweetflag, Grassy-leaved sweetflag
Origin: Asia, Japan
Habitat: Cultivated
Hardiness: Zones 6 through 9
Description: An acaulescent, cespitose, perennial herb with slender, nonaromatic rhizomes. Scape simple, leaflike, glabrous, trigonous, 6–18 in./1.5–4.5 dm high. Foliage dull dark green, fine in texture; leaves crowded at the base, erect, narrowly linear, ensiform, 4–6 in./1.0–1.5 dm long, 0.20–0.25 in./5–6 mm wide, without a distinct midrib. Inflorescence borne on an elongated spadix, subtended by a linear spathe, which is a flat prolongation of the scape; spadix dull green, linear-cylindric, 2–3 in./5–8 cm long, 0.1–0.2 in./3–5 mm broad; spathe linear, 2–6 in./0.5–1.5 dm long; flowers light green, dioecious; perianth of six scalelike, concave sepals; ovary superior, two-or-three-locular; fruit baccate, crowded, one-to-four-seeded. Flowering and fruiting occur sporadically, usually in late spring and early summer.

Uses: Japanese sweetflag and its cultivars are best used in warm climates. The plants provide an ideal ground cover in open woods, along wooded borders, or in partial shade of shrubbery; they are also useful for edging around ponds and pools, where their small size does not detract from the horizontal effect of the water. The lighter-colored variegated types are even more spectacular than ordinary green-leaved Japanese sweetflag; their color and texture add another dimension to the landscape in outdoor plantings. The small size and decumbent growth habit of these plants make them useful as specimen plantings in bog and water gardens. The fine-textured leaves of Japanese sweetflag and the variegated foliage of its variants remain attractive throughout the year, either in outdoor landscape plantings or indoors as house plants. These small, colorful plants are popular as potted plants indoors; they act as a good backdrop for other foliaceous plants.

Cultivation: Propagation is by plant division. Plants used in indoor plantings may be propagated at any time; early spring is the best time for outdoor landscape plantings. The plants grow best in a fertile, moist or wet soil. Japanese sweetflag requires medium to high light intensity and moist or wet soil when grown indoors. Ordinary potting soil or a mixture of equal parts of soil, sand, and peat moss are suitable media in which to grow plants indoors; the soil must be kept moist or slightly wet but well drained. Outdoor plantings should be located so as to be shaded somewhat in the middle of the day.

Cultivars: *Acorus gramineus* Ait. 'Albovariegatus'   This cultivar has leaves with alternate, longitudinal, green and white stripes.

Acorus gramineus Ait. 'Ogon' Golden variegated sweetflag   This cultivar is aromatic; it is 18–24 in./4.5–6.0 dm high; the variegated leaves have alternate, longitudinal stripes of green and gold. The plants thrive in mud at water's edge.

Acorus gramineus Ait. 'Pusillus' Dwarf sweetflag   The miniature plants, with vibrant green foliage, are 4–6 in./1.0–1.5 dm high. This small, attractive form is ideal for pool edgings; because of its small size, it could be used in aquariums and terrariums.

Acorus gramineus Ait. 'Variegatus'   This variant of Japanese sweetflag is aromatic and similar in size to the parent species; the longitudinally striped leaves of alternate green and white stripes arrange themselves like miniature folding fans.

***Butomus* L. (Flowering rush, Jonc fleuri).** A monotypic genus. An aquatic, erect, rhizomatous, perennial herb. Flowers perfect; perianth of three green or brightly colored, persistent sepals, three-colored petals, which are imbricate or involute in bud; stamens nine or more; carpels six or more, forming many-seeded follicles; seeds straight, curved, or folded, without endosperm. Leaves radical or clustered at remote nodes of the floating stem, ensiform or with deleted blades; flowers showy, solitary or in umbels, with large bracts (Fernald, 1970).

Latin name: *Butomus umbellatus* L.
Common names: Flowering rush, Grassy rush, Water gladiolus
Origin: Europe, Asia

Butomus umbellatus.
Habit, × 1/6;
inflorescence, × 1/2;
flower, × 1. *Source: Vascular
Plants of the Pacific Northwest.
Pt. 1.* Univ. of Washington
Press. 1969.

Habitat: Mud, shallow water, wet soil

Hardiness: Zones 4 and 5

Description: An erect, acaulescent, aquatic perennial herb with thick, fleshy rhizomes; the plants produce many very small tubers in the autumn. Scape erect, 2–4 ft/0.6–1.2 m high, smooth, more or less flat. Foliage medium green, coarse in texture; leaves densely tufted, two-ranked, erect, ensiform, trigonous at base, long attenuate, 2–3 ft/6–9 dm long, 0.7–1.0 in./18–25 mm wide, margins sharply serrate. Inflorescence a bracted terminal umbel, bracts three, leaflike, gladiate, purplish, terminating in a sharp point, 2–3 in./5–8 cm long, slightly retrorse; flowers numerous, perfect, 0.8–1.0 in./20–25 mm across, in scapose loose umbels, pedicellate, pedicels erect or ascending, slender, 2–3 in./5–8 cm long; perianth six-merous, segments persistent, more or less 0.8–1.0 in./20–25 mm broad, rose-colored, the petals deeply colored outside; androecium of nine stamens, with two-locular, basifixed, short anthers borne on linear-subulate filaments; gynoecium six-merous, carpels, barely coherent at base, verticillate, style persistent, stigma elongate, ovary superior, ovules many, young pistils and anthers dark red; fruit six inflated, long-beaked follicles, united at base, about 0.4 in./10 mm long, opening on the inner margin; seeds numerous, striate, straight. Flowering and fruiting occur from June through August.

Uses: Flowering rush is a useful addition to naturalized stands in and around the margins of lakes and ponds. It provides additional food and protection for migratory waterfowl. The umbels of pink or rose-colored flowers are an added attraction. This herb is also adaptable for use as a potted plant. The range of adaptation of flowering rush overlaps that of some other aquatic plants, such as *Typha* species, which are used primarily for the same purpose. The plants are well suited for naturalizing ponds and pools and for use in water gardens, where their long, linear, straplike leaves make interesting reflections on the water and provide contrast to the flat, horizontal leaves of various other aquatic plants, such as water lilies.

Cultivation: Propagation is by seeding and by plant division. The most expeditious method of establishing stands is by plant division and by planting the tubers produced in the autumn. Flowering rush is easily propagated, but the plants require some form of containment when grown outdoors, as they are very invasive. The plants grow in wet soil, in mud, or directly in shallow water.

Chlorophytum **Ker-Gawl. (St. Bernard's lily, Spider plant).** Type species, *Chlorophytum inornatum* Ker-Gawl. There are more than 200 species, native to all continents except Europe and North America. Succulent, rhizomatous herbs; leaves basal, sessile and narrowly linear or petiolate and lanceolate to ovate. Flowers small, regular, whitish or light greenish, disposed singly or in groups in bracted racemes or panicles; perianth segments six, separate; stamens six; fruit a loculicidal capsule, angled, lobed or three-winged (Hortus Third, 1977).

Latin name: *Chlorophytum amaniense* Engl.
Origin: Eastern Africa
Habitat: Cultivated
Hardiness: Zones 9 and 10
Description: A small, trailing, succulent herb. Foliage soft, tufted, pinkish, becoming orange at maturity, glossy, fine to medium in texture. Leaves

basal, grasslike, oblanceolate, 12–18 in./3.0–4.5 dm long, about 0.2–0.5 in./5–13 mm wide, long attenuate, 20-to-25-nerved, petiolate, petioles 4–6 in./1.0–1.5 dm long, channeled, pinkish orange like margins of the leaf blades. Flowers small, shorter than the subtending bracts, greenish, in dense, terminal racemes, 3–8 in./0.8–2.0 dm long, borne on scapes about 1–2 in./2.5–5.0 cm long.

Uses: Planted in flower beds and borders as accent, bedding, edging, or specimen plants in zones 9 and 10; used as a house plant in colder climates.

Cultivation: Chlorophytums are easy to propagate, grow, and maintain. They thrive in a soil-based mixture of one part sterilized, coarse-textured soil, one part peat moss or leaf mold, and one part coarse sand to which is added one part dehydrated cow manure or a balanced granular or powdered fertilizer. The fertilizer should be applied according to the instructions on the package. Propagation is by seeding and by plant division; the latter is most commonly employed. Usual propagation is by detaching several rooted plantlets from growing stems for planting in small (i.e., 3 in./8 cm) clay or plastic pots. When planting, leave enough space (1 in./25 mm) below the rim of the pot for root growth and expansion. When the root ball reaches the top of the pot, the plants should be transferred to larger pots, planters, or hanging baskets, or should be established in the garden. Usually a sufficient number of rooted plantlets is available as propagating stocks, thus making it unnecessary to attempt rooting plantlets. Should this not be the case, the plantlets may be rooted by applying a standard root-promoting substance to the lower portion and inserting them in a pot containing a peat-based mixture or equal parts of sand and peat moss. The plants should be planted in a soil-based mixture when the roots are about 1 in./25 mm long. Another method of propagation involves laying the growing stems of the parent plant with its attached plantlets on the ground (in the garden) or in adjacent pots and firming the soil around each clump of plantlets. After the plantlets have become well rooted and established, the stems should be severed from the parent plant. The space requirements may be a serious drawback to this method of propagation.

Chlorophytums require bright light when grown indoors, preferably some direct sunlight, especially during the short days of winter. During long, summer days, the plants thrive in indirect sunlight, or light or intermittent shade; the foliage, especially of variegated forms, scorches easily in direct midday sun. Normal room temperatures are adequate for most forms; they do not thrive in temperatures below about 45°F/7°C. Chlorophytums thrive best in moist warmth. Keep the potting mixture thoroughly moist during active growth. When the plants are in a resting state, water them only enough to keep the potting mixture moist, allowing the top portion to dry out between waterings. Insufficient watering results in permanently brown, unattractive, leaf tips. Apply standard liquid fertilizer at fortnightly intervals to actively growing plants. Chlorophytums may be enjoyed throughout the year when seasonally transferred indoors and outdoors in movable containers. The plants are easily maintained in the resting stage by removing a portion of the stems and accompanying plantlets, thereby reducing the stress for moisture and fertility.

Latin name: *Chlorophytum arundinaceum* Baker
Origin: East Himalayas
Habitat: Cultivated
Hardiness: Zones 8 through 10
Description: A small, trailing, succulent herb. Foliage soft, dull yellowish green, medium in texture. Leaves basal, grasslike, oblanceolate, 12–18 in./3.0–4.5 dm long, 0.4–0.6 in./10–15 mm wide, long attenuate, 20-to-30-nerved, petiolate, petioles channeled, 3–4 in./8–10 cm long. Flowers small, shiny, white, in dense terminal racemes, 6–8 in./1.5–2.0 dm long; borne on scapes 10–12 in./2.5–3.0 dm long.
Uses: Cultivated as a bedding or accent plant in flower beds or borders or in movable containers. This species is grown outdoors in zones 9 and 10. Most commonly grown in hanging baskets or other containers as a house plant in colder climates.
Cultivation: Propagation is by seeding and plant division.

Latin name: *Chlorophytum bickertii* (Karrer) Baker
Origin: Gabon
Habitat: Cultivated
Hardiness: Zones 9 and 10
Description: A small, evergreen, perennial herb. Foliage yellowish white, soft, fine in texture. Leaves basal, grasslike, linear-lanceolate, 6–8 in./1.5–2.0 dm long, 0.2–0.4 in./5–10 mm wide, long attenuate, striped yellowish white, particularly along the margins, distinctly petiolate. Flowers small, greenish white, in loose, terminal racemes shorter than the leaves; pedicellate, pedicels jointed below the middle.
Uses: This small, succulent herb is most commonly used as a house plant.
Cultivation: Propagation is by seeding and by plant division, usually the latter.

Latin name: *Chlorophytum capense* (L.) Voss
Synonym: *Chlorophytum elatium* (Ait.) R. Br.
Origin: South Africa
Habitat: Cultivated
Hardiness: Zones 9 and 10
Description: A small, trailing, succulent herb; barely proliferous. Foliage glaucous; leaves form a loose rosette. Leaves basal, 18–24 in./4.5–6.0 dm long, 0.5–0.7 in./13–18 mm wide, long attenuate, firm; scape compressed. Flowers small, white, borne in a loose, many-branched panicle; seeds 8–10 in each locule.

Uses: Grown as a bedding, accent, edging, or specimen plant in zones 9 and 10 and as a houseplant in colder climates.

Cultivation: Propagation is by seeding and by plant division, usually the latter.

Latin name: *Chlorophytum comosum* (Thunb.) Jacques
Synonym: *Chlorophytum sternbergianum* Steud.
Common names: Spider plant, Spider ivy, Ribbon plant, Walking antherium
Origin: South Africa
Habitat: Cultivated
Hardiness: Zones 9 and 10
Description: A small, succulent, proliferous herb. Foliage soft, medium green, more or less tufted. Leaves basal, grasslike, linear to linear-lanceolate, 12–18 in./3.0–4.5 dm long, 0.50–0.75 in./13–19 mm wide, arching, long attenuate; scape cylindrical. Flowers small, white, borne in a loose panicle; seeds three to five in each locule.
Uses: Spider plant is grown in the garden in zones 9 and 10 and as a house plant in colder climates. The variegated cultivars should always be grown in shaded locations. The spider plant, its cultivars, and all other chlorophytums are all useful in controlling pollution in the home. All other house plants are also useful for the same purpose.
Cultivation: Propagation is by seeding and by plant division.

Latin name: *Chlorophytum macrophyllum* (A. Rich.) Asch. ex Baker
Origin: Tropical Africa
Habitat: Cultivated
Hardiness: Zones 9 and 10
Description: A small, succulent herb. Foliage soft, medium green. Leaves basal, grasslike, lanceolate, 24–30 in./6.0–7.6 dm long, 0.6–0.8 in./15–20 mm wide, 30-to-40-nerved, narrowing into a winged, petiolelike base. Flowers small, white, borne in terminal racemes on scapes 12–14 in./3.0–3.5 dm long; pedicels jointed near the apex.
Uses: This species may be grown outside successfully in the warmer parts of zones 9 and 10; it is useful as a house plant in colder climates.
Cultivation: Propagation is by seeding and by plant division.

Latin name: *Chlorophytum nepalense* (Lindl.) Baker
Origin: Nepal
Habitat: Cultivated
Hardiness: Zones 9 and 10
Description: A small, succulent herb. Foliage soft, light green. Leaves basal, grasslike, sessile, linear-lanceolate, 12–18 in./3.0–4.5 dm long, 0.4–0.6 in./10–15 mm wide, light green above, glaucous beneath, long attenuate. Flow-

ers small, borne in panicles, 2–3 ft/6–9 dm long, white, pedicellate, pedicels jointed at or below the middle.

Uses: The plants may be grown outside in zones 9 and 10. They are usually grown as house plants in colder climates.

Cultivation: Propagation is by seeding and by plant division.

Latin name: *Chlorophytum orchidastrum* Lindl.
Origin: Sierra Leone
Habitat: Cultivated
Hardiness: Zones 9 and 10
Description: An evergreen, perennial herb. Foliage soft, medium glossy green, fine in texture. Leaves basal, grasslike, oblong to ovate-lanceolate, 8–10 in./2.0–2.5 dm long, 0.3–0.4 in./8–10 mm wide, long attenuate, 10-to-24-nerved, glossy green, tapering into a distinct channeled petiole 8–10 in./2.0–2.5 dm long. Flowers greenish white, small, borne in panicles.

Uses: The plants are grown outdoors in zones 9 and 10 and indoors as house plants in colder climates.

Cultivation: Propagation is by seeding and by plant division.

Commelina **L. (Dayflower, Widow's tears).** The name commemorating Kasper Commelin, a Dutch botanist. Lectotype, *Commelina communis* L. There are about 225 species, mainly in tropical and subtropical regions of both hemispheres. Herbaceous annuals or perennials with jointed subsucculent stems. Stems initially erect, in some species eventually decumbent. Leaves alternate, sheathing the stems below; leaf blades ovate to linear, leaf margins and throat of the sheath often lined with white to reddish trichomes. Inflorescence a cyme, closely subtended and enclosed by a closely folded, oblique spathe. Flowers borne inside a cymbiform spathe that is open across the top, three to five flowers in each spathe, the flowers open in succession three or four days apart. Flowers bluish, exserted above the spathe early in the morning, remaining so until midday, after which they usually recede into the spathe as a juicy mass. Sepals three, one subequal to the others; petals three, one of which is subequal to the others and often paler. Androecium six-merous, three regular stamens and three smaller staminodia, the lower fertile, the upper sterile. Ovary three-locular, the upper median locule smaller, with one ovule, abortive and empty, or obsolete, the lower two locules with one or two ovules each. Fruit a loculicidal capsule, one to three per spathe; seeds one to three per fruit (Fernald, 1970; Robinson and Fernald, 1908).

Latin name: *Commelina virginica* L.
Synonym: *Commelina elegans* Kunth
Common name: Day-flower
Origin: North and South American tropics

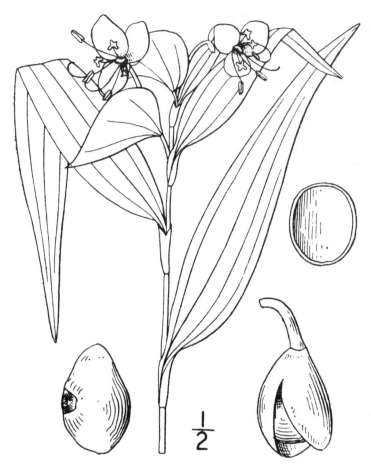

Commelina virginica. Source: *An Illustrated Flora of the Northern United States, Canada, and the British Possessions. Vol. 1.* Charles Scribner's Sons. 1896.

Habitat: Low boggy areas, around ponds and along streams
Hardiness: Zones 6 through 9
Description: A herbaceous perennial with slender rhizomes. Stems erect, usually unbranched or, if branched, usually few-branched above, 1–4 ft /0.3–1.2 m high. Foliage dull medium green, coarse in texture; leaf sheaths long-cylindric, usually closely clasping the stem, sometimes loose at the summit, pubescent on the surface, bearing numerous jointed, cellular, brownish trichomes at the summit; leaf blades lanceolate to broadly lanceolate, round to cuneate basely, the larger mostly acuminate apically, smaller ones acute; larger leaf blades 4–8 in./ 1–2 dm long, 0.4–1.0 in./10–25 mm wide, scabrous above. Inflorescence a

cyme, enclosed by a closely folded, oblique spathe; spathes congested, the base nearly vertical, horizontal to somewhat arched downward on the lower side, oblique on the upper, the margins united only along the vertical base; flowers rather small, petals blue; seeds 0.1–0.2 in./3–6 mm long, grayish brown or reddish, smooth or finely pubescent. Flowering and fruiting occur from June through September.

Uses: Day-flower is useful as ground cover in wet sites and in bogs and water gardens. The plants form compatible stands in sunny sites with other aquatic ornamentals. Day-flower is particularly useful with various sedges along and in streams, where the broad-leaved plants complement the sedges, and vice versa. The grasslike foliage is often mistaken for that of true grasses, particularly prior to the blossoming stage.

Cultivation: Propagation is by seeding and by plant division.

Convallaria L. (**Lily-of-the-valley**). From *convallis,* "valley." Lectotype, *Convallaria majalis* L. There are three species, native to temperate regions of Eurasia and North America. Low, acaulescent, glabrous herbs with slender rhizomes and simple scapes; rhizomes horizontal, the upright buds called *pips* are used for propagation. Angled scape bears a one-sided raceme of fragrant nodding flowers. Leaves basal, two or three, oblong. Flowers white to pink, in terminal bracted one-sided racemes; perianth white, globose-campanulate, with six retrorse lobes; androecium six-merous, stamens included, inserted at the base of the perianth; ovary three-locular, four or five ovules in each locule, tapering into a stout style; stigma trigonous; fruit a few-seeded berry, usually red (Fernald, 1970; Hortus Third, 1977).

Latin name: *Convallaria majalis* L.
Common name: Lily-of-the-valley
Origin: North America, Europe
Habitat: Cultivated
Hardiness: Zones 6 through 8
Description: A caulescent, deciduous, glabrous, perennial herb with slender, horizontal rhizomes with upright buds called *pips;* the plants form dense carpets. Scape simple, erect, elongate, usually angled, smooth, 6–12 in./1.5–3 dm high. Foliage medium to light green, coarse in texture; leaves basal, two or three together, erect, neither scalelike nor filiform; leaf blades lanceolate-ovate to elliptic, glabrous, 4–12 in./1–3 dm long, 3–4 in./8–10 cm wide, sheathing the glabrous scape. Inflorescence terminal, bracted, one-sided racemes bearing small, white to pink, fragrant, nodding flowers; bracts lanceolate, 0.2–0.4 in./5–10 mm long, shorter than the pedicels; perianth globose-campanulate, white, with six short retrorse lobes, 0.2–0.3 in./5–8 mm long; androecium six-merous, stamens, included, inserted on the base of the perianth; ovary three-locular, tapering into a stout style; ovules four to six in each locule; fruit a red berry, few-

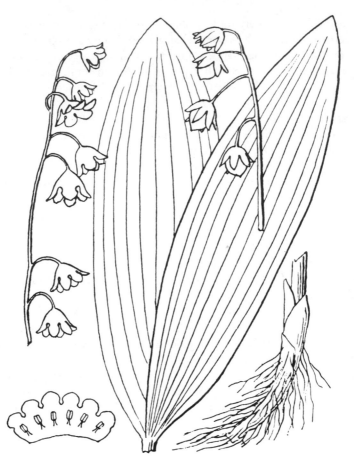

Convallaria majalis. Source: An Illustrated Flora of the Northern United States, Canada, and the British Possessions. Vol. 1. Charles Scribner's Sons. 1896.

seeded, 0.3–0.4 in./8–10 mm in diameter. Flowering and fruiting occur from May through June.

Uses: Lily-of-the-valley is commonly found in garden plantings, usually as ground cover in shaded locations. Its ornamental value lies in its use as a bedding plant in foreground borders, and particularly in naturalized areas in open woods. The plants are a valuable source of cut flowers and are also useful as house and greenhouse plants. Lily-of-the-valley usually blossoms following the usual spring bulbs and retains its foliage until frost. The plants reach their peak of excellence during the interim between the early spring bulbs and the midsummer blossoms. Lily-of-the-valley is frequently used in understory plantings in flower beds and among shrubs. The economic value of lily-of-the-valley is in its use as a perfume plant; the dry rhizomes have medicinal properties. Large quantities of plants are forced into blossom to provide cut flowers. The popularity and widespread distribution and use of lily-of-the-valley are indicative of its value as an ornamental.

Cultivation: Lily-of-the-valley should be established in the autumn. Single crowns or roots, called *pips,* are planted 3–4 in./8–10 cm apart, with the tips about 1.0 in./25 mm below the ground surface. The pips can be placed closer together when plantings are made in pots (i.e., 1 in./25 mm). For pot plantings, use a compost of equal parts of fibrous loam and leaf mold, shake the mixture among the roots, and firm the soil mixture thoroughly. Place the pots in a cold frame covered with ashes or peat moss until early spring. Then place the pots in a shaded location at about 50–60°F/10–16°C, and water freely as growth advances. Place the pots back in the cold frame after the plants have flowered and keep them there until the danger of frost is past before removing the plants and planting them in the garden. Blossoms may be had at any time by forcing the retarded crowns or roots. Retarded crowns or roots can be placed close together in 6 in./15 cm pots or flats, and light sandy soil or peat moss shaken among the roots and left fairly loose, the tips of the crowns remaining about 1 in./25 mm above soil level. The pots or flats should then be placed in a greenhouse at a temperature of 65–75°F/18–24°C and covered to exclude light for about two weeks; admit light gradually as growth commences, and remove the covering entirely as growth advances. Bottom heat causes the flower spikes to develop in advance of the leaves. Add water freely when growth is active. Retarded crowns can be forced into blossom in three to four weeks. Garden plantings should be left undisturbed as long as possible. After several years established stands may beome overcrowded and begin to deteriorate. When this occurs, some of the plants should be lifted and separated for replanting. This may be done by removing some of the plants and leaving others in the established stand. Lily-of-the-valley in the United States is apparently identical to the form in European gardens.

Equisetum **L. (Horsetail, Scouring rush).** The ancient name from *equus,* "horse," and *seta,* "bristle." Lectotype, *Equisetum arvense* L. There are about 35 species, widely distributed except in Australia and New Zealand. Primitive, sporogenous, rhizomatous, colonial perennials, the aerial stems annual or perennial. Stems hollow or solid, jointed, impregnated with silica, branches whorled; leaves scalelike, marginally united into a sheath around each node; sporophylls in a terminal spikelike cone composed of peltate sporangia-bearing structures; spores all alike (Hauke, 1963).

Latin name: *Equisetum hyemale* L.

Common names: Common horsetail, Horsetail, Scouring rush, Common scouring rush, Winter scouring rush

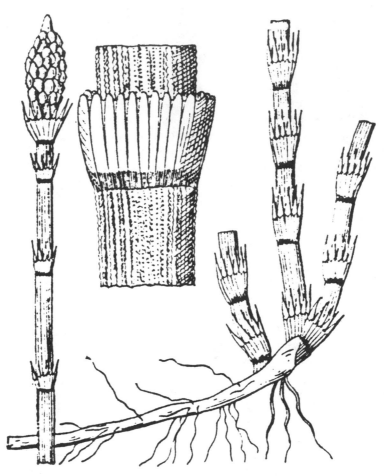

Equisetum hyemale. *Source: An Illustrated Flora of the Northern United States, Canada, and the British Possessions. Vol. 1.* Charles Scribner's Sons. 1896.

Origin: Eurasia, Pacific North America
Habitat: Moist, evergreen woods and low fields, cultivated
Hardiness: Zones 6 through 9
Description: A grasslike or rushlike, rhizomatous, evergreen perennial. Stems erect, all alike, few to many per tuft, mostly simple, 3–4 ft/0.9–1.2 m high, 0.4–0.6 in./10–15 mm thick, rough, with 14 to 40 biangulate ridges; stem nodes solid, each bearing a whorl of reduced leaves, joined by the edges into cylindrical sheaths; sheaths longer than broad, tight, with two black rings separated by an ashy one, teeth mostly deciduous. Centrum usually two-thirds to three-fourths the diameter of the stem; green parenchyma continuous over

the vallecular holes, separated by bast under the ridges. Fruit a pointed strobilus; prothallus dioecious, variously lobed, green; spores are produced from March through August.

Uses: Common horsetail is useful in naturalizing damp or wet sites adjacent to the formal garden. The gregarious growth habit of common horsetail makes it an ideal plant in low, moist or wet sites, either in full sun or light shade; it is also useful in the rock garden. Horsetail provides a diversified texture to the landscape and is often used in the water garden. It is often grown in Japanese-style gardens around pool margins. The growth habit and filiform stems of common horsetail make it appear to be somewhat grasslike. The siliceous stems are sometimes used in polishing.

Cultivation: Propagation is by plant or rhizome division; the plants are easily propagated. Common horsetail is prevalent in the eastern United States.

Latin name: *Equisetum scirpoides* Michx.
Common names: Dwarf horsetail, Dwarf scouring rush
Origin: Eurasia
Habitat: Moist evergreen woods and low fields, cultivated
Hardiness: Zones 5 and 6
Description: A grasslike or rushlike, evergreen, rhizomatous perennial. Stems decumbent or ascending, all alike, firm but somewhat flexuous, usually simple or with a few long branches near the base, 4–8 in./1–2 dm high, about 1–2 mm thick, solid at the center, six-grooved and angled, ridges round, alternating grooves shallow and deep, each ridge with a single row of tubercles, the stomates in two rows in each major furrow, sunken below the level of the epidermis, three well-developed, valleculae cavities; sheaths short, flaring, with a broad black band above the green base, usually thin and white-hyaline distally; teeth thin, filiform-tipped, about 1–2 mm long, with pale hyaline margins and a darker median band that is prolonged into a short, soft bristle; fruit a small, terminal strobilus, about 0.1–0.2 in./3–5 mm long.

Uses: The sprawling growth habit of dwarf horsetail makes it useful as a ground-cover plant in both sunny and shaded sites. The plants are grasslike or rushlike in appearance.

Cultivation: Propagation is by plant and rhizome division.

Other ornamental species: *Equisetum variegatum* Schleich. ex Weber & C. Mohr, Variegated horsetail, Variegated scouring rush A rushlike, evergreen, perennial with smooth rhizomes. Stems perennial, erect, tufted, slender, 1–2 ft/ 3–6 dm high, simple or variously branched, with center cavity and greenish, light yellow stripes; furrowed with 5 to 10 ridges; sheaths black above with persistent teeth; strobilus about 0.15–0.20 in./4–5 mm long. This species is perhaps more attractive than scouring rush because of its variegated coloration. Like other scouring rushes, it is useful around pools when planted in clumps or as ground cover in low, wet areas. The small size of the plants makes them ideal for use as potted specimens. The plants grow equally well in light or medium

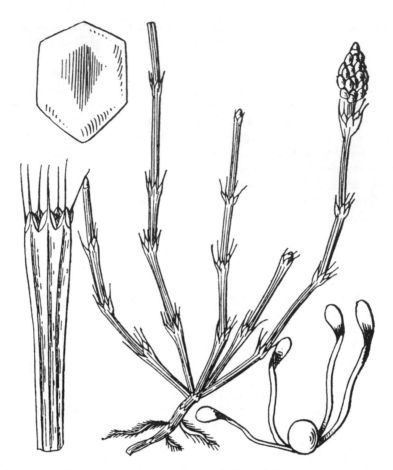

Equisetum variegatum. Source: *An Illustrated Flora of the Northern United States, Canada, and the British Possessions. Vol. 1.* Charles Scribner's Sons. 1896.

shade. Variegated horsetail is more decorative than common horsetail, *Equisetum hyemale,* and dwarf horsetail, *Equisetum scirpoides,* and consequently it is more popular as an ornamental. It is most useful in lightly shaded, low, wet sites in the garden. Propagation is easily accomplished by plant or rhizome division.

Hypoxis **L. (Stargrass, Yellow stargrass).** From Greek *upoxus,* "subacid," an old name for a plant having sourish leaves; also from *hypo,* "beneath," and *oxys,* "sharp," referring to the base of the capsule. Lectotype, *Hypoxis hirsuta* (L.) Cov. There are about 110 species, mostly native to and widespread in the Southern Hemisphere. Small, acaulescent, herbs with vertical corms. Scapes from a cormlike, short, vertical rhizome; slender, sometimes tufted, usually several-flowered. Leaves closely set basely, grasslike, narrowly linear with nearly filiform blades, usually hairy. Flowers borne terminally, solitary or in two-to-several-flowered irregular umbels, white or yellow. Perianth segments six, three in each of two series, surmounting the pilose floral tube, those of the two series nearly alike, spreading at anthesis, yellowish on the upper surface, greenish below, becoming erect at anthesis and converging above the developing fruit. Androecium of six stamens in one series, about one-half as long as the perianth lobes, filaments slender, adnate to the base of the perianth. Ovary inferior, glabrous or pilose, three-locular. Fruit an indehiscent or loculicidal capsule; seeds globose, with black pebbled or muricate seedcoat (Brackett, 1923).

Latin name: *Hypoxis hirsuta* (L.) Cov.
Synonym: *Hypoxis erecta* L.
Common names: Stargrass, Goldstar grass, Yellow stargrass
Origin: North America
Habitat: Dry, open woods on acid soils
Hardiness: Zones 5 through 10
Description: An acaulescent, scapose, semievergreen herb with cormlike rootstocks. Corms subglobose to ellipsoid, 0.2–0.8 in./5–20 mm thick, covered with pale brown membranous sheaths that do not become fibrillose. Foliage medium green, fine in texture; leaves closely set basely, grasslike, narrowly linear with filiform blades, usually hairy. Scapes slender, stiff, simple, ascending or reclining, 4–12 in./1–3 dm long, usually two-to-nine-flowered; flowers umbellate, bright golden yellow, star-shaped, 0.6–0.8 in./15–20 mm wide, petals subulate or linear-subulate, subtended by several setaceous, membranous, subulate bracts, 0.8–1.6 in./2–4 cm long; pedicels filiform, elongate, 0.4–0.8 in./10–20 mm long; peduncles 2–8 in./0.5–2.0 dm long; perianth of six separate segments, united only at the base, rotate lobes greenish outside, yellowish within, dorsally pubescent, 0.2–0.6 in./5–15 mm long, sepals lanceolate, elliptic, or elliptic-lanceolate; ovary short pilose; fruit an indehiscent or dehiscent, pubescent capsule, ovoid to ellipsoid, densely covered with pointed tubercles, 0.10–0.25 in./3–6 mm long; seeds black, lustrous, about 1 mm in diameter, closely covered with a black, crustaceous testa. Flowering and fruiting occur during the spring, summer, and fall.

Uses: This grasslike herb is beneficial as a ground cover in full sun on acid soils. Although the plants are tufted, they tend to grow together, forming a meadow effect, with the foliage forming a complete ground cover. Stargrass is grown for its thick, fine-textured foliage; it forms a good edging plant in foreground borders. Optimum results from stargrass may be achieved from its pure culture in massed plantings in the wild garden and as ground cover on impoverished, dry soils to which it is adapted. The plants have a prolonged flowering period and remain attractive throughout the summer.

Cultivation: Propagation is by seeding or by division of the offsets, which

Hypoxis hirsuta. *Source: An Illustrated Flora of the Northern United States, Canada, and the British Possessions. Vol. 1.* Charles Scribner's Sons. 1896.

are produced by the corms in the fall. Plant division and planting can be done either in the spring or fall. Stargrass prefers full sun or light shade in dry sites on acid, sandy soils. The quickest and most reliable way to establish stargrass is to purchase plants from a local nursery and plant them in the spring, thereby allowing the young plants to form corms and offsets by the following autumn.

Other ornamental species include *Hypoxis hemerocallidea, Hypoxis latifolia, Hypoxis stellata,* and *Hypoxis stellata* var. *elegans.*

***Liriope* Lour. (Lily turf).** The name from the nymph Liriope. Type species, *Liriope spicata* Lour. There are five species, native to China, Japan, and the Philippines. Acaulescent, evergreen, perennial herbs, tufted and rhizomatous. Leaves narrowly linear, grasslike, glabrous. Inflorescence axillary fascicles of flowers arranged in terminal spikes or racemes; flowers white or lilac blue; perianth six-merous; androecium six-merous; ovary superior; fruit baccate, black; seeds one or two, fleshy (Hortus Third, 1977).

Latin name: *Liriope muscari* (Decne.) L. H. Bailey
Synonym: *Liriope graminifolia* var. *densiflora* Baker
Common name: Lily turf
Origin: Japan, China, Philippines
Habitat: Cultivated
Hardiness: Zones 6 through 10
Description: An acaulescent, scapose, densely tufted, sod-forming perennial herb, very leafy, with stout, thick, tuberous roots. Scape 12–18 in./3.0–4.5 dm high, smooth, light green. Foliage dark green, coarse in texture; leaves numerous, basal, coriaceous, narrowly linear, smooth, firm, ascending to arching, 18–24 in./4.5–6.0 dm long, 0.5–0.8 in./13–20 mm wide. Inflorescence a terminal, dense, many-flowered raceme or spike, 2–3 in./5–8 cm long, 0.5–1.0 in./13–25 mm thick; flowers perfect, hypogynous, in axillary fascicles, small, bell-shaped, about 0.2–0.3 in./5–8 mm long, 0.25 in./6 mm wide at the mouth, dark violet; perianth six-merous, petaloid, segments separate; ovary three-locular, superior; fruit a small bluish green berry; seeds one or two, fleshy, black. Flowering and fruiting occur from May through August. There are cockscomb and fascicled forms of lily turf and other horticultural varieties which are of ornamental value.

Uses: Lily turf and its variants are unexcelled as accent-edging ground-cover plants, as they form sods or mats of varying densities in both sunny and shaded locations. Their most common use outdoors is for ground cover established in groups or in massed stands in light or medium shade; similarly, liriope is ideal in understory plantings in flower beds and among shrubbery if enough shade is provided. The waxy flowers of different colors among lily turf and its variants are an added attraction, although the primary ornamental value of the plants is their rich, usually dark green foliage. Lily turf and its variants are excellent rock garden plants. Liriopes make excellent potted plants or window plants, as they are small enough for indoor plantings and are enhanced by larger indoor ornamentals. The dark green leaves of lily turf and the variegated leaves of its variants are attractive during spring, summer, and fall.

Cultivation: Propagation is by plant division, usually in the spring following flowering. The plants prefer a moist but well-drained, ordinary garden soil and will tolerate some sun, but they perform better in light or medium shade. The only maintenance problem that may arise is that of containing the plants in their designated area, especially the rhizomatous forms of *Liriope exiliflora* and *Liriope spicata,* creeping lily turf. The plants have extended longevity once they are established. Liriopes require bright light when grown indoors; failure to provide adequate light results in the failure of the plants to flower. The plants will tolerate wide ranges in temperature and will withstand summer heat very well. Potted liriopes should be kept cool during the winter in indoor plantings, preferably not above 50–55°F/10–13°C, and for this reason they are excellent for cool rooms. During the active growth period, the plants should be watered moderately enough to maintain the potting mixture moist at each watering, but allowing the top 0.5 in./13 mm to dry out before watering again. During the winter rest period, water only enough to keep the potting mixture from drying out. The plants should be fertilized every fortnight during active growth periods by using any standard liquid fertilizer. Lily turf is propagated by breaking or cutting the thickened base into smaller pieces, each piece with some leaves attached. Plant the individual pieces in a soil-based potting mixture. As the plants become pot-bound, they should be either divided or placed in larger pots.

Some of the many variegated variants of lily turf include the cultivars 'Big Blue,' 'Grandiflora,' 'Majestic,' and 'Variegata.'

Other ornamental species: *Liriope exiliflora* (L. H. Bailey) Hume   A rhizomatous acaulesent herb. Scapes erect, purplish or violet brown, 1–2 ft/3–6 dm high. Foliage dark green, smooth, fine in texture. Leaves numerous, basal, grasslike, narrowly linear, 16–18 in./4.0–4.5 dm long, 0.2–0.3 in./5–8 mm wide. Flowers small, violet, borne in an open raceme; rachis violet. This exotic species is native to China and Japan.

Liriope spicata Lour. Creeping lily turf   A rhizomatous, acaulescent, semievergreen, perennial herb with grasslike leaves. Scapes erect, light violet brown, 4–12 in./1–3 dm high. Foliage medium to dark green, shiny, fine in texture. Leaves numerous, basal, grasslike 12–18 in./3.0–4.5 dm long, 0.20–0.25 in./5–6 mm wide, serrulate with translucent teeth. Inflorescence terminal racemes of small, pale, violet to nearly white flowers with a distinct tube; rachis violet. Creeping lily turf differs from lily turf, *Liriope muscari*, in having a shallow root system. Creeping lily turf is native to China and Vietnam.

Ophiopogon Ker-Gawl. (**Mondo grass, Lily turf**). Name from *ophis,* "snake," and *pogon*, "beard," and probably refers to the flower spike. Type species, *Ophiopogon japonicus* (L. f.) Ker-Gawl. There are about 10 species, native to Japan, India, and Korea. Acaulescent, evergreen, sod-forming perennial herbs. Leaves erect or ascending, glabrous, grasslike, narrowly linear. Flowers in simple racemes or in fascicles arranged in terminal racemes, white to pale purple, usually nodding. Perianth six-merous, segments separate; androecium six-merous, filaments extremely short; ovary inferior; fruit baccate, blue (Hortus Third, 1977).

Latin name: *Ophiopogon jaburan* (Sieb.) Lodd.
Synonym: *Mondo jaburan* (Sieb.) L. H. Bailey
Cultivars: 'Argenteo-vittatus,' 'Aureo-variegatus,' 'Caeruleus,' 'Variegatus,' 'Vittatus'

Common names: Mondo grass, Snakebeard, Lily turf, White lily turf
Origin: Japan, Korea
Habitat: Cultivated
Hardiness: Zones 6 through 10
Description: An acaulescent, sod-forming, perennial herb. Plants tufted, grasslike, 8–16 in./2–4 dm high; roots stout, cordlike, not tuberous. Foliage dark green, fine to medium in texture. Leaves erect to arching, grasslike, smooth, narrowly linear, 18–24 in./4.5–6.0 m long, 0.4–0.5 in./10–13 mm wide, margins smooth, long attenuate. Inflorescence racemose; flowers closely arranged in axillary fascicles, in short simple racemes on flattened stems, 9–15 in./2.3–3.8 dm long; flowers usually nodding, white or white tinged with lilac, 0.5–0.9 in./13–23 mm long; perianth six-merous, segments separate; ovary inferior; fruit baccate, violet blue, oblong, about 0.25 in./6 mm long. Flowering and fruiting occur from July through September.

Uses: Mondo grass makes a valuable ground-cover and rock garden plant in sunny or shaded sites in mild climates. It is good in understory plantings in the shade of other ornamentals in border plantings. It is useful as a potted plant in colder climates, where it is usually displayed on decks or terraces during the summer and moved inside during the winter. The plants made good edgings in greenhouses, especially under benches, and may, on occasion, be grown in hanging baskets. This small, sod-forming herb is useful as an accent plant in foreground borders.

Cultivation: Propagation is by plant division. Mondo grass grows well in ordinary garden soil, requiring minimum attention once established; it is easily propagated. The soil should be kept evenly moist at all times, whether grown indoors or in the garden. Moderate temperatures are required, and the plants thrive in full sun and light or medium shade. In addition to the dark green form, typical of the species, usually the cultivar Variegatus is most commonly available in the trade. The foliage of the green form is usually light green when plants are grown in full sun; shade-grown plants are usually dark green. Although the plants tolerate a wide range in temperature, they thrive best in relatively cool temperatures, usually about 55–65°F/13–18°C throughout the year. Indoor plantings should be watered regularly and enough to keep the potting mixture moist at all times; they should be watered more sparingly during the winter rest period. Apply standard liquid fertilizer every two weeks during periods of active growth. A good growing medium consists of a combination of one-third coarse sand and two-thirds soil-based potting mixture. Propagation is best done in the spring by dividing large clumps. Be sure to include as many roots as possible and 8 to 10 leaves on each section for planting. Plant the sections separately in 3 in./8 cm pots, and treat them as adult plants. Do not feed the new plants for the first few months, however. Mondo grass is quite often confused with lily turf, *Liriope muscari*. The flowers of mondo grass are slightly larger and droop rather more loosely on the flower stalk than do those of lily turf.

Cultivars: *Ophiopogon jaburan* (Sieb.) Lodd. 'Argenteo-vittatus,' 'Aureo-variegatus,' 'Caeruleus,' 'Variegatus,' 'Vittatus.' The foliage of these cultivars, with the exception of Caeruleus, is variegated. The leaves are longitudinally striped with white or yellow and green stripes. The variable variegated foliage usually makes it difficult to distinguish one cultivar from another. The cultivar Caeruleus has dark green leaves like the parent species and violet blue flowers.

Latin name: *Ophiopogon japonicus* (Thunb.) Ker-Gawl.
Synonym: *Mondo japonicum* (Thunb.) Farw.
Cultivars: 'Kioto' Dwarf mondo grass
Common names: Mondo grass, Dwarf lily turf
Origin: Japan, Korea
Habitat: Cultivated
Hardiness: Zones 7 through 10
Description: A grasslike, caulescent, perennial herb. Plants are sod-forming, 6–12 in./1.5–3.0 dm high, with tuberous roots that are somewhat rhizomatous. Foliage dark green, fine in texture. Leaves numerous, rather rigid, erect to ascending and curved, glabrous, narrowly linear, 8–12 in./2–3 dm long, 0.10–0.15 in./3–4 mm wide, margins smooth. Inflorescence racemose; flowers small, 2–3 mm long, light lilac to white, borne on a short, loose, few-flowered raceme; fruit blue, very small, baccate. Flowering and fruiting occur from June through July.
Uses: Mondo grass makes an excellent ground cover, as it is a good sod-forming plant. The small plants are ideal as potted specimens that may be enjoyed outside in the shade during the summer in moderate climates and indoors during the winter. Frequently it is used as edging or in groups in foreground borders, flower beds, and rock gardens. It is somewhat suited for growing in hanging baskets.
Cultivation: Propagation is by plant division. The plants are easily established and require only minimal maintenance. Any ordinary garden soil is adequate if it is kept moist. The color and vigor of the plants grown in shade surpass those of plants grown in full sun; the plants may not survive full sunlight in warmer climates.
Cultivars: *Ophiopogon japonicus* (Thunb.) Ker-Gawl. 'Kioto' Dwarf mondo grass A grasslike, acaulescent, perennial, sod-forming herb; the plants are about 4 in./10 cm high.

Latin name: *Ophiopogon plansicapus* Nakai
Common name: Black mondo grass
Origin: Japan
Habitat: Cultivated
Hardiness: Zones 7 through 10
Description: An acaulescent, grasslike, perennial herb. Plants are sod-forming, 1–2 ft/3–6 dm high, with thick rootstocks, often stoloniferous. Foliage

medium green, fine in texture. Leaves numerous, narrowly linear, ascending to arching, dark green, with several veins, 15–20 in./3.8–5.0 dm long, 0.1–0.3 in./3–6 mm wide, smooth throughout. Inflorescence small flowers borne on a loosely flowered raceme; flowers 0.2–0.3 in./5–8 mm long, pale purple, pink or white; fruit dull bluish green, baccate. Flowering and fruiting occur from June through July. The foliage becomes darker bluish black at maturity.

Uses: The mature bluish black foliage is the unique characteristic of this species. Black mondo grass is grown primarily as a curiosity both as a house plant and in the garden. Outdoor plantings usually include its use in foreground borders and in rock gardens. The curiosity aroused by its unique foliage color should induce more gardeners to include it in their plantings. The plants form a good ground cover and, in addition, produce a unique special effect by their bluish black foliage.

Cultivation: Black mondo grass is easy to propagate and maintain. Propagation is by plant division and by planting cuttings of the stolons. The plants are equally at home in full sun or light shade and do well in ordinary garden soil when it is maintained uniformly moist.

Cultivars: Two popular cultivars of black mondo grass include Arabicus and Ebony Knight, especially the latter.

Phormium **Forst. (Flax lily).** Name derived from *phormos,* "basket," and refers to the leaf fiber used for making baskets. Type species, *Phormium tenax* Forst. There are two species, native to New Zealand. Large caulescent, scapose, perennial herbs. Leaves basal, equitant, gladiate. Inflorescence a panicle on a leafless scape. Flowers tubular at the base, segments six, spreading; androecium six-merous; ovary superior, three-locular; fruit an erect trigonous capsule (Hortus Third, 1977).

Latin name: *Phormium tenax* Forst.
Common names: New Zealand flax, New Zealand hemp
Origin: New Zealand
Habitat: Cultivated
Hardiness: Zone 10
Description: A large, caulescent, scapose, deciduous, perennial herb, 5–15 ft/1.3–4.6 m high. Foliage variegated, grasslike, coarse in texture. Leaves basal, equitant, gladiate, 6–8 ft/1.8–2.5 m long, 3–5 in./0.8–1.3 dm wide, stiff but slightly arching, tough and coriaceous, splitting at the apex, margins with orange or red stripes. Inflorescence a panicle borne on a leafless scape; flowers tubular at base, dull red, 1–2 in./2.5–5.0 cm long, segments six, spreading, androecium six-merous; ovary superior, three-locular; fruit an erect trigonous capsule, 2–4 in./5–10 cm long. The aboveground parts of the plant die soon after flowering; however, plants grown indoors very seldom flower.

Uses: New Zealand flax and its cultivars are excellent pot plants for porches, decks, and terraces. The plants, with their variegated foliage of fanlike leaves, are attractive both in shape and color in specimen plantings. The economic importance of the plant is in the commercial manufacture of ropes, twine, and baskets. New Zealand flax and its cultivars may be used as specimen plants in shaded sites in zone 10.

Cultivation: Propagation is by seeding and by division of the rhizomes. A compost mixture of two parts leaf mold and one part decayed manure with a little sand is ideal for growing the plants in pots. Seeding indoors should be done at a temperature of about 60°F/16°C. Plants three or more years old may be divided for further expansion. Rooted pieces of plant divisions should be potted just before the plants initiate fresh growth in the spring. They should be kept indoors until all danger of frost is past. New Zealand flax is adapted to a wide range of soils; it requires a constant, moist environment and thrives best in full sun near water in sandy or loamy soils. Seeding should be done in early spring in the garden in zone 10 and in pots or flats when grown in colder climates. New Zealand flax is a tender perennial that does not withstand frost, but it is useful in outdoor plantings in the warmer parts of zone 10. The plants should be taken indoors before the danger of sharp frost. New Zealand flax may be grown in tubs or large flower pots in colder climates. These plants can be overwintered by being placed in a frostproof greenhouse or even in a cellar with sufficient light. Plants grown inside are usually much smaller than those grown outside.

Reineckea **Kunth.** The name commemorates J. Reinecke, a German horticulturist. A monotypic genus, native to warm regions of China and Japan. A rhizomatous perennial herb; stems form clumps, leaves tufted, basal, flowers pink, in dense scapose spikes, perianth six-merous, united into a tube; androecium six-merous, filaments arising from the perianth; fruit a berry.

Latin name: *Reineckea carnea* Kunth
Common name: Fangrass
Origin: China, Japan
Habitat: Wet to dry soils in shaded sites
Hardiness: Zones 9 and 10
Description: A rhizomatous, perennial, grasslike herb forming clumps. Scape green, smooth, 10–18 in./2.5–4.5 dm high. Foliage shiny green, medium in texture; leaves two-ranked, basal, grasslike, tufted, thin, tough, coriaceous and smooth, linear to lanceolate, 8–16 in./2.0–4.0 m long, 0.4–0.6 in./10–15 mm wide, arching from the base. Inflorescence dense, bracted, scapose spikes; spikes many-flowered; flowers fresh pink, fragrant, 0.4–0.6 in./10–15 mm long; perianth six-merous, segments united into a tube; androecium six-merous, filaments arising from the perianth; fruit a berry, red when mature. Flowering and fruiting occur from May through June.

Uses: The grasslike appearance and small size of fangrass make it ideal as a potted specimen for use in cold climates. It is useful as ground cover in shaded sites, as an edging plant in foreground borders, and in rock and water gardens in plant-hardiness zones 9 and 10.

Cultivation: Propagation is by seeding and by plant division. Plant division should be done in the spring, probably in April. The plants require moist, well-drained soil in full sun or partially shaded locations. Fangrass does quite well in any ordinary garden soil, but the soil must be kept moist by copious waterings in dry weather. The plants should be lifted, divided, and replanted every few years to keep them growing vigorously and to prevent overcrowding. Fangrass has been confused with *Ophiopogon* species.

Sisyrinchium **L. (Blue-eyed grass).** A meaningless name of Greek origin. Type species, *Sisyrinchium bermudiana* L. There are about 75 species, native to the Western Hemisphere. Perennial, usually cespitose, grasslike herbs with distinct or obsolete rootstocks and fibrous roots. Leaves basal, blades linear to lanceolate or cylindrical. Scape two-edged or two-winged, when branched each node furnished with a leaflike bract; flowers in terminal solitary or fascicled clusters arising from spathes of mostly two bracts each, blue, yellow, or white. Petals and sepals alike, spreading, usually apiculate or mucronate. Stamens three, filaments united at the top or nearly so, anthers clustered. Ovary three-locular, style branches filiform, alternate with the anthers, or styles entirely united, ovules few to many in each locule. Fruit a globular capsule, readily opening near the apex; seeds numerous and small (Shinners, 1957).

Latin name: *Sisyrinchium angustifolium* P. Mill.
Synonym: *Sisyrinchium idahoense* Bickn.
Common name: Blue-eyed grass
Origin: Eastern North America
Habitat: Wet meadows, thickets, and woods; lake banks
Hardiness: Zones 4 through 9
Description: A loosely cespitose, scapose, perennial herb with distinct, fibrous roots and one to several stems. Flowering stems erect or ascending, flexuous, or even geniculate, simple, or simple and branched on the same plant, distinctly broadly winged, 8–20 in./2–5 dm high, usually bearing a single terminal spathe, drying olive green, darkening to blackish with age. Foliage glaucous to dark green, stiff, fine in texture; basal leaves erect or ascending, 4–8 in./1–2 dm long, 0.1–0.2 in./3–5 mm wide, submembranous, about one-fourth to three-fourths as high as the flowering stems, lanceolate, long attenuate, almost straight; old leaf bases deciduous. Inflorescence terminal fascicled clusters, each cluster subtended by a spathe; spathes solitary, on stout, flattened peduncles, 2–6 in./0.5–1.5 dm long, each spathe two-bracted, the outer usually longer, 2-to-12-flowered, with margins united, 0.10–0.25 in./3–6 mm above the base,

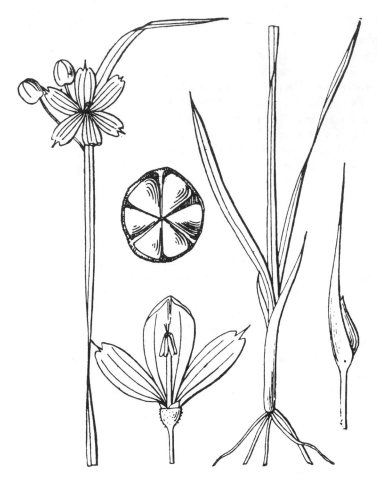

Sisyrinchium angustifolium. *Source: An Illustrated Flora of the Northern United States, Canada, and the British Possessions. Vol. 1.* Charles Scribner's Sons. 1896.

the inner 0.4–1.2 in./1–3 cm long; pedicels filiform, suberect, scarcely exceeding the inner bract, usually light green, or sometimes purple tinged; perianth pale blue turning to violet, rarely white, about 0.5 in./13 mm wide, actinomorphic; sepals and petals similar, separate to the base, oblanceolate, caudate at the apex; fruit a dull brown or purple-tinged, glabrous capsule, 0.15–0.25 in./4–6 mm long when mature, on an erect retrorse pedicel; seeds one to several per cell, globose, dark brown to black, obovoid-oblong, smooth with shallow pits. Flowering and fruiting occur from April through July.

   Uses: Blue-eyed grass has a home in rock and water gardens, and it is useful in accent plantings, in massed stands as ground cover in naturalized areas, and in foreground borders. It is particularly useful in edging foreground borders, as it has a long flowering period. The small, blue flowers are attractive in fresh cut-flower arrangements, though they are short-lived. Blue-eyed grass has the advantage of a rather long flowering season.

Cultivation: Propagation is by seeding and by plant division. The plants will reach maturity the first growing season when established by seeding, although flowering may be sporadic during late summer. Blue-eyed grass grows best in full sun or light shade in fertile, moist, or dry well-drained soil. Plant division should be made in the spring, as newly planted plants established in the fall may not survive the winter.

Other ornamental species: *Sisyrinchium californicum* (Ker-Gawl.) Dryand. Golden-eyed grass   A cespitose scapose deciduous perennial herb with distinct, fibrous roots. Flowering stems 6–24 in./1.5–6.0 dm high, simple, flat, broadly winged, dull green. Leaves alternate, basal, flat, mostly half as long as the scapes, 0.20–0.25 in./5–6mm wide; outer spathe valve longer than the inner; pedicels slender and very weakly winged, not much exserted beyond the spathe; perianth bright yellow, 0.8–1.0 in./20–25 mm wide, rotate, facing upward, segments elliptic, bluntly acute; calyx open, petals entire; fruit a linear, cylindrical capsule. Flowering and fruiting occur from May through July. Golden-eyed grass is adapted to zone 8; it is not hardy in the colder parts of the country. This species occurs in moist, coastal meadows along the Pacific coast.

Sisyrinchium douglasii A. Dietr. Purple-eyed grass (Synonym: *Sisyrinchium grandiflorum* Dougl.)   A cespitose, scapose, perennial herb, erect or ascending. Stems simple, leafy at base, 6–12 in./1.5–3.0 dm high, cylindrical, flexuous. Foliage dark green, fine in texture; leaves two or three, cauline, nearly cylindrical, bractlike, 4–8 in./1–2 dm long, 0.1–0.2 in./3–5 mm wide, lanceolate. Inflorescence terminal, solitary spathes, two-or-three-flowered; pedicels slender, flexuous; flowers nodding; perianth campanulate, 0.7–0.8 in./18–20 mm long, dark reddish purple; fruit a purplish brown capsule, 0.25–0.50 in./6–13 mm long. Flowering and fruiting occur from May through July. This hardy species occurs in the extreme western United States.

These so-called grasses, which are only grasslike in appearance, are best exhibited in large clumps, as are many other small ornamentals. The flowering period is rather long, and the appearance of new flowers each day enhances their ornamental value. Blue-eyed grasses are perhaps best used in naturalized areas surrounding the more formal garden; however, they do have some value as bedding plants. Establishment is easily accomplished by seeding.

There are other species of blue-eyed grass of ornamental value in addition to those described. They include the following tender or weak perennial species: *Sisyrinchium bermudiana,* with 18-in./4.5-dm stems and blue flowers; *Sisyrinchium chilense,* with 12-in./3-dm stems and purple flowers; *Sisyrinchium filifolium,* with 8-in./2-dm stems and white flowers; *Sisyrinchium micranthum,* with 8-in./2-dm stems and yellow flowers; and *Sisyrinchium striatum,* with 3-ft/9-dm stems and light yellow flowers.

Tradescantia **L. (Spiderwort).** Named for John, the elder Tradescant, gardener to Charles I of England. Type species, *Tradescantia virginiana* L. There are more than 35 species, native to the Western Hemisphere. Succulent, evergreen, perennial herbs. Stems mostly erect, mucilaginous, simple or branched, leafy; leaves distinctly keeled. Inflorescence terminal or terminal and axillary, paired, sessile, scorpioid cymes, each pair subtended by paired leaflike or spathelike bracts when terminal, or by one bract when axillary. Flowers in umbelled cymes, axillary and terminal, not surrounded by a folded spathe, regular, white, blue, purple, or rose; ephemeral, open only in the morning; sepals and petals separate, equal, the former herbaceous, the latter all similar, ovate, sessile; androecium of six fertile stamens, all alike, filaments bearded; ovary two-or-three-locular, each locule with one or two ovules. Fruit a two-or-three-locular capsule, each locule one- or two-seeded (Anderson and Woodson, 1935).

Latin name: *Tradescantia albiflora* Kunth
Synonym: *Tradescantia viridis* Hort.
Common name: Wandering Jew
Origin: South America
Habitat: Cultivated
Hardiness: Zones 8 through 10
Description: A succulent, evergreen, perennial herb. Stems decumbent to erect, rooting at the nodes, with a line of hairs on one side, 0.2–0.4 in./5–10 mm long, 5–12 in./1.3–3.0 dm high, the stems grow rapidly and change direction slightly at each node; they are branched and more or less mottled and widely spreading, smooth, with prominent nodes. Foliage green and shiny above and beneath, coarse in texture. Leaves alternate, keeled, sessile, oblong-acuminate or elliptic, 2–3 in./5–8 cm long, 0.8–1.0 in./20–25 mm wide, glabrous except for ciliate margins. Inflorescence terminal or terminal and axillary cymose clusters, the cymes subtended by an involucre of one to three leaflike bracts; flowers perfect, ephemeral, borne in clusters with few in cluster, corolla usually white or white and pink, three-petaled, 0.20–0.25 in./5–6 mm long; petals ovate, equal; stamens all fertile, filaments hairy, anthers with triangular connectives; calyx of ovate herbaceous sepals, sepals pilose along the green keel, 0.1–0.2 in./3–4 mm long; ovary three-locular; fruit a subglobose capsule, 1–3 mm long. Flowering and fruiting occur from April through August or sporadically throughout the year in warmer climates. New flowers, which blossom each morning, persist for only one day.
Uses: Wandering Jew is a tender perennial that has been a favorite house plant for centuries. Its trailing growth habit makes it an ideal plant in hanging baskets. It also forms a colorful ground cover and edging plant in shaded locations in the water garden and in understory plantings in flower beds and shaded borders.
Cultivation: Wandering Jew is easy to propagate and grow. This species is only one of a few succulents known by this name. Propagation is by planting

cuttings of the growing stems, by seeding, and by plant division. The plants may be propagated throughout the year in warm climates. It is naturalized in the southern United States. All *Tradescantia* species tend to lose their lower leaves with age and should be propagated regularly. *Tradescantia* requires bright light, with some direct sunlight each day. Plants grown in insufficient light will lose much of their decorative leaf color. Wandering Jew thrives best at 70°F/21°C or above and should not be subjected to temperatures below 50°F/10°C. The plants should be watered enough to keep the potting mixture thoroughly moist when they are actively growing. Apply some form of standard fertilizer once every two weeks from early spring to late fall. A soil-based potting mixture is usually best for most tradescantias. The plants are usually propagated by taking stem cuttings almost any time of the year; the cuttings should include the growing tip of the stem. Cuttings 3–5 in./0.8–1.5 dm long should be placed in pots containing equal parts of peat moss and sand as a rooting mixture, keep the pots in a warm place in bright light, watering enough to keep the rooting mixture moist. Roots should form in about two or three weeks, after which the plants should be transferred to pots containing a regular soil-based potting mixture. Wandering Jew requires watering on a regular basis. Alternatively, new plants could be started by placing the cuttings directly in pots containing a soil-based potting mixture. Outdoor plantings should be done in the same manner, making sure to water the new plantings regularly, particularly immediately following planting.

Latin name: *Tradescantia bracteata* Small
Synonym: *Tradescantia fluminensis* Vell.
Common name: Wandering Jew
Origin: North America, South America
Habitat: Cultivated
Hardiness: Zones 8 through 10
Description: A decumbent, succulent, evergreen, perennial herb with trailing, branched stems. The stems and branches are more or less matted and widely spreading, 36–40 in./0.9–1.0 m long, 8–12 in./2–3 dm high; stems and foliage smooth. Foliage dull green, shiny above, deep purple violet beneath, coarse in texture; leaves alternate, sheathed, keeled, leaf blades ovate-acuminate, 1.2–1.6 in./3–4 cm long, 0.70–0.75 in./18–19 mm wide, slightly acuminate; the sheaths long-ciliate. Inflorescence small terminal and axillary, cymose clusters, the cymes subtended by an involucre of one to three leaflike bracts; flowers perfect, few in a cluster, ephemeral, corolla white, 0.4–0.5 in./10–13 mm wide, petals similar, ovate, sessile; stamens all fertile, filaments bearded, anthers with rectangular connectives; calyx of ovate herbaceous sepals, 0.15–0.25 in./4–6 mm long, with a finely pubescent median keel; ovary three-locular; fruit a subglobose capsule, about 2–3 mm long. Flowering and fruiting occur from April through June or longer in zone 10. New flowers blossom each morning and persist for only a portion of the day.

Tradescantia bracteata.
Source: *Wild Flowers in Kansas.*
Kansas State Printing Plant.
1934.

Uses: Wandering Jew has long been a favorite house plant; it is most frequently used in hanging baskets. It is grown primarily for its colorful foliage, although its production of new, fresh flowers each day adds to the attractiveness of the plants. Another interesting aspect is that the foliage color is changeable; new growth from pruned plants may or may not be the same color as that of the original growth. The trailing, twining, leafy stems produce a cascade of color as they are suspended from hanging baskets. Wandering Jew is also useful as colorful ground cover in understory plantings in flower beds and in planters; it grows well under greenhouse benches as ground cover. It is an excellent ground cover in shaded sites.

Cultivation: Wandering Jew is easy to propagate and grow. Propagation is by stem cuttings, seeding, and plant division. Propagation is done throughout the year in warm climates. *Tradescantia bracteata* is propagated in the same manner as that described for *Tradescantia albiflora.*

Other ornamental species: *Tradescantia blossfeldiana* Mildb. Flowering inch-plant   A robust, vigorous, fast-growing, weak, evergreen perennial. Stems and branches smooth, more or less matted, trailing or ascending, widely spreading. A variant form has leaves that may be cream-colored, green, or striped half-green and half-cream, all on the same plant. The cream sections of this cultivar take on a strong pink hue when the plants are grown in bright light. In propagating the plants, it is essential to use stem cuttings with leaves containing a third or more green coloring in them. The stems bearing all cream-colored leaves will not root.

Tradescantia navicularis Ortg. Wandering Jew, Chain plant   A slow-growing, prostrate, weak, evergreen, perennial, succulent herb. The entire plant is succulent; the small, fleshy, coppery green, sessile leaves are closely packed, trigonous, about 1 in./25 mm long. The leaves have a crease along the central vein, with short hairs along the margins and purple dots beneath. The small flowers are bright pink to rose purple. This species is particularly suited to rather dry conditions similar to those in which cacti and other succulents are grown.

Tradescantia sillamontana Matuda 'White Velvet' Wandering Jew   The plants of this cultivar are white-villous throughout. Stems from stout rhizomes with fibrous roots, branched, loose, 6–8 in./1.5–2.0 dm long; branches breaking through leaf sheaths at lower nodes. Foliage is light green, coarse in texture; leaves at the base of stem reduced, upper leaves elliptic-ovate, 2–3 in./5–8 cm long, 0.8–1.0 in./20–25 mm wide, arranged in flattened ranks. Flowers small, rose-magenta; filaments glabrous.

Tradescantia virginiana L. Common spiderwort (Synonym: *Tradescantia brevicaulis* Raf.)   The wild plants of this semievergreen, erect species are 2–3 ft/6–9 dm high; flowers blue or purple. The garden cultivars and their hybrids are usually more compact and smaller than the wild type and have larger flowers in a wider range of colors. The following cultivars are popular among gardeners: 'Iris Pritchard' with white flowers tinged with violet; 'Osprey' with white flowers; 'Purple Dome' with brilliant purple flowers; 'James Stratton' with deep blue flowers; and 'J. C. Weguelin' with porcelain blue flowers.

Other native species are useful for plantings in wild gardens; all have grasslike leaves. The most popular ones include *Tradescantia humilis,* with pale blue or pink flowers; *Tradescantia micrantha,* a prostrate creeper with rose-purple flowers; *Tradescantia occidentalis,* the plants about 30 in./7.6 dm high, with blue or reddish flowers, and *Tradescantia subaspera,* the plants about 3 ft/9 dm high with bluish or white flowers. There are other *Tradescantia* species that are less grasslike in appearance that also have ornamental value.

Typha **L. (Cattail, Cattail flag, Bulrush, Reed mace, Down, Slag).** *Typha* for "tuphe," an ancient Greek name of the plant. Lectotype, *Typha latifolia* L. About 15 species of worldwide geographic distribution comprise the entire family. Paludal or subaquatic, large, upright-narrow herbs of tropical and tem-

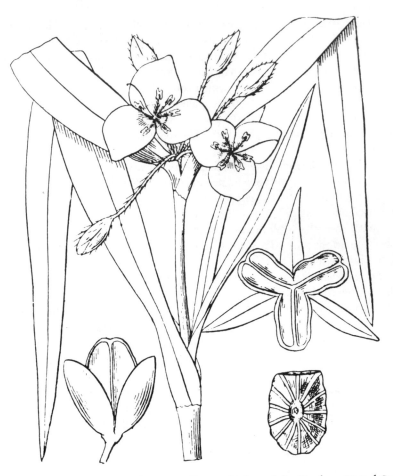

Tradescantia virginiana. Source: *An Illustrated Flora of the Northern United States, Canada, and the British Possessions.* 2nd ed., Vol. 1. Charles Scribner's Sons. 1913.

perate regions. Stems erect, simple, terete, jointless, sheathed, arising from stout, creeping rhizomes. Leaves few to many, sessile, erect, distichous, narrowly linear or strap-shaped, sheathing the base of the simple, jointless stems, rather thick, flat or slightly convex on the lower surface. Inflorescence monoecious flowers densely crowded in compact, cylindrical, spikelike racemes terminating the erect stem. Staminate portion of raceme terminal, separated from the pistillate portion or contiguous to it; each raceme subtended by a spathaceous fugacious bract; perianth comprised of bristles; flowers with one to seven stamens, filaments free or connate. Ovary of pistillate flowers one-locular, with single ovule. Fruit a subsessile or long-stipulate achene, subtended by capillary bristles; seeds subcylindrical or ellipsoid (Hotchkiss and Dozier, 1949).

Latin name: *Typha angustifolia* L.
Synonym: *Typha angustifolia* var. *calumetensis* Peattie
Common names: Cattail, Narrow-leaved cattail, Soft flag, Small bulrush, Reed mace
Origin: Eurasia, North America
Habitat: Roadside ditches, low swales, boggy sites, cultivated

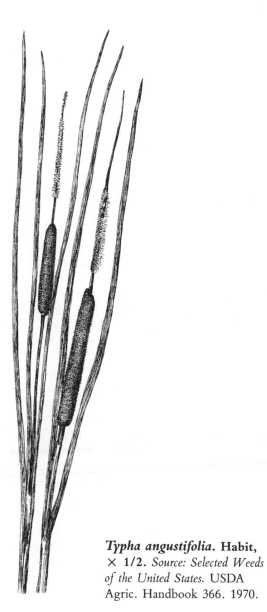

Typha angustifolia. **Habit,**
× 1/2. *Source: Selected Weeds of the United States.* USDA Agric. Handbook 366. 1970.

Hardiness: Zones 4 through 10

Description: An upright-narrow perennial herb with vigorous, creeping rhizomes. Culms sheathed, erect, slender, 4–8 ft/1.2–2.5 m high, jointless with white pith. Foliage yellowish green to dark green, medium in texture. Leaves distichous, sessile, thick, usually flat or convex on the back, slightly channeled on the upper surface, somewhat arching, firm or coriaceous, narrowly linear, 2–3 ft/6–9 dm long, 0.3–0.6 in./8–15 mm wide, much exceeding the inflorescence, sheaths tapering at the throat of the leaf blade, scarious-margined above, persistent. Inflorescence racemose, compact, cylindrical, spikelike, light brown racemes, borne on an erect, slender straight culm; the mature racemes are brownish black; staminate inflorescence terminal, buff, subtended by a fugacious bract, usually interrupted by as much as 3 in./8 cm from the lower, whitish brown pistillate portion; each portion of the raceme is 4–12 in./1–3 dm long, the pistillate portion is 0.5–1.0 in./13–25 mm thick in fruit; denuded rachis of the pistillate raceme roughened by short, rigid pedicels 1 mm long; perianth bristles accompanying the pistillate flowers with or without club-shaped tips, fruit a minute, subsessile, brownish, slightly furrowed nutlet, the mature spikes brownish black. A coarse, gregarious, perennial herb colonizing large areas. Flowering and fruiting occur from June through September or until frost in some regions.

Uses: This species is found in public parks, national forests, and in other areas where space is not limited. The leaves are used in making mats, and the hair or down of the fruits is used in stuffing pillows. The rootstocks are a source of aboriginal food. The spikes make ideal, interesting contributions to dried floral arrangements. To prevent the compact, spikelike racemes from shedding their numerous seeds, pick or cut the flowering stems before they mature and hang them upside-down in the shade to dry. Cattails provide excellent cover and protection for wildlife; they aid in preventing soil erosion and in building soils, an essential process necessarily long in fruition. The down is used in nest building by waterfowl.

Cultivation: Cattails are usually ubiquitous; they commonly occur advantageously in pools, ponds, highway ditches, along streams, and in marshes and swamps. Should propagation be necessary, it is usually accomplished by plant division or by seeding. Plant division is most successful when done in early spring before the appearance of stems or leaves or before they reach about 1 ft/3 dm in height. When planted in water in pools or ponds, cattails should be placed in a strong container and submerged about 6 in./1.5 dm below the surface to remain contained. Once cattails are established, their invasive growth competes vigorously with that of other aquatic perennials. They are difficult to contain, mainly because of their more or less inhospitable habitat. Digging or pulling out unwanted plants is a difficult and expensive operation. Careful consideration should be given to their use as aquatic ornamentals, as the plants are extremely gregarious. Where cattails are to be grown in a small pool or pond, the rhizomes should be planted in a large wooden tub to prevent their spread.

Alternatively, a portion of the pool may be partitioned off with wood or concrete to prevent the plants from spreading over the entire pool. This ubiquitous perennial, like *Typha latifolia,* is strongly invasive. Once it is established without any form of containment, it spreads rapidly at the expense of almost all other water plants. It is apparently infeasible and uneconomical to try to contain cattails in any specified areas in ponds, lakes, or pools.

Latin name: *Typha gracilis* Schur
Synonym: *Typha angustata* Bory & Chaub.
Common name: Cattail
Origin: Europe
Habitat: Low, wet sites in water, cultivated
Hardiness: Zones 4 through 10
Description: An upright-narrow perennial herb with stout, vigorously spreading rhizomes. Stems erect, slender, 3–4 ft/0.9–1.2 m high, greenish, sheathed, jointless. Foliage medium green or somewhat glaucous, medium in texture; leaves sessile, convex on the back, channeled on the upper surface, narrowly linear, 18–24 in./4.5–6.0 dm long, about 0.3–0.6 in./8–15 mm wide; sheaths tapering at the throat of the leaf blade. Inflorescence a solitary, spikelike, compact, cylindrical raceme; staminate portion of the raceme terminal, 1–2 in./2.5–5.0 cm long, buff, fugacious, interrupted from the pistillate portion by about 0.50–0.75 in./13–19 mm; pistillate portion dark brown, 4–5 in./1.0–1.3 dm long, 0.5–0.6 in./13–15 mm thick; pistillate flowers accompanied by short stiff bristles; fruit a very small, furrowed, light brown nutlet. Flowering and fruiting occur from July through September.
Uses: This small, refined cattail is useful in gardens smaller than those required for the giant species, *Typha angustifolia* and *Typha latifolia.* It provides a perfect foil for willows, *Salix* species, or any other broad-leaved plants, in addition to water lilies or various other water plants. The mature, cylindrical, colorful racemes, usually borne high above the foliage, provide a unique spectrum in shape and color not furnished by any other plants. The plant form, shape, and color of leaves and inflorescences of cattails and water lilies provide an interesting contrast in color and form when grown in the same pool or pond. Numerous other combinations of this nature are possible for the gardener who is a water-plant enthusiast. The availability of a wide range of cattails, including *Typha gracilis,* varying in cold hardiness, size, color, and shape provide the water gardener a wide choice in their use.
Cultivation: Propagation is by plant division and by seeding. Plant division is best accomplished in the spring soon after new growth has begun. This species does equally well in mud or in shallow water of ponds, pools, lakes, and streams. Planted cattails should be placed in a strong container when planted directly in pools or ponds, because of their invasive growth habit. The container should be placed in shallow water near the edge of the pool or pond and submerged about 3–4 in./8–10 cm below the surface. Either good loam soil or pond mud

will provide optimum growth. Cattails are easy to propagate and grow; their chief drawback is the effort required to keep the plants under control. Cattails are highly invasive and competitive and may quickly dominate the area where they are grown. This particular species, whose origin is Europe, may require introduction.

Latin name: *Typha latifolia* L.
Synonym: *Massula latifolia* Dulac
Common names: Common cattail, Great reed mace, Bulrush, Nail-rod, Cossack asparagus
Origin: Eurasia, North Africa
Habitat: Wet locations, often in water, cultivated
Hardiness: Zones 3 through 10
Description: An upright-narrow, perennial herb with vigorous, creeping rhizomes. Stems erect, slender, terete, jointless, sheathed, with a beige pith, 3–8 ft/0.9–2.5 m high. Foliage somewhat glaucous or grayish green, coarse in texture; leaves sessile, somewhat arching outward and glaucous, narrowly linear, 4–6 ft/1.2–1.8 m long, sometimes exceeding the stems, 0.5–1.0 in./13–25 mm wide, usually flat or convex on the back, slightly channeled on the upper surface; sheaths tapering at the throat of the leaf blade. Inflorescence a solitary, cylindrical, spikelike raceme terminating the erect stem, subtended by deciduous bracts; raceme with staminate and pistillate portions usually contiguous, the former about 3–5 in./0.8–1.3 dm long, the latter 2–8 in./0.5–2.0 dm long, about 0.5–1.5 in./1.3–3.8 cm thick in fruit, scarcely bristly; pistillate flowers devoid of bractlets among the bristles; naked axis of old spike retaining slender pedicels, pedicels of pistillate flowers bristlelike, bristles stiff, 2–3 mm long; fruit a minute, brownish, furrowed nutlet. Flowering and fruiting occur from June through August.
Uses: This species is too large except for the largest gardens. It is commonly found growing in the wild; common cattail is ubiquitous in temperate and tropical regions of the world. This course perennial has a strong, rhizomatous, invasive root system that makes the plants strongly competitive. The invasiveness, coupled with its enormous size, tends to reduce its usage to a large extent. This large species is commonly found in the wild in such places as state and national parks and forests. The tender, young shoots are highly esteemed as green vegetables by some people; the hair or down attached to the nutlets is used to stuff pillows. There are smaller forms, such as *Typha laxmannii* and *Typha minima,* available from the wild or from commercial sources for use by the home gardener.
Cultivation: Propagation is by plant division and by seeding. Plant division should be done in the spring when the plants are small and easily handled. Like other *Typha* species, the plants of common cattail are marginal; that is, they thrive in mud or in shallow water. When planted in water, the rootstocks should be placed in a strong container and submerged about 6 in./1.5 dm below the

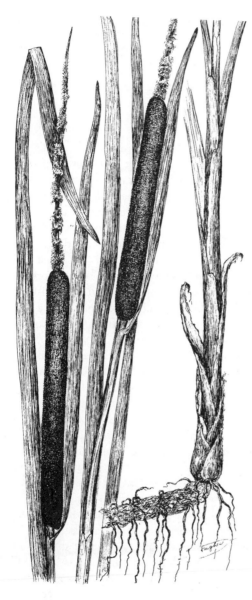

***Typha latifolia.* Habit,** ×
1/2. *Source: Selected Weeds of
the United States.* USDA
Agric. Handbook No. 366.
1970.

surface to remain contained. Good, heavy, clay soil or pond mud usually produces good growth. Common cattail colonizes large areas and is unsuited for the average home garden because of its excessive size and invasive growth habit; it may have a niche in large, expansive areas such as freshwater marshes and the largest water gardens. It is infeasible and uneconomical to attempt to control its growth and spread where it occurs in wet, marshy sites, including lakes and ponds.

> **Latin name:** *Typha laxmannia* Lepech.
> **Synonym:** *Typha stenophylla* Fisch. & B. Mey.
> **Common name:** Cattail
> **Origin:** Eurasia, China
> **Habitat:** Cultivated
> **Hardiness:** Zones 4 through 9
> **Description:** An upright-narrow, vigorous, strongly rhizomatous perennial. Stems slender, erect, 2–4 ft/0.6–1.2 m high, sheathed and jointless. Foliage medium green, fine in texture; leaves sessile, convex on the back, upper surface channeled, narrowly linear, 2–3 ft/6–9 dm long, 0.20–0.25 in./5–6 mm wide, outward arching, slightly glaucous. Inflorescence a solitary, compact, cylindrical, spikelike raceme, borne on a slender, erect stem, staminate portion of the raceme beige, about 1.6–2.0 in./4–5 cm long, interrupted by as much as 3–4 in./8–10 cm from the lower, foxy-red, pistillate portion; pistillate portion 4–5 in./1.0–1.3 dm long, 3–4 in./8–10 cm thick; perianth of short, stiff bristles; pistillate flowers with one-locular ovary; ovule pendulous, solitary; fruit a minute, furrowed, tan nutlet. Flowering and fruiting occur from July through September.
> **Uses:** This cattail is unique in having an orbicular, reddish, female spike in contrast to the thinner, cylindrical more or less beige spikes of other species. It is intermediate in size between *Typha minima,* dwarf cattail, and larger species such as *Typha latifolia.* This species is useful in most home gardens because of its reduced size. It is particularly attractive in a pool located below a rock garden, for example. When used in this setting, the plants act as a perfect foil for broad-leaved plants and particularly any low-growing, creeping, mat-forming grasses or other low, decumbent forms. The foxy-red, fat racemes are an attraction alone. This species of cattail provides an interesting and attractive sight in both form and color to any marsh, bog, or pond. It is particularly conspicuous in large clumps, keeping in mind the overall balance in size and color desired. The bright, foxy-red, orbicular racemes of this species are particularly attractive in dried arrangements. Their use, along with other cattails of different shapes and colors, adds diversity in shape and color to dried floral arrangements. All cattails are useful in dried arrangements. Some species retain their seedheads intact longer than others. Usually the racemes shatter their wind-blown seeds sporadically over a considerable period. The racemes should be collected before the initiation of shattering if they are to be used in dried arrangements. The seedheads are usually brownish green when mature, the brown or tan color becoming more pronounced with age. In harvesting the seedheads, be sure to leave enough stem below so that they may be arranged in floral displays. They usually shatter sooner or later, producing an attractive sight compounded by fluffy seeds (nut-

lets). Shattering may be prevented in part at least by spraying the racemes with hair spray or some similar product. Wild stands of this species provide wildlife protection.

Cultivation: Propagation is by plant division and by seeding. Plant division should be done in the spring when the plants are very small. Old stems may be cut to almost ground level in early fall and the plant crowns divided and planted the following spring. Cattails may be established in mud or directly in shallow water. The water level should not exceed 4–6 in./1.0–1.5 dm above the roots when planted in water. As with other cattail species, this species requires some form of containment to prevent its spread. The plant crowns or rhizomes should be placed in a strong container when planted either directly in water or in mud, because of their invasiveness. Cattails are highly competitive with other water plants and will exert their dominance rather quickly unless adequate control measures are followed for sustained periods.

Latin name: *Typha minima* Hoppe
Synonym: *Typha minor* Smirn.
Common names: Dwarf cattail, Dwarf reed mace
Origin: Caucasus, Asia
Habitat: Low wet locations, often in water, cultivated
Hardiness: Zones 4 through 8
Description: An upright-narrow, vigorous, rhizomatous perennial. Stems very slender, erect, 24–30 in./6.0–7.6 dm high, jointless, sheathed. Foliage medium green or slightly glaucous, fine in texture; leaves sessile, erect or arching outward, narrowly linear, 18–24 in./4.5–6.0 dm long, about 2–3 mm wide or reduced to somewhat inflated sheaths. Inflorescence a compact, orbicular raceme, borne on a very slender, simple, straight stem; staminate portion of the raceme terminal, beige, about 1–2 in./2.5–5.0 cm long; pistillate portion dark brown, almost spherical, 1.6–1.8 in./4.0–4.6 cm long, 0.4–0.6 in./10–15 mm thick; staminate and pistillate portions interrupted by a naked segment of the axis about 1 in./25 mm long; pistillate flowers accompanied by stout, short, stiff bristles; ovary one-locular, ovule solitary; fruit a subsessile, minute, furrowed nutlet. Flowering and fruiting occur from June through September.

Uses: Dwarf cattail is perhaps the most desired and sought-after of all cattails; it is slender and graceful in all its parts. This small species is superior in quality and beauty to all other species; for this reason it should be given priority when considering the use of cattails in the water garden, peat bog, or marsh. Its small size and foxy-red seedheads make it advantageous over larger forms for use in the home garden but perhaps disadvantageous in other situations. Dwarf cattail provides a perfect foil for other water and terrestrial plants. The mature racemes are useful in dried arrangements. The plants provide interesting contrasts in form and color to broad-leaved plants, including water lilies, and to mat-forming grasses. The form, size, and color of the plants are entirely different from those of any other water garden plants, thus adding a new and different dimension to such plantings. It may be somewhat difficult to locate in the trade, although it can be found in English plant catalogs.

Cultivation: Propagation is by seeding and by plant division. Plant division should be done in the spring when the plants are small and manageable. Dwarf cattail may be planted in low, marshy areas, in peat bogs, or in wet soil, mud, or directly in shallow water, where the roots may be submerged by as much as 2–4 in./5–10 cm below the surface. Dwarf cattail has vigorous rhizomes that produce a vigorous, gregarious growth like that of other cattails. For this reason, it must be controlled in some manner; otherwise, it will get out of hand very quickly.

Xerophyllum **Michx.** Name from Greek *xeros,* "arid," and *phyllon,* "leaf." Type species, *Xerophyllum asphodeloides* (L.) Nutt. There are four known species, native to North America. Perennial, tall, stout, rigid herbs with woody rootstocks. Stems simple, leafy; leaves basal, numerous, spreading, narrowly linear, grasslike. Flowers perfect, in dense terminal racemes, each subtended by one to three narrow branchlets. Perianth of six widely spreading, white segments, oval, distinct, without glands or claws, sepals and petals broad, five-to-seven-nerved, persistent, the latter longer than the former; androecium six-merous, filaments subulate, anthers two-locular; styles three, filiform, persistent, ovary three-locular, two to four ovules in each locule; fruit a loculicidal, three-locular capsule, obtuse; seeds collateral, trigonous (Hortus Third, 1977).

> **Latin name:** *Xerophyllum asphodeloides* (L.) Nutt.
> **Synonym:** *Xerophyllum setifolium* Michx.
> **Common names:** Beargrass, Turkey-beard, Mountain asphadel
> **Origin:** United States
> **Habitat:** Shaded, sandy soils; mountain wooded sites
> **Hardiness:** Zones 5 through 9
> **Description:** An upright-narrow to spreading, rigid herb from thick, tuberous, woody rhizomes. Stems simple, 18–48 in./0.5–1.2 m high. Foliage light green, medium in texture; leaves basal and cauline, basal leaves densely tufted, numerous, spreading and reclining, narrowly linear, grasslike, long attenuate, many-veined, stiff and wiry, rigid and dry, rough on the margins, upper cauline leaves reduced to bristlelike bracts. Inflorescence a dense, bracteate, racemelike, spike, 10–12 in./2.5–3.0 dm long, stout, many-flowered; flowers about 0.4 in./10 mm across, pedicellate, pedicels 1–3 in./2.5–8.0 cm long, perfect, creamy-white, showy, each flower subtended by one to three narrow branchlets; perianth six-merous, segments distinct, sepals pearl-like, white, oval, without glands or claws, petals and sepals broad, five-to-nine-nerved, the former longer than the latter, persistent, eventually withering, about the length of the filaments; fruit an obtuse, globular, three-locular capsule; ovules two to four in

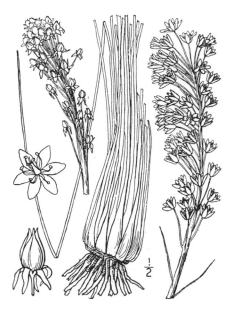

Xerophyllum asphodeloides.
Source: *An Illustrated Flora of
the Northern United States,
Canada, and the British
Possessions. 2nd ed., Vol. 1.*
Charles Scribner's Sons.
1913.

each cavity; seed trigonous. Flowering and fruiting occur from May through August.

Uses: This hardy, stout, rigid herb is noted for its light green, filiform foliage and its small, showy, white flowers. The plants form large, dense, light green mounds topped with prodigious white flowers borne on tall, slender stems far above the foliage. The grasslike foliage is deceiving upon casual observation; the true identity of beargrass is revealed by its bountiful flower production. Beargrass is useful in specimen plantings in middleground borders and around the periphery of the garden. Its tolerance of dry sites is conducive to its use in rock gardens, where it may be located on berms or other dry sites. The plants are attractive when grown in rather large colonies in the so-called wild garden.

Cultivation: Propagation is usually by plant division. The plants may be propagated most successfully in early spring, when new growth is still small. Beargrass is quite drought tolerant. The plants may be grown in full sun, but perhaps they perform better in light, shaded, wooded sites in moist or dry sandy soils relatively low in pH. Beargrass will survive winters in zone 5, provided it is properly mulched and planted in a protected location.

Other ornamental species: *Xerophyllum tenax* (Pursh) Nutt. Elk grass, Fire lily, Beargrass   An upright-narrow perennial with short, thick rhizomes. Stems simple, 4–5 ft/1.2–1.5 m high, copiously leafy, the leaves reduced upward. Basal leaves densely tufted, wiry and tough, scabrous, long attenuate, narrowly linear, 1–3 ft/3–9 dm long, 0.15–0.30 in./6–8 mm wide. Inflorescence a terminal pyramidal raceme, initially corymblike, but elongating to 12–18 in./ 3.0–4.5 dm long in late flower; flowers numerous, small, long-pedicellate, pedi-

Xerophyllum tenax. Source: An Illustrated Flora of the Pacific States. Vol 1. Stanford Univ. Press. 1923.

cels 1–2 in./2.5–5.0 cm long, creamy-white with purplish stamens; perianth sepals oblong, distinct, spreading, 0.2–0.4 in./5–10 mm long, persistent; stamens equaling or exceeding the perianth; fruit a three-locular capsule, 0.2–0.3 in./5–8 mm long; seeds two to six per locule. Elk grass is native to northwestern America; it is a stately, hardy, somewhat grasslike herb. It is not commonly cultivated, although it is easy to grow in its native range. The long, coriaceous leaves are useful in basketry. It is useful in borders and the wild garden as an ornamental. Flowering and fruiting occur from May through August. Propagation is usually by offsets.

Xyris L. (**Yellow-eyed grass**). From Greek *xyris,* name of a plant with two-edged leaves, from *xyron,* ''razor.'' Type species, *Xyris indica* L. There are about 245 species, native chiefly to warmer regions of the world, except Europe. Annual or perennial, acaulescent, rushlike, tufted herbs. Leaves basal, imbricate at the base of the scape, erect, narrow. Flowers borne singly in the axils of coriaceous, scalelike, imbricate bracts on leafless scapes. Sepals three; petals three, yellow, rarely white, fugacious, with claws. Androecium of three fertile stamens, inserted on the claws of the petals, alternating with three sterile filaments that are cleft, plumose, or bearded at the apex; style three-cleft. Fruit a free, ellipsoid capsule, one-locular with three-parietal placenta, three-valved, many-seeded (Kral, 1966).

Latin name: *Xyris arenicola* Small
Synonym: *Xyris torta* J. E. Smith
Common name: Yellow-eyed grass
Origin: North America
Habitat: Moist or wet sands and bogs
Hardiness: Zones 6 through 10
Description: An acaulescent, rushlike, perennial herb, base dark brown, bulbous and indurate. Bulbs 0.2–0.5 in./5–13 mm high, 0.15–0.40 in./4–14 mm thick, usually clustered, forming tufts. Scape somewhat compressed toward the summit, not winged, spirally twisted and flexuous, 12–28 in./3–7 dm high. Foliage grayish green or bluish green, fine in texture; leaves narrowly linear, stiff, with dark, dilated bases, thick and spirally twisted, 4–16 in./1–4 dm long, 0.1–0.2 in./3–5 mm wide. Inflorescence a subglobose to cylindric or conic-oblong, scaled spike, 0.2–0.7 in./5–18 mm long, 0.3–0.4 in./8–10 mm thick, often round at the summit; scales suborbicular, light brown, the greenish area small; lateral sepals fringed, conspicuous, keeled, 0.3–0.5 in./8–13 mm long, ciliolate on the keel, bearded at the apex; corolla yellow; fruit an oblong, one-locular, three-valved capsule with many seeds.
Uses: This grasslike herb is of little, if any, ornamental value alone. Its chief value is in its use in the water garden, around swimming pools, and for naturalizing low, wet sites surrounding, adjacent to, or near the formal garden. The small yellow flowers may come as a surprise, especially to the uninformed, who may have surmised a true grass to be present. Another location in which yellow-eyed grass and its larger relatives, *Xyris fimbriata* and *Xyris platylepis,* is useful is that of the so-called wild garden, provided that it is located in a low, wet site on acid soil.
Cultivation: Propagation is by seeding and by plant division, preferably the latter. This species, like other *Xyris* species, prefers wet places, chiefly on sandy, acid soils. The plants perform best in full sun, or in light or intermittent shade.

Latin name: *Xyris baldwiniana* Schult.
Synonym: *Xyris juncea baldwiniana* var. *tenuifolia* (Chapm.) Malme
Common names: St. Mary's grass, Yellow-eyed grass
Origin: North America
Habitat: Peat bogs, wet sand, pond margins
Hardiness: Zones 8 through 10
Description: An acaulescent, rushlike, paludal, perennial herb with stiff, narrow leaves sheathing the base of the naked scape; plants clustered. Scape nearly terete or one-angled, smooth, slender, 8–16 in./2–4 dm high. Foliage light green, fine in texture; leaves basal, numerous, equitant, filiform, terete, 2–8 in./0.5–2.0 dm long, 1–2 mm wide, becoming twisted. Inflorescence a compact, terminal spike, ovoid or subglobose, 0.15–0.25 in./4–6 mm long, turbinate at the base, with densely imbricate, scalelike bracts; lateral sepals 0.15–

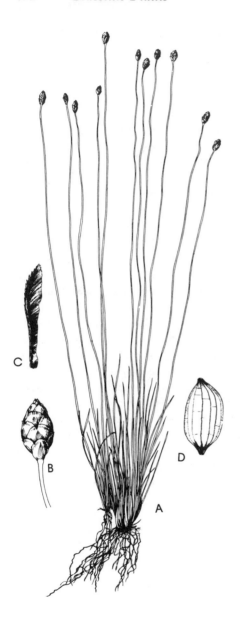

**Xyris baldwiniana. A,
Habit; B, head; C, lateral
sepal; D, seed.** *Source, A
and B: Aquatic and Wetland
Plants of Southeastern United
States. Univ. of Georgia Press.
(1979); C and D: Xyris
(Xyridaceae) of the Continental
United States and Canada.* Sida
2. 1966.

0.25 in./4–6 mm long, the upper half of the keel wing conspicuously serrate;
calyx of three sepals, glumaceous; flowers aggregate, corolla yellow, petals three,
fugacious; androecium of three stamens alternating with three staminodia, sterile
filaments glabrous, anthers extrorse; gynoecium three-merous; fruit a one-locular,
oblong, free capsule with many seeds. Flowering and fruiting occur throughout
the year.

Uses: This grasslike herb, with its filiform foliage, resembles some true grasses so closely that it is difficult to differentiate it by casual observation; usually it is only when the small, yellowish flowers appear that St. Mary's grass is easily distinguishable. The plants form rather dense clusters, producing a good ground cover on highly acid soils. This characteristic may be advantageous in certain situations, especially when plants of high tolerance of soil acidity are being sought. St. Mary's grass may have a place in water gardens and in naturalizing low, wet areas, such as wild gardens in warmer climates. It may be used along with other water-loving plants to form a meadowlike effect in small, wet sites.

Cultivation: Propagation is by plant division. Propagation is most successful in the spring; this allows the plants maximum duration during the growing season to become established. St. Mary's grass grows best in full sun or light shade in moist or wet, sandy, highly acid soils. The plants require only minimum maintenance once they are established.

Latin name: *Xyris fimbriata* Ell.
Common name: Yellow-eyed grass
Origin: North America
Habitat: Wet, sandy soils, pond margins, swamps
Hardiness: Zones 6 through 10
Description: An acaulescent, rushlike, paludal, perennial herb, base neither bulbous nor indurate, soft. Scape straight, erect, stiff, compressed, two-edged and roughened on the edges toward the summit, 20–48 in./0.6–1.2 m high. Foliage dull light green, medium in texture; leaves basal, equitant, lorate, not lustrous, broadly linear, 1–2 ft/3–6 dm long, 0.4–0.5 in./10–13 mm wide, larger leaves tawny. Inflorescence an ovoid to ellipsoid spike, 0.5–1.0 in./13–25 mm long, 0.3–0.5 in./8–13 mm wide, with loosely imbricate bracts; lateral sepals 0.3–0.4 in./8–10 mm long, much exceeding the subtending bracts, relatively broad, keel conspicuously fringed with long, spreading segments from about the middle to the apex; flowers aggregate, corolla yellow; androecium of three fertile stamens and three staminodia; gynoecium three-merous; fruit an oblong, one-locular, three-valved capsule. Flowering and fruiting usually occur during the spring, but occasionally in the fall or throughout the year in zones 9 and 10.

Uses: This rushlike, rather large, perennial herb is useful in naturalizing areas that are low, wet, sandy, and highly acidic. It is useful, along with other water plants such as sedges, *Cyperus* species, and cattails, *Typha* species, along the margins of ponds, lakes, pools, and streams. A carefully balanced combination of such plants will improve the appearance of many low, swampy, unsightly places around the periphery of the formal garden. The plants have no outstanding ornamental value, although they do add variety and yet another dimension in improving the landscape in some locations, such as the wild garden.

Cultivation: Propagation is by seeding and by plant division, usually the

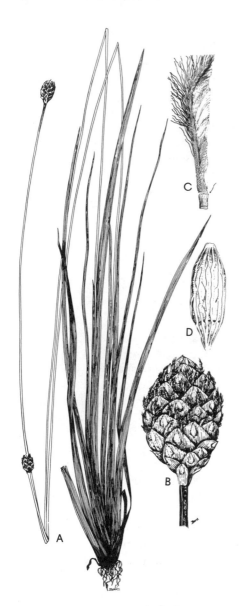

Xyris fimbriata. **A, Habit;
B, head; C, lateral sepal;
D, seed.** *Source, A and B:
Aquatic and Wetland Plants of
Southeastern United States.
Univ. of Georgia Press. (1979);
C and D: Xyris (Xyridaceae) of
the Continental United States
and Canada.* Sida 2. 1966.

latter. The plants thrive equally well in full sun or light shade on damp or wet,
highly acidic, sandy soils.

Latin name: *Xyris montana* Ries
Synonym: *Xyris flexuosa* var. *pusilla* R. Br.
Common name: Yellow-eyed grass

Origin: North America
Habitat: Chiefly in peat bogs and shallow water around pond borders
Hardiness: Zones 4 through 6
Description: A dwarf, acaulescent, rushlike, cespitose or matted herb with more or less branching rhizomes, bases soft and flattened. Scape erect, straight or spiraling, filiform, 6–12 in./1.5–3.0 dm high, usually with metallic luster, readily disarticulating at the base. Foliage soft, light green, fine in texture; leaves basal, equitant, narowly linear, 2–6 in./0.5–1.5 dm long, less than 0.1 in./3 mm wide. Inflorescence a narrow ovoid spike with few (i.e., four to seven) appressed, floriferous scales, greenish, becoming dark brown at maturity, 0.4–0.5 in./10–13 mm long, 0.20–0.25 in./5–6 mm thick; lateral sepals projecting beyond the bracts, with purple tips, keel slightly toothed at the summit; flowers small, yellow, with purple tips; androecium of three fertile stamens and three staminodia; gynoecium three-merous; fruit an oblong, one-locular, three-valved capsule; seeds subcylindric, spindle-shaped, regularly ribbed. Flowering and fruiting occur from July through September.
Uses: This dwarf yellow-eyed grass is at home in the peat bog or the wild garden. It is a cool-season herb adapted to the north-central and northeastern United States.
Cultivation: Propagation is usually by plant division or, occasionally, by seeding. The plants prefer full sun or partial shade on an acid, wet soil or a peat bog.

Latin name: *Xyris platylepis* Chapm.
Common name: Yellow-eyed grass
Origin: North America
Habitat: Moist, sandy soils, bogs, savannas
Hardiness: Zones 8 through 10
Description: An acaulescent, rushlike, coarse, perennial herb with a bulbous base. Scape 2–3 ft/6–9 dm high, twisted, sometimes slightly roughened on the margins, two-ridged above. Foliage light green, fine in texture; leaves basal, equitant, lowest leaves are firm, short scales surrounding the bulbous base, elongate leaves coriaceous, 1–3 ft/3–9 dm long, 0.25–0.50 in./6–13 mm wide. Inflorescence a terminal ellipsoid or cylindrical spike, 0.6–1.0 in./15–25 mm long, 0.3–0.7 in./8–18 mm thick, bracted, bracts firm, brown, very broad and broadly truncate or nearly so at the apex; lateral sepals keeled, lacerate toothed; flowers small, yellow; androecium of three fertile stamens and three staminodia; gynoecium three-carpellate; fruit an oblong, one-locular, three-valved capsule. Flowering and fruiting occur from April through June in the spring and occasionally in the fall.
Uses: This acaulescent, grasslike herb, which is slightly smaller than *Xyris fimbriata,* is useful for the same purposes as the latter. The natural habitat of this herb is usually sites where moisture is available on a more or less constant basis. For this reason, it may be used, along with other water-loving plants, in natural-

Xyris platylepis. **A, Habit; B, head; C, lateral sepal; D, seed.** *Source, A and B: Aquatic and Wetland Plants of Southeastern United States. Univ. of Georgia Press. (1979); C and D: Xyris (Xyridaceae) of the Continental United States and Canada.* Sida 2. 1966.

izing low, wet, boggy sites. These stiff herbs, like the sedges, aid in soil and sand stabilization along stream banks and around the margins of lakes, ponds, and pools. The plants are not too large for use in large water gardens. Yellow-eyed grass is useful in improving the landscape by providing variety to its structure, color, and texture.

Cultivation: Propagation is by seeding and by plant division, preferably the latter. The plants are equally adapted to full sun or light shade, in damp or preferably wet, sandy soils of very low pH. These grasslike or rushlike herbs are usually compatible with other water-loving plants, such as sedges and cattails. These plants are not as gregarious as other rhizomatous forms; however, they may become weedy.

Yucca L. (**Spanish bayonet, Beargrass**). The native Haitian name for the root of the cassava plant, *Jatropha manihot.* Lectotype, *Yucca aloifolia* L. There are about 40 species, native to the warmer regions of North America. Acaulescent or erect, woody trunks; leaves gladiate or rarely stilettolike; inflorescence racemose or paniculate. Flowers violet or white; perianth cup-shaped or saucer-shaped; segments six, separate or partly united; androecium six-merous. Ovary superior, three-locular, each locule with numerous ovules. Fruit sometimes dry or dehiscent and capsular or indehiscent and fleshy; seeds usually black, thickened and rough or smooth, thin and winged or wingless (Small, 1933; Hortus Third, 1977).

Latin name: *Yucca aloifolia* L.
Common names: Spanish dagger, Spanish bayonet, Beargrass
Origin: North America
Habitat: Cultivated
Hardiness: Zones 8 through 10
Description: An erect, woody, evergreen perennial. Caudex usually simple, occasionally branched, often 3–9 ft /0.9–2.8 m high, about 2 in./5 cm thick, copiously leafy, brown, rough. Foliage dark green, coarse in texture. Leaves alternate, clustered near the top of the stem, erect and spreading above, reflexed and deciduous below, margins denticulate, very firm and rigid, coriaceous, gladiate with a very sharp tip, 18–24 in./4.5–6.0 dm long, 1.0–1.6 in./2.5–4.0 cm wide. Inflorescence a showy, oval or broadly elliptical panicle terminating a scapelike stem, 12–18 in./3.0–4.5 dm long, about 12 in./3 dm across at its widest point, many-flowered. Flowers perfect, whitish, often purple tinged, 3–4 in./8–10 cm across, campanulate, sepals and petals each about 1.6–2.4 in./4.0–6.0 cm long, several-veined, deciduous; calyx of three greenish white sepals; corolla of three petals very similar to the sepals; fruit an indehiscent loculicidal capsule, 3.0–3.6 in./8–9 cm long, with purple pulp and no core; seeds thick. Flowering and fruiting may not occur annually in plant-hardiness zones 8 and 9; flowering and fruiting usually occur from October through January in zone 10; flowers are not normally produced on plants grown indoors.
Uses: Spanish dagger is grown for its unique architecture, stiff, dark green foliage and showy, white-flowering panicles. Its size limits its use somewhat, but the plants offer an interesting contrast to all other ornamentals when used in background or in specimen plantings. Spanish dagger is often grown in large

greenhouses and terrariums. The plants are a perfect foil for some of the taller, ornamental, perennial grasses, such as giant reed, pampas grass, and plumegrass. The economic value of Spanish dagger consists of its use in making ropes, lines, and strings from its fibrous leaves.

Cultivation: Propagation is by seeding and by planting offsets or stem cuttings. The fastest method of propagation involves planting stem cuttings or offshoots. Spanish dagger is a slow grower, although it is fairly easily propagated. Proper and adequate spacing of the plants in the garden or landscape is perhaps the paramount consideration in their establishment and use; plants of this size and form are used most advantageously in spacious surroundings in large gardens. Spanish dagger is quite drought tolerant; although the plants grow and develop comparatively slowly, they are more than worth the wait. Yuccas are tolerant of extremely low humidity and will thrive in conditions that are unsuitable for many other ornamentals. This is to their advantage when grown in homes with forced-air heating systems. The plants are tolerant of wide temperature ranges; however, temperatures below about 50°F/10°C are harmful. Plants grown indoors require light of high intensity. Spanish dagger in active growth requires enough watering to keep the potting mixture thoroughly moist, but the containers should never be allowed to stand in water. As with most house plants, apply standard liquid fertilizer every two weeks during periods of active growth. Yuccas grown indoors may become top-heavy; for this reason, it is best that they be grown in clay pots rather than in lighter, plastic pots. The plants may become large enough to require 12-in./3-dm pots or tubs. Indoor plants do best when kept outside during summer months. They require at least three or four hours of direct sunlight or artificial light of high intensity per day.

> **Latin name:** *Yucca filamentosa* L.
> **Common names:** Adam's needle, Curly-hair yucca, Needle palm
> **Origin:** North America
> **Habitat:** Cultivated
> **Hardiness:** Zones 6 through 9
> **Description:** An erect, woody, evergreen perennial. Caudex simple, 3–6 ft/0.9–1.8 m high, with copious leaves from a running rootstock. Foliage dark green, coarse in texture. Leaves numerous, spatulate, abruptly narrowed to a stout, terminal spine, stiff and spreading above, reflexed and tardily deciduous below, coriaceous, long attenuate, rough on the back, filiferous on the margins, 16–24 in./4–6 dm long, 0.8–1.6 in./2–4 cm wide. Inflorescence a large pyramidal, branched panicle, 10–18 in./2.5–4.5 dm long, 8–10 in./2.0–2.5 dm wide, terminating a stout, bracteate scape, branches glabrous. Flowers large, about 2 in./5 cm long, perfect, campanulate, greenish white, petals broadly ovate, 1.0–1.6 in./2.5–4.0 cm long; fruit an ellipsoid, dry, dehiscent capsule, 2.0–2.4 in./5.0–6.0 cm long; seeds black, elongate, sometimes angulate. Flowering and fruiting occur irregularly in cooler climates, usually from July through August

Yucca filamentosa. Source: *An Illustrated Flora of the Northern United States, Canada, and the British Possessions. 2nd ed., Vol. 1.* Charles Scribner's Sons. 1913.

and from October through January in the subtropics and in the warmer parts of zone 10.

   Uses: The ornamental value of Adam's needle is its dark-green, rigid, erect foliage and its large, terminal, flowering panicles. The plants are generally smaller than those of Spanish dagger and, consequently, are useful in middle-ground borders and in group and specimen plantings. They are a perfect foil for some of the intermediate ornamental grasses in middleground border plantings. In cooler climates, Adam's needle may be grown indoors, provided sufficient space and adequate light are available. Specimen plantings in rock gardens and in perennial borders aid in diversifying and improving the landscape.

Cultivation: Propagation is by seeding and by planting stem cuttings, off-shoots, and the tuberous rootstocks. The plants are adapted to a wide range of soils, including poor, undrained, and dry, rocky types. Full sun and sufficient space are required for maximum growth and development. Yucca species grown in cooler climates, usually beyond their natural distribution range, tend to be smaller than those grown in their natural habitat.

Other ornamental species: *Yucca baccata* Torr. Blue yucca   A woody perennial; stems short, prostrate, very leafy. Foliage dark green, coarse in texture; leaves coriaceous, gladiate, 12–28 in./3.0–7.1 dm long, 1.8–2.2 in./4.5–5.5 cm wide, erect, stiff, often coarsely curly filiferous. Inflorescence an erect, terminal panicle, 18–24 in./4.5–6.0 dm long, 6–12 in./1.5–3.0 dm thick, densely many-flowered. Flowers perfect, campanulate, whitish or cream, often tinged with purple; sepals and petals essentially separate, equal, pistil 2–3 in./5–8 cm long; fruit an indehiscent, loculicidal capsule, 8–10 in./2.0–2.5 dm long, fleshy; seeds wingless, thick, rough, dark brown, or black. Blue yucca is propagated in the same manner as other yuccas. It is adapted to zones 9 and 10. Its ornamental use usually involves specimen plantings.

Yucca constricta Buckl.   A short, prostrate form; stems, if present, are short, decumbent. Foliage dark green, medium in texture; leaves stiff, coriaceous, erect, linear, 24–26 in./6.0–6.5 dm long, 0.5–0.6 in./13–15 mm wide, flat or slightly trigonous, striate, margins white or green, filiferous. Inflorescence an erect, simple, many-flowered panicle, borne on scapes 6–8 ft/1.8–2.5 m high; flowers campanulate, perfect, greenish white, 1.6–2.0 in./4–5 cm long, segments united basely; fruit a constricted, loculicidal, dehiscent capsule. This species is commonly used in specimen plantings; it is adapted to zones 9 and 10. It is propagated in the same manner as other yuccas.

Yucca glauca Nutt. ex Fraser Soapweed, Soapwell (Synonym: *Yucca angustifolia* Pursh)   A woody, hardy perennial; stems short, prostrate, copiously leafy, 2–3 ft/6–9 dm high. Foliage dark green, medium in texture. Leaves erect, very stiff, coriaceous, pungent, gladiate, 16–28 in./ 4.0–7.0 dm long, 0.15–0.50 in./4–13 mm wide, margins whitish or greenish white, filiferous, rigidly sharp-pointed. Inflorescence a terminal raceme, nearly sessile, many-flowered, 1–4 ft/0.3–1.2 m long, 8–12 in./2–3 dm thick, with few basal branchlets, tardily deciduous; perianth greenish white, chartaceous; flowers perfect, greenish white, often tinged rosy-brown, 1.6–2.4 in./4–6 cm long, segments separate or briefly united basely, fragrant; fruit a six-sided ellipsoid capsule, scarcely constricted, dehiscent, 2.4–2.8 in./6–7 cm long; seeds black, 0.4–0.5 in./ 10–13 mm broad. Flowering and fruiting occur from May through June. Propagation is by seeding and by planting stem or root cuttings or offshoots. This species is probably the most cold tolerant of all yuccas; it occurs in zones 4–9. The exceptional cold tolerance is its chief advantage as an ornamental; flowering and fruiting occur from May through July.

Yucca gloriosa L. Spanish bayonet, Spanish dagger, Palm lily, Roman candle, Lord's candlestick   A woody perennial, stems 6–8 ft/1.8–2.5 m high, trunks

½

Yucca glauca. **Habit,** ×
1/12; leaf × 1/2; flowers
× 1/2. *Source: Vascular*
Plants of The Pacific Northwest.
Univ. of Washington Press.
1969.

short. Foliage dark green, coarse in texture; leaves coriaceous, stiff, gladiate, 24–
30 in./6.0–7.6 dm long, 1–2 in./2.5–5.0 cm wide, terminating in a stiff, spine-
like tip. Inflorescence a terminal, many-flowered panicle. Flowers campanulate,
white to greenish white to reddish, 3–4 in./8–10 cm wide; fruit a scarcely fleshy,
six-ribbed, indehiscent capsule; seeds shiny, thin. Spanish bayonet is adapted to
plant hardiness zones 7–10. Like other yuccas, it is used primarily in large,

expansive areas in specimen and background plantings. Propagation is similar to that of other yuccas.

Zebrina **Schnizl. (Wandering Jew).** Type species, *Zebrina pendula* Schnizl. There are two or more species, native to Mexico and Central America. Trailing, succulent herbs with diffusely branching stems, branches breaking through leaf sheaths. Leaves alternate; leaf blades rather broad. Inflorescence paired cymes borne in involucres of leaflike bracts with saccate bases. Sepals united into a hyaline, unequally lobed tube; corolla white or rose purple, petals united into a tube with spreading lobes; androecium six-merous, filaments bearded; ovary three-locular, each locule with two ovules. Fruit a slender pedicellate capsule.

> **Latin name:** *Zebrina pendula* Schnizl.
> **Common names:** Wandering Jew, Inch plant
> **Origin:** Mexico, Guatemala
> **Habitat:** Cultivated, escape from cultivation
> **Hardiness:** Zones 9 and 10
> **Description:** A decumbent, succulent, evergreen, perennial herb with diffusely branched creeping stems; stems and branches usually very weak, smooth, rooting at the nodes, 1–3 ft/3–9 dm long, 6–12 in./1.5–3.0 dm high. Foliage coarse in texture, variable in color; leaves usually striped, with longitudinal whitish stripes above, purple beneath in the typical form; or variegated, with two marginal, glistening, silvery green stripes surrounding a medium green, central portion, or with alternate dark green or reddish green stripes; sessile, sheathed, blades ovate or elliptic-ovate, 1–3 in./2.5–8.0 cm long, 1.0–1.2 in./2.5–3.0 cm wide. Inflorescence cymes borne in involucres of leaflike bracts, nearly glabrous to villous at base or throughout, with saccate bases; flowers perfect, ephemeral; calyx coralloid, lobes lanceolate; sepals united into a hyaline, unequally lobed tube; corolla rose purple, petals united into a tube with spreading lobes 0.2–0.3 in./5–8 mm long; androecium six-merous, filaments bearded; gynoecium a three-carpellate ovary, styles united; fruit an ovoid or ellipsoid-ovoid capsule, 1–2 mm long. Flowering and fruiting throughout the year; new flowers, which blossom each morning, persist for only a portion of the day. This is one of several plants known as wandering Jew.
> **Uses:** Wandering Jew has been a favorite house plant for many, many years and still remains a favorite. It is grown primarily for its colorful foliage, which, when allowed to cascade over the sides of hanging baskets, in which it is usually grown, makes a spectacular statement. The plants are equally attractive when different-colored zebrinas are trained on a fan-shaped or rectangular trellis. The rose-colored flowers, of which new ones blossom each morning, add to the attractiveness of this viny, succulent herb. It is often grown in warm climates as a colorful ground cover in understory plantings in shaded sites among shrub-

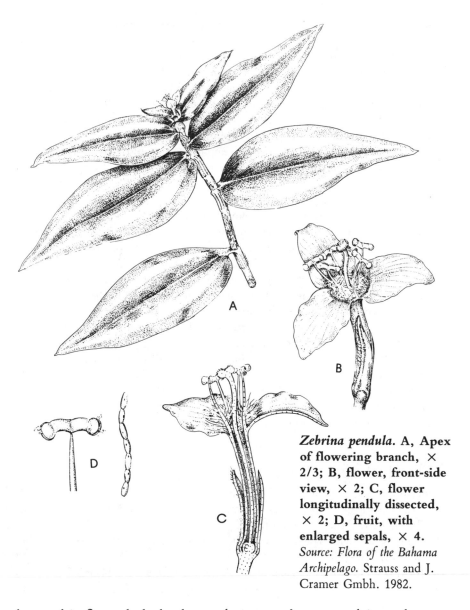

A

B

D

C

***Zebrina pendula.* A, Apex of flowering branch, × 2/3; B, flower, front-side view, × 2; C, flower longitudinally dissected, × 2; D, fruit, with enlarged sepals, × 4.**
Source: *Flora of the Bahama Archipelago.* Strauss and J. Cramer Gmbh. 1982.

bery and in flower beds, borders, and water gardens as an edging and accent plant.

Cultivation: Propagation is by stem cuttings, seeding, and plant division. Wandering Jew is easily propagated and maintained. It may be propagated throughout the year in warm climates. The growing tips of stems may be rooted readily, either in water or potting soil; if water is used, it should be changed regularly for best results, although the cuttings will root without water changes. When rooting is done in potting soil, the soil should be kept moist until rooting is complete. Stem cuttings may be successfully established by being planted directly in the pots in which they are to be grown and maintained. It is advisable to propagate wandering Jew fairly frequently because the older leaves dry up and become brown and unattractive, leaving bare stems. Stem-tip cuttings are easily rooted in a mixture of equal parts of peat moss and sand, or soil and sand. Maintain the cuttings in bright, filtered light, providing just enough water to keep the mixture moist but not wet. The cuttings should root in about three or four weeks, after which they should be transferred to pots, hanging baskets, trellises, or wherever they are to be grown, and treated as mature plants.

Wandering Jew requires continuous bright light to produce vigorous compact growth with brilliant foliage color. This warm-season succulent herb performs best at normal room temperatures of 70–75°F/21–24°C; the plants grow very slowly at cooler temperatures; they can tolerate temperatures as low as about 55°F/13°C. Plants in an active growth state require moderate watering; the top portion of the potting mixture should be allowed to dry out between waterings. The plants require watering less frequently when in the resting stage. Best foliage color is produced by plants grown in slightly dry soils. Fertilize actively growing plants with standard liquid fertilizer every two weeks. The plants become spindly and unattractive if their growing points are not pinched off regularly. Pinching off the growing tips of lengthy shoots encourages the production of side branches, which increases the attractiveness of the plants by new, fresh growth. The popularity of this species as a house plant perhaps exceeds that of *Tradescantia albiflora* and *Tradescantia bracteata,* which are known and grown under the same name.

REFERENCES

Anderson, Edgar, and Robert E. Woodson. 1935. *The Species of Tradescantia Indigenous to the United States.* Contributions to Arnold Arboretum. Jamaica Plain, MA: Arnold Arboretum.

Brackett, Amelia. 1923. Revision of the American species of Hypoxis. *Rhodora* 25(296):120–163.

Buell, M. F. 1935. Acorus calamus in America. *Rhodora* 37(442):367–369.

Fernald, M. L. 1970. *Gray's Manual of Botany.* 8th ed. New York: D. Van Nostrand.

Hauke, R. L. 1963. A taxonomic monograph of the genus Equisetum subgenus Hippochaete. Beich. Nova Hedwigia 8:1–123.

Hortus Third. 1977. *A Concise Dictionary of Plants Cultivated in the United States and Canada.* New York: Macmillan.

Hotchkiss, N., and H. L. Dozier. 1949. Taxonomy and distribution of North American cat-tails. *American Midland Naturalist* 41:237–254.

Kral, Robert. 1966. Xyris (Xyridaceae) of the continental United States and Canada. *Sida* 2(3):177–260.

Robinson, B. L., and M. L. Fernald. 1908. *Gray's New Manual of Botany.* 7th ed. New York: American Book Company.

Shinners, L. H. 1957. Sisyrinchium Bermudiana L. instead of Sisyrinchium angustifolium Miller. *Rhodora* 59(702):159–160.

Small, J. K. 1933. *Manual of the Southeastern Flora.* New York: J. K. Small.

4

Rushes and Sedges

Two monocotyledonous plant families, Cyperaceae, or sedge family, and Juncaceae, or rush family, consist mainly of perennial, grasslike herbs, some of which are of ornamental value. The very large and diverse Cyperaceae family includes about 3,000 species distributed among some 80 genera of caulescent or scapose, grasslike herbs. These plants are of widespread geographic distribution and often occur in wet locations. They comprise aquatic, semiaquatic, and terrestrial forms. The smaller Juncaceae family consists of some 300 species distributed among eight genera of perennial, or sometimes annual, herbs, some of which are grasslike in habit. Included in this family are (1) the aquatic true rushes found growing in wet places and directly in water and (2) the terrestrial wood-rushes occurring in shaded woods in moist or more or less dry sites.

The similarities of the ornamental types in these two plant families to one another and to true grasses by far overshadow their dissimilarities. For this reason, among others, representatives of these two plant families are included together. The genera, species, and cultivars that are included represent only a very small portion of the Cyperaceae and Juncaceae. There are certainly many more types in both plant families of equal stature and ornamental value that also require recognition and consideration.

COMPOSITION, CHARACTERISTICS, AND DISTRIBUTION

The Cyperaceae, or sedge family, is more closely related to the Gramineae, or grass family, than is the Juncaceae, or rush family. The monocotyledonous Cyperaceae contains several genera and many species of annual, but many more perennial, grasslike herbs of ornamental value. Because of their similarities to each other, representatives of Cyperaceae are included with ornamental grasses.

Most large nurseries include many of these grasslike herbs in their inventories. Such stocks are usually available as live plants, stolons, rhizomes or so-called offshoots, rather than seeds. Seed stocks are usually available only from the larger seed companies. Plants found growing in the wild often provide an excellent source of these ornamentals, as many of them are native to the United States and North America. Exchanging plants and planting materials among neighbors, relatives, and friends is also an excellent way to acquire these ornamental herbs.

Many sedges appear grasslike upon casual observation; this is probably why they are often included in ornamental grass literature and why many nurseries include them in the trade for use as "false" ornamental grasses. Indeed, it is often extremely difficult to distinguish certain sedges from true grasses, especially when the plants are in a juvenile growth stage. The following characteristics aid in a quick, easy, and fairly reliable means of distinguishing sedges from true grasses:

1. Culms of sedges are usually trigonous; this is easily established by rubbing them between the fingers.
2. Culms have no nodes.
3. Culms are usually solid, not hollow.
4. Leaves are three-ranked.
5. Lower leaves are often reduced to sheaths.
6. Sheaths are usually closed, not open.
7. Ligules, if present, are not visible.

Grasses usually have cylindrical hollow culms with nodes, whereas the angular solid culms of sedges are without nodes. Although the leaves of both grasses and sedges are quite similar, they are two-ranked on grasses and three-ranked on sedges; the lower leaves of sedges are quite often greatly reduced. The sheaths of grasses are usually open, as opposed to the sheaths of sedges, which are usually closed. Grass ligules are usually conspicuous, whereas those of sedges are obsolete or absent. Grass scales consist of glumes, lemmas, and paleas, whereas those of sedges are pistillate and staminate. The perianth of some grasses is absent; on other grasses, it may be comprised of one to three glumaceous segments. The perianth of sedges usually consists of small scales or bristles, sometimes numerous. Grass flowers have one to six stamens, usually three, whereas sedges usually have only one to three stamens. The fruit of grasses is a caryopsis, as opposed to that of sedges which is an achene, usually trigonous. More detailed observations reveal several distinct differences between grasses and sedges in their plant structure and morphology. The foliage—basal and cauline leaves and sheaths—

is perhaps the most conspicuous feature of sedges leding to their misidentification as grasses. Usually, the larger basal leaves are present before culms or scapes form. The leaves of many sedge species are filiform or narrowly linear and long attenuate, just as those of many grasses. The presence of culms or scapes and inflorescences provides a sound basis for differentiating grasses and sedges.

CYPERACEAE OR SEDGE FAMILY

Cyperaceae is a large and diverse plant family of widespread geographic distribution. It is variously reported to contain 3,200 to more than 4,000 species, included in about 75 to 90 genera. Only a few genera are included in ornamental horticulture; among these are *Carex, Cladium, Cymophyllus, Cyperus, Eleocharis, Eriophorum, Fuirena,* and *Scirpus.* Certain species of ornamental value among these genera are commonly used in landscape development and improvement. Several species supply products of some economic value, in addition to having ornamental value. The nutlets and rootstocks of certain species supply food for primitive peoples; the culms of other types are used in thatching. Papyrus made from *Cyperus* is of paramount historical significance and importance. Sedges play a major role in conserving soils by preventing and reducing soil erosion. Their presence in low, wet marshes and floodplains aids in building soils, a very slow but essential process; sedges also provide food and protection for wildlife.

Certain species of Cyperaceae have characteristics that very closely resemble those of grasses. They are grasslike or rushlike, caulescent or scapose, tufted herbs comprising aquatic, semiaquatic, and terrestrial forms. Numerous aquatic, semiaquatic, and terrestrial herbs distributed among several genera of the sedge family have some ornamental value; yet other genera and species have potential ornamental value. Some of these plants have a definite place in the home garden and in general landscape improvement. Their judicious use supplements that of other ornamentals used in landscape improvement. These perennial, grasslike herbs include a vast array of true sedges in the genera *Carex* and *Cymophyllus.*

True sedges are widespread in distribution; they occur at low, medium, and high elevations from the arctic to the tropics. Their natural habitat includes damp soils, mud, or water in full sun or lightly shaded locations. Sedges are found in bayous, bogs, marshes, peat beds, lakes, and swamps, and along canals and streams, in addition to occurring naturally in artificially made pools, ponds, lakes, and reservoirs. They are found growing in still and stagnant water and in slow-flowing streams. Sedges are adapted to rather wide ranges in soil and water pH values; most species occur in acid or slightly acid situations. However, some species prefer either neutral or slightly alkaline environments. There is also considerable diversity among species in drought and water tolerance; some forms thrive best in open woods in moist soil, whereas others prefer wet, undrained sites, growing either in mud or directly in water.

WINTER HARDINESS, SIZE, FORM, COLOR, AND GROWTH HABIT

Considerable variation exists among ornamental sedges in winter hardiness, size, form, color, and growth habit. Fortunately, the diversity among species provides a wide choice of types for use in the garden or for other landscape improvement.

The widespread distribution of sedges indicates that considerable differences in winter hardiness exist among species. Most *Carex* species inhabit temperate regions; however, some species are more winter hardy than others. Jet sedge, *Carex atrata,* graceful sedge, *Carex acuta,* and palm sedge, *Carex muskingumensis,* are more cold tolerant, for example, than lesser pendulous wood sedge, *Carex sylvatica,* Morrow's sedge, *Carex morrowii,* and Fraser's sedge, *Cymophyllus fraseri.* Differences in winter hardiness among sedge species determine, to some degree, the choice of types for use in specific regions or plant hardiness zones.

Some sedges of ornamental value, listed in ascending order of size, include the miniature types of *Carex nigra* and *Carex sylvatica,* 4–8 in./1–2 dm high; intermediate types of *Carex flacca* and *Carex morrowii,* 12–24 in./3–6 dm high, and large types of *Carex acutiformis* and *Carex capillaris,* 2–3 ft/6–9 dm high. Some species are tufted, with fibrous roots, such as *Carex brunnea* and *Carex plantaginea,* whereas others, such as *Carex arenaria, Carex flava,* and *Carex X stipata* have strong, rhizomatous roots. Pond sedge, *Carex lacustris,* is equipped with strong, long stolons and stout rhizomes.

Plant size and texture may influence the choice and use of sedges in landscape improvement. These characteristics are important considerations when using sedges along with grasses, grasslike plants, rushes, and broad-leaved ornamentals to produce a harmonious, practical, and pleasing design in landscape improvement. The texture of ornamentals included herein is described as fine, medium, or coarse, based primarily on leaf width, although the thickness of the scape or culm is also considered. Examples of small sedges up to 12 in./3 dm high of fine texture (i.e., leaf width up to 0.4 in./10 mm wide) include *Carex nigra* and *Scirpus cernuus;* large types, 2–9 ft/0.6–2.8 m high, include *Scirpus tabernaemontani* and its cultivar 'Zebrinus.' Sedges of 1–4 ft/0.3–1.2 m high, of medium texture (i.e., leaf width 0.4–0.6 in./10–15 mm) include *Carex acuta* and *Cyperus vegetus.* Sedges of 1–12 ft/0.3–3.8 m high, of coarse texture (i.e., leaf width 0.7 in./15 mm or greater) include *Carex conica, Cyperus albostriatus,* and *Cyperus papyrus.* The combination of plant size and texture becomes important in the choice of sedges when they are used in conjunction with other aquatic or semi-aquatic ornamentals in landscape improvement.

The outline of most densely tufted sedges, such as *Carex stricta,* is upright-narrow, with erect, straight culms, in contrast to loosely tufted *Carex arenaria,* with scattered, curved culms, or *Carex capillaris,* with culms nodding at the top. The vernacular name of *Carex acuta,* graceful sedge, is associated with plant form.

Differences in color provide for a wide choice in the use of sedges for garden

and landscape improvement. Petrie's sedge, *Carex petriei,* exemplifies intraspecific color differences about as well as any other type. The foliage is usually
reddish brown or brilliant copper red; however, its color is variable, depending
on whether the plants are grown from seed or propagated by plant division,
grown in sun or shade, and grown in acid or alkaline soil. Petrie's sedge provides a spectacular color contrast when grown in association with blue-green
grasses. The seedheads are usually dark brown, becoming black at maturity, and
the foliage is variably colored. The color of stems, basal and cauline leaves,
sheaths, involucral leaves, or bracts, and seedheads all contribute to the attractiveness of sedges as ornamentals. The ornamental value of sedges lies in their
color, shape, texture, and especially in the many shapes and colors of the inflorescences and mature seedheads. Color of culms and foliage is variable among species and, to some degree, within species. A few examples are *Carex comans,* with
whitish green or yellowish green foliage; *Carex conica,* with dark green foliage;
and *Carex buchananii,* with reddish green or coppery brown leaves. Variable
coloration exists among other species. The common names of some species are
derived from or associated with their foliage color—for example, blue sedge,
Carex flacca, orange sedge, *Carex flagellifera,* and yellow sedge, *Carex flava;* or
the color of their mature seedheads, such as black sedge, *Carex nigra,* and jet
sedge, *Carex atrata,* both with black seedheads. Forms with variegated foliage
are usually the most interesting and popular. Many species have multicolored or
variegated forms from the species type.

The color and color patterns of the longitudinally striped leaves varies
among species and among plants within species. Some species have alternate
white-green stripes; others have yellow-green stripes. The leaf margins of some
species are white or yellow, while those of other species have green margins.
Stripe width is also variable among species, as well as among individual plants
within species. Species with cultivars of outstanding variegated foliage include
Carex acuta, Carex morrowii, Carex stricta, and *Scirpus tabernaemontani.*

Seedheads are the most conspicuous and visible outstanding characteristic of
sedges; they vary in size, shape, and color. The seedheads are conspicuous because
they are usually borne on elongated culms high above the foliage. Their variable
shapes and colors add interest to these semiaquatic and aquatic herbs. The persistence of colorful, mature seedheads into late fall and winter adds to the longevity
of attractiveness of the plants. Examples of seedheads of different color include
those of *Carex capillaris* (grayish brown), and *Carex nigra* (dark brown or black).
Leaves of sedges are often reduced to sheaths, some of which are quite colorful,
such as the purplish sheaths of *Carex plantaginea.* The bracts or involucral leaves,
which subtend the inflorescences of some species, are colorful and add to the
attractiveness of the plants.

The growth habit and resulting stands of some carexes are quite different.
Gray's sedge, *Carex grayii,* a densely cespitose, upright-narrow form, produces
large colonies, in contrast to *Carex muskingumensis,* with numerous solitary
culms or small tufts. Tufted sedge, *Carex stricta,* produces dense, comparatively

small tufts of plants that are upright-narrow in outline, whereas *Carex morrowii* forms large mounds, and *Carex kobomugi,* a low-growing species, is more or less mat-forming. Rhizomatous, loosely cespitose *Carex atrata* is an intermediate form. Some species are invasive, such as mat-forming *Carex kobomugi,* with both stout rhizomes and stolons, in contrast to densely cespitose, noninvasive *Carex brunnea.* The potential invasiveness of sedges should be carefully considered in their selection and use as ornamentals. Sedges, like bamboos, are difficult and expensive to eradicate once they are established. When invasive types are used, necessary precautionary measures should be employed to prevent their spread into unwanted sites. One way to surmount this problem is to substitute a noninvasive species or one that is less invasive.

Most sedges are deciduous perennials (e.g., *Carex flava),* whereas others are either semievergreen (e.g., *Carex grayii)* or evergreen (i.e., *Carex brunnea).* Evergreen and semievergreen types usually remain so when grown in their areas of adaptation; however, when grown in colder climates, they may be winter-killed. When given a choice of using deciduous or evergreen types, the latter are usually chosen. The habitat and use of sedges and related plants as ornamentals may be determined from an examination of Appendix 4.

Other aquatic and semiaquatic sedges and related plants in the sedge family deserve attention as ornamentals in addition to carexes. These species serve as soil-building and erosion-control plants and provide food and protection for wildlife, in addition to having ornamental value. They, like carexes, are adapted to more or less aquatic environments. Perennial, or rarely annual, caulescent herbs, including twig rush *(Cladium)* and spike rush *(Eleocharis)* deserve attention, as do cotton grass *(Eriophorum)* and *Fuirena* species. Some annual or perennial *Scirpus* species deserve consideration as ornamentals. Other plants that warrant consideration as ornamentals are annual *Cyperus* herbs with fibrous roots or rhizomatous perennial types.

Twig rushes, one indigenous, wild, and invasive, *Cladium mariscoides,* and one exotic, cultivated, and noninvasive, *Cladium sinclairii,* are useful in bogs and pools, and in wet wooded areas, respectively. Although the former species is wild and invasive, it has its niche in landscape improvement if it is properly located and safeguarded against encroachment on other aquatics. The large, brilliantly colored flower heads of *Cladium sinclairii,* borne in a reddish panicle high above the foliage on tall, gracefully arched culms, are a beautiful sight in summer and likewise in winter, when the reddish brown seedheads are reflected on snow. Although this species may not be available in the trade, the difficulty in obtaining it from New Zealand may be more than worthwhile.

Certain species of *Eriophorum,* cotton grass, are worthy as ornamentals in naturalized, usually cold, bogs, marshes, swales, and swamps. They are also useful in and around pools and ponds in the water garden. The selection and use of cotton grasses should be carefully considered in terms of their potential invasiveness. Small, cold-tolerant hare's-tail, *Eriophorum callitrix,* is noninvasive, as opposed to upright-open to spreading cotton grass, *Eriophorum polystachion.*

Cotton grasses are most impressive when planted in large drifts or in massed stands in full sun. They are grown primarily for their fluffy, feathery seedheads with long, whitish, stringy threads hanging from the seedheads in late summer or early fall. The whitish, dense seedheads, borne above the foliage with their white, stringy threads blowing in the slightest breeze, make a spectacular sight, especially when the plants are grown in massed stands. Cotton grasses are adapted to a wide climatic range—zones 2 through 9. The main differences among species are plant size, inflorescence color, and color of the seedheads. Cotton grasses, along with other aquatics and semiaquatics, play an important role in their niche in home gardens and landscape improvement.

Umbrella grasses, *Fuirena* species, deserves consideration for the water garden, for naturalizing open, wet areas, and for planting in and around pools, ponds, and lakes. One small, caulescent, perennial species, *Fuirena simplex,* is ideal for the water garden and for pool plantings. Its rusty-brown seedheads and yellowish green culms are attractive in early to late fall and winter. The plants are useful in naturalizing low, wet sites on acid soils and are capable of growing directly in water. Two forms of spike rush—*Eleocharis acicularis* and *Eleocharis cellulosa*—are at home in wet soil or directly in water. Hardy, slender spike rush, used most commonly in aquariums, is also useful in the water garden over a wide climatic range—zones 4 through 10. Slender spike rush and a related form, round-stemmed spike rush, *Eleocharis cellulosa,* are both useful in ground-cover plantings or in naturalizing aquatic sites.

Bulrush (of the Bible), *Cyperus papyrus,* has been cultivated as an aquatic ornamental from time immemorial. Egyptian reed is a weak perennial, with its range of adaptation restricted to the tropics. Despite its limited winter hardiness, it still remains a favorite among gardeners and horticulturists alike. Its lack of winter hardiness restricts its outdoor use to zone 10. It may be grown indoors in a warm, humid environment, but the plants usually do not attain normal size. Two cultivars, one much smaller than the type—'Nanus' and 'Variegatus,' a variegated form about the size of the type—are also useful for indoor plantings. Dwarf papyrus, *Cyperus haspan,* is highly regarded as an indoor, decorative plant. Like Egyptian reed, it is of tropical origin and consequently is adapted only for outdoor plantings in zone 10. Broadleaf umbrella palm, *Cyperus albostriatus,* and umbrella palm, *Cyperus alternifolius,* are likewise used in the same manner as Egyptian reed in zone 10. Umbrella palm and its cultivars are more cold hardy than broadleaf umbrella palm; however, they may be cultivated successfully in zones 8 through 10. Two additional hardy representatives of flat sedge are also useful as aquatic ornamentals—*Cyperus longus* and *Cyperus vegetus.* Both species, 2–4 ft/0.6–1.2 m high, are ideal aquatic, pond, or pool plants and are equally adapted for use as house plants. Perennial forms of flat sedge are more likely to be found in the trade and used as aquatic ornamentals than annual forms. History has recorded their value as ornamental aquatics.

Bulrush, *Scirpus* species, like flat sedge, *Cyperus* species, is commonly used in both indoor and outdoor plantings. Ornamental bulrushes range in size from miniature bulrush, *Scirpus cernuus* (6–12 in./1.5–3.0 dm high) to great bulrush, *Sirpus tabernaemontani* (ranging up to 9 ft/2.8 m high). Ranked in increasing order of winter hardiness, the species included are *Scirpus flaccidus, Scirpus nodulosus* (zone 10), and *Scirpus cernuus* and *Scirpus cyperinus* (zones 5–7). The largest form, great bulrush, is more widely adapted than the other species, being suitable for zones 4–10. Great bulrush, *Scirpus tabernaemontani,* is perhaps the most notable of native water plants. It is well known, well liked, and extensively used as an ornamental both indoors and outdoors. Striped bulrush, *Scirpus tabernaemontani* 'Zebrinus,' is an outstanding water ornamental. The scapes and foliage of this cultivar are transversely banded green, yellow, and white, resembling zebragrass, *Miscanthus sinensis* var. *zebrinus.* The variegated foliage of striped bulrush provides a perfect foil for all other green-leaved aquatic and terrestrial plants. It has two important advantages over zebragrass as an ornamental: (1) it is semievergreen; and (2) it is capable of growing directly in water, whereas zebragrass is deciduous and terrestrial, although it does thrive in moist or wet soil. Bulrushes are used in the same manner and for the same purposes as other sedges. They, too, have a place in ornamental horticulture, along with other water and terrestrial ornamentals.

THE RUSH FAMILY, JUNCACEAE

The Juncaceae, or rush family, is much smaller than the Cyperaceae or sedge family; it is less closely related to the Gramineae or grass family than is Cyperaceae. The Juncaceae family consists of more than 400 species distributed among eight genera, of widespread geographic distribution, but mostly in cold or temperate wet regions. These perennial or sometimes annual sedgelike herbs are somewhat grasslike in appearance and habit. At least two genera contain some species of ornamental value; they include aquatic true rushes, *Juncus* species, found growing in wet places and directly in water, usually in full sun, and terrestrial woodrushes, *Luzula* species, occurring in shaded woods in moist or dry sites. The larger genus, *Juncus,* of about 250 species of stiff, glabrous herbs, is native mostly to temperate regions. The smaller genus *Luzula* consists of about 80 species of usually perennial, hairy herbs native to temperate or cold regions. The few ornamental species included herein represent only a small portion of those that are of real or potential value as ornamentals.

True rushes, *Juncus* species, and woodrushes, *Luzula* species, are among the genera of ornamental value in Juncaceae. Natural stands occur in temperate regions, usually in wet meadows, bogs, and tidelands, including freshwater, brackish-water, and saltwater marshes, usually in full sun or light shade. True rushes usually require more water and less shade than woodrushes. Rushes are easily propagated and maintained. They should be used along with aquatic or semiaquatic, grasslike plants, water-loving ornamental grasses, and sedges in landscape design and improvement. Each of these groups of water-loving plants has its own particular niche and makes its own contribution to landscape improvement, particularly in bogs, peat beds, and water gardens. The plant form, texture, and color of rushes add diversity and attractiveness to the landscape.

Common rush and its variants are useful in beautifying the water garden, where they are used in its pools and ponds or along its streams (Appendix 4). The home of these plants is in bog and water gardens and in marshes and sloughs. They thrive in full sun or light shade, with their feet in water. Common rush is likewise useful as a decorative plant in large planters, city fountains, or pools and lakes. It occurs spontaneously or is planted in public parks, golf courses, playing fields, and zoos. The variegated, smaller forms are more attractive and consequently are more in demand than the common yellowish green form. These are the types most frequently used in home gardens. They are used in outdoor plantings in the same manner as common rush, although they require shaded sites to prevent their leaves from becoming blistered in full sun. The small, variegated cultivars are popular as house plants, in addition to being attractive and useful in outdoor plantings.

Spiral rush, *Juncus effusus* 'Spiralis,' is perhaps the most interesting of all cultivated rushes. The living stems of this medium-sized rush are curled in a spiral or corkscrew fashion, usually producing a jumbled mass. Spiral rush is grown chiefly as a curiosity because it has a unique growth form. Soft rush, *Juncus effusus* var. *solutus,* a giant form (i.e., 5–10 ft/1.5–3.1 m high), is useful only in the largest gardens containing large pools, ponds, or lakes. It is most commonly used in naturalizing the wild garden or marshes and swamps that are contiguous to or bordering the formal garden. Japanese mat, *Juncus effusus* var. *compactus,* is used in a manner similar to soft rush. Important economic uses of Japanese mat and common rush and perhaps soft rush in Japan involve weaving tatami, the standard floor covering in Japanese homes. Many years ago, the pith of both common rush and soft rush was soaked with grease and used as rush candles. The pith of these rushes was also used for candlewicks. The economic value of true rushes lies in their ability to control erosion and build soils; the latter, although very, very slow in fruition, is especially essential. Large forms provide food and shelter for wildlife, a benefit as important as their ornamental value. The ornamental value of true rushes lies in their plant form, texture, and color; the perennial evergreen forms such as common rush and its cultivars are attractive and decorative throughout the year. True rushes are grown primarily for their colorful culms rather than their flowers, although the flowers and fruits of some forms are attractive. The mature seedheads are usually the crowning glory of *Juncus* species. The culms remain upright into winter, topped by their persistent, mature, and decorative seedheads of various colors, shapes, and sizes. They are often used alone and in combination with other ornamentals in dried floral arrangements. Common rush, with its yellowish green culms and persistent decorative seedheads, is essential for any gardener with a bog or water garden or peat bed. The variegated cultivars of common rush, which are more colorful and interesting than the common green form, are used in the same manner as the type. True rushes are not necessarily attractive as individual plants; they are much more decorative and showy when grown in large clumps and are even more spectacular in massed stands. True rushes, like cattails, sedges, water grasses, and other water-loving plants, should not be grown alone but in combination with other aquatics. Each of these types of water-loving plants grown alone is of some value, although when grown together in harmonious, compatible combinations, they complement each other, thereby becoming more decorative, useful, and valuable in landscape development and improvement.

Any number of combinations are possible with other water-loving plants in the garden and its environs. A dramatic contrast in plant form, size, and color is afforded by growing large, tufted maidengrass, *Miscanthus sinensis* var. *gracillimus* (5–7 ft/1.5–2.2 m high), with dark green foliage, near a pool in which *Juncus effusus* 'Aureus Striatus' (2–3 ft/6–9 dm high), with striped, yellowish green stems, occurs. Large clumps are necessary to emphasize the effect. Any of the variegated forms such as *Juncus effusus* 'Vittatus' grown in the same small pool or pond with cattails, *Typha minima,* with foxy-red seedheads would produce a pleasing contrast. Water-loving ornamental grasses, such as creeping softgrass, *Holcus mollis,* with greenish gray foliage, or milletgrass, *Milium effusum,* with light, yellowish green leaves, provide a more subtle contrast in color. Giant reed, *Arundo donax,* a tall, upright-narrow, green-leaved reed, 10–26 ft/3.1–8.0 m high, near a large pond containing soft rush 5–10 ft/1.5–3.1 m high, provides a compatible combination of "giants" in plant form, if not in color. Perhaps a more pleasing combination, in color at least, is striped giant reed, *Arundo donax* var. *versicolor* (6–10 ft/1.8–3.1 m high), in wet soil near a stream containing common rush and cattails, *Typha* species. Combinations of common rush or its variants with various sedges also are possible; examples include umbrella palm, *Cyperus alternifolius,* with dark green leaves and stems, and *Juncus effusus* 'Zebrinus,' with white-green striped leaves, in zones 8 and 9 only, as the former is a weaker perennial than the latter. Many other compatible and pleasing combinations may be made by matching or, for contrast, not matching, plant size, color, shape, hardiness, and habitat of true rushes with ornamental grasses, sedges, cattails and other broad-leaved ornamentals, all of which have forms that are tolerant of wet, soggy soils or mud, or that grow directly in water. It is easy to ascertain any desired combination of plants for the bog or water garden, peat bed, marshes, and swamps or for low, wet, soggy soils by examining the characteristics of the various groups of plants adapted to such sites and conditions (Appendixes 1, 3, and 4). All types of plants are needed for improving the landscape of pools, ponds, lakes, streams, and low, wet sites.

Woodrushes are plants for wooded areas. These low-growing, hairy, hardy perennials occur in temperate and cold regions, usually in shaded, wooded sites. The ornamental value of woodrushes is primarily in their colorful foliage and secondarily in their small flowers of various colors and hues. Their utilitarian value lies in their ability to prevent soil erosion by forming a complete, impenetrable ground cover and by their extensive, rhizomatous root systems; woodrushes also act as protection for wildlife.

Woodrushes possess three outstanding attributes that render them useful for naturalizing wooded areas, in understory plantings among shrubbery, and as lawn substitutes: tolerance of shade, drought, and acid soils. Woodrushes usually produce good ground cover in shaded locations, although the stands of some types are more dense than others. Differences in shade tolerance also exist among species. Snowy woodrush, *Luzula nivea,* adapted as far north as zone 4, thrives in full sun or light shade, in contrast to colorful, gold-margined woodrush, *Luzula sylvatica* 'Marginata,' a weak perennial, which prefers deep shade; the latter makes an ideal house plant. The densely cespitose types of hairy woodrush, *Luzula pilosa,* and greater woodrush, *Luzula sylvatica,* are ideal as substitute lawns in difficult sites in shaded areas (Appendix 4). The plants form an attractive, almost impenetrable, ground cover that withstands light traffic and prevents or reduces soil erosion. The chestnut-brown flowers of hairy woodrush and greater woodrush are an added attraction in massed stands. For a substitute lawn of a different color, try purple woodrush, *Luzula purpurea,* with its purplish green foliage. These species are also ideal as ground cover for naturalizing wooded areas, as they are somewhat tolerant of drought and acid soils. Some of the smaller types are useful in understory plantings among shrubbery in mixed perennial borders. Greater woodrush is ideally suited for woodlot sites, since the plants attain their maximum size and come into blossom following the flush of spring bulbs. Woodrushes are unsurpassed as ground-cover and erosion-control plants in moist, acid soils in shaded locations.

The value and use of rushes and sedges in ornamental horticulture are being increasingly recognized, and their further use should be encouraged. Their use adds a different and interesting dimension to this science.

SELECTED SPECIES

The following species, arranged alphabetically by genera and by species within genera, are discussed in terms of their habitat, description, uses, and cultivation.

Carex L. **(Sedge, Laiche).** The classical Latin name of obscure significance. Type species, *Carex hirta* L. There are about 2,000 species, cosmopolitan, most common in temperate and cold regions. Grasslike herbs, perennial by rootstocks; the plants usually monoecious, occasionally dioecious. Culms mostly trigonous, rarely terete, solid or occasionally hollow, the flowering culms often strongly phyllopodic (i.e., lower leaves with well-developed blades) or aphyllopodic (i.e., the lower leaves bladeless or nearly so); making growth in one year and then without dry leaves at base at flowering time, or making growth in two years, leaving dry leaves at the base at flowering time, arising centrally or laterally; sterile shoots only occasionally well developed, often resembling the fertile culms, the leaves are often much longer and wider. Leaves three-ranked, the upper bracts subtending the spikes, short or elongate or occasionally wanting. Flowers arranged in one to many spikes, the spikes much reduced in some species. Spikes are either sessile or pedunculate; when pedunculate, the base of the peduncle is often surrounded by the perigynium or a spathaceous organ. Spikes are entirely staminate, pistillate, androgynous, or gynecandrous. Androgynous spikes have the staminate flowers above the pistillate flowers. Gynecandrous spikes have the pistillate flowers above the staminate flowers. Flowers unisexual, solitary in the axils of scales; perianth absent. Staminate flowers usually of three stamens. Pistillate flowers surrounded by a scalelike organ (i.e., perigynium) and consisting of a single pistil, branched style usually consisting of three stigmas. Style either jointed with the achene and withering and at length deciduous, or continuous with the achene, persistent, indurate, and not withering. Achenes trigonous, denticular or plano-convex, sessile or stipitate, rarely constricted at the base, completely surrounded by the perigynium or rarely rupturing it; stigmas and usually part of the style protruding through the small, terminal orifice. Perigynia chartaceous, membranous, or coriaceous, from closely enveloping the achene and not inflated to strongly inflated, sessile or stipitate, nerved or nerveless, glabrous or pubescent or hispid or rarely papillose, frequently puncticulate, occasionally spongy at the base, flattened and more or less winged, beakless or strongly beaked, the beak entire, obliquely cleft or bidentate at apex, the dorsal suture developed and conspicuous in some species, in others entirely absent (Mackenzie, 1931–1935).

Latin name: *Carex acuta* L.
Synonym: *Carex acuta* var. *nigra* L.
Common name: Graceful sedge
Origin: North America
Habitat: Bogs, wet meadows near the coast, cultivated
Hardiness: Zones 3 through 5
Description: A loosely to densely cespitose perennial with long, horizontal, slender, brownish, scaly stolons. Culms erect or somewhat curved, stiff to slender, sharply trigonous, 12–20 in./3–5 dm high, papillate, smooth to strongly roughened above, usually exceeding the leaves but occasionally shorter, brownish and usually fibrillose at base, strongly phyllopodic; sterile shoots phyllopodic. Foliage light green, fine in texture; leaves five to eight per fertile culm, the lower clustered near the base, blades erect, ascending, spreading or even retrorse, flat or channeled toward the base, 2–12 in./0.5–3.0 dm long, 2–3 mm wide, thin but firm, or sometimes stiff, papillate, long attenuate, roughened toward the apex; sheaths round and smooth dorsally, white hyaline; the ligule wider than long. Inflorescence staminate and pistillate spikes, terminal spikes staminate, often with one or two smaller ones at base, short-pedunculate to long-

pedunculate, linear, 0.6–1.5 in./1.5–4.0 cm long, 2–3 mm wide, the scales oblong-obovate, very obtuse to acute, brownish with lighter midrib and hyaline margins; pistillate spikes two to four, often staminate above, erect, all sessile or the lower pedunculate, contiguous or more or less separate, oblong to linear-oblong, 0.4–2.0 in./1–5 cm long, about 0.2 in./5 mm wide, densely flowered except toward the base, containing 30 to 100 appressed, ascending perigynia in many rows; lowest bract leaflike, usually shorter but frequently more or less exceeding the culm, sheathless but biauriculate, the upper reduced, strongly auricled; scales ovate to oblong-ovate, narrower and shorter than the perigynia, dark brown with lighter midrib and inconspicuous hyaline margins; perigynia plano-convex, strongly flattened, obovate, ovate, oval or suborbicular, 2–3 mm long, about 2 mm wide, green at apex, membranous, puncticulate, two-ribbed and lightly several-nerved on both sides, short to long stipitate, round at the base and apex, minutely apiculate-beaked, the beak very short, ciliolate at tip; fruit a lenticular, suborbicular achene, 1–2 mm long, almost as wide, broadly substipitate, rather loosely enveloped in the lower half of the perigynium body, short-apiculate, obscurely jointed with the straight, slender style. Flowering and fruiting occur from June through August.

Uses: Graceful sedge is useful as ground cover in wet, shaded sites and in water gardens.

Cultivation: Propagation is by plant division and by seeding. Plants should be divided in the spring, and seeding should be done in the fall. The plants require ample light and a constant moisture supply when grown indoors.

Latin name: *Carex acutiformis* Ehrh.
Synonym: *Carex spadicea* Roth
Common name: Lesser marsh sedge
Origin: Europe
Habitat: Bogs, wet meadows near the coast
Hardiness: Zones 5 through 7
Description: An upright-narrow, loosely cespitose, stoloniferous perennial; the stolons stout, scaly, horizontal. Culms erect, 2–4 ft/0.6–1.2 m high, exceeding the leaves, sharply trigonous, much roughened above, stout and thick below. Foliage light green, fine in texture. Leaves well developed, 5 to 12 per fertile culm, the lower clustered, 8–16 in./2–4 dm long, 0.15–0.30 in./4–8 mm wide, blades channeled below, flat above with revolute margins, firm; sheaths smooth, thin deeply concave at the mouth; ligule as wide as long; sterile shoots elongate, aphyllopodic. Inflorescence staminate and pistillate spikes, staminate spikes two to four, sessile or the uppermost pedunculate, 1.0–2.5 in./2.5–6.3 cm long, 0.10–0.15 in./3–4 mm wide, scales oblong-oblanceolate, obtuse to awned, purplish with lighter center and narrow hyaline margins; pistillate spikes three or four, widely separate, erect, the upper sessile and staminate at the apex, the lower pedunculate, linear or linear-oblong, 2–5 in./0.5–1.3 dm long, 0.2–0.3 in./5–8 mm wide, densely flowered, containing 50 to 100 appressed but ascend-

ing perigynia in rows; lower bracts leaflike, not sheathing, equaling or exceeding the inflorescence, the upper reduced, scales awned, lanceolate, acuminate or acute, purplish with lighter, three-nerved center and narrow hyaline margins; perigynia ovoid, 0.10–0.15 in./3–4 mm long, flattened, oval in cross section or obtusely trigonous at maturity, inflated, subcoriaceous, several-ribbed, stipitate, tapering at the apex into a short, conic beak; fruit a trigonous, indehiscent achene, oblong-ovoid, 2 mm long, sides slightly concave, somewhat loosely enveloped, tapering at apex and continuous with the style. Flowering and fruiting occur from June through August.

Uses: Lesser marsh sedge is useful as ground cover in water gardens or around the margins of pools and streams, in addition to naturalized, wet, shaded locations. The plant form provides a perfect foil for other broad-leaved ornamentals and for water plants such as water lilies, whose foliage is almost perpendicular to the flowering culms of the sedge. The mature seedheads are often used in dry floral bouquets.

Cultivation: Propagation is by plant division. The plants require constant moisture and may be grown in shallow water. Lesser marsh sedge is adventive from Europe.

Latin name: *Carex arenaria* L.
Synonym: *Carex arenaria* var. *typica* Asch. & Graebn.
Origin: Europe
Habitat: Sandy beaches near the sea
Hardiness: Zones 6 through 9
Description: A grasslike perennial with strong, extensively creeping, monopodial rhizomes, slender 0.1–0.2 in./3–5 mm thick, elongate, becoming slender stolons at base, clothed fibrillose scales. Culms erect, 6–20 in./1.5–5.0 dm high, slender, sharply trigonose, smooth or slightly roughened above, exceeding the leaves, arising one to few together. Foliage light green, fine in texture; leaves three to six per fertile culm, or rather more on the sterile culms, well developed, clustered toward the base, blades flat or slightly channeled, 2–8 in./0.5–2.0 dm long, 1–3 mm wide, erect or retrorse, thick, long attenuate, smooth toward the base, scabrous toward the apex; sheaths tight, yellowish hyaline ventrally, thickened at mouth, truncate or concave, scarcely prolonged beyond the base of the blade; ligule as long as wide. Inflorescence an oblong or linear-oblong head, 1–2 in./2.5–5.0 cm long, 0.3–0.8 in./8–20 mm thick, containing numerous, closely aggregate spikes or the lower somewhat distant; spikes androgynous, pistillate or staminate, 0.3–0.5 in./8–13 mm long, 0.1–0.3 in./3–8 mm wide, the upper usually oblong-elliptic and staminate, the middle spikes androgynous, the lower ones ovoid and pistillate; the lower spikes provided with a scalelike bract usually much shorter or longer than the head; scales ovate-trigonous, brownish, thin, the margins hyaline, the center green, three-nerved, acuminate-aristate, about as long and concealing the perigynia; the perigynia appressed or spreading-ascending, flattened, 0.15–0.20 in./4–5 mm long,

1–2 mm wide, coriaceous, stramineous, the body ovate-lanceolate, flat and many-striate ventrally, round and many-striate dorsally, minutely stipitate, abruptly strongly wing-margined above from below the middle, the wings serrulate, green, wingless toward the base, abruptly contracted into serrulate beak, hyaline at the mouth, very strongly bidentate, the teeth subulate; fruit a lenticular, broadly oblong-quadrate achene, about 2 mm long and 1 mm wide, substipitate, slightly ridged, minutely apiculate, jointed with the style. Flowering and fruiting occur from June through August.

Uses: This small sedge, with its small, brown seedheads, is ideal for the water garden and for stabilizing sand dunes. This species is equally adaptable as a house plant, where its invasiveness is easily controlled. The mature, brown seedheads are used occasionally in dried floral arrangements.

Cultivation: Propagation is by plant division and by seeding. Plant division is usually most successful in the spring, whereas seeding should be done in the autumn. This sedge is very invasive and should not be used in areas where it will become a nuisance. The plants grow equally well in full sun or light shade in low, poorly drained, heavy clay, or muck soils, directly in water or on sandy beaches. This sedge is adventive from Europe.

> **Latin name:** *Carex atrata* L.
> **Synonym:** *Carex atrata* var. *varia* Gaudin
> **Varieties:** *Carex atrata* var. *ovata* (Rudge) F. Boott
> **Common name:** Jet sedge
> **Origin:** Europe
> **Habitat:** Arctic or alpine meadows in calcareous districts, cultivated
> **Hardiness:** Zones 3 through 5
> **Description:** A dwarf, loosely cespitose perennial from short to elongated

rhizomatous rootstocks. Culms slender, stiff below and nodding above, sharply trigonous, smooth below, but somewhat roughened above, much exceeding the leaves, 6–20 in./1.5–5.0 dm high, papillose, fibrillose at base; foliage light green, fine in texture; leaves 7 to 15 per fertile culm, mostly clustered near the base, blades 2–8 in./0.5–2.0 dm long, 0.1–0.3 in./3–8 mm wide, flat with revolute margins and channeled above, stiff, papillose, roughened toward the attenuate apex; sheaths hyaline, strongly convex at mouth, brownish; the ligule is as long as wide. Inflorescence three to seven approximate or somewhat separate spikes, the upper weakly erect, short-pedunculate, the lower pedunculate, peduncles about the length of the spikes, trigonous, erect to nodding, slender, smooth, terminal spike gynecandros, the upper largely pistillate, ovoid or oblong-ovoid, 0.5–1.0 in./13–25 mm long, 0.3–0.4 in./8–10 mm wide, lateral spikes similar, slightly narrower, pistillate throughout, densely flowered, 15 to 50 perigynia closely appressed in many rows; lowest bract not sheathing, leaflike with blackish auricle, shorter than or exceeding the inflorescence, the upper much reduced; scales ovate to oblong-ovate, brownish black with lighter midrib extending to the apex and whitish hyaline tip and narrow margins, strongly acute to obtuse, longer but about as wide as the perigynia; the perigynia oval to obovate, 0.10–0.15 in./3–4 mm long, 1–2 mm wide, two-ribbed, more or less flattened, papillose, round-tapering and substipitate at base, round at apex and abruptly beaked, beak apiculate, less than 1 mm long, emarginate; fruit a trigonous achene, narrowly oblong-obovoid, 2–3 mm long, about 1 mm wide, sides concave below, short stipitate, apiculate, jointed with the straight slender style. Flowering and fruiting occur from June through August.

Uses: Jet sedge is adapted to wet, cool, shaded sites in naturalized areas, where the plants form a good ground cover. The almost-black seedheads are the main attraction of jet sedge, although another sedge of approximately the same size, black sedge, *Carex nigra,* produces fruits of the same color. The seedheads are attractive on the plants and in dried floral arrangements.

Cultivation: Propagation is by seeding and by plant division. Plant division should be done in the spring and seeding in the autumn. Jet sedge may be grown successfully in full sun and light shade in all but the driest soil, although the plant size depends largely on the amount of soil moisture available.

Varieties: *Carex atrata* var. *ovata* (Rudge) F. Boott A loosely cespitose perennial with purple bases. Culms slender, erect, roughish above, sharply trigonous, 8–18 in./2.0–4.5 dm high, flexuous at the tip. Foliage dull green, fine in texture; leaves flat, 6–24 in./1.5–6.0 dm long, 0.1–0.2 in./3–5 mm wide, long attenuate; lower sheaths leafless, dark brown, persistent. Inflorescence three to six reddish brown to purple-black spikes, the terminal staminate only at the base, the others pistillate, on slender, arching, curving peduncles, cylindrical or ellipsoid, 0.4–1.0 in./10–25 mm long; scales acuminate or blunt, 0.10–0.15 in./3–4 mm long, about equal to or longer than the perigynia; the perigynia ovoid or broadly ellipsoid, thin and puncticulate, very dark, 2–3 mm long, very short beak with barely notched orifice; fruit a trigonous achene. Flowering and fruiting occur from June through August. This variety is adapted to zones 4 and 5.

Latin name: *Carex aurea* Nutt.
Synonym: *Carex mutica* R. Br.
Origin: Europe
Habitat: Wet meadows, along and in slow-moving streams, lakes, and ponds, mostly in calcareous regions
Hardiness: Zones 5 and 6
Description: A loosely cespitose, stoloniferous perennial, stolons very slender, horizontal, very long, brownish, the clumps small to medium-sized. Culms erect, slender, trigonous, more or less roughened above, from very short to exceeding the leaves, 10–22 in./2.5–5.5 dm high, brownish at base. Foliage light green, fine in texture; leaves four to seven per fertile culm, three-ranked, more numerous on sterile culms, inserted toward the base, blades stiff, flat above, channeled at base, attenuate, roughened toward the apex, 2–10 in./0.5–2.5 dm long, 0.10–0.15 in./3–4 mm wide; sheaths concave at the mouth; the ligule about as long as wide. Inflorescence staminate and pistillate spikes, stami-

nate spikes erect, sessile or short-pedunculate, linear, 0.1–0.4 in./3–10 mm long, 1–3 mm wide, occasionally with a few perigynia, scales oblong-obovate, acute or obtuse, brownish with greenish center and hyaline margins; pistillate spikes three to five, erect, the upper approximate, sessile or short-pedunculate, the lower widely distant, usually nearly basal, occasionally on peduncles 1–2 in./ 2.5–5.0 cm long; the spikes linear-oblong or oblong, 0.2–0.8 in./5–20 mm long, 0.1–0.2 in./3–5 mm wide, 5-to-20-flowered, the perigynia ascending or spreading in age in few rows, alternate below or imbricate above; bracts conspicuously sheathing at base, leaflike, erect, the blades much exceeding the inflorescence, the sheaths concave at mouth; scales ovate or ovate-orbicular, widely spreading at maturity, shorter than the perigynia, short-cuspidate to obtuse, reddish brown with conspicuous greenish yellow three-nerved center and white hyaline margins; perigynia orbicular-obovoid, not inflated, 2–3 mm long, about 1 mm wide, coriaceous, coarsely ribbed, brownish at maturity, densely puncticulate, broadly short-stipitate, round at base, apex round and nearly beakless; fruit a lenticular achene with suborbicular face 1–2 mm long, 1 mm wide, brownish, closely enveloped, minutely densely puncticulate, abruptly short-apiculate, jointed with short slender style. Flowering and fruiting occur from June through August.

Uses: This relatively small sedge is grown primarily for its rich brown spikes, usually borne above its light green foliage. It forms dense colonies in wet areas around ponds and pools and along streams and ditches; the colorful spikes are an added attraction in late summer and early fall. All sedges, including this one, are also useful as ground cover and erosion control. The water garden is the correct place for this small sedge.

Cultivation: Propagation is by seeding and by plant division. Seeding should be done in the fall; plant division is most successful in the spring. The plants thrive equally well in full sun or light shade in calcareous soils, unlike most other sedges.

Latin name: *Carex brunnea* Thunb.
Origin: Australia, Southeast Asia
Habitat: Cultivated
Hardiness: Zones 5 through 8
Description: A densely cespitose, noninvasive, evergreen perennial. Culms slender, weak, rough, trigonous, 1–3 ft/3–9 dm high, usually about half this height. Foliage medium to dark green, fine in texture; leaves somewhat rough, stiff, sharply keeled, 8–24 in./2–6 dm long, 0.15–0.25 in./4–6 mm wide. Inflorescence four to eight slender spikes, all pistillate, usually with staminate tips, nodding when mature, 0.4–0.8 in./10–20 mm long, brownish, the entire inflorescence rather long and loose; perigynia dark green when young, 2–3 mm long, 1–2 mm broad, long beaked, serrulate at the base of the small distinct beak, costate, hispid, loosely spreading when mature; fruit a brownish, trigonous achene. Flowering and fruiting occur from June through September.

Uses: This sedge is ideal as a potted plant in the house or greenhouse. The plants also make good garden specimens when grown in clumps in middle-ground borders and water gardens, because they are not invasive.

Cultivation: Propagation is by seeding and by plant division. Seeding should be done in the fall, and plant division in the spring. The plants thrive best in shaded, wet or damp sites in acid soils. This sedge and its variegated form very closely resemble graceful sedge, *Carex acuta,* and its variants, although they are adapted to entirely different climates. This weak perennial, native to Southeast Asia, may be difficult to locate in the trade.

Latin name: *Carex buchananii* C. B. Clarke
Common names: Leatherleaf sedge, Leatherleaf sedgegrass
Origin: Europe, New Zealand
Habitat: Cultivated
Hardiness: Zones 6 through 9
Description: A densely cespitose, rhizomatous, erect to arching perennial. Culms cylindrical or indistinctly trigonous, erect, 18–24 in./4.5–6.0 dm high. Foliage reddish green or coppery brown, fine in texture; leaves mostly basal, tough, coriaceous; indistinctly trigonous but appearing cylindrical, erect to arching, 10–12 in./2.5–3.0 dm long, about 2 mm wide, with a long, attenuate, curled tip. Inflorescence several distinct spikes ranging in ascending order of size from 0.15 in./4 mm to 0.6 in./15 mm long from uppermost to lowest, the uppermost staminate and dull green; scales dark brown or purplish; perigynia whitish, dry, and firm, puberulent, tapering to a short tip; fruit an indehiscent, lenticular achene. Flowering and fruiting usually occur from June through July, but sometimes rather erratically.

Uses: Leatherleaf sedge is grown for its colorful reddish bronze or coppery brown foliage, which persists throughout the year and provides a distinct and interesting contrast to plants with dark green or bluish green foliage. The narrow, upright growth habit and unusual, curled, colorful foliage provide a perfect foil for mat-forming plants in the water garden. Leatherleaf sedge is grown outdoors in specimen plantings in rock and water gardens and shaded foreground borders and indoors as potted specimens. The plants are most conspicuous when grown in large clumps, where they provide good fall and winter color. Leatherleaf sedge shows to maximum advantage when grown adjacent to grasses with blue foliage, such as *Elymus arenarius* and *Helictotrichon sempervirens.* Similarly, *Dactylis glomerata* 'Variegata' and *Glyceria maxima* 'Variegata' provide a pleasing contrast in color. The erect growth of leatherleaf sedge and its colorful foliage provide a perfect foil for many mat-forming plants with bluish green foliage in the water garden; it is also adapted to the peat bed.

Cultivation: Propagation is by seeding and by plant division, preferably the latter. The plants may be slow in becoming established following transplanting; they prefer medium shade in soil that is provided with a continuous moisture supply. It is grown as an annual in plant-hardiness zone 5 and as a weak perennial in zones 6–9. Mulching may become necessary for the plants to peren-niate in cooler climates. The plants require either snow cover or a winter mulch for protection when the temperature falls below about 50°F/10°C. Good light, constantly moist soil, and relatively high humidity are required for success in growing leatherleaf sedge indoors. Leatherleaf sedge may be difficult to find in the trade in the United States.

Latin name: *Carex capillaris* L.
Synonym: *Carex pendula* Huds.
Common names: Drooping sedge, Sedgegrass, Pendulous sedge
Origin: Europe
Habitat: Dry, sunny places in calcareous districts, cultivated
Hardiness: Zones 2 through 5
Description: A stoloniferous perennial with short rootstocks, the stolons ascending, very short. Culms erect or decumbent, 4–24 in./1–6 dm high, usu-ally very slender, weak, and drooping, much exceeding the leaves, obtusely tri-gonous, phyllopodic, smooth, brownish, and more or less fibrillose at the base, dry leaves from previous year conspicuous. Foliage dark green, fine in texture; leaves five to eight per fertile culm, clustered near the base, blades flat or chan-neled toward the base, thin, firm, 1–4 in./2.5–10.0 cm long, 1–3 mm wide, roughened at the apex; sheaths tight, truncate at the mouth, the ligule very short. Inflorescence staminate and pistillate spikes, terminal spikes usually stami-nate, occasionally gynecandros, very slender, 0.2–0.3 in./5–8 mm long, less than 1 mm wide, several-flowered, sometimes overtopped by the uppermost pistillate spike, peduncle short, slender, rough, the scales oblong-obovate to lanceolate, acute or obtuse, stramineous with greenish midrib and white, hyaline margins; pistillate spikes two or three, borne on very slender, weak, smooth, elongate, drooping peduncles, approximate to widely distant, linear-oblong, 0.2–0.6 in./ 5–15 mm long, 0.10–0.15 in./3–4 mm wide, containing 5 to 20 ascending perigynia loosely arranged in few rows; bracts tubular, long-sheathing, the sheaths green, the blades leaflike, rather short, usually exceeding the culm; scales orbicular-ovate, closely appressed, obtuse or acute, wider but much shorter than the perigynia, thin, smooth, deciduous, light brown with lighter midrib and white hyaline apex and less conspicuous margins; perigynia ovoid-lanceolate, 2–3 mm long, almost 1 mm wide, obtusely trigonous in cross section, slightly inflated, barely ciliate, membranous, serrulate, brownish, two-ribbed, otherwise nerveless, round at base and strongly stipitate, contracted into a minute, conic, entirely or nearly so, straight beak about 1 mm long, orifice oblique; fruit a trigonous, brownish achene with concave sides and blunt angles, closely envel-oped by the perigynium, substipitate, short-apiculate, jointed with the short, slender style. Flowering and fruiting occur from July through August.
Uses: Drooping sedge is popular among middle-sized sedges. It is good in

specimen plantings in moist, shaded, naturalized areas and as ground cover in shaded sites in the water garden, where its pendulous growth can be fully appreciated. The plants remain attractive throughout the growing season. Mature plants form a mound of bright green foliage, with the brownish green spikes borne on their graceful, arched culms. Drooping sedge is also attractive as ground cover among other lower-growing plants, such as lilies and foxgloves, and other shade-loving plants in shaded, wooded locations. The mature seedheads are used in dried floral arrangements. Its size is conducive to its use in middle borders or as a hedge.

Cultivation: Propagation is by seeding and by plant division. Seeding should be done in the fall and plant division in the spring. The plants are slow in becoming established, although their ultimate beauty soon overshadows their tardiness. Drooping sedge grows well in full sun or light shade. Ordinary garden soil with high moisture-retention capacity is necessary for maximum growth. This handsome sedge is easily recognized by its large size, narrow leaves, and long drooping spikes.

Latin name: *Carex comans* Bergg.
Synonym: *Carex vilmorinii* Mottet
Cultivars: 'Bronze Form'
Common names: New Zealand hair sedge, Green wig
Origin: New Zealand
Habitat: Cultivated
Hardiness: Zones 7 through 9
Description: A densely cespitose, upright-narrow, evergreen, perennial herb. Culms erect, indistinctly trigonous, rather thin, 15–18 in./3.8–4.5 dm high. Foliage whitish green or yellowish green, fine in texture; leaves very thin and flexible, almost tubular in section, initially erect, then gracefully arching to the ground, 12–15 in./3.0–3.8 dm long, about 1 mm wide. Inflorescence five or more spikes borne in the axils of bracts or scales; spikes usually oblong to cylindrical, largely obscured by the foliage, the longest spike 0.8–1.0 in./20–25 mm long, about 0.1 in./3 mm wide; perigynia narrowly ovoid, many-nerved, glabrous, minutely beaked; fruit an indehiscent, trigonous achene. Flowering and fruiting occur from June through August.

Uses: The cultivar Bronze Form is grown for the color of its foliage, as is that of the parent species. New Zealand hair sedge and its variant are useful in group plantings in rock gardens outdoors, and indoors as potted plants. The plants form a mound of mangled, hairlike leaves when grown as ground cover in partial shade. The drooping growth habit, much like that of nodding scirpus, *Scirpus cernuus,* is ideal for its indoor use in hanging baskets. Constant watering is necessary when it is grown in this manner, however. This species and its cultivar are best exhibited in hanging baskets, although they are also attractive as potted specimens.

Cultivation: Propagation is by plant division in the spring and by seeding in the fall. Dead growth should be removed periodically to keep the planting tidy. The plants prefer locations with light shade in moist or wet soil.

Cultivars: *Carex comans* Bergg. 'Bronze Form' The plant size and all its parts are smaller than those of New Zealand hair sedge (i.e., 5–8 in./1.3–2.0 dm high). The foliage of this cultivar is dull brown or bronze.

Latin name: *Carex communis* L. H. Bailey
Synonym: *Carex varia* Muhl.
Origin: North America
Habitat: Open dry woods, mountainous areas, rocky ledges
Hardiness: Zones 2 through 7
Description: A loosely cespitose, rhizomatous perennial, rhizomes short, ascending, branched and scaly, purplish red. Culms weak, slender, 6–20 in./1.5–5.0 dm high, rarely very short, mostly lateral and aphyllopodic but the terminal central and phyllopodic, sharply trigonous, usually exceeding the leaves, not conspicuously fibrillose at base; sterile shoots strongly aphyllopodic, numerous. Foliage light green, fine in texture; leaves several per culm, clustered near the base, well developed, blades flat, thin and flaccid, 1–2 in./2.5–5.0 cm long, 0.1–0.2 in./3–5 mm wide, rough on the margins and at the apex; sheaths concave at the mouth, the lower breaking and becoming filamentose; the ligule longer than wide; leaf sheaths of sterile shoots 3–12 in./0.8–3.0 dm long, 0.10–0.15 in./3–4 mm wide. Inflorescence staminate and pistillate spikes, staminate spike solitary, linear, from sessile to conspicuously pedunculate, 0.15–0.70 in./4–18 mm long, 1–3 mm wide, scales obovate-oblong; obtuse to acute, the margins white hyaline, the center three-nerved, green; pistillate spikes two or three per culm, the upper one or two approximate and sessile, the lowermost somewhat distant and short-pedunculate, none sessile, the spikes oblong-orbicular, 0.2–0.3 in./5–8 mm long, 0.1–0.2 in./3–5 mm wide, densely flowered, usually containing 3 to 12 ascending perigynia in several rows; lowest bract leaflike, nearly sheathless, well developed, usually from shorter than to exceeding the inflorescence, margins hyaline, purplish at base; upper bracts scalelike or much reduced; scales ovate to ovate-lanceolate, acuminate to obtuse, exceeded by or exceeding the perigynia, purplish with narrow hyaline margins and three-nerved green center; perigynia obovoid, 0.1–0.2 in./3–5 mm long, 1 mm wide, the body puberulent, two-keeled but otherwise nerveless, membranous, closely enveloping the achene, the body suborbicular, stipitate, abruptly contracted into a bidentate beak about 1 mm long; fruit an indehiscent, trigonous achene, broadly obovoid with convex sides, minutely pitted, 1–2 mm long, about 1 mm wide, short attenuate at base, truncate and bent-apiculate at apex; style jointed with the achene. Flowering and fruiting occur from June through August.

Uses: This hardy sedge is useful in naturalizing shaded, wooded sites in massed plantings. It may be considered as ground cover, or as a substitute lawn in moderately shaded areas.

Cultivation: Propagation is by plant division, usually in the spring or summer.

Latin name: *Carex conica* F. Boott
Cultivars: 'Variegata'
Origin: Japan, Korea
Habitat: Cultivated
Hardiness: Zones 5 through 9
Description: An upright-narrow, cespitose perennial. Culms mostly smooth, indistinctly trigonous, erect, 8–20 in./2–5 dm high. Foliage dark green, coarse in texture; leaves erect, stiff, flat, 0.8–1.6 in./2.0–4.0 cm wide; bracts short, with long, inflated, often purplish brown sheaths. Inflorescence three to five erect spikes, the terminal ones staminate, brown, the others pistillate, short cylindrical, 0.5–1.0 in./13–25 mm long, many-flowered, aggregate; perigynia light green, with an abruptly retrorse beak, firm and tough, closely investing the achene; scales longer than the perigynia; fruit an indehiscent, trigonous achene, completely surrounded by the persistent perigynium. Flowering and fruiting occur from May through July.

Uses: This species and its cultivars are used indoors as house plants. These forms do not require as much moisture as some other sedges and are useful in open, wooded areas, the wild garden, and along streams. The smaller variegated cultivar, Variegata, is useful in shaded borders around pools, ponds, and lakes. Ample light and moisture must be provided when the plants are grown indoors. Like other sedges, these small forms serve as food and cover for wildlife and in all-important erosion control.

Cultivation: Propagation is by plant division and by seeding, preferably the latter. Seeding should be done in the fall, and plant division in the spring. The plants prefer light to medium shade and will thrive in a wide range of soils.

Cultivars: *Carex conica* F. Boott 'Variegata' The cultivar is 2–4 in./5.0–10 dm high; the leaves are variegated with longitudinal green and whitish stripes. It prefers light to medium shade and is adapted to zones 7–9.

Latin name: *Carex flacca* Schreb.
Synonym: *Carex glauca* Scop.
Common name: Blue sedge
Origin: Europe
Habitat: Dry fields, waste grounds, cultivated
Hardiness: Zones 5 and 6
Description: A loosely cespitose, upright-narrow, stoloniferous perennial, stolons long, slender. Culms erect, stiff, slender, phyllopodic, 8–24 in./2–6 dm high, exceeding the leaves, sharply trigonous with flat sides, rough above. Foliage glaucous or bluish green, fine in texture; leaves 8 to 15 per fertile culm, mostly clustered near the base, the blades keeled below, flat above with revolute margins, thick, 6–16 in./1.5–4.0 dm long, 0.1–0.2 in./3–5 mm wide, rough

Carex flacca. *Source: North American Cariceae. Vol. 2.* The New York Botanic Garden. 1940.

serrulate on margins; sheaths tight, copper-colored ventrally, concave at mouth; the ligule much wider than long; sterile shoots aphyllopodic, the lower sheaths splitting and becoming sparingly filamentous. Inflorescence staminate and pistillate spikes, staminate spikes one to three, approximate, the uppermost short-pedunculate, the lateral sessile, linear, 1–2 in./2.5–5.0 cm long, 0.10–0.15 in./3–5 mm wide, scales oblong-obovate, obtuse, brownish with lighter midrib and hyaline margins; pistillate spikes two or three, not aggregate, erect initially, soon nodding on slender, rough peduncles, usually shorter than the spikes, usually staminate at the apex, linear or oblong-cylindric, 0.4–1.5 in./1–4 cm long, 0.2–0.3 in./5–8 mm wide, containing 50 to 100 ascending to somewhat spreading perigynia, approximate, in several rows; bracts leaflike, the lowest equaling or exceeding the inflorescence, partially sheathing; scales ovate-lanceolate, acute, acuminate or usually short-mucronate, dark brown with lighter center and hyaline margins, usually equaling the perigynia; the perigynia ovoid-oval or obovoid, suborbicular, about 0.1 in./3 mm long and 2 mm wide, nerveless except the two marginal nerves, sparingly appressed-hispid above, coriaceous, stramineous, round and substipitate at base, round at apex, abruptly minutely beaked; fruit a trigonous achene, the angles round, obovoid, about 0.1 in./3 mm long, 1 mm wide, the sides convex below, brownish puncticulate, jointed with the abruptly bent, slender style. Flowering and fruiting occur from June through July.

Uses: Blue sedge is useful as ground cover in naturalized areas. It is more drought tolerant than many other forms. It forms compatible combinations with tufted prairie grasses. The bluish or glaucous color of blue sedge makes it useful as a lawn substitute in lightly shaded sites.

Cultivation: Propagation is by seeding and by plant division. Plant division is best done in the spring after new growth has begun. Blue sedge thrives best in full sun.

Latin name: *Carex flava* L.
Synonym: *Carex foliosa* All.
Common name: Yellow sedge
Origin: Great Britain, North America
Habitat: Cultivated, escape from cultivation
Hardiness: Zones 5 through 9
Description: A densely cespitose, upright-narrow perennial, clumps small to medium-sized, rootstocks short. Culms erect, stiff, trigonous, sharply angled at the summit, leafy, 8–30 in./2.0–7.6 dm high, usually exceeding the leaves, sometimes shorter, more or less smooth and fibrillose at base; sterile shoots elongate, conspicuous. Foliage yellowish green, fine in texture; leaves four to eight per fertile culm toward the base, but not clustered, the blades flat or somewhat canaliculate at base, thick, stiff, 6–18 in./1.5–4.5 dm long, 0.1–0.2 in./3–5 mm wide, somewhat roughened toward the apex, long attenuate; sheaths whitish ventrally, thin and truncate at the mouth; the ligule mostly

longer than wide. Inflorescence staminate and pistillate spikes, terminal spike staminate or occasionally partially pistillate, sessile or pedunculate, linear, 0.2–0.8 in./5–20 mm long, 2–3 mm wide, the scales oblong-lanceolate, closely appressed, obtuse to acute, brownish with narrow hyaline margins and three-nerved, lighter center; pistillate spikes usually two to five, occasionally staminate at the apex, erect, contiguous or the lower more or less distant, the uppermost nearly sessile, the lower more or less strongly short-pedunculate, oblong or suborbicular, 0.4–0.7 in./10–18 mm long, 0.4 in./10 mm wide, densely flowered with 15 to 35 perigynia in several to many rows, obliquely attached, the conspicuous beaks reflexed in all except the uppermost; bracts leaflike, conspicuous, erect or abruptly retrorse, usually exceeding the inflorescence, the lower sheath short to strongly developed, 0.1–0.8 in./3–20 mm long, more or less prolonged ventrally at the mouth; scales ovate to ovate-lanceolate, acute to short-cuspidate, narrower and about one-half the length of the perigynia, reddish brown with narrow hyaline margins and three-nerved lighter center; perigynia 0.15–0.25 in./4–6 mm long, 1–2 mm wide, yellowish green, membranous, puncticulate, strongly many-ribbed, slightly inflated, round at base, obliquely contracted into a slender, conic, serrulate, bidentate, reddish beak; fruit a broadly obovoid achene, 2–3 mm long, 1 mm wide, trigonous, jointed with the slender style. Flowering and fruiting occur from June through August.

Uses: Yellow sedge and its varieties are ideally suited for water gardens, peat bogs, and damp or wet shaded sites in the flower garden. The small size of the plants makes them useful as specimen plantings in shaded foreground borders. Their shape, size, and yellowish color provide a perfect foil for broad-leaved ornamentals with dark green or bluish green foliage and for mat-forming plants like water lilies in water gardens. These small plants are equally at home when grown indoors as potted specimens. The rhizomatous root system of yellow sedge is conducive to building soil upon which other plants depend. This process, although extremely slow in fruition, is essential in the critical areas in which sedges are adapted.

Cultivation: Propagation is by seeding and by plant division. Seeding should be done in the fall and plant division in the spring. Yellow sedge and its smaller varieties grow best in medium-shaded, wet sites along the margins of pools, ponds, and streams; they will also grow directly in shallow water. Ample light, humidity, and moisture are required for the survival and growth of plants grown indoors. Yellow sedge naturalizes very easily, spreading by creeping rhizomes.

Latin name: *Carex grayii* J. Carey
Synonym: *Carex grayii* var. *hispidula* A. Gray
Common name: Gray's sedge
Origin: Canada
Habitat: Rich, alluvial woods in calcareous districts, cultivated
Hardiness: Zones 2 through 8

Carex grayii. *Source: North American Cariceae. Vol. 2.* The New York Botanic
Garden. 1940.

Description: A cespitose, upright-narrow, semievergreen perennial with short, thick, tough rootstocks. Culms erect, 1–4 ft /0.3–1.2 m high, stout, leafy throughout, sharply trigonous, exceeded by upper leaves, roughened immediately below the head, purplish at base; sterile shoots elongated. Foliage light green, medium in texture; leaves 8 to 16 per fertile culm, the lower clustered, the upper scattered and exposing the internodes, blades erect or ascending, flat, thin but firm, 4–12 in./1–3 dm long, 0.2–0.6 in./5–15 mm wide, the upper portion very rough on the margins; sheaths rather loose, whitish hyaline ventrally, concave and brownish at the mouth; the ligule about as long as wide. Inflorescence staminate and pistillate spikes, staminate spike solitary, short- to long-pedunculate, usually with a bract, narrowly linear, 0.4–2.0 in./1–5 cm long, about 2 mm wide, the peduncle rough, the scales from oblong-obovate and obtuse to lanceolate and acuminate, yellowish with green center and hyaline margins; pistillate spikes one or two, erect, aggregate, pedunculate, peduncles about as long as the spikes or nearly sessile, globose or subglobose, 0.8–2.0 in./ 2–5 cm long and as wide, containing 10 to 30 perigynia, spreading; bracts leaf-like, much exceeding the culm, sheathless or short-sheathing, the sheath not prolonged upward at mouth beyond the base of the blade; scales broadly ovate, three-nerved, obtuse to slightly cuspidate, white-hyaline with green center, narrower than the perigynia and about half as long, usually completely concealed by the ripening perigynia; the perigynia ovoid-lanceolate, 0.4–0.7 in./10–18 mm long, 0.25–0.30 in./6–8 mm wide, strongly inflated, usually more or less hispidulous, subcoriaceous, strongly ribbed, about 15 ribs, cuneate at base and broadly stipitate, tapering to a smooth or serrulate, broad, conic, bidentate beak, 1–2 mm long; fruit a trigonous, obovoid achene, 0.15–0.25 in./4–6 mm long, 0.10–0.15 in./3–4 mm wide, with blunt angles and sides concave below, loosely enveloped, sessile, yellowish white, abruptly conic-apiculate tipped and continuous with the slender, straight style. Flowering and fruiting occur from June through September.

Uses: Gray's sedge makes excellent stands in large groups around pools and ponds and in water gardens, where it is used for accent. The plants are tall enough when planted near water to form curious reflections on the surface. The foliage remains green well into the fall. The fruits, which remain on the plants into winter, are interesting, especially when their shadows are reflected on a snowy background; they are useful in dried arrangements.

Cultivation: Propagation is by seeding and by plant division. Seeding should be done in the fall, and plant division in the spring. The plants thrive best on deep, fertile, moist or wet soil. Unlike many sedges, Gray's sedge grows well in full sun but will tolerate light shade. It is often found growing in the wild.

Latin name: *Carex kobomugi* Ohwi
Common name: Japanese sedge
Origin: Japan

Habitat: Sand dunes, cultivated

Hardiness: Zones 6 through 8

Description: A low-growing, extensively creeping perennial with stout rhizomes and stolons. Culms arise from among old, persistent leaves, coarse, subcylindric, smooth, 4–12 in./1–3 dm high. Foliage medium green, fine in texture; leaves coriaceous, papillate-serrulate, 4–6 in./1.0–1.5 dm long, 0.15–0.30 in./4–8 mm wide, pungent. Inflorescence numerous spikes crowded into an ellipsoid or ovoid head, 1–2 in./2.5–5.0 cm long, 0.8–1.6 in./2–4 cm thick; scales and bracts herbaceous, green becoming beige, serrate at base; perigynia coriaceous, orbicular-ovate, 0.4–0.6 in./10–15 mm long, erose near base, soon divergent; fruit a small trigonous achene. Flowering and fruiting occur from May through July.

Uses: The primary use of this sedge is for sand dune stabilization. It has been established successfully by being interplanted with existing stands of American beachgrass, *Ammophila breviligulata.* It is adapted to areas that are subject to heavy traffic on fore dunes and thrives in full sun.

Cultivation: Propagation is by seeding and by rhizome or plant division. Plant division may be done in the spring, summer, or fall. The mortality rate is sometimes high following transplanting. The plants spread slowly, eventually forming dense stands. The plants prefer full sun in sand or sandy soils.

Latin name: *Carex lacustris* Willd.

Synonym: *Carex riparia* var. *lacustris* (Willd.) Kunth

Common name: Pond sedge

Origin: Europe

Habitat: Calcareous soils, circumneutral swamps, cultivated

Hardiness: Zones 5 through 8

Description: A cespitose, stoloniferous perennial, stolons horizontal, slender, scaly. Culms erect, stiff, thick at base, 2–4 ft/0.6–1.2 m high, usually exceeding the leaves, aphyllopodic, sharply trigonous and rough above, dark purple at base, the basal sheaths breaking and becoming filamentous ventrally; sterile shoots elongate, the leaves clustered at the apex. Foliage glaucous or glaucous green, medium in texture; leaves three to five per fertile culm, not clustered at base, leaf blades firm, flat, with revolute margins, 8–20 in./2–5 dm long, 0.2–0.6 in./5–15 mm wide, the two midlateral nerves conspicuous above and the inconspicuous septa evenly distributed, attenuate, strongly roughened on the margins, sheaths yellowish brown and thin at mouth, breaking and becoming filamentous; the ligule much longer than wide, conspicuous. Inflorescence staminate and pistillate spikes, staminate spikes two or three, linear, the lateral sessile, the terminal pedunculate, 2–3 in./5–8 mm long, 0.15–0.20 in./4–5 mm wide, the scales oblong-obovate, obtuse, retuse or emarginate, mucronate or abruptly awned, purplish with lighter center and hyaline margins; pistillate spikes two or three, strongly septate, erect, sessile or the lower short-pedunculate with rough peduncles, oblong-cylindric, 1–4 in./2.5–10.0 cm long, 0.4–0.6 in./10–

15 mm wide, densely flowered above, somewhat loosely at base, containing 50 to 150 ascending spreading perigynia in several to many rows; lowest bract leaflike, usually exceeding the culm, sheathless or nearly so, not thickened at mouth, the upper reduced; scales ovate, awned or acuminate, purplish with three-nerved green center and narrow hyaline margins, narrower than and half as long as the perigynia; the perigynia oblong-ovoid, 0.2–0.3 in./5–8 mm long, 2 mm wide, slightly inflated, coriaceous, glabrous not papillate, round at base and strongly many-nerved, sessile or nearly so, tapering at apex into a glabrous, short, flattened, bidentate beak, 1 mm long, the teeth smooth, short, erect; fruit a broadly oval, obovoid achene, 2–3 mm long, 1 mm wide, trigonous with slightly concave sides, loosely enveloped, sessile and continuous with the slender, persistent, abruptly bent or flexuous style. Flowering and fruiting occur from June through August.

Uses: Pond sedge is useful in specimen plantings in and around pools, along streams, and in water gardens. The plants provide ground cover in shaded moist or wet areas, where they make a remarkable display. The plants of pond sedge remain attractive throughout the year when grown in the garden, where it is compatible with low, mat-forming plants. The plants, which usually form a good ground cover, are particularly attractive when surrounded by pavement or any other extensive barricade. Pond sedge could be considered as a lawn substitute or running ground cover in wooded areas; it is occasionally used as a hedge or border because of its large size. Pond sedge may be grown indoors, where it remains evergreen.

Cultivation: Propagation is by plant division and by seeding. Plant division should be done in the spring and seeding in the autumn. Pond sedge is very invasive; therefore, careful consideration should be given to its location in the garden—it must be grown where it can be controlled. The plants prefer cool, moist or wet sites in shaded areas; they thrive in shallow water.

Latin name: *Carex montanensis* L. H. Bailey
Synonym: *Carex podocarpa* R. Br.
Common name: Mountain sedge
Origin: North America
Habitat: Meadows and along streams in mountainous areas
Hardiness: Zones 3 through 5
Description: A loosely cespitose perennial with slender, elongate, brownish rootstocks, the new shoots at the base of the old. Culms 8–20 in./2–5 dm high, central culm rather slender at base, stiff below, more or less nodding above, obscurely papillose, bluntly trigonous, exceeding the leaves, slightly to strongly roughened above, somewhat fibrillose, strongly aphyllopodic; sterile shoots aphyllopodic, elongate. Foliage dark green, fine in texture; leaves two to four per fertile culm, with well-developed blades, the upper much longer, widely distant below, not at all clustered, erect, thin but firm, flat, 3–12 in./0.8–3.0 dm long, longer on sterile shoots, 0.10–0.15 in./3–4 mm wide, roughened

toward the apex, short attenuate; sheaths round and smooth dorsally, brownish ventrally, not filamentous, lower sheaths long and conspicuous; the ligule much longer than wide. Inflorescence staminate and pistillate spikes, staminate spike solitary, occasionally with small sessile one at its base, erect, oblong or oblong-obovoid, pedunculate, 0.7–1.0 in./18–25 mm long, 0.1–0.2 in./3–5 mm wide, the scales black, obtuse, oblong-obovate, the lighter midrib inconspicuous, the margins not hyaline; pistillate spikes two to four, occasionally slightly staminate at the apex, approximate or slightly distant, weakly erect or drooping on slender, smooth peduncles that are either shorter or twice the length of the spikes, the spikes oblong to linear-oblong, 0.4–0.8 in./10–20 mm long, 0.1–0.3 in./3–5 mm wide, closely flowered, the 15 to 30 perigynia appressed-ascending in several rows; bracts sheathless with blackish auricles, usually much shorter than the culm; scales obtuse to acute, oblong-obovate, thin, closely appressed, black, much narrower and shorter than the perigynia, the margins not hyaline, midvein obsolete or sometimes with lighter midvein not extending to the apex; perigynia oblong-ovate or elliptical, much flattened, about 0.2 in./5 mm long, 2 mm wide, two-ribbed, otherwise nerveless, very membranous, stramineous at base, blackish above, round at base, substipitate, round at apex and minutely beaked, the beak less than 1 mm long, black, entire or becoming bidentate; fruit a trigonous, obovoid achene with concave sides, very small, about 1 mm long, about one-fourth the width and half the length of the perigynium, long stipitate, apiculate, brownish, jointed with the straight exserted style. Flowering and fruiting occur from June through August.

Uses: Mountain sedge is useful in naturalizing the water garden in cold climates. It thrives in full sun or light shade, where it is compatible with other water-loving plants, despite the fact that it is terrestrial. The plants provide ground cover in naturalized areas along streams, and around pools, ponds, and lakes.

Cultivation: Propagation is by plant division and by seeding, preferably the former. Mountain sedge is more or less invasive, and control measures are necessary to keep the plants contained in the desired area.

Latin name: *Carex morrowii* F. Boott
Synonym: *Carex japonica* Thunb.
Cultivars and varieties: 'Aureo-variegata,' 'Nana,' 'Old Gold,' 'Variegata'; *Carex morrowii* var. *expallida* Ohwi Japanese sedgegrass
Common name: Morrow's sedge
Origin: Japan
Habitat: Wet meadows, cultivated
Hardiness: Zones 6 through 9
Description: A densely cespitose, mound-forming, stoloniferous, evergreen perennial. Culms indistinctly trigonous, erect or slightly arching, 12–18 in./3.0–4.5 dm high. Foliage dark lustrous green, fine in texture; leaves clustered near the base of the culms, flat or U-shaped, appearing cylindrical, thick,

stiff, 8–12 in./1–2 dm long, 0.3–0.4 in./8–10 mm wide, long attenuate; bracts with short blades, inflated and long-sheathing basally. Inflorescence four to six staminate and pistillate spikes, distant, on long erect peduncles, fugacious, brownish, slender, 1–2 in./2.5–5.0 cm long, the uppermost staminate, the lower pistillate; perigynia glabrous, spreading or divergent, narrowly ovoid, 0.10–0.15 in./3–4 mm long, beaked, strongly many-nerved, the short beak slightly toothed; scales with rough awns and longer than the perigynia; fruit a brownish, trigonous achene. Flowering and fruiting occur from April through July.

Uses: The typical, green-leaved form is rarely cultivated. The smaller, mound-forming, variegated cultivars are grown indoors as potted plants and also outdoors. They are grown primarily for their mound-forming growth habit and for their spectacular variegated foliage. The plants are useful as edging in foreground borders and as specimens and ground cover in water gardens. The plants remain attractive throughout the year, affording good fall and winter color. The variegated cultivars form a low mound of striped leaves, green and creamy-white. They are useful as border edgings or in foreground plantings of perennial mixed borders. They are best demonstrated in large clumps in border plantings and, better still, in massed plantings. The variety *Carex morrowii* var. *expallida* is used in the same manner. The distinctly variegated forms are useful as potted plants indoors, provided the potting soil is kept constantly moist or wet. The erect plant forms and colorful, variegated foliage are a perfect foil for low-growing, green-leaved plants.

Cultivation: Propagation is by seeding and by plant division. Seeding should be done in the autumn, and plant division in the spring. The plants prefer soil with a constant moisture supply in shaded locations. Morrow's sedge thrives in full sun in zone 6 but requires shaded sites in warmer climates. Whether grown indoors or outdoors, the plants require a constant moisture supply at their roots. Adequate light must be provided when Morrow's sedge and its cultivars are grown indoors. The plants perform well in a mixture of one-half peat moss and one-half moist, fertile soil. Potted plants must be kept constantly moist but well drained. Water may be applied at either the top or the bottom of the containers. Vermiculite, when used in soil mixtures, tends to work its way to the top of the container upon repeated watering. It is lightweight and floats to the top of the container when it is overwatered or flooded, thus creating an untidy appearance. The use of sand, pebbles, or small stones on the soil surface improves the appearance of the potted plants.

Cultivars: *Carex morrowii* F. Boott 'Aureo-variegata' The plant and all its parts are smaller than the parent species (i.e., about 12 in./3 dm high). The leaves are brilliantly variegated, with longitudinal, broad, golden-yellow stripes down their middle, with green margins. This evergreen perennial is adapted to shaded sites in zones 6–9.

Carex morrowii F. Boott 'Nana' This semievergreen form produces a dense dwarf mat. The curled and twisted leaves are only 2–3 in./5–8 cm long. This cultivar is smaller than Morrow's sedge or its cultivar Aureo-variegata; it is adapted to shaded sites in zones 6–9.

Carex morrowii F. Boott 'Old Gold'   The variegated foliage of this cultivar is comprised of leaves with green and gold longitudinal stripes. This cultivar is 8–12 in./2–3 dm high; it is adapted to shaded sites in zones 7–9.

Carex morrowii F. Boott 'Variegata'   This semievergreen cultivar is slightly smaller than the parent species (i.e., 6–10 in./1.5–2.5 dm high). The variegated leaves have a broad, pure white midvein or longitudinal stripe down the middle of the leaf, with green margins. It is used as a colorful ground cover in shaded locations in zones 5–9.

Carex morrowii var. *expallida* Ohwi Japanese sedgegrass   This evergreen perennial herb is 6–12 in./1.5–3.0 dm high with gracefully arched, very narrow leaves. The foliage persists into winter, and flowering occurs in very early spring. The leaves have creamy-white and green longitudinal stripes. This variety thrives in shaded locations in zones 5–9.

Latin name: *Carex muskingumensis* Schwein.
Synonym: *Carex arida* Schwein. & Torr.
Common name: Palm sedge
Origin: Europe
Habitat: Moist woods and thickets, cultivated
Hardiness: Zones 2 through 6
Description: A cespitose, rhizomatous perennial with short, fibrillose rootstocks. Sterile culms numerous, fertile culms few, 24–40 in./0.6–1.0 m high, exceeding the leaves, slender to base, roughened on the angles above, sharply trigonous with concave sides, brownish below, lower nodes bladeless and exposed; sterile culms very leafy, the blades spreading widely. Foliage light green, fine in texture. Leaves 7 to 12 per fertile culm, well developed, regularly disposed on the lower half, blades flat, thin but stiff, usually spreading, 6–10 in./1.5–2.5 dm long, 0.1–0.2 in./3–5 mm wide, roughened on the margins toward the apex; sheaths loose, green striate ventrally, very firm, deeply concave at mouth; the ligule as wide as long, thick; blades of sterile shoots wider. Inflorescence 5 to 12 approximate linear-elliptic spikes forming a linear-oblong to oblong head 2–3 in./5–8 cm long, 0.6–0.8 in./15–20 mm thick, the spikes gynecandros, stramineous or brownish, 0.6–1.0 in./15–25 mm long, 0.2–0.3 in./5–8 mm wide, tapering to a blunt apex and to a subclavate base, the basal flowers not conspicuous, staminate, rarely numerous and conspicuous; perigynia numerous, erect, closely appressed with closely appressed beaks; bracts scalelike or the lowest prolonged; scales oblong-ovate, acute or obtuse, brownish with hyaline margins, the three-nerved center is lighter, narrower and about half the length of the perigynia; the perigynia flat, scalelike, somewhat distended over the achene, narrowly oblong-lanceolate, 0.2–0.4 in./5–10 mm long, about 2 mm wide, strongly wing-margined and serrulate to below the middle, somewhat con-

Carex muskingumensis.
Source: *North American
Cariceae. Vol. 1.* The New
York Botanic Garden. 1940.

tracted into a narrower wing margin to the base, membranous, stramineous,
the margins pellucid above, finely several-to-many-nerved both dorsally and ventrally, round at base, tapering at apex into a beak about one-third the length of
the whole, flat, obliquely cut dorsally, deeply bidentate; fruit a lenticular-oblong
achene, about 0.1 in./3 mm long, less than 1 mm wide, brownish, short-stipi-

tate, apiculate; style straight, slender, jointed to the achene, ultimately deciduous. Flowering and fruiting occur from June through September.

Uses: Palm sedge makes an excellent ground cover in shaded water gardens. Its texture contrasts with that of true grasses and broad-leaved ornamentals. Although it is not as colorful as other forms, with brownish, golden, or variegated foliage, this sedge forms small, interesting colonies, offering a foil for other ornamentals. Palm sedge is a good ground cover or substitute lawn in medium or deep shade.

Cultivation: Propagation is by seeding and by plant division; plant divisions should be made in the spring; seeding should be done in the fall. The plants do best in medium- to darkly shaded sites in wet locations and are quite winter hardy.

Latin name: *Carex nigra* (L.) Reichard
Synonym: *Carex goodenowii* J. Gay
Common name: Black sedge
Origin: Eurasia
Habitat: Wet soils in full sun or light shade, cultivated
Hardiness: Zones 4 through 8
Description: A loosely cespitose, strongly stoloniferous perennial. Culms smooth, or rough at the summit, sharply angled, 1–2 ft/3–6 dm high. Foliage glaucous or dark bluish green, fine in texture; leaves 3–4 in./8–10 cm long, less than 0.1 in./3 mm wide, filiform, margins involute in drying. Inflorescence staminate and pistillate spikes, staminate spike solitary, pedunculate, or with smaller basal spikes; pistillate spikes two or three, erect, distant to approximate, cylindric, 0.5–1.0 in./13–25 mm long, 0.10–0.25 in./3–6 mm thick, densely flowered above, loosely so below, often staminate at the tip, the lower subtended by a bract, 1–4 in./2.5–10.0 cm long; scales purplish to blackish, with slender green midrib, obtuse, ovate, shorter and narrower than the perigynia; the perigynia usually oval or orbicular-ovate, mostly fine striate toward the base, 2–3 mm long, bright green to tawny, short beak nearly entire; fruit a small lenticular achene. Flowering and fruiting occur from May through September.

Uses: Black sedge is unique for the color of its scales; as such, it is highly prized as an ornamental. This colorful sedge adds diversity of color and shape to foreground borders among green-leaved plants; it is also very much in demand as a specimen plant in pots or other containers. Black sedge occurs naturally fairly near the sea. Although it may be somewhat difficult to locate in the trade, it is well worth the effort.

Cultivation: Propagation is by seeding and by plant division. Plant division is most successful when done in the spring.

Latin name: *Carex petriei* Cheesem.
Common name: Petrie's sedge
Origin: New Zealand

Habitat: Cultivated
Hardiness: Zones 5 through 7
Description: A densely cespitose, evergreen, perennial herb. Culms trigonous, thin, erect, 12–18 in./3.0–4.5 dm high. Foliage fine in texture, color is variable depending upon whether or not the plants are grown from seed or propagated by plant division, grown in sun or shade, or in acid or alkaline soil; usually the color is a rich reddish brown to a brilliant copper red; leaves cylindrical or indistinctly trigonous, somewhat U-shaped, erect or slightly arching, 8–12 in./2–3 dm long, about 0.10–0.15 in./3–4 mm wide, long attenuate. Inflorescence five to seven separate spikes borne on short peduncles; terminal spikes staminate; pistillate spikes, three to five, flat, almost globose, 0.6–0.7 in./15–18 mm long, extremely dark brown, usually becoming black; perigynia glabrous, ovoid, many-nerved, 2–3 mm long, almost as thick; fruit a hard, trigonous achene. Flowering and fruiting occur from June through August.

Uses: This small, grasslike, perennial herb is grown primarily for its unusual, rich brown foliage. The plants remain attractive throughout the growing season; the colorful foliage provides an interesting contrast to plants with variegated foliage, particularly to those with dark green or bluish green foliage. The plants are especially attractive when grown in massed stands as ground cover in small areas or in foreground borders, water gardens, or the peat bed. Petrie's sedge is among the most colorful and interesting sedges for the garden, especially when grown in contrast to any blue grass. Petrie's sedge provides an excellent foil for mat-forming plants in the water garden.

Cultivation: Propagation is by plant division and by seeding, preferably the former. Plant division should be done in the spring, and seeding in the fall; vegetative propagation is most expeditious. The plants prefer moist or wet soil at all times; they thrive best in light to medium shade but will withstand full sun. Factors such as amount of light, method of propagation, and soil pH influence foliage color. The massive colorful effect resulting from altering these variables in growing Petrie's sedge places it among the most desirable of garden sedges.

Latin name: *Carex plantaginea* Lam.
Synonym: *Carex latifolia* Moench
Cultivars: 'Dr. Richard Lighty'
Common name: Plantain-leaved sedge
Origin: Europe
Habitat: Dry rich woods, cultivated
Hardiness: Zones 4 through 8
Description: A cespitose, evergreen perennial with very short rootstocks. Culms erect or ascending, lateral, 10–24 in./2.5–6.0 dm high, asperulous, not winged, sharply trigonous, exceeding the leaves, purplish at base, lower bladeless sheaths conspicuous, purplish; sterile shoots erect, elongate. Foliage medium green, not glaucous except in age, coarse in texture; basal leaf blades and those

Carex plantaginea. *Source: North American Cariceae. Vol. 2.* The New York Botanic Garden. 1940.

of the sterile culms persistent, 6–14 in./1.5–3.6 dm long, 0.5–1.0 in./13–25 mm wide, flat, thin, the midnerve well developed on the lower and two of the lateral nerves on the upper surface, acute or acuminate, rough on the margins and hispidulous on the veins toward the apex; fertile culm leaves reduced or bladeless; sheaths acuminate, 1–2 in./2.5–5.0 cm long, deeply concave at mouth, purplish, the upper portion free but not expanding into a blade; the ligule long.

Inflorescence staminate and pistillate spikes, staminate spikes solitary, oblong-clavate, pedunculate, 0.4–0.8 in./10–20 mm long, 0.1–0.2 in./3–5 mm wide, scales broadly obovate, obtuse to acuminate, purplish, the midvein almost obsolete; pistillate spikes two or three, distant, the lower on erect, slender, asperulous peduncles, the upper more or less sessile, linear, 0.6–1.0 in./13–25 mm long, 0.15–0.20 in./4–5 mm wide, loosely flowered, alternately, 4 to 12 flowers; bracts bladeless, long-sheathed, purplish, spathaceous; scales broadly ovate-trigonous, white hyaline with green midrib, purplish, the lower cuspidate, the upper acuminate, shorter and narrower than the perigynia; the pergynia oblong-obovoid, sharply trigonous, 0.1–0.2 in./3–5 mm long, about 2 mm wide, not inflated, asperulous, many-nerved, substipitate, shortly tapered at the base, contracted at the apex into an erect, short, slightly curved beak about 1 mm long, with entire hyaline orifice; fruit a sharply trigonous, broadly oval achene with deeply concave sides, closely enveloped in the perigynium, about 0.1 in./3 mm long, 2 mm wide, brownish, short-apiculate, substipitate, jointed with the slender style. Flowering and fruiting occur from June through August.

Uses: This hardy evergreen herb is grown for its evergreen foliage, which provides some summer color in midwinter. Its dark green leaves and culms provide some promise of spring; the plants flower before their leaves form. Water gardens, pools, ponds, and streams in shaded locations are the places where this sedge is most adapted. The mature flower heads are often employed in dried arrangements. The plants are conspicuous by their broad evergreen leaves and rather large, purple sheaths; they provide good ground cover in massed plantings in shaded woods. The semievergreen plants are particularly useful as a substitute lawn in shaded sites.

Cultivation: Propagation is by seeding and by plant division. Seeding should be done in the fall, and plant division in the spring. The plants prefer medium shade in wet sites in calcareous soils.

Cultivars: *Carex plantaginea* Lam. 'Dr. Richard Lighty'   This cultivar differs from the type only in plant size (i.e., the culms are 10–12 in./2.5–3.0 dm high). It is adapted to the same plant-hardiness zones as that of the species and is used in the same manner.

Latin name: *Carex stricta* Lam.
Synonym: *Carex acuta* L.
Cultivars and varieties: 'Bowles's Golden'; *Carex stricta* var. *angustata* (F. Boott) L. H. Bailey; *Carex stricta* var. *curtissima* Peck; *Carex stricta* var. *decora* L. H. Bailey
Common name: Tufted sedge
Origin: Europe
Habitat: Swampy meadows and wooded sites, cultivated
Hardiness: Zones 4 through 9
Description: A densely cespitose, stoloniferous perennial, rootstocks descending obliquely, stolons usually not conspicuous, horizontal, stout, brown-

ish, scaly. Culms slender, 1–3 ft/3–9 dm high, exceeding the leaves, sharply trigonous, papillate, very rough above, sides concave, aphyllopodic and not arising from the center of dry leaves of previous year, brownish at the base, basal sheaths subcarinate dorsally; sterile shoots aphyllopodic. Foliage dark green, fine in texture; leaves three to five per fertile culm, usually clustered near the base, the blades 4–12 in./1–3 dm long, 2–3 mm wide, strongly roughened, long attenuate, thin but stiff, papillate, channeled and keeled toward the base, margins revolute; sheaths thick, concave, without a jagged margin at the mouth, glabrous or dorsally slightly hispidulous, brownish ventrally and breaking and strongly filamentous; the ligule much longer than wide. Inflorescence staminate and pistillate spikes, staminate spike usually solitary or with one or two smaller, sessile ones near its base, pedunculate, erect, 1–2 in./2.5–5.0 cm long, 2–3 mm wide, the scales oblong-obovate, obtuse, reddish brown with lighter center and hyaline margins; pistillate spikes two or three, erect, the upper usually staminate above, sessile, or the lower short-pedunculate, more or less distant, 1–2 in./2.5–5.0 cm long, 0.1–0.2 in./3–5 mm wide, densely flowered or somewhat attenuate toward the base; perigynia 50 to 150, ascending and appressed in several rows; bracts sheathless, lower bract 1–3 mm long, with inconspicuous auricles or lacking, shorter than the culm, the upper reduced, biauriculate; scales oblong-obovate to lanceolate, obtuse to acuminate, reddish brown with lighter center and narrow hyaline margins, appressed, narrower and shorter than the perigynia; the perigynia are broadly to narrowly ovate or oval-ovate, 2–3 mm long, 2 mm wide, usually biconvex, closely enveloping the achene, two-edged, not inflated, puncticulate, two-ribbed and obscurely few-nerved dorsally, almost nerveless ventrally, round and substipitate at base, tapering to the nearly beakless, white-tipped apex, style short-exserted; fruit a lenticular obovate, substipitate achene, about 2 mm long and 1 mm wide, filling most of the perigynium body, apiculate, jointed with the straight, short, slender style. Flowering and fruiting occur from June through August.

Uses: Tufted sedge, an introduction from Europe, along with the botanical varieties *angustata, curtissima,* and *decora* have become naturalized in southern Canada and in the United States as far south as plant-hardiness zone 6. The varieties occur farther south than does the species. Tufted sedge, occurring in extensive, dense stands in swampy meadows and woods, is of little ornamental value itself, although the smaller varieties are useful in naturalizing such areas. They are useful in water gardens and in wet and shaded middleground borders. The cultivar Bowles's Golden is the best known and most attractive as an ornamental. This cultivar is almost unexcelled in color and beauty among ornamental sedges. It makes a striking appearance, with its variegated golden foliage, in shaded locations in mud around the margins of pools and ponds and along streams. The plants exhibit their maximum effectiveness when grown in large, bold clumps. Tufted sedge is grown primarily for its colorful foliage, although the mature seedheads are used occasionally in dried floral arrangements.

Cultivation: Propagation is by seeding and by plant division. Seeding should be done in the autumn, and plant division in the spring. The cultivar 'Bowles's Golden' prefers acid soil and some shade and some sun—that is, medium to light shade; it does not thrive in deep shade. These sedges, including 'Bowles's Golden,' may be grown successfully directly in shallow water, in addition to mud or wet soil around the margins of pools, ponds, and streams. The cultivar Bowles's Golden may be difficult to obtain in the United States and may require being introduced; its ornamental value is well worth any extra effort in obtaining it.

Cultivars and varieties: *Carex stricta* Lam. 'Bowles's Golden'   A densely cespitose, perennial herb. Culms slender, erect, 24–30 in./6.0–7.6 dm high. Foliage variegated, fine in texture; leaves with brilliant, golden yellow longitudinal stripes and thin green margins, rather glaucous, sharply keeled, 18–24 in./4.5–6.0 dm long, 0.15–0.25 in./4–6 mm wide; lowest sheaths leafless. Inflorescence three to five spikes, the terminal one staminate, pistillate spikes 0.5–1.0 in./13–25 mm long, 0.15–0.25 in./4–6 mm thick; perigynia tawny or chocolate brown, more or less trigonous; fruit a trigonous, indehiscent achene. Flowering and fruiting occur from May through July.

Carex stricta var. *angustata* (F. Boott) L. H. Bailey   This variety has loose, pistillate spikes, long attenuate at the base, 1.2–2.4 in./3–6 cm long, 0.10–0.15 in./3–4 mm thick, more approximate than those of the species, usually with long, staminate tips; scales acute, narrower, mostly longer than the perigynia; the perigynia are similar to those of the species.

Carex stricta var. *curtissima* Peck   This variety has very short, pistillate spikes; the scales are 0.2–0.6 in./5–15 mm long, much shorter than the perigynia; the elliptic perigynia taper equally to the apex and base.

Carex stricta var. *decora* L. H. Bailey   This variety is usually smaller than the species. The basal sheaths are less fibrillose; spikes 0.4–1.6 in./1–4 cm long, 0.15–0.30 in./4–8 mm thick, usually sessile, rarely attenuate at the base, slightly staminate at the tip; scales spreading and very sharp, longer than the perigynia.

Latin name: *Carex X stipata* Muhl. ex Willd.
Common name: Tussock sedge
Habitat: Cultivated
Hardiness: Zones 5 and 6
Description: A densely cespitose, perennial herb with short, thick rhizomes. Culms arising from rhizomes in clumps, rather weak and soft but stout at the base, sharply trigonous, slightly winged, smooth below, strongly serrulate above, 12–40 in./0.3–1.0 m high. Foliage medium green, medium in texture; leaves flat and soft, 6–12 in./1.5–3.0 dm long, 0.2–0.6 in./5–15 mm wide, long attenuate. Inflorescence a terminal head, 0.8–4.0 in./2–10 cm long, often somewhat compound at base, interrupted; spikes numerous, the lowest 0.4–0.8 in./10–20 mm long, bracts inconspicuous; scales ovate to lanceolate, acuminate, much shorter than the perigynia; the perigynia yellowish or brownish, prominently enlarged and spongy at the base, conspicuously nerved, lanceolate, 0.15–

Table 4.1   Additional Ornamental Sedges in the Genus *Carex*

Latin Name	Plant Height (in./dm)	Shade Tolerance[a]	Plant-Hardiness Zones
C. baldensis	10–14/2.5–3.6	MS	5–9
C. concinna 'Variegata'	4/1	LS	5–7
C. digitata	4–8/1–2	MS	6–9
C. flagellifera	24–36/6–9	MS	7–9
C. speciosa 'Velebit Humilis'	4–6/1.0–1.5	MS	7–9
C. sylvatica	4–6/1.0–1.5	MS	7–9
C. umbrosa	4–8/1–2	MS	7–9
C. uncinifolia	4/1	MS	5–9

[a]MS = Medium shade; LS = Light shade.

0.20 in./4–5 mm long, gradually tapering from the base to the tip, the beak toothed and rough, about twice the length of the body and much longer than the scale; fruit a lenticular, brownish achene. Flowering and fruiting occur from May through August.

Uses: The ornamental value of this sedge is its yellowish or brownish seedheads. The attractive brown seedheads are borne high above the foliage on attractive, slender, green culms; they persist into winter, providing good fall color. The plants provide a perfect foil for other ornamentals of different texture and color. When grown in pools or ponds, the plants provide a pleasing contrast, especially to broad-leaved plants such as water lilies, whose foliage is more or less perpendicular to that of the sedge culms, and usually a different shade of green; the brownish seedheads are a contrasting, added attraction. This sedge, among others, is useful in water garden or in group plantings in shaded damp or wet sites. The brown, mature seedheads are used in dried floral arrangements.

Cultivation: Propagation is by seeding and by plant division. Seeding should be done in the autumn, and plant division in the spring. The plants grow equally well in wet soil, mud, or shallow water in medium shade. Most sedges prefer moist, acid soils; this species does well on neutral soils.

Additional ornamental sedges in the genus *Carex* are given in Table 4.1.

***Cladium* P. Br. (Twig rush, Pond rush).** Diminuitive of Greek *kladion*, "branchlet," from the repeatedly branched cyme of the original species. Type species has not been designated. There are about 55 species, of worldwide distribution, but most abundant in warm regions. Caulescent perennials, often tall herbs with thick rhizomes. Culms angular or flattened, mostly solid with closed sheaths. Leaves few, not crowded; leaf blades elongate, flat, or revolute with age, sometimes with spinulose-serrulate margins. Spikelets of several loosely imbricate, oblong or ovoid scales; lowest scales empty, one or two above bearing an imperfect or staminate flower, terminal flower perfect and fertile. Perianth none. Androecium two-merous; ovary sessile, style two- or three-cleft, deciduous. Achene short, usually ovoid, lenticular or obscurely trigonous, striate or wrinkled, not tuberculate, without bristles.

Latin name: *Cladium mariscoides* (Muhl.) Torr.
Synonym: *Mariscus mariscoides* (Muhl.) Kuntze

Cladium mariscoides. *Source: An Illustrated Flora of the Northern United States, Canada, and the British Possessions. 2nd ed., Vol. 1. Charles Scribner's Sons. 1913.*

Common names: Twig rush, Pond rush
Origin: North America
Habitat: Brackish-water or freshwater marshes, sandy shores, cultivated
Hardiness: Zones 5 through 9
Description: A loosely cespitose, semievergreen, stoloniferous perennial. Culms glabrous, branched, yellowish green, obscurely trigonous, stout, 20–40 in./0.5–1.0 m high. Foliage light green or yellowish green, fine in texture; leaves sparse, nearly smooth, margins scabrous, narrowly linear, 8–12 in./2–3 dm long, 1–3 mm wide, channeled, erect or ascending, not crowded; sheaths loose, smooth, hyaline ventrally. Inflorescence two to four umbelliform branched cymes, 0.25–0.50 in./6–13 mm broad, the rays rigidly ascending, peduncles flat to terete, glabrous, on rigidly erect or ascending, stiff branches, the entire panicle is 4–12 in./1–3 dm long, 0.8–2.0 in./2.0–5.0 cm broad; spikelets clustered in heads, 3 to 10 together on few peduncles, 0.15–0.25 in./4–6 mm long, one-to-four-flowered; scales reddish, 0.1–0.2 in./3–5 mm long, loosely imbricate; fruit a brownish, lustrous achene, ovoid, 0.10–0.15 in./3–4 mm long including the beaklike tip, longitudinally striate, the flat base often with a flaring edge. Flowering and fruiting occur from August until frost.
Uses: The colorful, reddish seedheads borne high above the foliage on long, erect, yellowish green culms make this sedge outstanding for plantings in bogs, in low wet sites, and in the shallow water of pools and streams. Its size determines its exact location in the garden in relation to other plants, to keep the entire landscape in harmony and to scale.
Cultivation: Propagation is by plant division; twig rush is easily established. The plants require fertile, moist or wet soil in light shade or full sun. This rush is invasive and requires careful consideration as to its location in the water garden to prevent it from becoming a problem.

Latin name: *Cladium sinclairii* Hook. f.
Origin: New Zealand
Habitat: Cultivated, escape from cultivation
Hardiness: Zones 7 through 9
Description: A vigorous, densely cespitose, caulescent, evergreen perennial. Culms erect, becoming arched, stout, glabrous, 30–36 in./7.6–9.0 dm high, obtusely angled, laterally compressed. Foliage light green, coarse in texture; basal leaves flat, 3–4 in./0.8–1.0 dm long, 1.0–1.2 in./2.5–3.0 cm wide, long attenuate, margins smooth; sheaths glabrous, hyaline ventrally. Inflorescence cymose clusters in a many-branched, reddish or brownish panicle, 10–16 in./2.5–4.0 dm long, 4–8 in./1–2 dm wide; cymes sessile or pedunculate, peduncles more or less terete, glabrous, on ascending branches; spikelets clustered, 0.1–0.2 in./3–5 mm long, one-to-four-flowered; scales reddish brown, ovate, many-nerved, about as long as the spikelets, spirally imbricate; fruit an apiculate, rich brown achene, smooth, lustrous, truncate basally, cylindric, 1–3 mm long. Flowering and fruiting occur from July through September.

Uses: The architectural value and large colorful brilliant flower heads make this sedge an outstanding value. The large, brownish flower heads, borne high above the foliage on long, graceful, arched culms, are a beautiful sight in the fall and winter when the seedheads are reflected on snow. It may be used effectively in a naturalized, wet, sheltered corner of a woodlot.

Cultivation: Propagation is by plant division. The plants require fertile, moist, garden soil in light shade. This sedge is easily established and maintained, as it is not invasive.

Cymophyllus **Mackenz. ex Britton and Brown (Fraser's sedge).** A monotypic genus, native to southern Appalachian Mountains. Named for its discoverer, John Fraser. Name from the Greek *cyma,* "wave," and *phyllon,* "leaf," from the minutely undulate margin. A perennial sedge with short rootstocks and flattened culms. Culms with 4–6 imbricate, striate, bladeless sheaths, and after flowering bearing one large, blade-bearing leaf without sheath, ligule, or midrib, with umbellate margins appearing minutely serrulate. Spike solitary, bractless, androgynous; flowers monoecious, solitary in the axils of the scales; perianth none. Staminate flowers with three stamens, filaments filiform. Pistillate flowers of a single pistil, a style and three stigmas, stigmas exserted, clavate, the pistil and style enveloped by the somewhat tumid perigynium. Achenes trigonous, jointed with the slender style.

Latin name: *Cymophyllus fraseri* (Andr.) Mackenz.
Synonym: *Carex fraseri* Andr.
Common names: Fraser's sedge, Lily-leaf sedge
Origin: North America
Habitat: Cultivated, escape from cultivation
Hardiness: Zones 7 and 8
Description: A monopodial perennial with short branching rhizomes. The stems of each branch of the rhizome consist of four or five membranous, closed, imbricate, basal sheaths and a single, broad, convolute blade without sheath, ligule, or midrib. Culms erect or arching, slender, 8–20 in./2–5 dm high, stiff, smooth on the lower portion, included in the imbricate, closed basal sheaths; sterile shoots none. A single, light green, coriaceous, evergreen leaf appears directly from the rhizome after flowering, flat or U-shaped, very persistent, widening along its length, terminating in a blunt round tip, 12–20 in./3–5 dm long, 1–2 in./2.5–5.0 cm wide, closely many-veined, margins cartilaginous, undulating, toothed or serrulate, sheaths (not of leaf) loose, thick, persistent. Inflorescence a singular, androgynous, bractless, globular spike, 0.5–1.0 in./13–25 mm long, about 1 in./25 mm in diameter at the base, becoming smaller near the apex, usually borne above the foliage, the upper portion staminate, oblong, the oblong-obtuse staminate scales white, midrib faint, filaments elongate, yellow; pistillate portion of spike ovoid-globose, very dense, 20 to 30 perigynia in

many rows, ascending or spreading, scales ovate-orbicular, obtuse to acute, half the length of the perigynia, the midvein faint; perigynia elliptic-ovoid, inflated, compressed-orbicular in section, 0.20–0.25 in./5–6 mm long, 2–3 mm wide, obscurely nerved, white, very membranous, glabrous and shining, gradually tapering at base and above, apex a very short, cylindric tip; fruit an ovoid or obovoid achene, trigonous, loosely enveloped in the lower part of the perigynium, strongly stipitate, jointed with the persistent style. Flowering and fruiting occur from May through July.

Uses: This native sedge is unique in having white "snowball" flowers in contrast to the usual brownish seedheads of other sedges. Fraser's sedge is useful in small areas in peat beds, or bogs, in or near water in water gardens and naturalized areas. The foliage is also attractive, as the leaves are much wider than those of other sedges. When grown as ground cover, the plants are compatible with spring-flowering bulbs and larger plants such as rhododendrons and azaleas. In shaded areas, it produces a good contrast in color to various woodrushes, *Luzula* species.

Cultivation: Propagation is by seeding and by plant division. Fraser's sedge is not invasive, despite its rhizomatous root system. Fraser's sedge is easily grown in shaded locations in rich, wet, peaty soil, as the roots require a constant moisture supply.

Cyperus **L. (Flat sedge, Umbrella sedge, Galingale, Sweet rush, Souchet)**. From Greek *Cypeiros,* the ancient name. Lectotype, *Cyperus esculentus* L. There are about 600 species, native chiefly to the tropics and temperate regions. Annual herbs with fibrous roots or perennial herbs with rhizomes. Leaves basal, with elongate narrow blades or rarely mere sheaths. Culms simple or compound, usually trigonous, with terminal involucre of one or several bracts that subtend the simple or compound inflorescence. Inflorescence branches, when present, sheathed at the base, usually very unequal. Spikelets few-to-many-flowered, flat or nearly terete, borne in clusters or heads on a simple or compound umbel; scales two-ranked and enclosing a single, bisexual flower; deciduous or persistent and falling away with the rachis, which disarticulates above the lower pair of scales or with each joint of the rachis when it breaks into one-fruited sections, the internodes of the rachis often winged. Flowers perfect; perianth absent; androecium of one to three stamens; style simple or two- or three-cleft, deciduous; stigmas two or three. Fruit a lenticular or trigonous achene, naked at the apex (Fernald, 1970).

Latin name: *Cyperus albostriatus* Schrad.
Synonym: *Cyperus laxus* Lam.
Cultivars: 'Variegatus'
Common name: Broadleaf umbrella palm
Origin: South Africa

Habitat: Low, wet places, cultivated
Hardiness: Zone 10
Description: A densely cespitose, evergreen, perennial herb with woody rhizomes. Culms solitary or several, slender, distinctly obtusely trigonous, finely striate, glabrous, 1–2 ft/3–6 dm high, bearing a whorl of leafy bracts at the summit. Foliage bright light green, coarse in texture. Basal leaves numerous, V-shaped, 12–18 in./3.0–4.5 dm long, 0.3–0.7 in./8–18 mm wide, some as long as the stems, rough on the margins, with three rather prominent, pale nerves; sheaths purple; involucral bracts many, leaflike, spreading, flat, 12–15 in./3–4 dm long, 0.4–0.5 in./10–13 mm wide, overtopping the inflorescence. Inflorescence a terminal compound umbel, rays 8 to 24, slender, 1–4 in./2.5–10.0 cm long; spikes two to four, clustered, 8-to-24-flowered, light brown or beige; spikelets few to many per spike, pedunculate, several-flowered, linear, 0.2–0.3 in./5–8 mm long, 1–2 mm wide; scales greenish or brownish, acute, appressed, 1–2 mm long; fruit a small, oblong, trigonous achene, slightly shorter than the scale. Flowering and fruiting occur from July through September.
Uses: Broadleaf umbrella palm and its variegated cultivar are grown for their curious umbrella effect produced by the radial whorl of leaves at the top of the stems. This species and its variegated cultivar are ideal as house plants and outdoors as accent and specimen plants in pools and in water gardens in zone 10 only.
Cultivation: Broadleaf umbrella palm is semiaquatic. Propagation is by seeding and by detaching plantlets grown from old, leafy heads that have been placed upside-down in water. The latter method of propagation may be successful with the species; however, its variegated cultivar may be difficult to propagate in this manner. The variegated cultivar should preferably be propagated by plant division. Potted plants must be placed in a container of water at all times to keep the roots wet. Sufficient light is necessary when the plants are grown indoors. Shaded locations and fertile, moist, garden soil are necessary requirements for outdoor plantings. When grown in pots, the plants should be watered only as much as is necessary to keep the potting mixture moist; the pot should not be kept standing in water. Cyperus plants usually require rather high humidity. The bracts are likely to dry out and develop brown tips if the plants are allowed to dry out for short periods. House-grown plants are usually much smaller than those grown outside. The leaves and stems are easily scorched by direct sunlight, even indoors.
Cultivars: *Cyperus albostriatus* Schrad. 'Variegatus' This cultivar is brilliantly variegated; its leaves are longitudinally striped pale yellow or whitish, and less so on the culms. The plant size and all its parts are identical to those of broadleaf umbrella palm. This cultivar is adapted to zone 10.

Latin name: *Cyperus alternifolius* L.
Cultivars: 'Flabelliformis,' 'Gracilis' Dwarf umbrella palm, 'Variegatus'

Cyperus alternifolius. **A, Inflorescence; B, spikelet; C, scale; D, achene.**
Source: Aquatic and Wetland Plants of Southeastern United States. Univ. of Georgia
Press. 1979.

Common names: Umbrella palm, Umbrella plant, Umbrella sedge, Nilegrass

Origin: Malagassy Republic, Africa, West Indies

Habitat: Low wet sites in water, cultivated

Hardiness: Zones 8 through 10

Description: A densely cespitose, scapose, evergreen perennial with short, stout rootstocks. Culms erect, becoming arching, obtusely trigonous to round, finely striate, smooth, bright dark green, 1–3 ft/3–9 dm high. Foliage bright dark green, medium in texture; basal leaves linear, usually reduced to lanceolate, acuminate, reddish brown sheaths, trigonous in section; involucral bracts 10 to 20, borne in a radial whorl near the tip of the scape, spreading, 4–10 in./1.0–2.5 dm long, 0.5–0.6 in./13–15 mm wide, leaflike, flat, acuminate, spreading and drooping, longer than the inflorescence. Inflorescence a compound umbel, 4–6 in./2.5–10.0 cm broad, primary rays filiform, 1–2 in./2.5–10.0 cm long, as many as the bracts and arising from their axils, with very short raylets; spikes 3 to 12, clustered, dull brown; spikelets few per spike, digitate, linear, many-flowered, ovate to elliptic, 0.2–0.4 in./5–10 mm long, 2–3 mm wide, rachis narrowly membranous-winged, scales greenish yellow or brownish, ovate or ovate-lanceolate, acute, obscurely nerved, appressed, 1–2 mm long, ascending or spreading. Fruit an oblong, trigonous, black achene, narrowed at each end, slightly shorter than the scale. Flowering and fruiting occur from July through September. The plants are greenish yellow at times, and they copiously reseed themselves.

Uses: Umbrella palm or nilegrass and its cultivars are grown in the home and in greenhouses as potted plants in colder climates and outdoors in warmer areas. They are used as specimen and accent plants in and around indoor and outdoor pools. Nilegrass is ideally suited for use with other water-loving plants in water gardens. It is commonly found in suburban parks and in city beautification plantings. The plants are an excellent foil for other broad-leaved water plants, including erect types with foliage above the water, and for all plant types with floating foliage or blossoms on the water. Another good setting for umbrella palm is along streams in the garden. It is widely used as an indoor plant in decorating homes, offices, and public buildings. Umbrella palm or nilegrass has been cultivated for more than two centuries in water gardens and as a potted plant.

Cultivation: Propagation is by seeding in spring or early autumn, by plant division, or by removing the leafy heads and placing them upside-down in water until young plants emerge. The young plants can be detached, planted, and grown in water or a soil-based mixture. Any good growing mixture is sufficient, when grown indoors as a potted plant. The potted plant should be placed in a flat container, which holds water at all times, with sufficient natural or artificial light. The plants must be established and grown in mud or directly in water when grown outside, preferably in light or medium shade, as the sun will blister the leaves, even indoors sometimes. All plants in this genus do best in light shade. The cultivar Variegatus requires brighter light than most other forms. When few new stems are produced, it is usually indicative that the plants are not receiving enough light. Most cyperus species tolerate moist or wet soil and temperatures as low as about 50°F/10°C, although *Cyperus papyrus* requires a minimum temperature of 60–65°F/16–18°C. Umbrella palm, *Cyperus alternifolius,* and *Cyperus papyrus* require a constant water supply. The root ball should be kept moist at all times. This may be accomplished by standing the pot containing the plant in a container of water; the plant will then draw up the water that it needs. The pots must not be completely immersed, because the stems will rot if they are below the water line. *Cyperus alternifolius* may also be grown in watertight containers filled with water and pebbles. Apply standard liquid fertilizer at monthly intervals during active growth. A soil-based potting mixture is adequate for cyperus species. The young plants should be started in small (3 in./8 cm) pots, then removed to larger (5 in./13 dm) pots. Most species look best in 5 in./1.3 dm pots; they appear completely out of scale in oversize containers.

Cultivars: *Cyperus alternifolius* L. 'Flabelliformis' A vigorous rhizomatous perennial; culms 3–4 ft/0.9–1.2 m high. The thick, spongy leaves and strong, spreading rhizomes differentiate this cultivar from the species.

Cyperus alternifolius L. 'Gracilis' Dwarf umbrella palm The small size and very narrow leaves differentiate this cultivar from the species. The plants are 12–18 in./3.0–4.5 dm high with dark green bracts; they rarely flower.

Cyperus alternifolius L. 'Variegatus' The culms and foliage of this cultivar are distinctly variegated, with longitudinal white and yellowish green stripes. The bracts are soft and pliable, either striped white-green or totally white; occasionally there is some white on the culms. Quite often, the ephemeral variegation reverts to green as the plants age, making them difficult to maintain in their most elegant color. Stems that revert to green should be removed at the rootstocks.

Latin name: *Cyperus haspan* L.
Synonym: *Cyperus haspan* var. *americanus* Boeckl.
Cultivars: 'Viviparous' Pygmy papyrus
Common name: Dwarf papyrus
Origin: Pantropics
Habitat: Low wet areas, swamps, cultivated
Hardiness: Zone 10
Description: A densely cespitose or gregarious scapose perennial herb with short rhizomes. Culms from a short rhizome, tufted, soft, weak, smooth, simple, 12–40 in./0.3–1.0 m high, usually smaller, sharply trigonous; upper sheaths bladeless; lower sheaths blade-bearing. Foliage medium green, fine in texture; basal leaves filiform, linear, 4–6 in./1.0–1.5 dm long, often reduced to sheaths; involucral leaves usually two, erect or ascending, commonly shorter than the filiform elongate rays of the open, compound umbel. Inflorescence few spikelets

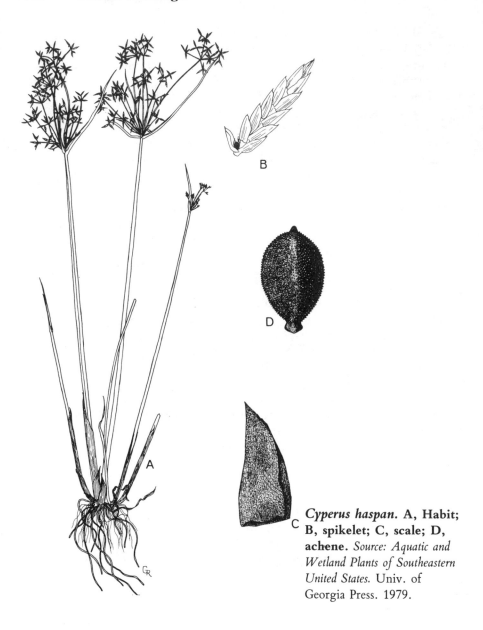

Cyperus haspan. A, Habit; B, spikelet; C, scale; D, achene. *Source: Aquatic and Wetland Plants of Southeastern United States.* Univ. of Georgia Press. 1979.

together in glomerules on numerous lax spikes on stiff stalks, linear to linear-lanceolate, 0.25–0.50 in./6–13 mm long, about 1 mm wide, mostly reddish brown; scales elliptic, elliptic-lanceolate or ovate, about 1–2 mm long, often mucronate, loosely appressed, three-nerved, membranous, tinged with red or purple; fruit a lenticular achene, pale, the body oval, suborbicular, or broadly ovate, less than 1 mm long, pearly white, minutely papillate. Flowering and fruiting occur from August through October. A pantropical and highly variable species.

Uses: Dwarf papyrus is best known and used as a potted house plant in homes, offices, and public buildings. It is the most delicate and finest of the so-called umbrella plants. It is useful in water gardens in warm climates, where it will thrive in shallow water.

Cultivation: Propagate dwarf papyrus by inverting the seedheads in water until new plantlets are produced, then plant in pots in a good soil mixture, and keep the base of the pots in water. The plants may be grown outside in light shade in moist or wet soil. The viviparous form is propagated by potting the viviparous plantlets.

Cultivars: *Cyperus haspan* L. 'Viviparous' Pygmy papyrus   This small species is only about 12–18 in./3.0–4.5 dm high. It is usually grown indoors as a house plant for its unique, viviparous propagation. Pygmy papyrus is a tender perennial adapted to zone 10.

Latin name: *Cyperus papyrus* L.
Cultivars: 'Nanus,' 'Variegatus'
Common names: Egyptian reed (Bulrush of the Bible), Paper plant
Origin: Africa
Habitat: Ponds, lakes, slow-moving streams, cultivated
Hardiness: Zone 10
Description: A cespitose, weak, evergreen perennial with stout, thick, woody, rhizomes. Culms four to eight, not jointed, stout, smooth, bluntly trigonous, 10–12 ft/3.1–3.7 m high and 0.8–1.0 in./20–25 mm thick near the base. Foliage medium to dark green, coarse in texture; basal leaves numerous, trigonous in section, usually reduced to brownish sheaths, 1–2 ft/3–6 dm long, 0.7–0.9 in./18–23 mm wide, scabrous on the margins, otherwise smooth; sheaths hyaline, smooth, closed ventrally. Involucral bracts numerous, flat, brownish, spreading, lanceolate-acuminate, 2–3 in./5–8 cm long, 0.25–0.50 in./6–13 mm wide. Inflorescence a terminal, compound umbel, primary rays often more than 100, 4–12 in./1–3 dm long, slender, drooping, each enclosed at the base by a brown sheath about 1 in./25 mm long and topped by three to five threadlike bracts subtending three to five spikes; spikes brownish, 0.2–0.4 in./5–10 mm long, 2–3 mm wide, each containing 20 to 30 spikelets, central spike usually sessile, axillary spikes pedunculate; spikelets terete or flattened, spreading, slender, digitate, 6-to-16-flowered, 0.2–0.3 in./5–8 mm long, 1–2 mm wide, light tan; scales acute, ovate, keeled, 1–2 mm long, appressed; fruit a light tan, lenticular achene, about half or three-quarters the length of the scale. Flowering and fruiting occur from June through September.

Uses: Egyptian reed and its variegated form make marvelous plantings in large ponds or lakes, where the tall culms form graceful arches under the weight of the round umbels of leaves at their summits. Its range when grown outside is limited by its lack of winter hardiness. Despite its size when grown outside, Egyptian reed may be grown in greenhouse ponds.

Cultivation: Egyptian reed is propagated by dividing overcrowded clumps, usually in the spring. It is a tender, aquatic ornamental that requires a tropical climate and adequate soil moisture to flourish. This perennial is a tropical plant in every respect. Egyptian reed may be grown outside in zones 9 and 10, provided it is brought indoors during the winter. Egyptian reed and its cultivars are a success indoors if the temperature is maintained above about 60°F/16°C with relatively high humidity. A growing medium of three parts heavy clay soil and one part well-rotted manure is adequate for good growth. The plants should be grown in large pots or containers, which may be transferred indoors during the winter. Fill the pots to about 2 in./5 cm from the top with the growing mixture; then place crushed stone, sand, or gravel above the soil to prevent the water from becoming muddy. The containers should be kept submerged in water at least 3 in./8 cm above the container. If this is not possible, use a container that does not drain, and keep the roots under water constantly. The water should be changed periodically to keep the plants healthy and in an active growth state; even so, the lack of drainage may cause the plants to die. In repotting Egyptian reed, be sure to set the plants in the new pot at the same level in the potting mixture as they were before. Humid warmth is essential to success in growing Egyptian reed indoors. Outdoor plantings thrive best when grown directly in water; however, mud is the next-best growing medium.

Cultivars: *Cyperus papyrus* L. 'Nanus'   This miniature papyrus is about 2 ft/6 dm high; otherwise, it resembles Egyptian reed.

Cyperus papyrus L. 'Variegatus'   This cultivar is approximately the same size as Egyptian reed or bulrush. It is very tender and not cold tolerant (i.e., adapted to warmer parts of zone 10). The leaves of this cultivar are distinctly and boldly variegated, with longitudinal white-green stripes.

Latin name: *Cyperus vegetus* B. Mey.
Synonym: *Cyperus eragrostis* Lam.
Habitat: Low wet sites, occasionally in water, cultivated
Hardiness: Zones 4 through 7
Description: A loosely cespitose, semievergreen, perennial herb. Culms erect to slightly arching, indistinctly trigonous, stout, light green, rough, 2–4 ft/0.6–1.2 m high, occasionally smaller. Foliage medium green, medium in texture; leaves basal, acutely V-shaped in section, 12–18 in./3.0–4.5 dm long, 0.4–0.5 in./10–13 mm wide, long attenuate, somewhat rough on the margins, finely veined above; involucral bracts numerous, bright green, flat, leafy, up to 6 in./1.5 dm long, usually straight or sometimes drooping, borne on peduncles 1–2 in./2.5–5.0 cm long which are perpendicular to the stem. Inflorescence a terminal, loose umbel surrounded by many leafy, bright green bracts. Spikes in dense clusters, greenish white, borne at right angles to the culm; spikelets linear, pedunculate, several-flowered, 0.1–0.2 in./3–5 mm long, 1–2 mm wide, bright

Cyperus vegetus. *Source: An Illustrated Flora of the Pacific States. Vol. 1.* Stanford Univ. Press. 1923.

green or yellowish becoming tan; scales acute, greenish brown, 1–3 mm long; fruit a small, trigonous achene, about half the length of the scale. Flowering and fruiting occur from July through September.

Uses: The umbrella-type inflorescence of this freshwater sedge is interesting both on the plant and as a dried specimen. It is useful and decorative around and in pools and in the water garden. This hardy species is also useful as a house plant.

Cultivation: Propagation is by seeding and by plant division, preferably the latter. The plants reseed themselves copiously. This curious plant thrives best in light shade but will withstand some direct sun. It thrives equally well in ordinary moist or wet garden soil or with its feet in shallow water; the roots should always be kept moist or wet. This sedge is ideal for naturalizing freshwater marshes.

Other ornamental species: *Cyperus longus* L. This hardy species, adapted to zones 5–8, attains a height of about 4 ft/1.2 m. This species may be planted in spring or autumn in shallow water of lakes and slow-moving streams or in bogs or boggy grounds; it is also useful as a houseplant.

Eleocharis **R. Br. (Spike rush).** Name from Greek, *elos,* "marsh," and *charis,* "grace," since many species grow in marshes. A cosmopolitan genus of about 200 species. The type species has not been designated. Annual cespitose herbs or chiefly rhizomatous or stoloniferous perennials from creeping or matted rhizomes, usually in aquatic environments. Culms simple, ascending or upright, three-to-four-angled or compressed. Leaves reduced to bladeless sheaths. Inflorescence terminal, spiciform with the bract reduced to a basal scale or usually absent, bearing few to many perfect flowers crowded into three or more ranks in the axils of the scales. Scales usually spirally imbricate, of various textures, usually crowded, remaining so even when the achenes mature in some species, but in others serially deciduous beginning at the base of the spike. Perianth of six to nine retrorsely barbed bristles or in some species, reduced or absent. Stamens usually three, in some species reduced to one or two; styles two- or three-cleft, basally enlarged into a persistent tubercle capping the trigonous achene. Tubercle variously shaped and textured. Fruit an achene, achene body nearly terete or plano-convex, of various shapes, textures, and colors (Svenson, 1929, 1957b).

Latin name: *Eleocharis acicularis* (L.) Roem & Schult.
Synonym: *Scirpus acicularis* L.
Common names: Slender spike rush, Least spike rush, Hairgrass
Origin: Asia, North America
Habitat: Wet ground, marshes, often growing in water
Hardiness: Zones 4 through 10
Description: A hardy, perennial rush, with capillary branching rhizomes, that forms tufted mats. Culms capillary, green, erect, 2–8 in./0.5–2.0 dm high, usually angular and sulcate; rootstocks capillary, with abundant stolons. Sheaths loose and membranous, reddish striate at base, the apex somewhat inflated, scarious. Inflorescence a columnar spike; spikelets flattened, ovate lanceolate to linear, 0.1–0.3 in./3–8 mm long, 3-to-12-flowered; scales keeled, 1–2 mm long, membranous, usually only a few subtending the mature fruit, ovate-lanceolate, acute, green with reddish sides and scarious margins; bristles three or four, capillary, brownish, equaling the achene, often lacking; fruit an obscurely trigonous achene, narrowly elliptic-obovate with about 40 to 50 ribs; style base or tubercle narrow, compressed. Flowering and fruiting occur during June through September.
Uses: Slender spike rush is commonly used in aquariums. The hardiness of this small spike rush renders it useful in peat bogs and water gardens over a wide climatic range.

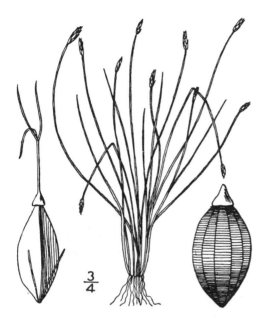

Eleocharis acicularis. Source: An Illustrated Flora of the Northern United States, Canada, and the British Possessions. Vol. 1. Charles Scribner's Sons. 1896.

Cultivation: Propagation is by plant division. Young plants or rhizomes may be planted directly in mud or water.

Latin name: *Eleocharis cellulosa* Torr.
Synonym: *Scirpus dictyospermus* C. Wright
Common name: Round-stemmed spike rush
Origin: North America, Asia
Habitat: In mud and fresh water in shallow depressions
Hardiness: Zones 7 through 10
Description: A tufted, perennial, rhizomatous rush; culms erect, simple, terete, rarely trigonous, 1–3 ft/4–9 dm high, 1–2 mm wide, greenish to greenish yellow; rootstocks rhizomatous; sheaths normally reddish, upper sheaths rigid, purplish, oblique with a long mucronate tip, lowest membranous, leaflike. Inflorescence a cylindrical spike, 8–14 in./2–4 dm long, 0.1–0.2 in./3–5 mm thick with 50 to 100 small flowers; spikelets cylindrical, obtuse, 1–2 in./2.5–5.0 cm long, thicker than the culm; scales broadly ovate to obovate, 0.2–0.3 in./5–8 mm long, 0.1–0.2 in./3–5 mm broad medially, stramineous with prominent midrib and brownish borders and white, scarious margins; bristles five or six, involute, without teeth, capillary, mostly equaling or exceeding the achene and not serrulate, brownish; fruit biconvex brownish achene, about 2 mm long, the surface apically umbonate, forming a base that is the podium for and merges into the tubercle; tubercle, about 1 mm long. Flowering and fruiting occur from June through September.

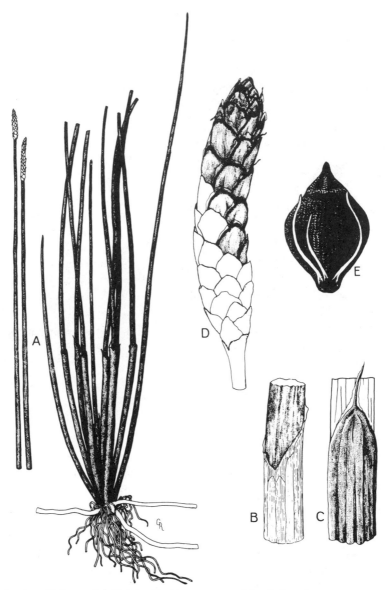

Eleocharis cellulosa. **A, Habit; B–C, summit of leaf sheath (two views); D, spike; E, achene.** *Source: Aquatic and Wetland Plants of Southeastern United States.* Univ. of Georgia Press. 1979.

Uses: Round-stemmed spike rush is used as ground cover in naturalizing low, wet sites. It forms compatible stands with other sedges and aquatics around and in shallow water of pools, ponds, and lakes. This tufted perennial is equally useful in the bog or water garden.

Cultivation: Propagation is by plant division. Round-stemmed spike rush is adapted to warmer temperate and subtropical regions. It is not as hardy as slender spike rush.

Eriophorum **L. (Cotton grass, Bog cotton, Linaigrette).** Name from Greek, *erion,* "wool" or "cotton," and *phoros,* "bearing," referring to the cottony spikelets. Lectotype, *Eriophorum vaginatum* L. There are about 15 species, native to the Northern Hemisphere. Erect, caulescent herbs with fibrous roots, with or without rhizomes, culms erect, simple, densely cespitose, more or less terete or obtusely angled. Basal leaves mostly filiform, leaf blades narrowly linear, smooth or scabrous. Cauline leaves mostly reduced to bladeless sheaths. Spikelets solitary, umbellate or clustered, often subtended by an involucre of one to several leaflike bracts on a leafy or naked stem. Scales spirally imbricate, membranous, one-to-five-nerved, usually all fructiferous or some of the lower ones empty; perianth of numerous, naked capillary, greatly elongated, silky bristles. Flowers perfect; androecium three-merous, style very slender and elongated, three-cleft, not tumid, deciduous; gynoecium three-merous; fruit an acutely trigonous achene.

Latin name: *Eriophorum callitrix* Cham.
Common name: Hare's-tail
Origin: Asia
Habitat: Calcareous peat bogs, mountain slopes
Hardiness: Zones 2 through 6
Description: A caulescent, upright-open, perennial herb with fibrous roots. Culms numerous, densely cespitose, stout, stiff, trigonous and scabrous at the tip, 4–8 in./1–2 dm high. Foliage medium green, fine in texture; basal leaves filiform-trigonous, stiff, scabrous; sheaths borne mostly below the middle of the culm, the upper inflated and often with a short blade; spathe ovate and ribbed nearly to the margin. Inflorescence a dense, terminal head; flowering spikelets obovoid or globose, 0.3–0.6 in./8–15 mm long; scales castaneous, margins pale, ovate to ovate-lanceolate, long attenuate; perianth bristles numerous, smooth, silky and becoming elongated, bright white; fruit a small, brownish, acutely trigonous achene, ellipsoid-obovoid. Flowering and fruiting occur from May through July.

Uses: Hare's-tail is a typical aquatic plant, useful in swamps, marshes, and bogs. Like cotton grass, *Eriophorum polystachion,* it is grown for its feathery, whitish seedheads, with their silky, smooth, long, white bristles or threads that sway and oscillate in the slightest breeze. The plants are ideally suited for poolside plantings and around the margins of ponds and in water gardens. Unlike cotton grass, hare's-tail is noninvasive, which is advantageous in its use in outdoor plantings.

Cultivation: Propagation is by plant division. The plants require a moist or wet site in shaded, cool locations. Hare's-tail is most impressive when grown in clumps or massed stands; it will remain fairly stable in size, as the plants are not invasive. Hare's-tail thrives in full sun.

Latin name: *Eriophorum polystachion* L.
Synonym: *Eriophorum angustifolium* Honck.
Common names: Cotton grass, Cotton rush

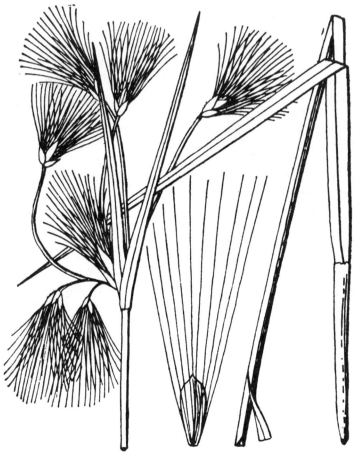

Eriophorum polystachion. *Source: An Illustrated Flora of the Northern United States, Canada, and the British Possessions. Vol. 1.* Charles Scribner's Sons. 1896.

Origin: Eurasia
Habitat: Wet meadows, bogs, swamps, cultivated
Hardiness: Zones 4 through 6
Description: A caulescent, upright-open to spreading perennial herb with strong rhizomes, extensively colonial. Culms erect, soft, slender, glabrous, subterete, obtusely angled, 1–3 ft/3–9 dm high. Foliage medium green, fine in texture; leaves basal and cauline, basal leaves few, soft, elongate, flat near the base, usually conduplicate above the middle, 10–12 in./2.5–3.0 dm long, 0.15–0.25 in./4–6 mm wide, margins scabrous, cauline leaves 0.10–0.15 in./3–4 mm wide, the uppermost cauline leaf with well-developed blade usually exceeding the sheath; sheaths glabrous, hyaline near the ventral orifice, dark purple at the base; involucral bracts several, unequal, some foliaceous above the base, the longest about equaling the inflorescence. Inflorescence two to several spikelets in a terminal, compact to open, umbellate cyme subtended by several leafy or scale-like, unequal bracts, the peduncles strongly compound, smooth or sometimes scabrid; scales castaneous, more or less hyaline, especially distally, bristles numerous; fruit an oblanceolate blackish achene, 1–3 mm long, twice as long as wide. Flowering and fruiting occur from June through August.

Uses: Cotton grass is an ideal water plant, adapted for naturalizing cold bogs, marshes, and swamps. It is grown for its whitish, fluffy, feathery seedheads. Although the seedheads are rather dense, the long, white threads are subject to being windblown. The whitish, dense seedheads, with their stringy threads blowing in the wind, make a spectacular sight. The plants are useful outdoors in clump plantings in the water garden, usually on the margins of pools and ponds and along streams. Cotton grass is unsurpassed for use in adding diversity and attractiveness to difficult wet sites in the water garden.

Cultivation: The plants require severe control measures to prevent or reduce their invasion into undesired areas by their strong, spreading rhizomes. This may be accomplished by sinking some form of containing barrier into the soil about 6 in./1.5 dm deep to control their invasiveness. Perhaps a better method of control involves establishing the plants in 55-gallon steel drums that have been reduced to about 2–3 ft/6–9 dm high and placed in shallow water or mud near or in pools or ponds. The plants require moist or wet soils and grow best in light shade or full sun. Propagation is by seeding and by plant division, preferably the latter. Like many other ornamentals, to achieve maximum effectiveness, the plants should be established in rather large clumps or in massed stands. It thrives best in bogs, marshes, and sloughs, where the roots are constantly wet. This is the only species of so-called cotton grass that is commercially available.

Latin name: *Eriophorum virginicum* L.
Common name: Tawny cotton grass
Origin: North America
Habitat: Acid bogs, meadows and swamps, cultivated

Eriophorum virginicum. *Source: An Illustrated Flora of the Northern United States, Canada, and the British Possessions. Vol. 1.* Charles Scribner's Sons, 1896.

Hardiness: Zones 5 through 9

Description: A caulescent, upright-open to spreading perennial herb with strong rootstocks. Culms wiry, smooth, terete below, trigonous above, 2–4 ft / 0.6–1.2 m high. Foliage medium green, fine in texture; basal leaves flat, stiff, elongate-linear, the uppermost 4–10 in./1.0–2.5 dm long, 0.10–0.15 in./3–4 mm wide, with closed sheaths; involucral bracts two to five, divergent, the longest 2–5 in./0.5–1.3 dm long. Inflorescence a dense, terminal glomerule; spikelets two to several, crowded in a dense glomerule, 0.6–2.4 in./1.5–6.0 cm in diameter, in anthesis ellipsoid and 0.25–0.40 in./6–10 mm long, in fruit 0.4–0.8 in./10–20 mm long; scales ovate-oblong, with strongly striate-ribbed green-ish or stramineous body and thin, nerveless, reddish brown margins; bristles numerous, tawny or copper-colored; fruit an ellipsoid-obovoid, trigonous achene, 0.10–0.15 in./3–4 mm long, short beaked, stipitate. Flowering and fruiting occur from August until frost.

Uses: This species, native to North America, is more widely distributed than cotton grass, *Eriophorum polystachion,* occurring along the Atlantic coast from Newfoundland to Florida. It is used in the same manner as cotton grass, although it is not quite as showy. The plants are about twice the size of cotton grass. Tawny cotton grass is useful in large areas, including freshwater bogs and swamps. Its ideal garden site is around swimming pools or in acid soils in water gardens.

Cultivation: The gregarious growth habit of tawny cotton grass makes it particularly useful in naturalizing extended areas of low, wet sites, including ponds and pools, and along streams. Propagation is by seeding and by plant division. The plants should be established over rather large areas to maximize their effectiveness. Tawny cotton grass thrives in full sun.

Other ornamental species: *Eriophorum vaginatum* L. Hare's-tail This small, cespitose, perennial herb is a smaller version of cotton grass, *Eriophorum polystachion.* The glabrous culms are terete below, trigonous above, 12–18 in./3.0–4.5 dm high. Foliage is medium green, fine in texture; basal leaves lanceolate, sharply trigonous or enrolled near the base, 6–12 in./1.5–3.0 dm long, 0.2–0.4 in./5–10 mm wide, very bristly, cauline leaves much shorter and cylindrical; sheaths cylindrical, loose, narrow at the throat, glabrous, membranous. Inflorescence solitary, compact, white flower heads about 0.5–1.6 in./1.3–4.0 cm thick; mature flower heads with numerous whitish bristles 1.0–1.6 in./2.5–4.0 cm long. Flowering and fruiting occur from May through July. The plants produce a profusion of small, whitish flowers when grown in massed stands or in large clumps. They are ideal for small, naturalized areas in bogs and water gardens and near pools and streams. Propagation is by plant division. The plants thrive best in muddy, acid soils in full sun near pools, lakes, and streams. This species is also valuable as a house plant; it is adapted to zones 4–6.

Fuirena **Rottb. (Umbrella grass).** Named for G. Fuiren, a Danish botanist. Type species, *Fuirena umbellata* Rottb. There are about 40 species, most abundant in the warmer regions of low latitudes. Erect perennial or rarely annual caulescent herbs. Culms usually leafy, obtusely trigonous, usually from a perennial rootstock. Leaves sometimes reduced to mere trigonous sheaths. Spikelets axillary and terminal, clustered or rarely solitary, terete, many-flowered, often burlike. Scales spirally imbricate in many ranks, awned below the apex, all floriferous. Perianth usually of six bristles, the inner three inflated and scalelike, ovate at the apex, alternating with three retrorsely barbed bristles. Flowers perfect; style three-cleft, or swollen at the base, deciduous; stamens and stigmas three each; ovary stipitate or merely sessile, smooth. Fruit a sharply trigonous smooth achene, stipitate or nearly sessile, whitish becoming brown when mature, often

Eriophorum vaginatum. *Source: An Illustrated Flora of the Northern United States, Canada, and the British Possessions. Vol. 1.* Charles Scribner's Sons. 1896.

prolonged into a slender beak as long as the body of the achene, surrounded by three bristles alternating with three stalked broadened scales (Svenson, 1957a).

> **Latin name:** *Fuirena simplex* Vahl
> **Synonym:** *Fuirena primiera* M. E. Jones
> **Common name:** Umbrella grass
> **Origin:** North America
> **Habitat:** Moist meadows and margins of ponds and lakes
> **Hardiness:** Zones 7 through 10
> **Description:** A cespitose, perennial herb with thick rhizomes. Culms slender, hispid-ciliate, 4–24 in./1–6 dm high, from tuber-bearing rootstocks, leafy,

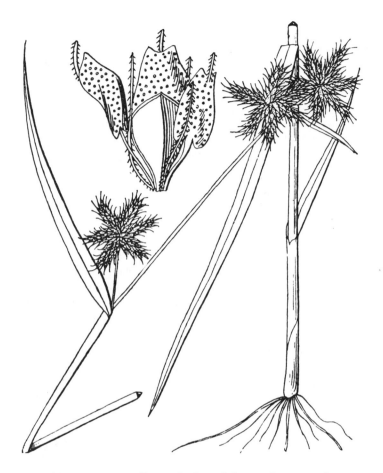

Fuirena simplex. *Source: An Illustrated Flora of the Northern United States, Canada, and the British Possessions. 2nd ed., Vol. 1.* Charles Scribner's Sons. 1913.

but almost entirely covered by sheaths, obtusely trigonous, yellowish green. Foliage light to yellowish green, fine in texture; leaf blades oblong to lanceolate-linear, flat, 2–6 in./0.5–1.5 dm long, 0.2–0.4 in./5–10 mm wide, shining above, hispid-ciliate; sheaths 4–6 in./1.0–1.5 dm long, slightly inflated upward, sparsely pubescent, eventually nearly glabrate; ligule short, hyaline, rather densely villous-ciliate. Inflorescence one to several terminal and axillary pedunculate clusters of 3 to 10 spikelets; spikelets 0.2–0.4 in./5–10 mm long, 0.10–0.15 in./3–4 mm wide; spikelet scales floriferous, imbricate in many ranks, broadly ovate to obovate, rusty-colored with a greenish midrib, 2–3 mm long, midrib excurrent as a curved awn about 1 mm long, blades ovate to oblong, less than 1 mm long, set on a slender, short claw, emarginate, with a smooth or retrorsely barbed bristle set on the back just below the apex, round at the base; perianth scales ovate-oblong, the retrorsely barbed awns arising from below the tip, the alternating bristles retrorsely barbed, equaling or exceeding the achene; fruit a light yellowish or whitish, strongly trigonous, obovoid achene about 1 mm long, acute at each end. Flowering and fruiting occur from July until frost.

Uses: Umbrella grass is best suited for the water garden, bogs, or other low, wet sites. The rusty-brownish seedheads and yellowish green culms are attractive in early fall and persist into winter. The structure and color of the plants provide a perfect foil for other water plants such as water lilies, with their flat horizontal leaves.

Cultivation: Propagation is by plant division. Umbrella grass prefers wet, acid soil in light shade or full sun; the plants are easily propagated and will thrive directly in water.

Juncus L. (**Rush, Bog rush, Jonc**). The classical name, from *jungere,* "to join," alluding to the use of the stems for bands. Lectotype, *Juncus acutus* L. There are about 300 species, cosmopolitan but native mostly to temperate regions. Caulescent, rather stiff, rhizomatous, glabrous annual or chiefly perennial herbs, the latter with rhizomes. Flowering stems usually simple, rarely branching, pithy or hollow, terete. Leaves bladeless or bearing blades, blades terete in section, narrow to filiform, rarely hairy, sometimes reduced to basal, open sheaths. Inflorescence terminal, cymose or clustered, some forms with a subtending bract that appears to be a continuation of the stem, the inflorescence thus appearing lateral. Flowers in simple or compound cymes, in many the ultimate cymes glomerate. Flowers hypogynous, green to brown or reddish black, small, not showy; perianth of two whorls of three distinct but similar, bractlike, persistent segments. Gynoecium three-merous, carpels fused, style short, bearing three recurved stigmas; stamens three or six. Ovary one-locular or three-locular by intrusion of the parietal placenta. Fruit a loculicidal, three-valved capsule; seeds numerous, very small (Fernald, 1970).

Latin name: *Juncus effusus* L.
Synonym: *Juncus polyanthemus* Buchenau
Cultivars and varieties: 'Aureus Striatus,' 'Spiralis' Spiral rush, 'Vittatus,' 'Zebrinus'; *Juncus effusus* var. *compactus* Lej. & Courtois Japanese mat; *Juncus effusus* var. *solutus* Fern. & Wieg. Soft rush
Common names: Common rush, Soft rush
Origin: Europe, North Africa
Habitat: Shaded, moist to wet, open woods, cultivated
Hardiness: Zones 4 through 8
Description: A densely cespitose, caulescent, evergreen, perennial herb with strong rhizomes. Culms many, terete, from creeping rootstocks in dense tufts, 18–60 in./0.5–1.5 m high, arching or ascending, simple, rarely branched,

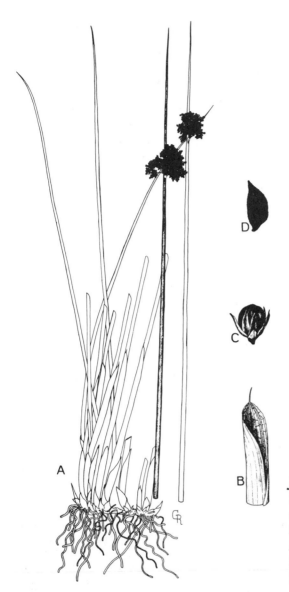

**Juncus effusus. A, Habit;
B, leaf sheath; C, perianth
and capsule; D, seed.**
Source: *Aquatic and Wetland
Plants of Southeastern United
States.* Univ. of Georgia
Press. 1979.

smooth along their length, striate near the top, soft to firm, light yellowish green, not glaucous, pithy, pith continuous, glossy. Foliage mostly absent; leaves rudimentary or absent; open sheaths near the base, 2–4 in./5–10 cm long, reddish or brown, chartaceous, strictly erect, more or less clasping bases of the culms, mucronate, inner sheaths awned. Inflorescence a loose, diffusely branched, many-flowered cyme, about one-third the distance from the top of the culm, branching open or congested, it appears lateral; the involucral bract terete, erect or ascending, similar to and continuing the naked or essentially naked scape; flowers bracteolate, borne singly on the branches of the cyme, greenish brown, 0.10–0.15 in./3–4 mm long, perfect, sepals and petals lanceolate, acute or acuminate, about as long as the capsule, mature perianth about 0.1 in./3 mm long; androecium three-merous, styles minute, very short; ovary superior, three-celled; fruit a three-celled, many-seeded, greenish brown, obovoid capsule, round at the apex, readily dehiscent; seeds less than 1 mm long, ribbed and reticulate. Flowering and fruiting occur from June through September.

Uses: Common rush is a highly variable species; included among its variants are two botanical varieties, three variegated cultivars, and the cultivar Spiralis. They are truly water plants of ornamental value. The home of these ornamentals is in bog and water gardens, around the margins of pools and ponds, and along streams. All forms of common rush are useful, along with other water-loving plants, in naturalizing bogs, pools, or other low, wet areas in or surrounding the garden. Their unique architectural beauty, plant form, color, and texture add diversity and attractiveness to the landscape not provided by other aquatics. Common rush and its variants are attractive throughout the year; the plants remain stiff and upright into winter; the colorful foliage and stems of the variegated forms provide good fall color. The mature seedheads, which turn rust-red or brownish in the fall, and remain into winter, are the center of attraction of these water plants. The evergreen plants persist through the winters in zones 4–8, although they may turn somewhat yellowish or brownish. The drastic contrast in color of the bright yellow-green striped stems of 'Aureus Striatus' are particularly attractive, as are those of the narrow, white-green stripes of 'Vittatus' and the broad, greenish white or white-green stripes of 'Zebrinus.'

The variegated cultivars are far more attractive than common rush, and, consequently, more popular. They are a perfect foil for green-leaved ornamental grasses, cattails, and other aquatics in pools and ponds and along streams. Common rush and its variants thrive in wet soils, mud, and shallow water. They are particularly beneficial in naturalizing low, wet sites, including bog gardens and marshes. The larger forms of common rush and soft rush, *Juncus effusus* var. *solutus,* occur spontaneously in marshes and swamps, in which they are useful in naturalizing. These large forms require considerable space and are useful only in the largest of gardens. The smaller, more colorful, variegated types are popular and useful as potted house plants, in addition to being attractive and useful in outdoor plantings. Common rush and its variants are generally found in public parks, golf courses, and sports and playing fields, in which pools and ponds are found and through which streams flow. They, along with other aquatics, are used in urban areas and cities in large planters or along streams and canals. Spiral rush, *Juncus effusus* 'Spiralis,' deserves a prominent place in the garden as a curiosity because of its unique spiral growth habit. The living, slender stems fall to the ground and curl and twist in corkscrew fashion in all directions, forming a jumbled mass. Spiral rush is equally deserving, whether grown in a bog area or wet part of the peat garden, or as a border specimen in a wet, shaded location. It also does well as a house plant in a well-lighted room.

Cultivation: True rushes are water plants. They thrive in moist or wet soils, in and surrounding ponds and pools, and along streams and canals; they are also equally at home in shallow water. For those who have a stream, pool, or pond in their garden, common rush may be present naturally, as it is ubiquitous. Potted plants grown indoors require that water be maintained above the soil level in the containers. The excess water should be drained off occasionally and replaced with fresh water to prevent the soil from becoming sour, resulting in reduced growth, vigor, and attractiveness of the plants. The appearance of indoor plantings may be improved by placing sand, gravel, pebbles, or crushed stone above the soil in the containers. The plants will grow in ordinary garden soil, provided it is kept constantly wet, although they prefer muddy areas surrounding pools and along streams or in shallow water. Propagation is by seeding and by plant division, usually the latter. Plant division is more successful in the spring than in the autumn, although autumn plantings are not discouraged. Green-leaved rushes, including common rush, thrive equally well in full sun or in light or partial shade. The variegated cultivars of common rush prefer light or partial shade, as full sun will blister their leaves.

Cultivars: *Juncus effusus* L. 'Aureus Striatus' This cultivar differs from the species in its smaller size and color. It is 30–36 in./7.6–9.0 dm high and more intensely yellow than the species; the stems are striped yellow-green. This cultivar is adapted to the same plant-hardiness zones as common rush.

Juncus effusus L. 'Spiralis' Spiral rush This most interesting cultivar is 2–3 ft/6–9 dm high. The slender, living stems are curled in a spiral or corkscrew fashion, usually producing a jumbled mass. Spiral rush is often grown as a curiosity in zones 4–8.

Juncus effusus L. 'Vittatus' This cultivar is 2–3 ft/6–9 dm high; the stems are narrowly striped white-green. It is adapted to the same plant-hardiness zones as common rush.

Juncus effusus L. 'Zebrinus' This cultivar is 24–30 in./6.0–7.6 dm high; the stems are broadly striped greenish white. It is adapted to the same plant-hardiness zones as spiral rush.

Juncus effusus var. *compactus* Lej. & Courtois Japanese mat This variety is less common than *Juncus effusus,* common rush. It occurs in bogs, swamps, and wet thickets in zones 5–7. A densely cespitose, perennial herb. Culms firm, dark green, relatively stout. Inflorescence a dense, lobulate or subglobose head, 0.4–2.0 in./1–5 cm in diameter; perianth greenish, often tinged brown; capsule darker brown than the perianth.

Juncus effusus var. *solutus* Fern. & Wieg. Soft rush A densely cespitose, caulescent, evergreen perennial with short, thick rhizomes; the plants become crowded, forming thick stands. Culms strictly erect, essentially terete, 5–10 ft/1.5–3.1 m high, 0.1–0.2 in./3–5 mm thick at the base. Leaves absent; open, basal, brown sheaths bladeless, apically round, inner sheaths slightly awned. Inflorescence bracteate, 30 to 100 flowers, cymose, appearing as if emerging subterminally from the side of the culm, many-branched, branches unequal; perianth parts 1–3 mm long, greenish brown, each flower is subtended by three bracteoles; fruit an obovoid, apically obtuse capsule, three-locular, many-seeded, truncate or depressed or slightly exceeding the perianth; seeds spherical, very small, less than 1 mm in diameter, brownish and indistinctly ribbed. Flowering and fruiting occur from July through September. Soft rush is adapted to zones 5–9, where it occurs in swamps and marshes.

Luzula **DC. (Woodrush).** Name from Latin, *luciola,* or "glow-worm," referring to the sparkling dew that adheres to the small hairs on the summit of the stems and on the leaves. Type species, *Luzula campestris* (L.) DC. There are about 80 species, native to temperate or cold regions, especially Eurasia. Erect, cespitose, perennial herbs, often hairy. Stems simple, usually hairy; leaves flat, soft, pliant, usually more or less hairy. Flowers in spikes, umbels or heads, crowded. Sepals and petals three each, scalelike; androecium six-merous; ovary one-locular; fruit a one-locular, three-seeded capsule (Fernald, 1970).

Latin name: *Luzula acuminata* Raf.
Synonym: *Luzula pilosa* (L.) Willd.
Origin: Eurasia
Habitat: Shaded, moist woods, cultivated
Hardiness: Zones 5 through 10
Description: A loosely cespitose perennial, sometimes with short rhizomes or sometimes with scaly stolons, 16–24 in./4–6 dm long. Stems 4–16 in./1–4 dm high. Foliage dull green, medium in texture; leaf blades elliptic-linear to lance-linear, variously pilose on the margins, with a terete, callused tip; basal leaves variable in length, 8–12 in./2–3 dm long, usually much shorter, 0.2–0.4 in./5–10 mm wide. Inflorescence a simple umbel with loosely ascending, or drooping, filiform rays, 1–2 in./2.5–5.0 cm long, loosely spreading with a single terminal flower, or some with a lateral flower, or others cymosely branched and bearing three or four flowers; perianth segments nearly equal, ovate to lance-ovate, apically acuminate, light brown or chestnut brown medially, the margins scarious, 0.1–0.2 in./3–5 mm long, about equaling the capsule or somewhat shorter; fruit an oval capsule, apiculate, usually light green, about 0.3 in./8 mm long; seeds about 1 mm long and about equally broad, with a terminal appendage. Flowering and fruiting occur from June to August. Plants with branched umbels bearing three or four flowers are referred to as *Luzula acuminata.*
Uses: This species, like that of other *Luzula* species, is ideal as ground cover in shaded sites. It is equally useful as a house plant. It is often used in underplanting as ground cover in borders.
Cultivation: Propagation is by plant division and by detaching the offsets.

The plants thrive equally well in dry or moist, shaded sites in acid soils. When grown as house plants, they should be provided with an ample, constant, moisture supply and ample light, although not necessarily of high intensity.

Latin name: *Luzula campestris* (L.) DC.
Synonym: *Juncus campestris* L.
Common names: Common woodrush, Field woodrush
Origin: Eurasia
Habitat: Shaded, moist or dry woods on acid soils, cultivated
Hardiness: Zones 5 through 10
Description: An upright-arching, loosely cespitose, perennial herb with stout stolons and rhizomes; the tufts are small and scattered, connected by sto-

Lazula campestris. *Source: An Illustrated Flora of the Northern United States, Canada, and the British Possessions. Vol. 1.* Charles Scribner's Sons. 1896.

lons and slender rhizomes 0.4–1.2 in./1–3 cm long. Flowering stems usually solitary, 4–8 in./10–20 cm high, solid, cylindrical, decumbent or spreading ascending, with three small, cauline leaves. Foliage soft, dull medium green, fine in texture; basal leaves flat, very hairy, linear, 4–5 in./10–13 cm long, 0.10–0.25 in./3–6 mm wide, with blunt callus tips, cauline leaves two to four, generally pilose, about 0.10–0.25 in./3–5 mm wide; sheaths closed. Inflorescence irregularly umbeled, umbels of two to six subglobose, dark brown spikes, 0.25–0.30 in./8–10 mm in diameter, all but the central sessile one on horizontal divergent to arched retrorse rays 0.4–0.8 in./10–20 mm long; peduncles mostly recurved; perianth about 3 mm long; sepals lanceolate, dark brown with pale margins; petals similar and subequal; flowers aggregate, brown or stramineous, about 0.1 in./3 mm long; calyx sepals bristle-pointed, longer than the obtuse capsule; androecium six-merous; ovary one-locular; fruit a one-celled, three-seeded capsule tapering at tip but equaling the perianth; seeds with a conical appendage at base. Flowering and fruiting occur from May through July.

Uses: Common woodrush is ordinarily used as ground cover in naturalizing areas located in shaded woodland. The plants form a fairly dense ground cover. They are also useful in group or massed plantings among shrubbery in mixed perennial borders and occasionally as potted specimens.

Cultivation: Propagation is by seeding and by plant division. Plant division is best made in the spring. The plants are easily propagated and grown. Common woodrush, native to Eurasia, has become naturalized in North America. This rush performs best in light to medium shade. Woodrushes are more tolerant of dry soils than the true rushes.

Latin name: *Luzula nemorosa* (Poll.) B. Mey.
Synonym: *Luzula luzuloides* (Lam.) Dandy & A. Wilm.
Common name: Woodrush
Origin: Europe
Habitat: Roadsides, shaded woods
Hardiness: Zones 4 through 6
Description: A loosely cespitose, perennial herb with slow-spreading stolons; the plants form a dense mat. Culms solid, cylindrical, 15–24 in./3.8–6.0 dm high. Foliage light bright green, fine in texture; basal leaves erect, linear, 10–14 in./2.5–3.6 dm long, 0.1–0.2 in./3–5 mm wide, cauline leaves much shorter, more or less hairy with long, white hairs. Inflorescence diffusely corymbiform, 1–8 in./2.5–20.0 cm long, the ultimate branchlets terminated by off-white flowers, flowers in glomerules of three to eight; sepals and petals lanceolate, acute, the sepals distinctly shorter; androecium six-merous; fruit a one-celled, three-seeded capsule, about equaling the perianth. The flowering stems are slender and weak, and the plants have a sprawling growth habit. Flowering and fruiting occur from June through July.

Uses: The plants are not outstanding as individuals, but they are highly effective when used in massed stands as ground cover. They are most useful over large, naturalized areas among shrubs in large gardens. Woodrush has a sprawling growth habit, forming a dense, impenetrable mat that makes an excellent ground cover. The seedheads are ideal in dried floral arrangements.

Cultivation: Propagation is by seeding and by plant division. The plants are widely adapted; they grow equally well in light to medium shade on a wide range of soils, including dry, acid types. Woodrush is invasive in growth habit; for this reason, it should not be used in rock gardens.

Latin name: *Luzula sylvatica* (Huds.) Gaud.-Beaup.
Synonym: *Luzula maxima* (Reichard) DC.
Cultivars: 'Marginata' Gold-margined woodrush
Common name: Greater woodrush
Origin: Europe
Habitat: Shaded open woods, cultivated
Hardiness: Zones 5 through 9
Description: A robust, densely cespitose, perennial herb with a short, ascending rootstock and short, stout stolons. The plants form bright green tussocks. Culms erect or somewhat oblique, solid, cylindrical, thick, stout, 10–14 in./2.5–3.6 dm high, glabrous in the lower portion, hairy at the summit, with four cauline leaves. Foliage bright green, medium in texture; basal leaves flat, broadly linear, short attenuate, 10–12 in./2.5–3.0 dm long, 0.4–0.5 in./10–13 mm wide, glossy, sparsely hairy with long, white hairs and filamentous on the margins, spreading, cauline leaves somewhat shorter, 1–2 in./2.5–5.0 cm long, 0.3–0.4 in./8–10 mm wide. Inflorescence a terminal, lax, branched cyme, the branches wide-spreading, the cymose chestnut-brown flowers borne three or four together, with conspicuous yellow stamens; sepals and petals lanceolate and acute; androecium six-merous; fruit a dark brown ovoid or obovoid one-celled, three-seeded capsule. Flowering and fruiting occur from May through July.

Uses: Greater woodrush and its cultivars are useful ornamental groundcover plants. Their plant form, texture, and color add diversity and attractiveness to the landscape. Woodrushes are completely at home in wooded areas. This species and its variant are far superior to other woodrushes as ground cover in shaded woodland. The plants thrive best in light to medium shade, where they form a dense, impenetrable ground cover. Greater woodrush and its cultivar are often used in understory plantings among shrubbery and other ornamentals; they also have a niche in shaded borders that are out of direct sunlight for most of the day. The individual plants are not of outstanding ornamental value; however, their attractiveness is maximized when grown in colonies or in massed stands over extensive areas. Greater woodrush and its variant are ideal for naturalizing wooded areas where the plants are shaded most of the time. The variegated types are far more attractive than the species. The brownish seedheads are quite often used in dried floral arrangements. Greater woodrush and its variant are both adapted for use as indoor, potted specimens. Greater woodrush forms compatible combinations with spring bulbs in shaded woods. The plants approach their maximum size and attractiveness following the flush of spring bulbs. Like true rushes and sedges, greater woodrush aids in the prevention of soil erosion by the ground cover it produces.

Cultivation: Propagation is by plant division and by detaching the offsets. Establishing the plants in early spring allows ample time for them to get a good root system established before winter. Greater woodrush and its cultivar are easily planted and maintained. The plants prefer moist, acid soils in shaded sites, although they will thrive in somewhat dry locations. When grown indoors, the plants should be provided with a constant moisture supply and ample light, not necessarily of high intensity.

Cultivars: *Luzula sylvatica* (Huds.) Gaud.-Beaup. 'Marginata' Gold-margined woodrush   This cultivar is approximately 1 ft /3 dm high. The variegated foliage is comprised of leaves with longitudinal stripes of green-white or green-yellow-white; the margins are usually either white or yellow. Gold-margined woodrush thrives best in deep-shaded locations in moist soil; it is also somewhat drought tolerant. This variegated cultivar is useful as a house plant.

Other ornamental species: *Luzula nivea* (L.) Lam. & DC. Snowy woodrush   A loosely cespitose, hairy, perennial herb with short stolons. Flowering stems are 8–24 in./2–6 dm high, slender, flexuous. Foliage dark green, fine in texture. Basal leaves nearly as long as the stems, 8–18 in./2.0–4.5 dm long, 0.2–0.3 in./5–8 mm wide, thin, margins pilose; the cauline leaves are considerably shorter. Inflorescence umbellate, a loose, lax corymb of many bright-white flowers; perianth segments twice as long as the capsule; fruit a trigonous capsule. Snowy woodrush is native to the cold regions of Eurasia and central Europe; it is adapted to plant-hardiness zones 4–8. This species, like *Luzula nemorosa,* is invasive and is not recommended for rock gardens because of its invasiveness. The plants are ideal in ground-cover and group plantings in naturalized areas with light shade and as understory among shrubs. The tan seedheads are quite showy during the fall and into the winter; they are also useful in dried arrangements. Propagation is by seeding and by plant division. The plants prefer full sun to light shade and are exhibited most effectively in group or massed plantings. Flowering and fruiting occur from June through July.

Luzula nivea (L.) Lam. & DC. 'Marginata'   The plants and plant parts of this variegated cultivar are approximately the same size as those of the species. It differs from the parent species in its variegated foliage; the leaves have cream-colored margins. This variant makes a more colorful ground cover than does the species, because of its variegated foliage; it prefers light to medium shade. Propagation is by seeding and by plant division. This cultivar is adapted to zones 4–8.

Luzula nivea (L.) Lam. & DC. 'Nana' Dwarf snowy woodrush   This miniature cultivar is 2–4 in./5–10 cm high. This small variant is useful in rock gardens in light to medium shade and as a potted specimen plant indoors; it is adapted to zones 5–9.

Luzula nivea (L.) Lam. & DC. 'Schneehaeschen' Snow hare   This cultivar is 10–14 in./2.5–3.0 dm high. Like that of snowy woodrush and other *Luzula* species, it is most useful as ground cover for shaded borders or in wooded sites bordering the formal garden and in understory plantings among shrubbery. Snow hare is adapted to zones 5–9.

Luzula pilosa (L.) Willd. Hairy woodrush A hairy, densely cespitose, perennial herb with slender rhizomes and stolons. Culms solid, cylindrical, 6–12 in./1.5–3.0 dm high. Foliage dark green, fine in texture; basal leaves narrowly linear, 6–8 in./1.5–2.0 dm long, 0.15–0.25 in./4–6 mm wide, tapering to a truncate swelling at the tip, very hairy. Inflorescence a large, lax, terminal cyme, borne above the foliage; flowers dark chestnut brown, borne in aggregate glomerules; fruit a one-celled, three-seeded capsule; seeds with long, hooked appendages. Flowering and fruiting occur from April through June. Hairy woodrush

Luzula pilosa. *Source: An Illustrated Flora of the Northern United States, Canada, and the British Possessions. Vol. 1.* Charles Scribner's Sons. 1896.

makes an ideal lawn substitute or ground cover in wooded, shaded locations. It is also useful in understory plantings among shrubbery. Like most *Luzula* species, the plants exhibit their maximum effectiveness when grown in massed stands or in large clumps as ground cover. The brown flowers are most interesting and conspicuous when the plants are grown in massed stands. Hairy woodrush makes an interesting indoor specimen plant; the flowers are excellent for dried arrangements. Propagation is by seeding and by plant division. The plants reseed themselves readily and may be a weed in some gardens. Hairy woodrush is adapted to zones 4–8.

Luzula purpurea Link Purple woodrush   Purple woodrush is 5–8 in./1.3–2.0 dm high. The purplish green foliage makes an attractive ground cover in shaded locations and provides good fall color. Purple woodrush makes an interesting substitute lawn of a uniquely different color in shaded woods. This species is used occasionally indoors as potted specimens and outdoors in the rock garden.

Scirpus **L. (Bulrush).** Scirpus is the old Latin name for bulrush, although this is a sedge. Lectotype, *Scirpus sylvaticus* L. There are about 300 species, widely distributed in temperate and warm regions. Annual or perennial caulescent or scapose herbs. Culms erect, simple, sheathed at base. Leaves filiform with blades or mere sheaths. Inflorescence umbellate or usually involucrate, the involucre, when simple, somewhat flattened; spikelets few-to-many-flowered, solitary or few to many in a terminal cluster when it is subtended by a one-to-several-leaved involucre; scales spirally imbricate in several ranks or rarely inclining to be two-ranked; flowers to all the scales, or to all but one or two of the lowest, all perfect; perianth rarely wanting or one-to-eight-barbed or smooth, sometimes pubescent, short, stiff bristles; androecium of two or three stamens; style two- or three-cleft, simple, not tumid, wholly deciduous or the base persistent; stigmas two or three; fruit a trigonous or lenticular achene, beaked or beakless, not tubercled (Fernald, 1970).

> **Latin name:** *Scirpus cernuus* Vahl
> **Synonym:** *Scirpus gracilis* Rudge
> **Common names:** Club grass, Nodding scirpus
> **Origin:** Europe
> **Habitat:** Low wet sites, freshwater, brackish-water, or saline marshes
> **Hardiness:** Zones 4 through 7
> **Description:** A densely cespitose annual producing numerous filiform stems 6–12 in./1.5–3.0 dm high. Culms arching or drooping, smooth, glabrous, bright green, sheathed at the base, basal sheaths usually bladeless. Foliage soft, bright green, fine in texture; leaves one to few near the base, variously developed, erect initially, later arching, filiform, 8–10 in./2.0–2.5 dm long, 0.15–0.25 in./4–6 mm wide. Inflorescence, solitary or twin flower heads, terminal or sometimes subterminal, flowers white or cream-colored; bracts usually absent

or sometimes one, or if present, very small, bristles about equaling the achene; spikelets solitary, 0.1–0.2 in./3–5 mm long; scales about 1–2 mm long; fruit a broad trigonous achene about 1 mm long, somewhat subcapitate. Flowering and fruiting may occur at any time.

Uses: Club grass is ideal in a hanging basket or as a potted plant indoors, provided the soil is kept constantly wet. The main attractions of this small plant are its rich, green foliage, its weeping, trailing growth habit, and its small whitish or cream-colored flowers. The plants are ideal for use in water gardens, where they provide a perfect foil for other plants of different structure and growth habit. Its bright green foliage and weeping form are ideally suited for the rock garden, where the plants trail over the rocks. Nodding scirpus is especially attractive in the rock garden when grown in conjunction with erect grasses, such as *Festuca* species, which are adapted to the same habitat. Any number of combinations of nodding scirpus with rock garden plants are possible, providing subtle contrasts in color and more dramatic contrasts in plant form. Nodding scirpus is also handsome as a house plant when grown in a sandy soil with the pot standing in a container of water. Its graceful, grasslike tufts, topped with tiny white or cream-colored flowers, cascade over the sides of the container, providing an interesting statement resembling lush, green hair. Scirpuses are attractive as potted plants. Nodding scirpus is used as edging on greenhouse benches and is ideally suited for naturalizing wet shaded sites. The common name, club grass, is derived from the presence of the tiny flower heads borne near the tips of the scapes.

Cultivation: Propagation is by plant division. Plant division is accomplished by dividing the plants in overcrowded pots into smaller clumps, preferably in the spring. Plant the clumps in small 3 in./8 cm pots and keep them constantly moist or wet. As the pots become overcrowded, transfer the plants to larger pots (i.e., not over 5 in./1.3 dm). Any soil-based potting mixture is sufficient to produce good growth if it is kept sufficiently moist or wet. Nodding scirpus may also be grown in a planting mixture without soil that is kept constantly wet. The reduced plant size of nodding scirpus enhances its use in indoor plantings, although when grown outside, close attention should be given to the overall scale of plants used so that a well-balanced garden can be maintained. Unlike many other house plants, nodding scirpus thrives in a location in windows that are somewhat obscured from sun or at a window that faces north. Nodding scirpus requires a plentiful and constant water supply at all times; the potting mixture should be kept constantly moist. Hanging baskets of scirpuses dry out rapidly and may require watering daily. Pots could be placed in a container holding water if necessary. When temperatures fall below about 55°F/ 13°C for any length of time, the plants should be encouraged to take a rest period by being watered very sparingly; they should be watered only enough to prevent the potting mixture from drying out completely. Fertilize actively growing plants with a standard fertilizer once a month. Plants grown outside prefer sandy soils in shaded locations. Outdoor plantings are made simply by pushing the roots into the mud near streams, ponds, pools, or lakes, where they quickly become established.

Latin name: *Scirpus tabernaemontani* C. C. Gmel.
Synonym: *Scirpus validus* Vahl
Cultivars: 'Zebrinus' Striped bulrush, Porcupine plant
Common names: Great bulrush, Cattail flag, Soft-stem bulrush
Origin: North America
Habitat: Freshwater, brackish-water, saltwater marshes, cultivated
Hardiness: Zones 4 through 10
Description: An upright-narrow, gregarious, caulescent perennial with stout, scaly, horizontal rhizomes 0.1–0.3 in./3–8 mm in diameter. Culms erect, soft, and easily compressed, terete, stout, light green, 7–9 ft/2.2–2.8 m high, 0.8–1.2 in./2–3 cm thick at base, borne at intervals along the horizontal rhizomes, sheathed at base; basal sheath membranous, soft, with lacerate hyaline margins, mostly bladeless. Foliage dark green, fine in texture; basal leaves may be partially submerged, leaves linear, 12–18 in./3.0–4.5 dm long, 0.2–0.3 in./ 5–8 mm wide. Inflorescence a stiffly branched panicle, the branches and pedicels minutely pilose, thin-edged; flowers brownish; spikelets ovoid, fulvous, occurring in glomerules of two or more, 0.2–0.4 in./5–10 mm long; scales ovate, with prominent green keel slightly excurrent, pilose to glabrate on back with fimbriate-ciliate margins, minutely pubescent, much longer and broader than the achene (i.e., up to 0.15 in./4 mm long); perianth bristles four to six, about equaling the achene, slender, remotely setulose above the naked basal portion, overtopping the obovate finally brown achene; fruit a lenticular, abruptly mucronate achene, 1–2 mm long, brown, reddish, or dull black. Flowering and fruiting occur from June through August.

Uses: The plants are a perfect foil for other broad-leaved plants growing either in the water, such as water lilies, or on land, such as rhododendrons, *Rhododendron* species. Their tall, yellowish green stems, terminated with clusters of brown or reddish achenes, provide an interesting contrast in color, shape, and texture to broad-leaved plants. Great bulrush is an interesting plant for the water garden, where a single specimen in a small pool produces a striking sight. It provides an interesting companion plant to striped bulrush, *Scirpus tabernaemontani* 'Zebrinus,' a smaller plant with transversely banded leaves; the two species, which differ in size and the color of their achenes, provide an interesting contrast in color and size, as their flowering and fruiting periods more or less coincide. Great bulrush is among the most noble of native water plants.

Cultivation: Great bulrush is easily grown in water garden pools, ponds, and lakes. The gregarious plants should be contained in some manner to prevent their spread, should this be desired. Propagation is by seeding or by plant division. Rhizomes of young, small plants may be placed in a washtub, a 55-gallon steel drum, or any other suitable container, and sunk below water level near the edge of the pool or pond. Mature plants may be divided, cut back, or planted almost year-round in mild climates, and in the spring or early summer in cooler climates. Plants may be found in native stands or purchased from reputable sources. If native stands are used as propagating stocks, make certain that they are properly identified, as it is difficult to distinguish among scirpus species, especially with immature plants. Great bulrush, like Egyptian reed, may also be grown indoors in greenhouse pools; plants grown indoors are usually much smaller than those grown outdoors. Potted plants should be buried in the garden to carry them over winter; the pot containing the rootstock should be covered with about 4–6 in./1.0–1.5 dm of soil. Although great bulrush occurs naturally in salt marshes and lagoons, it also thrives in freshwater marshes.

Cultivars: *Scirpus tabernaemontani* C. C. Gmel. 'Zebrinus' Striped bulrush, Porcupine plant The culms and leaves of this cultivar are transversely banded green-yellow or green-white, somewhat similar to zebragrass, *Miscanthus sinensis* var. *zebrinus.* The plants differ from blue bulrush in being smaller in size and of different color (i.e., variegated versus light green); usually the plants are 2–4 ft / 0.6–1.2 m high. Striped bulrush is adapted to zones 6–8. Propagation is by plant division. Striped bulrush is smaller than zebragrass, *Miscanthus sinensis* var. *zebrinus;* it differs from it in that it will grow directly in shallow water, in addition to wet soil in marshy areas. The plants thrive equally well in shallow water and in wet, muddy areas surrounding pools, ponds, lakes, and streams. Striped bulrush thrives best in light to medium shade, whereas great bulrush performs best in full sun. The plants may be grown indoors in large greenhouses and terrariums, where light of moderate intensity is required. Sand, gravel, or pebbles are recommended for covering the top of the soil in pots when striped bulrush is grown indoors. The plant containers may be watered from the top or from the bottom; the important thing to remember is that they must be kept constantly wet. Any green stems that appear in striped bulrush should be removed at the rhizome. The unique color of striped bulrush make it an outstanding plant for water gardens, naturalized marshes, in or around pools, and ponds, or along slow-moving streams. The banded foliage persists throughout the growing season, providing good early fall color. Striped bulrush is an ideal house plant because of its variegated foliage.

Other ornamental species: *Scirpus cyperinus* (L.) Kunth Woolgrass (Synonym: *Eriophorum cyperinum* L.) A gregarious, cespitose perennial without rhizomes. Culms nearly terete, leafy, 4–6 ft/1.2–1.8 m high. Foliage bright green, fine in texture; leaves curved, narrowly linear, rigid, long attenuate, 1–2 ft/3–6 dm long, 0.10–0.25 in./3–6 mm wide, involucral leaves three to five, up to 12 in./3 dm long; tips of the rays eventually drooping; perianth bristles elongate, much exserted, exceeding the achenes and scales, curled at maturity, brownish or rust-colored. Inflorescence a terminal, compound cyme consisting of slender, pedunculate spikes, subtended by several unequal, leaflike bracts; scales numerous, 1–2 mm long, blunt; bristles six, slender, flexuous, tawny, longer than the scales; spikelets many, in small heads or clusters of 3 to 15, sessile, ovoid, 0.10–0.25 in./3–6 mm long; fruit an ellipsoid, oval or obovoid achene, about 1 mm

Scirpus cyperinus. **A, Habit; B, scale; C, achene.** *Source: Aquatic and Wetland Plants of Southeastern United States. Monocotyledons.* Univ. of Georgia Press. 1979.

long, short-pointed, pale or almost white. Flowering and fruiting occur from August through September.

Woolgrass occurs in wet meadows and swamps; it is adapted to zones 5–7. The graceful, long leaves of woolgrass wave in the wind, and the seedheads, which persist, add interest in the fall. Flower heads have many rays. The spikelets are eventually covered with wool threads; the seedheads are excellent for dried arrangements. Although woolgrass is not adapted for use in the formal garden, it does have a niche in naturalized plantings in the wild garden, or in poor damp or wet soils, where it is allowed to grow rampant. The ornamental value of woolgrass is best demonstrated in massed stands, where the woolly spikelets of the flower heads are allowed to blow in the breeze. Propagation is by seeding and by plant division, preferably the latter.

Scirpus flaccidus (Rchb.) Urban   A loosely cespitose, caulescent, perennial herb with very slender rhizomes. Culms very slender or filiform, somewhat trigonous, 8–12 in./2–3 dm high, sheathed, upper sheath with a hyaline membranous limb. Foliage medium green, fine in texture; leaves mostly reduced to sheaths. Inflorescence a terminal, rather dense, solitary flower head; perianth bristles about as long as the achene or longer, retrorsely barbed, sometimes wanting; spikelets several-flowered, oblong or ovoid, 0.15–0.25 in./4–6 mm long, two to three times as thick; scales elliptic to oblong-lanceolate, thin, light green with a faint midvein; fruit an obovate, plano-convex, smooth, dark brown achene, about 0.5 mm long, two to four times as long as the acute conic tubercle. Flowering and fruiting occur from July through September. Propagation is by plant division. This species, like other scirpus species, is easily grown as a potted specimen in colder climates. It requires constant moisture and will perform admirably during the summer on the patio, deck, or porch, after which time it may be moved indoors. It is also useful in freshwater swamps in warmer climates. The size and growth habit of this species make it useful in water gardens, where it performs equally well in full sun or light shade. This pantropic species is adapted to zone 10.

Scirpus nodulosus Roth   A tufted, caulescent perennial with long, strong stout rhizomes. Culms rather stout, terete, or nearly so, pseudoseptate, 16–24 in./4–6 dm high, sheathed, the upper sheath truncate or one-toothed. Foliage medium green, fine in texture; leaves filiform, if present, otherwise reduced to sheaths. Inflorescence a dense, branched flower head; spikelets densely many-flowered, erect, 0.4–1.0 in./10–25 mm long, 0.15–0.20 in./4–5 mm thick, ovoid-cylindric, acute; scales ovate-oblong, obtuse, brown or purplish brown, margins scarious; perianth bristles brown, about as long as the achene or longer; fruit an ovate plano-convex, brown achene, 1 mm long, much longer than the black, acute tubercle. Flowering and fruiting occur from July through September. The adaptation (i.e., zone 10), propagation, and uses of this species are quite similar to those of *Scirpus flaccidus*. This species may be grown as a potted plant in colder climates.

REFERENCES

Fernald, M. L. 1970. *Gray's manual of botany.* (Corrected printing) 8th ed. New York: D. Van Nostrand.

Mackenzie, K. K. 1931–1935. Cyperaceae-Cariceae. *North American Flora* 18:1–478. New York: The New York Botanical Garden.

Svenson, H. K. 1929. Monographic studies in the genus Eleocharis. *Rhodora* 31(68):152–163; 31(369):169–191.

———. 1957a. Cyperaceae (Fuirena). *North American Flora* 18(9):505–507.

———. 1957b. Eleocharis R. Br. *North American Flora* 18(9):509–540.

Appendix 1
Uses of Ornamental Grasses

	Accent plants	Specimen plants	Groups	Edging (E)/Massing (M)	Ground cover—Dry sites	Ground cover—Wet sites	Borders*	Hedges**	Screens**	Windbreaks**	Naturalized	Pebble/Rock gardens	Bog/Water gardens	Lawn/Lawn substitute	Shade	Full sun	Flowers on plants	Cut flowers	Dried arrangements	Foliage	Foliage and flowers	Fall color	House plants	Seashore/Saline soils	Bird feed/Wildlife protection	Dyed specimens
Agropyron caninum				M							•				•											
Agropyron junceum				M	•											•			•					•		
Agropyron pungens				M		•										•			•					•		
Agrostis nebulosa		•					A					•				•	•	•	•	•			•			
Agrostis stolonifera				M		•							•	•						•						
Alopecurus aequalis				M		•				•			•			•				•						
Alopecurus alpinus				M		•							•			•										
Alopecurus lanatus		•					A			•						•				•						
Alopecurus pratensis	•	•	•	M	•	•	B					•				•	•			•						
Alopecurus pratensis 'Aureo-variegatus'	•	•	•	M		•	B									•	•			•						
Alopecurus pratensis 'Aureus'		•	•	M		•	A									•				•						
Alopecurus pratensis 'Glaucus'		•	•	M		•	A									•				•						
Ammophila arenaria				M						M						•	•			•	•			•		
Ammophila breviligulata				M						M						•				•						
Ampledesmos mauritanicus				E			C	T	T	T						•	•	•	•							•
Andropogon barbinodis				M	•					•						•										
Andropogon gerardi	•	•		M	•		C		T	T	•		•			•				•		•		•		

	Accent plants	Specimen plants	Groups	Edging (E)/Massing (M)	Ground cover—Dry sites	Ground cover—Wet sites	Borders*	Hedges**	Screens**	Windbreaks**	Naturalized	Pebble/Rock gardens	Bog/Water gardens	Lawn/Lawn substitute	Shade	Full sun	Flowers on plants	Cut flowers	Dried arrangements	Foliage	Foliage and flowers	Fall color	House plants	Seashore/Saline soils	Bird feed/Wildlife protection	Dyed specimens
Andropogon stolonifer				M					M	M						•	•								•	
Andropogon virginicus		•		M	•						•	•				•	•			•		•				
Anthoxanthum odoratum	•	•					A					•	•			•										
Aristida purpurascens				M	•							•				•										
Aristida purpurea		•		M	•		B					•				•	•									
Aristida wrightii	•						A					•				•	•		•							
Arrhenatherum elatus		•		M	•		B	M	M	•						•		•	•	•					•	
Arrhenatherum elatus var. *bulbosum*		•			•		A						•	•				•				•				
Arrhenatherum elatus var. *bulbosum* 'Variegatum'	•	•	•	M		•	A						•	•				•				•				
Arundo conspicua 'Toe-toe'		•	•						T	T						•	•	•								•
Arundo donax		•	•			•	C	T	T	T		•	•			•	•	•	•	•	•					•
Arundo donax var. *versicolor*	•	•	•			•	C		T	T		•	•			•	•		•			•				•
Arundo fulvida 'Kakaho'		•	•													•	•		•		•					•
Avena sativa		•					B					•				•	•		•							•
Avena sterilis		•					B									•	•	•	•							•
Axonopus compressus			M		•									•		•										
Bouteloua breviseta		•					A									•	•	•	•							
Bouteloua curtipendula	•	•	M								•					•	•	•	•							
Bouteloua gracilis	•	•	M				A				•	•				•	•	•	•							
Bouteloua hirsuta			M	•							•					•										
Brachypodium sylvaticum											•			•	•	•				•						
Briza maxima		•		•			A					•				•	•	•	•							•
Briza maxima var. *rubra*	•	•					A					•				•	•	•	•	•						•
Briza media		•	M				A				•	•				•	•	•	•							•
Briza minor		•					A					•				•	•	•	•							•
Bromus brizaeformis		•		•			A				•					•	•		•							•
Bromus inermis			M	•							•					•			•					•		

	Accent plants	Specimen plants	Groups	Edging (E)/Massing (M)	Ground cover—Dry sites	Ground cover—Wet sites	Borders*	Hedges**	Screens**	Windbreaks**	Naturalized	Pebble/Rock gardens	Bog/Water gardens	Lawn/Lawn substitute	Shade	Full sun	Flowers on plants	Cut flowers	Dried arrangements	Foliage	Foliage and flowers	Fall color	House plants	Seashore/Saline soils	Bird feed/Wildlife protection	Dyed specimens
Bromus secalinus				•						•						•	•	•			•					
Bromus unioloides				•				M	M							•	•				•			•		
Calamagrostis arundinacea			M		•			T	T	•		•				•			•			•				
Calamagrostis canadensis			M		•	C		T		•	•	•				•			•			•		•		
Calamagrostis canescens		•								•	•	•				•	•	•	•					•		
Calamagrostis canescens 'Variegata'	•	•				•	B			•		•							•	•	•	•		•		
Calamagrostis epigejos		•				•		M	M	•		•				•	•	•		•	•	•		•		
Calamagrostis epigejos 'Hortorum'	•	•				•	B	M	M			•				•	•			•	•			•		
Cenchrus ciliaris			•	M	•		B				•					•	•									
Chasmanthium latifolium	•	•	•	E			B				•	•			•	•	•	•	•	•	•	•		•		
Chloris cucullata			•	M	•						•	•				•	•	•	•			•				
Chloris distichophylla	•	•	•			•	B				•					•	•	•	•			•				
Chloris gayana				M							•					•	•									
Chloris glauca				M							•					•	•			•				•		
Chloris verticillata		•	•				A				•					•	•									
Coix lacryma-jobi		•				•	C									•	•		•			•				
Coix lacryma-jobi 'Aurea Zebrina'	•	•	•				B						•		•	•	•				•	•				
Cortaderia fulvida 'Kahaho'	•	•	•				C				•					•	•	•	•							•
Cortaderia richardii	•	•	•				C	T			•					•	•	•	•	•	•					•
Cortaderia selloana	•	•	•	M			C	T	T	•	•					•	•	•	•	•	•	•				•
Cortaderia selloana 'Argenteum'	•	•	•	M			C	T	T	•	•					•	•	•	•	•	•	•		•		•
Cortaderia selloana 'Bertini'	•	•	•	M			B	M	M	•	•					•	•	•	•	•	•	•		•		•
Cortaderia selloana 'Carminea Rendadleri'	•	•	•	M			C	T	T	•	•					•	•	•	•	•	•	•		•		•
Cortaderia selloana 'Carnea'	•	•	•	M			C	T	T	•	•					•	•	•	•	•	•	•		•		•

	Accent plants	Specimen plants	Groups	Edging (E)/Massing (M)	Ground cover—Dry sites	Ground cover—Wet sites	Borders*	Hedges**	Screens**	Windbreaks**	Naturalized	Pebble/Rock gardens	Bog/Water gardens	Lawn/Lawn substitute	Shade	Full sun	Flowers on plants	Cut flowers	Dried arrangements	Foliage	Foliage and flowers	Fall color	House plants	Seashore/Saline soils	Bird feed/Wildlife protection	Dyed specimens
Cortaderia selloana 'Elegans'	•	•	•				C		T	T	•	•				•	•	•	•	•	•	•	•			•
Cortaderia selloana 'Gold Band'	•	•	•	M			B		M	M	•	•				•	•	•	•	•	•	•	•			•
Cortaderia selloana 'Marabout'	•	•	•	M			C		T	T	•	•				•	•	•	•	•	•	•	•			•
Cortaderia selloana 'Monstrosa'	•	•	•	E			C		T	T	•	•				•	•	•	•	•	•	•	•			•
Cortaderia selloana 'Pumila'	•	•	•	E			B		M	M	•	•				•	•	•	•	•	•	•	•			•
Cortaderia selloana 'Rosa Feder'	•	•	•	E			C		T	T	•	•				•	•	•	•	•	•	•	•			•
Cortaderia selloana 'Rosea'	•	•	•	M			C		T	T	•	•				•	•	•	•	•	•	•	•			•
Cortaderia selloana 'Silver Stripe'	•	•	•	M			B		M	M	•	•				•	•	•	•	•	•	•	•			•
Cortaderia selloana 'Sunningdale Silver'	•	•	•	E			C		T	T	•	•				•	•	•	•	•	•	•	•			•
Cortaderia selloana Violacea'	•	•	•	M			C		T	T	•	•				•	•	•	•	•	•	•	•			•
Ctenium aromaticum			M		•						•		•			•	•	•	•					•		
Cymbopogon citratus		•	•				B			M						•			•					•		
Cymbopogon nardus		•	•				B	M								•			•					•		
Cynodon dactylon			M		•							•		•		•									•	
Cynosurus cristatus			M									•				•	•	•								
Dactylis glomerata		•	•			•	B					•				•				•	•					
Dactylis glomerata 'Elegantissima'		•	•				A					•	•	•		•				•						
Dactylis glomerata 'Variegata'		•	•	E								•	•	•		•				•						
Deschampsia alpina		•				•	A					•				•				•						
Deschampsia caespitosa		•				•	A					•				•				•						
Deschampsia caespitosa 'Bronzeschleier'	•	•				•	B						•			•	•	•	•							

	Accent plants	Specimen plants	Groups	Edging (E)/Massing (M)	Ground cover—Dry sites	Ground cover—Wet sites	Borders*	Hedges**	Screens**	Windbreaks**	Naturalized	Pebble/Rock gardens	Bog/Water gardens	Lawn/Lawn substitute	Shade	Full sun	Flowers on plants	Cut flowers	Dried arrangements	Foliage	Foliage and flowers	Fall color	House plants	Seashore/Saline soils	Bird feed/Wildlife protection	Dyed specimens
Deschampsia caespitosa 'Goldgehaenge'		•	•			•	B						•			•	•	•	•	•						
Deschampsia caespitosa 'Goldschleier'		•	•	E		•	B						•			•	•	•	•	•						
Deschampsia caespitosa 'Goldstaub'		•	•	E		•	B						•			•	•	•	•	•						
Deschampsia caespitosa 'Schottland'		•	•	E		•	C						•			•	•	•	•	•						
Deschampsia caespitosa 'Tardiflora'		•	•	E		•	B						•			•	•	•	•	•						
Deschampsia caespitosa 'Tautraeger'		•	•	E		•	B						•			•	•	•	•	•						
Deschampsia caespitosa var. *vivipara*		•	•	E												•	•			•						
Deschampsia flexuosa		•	•				B				•	•				•	•	•	•							
Distichlis spicata					•											•								•	•	
Elymus arenarius		•	•										•			•			•					•		
Elymus canadensis	•	•	•			•	B						•			•				•	•					
Elymus condensatus				M					T	T	•													•		
Elymus giganteus									•	•																
Elymus glaucus	•	•	•		•		B									•			•					•		
Elymus villosus				M							•				•	•			•							
Elymus virginicus	•	•	•		•		B								•	•	•	•	•	•						
Eragrostis capillaris		•			•		A				•					•		•								
Eragrostis curvula		•	•	M	•		B	M	M	•	•					•	•	•	•	•				•		
Eragrostis spectabilis		•			•		A	M	M	•	•					•	•	•	•							
Eragrostis tef	•	•			•		B						•			•	•	•	•			•				
Eragrostis trichodes	•	•		M	•		B						•			•										
Erianthus alopecuroides	•	•		E		•	C		T	T						•	•	•	•							
Erianthus contortus	•	•		E		•	C				•				•	•	•	•	•						•	
Erianthus giganteus	•	•				•	C		T	T			•			•	•	•	•							
Erianthus ravennae	•	•	•			•	C		T	T			•			•	•	•	•					•	•	
Erianthus ravennae var. *purpurascens*		•	•			•			T	T						•	•	•	•					•	•	

	Accent plants	Specimen plants	Groups	Edging (E)/Massing (M)	Ground cover—Dry sites	Ground cover—Wet sites	Borders*	Hedges**	Screens**	Windbreaks**	Naturalized	Pebble/Rock gardens	Bog/Water gardens	Lawn/Lawn substitute	Shade	Full sun	Flowers on plants	Cut flowers	Dried arrangements	Foliage	Foliage and flowers	Fall color	House plants	Seashore/Saline soils	Bird feed/Wildlife protection	Dyed specimens
Erianthus strictus		•	•	E		•	C	M			•					•	•	•	•		•			•		
Festuca alpestris			•	E								•				•				•						
Festuca alpina			•	E								•				•				•						
Festuca amethystina	•	•	•	E								•	•	•		•				•						
Festuca elegans		•		E	•		A					•	•			•										
Festuca gigantea		•					B					•			•	•				•						
Festuca mairei			•	E	•		B					•	•			•										
Festuca muelleri			•	E	•		A					•	•			•										
Festuca ovina var. *glauca*	•	•	•	M			A					•	•	•		•				•		•				
Festuca pallens				E	•							•				•				•						
Festuca pseudoeskia			•	E	•							•				•				•						
Festuca pulchella				E	•							•	•			•										
Festuca rubra					•							•	•	•	•	•				•						
Festuca rubra var. *heterophylla*					•									•	•											
Festuca rupicaprina				E	•							•				•										
Festuca scoparia			•	E	•							•	•			•										
Festuca scoparia 'Pic Carlit'	•			E	•							•				•										
Festuca tenuifolia			•	E	•							•	•							•						
Festuca varia			•	E	•							•				•										
Festuca vivipara		•			•							•				•										
Fingerhuthia sesleriaeformis		•				•	B									•	•	•	•							•
Glyceria canadensis				M	•								•			•						•				
Glyceria fluitans				M	•								•			•									•	
Glyceria maxima				M	•																					
Glyceria maxima 'Pallida'	•	•	•	M	•								•			•				•					•	
Glyceria maxima 'Variegata'	•	•	•	M	•								•			•				•					•	
Gynerium sagittatum			•	M	•					T	•					•	•	•	•						•	•

	Accent plants	Specimen plants	Groups	Edging (E)/Massing (M)	Ground cover—Dry sites	Ground cover—Wet sites	Borders*	Hedges**	Screens**	Windbreaks**	Naturalized	Pebble/Rock gardens	Bog/Water gardens	Lawn/Lawn substitute	Shade	Full sun	Flowers on plants	Cut flowers	Dried arrangements	Foliage	Foliage and flowers	Fall color	House plants	Seashore/Saline soils	Bird feed/Wildlife protection	Dyed specimens
Hakonechloa macra		•	•	M			A					•	•	•	•	•				•						
Hakonechloa macra 'Albo-aurea'	•		•	E								•	•	•						•						
Hakonechloa macra 'Albo-variegata'	•		•	E											•					•						
Hakonechloa macra 'Aureola'			•	E			A					•	•	•	•					•						
Helictotrichon pubescens		•	•		•		B					•				•			•							
Helictotrichon sempervirens			•	E								•				•		•		•		•				
Hemarthria altissima				M							•			•		•				•						
Hierochloa odorata			•	E		•	A					•				•								•	•	
Holcus lanatus			•	M			B									•				•	•	•				
Holcus lanatus 'Variegatus'		•	•	M			A				•	•		•	•	•				•						
Holcus mollis				M	•		A				•					•				•						
Holcus mollis 'Albo-variegatus'		•	•	M			A				•				•	•				•						
Holcus mollis 'Variegatus'		•	•	M			A				•				•	•				•						
Hordeum jubatum			•	M	•		A				•						•	•	•	•						
Hordeum vulgare			•				B										•	•	•	•						•
Hystrix patula			•													•	•	•	•	•						
Imperata brasiliensis		•	•		•						•						•	•		•					•	
Imperata cylindrica 'Rubra'	•	•	•	M								•				•	•			•						
Koeleria cristata		•	•	M			A					•	•			•	•		•	•		•				
Lagurus ovatus	•	•	•	E			A					•				•	•	•	•				•			•
Lagurus ovatus 'Nanus'		•	•				A					•				•	•	•	•				•			•
Lamarckia aurea		•					A									•	•	•								
Lasiacis divaricata		•		M							•					•	•							•		
Leersia oryzoides				M	•								•			•			•					•		

	Accent plants	Specimen plants	Groups	Edging (E)/Massing (M)	Ground cover—Dry sites	Ground cover—Wet sites	Borders*	Hedges**	Screens**	Windbreaks**	Naturalized	Pebble/Rock gardens	Bog/Water gardens	Lawn/Lawn substitute	Shade	Full sun	Flowers on plants	Cut flowers	Dried arrangements	Foliage	Foliage and flowers	Fall color	House plants	Seashore/Saline soils	Bird feed/Wildlife protection	Dyed specimens
Melica altissima			•	M			B				•					•	•	•		•						
Melica altissima 'Atropurpurea'			•	M							•				•	•	•	•		•						
Melica ciliata			•			•	A									•	•	•		•						
Melica uniflora	•	•	•	M											•	•				•						
Melica uniflora 'Variegata'	•	•	•	M											•	•				•						
Milium effusum			•			•									•		•			•	•					
Milium effusum 'Aureum'			•				B						•		•		•			•	•					
Miscanthus floridulus			•			•	C					•	•			•	•	•	•							•
Miscanthus oligostrechys	•		•			•	B					•	•			•	•	•	•							•
Miscanthus sacchariflorus	•	•		E			B					•	•		•		•	•	•	•	•					•
Miscanthus sacchariflorus 'Aureus'	•	•		E			B					•	•	•		•		•	•	•	•	•				•
Miscanthus sacchariflorus 'Dwarf'			•			•	B						•			•			•	•		•	•			•
Miscanthus sacchariflorus 'Giganteus'			•	E		•		T	T	T	•		•			•		•	•							•
Miscanthus sacchariflorus 'Robustus'	•	•		E		•	C	T	T			•	•			•		•	•							•
Miscanthus sacchariflorus 'Variegatus'	•	•		E	•	•	B		M		•	•	•		•	•	•	•	•	•						•
Miscanthus sinensis	•	•		E		•	C	T	T		•	•	•			•	•	•	•	•	•	•				•
Miscanthus sinensis 'Autumn Light'	•	•		E		•	C					•	•			•	•	•	•	•	•	•				•
Miscanthus sinensis 'Herbstfeuer'	•	•		E		•	B					•	•		•	•	•	•	•	•	•	•				•
Miscanthus sinensis 'Natsubo'	•	•		E		•	B					•	•			•	•	•	•	•	•	•				•
Miscanthus sinensis 'November Sunset'	•	•		E		•	C					•	•			•	•	•	•	•	•	•				•
Miscanthus sinensis 'Purpurascens'	•	•		E		•	B					•	•			•	•	•	•	•	•	•		•		•

	Accent plants	Specimen plants	Groups	Edging (E)/Massing (M)	Ground cover—Dry sites	Ground cover—Wet sites	Borders*	Hedges**	Screens**	Windbreaks**	Naturalized	Pebble/Rock gardens	Bog/Water gardens	Lawn/Lawn substitute	Shade	Full sun	Flowers on plants	Cut flowers	Dried arrangements	Foliage	Foliage and flowers	Fall color	House plants	Seashore/Saline soils	Bird feed/Wildlife protection	Dyed specimens
Miscanthus sinensis 'Silberfeder'	•	•		E		•	C									•	•	•	•	•	•					•
Miscanthus sinensis 'Strictus'	•	•		E		•	C			•						•	•	•	•	•						•
Miscanthus sinensis 'Univittatus'	•	•				•	C				•	•	•			•	•	•	•	•						•
Miscanthus sinensis 'Yaku Jima'	•	•		E		•	B					•	•			•	•	•	•	•	•	•				•
Miscanthus sinensis 'Yima Yuma'	•	•		E		•	B					•	•			•	•	•	•	•	•					•
Miscanthus sinensis var. *condensatus*	•	•				•	C					•	•			•	•	•	•	•						•
Miscanthus sinensis var. *condensatus* 'Silberpfeil'	•	•				•	C					•	•			•	•	•	•	•						•
Miscanthus sinensis var. *gracillimus*	•	•		E		•	C		T	T	•	•	•			•	•	•	•	•	•					•
Miscanthus sinensis var. *variegatus*	•	•		E		•	C		T	T	•	•	•			•	•	•	•	•	•					•
Miscanthus sinensis var. *zebrinus*	•	•		E		•	C		T	T	•	•	•			•	•	•	•	•	•					•
Miscanthus transmorrisonensis	•	•		E		•	B		M	M	•	•	•			•	•	•	•	•	•					•
Molinia caerulea	•	•				•	B									•	•					•	•			
Molinia caerulea 'Bergfreund'	•	•				•										•	•					•	•			
Molinia caerulea 'Heidebraut'		•				•										•	•					•	•			
Molinia caerulea 'Karl Foerster'	•	•				•										•	•					•	•			
Molinia caerulea 'Moorhexe'		•				•	B									•	•					•	•			
Molinia caerulea 'Skyracer'		•				•	C									•	•					•	•			
Molinia caerulea 'Staefa'	•					•	C									•	•					•	•			

	Accent plants	Specimen plants	Groups	Edging (E)/Massing (M)	Ground cover—Dry sites	Ground cover—Wet sites	Borders*	Hedges**	Screens**	Windbreaks**	Naturalized	Pebble/Rock gardens	Bog/Water gardens	Lawn/Lawn substitute	Shade	Full sun	Flowers on plants	Cut flowers	Dried arrangements	Foliage	Foliage and flowers	Fall color	House plants	Seashore/Saline soils	Bird feed/Wildlife protection	Dyed specimens
Molinia caerulea 'Strahlenquelle'		•				•	C									•	•				•		•			
Molinia caerulea 'Transparent'		•				•	C									•	•				•		•			
Molinia caerulea 'Variegata'		•	•	E		•	B					•			•	•	•			•			•	•		
Molinia caerulea 'Windspiel'		•				•	C									•	•				•		•			
Oplismenus hirtellus			•				•								•								•			
Oplismenus hirtellus 'Vittatus'			•				•								•					•			•			
Oplismenus setarius			•				•								•					•						
Oryza sativa		•	•										•			•		•					•			
Oryza sativa 'Nigrescens'	•	•	•										•					•	•	•			•			
Oryzopsis miliacea			•			•	B									•										
Panicum clandestinum			•	M							•	•		•	•	•			•							
Panicum miliaceum	•	•			•		B				•					•	•		•							
Panicum virgatum			•	M		•	B		M	M	•					•	•	•	•	•		•		•	•	•
Panicum virgatum 'Haense Herms'			•	M		•	B			M			•			•	•	•	•			•		•		
Panicum virgatum 'Rehbraun'			•	M		•	B			M			•			•	•	•	•			•		•		
Panicum virgatum 'Rostrahlbusch'						•	B									•	•	•				•				
Panicum virgatum 'Rubrum'		•	•	M		•	B				•	•				•	•	•		•		•				
Panicum virgatum 'Strictum'				M		•	B				•					•	•	•		•		•				
Paspalum dissectum				M		•					•					•								•		
Paspalum notatum				M	•	•					•					•								•		
Pennisetum alopecuroides	•	•	•	E			B		M		•	•				•	•	•	•	•	•	•		•		
Pennisetum alopecuroides 'Hameln'		•	•	E			A				•	•				•		•	•	•	•	•				

	Accent plants	Specimen plants	Groups	Edging (E)/Massing (M)	Ground cover—Dry sites	Ground cover—Wet sites	Borders*	Hedges**	Screens**	Windbreaks**	Naturalized	Pebble/Rock gardens	Bog/Water gardens	Lawn/Lawn substitute	Shade	Full sun	Flowers on plants	Cut flowers	Dried arrangements	Foliage	Foliage and flowers	Fall color	House plants	Seashore/Saline soils	Bird feed/Wildlife protection	Dyed specimens
Pennisetum alopecuroides 'Weserbergland'	•	•		E			B				•	•				•		•	•	•						
Pennisetum alopecuroides var. *viridescens*	•	•		E			A				•					•	•	•	•	•	•	•				
Pennisetum alopecuros	•	•					B						•			•	•	•	•							
Pennisetum latifolium	•	•														•										
Pennisetum macrostachyum	•	•				•	C								•	•	•			•			•			
Pennisetum nervosum	•	•					C		T			•				•	•	•	•							
Pennisetum orientale		•					B					•				•	•									
Pennisetum orientale var. *triflorum*	•	•		E			B					•				•	•									
Pennisetum setaceum	•	•		E	•		B		M		•	•				•	•	•	•	•	•	•				
Pennisetum setaceum 'Astrosanguineum'	•	•		E	•		B				•	•				•	•	•	•	•	•					
Pennisetum setaceum 'Cupreum'	•	•		E	•		B				•	•				•	•	•	•	•	•	•				
Pennisetum setaceum 'Rubrum'	•	•		E	•		B				•	•				•	•	•	•	•	•	•				
Pennisetum villosum	•	•			•		B					•				•	•	•	•							
Phalaris arundinacea				M	•						•					•										
Phalaris arundinacea 'Dwarf's Garters'	•	•		E	•		A					•	•			•				•		•				
Phalaris arundinacea 'Feesey's Form'	•	•		E			A					•	•			•				•		•				
Phalaris arundinacea var. *picta*	•	•		E		•	B				•	•	•	•		•			•	•		•		•		
Phalaris arundinacea var. *variegata*	•	•		E		•	A					•	•	•		•				•		•	•	•		
Phalaris canariensis		•		M			B				•					•	•		•						•	•
Phalaris minor		•		M			A				•					•	•	•	•						•	
Phleum pratense				M							•					•		•								
Phragmites australis		•		M		•	C		T	T	•		•			•	•	•	•			•		•		•
Poa alpina					•											•										

	Accent plants	Specimen plants	Groups	Edging (E)/Massing (M)	Ground cover—Dry sites	Ground cover—Wet sites	Borders*	Hedges**	Screens**	Windbreaks**	Naturalized	Pebble/Rock gardens	Bog/Water gardens	Lawn/Lawn substitute	Shade	Full sun	Flowers on plants	Cut flowers	Dried arrangements	Foliage	Foliage and flowers	Fall color	House plants	Seashore/Saline soils	Bird feed/Wildlife protection	Dyed specimens
Poa bulbosa	•	•	•	M	•		A					•				•			•	•						
Poa chaixii		•		M	•							•	•	•		•				•						
Poa colensoi	•	•	•	M			A					•				•				•		•				
Poa compressa				M								•				•				•						
Poa confinis				M	•							•				•								•		
Poa glauca		•	•		•							•				•										
Poa labillardieri		•	•				B					•				•										
Poa macrantha				M	•							•				•								•		
Poa nemoralis				M	•							•		•	•	•		•								
Poa pratensis				M								•		•	•	•				•		•				
Polypogon monspeliensis		•					B									•	•	•	•							
Puccinellia fasciculata				M								•				•				•				•	•	
Puccinellia maritima				M								•				•				•				•	•	
Rhynchelytrum repens	•	•		M	•		B					•	•			•	•	•								
Schizachyrium scoparium				M	•							•				•	•	•	•			•			•	
Setaria geniculata				M								•				•								•	•	
Setaria italica				M								•				•		•	•					•	•	
Setaria palmifolia f. variegata		•	•			•	C						•			•	•			•			•			
Sitanion hystrix				M	•							•				•	•	•				•				
Sorghastrum nutans		•		M	•	C				T		•				•	•	•	•			•			•	
Spartina alterniflora				M		•						•				•								•	•	
Spartina cynosuroides				M		•						•				•								•	•	
Spartina gracilis				M	•							•				•										
Spartina patens				M		•						•				•								•	•	
Spartina pectinata		•		M		•			M			•	•			•									•	
Spartina pectinata 'Aureo-marginata'		•		M		•	C			T		•	•			•				•		•			•	
Spartina spartinae				M		•						•				•			•						•	
Sporobolus heterolepis				M	•							•				•									•	
Sporobolus virginicus				M		•						•				•								•	•	
Stenotaphrum secundatum				M		•						•	•	•												

	Accent plants	Specimen plants	Groups	Edging (E)/Massing (M)	Ground cover—Dry sites	Ground cover—Wet sites	Borders*	Hedges**	Screens**	Windbreaks**	Naturalized	Pebble/Rock gardens	Bog/Water gardens	Lawn/Lawn substitute	Shade	Full sun	Flowers on plants	Cut flowers	Dried arrangements	Foliage	Foliage and flowers	Fall color	House plants	Seashore/Saline soils	Bird feed/Wildlife protection	Dyed specimens
Stenotaphrum secundatum 'Variegatum'	•	•		M		•	A						•			•	•						•			
Stipa arundinacea	•	•	•	M	•		B					•	•			•				•		•				
Stipa calamagrostis		•	•		•		B						•			•	•	•	•							
Stipa capillata		•			•		B									•										
Stipa comata			•	M	•		B					•	•			•	•	•	•							
Stipa elegantissima		•					B						•			•										
Stipa extremoirentalis		•					B									•										
Stipa gigantea	•	•			•		C									•	•									
Stipa pennata	•	•			•		B						•			•	•	•	•							
Stipa rubens		•			•		A									•										
Stipa spartea	•	•			•		B					•	•			•	•									
Stipa tenuissima	•	•			•		B									•	•									
Trichloris crinita		•			•		B			•						•	•									
Tripsacum dactyloides	•	•				•	C	T					•			•										
Triticum aestivum		•					B									•	•		•							•
Triticum turgidum		•					B									•	•	•	•							•
Uniola paniculata				M							•					•	•					•		•	•	
Vetiveria zizanioides		•		M			C	T	T	T			•			•	•	•	•	•						•
Zea mays		•				•	B									•			•	•						
Zea mays 'Harlequin'		•	•				B									•			•	•						
Zea mays 'Indian Corn'		•	•				B									•				•						
Zea mays 'Multicolored'		•	•				B									•			•							
Zea mays 'Strawberry Corn'		•					B									•			•							
Zea mays var. *japonica*		•					B									•			•	•						
Zea mays var. *japonica* 'Quadricolor'		•	•				B									•			•	•						

	Accent plants	Specimen plants	Groups	Edging (E)/Massing (M)	Ground cover—Dry sites	Ground cover—Wet sites	Borders*	Hedges**	Screens**	Windbreaks**	Naturalized	Pebble/Rock gardens	Bog/Water gardens	Lawn/Lawn substitute	Shade	Full sun	Flowers on plants	Cut flowers	Dried arrangements	Foliage	Foliage and flowers	Fall color	House plants	Seashore/Saline soils	Bird feed/Wildlife protection	Dyed specimens
Zea mays var. *japonica* 'Variegata'	•	•					B									•			•	•						
Zea mays var. *praecox*		•					B									•			•							
Zea mays var. *tunicata*		•					B									•			•							
Zizania aquatica			•			•	B						•			•	•	•		•	•			•		

*A = Foreground (1–20 in./0–5 dm); B = Middleground (21–60 in./0.5–1.5 m); C = Background (>60 in./1.5 m)
**M = Medium (20–60 in./0.5–1.5 m); T = Tall (>60 in./1.5 m)

Appendix 2
Uses of Bamboo

	Plant-hardiness Zone	Ground cover	Hedge	House plants	Screen	Shade	Sound barrier	Specimen	Windbreak
Hardy Running Bamboo Adapted to Zones 5–8									
Dwarf Forms (1–3 ft/0.3–0.9 m)									
Arundinaria argenteostriata	7–8		•					•	
Arundinaria disticha	7–8	•		•					
Arundinaria humilis	7	•		•					
Arundinaria pumila	8	•		•				•	
Arundinaria pygmaea	8	•		•					
Arundinaria pygmaea 'Variegata'	8	•		•				•	
Arundinaria variegata	6–7	•		•					
Arundinaria viridistriata	7	•		•				•	
Sasa bicolor	8	•		•				•	
Sasa tessellata	6	•		•				•	
Sasa veitchii	7	•		•				•	
Semidwarf Forms (3–15 ft/0.9–4.6 m)									
Arundinaria gigantea ssp. *tecta*	6–9		•		•				
Arundinaria graminea	8							•	
Arundinaria nitida	5–6		•					•	
Chimonobambusa marmorea	8	•						•	
Sasa chrysantha	8	•		•				•	
Sasa palmata	6		•					•	
Shibataea kumasaca	6–7	•						•	
Intermediate Forms (15–35 ft/4.6–10.8 m)									
Arundinaria gigantea	6–7		•		•			•	
Arundinaria simoni	7		•		•			•	

	Plant-hardiness Zone	Ground cover	Hedge	House plants	Screen	Shade	Sound barrier	Specimen	Windbreak
Hardy Running Bamboo Adapted to Zones 5–8									
Intermediate Forms (15–35 ft/4.6–10.8 m)									
Arundinaria simoni var. *variegata*	7–8		•					•	
Chimonobambusa falcata	6		•	•				•	
Chimonobambusa quadrangularis	8							•	
Phyllostachys aurea	7–8			•				•	
Phyllostachys aureosulcata	6–7		•	•				•	
Phyllostachys bambusoides 'Allgold'	7–8				•		•	•	
Phyllostachys bambusoides 'Castillon'	7–8				•		•	•	
Phyllostachys flexuosa	7				•				
Phyllostachys meyeri	7		•		•				
Phyllostachys nigra	7–8			•				•	
Phyllostachys nuda	5–6			•				•	
Phyllostachys viridi-glaucescens	7				•		•		
Pseudosasa japonica	6–7		•	•	•				
Semiarundinaria fastuosa	6			•				•	
Large Forms (35–50 ft/10.8–15.4 m)									
Arundinaria amabilis	8				•	•	•		•
Arundinaria falconeri	8				•		•	•	•
Phyllostachys dulcis	7–8				•	•	•		
Phyllostachys nigra 'Henon'	7–8				•		•	•	•
Phyllostachys viridis	7–8				•		•		•
Phyllostachys vivax	7–8				•		•		•
Giant Forms (50–100 ft/15.4–30.8 m)									
Phyllostachys bambusoides	7–8						•	•	•
Phyllostachys pubescens	8						•		•
Warm-season Clump Bamboo Adapted to Zones 9–10									
Semidwarf Forms (3–15 ft/0.9–4.6 m)									
Bambusa multiplex 'Silverstem Fernleaf'	9–10		•	•	•			•	
Bambusa multiplex var. *rivierorum*	9–10		•	•				•	
Intermediate Forms (15–35 ft/4.6–10.8 m)									
Bambusa multiplex 'Fernleaf'	9–10		•		•			•	
Bambusa multiplex 'Silverstripe Fernleaf'	9–10		•		•			•	
Bambusa multiplex 'Willowy'	9–10							•	

	Plant-hardiness Zone	Ground cover	Hedge	House plants	Screen	Shade	Sound barrier	Specimen	Windbreak
Large Forms (35–50 ft/10.8–15.4 m)									
Bambusa beecheyana	9–10				•		•		•
Bambusa longispiculata	9–10				•		•		•
Bambusa multiplex	9–10		•		•		•		•
Bambusa multiplex 'Alphonse Karr'	9–10							•	
Bambusa multiplex 'Silverstripe'	9–10	•						•	
Bambusa textilis	9–10						•	•	•
Bambusa tuldoides	9–10				•		•		•
Dendrocalamus strictus	10						•		•
Giant Forms (50–100 ft/15.4–30.8 m)									
Bambusa arundinacea	10				•		•		•
Bambusa oldhamii	9–10					•	•		•
Bambusa polymorpha	10					•	•		•
Bambusa tulda	9–10					•	•		•
Bambusa ventricosa	9–10			•	•	•	•	•	•
Bambusa vulgaris	10					•	•	•	•

Appendix 3
Uses of Grasslike Plants

	Accent plants	Specimen plants	Groups	Edging (E)/Massing (M)	Ground cover—Dry sites	Ground cover—Wet sites	Borders*	Naturalized	Pebble/Rock gardens	Bog/Water gardens	Shade	Full sun	Flowers on plants	Cut flowers	Dried arrangements	Foliage	Foliage and flowers	House plants	Seashore/Saline soils	Bird feed/Wildlife protection
Acorus calamus		•				•				•		•				•				
Acorus calamus 'Variegatus'		•				•				•	•					•				
Acorus gramineus		•	•	E		•	A	•		•	•					•		•		
Acorus gramineus 'Albovariegatus'		•	•	E		•	A			•	•					•		•		
Acorus gramineus 'Ogon'		•	•	E		•	B			•	•					•		•		
Acorus gramineus 'Pusillus'		•	•	E		•	A			•	•					•		•		
Acorus gramineus 'Variegatus'		•	•	E		•	A			•	•					•		•		
Butomus umbellatus			•	M		•		•		•	•		•			•				•
Chlorophytum amaniense	•	•	•	E			A					•				•		•		
Chlorophytum arundinaceum	•	•	•	E			A					•				•		•		
Chlorophytum bickertii	•	•	•	E			A					•				•		•		
Chlorophytum capense	•	•	•	E			A					•				•		•		
Chlorophytum comosum	•	•	•	E			A							•		•		•		
Chlorophytum macrophyllum	•	•	•	E			B					•				•		•		
Chlorophytum nepalense	•	•	•	E			A					•				•		•		
Chlorophytum orchidastrum	•	•	•	E			A					•				•		•		
Commelina virginica						•		•		•		•								
Convalleria majalis			•	E	•		A	•			•			•	•			•	•	
Equisetum hyemale				M		•		•	•	•	•	•								
Equisetum scirpoides				M		•		•		•	•	•								
Equisetum variegatum				M		•		•		•	•	•								

	Accent plants	Specimen plants	Groups	Edging (E)/Massing (M)	Ground cover—Dry sites	Ground cover—Wet sites	Borders*	Naturalized	Pebble/Rock gardens	Bog/Water gardens	Shade	Full sun	Flowers on plants	Cut flowers	Dried arrangements	Foliage	Foliage and flowers	House plants	Seashore/Saline soils	Bird feed/Wildlife protection
Hypoxis hirsuta		•		E	•		A	•			•	•	•							
Liriope exiliflora	•	•		E	•	•	A		•		•					•		•		
Liriope muscari	•	•		E	•	•	A		•		•					•		•		
Liriope spicata	•	•		E	•	•	A				•					•		•		
Ophiopogon jaburan	•	•		E		•	A		•		•	•				•		•		
Ophiopogon jaburan 'Argenteo-vittatus'	•	•		E		•	A		•		•					•		•		
Ophiopogon jaburan 'Aureo-variegatus'	•	•		E		•	A		•		•					•		•		
Ophiopogon jaburan 'Caeruleus'	•	•		E		•	A		•			•				•		•		
Ophiopogon jaburan 'Variegatus'	•	•		E		•	A				•					•		•		
Ophiopogon jaburan 'Vittatus'	•	•		E		•	A				•					•		•		
Ophiopogon japonicus		•		E		•	A		•		•					•		•		
Ophiopogon japonicus 'Kioto'		•		E		•	A				•					•		•		
Ophiopogon plansicapus		•		E		•	A		•		•	•				•		•		
Phormium tenax		•	•									•				•		•		
Reineckea carnea		•		E			A		•	•	•									
Sisyrinchium angustifolium	•		•	E	•	•	A	•	•	•	•	•		•						
Sisyrinchium californicum		•		E	•	•	A	•	•	•	•	•				•				
Sisyrinchium douglasii		•		E	•	•	A	•	•	•	•	•				•				
Tradescantia albiflora		•		M	•	•	A			•	•					•		•		
Tradescantia blossfeldiana		•		M	•	•				•	•					•		•		
Tradescantia bracteata					•	•					•		•			•		•		
Tradescantia navicularis		•		M	•				•		•	•				•				
Tradescantia sillamontana		•		M	•				•		•					•		•		
Tradescantia virginiana		•		M	•				•		•					•		•		
Typha angustifolia		•				•				•		•	•		•		•			•
Typha gracilis		•				•				•		•	•		•		•			
Typha latifolia						•		•		•		•	•		•		•			•
Typha laxmannia		•				•				•		•	•		•		•			•
Typha minima		•				•				•		•	•		•		•			
Xerophyllum asphodeloides		•		E	•		B	•	•		•	•					•			

	Accent plants	Specimen plants	Groups	Edging (E)/Massing (M)	Ground cover—Dry sites	Ground cover—Wet sites	Borders*	Naturalized	Pebble/Rock gardens	Bog/Water gardens	Shade	Full sun	Flowers on plants	Cut flowers	Dried arrangements	Foliage	Foliage and flowers	House plants	Seashore/Saline soils	Bird feed/Wildlife protection
Xerophyllum tenax						•	C					•								
Xyris arenicola			•	M			•		•	•	•								•	
Xyris baldwiniana				M			•		•	•	•								•	
Xyris fimbriata				M			•		•	•	•								•	
Xyris montana				M			•		•	•	•								•	
Xyris platylepis				M			•		•	•	•								•	
Yucca aloifolia		•	•				C	•			•	•					•			
Yucca baccata		•	•				B	•			•	•					•			
Yucca constricta		•	•				B	•			•	•					•			
Yucca filamentosa		•	•				B	•			•	•						•		
Yucca glauca		•	•				C	•			•	•					•			
Yucca gloriosa		•	•				C	•			•	•					•			
Zebrina pendula	•		•	E			A				•	•				•		•		

*A = Foreground (1–20 in./0–5 dm); B = Middleground (21–60 in./0.5–1.5 m); C = Background (>60 in./1.5 m)

Appendix 4
Uses of Rushes and Sedges

	Accent plants	Specimen plants	Groups	Edging (E)/Massing (M)	Ground cover—Dry sites	Ground cover—Wet sites	Borders*	Hedges	Naturalized	Pebble/Rock gardens	Bog/Water gardens	Lawn/Lawn substitute	Shade	Full sun	Flowers on plants	Dried arrangements	Foliage	Foliage and flowers	Fall color	House plants	Seashore/Saline soils
Carex acuta			•	M	•				•		•			•						•	
Carex acutiformis				M	•				•		•		•	•			•				
Carex arenaria				M	•				•		•		•	•			•			•	•
Carex atrata				M	•				•		•		•	•	•	•					
Carex atrata var. *ovata*				M	•				•		•		•	•				•			
Carex aurea				M	•				•		•		•			•			•		•
Carex baldensis				E		•	A		•				•								
Carex brunnea			•	M		•	B			•	•		•							•	
Carex buchananii		•	•	M		•	A			•	•	•	•				•		•	•	
Carex capillaris		•	•	M		•	B		•				•				•				
Carex comans			•	E		•	A			•			•				•				
Carex comans 'Bronze Form'			•	E		•	A		•				•				•				
Carex communis				M	•				•		•	•	•								
Carex concinna 'Variegata'			•	E		•	A									•	•				
Carex conica			•	M	•				•				•								
Carex conica 'Variegata'			•	M		•	A						•				•			•	•
Carex digitata			•	E		•	A			•			•								
Carex flacca				M	•				•		•	•									
Carex flagellifera			•	M		•	B						•								
Carex flava			•	E		•	B		•	•	•		•						•		
Carex grayii	•	•	•	M	•				•		•		•	•	•	•			•		

	Accent plants	Specimen plants	Groups	Edging (E)/Massing (M)	Ground cover—Dry sites	Ground cover—Wet sites	Borders*	Hedges	Naturalized	Pebble/Rock gardens	Bog/Water gardens	Lawn/Lawn substitute	Shade	Full sun	Flowers on plants	Dried arrangements	Foliage	Foliage and flowers	Fall color	House plants	Seashore/Saline soils
Carex kobomugi				M										•							•
Carex lacustris		•	•	M		•	B	•	•		•	•	•								
Carex montanensis			•	E		•	A					•									
Carex morrowii			•	M		•			•				•								
Carex morrowii 'Aureo-variegata'			•	M		•			•	•		•					•				
Carex morrowii 'Nana'		•	•	E		•	A		•	•	•		•				•		•		
Carex morrowii 'Old Gold'		•	•	E		•	A		•	•	•		•				•		•		
Carex morrowii 'Variegata'		•	•	E		•	A		•	•	•		•				•		•		
Carex morrowii var. *expallida*		•	•	E		•	A		•	•	•		•				•				
Carex muskingumensis			•	M		•			•		•	•	•								
Carex nigra			•	E		•	A			•			•								
Carex petriei			•	E		•	A			•	•		•	•			•				
Carex plantaginea				M		•			•	•	•	•					•	•			
Carex plantaginea 'Dr. Richard Lighty'				M		•			•	•	•	•									
Carex speciosa 'Velebit Humilis'			•	E		•	A						•								
Carex stricta				M		•			•			•	•								
Carex stricta 'Bowles's Golden'			•	M		•	B		•	•		•					•	•			
Carex stricta var. *angustata*			•	M		•	B		•	•		•									
Carex stricta var. *curtissima*			•	M		•	B		•			•									
Carex stricta var. *decora*			•	M		•	B		•			•									
Carex sylvatica			•	E		•	A		•			•									
Carex umbrosa			•	E					•			•									
Carex uncinifolia			•	E		•	A		•			•									
Carex X *stipata*			•	M			B		•		•			•	•				•		
Cladium mariscoides			•	M		•			•		•		•	•				•			
Cladium sinclairii			•	M					•		•		•					•			
Cymophyllus fraseri			•	M					•	•		•	•	•			•	•			
Cyperus albostriatus	•	•	•								•		•				•			•	
Cyperus albostriatus 'Variegatus'	•	•	•								•		•				•			•	
Cyperus alternifolius	•	•	•								•		•				•			•	
Cyperus alternifolius 'Flabelliformis'	•	•	•								•		•				•			•	

	Accent plants	Specimen plants	Groups	Edging (E)/Massing (M)	Ground cover—Dry sites	Ground cover—Wet sites	Borders*	Hedges	Naturalized	Pebble/Rock gardens	Bog/Water gardens	Lawn/Lawn substitute	Shade	Full sun	Flowers on plants	Dried arrangements	Foliage	Foliage and flowers	Fall color	House plants	Seashore/Saline soils
Cyperus alternifolius 'Gracilis'	•	•	•								•			•			•			•	
Cyperus alternifolius 'Variegatus'	•	•	•								•			•			•			•	
Cyperus haspan			•	M	•						•			•						•	
Cyperus haspan 'Viviparous'			•		•									•						•	
Cyperus longus			•	M	•				•					•							
Cyperus papyrus			•	M	•				•		•			•	•		•				
Cyperus papyrus 'Nanus'			•	M	•				•		•			•			•			•	
Cyperus papyrus 'Variegatus'			•	M	•				•		•			•			•				
Cyperus vegetus			•	M	•				•		•		•	•	•	•	•			•	
Eleocharis acicularis						•					•		•								
Eleocharis cellulosa						•			•		•		•								
Eriophorum callitrix			•	M	•				•		•		•	•							
Eriophorum polystachion			•	M	•				•		•		•	•							
Eriophorum vaginatum			•	M	•				•		•			•	•				•		
Eriophroum virginicum			•	M	•				•		•		•	•							
Fuirena simplex			•	M	•				•		•		•	•	•		•	•			
Juncus effusus			•	M	•				•		•		•	•						•	
Juncus effusus 'Aureus Striatus'			•	M	•				•		•		•	•		•	•				
Juncus effusus 'Spiralis'			•	E	•				•		•		•							•	
Juncus effusus 'Vittatus'			•	M	•				•		•		•				•	•			
Juncus effusus 'Zebrinus'			•	M	•				•		•		•				•				
Juncus effusus var. *compactus*			•	M	•				•		•		•	•			•				
Juncus effusus var. *solutus*			•	M	•				•		•		•	•			•				
Luzula acuminata				M					•	•			•				•				
Luzula campestris			•	M	•				•				•								
Luzula nemorosa				M	•				•				•					•			
Luzula nivea			•	M	•				•	•			•	•				•			
Luzula nivea 'Marginata'			•	M	•				•	•			•				•				
Luzula nivea 'Nana'			•	M	•				•	•			•							•	
Luzula nivea 'Schneehaeschen'			•	E		•	A		•				•								
Luzula pilosa		•	•	M					•			•	•		•	•				•	

	Accent plants	Specimen plants	Groups	Edging (E)/Massing (M)	Ground cover—Dry sites	Ground cover—Wet sites	Borders*	Hedges	Naturalized	Pebble/Rock gardens	Bog/Water gardens	Lawn/Lawn substitute	Shade	Full sun	Flowers on plants	Dried arrangements	Foliage	Foliage and flowers	Fall color	House plants	Seashore/Saline soils
Luzula purpurea			•	M	•				•	•			•	•						•	•
Luzula sylvatica			•	M	•				•				•				•			•	•
Luzula sylvatica 'Marginata'			•	M	•				•				•					•		•	
Scirpus cernuus			•	M	•						•		•					•		•	
Scirpus cyperinus			•	M	•				•				•		•			•	•	•	
Scirpus flaccidus				M	•						•		•	•	•						
Scirpus nodulosus			•	M	•								•							•	
Scirpus tabernaemontani				M	•				•		•		•		•	•			•		
Scirpus tabernaemontani 'Zebrinus'				M	•				•				•			•			•	•	

*A = Foreground (1–20 in./0–5 dm); B = Middleground (21–60 in./0.5–1.5 m); C = Background (> 60 in./1.5 m)

Appendix 5
Plant Hardiness Zones Map

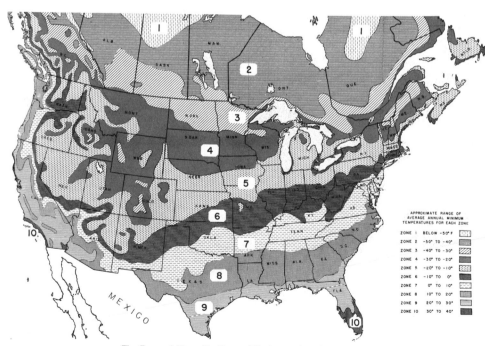

The Zones of Plant Hardiness—This is an adapted version of the color map on the reverse side. It may be useful for small-scale reproduction in books, magazines, and nursery catalogs. This map is not copyrighted, and permission for reproducing it is not required.

Glossary

Abortive Imperfectly developed.

Acaulescent Without an evident leafy stem.

Accent plant A plant with outstanding characteristics used to enhance other plants.

Achene A small, dry, indehiscent, one-seeded fruit having a thin pericarp that is free from the seed.

Actinomorphic Regular, radially symmetrical, capable of being divided vertically in more than one plane into two essentially equal halves.

Acuminate Long-tapering to a pointed apex.

Acute Sharp pointed; applies to apex.

Adaxial Facing toward the axis.

Adnate Fusion of unlike structures.

Aggregate Crowded into a cluster; a number of separate fruits from one flower.

Androecium The stamens collectively.

Androgynous Having staminate flowers above the pistillate flowers in the same inflorescence.

Annual Life cycle completed in one year or one season.

Anther The pollen-bearing part of the stamen.

Anthesis Time of flowering.

Antrorse Directed upward or forward.

Apex *(pl.* **apices)** The tip, the distal end.

Aphyllopodic With the lowest leaves reduced to scales, the first foliage leaves are well above the base of the plant.

Apicula A short, sharp, flexible point.

Apiculate Terminated by an apicula.

Apomictic Reproduced asexually, without fertilization.

Appendage An attached subsidiary or secondary part, as a projecting or hanging part.

Appressed Closely pressed against.

Approximate Close to each other but not united.

Arcuate Curved or bowed.

Aristate Bearing a stiff, bristlelike awn or seta; tapered to a very narrow, much-elongated apex.

Articulate   Jointed; joined by a line of demarcation between two parts that, at maturity, separate by a clean-cut scar.

Ascending   Rising obliquely or indirectly upward.

Asperulous   Slightly rough to the touch.

Attenuate   Elongate, tapering, usually, but not always, applied to base or tip.

Auricle   An ear-shaped appendage or lobe.

Auriculate   Bearing an auricle or auricles.

Awl-shaped, awl-tipped   Slender and sharp-pointed.

Awn   A bristle or slender, stiff appendage, usually terminal.

Axil   The angle between any two organs or structures.

Axillary   In the axil; designating flowers borne in the axils of leaves, or seeds produced in the angles formed by partitions in the ovary of a compound pistil.

Axis   The central stem along which parts or organs are arranged; the central line of any organ or structure.

Baccate   Berrylike, pulpy or fleshy.

Barbed   With rigid points that are retrorse, as in a fishhook.

Basifixed   Attached or fixed by the base.

Bast   The fibrous portion of the inner bark.

Beak   A long, prominent, and relatively thickened point.

Beard   A group of long awns or bristlelike trichomes.

Bearded   With rather long hairs.

Berry   A fleshy or pulpy fruit developed from a single ovary, with one or more seeds.

Bi-, Bis-   A prefix signifying two, twice, or doubly.

Bidentate   Having two teeth.

Biennial   Life cycle completed in two years or seasons.

Bifid   With two lobes or segments, as apices of some petals or leaves.

Bisexual   Having both sexes, stamens and ovary, present in the same floret or spikelet.

Blade   The expanded portion of a leaf, petal, or other structure.

Bloom   Bluish, whitish, or grayish powder, very fine, often waxy, on the surface of some leaves, stems, fruits, or other organs, easily rubbed off.

Bract   A more or less modified leaf subtending a flower or flower cluster.

Bracteate   Bearing or subtended by bracts.

Bracteolate   Having bracteoles, as the bracteolate pedicel of a flower.

Bracteole   A secondary or very small bract, a bractlet.

Bractlet   A secondary bract.

Branch   A lateral stem.

Branchlet   A branch of the second or higher order.

Bristle   A stiff, strong, but slender hair or trichome.

Bulb   A short, underground stem surrounded by fleshy leaves or scales.

Bulbil, bulblet   A small bulb or bulblike structure.

Bulbous   Having true bulbs; any structure having a swollen base.

Bur Numerous tightly coalesced bristles (sterile branchlets), usually subglobose; as in Cenchrus.

Callus A hard protuberance; the tough, swollen point of insertion of the lemma or palea in the Poaceae.

Calyx The outer part of the floral envelope, composed of sepals.

Campanulate Bell-shaped.

Canaliculate With a longitudinal channel or groove.

Cane Dead culm of bamboo.

Canescent Grayish white, pubescent, hoary, densely covered with short, fine, whitish or gray hairs.

Capillary Hairlike, very slender.

Capitate Head or headlike.

Capsule A simple, dry, dehiscent fruit of two or more carpels, and usually several-to-many-seeded.

Carinate Keeled, provided with a projecting central longitudinal line or ridge.

Carpel One member of a compound pistil; a simple pistil.

Carpellate Possessing or composed of carpels.

Cartilaginous Tough and hard but not bony; gristly.

Caryopsis The grain or fruit of grasses, seedlike, with a thin pericarp adherent to the seed.

Castaneous Dark brown or chestnut-colored.

Caudate Bearing a tail-like appendage as the apex of some leaves, the spadix of some Araceae.

Caudex The thickened, persistent base, usually of a herbaceous perennial.

Caulescent With an evident stem aboveground.

Cauline Pertaining to or belonging to an evident stem or axis, as opposed to basal.

Centrum The central air space in hollow-stemmed plants, especially of Equisetum.

Cespitose, caespitose Tufted, in clumps.

Chartaceous Of papery texture.

Ciliate Fringed with hairs on the margin.

Ciliolate Minutely ciliate.

Clavate Club-shaped; an elongate structure gradually thickened toward the apex.

Claw The narrow, petiolelike base of some petals or sepals.

Cleistogamous A type of self-pollinated flower that does not open.

Clump A single plant with two-to-many more or less crowded stems arising from a branched rootstock or short rhizome.

Cob Thickened, woody axis on which spikelets of *Zea mays* are borne.

Cockscomb Having the shape of a cockscomb.

Collar The area on the outer side of a leaf at the junction of sheath and blade.

Colony A stand, group, or population of plants of one species; may be colonial, seedling, or both in origin.

Compact   Said of closely flowered inflorescences.

Competitiveness   The ability of a species to coexist with other species in an area in which they occur together.

Compound   Composed of two or more similar and united parts.

Compressed   Flattened laterally, as the compressed spikelets of Chasmanthium latifolium.

Conduplicate   Folded together lengthwise, with the upper surface within, as in the blades of many grasses.

Conic, conical   Cone-shaped.

Conjugate   Joined.

Connate   United or joined; in particular, of like or similar structures joined as one body or organ.

Connective   The tissue connecting the two cells of an anther, particularly when the cells are separated.

Continuous   Said of the rachis or other organ that does not disarticulate.

Convex   Rounded on the surface. Said especially of glumes and lemmas that are rounded on the back instead of keeled.

Convolute   Rolled up lengthwise, as in leaves.

Coralloid   Coral-like.

Cordate   Heart-shaped; with a rounded lobe on each side of the base.

Coriaceous   With a leathery texture.

Corm   A bulblike structure in which the fleshy portion is predominantly stem tissue covered by membranous scales.

Cormatose   Corm-bearing.

Corolla   The inner set of floral leaves, consisting of petals.

Corymb   A short and broad, more or less flat-topped, indeterminate inflorescence, the outer flowers opening first.

Corymbiform   Corymblike, the shape of a corymb.

Costate   With a strongly pronounced midrib.

Crown   A corona, a crownlike extension of basal portions of perianth segments.

Crustaceous   Hard and brittle in texture.

Culm   The flowering stem of a grass or sedge.

Cultivar   A group of cultivated plants clearly distinguished by any characters and which, when reproduced sexually or asexually, retains its distinguishing characters.

Cuneate   Wedge-shaped; triangular.

Cuspidate   With an apical cusp.

Cylindric, cylindrical   Elongated and circular in cross-section.

Cymbiform   Cymelike, boat-shaped.

Cyme   A broad, flattish, determinate inflorescence, the central flowers maturing first.

Cymose   Like a cyme, or derived from a cyme; bearing or pertaining to a cyme.

Deciduous Not persistent or evergreen.

Decumbent With the base prostrate but the upper parts erect ascending.

Decurrent Adnate to the stem or petiole, and extending downward beyond the point of attachment.

Dehiscent Opening, not indehiscent or closed.

Dense Said of inflorescences in which the spikelets are crowded.

Dentate Toothed, the sharp or coarse teeth perpendicular to the margin.

Denticular, denticulate Minutely or finely dentate.

Diffuse Open and much-branched.

Digitate Having parts or segments diverging from a common point.

Dilated Widened or enlarged.

Dioecious Having staminate and pistillate plants.

Disarticulate Fracturing and separating at maturity.

Distichous Two-ranked, on opposite sides of a stem and in the same plane.

Divaricate Spreading broadly, at an angle of more than 50 degrees with the axis.

Divergent Spreading but less broadly than divaricate.

Dorsal Relating to, or attached to, the back or outer surface of a part or organ, facing away from the axis.

Dorsiventral Flattened and provided with a definite dorsal and ventral surface, laminate, as a leaf blade.

Downy Covered with very short, weak, soft hairs.

Drooping Erect to spreading at base but inclining downward above, as the branches of a panicle.

Ear The fruiting spike of a cereal, as corn or wheat.

Ellipsoid An elliptic solid. Said of the shape of panicles, spikelets, and fruits.

Elliptic Narrowed to relatively rounded ends and widest at or near the middle; two-dimensional.

Elongate Narrow, the length many times the width or thickness.

Emarginate Having a shallow notch at the extremity or apex.

Endosperm The starch- and oil-containing tissue of seeds.

Ensiform Sword-shaped, as in the leaf of Calamus.

Ephemeral Lasting for only a day or less, as flowers of Tradescantia.

Epidermis The true cellular covering of a plant below the cuticle.

Equitant Distichous, the bases overlapping.

Erose With irregular margin, as though chewed.

Evergreen Plants that remain green and functional through more than one growing season.

Excurrent Projecting or extending beyond a margin or apex, as a midrib extended into a mucro or awn.

Exserted Projecting out of, beyond.

Extravaginal Bursting through an enclosing sheath as the innovations of some grasses.

Extrose Facing or directed outward, as the dehiscence of an anther.

Falcate   Sickle-shaped, strongly curved.

Farinose   Covered with a whitish, mealy or granular coating.

Fascicle   A bundle, a close cluster.

Fascicled   Grouped in a fascicle or fascicles.

Fertile   Capable of bearing viable seeds, or, in the case of stamens, viable pollen.

Fibrillose   Furnished with fibers.

Filament   The stalk of the stamen; any threadlike structure.

Filamentous   Composed of threads.

Filiferous   Bearing threadlike appendages.

Filiform   Threadlike, slender, and usually terete in cross-section.

Fimbriate   With narrow or filiform appendages, fringed.

Fistulose   Hollow and cylindrical, as the culms of some bamboos.

Flabellate   Fan-shaped; broadly wedge-shaped.

Flaccid   Weak and limp.

Flexuous   Wavy, as the branches of some panicles.

Floret   The lemma and palea with included flower (stamens and pistil). Florets may be perfect, staminate, pistillate, neuter or sterile.

Floriferous   Flower-bearing.

Flower   An axis bearing one or more pistils or one or more stamens or both. When only the former, it is a pistillate (female) flower; when only the latter, it is a staminate (male) flower. When both, it is a perfect (bisexual), hermaphroditic flower.

Flower head   A simple or compound inflorescence at anthesis.

Folded   Applied to leaf blades lengthwise about the midrib, the upper surface within.

Foliaceous   Leaflike; said of sepals, calyx lobes, or bracts that resemble leaves in size, color, and texture.

Foliage   The leaves of a plant collectively.

Follicle   A dry, dehiscent, one-carpelled fruit usually with more than one seed and opening only along the ventral suture.

Fruit   A ripened ovary.

Fructiferous   Bearing fruit.

Fugacious   Falling or withering away very early.

Fulvous   Tawny, dull yellow.

Fuscous   Grayish brown.

Fusiform   A long, narrow ellipse with pointed ends.

Geniculate   Sharply or abruptly bent.

Gibbous   Swollen on one side, usually basally.

Glabrate   Becoming glabrous with age.

Glabrescent   Nearly glabrous, or becoming glabrous with maturity or age.

Glabrous   Without hairs or trichomes.

Gladiate   Sword-shaped.

Gland A protuberance, depression, or appendage on the surface of an organ, that secretes a usually sticky fluid.

Glandular Having or bearing secreting organs, glands, or trichomes.

Glaucescent Slightly glaucous.

Glaucous Whitened with bloom, often lost on heating or rubbing.

Globose Spherical.

Globular Globose or spherical.

Glomerate In a dense or compact cluster.

Glomerule A compact, capitate cyme.

Glumaceous Resembling a glume in texture; dry and chaffy.

Glume A bract at the base of the spikelet in the Gramineae; a chaffy bract.

Gregarious Growing together in colonies; spreading as in rhizomatous plants.

Gynecandros Having pistillate flowers above the staminate flowers in the same inflorescence.

Gynodioecious With perfect (bisexual) flowers on some plants, and only pistillate (female) flowers on others.

Gynoecium The collective term for the female parts of a flower, the pistil or pistils.

Head A capitulum, or dense, short cluster of sessile flowers.

Herb A vascular plant lacking a persistent woody stem.

Herbaceous Not woody; green and of soft texture.

Hirsute Pubescent with straight, rather stiff hairs.

Hispid Provided with stiff or bristly hairs.

Hispidulous Diminutive of hispid; somewhat or minutely hispid.

Horticultural annual A perennial from warm climates grown as an annual in cold climates.

Husk Foliaceous bract, as in husks of Zea mays.

Hyaline Translucent or transparent.

Hypogynous Borne on the receptacle.

Imbricate Overlapping.

Included Not exserted, within.

Indehiscent Not regularly opening, as a fruit or anther.

Indurate Hardened.

Inflated Puffed up, bladdery.

Inflorescence The flowering part of a plant.

Innovation The basal shoot of a perennial grass.

Inrolled Rolled inward, as in leaves.

Internode The portion of a stem between two nodes.

Interrupted The continuity broken. Said especially of dense inflorescences like those of Typha, whose continuity is broken by gaps.

Invasiveness The ability of a species to invade an area in which it was not planted or established.

Involucre   A whorl or collection of bracts surrounding or subtending a flower cluster or a single flower.

Involute   Rolled inward or toward the upper side, as in some leaves or petals.

Joint   The node of a grass culm. The internode of an articulate rachis.

Jointed   With nodes, as in grass stems; with points of articulation.

Keel   Sharp fold or ridge at the back of a compressed sheath, blade, glume, lemma, or palea.

Kernel   The whole seed of a cereal, as in corn or barley.

Lacerate   Torn, irregularly cleft or cut.

Laciniate   Slashed into narrow, pointed lobes.

Lanceolate   Lance-shaped, widest in the lowest third and gradually narrowed upwards; length to breadth in a ratio of about 3:1; if narrower or wider, it is described as narrowly or broadly lanceolate.

Lanose   Woolly.

Leaf   The lateral organ of a stem, in grasses consisting of sheath and blade.

Leaflet   A segment of a compound leaf.

Lectotype   A specimen of the original species, chosen after the original description to be the type.

Lemma   The lower bract enclosing the flower in the Poaceae.

Lenticular   Lens-shaped.

Ligule   The thin appendage or ring of hairs on the inside of a leaf at the junction of sheath and blade.

Linear   Long and narrow with essentially parallel margins, as the blades of most grasses.

Lobe   A usually major segment of an organ, representing a division halfway to the middle of the organ, as a leaf.

Lobulate   Divided into small lobes.

Locule   A chamber cavity, cell of an anther, ovary, or fruit.

Loculicidal   The method or process of opening of a seed, capsule, or anther.

Lodge   To bend or break down, as the culms of plants.

Lorate   Strap-shaped.

Maculate   Marked with spots, blotched.

Membrane   A thin, pliable layer of animal or plant tissue.

Membranous, membranaceous   With a thin and usually pliable texture, and more or less translucent.

-merous   A suffix signifying having parts, as three-merous, having three parts of each kind.

Midrib   The central or main rib of a leaf or other, similar structure.

Monocotyledonous   A plant bearing only one cotyledon or seed leaf.

Monoecious   With staminate and pistillate flowers on the same plant.

Monopodial   Having growth and prolongation of the stem or rhizome continuing indefinitely, usually without branching.

Monotypic   One type, as only one species in a genus such as *Zea mays*.

Mucilaginous   Slimy or mucilagelike.

Mucro (*pl.* **mucrones**) A short, sharp, abrupt spur or spiny tip.

Mucronate Having a short, sharp point at the apex.

Muricate A surface roughened by broad or fleshy, pointed spines.

Naked Without scales or hairs; a naked flower lacks a perianth.

Narrow A qualitative term; slender, thin.

Nerve One of the principal veins of a parallel-veined leaf or other part.

Neuter Without sex or sex organs, sterile. A neuter flower, lacking both pistils and stamens.

Node The place upon the stem which normally bears one or more leaves.

Nutlet A small nut, similar to an achene but with a harder and thicker wall.

Ob- A prefix signifying inversion, as obovoid.

Oblanceolate Inversely lanceolate, with the broadest width above the middle, and tapering to the base.

Oblong Elongate and with more or less parallel sides, the length usually less than 10 times the width.

Obovate Inversely ovate, broader above rather than below the middle.

Obovoid Inversely ovoid, with the point of attachment at the narrower end.

Obsolete Almost wanting, applied to organs usually present.

Obtuse Rounded at the apex; contrasted with acute.

Orbicular, orbiculate Circular or nearly so.

Orifice A mouthlike opening.

Orthotropus (ovule or seed) Erect, with the orifice or micropyle at the apex and the hilum at the base.

Oval Broadly elliptical.

Ovary The basal part of the pistil that encloses the ovules.

Ovate Outlined like a hen's egg; the broadest part below the middle, two-dimensional.

Ovoid A three-dimensional structure with an oval outline.

Ovule The body that, after fertilization, becomes the seed; the egg-containing unit of the ovary.

Palea The upper bract that subtends the flower in the Gramineae.

Palmate Digitate, with parts diverging from a common base.

Paludal Of or growing in marshes.

Panicle Branched flower head, with main axis, divided branches and stalked spikelets, ranging from very dense and spikelike to very diffuse.

Paniculate Resembling a panicle.

Papillate, papillose Bearing papillae or short, rounded, wartlike protuberances.

Parenchyma A plant tissue made up of undifferentiated and, usually, unspecialized cells.

Parietal Borne on or pertaining to the wall or inner surface of a capsule.

Pectinate Divided into long, linear, equal, lateral divisions; comblike.

Pedicel The stalk of a single flower in an inflorescence.

Pedicellate Having a pedicel.

Peduncle The stalk of a whole inflorescence, or of a solitary flower when that flower is the only member of the inflorescence.

Pedunculate Borne upon a peduncle.

Pellucid Clear, transparent.

Peltate An organ more or less circular in outline and attached near the center or inside its margin.

Pendulous Drooping, hanging downward.

Perennial Lasting from year to year.

Perenniate To live over from one year to another.

Perfect Applied to flowers having both stamens and pistils.

Perianth A collective term for the corolla and calyx.

Perigynia Perigynium collectively.

Perigynium The papery sheath that envelops the nutlet or ovary in Carex and Cymophyllus.

Persistent Remaining attached; not falling off.

Petal One of the parts of the corolla, or inner, leaflike parts of a flower.

Petaloid As an adjective, petal-like, in color and shape resembling a petal; as a noun, an organ that is petal-like.

Petiolate Having a petiole.

Petiole The stalk of a leaf blade.

pH A symbol denoting the negative logarithm of the hydrogen ion concentration in grams per liter of a solution; used in expressing relative acidity or alkalinity.

Phyllopodic With the lowest leaves well developed instead of reduced to scales.

Pilose Covered with long, soft trichomes.

Pistil A unit of the gynoecium, composed of ovary, style, and stigma.

Pistillate With pistils and without fertile stamens; female.

Pith The soft, spongy, central tissue of most angiosperm stems.

Placenta A zone of tissue to which the ovules are attached within the ovary.

Plano-convex Plane on one side and convex on the other.

Plantlet Juvenile, miniature plant.

Plumose Feathered, having fine hairs on each side. Said chiefly of awns and slender teeth.

Proliferous Producing numerous new individuals or parts of the same kind.

Prostrate A general term for lying flat on the ground.

Prothallus The gametophyte stage or generation of ferns and some other cryptogams; a small, delicate, flattened, thalluslike structure growing on the ground, bearing the sexual organs.

Puberulent Minutely pubescent.

Pubescent Covered with short, soft, downy hairs or trichomes.

Punctate Marked with translucent or colored dots, depressions, or pits.

Puncticulate Minutely punctate, diminutive of punctate.

Pyramidal Shape of a pyramid.

Raceme   A simple, elongated, indeterminate inflorescence with pedicellate or stalked flowers.

Racemose   In racemes or racemelike.

Rachilla   A secondary axis; the floral axis in the Gramineae and Cyperaceae.

Rachis   An axis bearing flowers or leaflets.

Radiate   Standing on or spreading from a common center.

Radical   Arising from the root or its crown, i.e., leaves that are basal or rosulate.

Ray   A branch of an umbel or an umbel-like inflorescence; a ray flower, or the corolla of a ray flower.

Raylet   Petal of a ray flower.

Receptacle   The enlarged or elongated end of the stem or flower axis on which some or all of the flower parts are borne.

Reniform   Kidney-shaped.

Reticulate   Netted, netlike.

Retrorse   Bent or turned backward or downward.

Retuse   Notched slightly at a usually obtuse apex.

Revolute   Rolled backward, with the margin rolled toward the lower side.

Rhizomatous   Producing or possessing rhizomes.

Rhizome   Rootstock, a usually horizontal stem on or under the ground that sends up a succession of leaves or stems at the apex.

Rhomboid   Pertaining to or having the shape of a rhombus.

Rib   The primary vein of a leaf or other similar organ; also any prominent vein or nerve.

Rigid   Stiff, not flexible.

Rootstock   Subterranean stem, rhizome.

Rosette   A cluster of leaves or other organs in a circular arrangement, usually close to the ground.

Rotate   Wheel-shaped, said of a gamopetalous corolla with a flat, circular limb at right angles to the short or obsolete tube.

Rudiment   An imperfectly developed organ or part; underdeveloped.

Rugose   Wrinkled, the venation seemingly impressed into the surface.

Saccate   Bag-shaped, pouched.

Scaberulous   Minutely scabrous.

Scabrid   Roughened with minute points, scurfy.

Scabridity   Roughness.

Scabrous   Rough, feeling rough or gritty to the touch.

Scale   A minute leaf without blade, found at the base of stems and on rhizomes.

Scaly   With scales.

Scape   A leafless, flowering stem.

Scapose   Resembling a scape; having a scape.

Scarious   Thin, dry, and membranous, often more or less translucent.

Scorpioid cyme or cincinnus   A coiled, determinate inflorescence similar to a helicoid cyme, but the flowers or branches developing alternately to left and right rather than only in one direction.

Scree   An accumulation of small pebbles or stones.

Secund   One-sided; said of inflorescences when the flowers appear as if borne from only one side.

Seed   A mature ovule, consisting of an embryo, with or without endosperm and a surrounding protective coat.

Seedhead   A simple or compound inflorescence at maturity.

Sepal   One of the separate units of a calyx.

Septate   Partitioned, divided by partitions or septa.

Septum (*pl.* **septa**)   A partition or cross wall.

Serrate   With sharp teeth pointing forward.

Serrulate   Minutely serrate.

Sessile   Without a pedicel or stalk.

Setaceous   Bristlelike; especially of slender teeth attenuate to an awn.

Setose   Bristly, covered with bristles.

Setulose   Diminutive of setose, minutely setose.

Shatter   To disperse or scatter, as seeds from a seedhead.

Sheath   Any more or less tubular structure surrounding an organ or part.

Shoot   A young plant, as bamboo.

Shrub   A woody plant that remains relatively low and produces shoots or trunks from the base.

Siliceous   Containing minute particles of silica, as the stems of Equisetum.

Simple   An unbranched stem, inflorescence or leaf that is not compound.

Sinus   The cleft or recess between two lobes.

Spadix   The thick or fleshy flower spike of certain plants, usually surrounded or subtended by a spathe, as in members of the Araceae.

Spathaceous   Spathelike.

Spathe   A large bract enclosing or surrounding an inflorescence.

Spatulate   Spatula-shaped, oblong with the basal end narrowed and the apical end rounded.

Specimen plant   A plant or plant clump representative of the species or cultivar.

Spiciform   Having the form of a spike.

Spike   Usually an unbranched, elongated, indeterminate inflorescence in which the flowers are sessile or subsessile.

Spikelet   The unit of the inflorescence in grasses, consisting of two glumes and one or more florets.

Spine   A strong, stiff, sharp-pointed outgrowth on a stem, leaf, or other organ.

Spinulose   With small spines.

Sporangium (*pl.* **sporangia**)   A spore case.

Spore   A simple reproductive body; used particularly in reference to ferns, fernlike allies and lower plants.

Sporogenous Spore-bearing, producing spores.

Sporophyll A leaflike organ which bears spores.

Stamen The pollen-bearing organ of a seed plant; the anther and filament.

Staminate Having stamens and no functional pistils; male.

Staminode, staminodium (*pl.* **staminodia**) A sterile stamen or stamens.

Stem The axis of a plant arising from its roots.

Sterile Nonfunctional; without functional sex organs, not bearing flowers, not subtending flowers, as sterile bracts, not producing fruit.

Stigma The apical part of the pistil.

Stipe The stalk of a pistil; also the petiole of a fern leaf.

Stipitate Borne on a stipe or short stalk, as stipitate glands.

Stolon A modified, horizontal, above-ground stem creeping and rooting at the nodes or curved over and rooting at the tip.

Stoloniferous Bearing stolons.

Stomate A breathing pore or aperture in the epidermis.

Stramineous Straw-colored, pale yellow.

Striate With fine, longitudinal lines, channels or ridges.

Strigose With sharp, stiff, straight or appressed hairs often basally swollen and usually directed forward.

Strobilus A conelike structure consisting of sporophylls more or less densely arranged on a central axis.

Style The elongated part of the pistil between the ovary and the stigma.

Sub- Prefix generally signifying under, below, beneath, slightly, almost, about.

Subtend To occur immediately below, as a bract subtending a flower.

Subulate Very narrow and pointed.

Succulent Juicy, fleshy, and usually also rather thick.

Sulcate Grooved or furrowed lengthwise.

Sulcus A groove or furrow, a channel or fissure.

Superior Above, upper.

Synonymy The series of discarded names for identical species.

Tassel The staminate flower cluster of corn, Zea mays.

Tawny Brownish yellow; fulvous.

Terete Round in cross section.

Tessellate The surface marked with checkered depressions.

Testa The outer seedcoat.

Texture The visual characteristics and appearance of a plant; overall structure, coarseness or fineness.

Thorn A stem modified as a spine.

Thorny With thorns.

Three-eye seedpiece Section of grass culm consisting of three nodes.

Tomentose Densely woolly, covered with curly, matted hairs.

Triad A group of three.

Trichomes Minute hairs or bristles.

Trifid   Divided into three parts or sections.

Trigonous   Having three angles or corners; triangular.

Truncate   Appearing as if cut off nearly or quite straight across the end.

Tuber   A short, thick, stem or branch bearing buds and serving as a storage organ, usually subterranean.

Tubercle   A small, tuberlike structure; small, rounded protuberance from a surface.

Tuberculate   Bearing tubercles.

Tuberous   Bearing or producing tubers; tuberlike.

Tuft   A cluster or fascicle of trichomes, leaves, or other elongate structures.

Tufted   Cespitose; in clumps.

Tumid   Swollen, inflated.

Turbinate   Inversely conical, shaped like a top.

Turgid   Swollen but solid or full.

Tussock   A tuft or clump of grass or sedge.

Twig   A shoot of a woody plant representing the growth of the current season.

Type specimen   The original specimen from which a description was drawn up.

Umbel   An inflorescence with pedicels or peduncles (rays) or both arising from a common point.

Umbellate   In an umbel, umbellike.

Umbelliform   Umbellike, resembling an umbel.

Umbo   A conical projection arising from a surface, usually centrally.

Umbonate   Bearing umbos.

Undulate   Having a wavy margin.

Unisexual   Of one sex, staminate only or pistillate only.

Upright   Erect.

Vallecula   A depression, groove, or furrow.

Variant   Differing in some way from others of the same kind, or from some standard or type.

Variegated   Of different colors, as green-yellow stripes of leaves.

Vein   Strands of fibrovascular tissue in a leaf or other laminar structure.

Ventral   Relating to, or attached to the front or inner surface of a part or organ, facing toward the axis, adaxial; the opposite of dorsal.

Verticil   A whorl, a ring of three or more.

Verticilate   Arranged in a whorl.

Vestigial   Imperfectly developed, said of a part or organ that was fully developed and functional in ancestral forms but is now a degenerate relic, usually smaller and less complex than its prototype.

Vesture   Pubescence, any covering of a surface causing it to be other than glabrous.

Villous   Provided with long, soft, shaggy hairs.

Viscid   Glutinous, sticky.

Viviparous   Having seeds that germinate or buds that sprout and form plantlets while remaining on the parent plant; sometimes bearing such seeds or
buds.

Whorl   A cluster of several branches around the axis of an inflorescence.

Wing   A thin membranous or flat extension.

Winged   Having a thin membranous or flat extension.

Bibliography

Beetle, A. A. 1947. Scirpus L. *North American Flora* 18(8):481–504.

Blomquist, H. L. 1948. *The grasses of North Carolina.* Durham, NC: Duke Univ. Press.

Britton, N. L., and Percy Wilson. 1923–30. *Botany of Porto Rico and the Virgin Islands and Suppl.* Vols. 5–6. New York: New York Acad. Sci.

Bor, N. L. 1960. *The grasses of Burma, Ceylon, India and Pakistan.* New York: Pergamon Press.

Bruggeman, L. 1957 *Tropical plants and their cultivation.* London: Thames and Hudson.

Corley, W. L. 1975. *Ornamental grasses for Georgia.* Athens, GA: Georgia Agric. Expt. Sta. Res. Rept. 217.

Correll, D. S., and Helen B. Correll. 1972. Aquatic and wetland plants of southwestern United States. Vols. 1 and 2. Stanford, CA: Stanford Univ. Press.

Correll, D. S., Helen B. Correll, and M. C. Johnston. 1970. *Manual of the vascular plants of Texas.* Renner, TX: Texas Res. Foundation.

Cox, Jeff, and Marilyn Cox. 1985. *The perennial garden.* Emmaus, PA: Rodale Press.

Creech, John L. 1957. Hardiness of the running bamboos. *Natl. Hort. Mag.* 36(4):335–339.

Deam, C. C. 1929. *Grasses of Indiana.* Indianapolis, IN: Indiana Dept. of Conservation.

———. 1940. *Flora of Indiana.* Indianapolis, IN: Indiana Dept. of Conservation.

Eldridge, Joan. 1975. Bush medicine in the Exumas and Long Islands, Bahamas: A field study. *Econ. Bot.* 29(4):307–332.

Everett, T. H., Ed. 1964. *New illustrated encyclopedia of gardening.* Vols. 3, 5, 6, 7, 8, 10, 11, and 13. New York: Greystone Press.

Fassett, N. C. 1951. *Grasses of Wisconsin.* Madison, WI: Univ. of Wisconsin Press.

Fernald, M. L. 1970. *Gray's Manual of Botany.* (Corrected printing) 8th ed. New York: D. Van Nostrand Company.

Foster, Maureen. 1973. *Preserved flowers.* London: Pelham Books Ltd.

Frederick, W. H. 1972. Use of this ornamental grass in your garden. *Hort. Soc. of New York Bull.* 3(2):2, 6. New York: New York Soc. of Hort.

Frederick, W. H., and R. A. Simon. 1965. *Grass. Horticulture* 63 (8):14–15, 26.

Gates, F. C. 1934. *Wild flowers in Kansas.* Kansas State Board of Agriculture Rept. Vol 51, No. 204-B. Topeka, KS: Kansas State Printing Plant.

Gould, Frank W. 1968. *Grass systematics.* New York: McGraw-Hill Book Company.

Grisebach, A. H. R. 1864. *Flora of the British West Indian Islands.* London: Lovell Reeve and Company.

Grounds, Roger. 1981. *Ornamental grasses.* New York: Van Nostrand Reinhold.

Growing ornamental bamboo. Home and Garden Bull. 76 USDA. Washington, DC.: Govt. Printing Office.

Harrington, H. D. 1977. *How to identify grasses and grasslike plants.* Chicago, IL: The Swallow Press Inc.

Hodge, W. H., and D. A. Bisset. 1957. Running bamboos for hedges. *Natl. Hort. Mag.* 36(4):335–339.

Holm, Le Roy G., Donald L. Plucknet, Juan V. Pancho, and James P. Herberger. 1977. *The world's worst weeds.* Honolulu, HI: Univ. of Hawaii Press.

Howard, R. A. 1979. *Flora of the Lesser Antilles. Vol. 3. Monocotyledoneae.* Jamaica Plain, MA: Arnold Arboretum.

Hubbard, C. E. *Grasses.* Rev. ed. 1968. Baltimore, MD: Penguin Books.

Hutchinson, J. 1959. *The families of flowering plants. Vol. 2 Monocotyledons.* London: Oxford Univ. Press.

Kartesz, J. T., and Rosemarie Kartesz. 1980. A synonymized checklist of the vascular flora of the United States, Canada, and Greenland. Vol. 2. Raleigh, NC: Univ. of North Carolina Press.

Knowles, E. 1967. Grasses. *Gardeners Chronical and New Horticulturist* 162(2):14.

Kuekenthal, Georg. 1955–56. *Cyperaceae-Scirpoideae-Cypereae. Engl. Pflanzenr.* IV, 20 (Heft 101). Stuttgart: Engelman.

Leithead, H. L., L. L. Yarlet, and T. N. Shiflet. 1971. *100 Native forage grasses in 11 southern states.* USDA Handbook No. 389. Washington, DC: Govt. Printing Office.

Loewer, H. Peter. 1977. *Growing and decorating with grasses.* New York: Walker and Company.

Long, R. W., and Olga Lakela. 1971. *A flora of tropical Florida.* Miami, FL: Univ. of Miami Press.

Mason, Herbert L. 1957. *Flora of the marshes of California.* Berkeley, CA: Univ. of California Press.

McClure, F. A. 1956a. Bamboo in the economy of oriental peoples. *Econ. Bot.* 10(4):335–361.

McClure, F. A. 1956b. Bamboo culture in the South Pacific. *South Pacific Comm. Qtrly. Bull.* 6:38–40.

Meyer, M. H. 1975. Ornamental grasses. *Decorative plants for home and garden.* New York: Charles Scribner's Sons.

Meyer, M. H., and R. G. Mower. 1973. *Ornamental grasses for home and garden.* Cornell Univ. Info. Bull. 64.

Mosher, E. 1918. *The grasses of Illinois.* Univ. of Illinois Agric. Expt. Sta. Bull. 205.

National List of Scientific Plant Names. 1982. Vol. 1. List of plant names; Vol. 2.

Synonymy. SCS-TP-159, Soil Conservation Service, USDA. Washington, DC: Govt. Printing Office.

Norton, J. B. S. 1930. *Maryland grasses.* Maryland Agric. Expt. Sta. Bull. 323.

Oakes, A. J. 1979. *Winter hardiness in limpograss.* Hemarthria altissima (Poir). Stapf & C. E. Hubb. Soil and Crop Science Soc. Florida Proc. 86–88.

Paterson, A. 1964. Grasses for the flower garden. *Gardners Chronicle and New Horticulturist* 155(14):301–302.

———. 1969. Decorative grasses. *Annual of Amateur Gardening:* 32–33.

Pesch, Barbara B., Ed. 1988. *Ornamental grasses.* Brooklyn Bot. Garden Record 44, No 3. New York: Brooklyn Bot. Garden.

Plant Hardiness Zone Map. 1972. USDA Misc. Pub. No. 814. Washington, DC: Govt. Printing Office.

Pohl, R. W. 1954. *How to know grasses.* Dubuque, IA: Wm. C. Brown & Co.

Polunin, O. 1969. *Flowers of Europe.* London: Oxford Univ. Press.

Porter, C. L. 1967. *Taxonomy of flowering plants.* San Francisco, CA: W. H. Freeman & Company.

Radford, A. E., H. E. Ahles, and C. R. Bell. 1968. *Manual of the vascular flora of the Carolinas.* Raleigh, NC: Univ. of North Carolina Press.

Richards, L. A., Ed. 1969. Salt tolerance of grasses. *Diagnosis and improvement of saline and alkali soils.* USDA Handbook No. 60. Washington, DC: Govt. Printing Office.

Silveus, W. A. 1933. *Texas grasses.* San Antonio, TX: The Clegg Company.

Sineath, H. H., P. M. Daugherty, R. N. Hutton, and T. A. Wastler. 1953. *Industrial raw materials of plant origin. V. A survey of the bamboos.* Georgia Institute Technology, Engineering Expt. Sta. Bull. 18. (Processed).

Steinegger, D. H., R. C. Sherman, and D. E. Janssen. 1979. *An evaluation of native and exotic grass species for ornamental use in Nebraska.* Nebraska Agric. Expt. Sta. SB 546.

Steyermark, Julian A. 1963. *Flora of Missouri.* Ames, IA: Iowa State Univ. Press.

Terrell, E. E. 1977. A checklist of names for 3,000 vascular plants of economic importance. USDA Handbook No. 505. Washington, DC: Govt. Printing Office.

Tidestrom, Ivar. 1925. *Flora of Utah and Nevada.* U.S. Natl. Herb. Vol. 25.

Tracy, S. M. 1922. *Natalgrass: A southern perennial hay crop.* USDA Farmer's Bull. 726 rev. Washington, DC: Govt. Printing Office.

Velez, Ismael. 1957. *Herbaceous angiosperms of the Lesser Antilles.* Lajas, P. R.: Inter-American Univ. of Puerto Rico.

Velez, Ismael, and van Overbeck. 1950. *Plantas indeseables en los cultivos tropicales.* Rio Piedras: Univ. of Puerto Rico Press.

Voss, Edward G. 1972. *Michigan flora. Pt. 1. Gymnosperms and monocots.* Cranbrook Institute of Sci. Bull. 55.

Willis, J. C. 1966. *A dictionary of the flowering plants and ferns.* Cambridge, MA: Cambridge Univ. Press.

Index

Accent plants
  grass, 21, 28–29
  grasslike plants, 401
Acid soil, grasses for, 14, 15(*table*)
Acorus americanus (Raf.) Raf., 49, 408
Acorus calamus L., 399, 408, *409*, 410
Acorus gramineus Ait. (Japanese sweetflag),
    398, 402, 404, 407, 409, 410–411
  cultivars, 411
Acorus L., 399, 400, 404, 406, 408–411
Adam's needle, 407. *See also Yucca filamentosa*
    L.
Adlay. *See Coix lacryma-jobi* L.
Aegilops hystrix. See Sitanion hystrix (Nutt.)
    J.G. Smith
Agropyron caninum (L.) Beauv., 20, 34, 36,
    52, 56–57
Agropyron cristatum (L.) Gaertn., 56
Agropyron Gaertn., 56–58
Agropyron junceum (L.) Beauv. (Sand couch),
    19, 57–58
Agropyron pungens Pers. (Sea couch), 16, 19,
    20, 58

Agrostis alba L., 58. *See also Agrostis stolonifera*
    L.
Agrostis L., 58–60
Agrostis miliacea. See Oryzopsis miliacea (L.)
    Benth. & Hook. f.
Agrostis nebulosa Boiss. & Reut. (Cloudgrass),
    23, 24, 36, 41, 59
Agrostis stolonifera L., 18, 19, 60
Agrostis virginica. See Sporobolus virginicus (L.)
    Kunth
Aira caerulea. See Molinia caerulea (L.) Moench
Aira cespitosa. See Deschampsia caespitosa (L.)
    Beauv.
Aira flexuosa. See Deschampsia flexuosa (L.)
    Trin.
Aira holcus-lanata. See Holcus lanatus L.
Aira mollis. See Holcus mollis L.
Alkali cordgrass. *See Spartina gracilis* Trin.
Alkaligrass. *See Distichlis* Raf.; *Distichlis
    spicata* (L.) Greene; *Puccinellia* Parl.
Alkaline soils, grasses for, 14, 15(*table*)
Allgold bamboo. *See Phyllostachys bambusoides*
    Sieb. & Zucc. 'Allgold' McClure

589